T0348754

ADVANCED SOFTWARE APPLICATIONS IN JAPAN

ADVANCED
SOFTWARE APPLICATIONS
IN JAPAN

Principal Authors

Edward Feigenbaum
Gio Wiederhold

Stanford University

Elaine Rich

Microelectronics and
Computing Consortium (MCC)

Michael Harrison

University of California
at Berkeley

Advanced Computing
and
Telecommunications Series

NOYES DATA CORPORATION
Park Ridge, New Jersey, U.S.A.

Published in the United States of America by
Noyes Data Corporation
Mill Road, Park Ridge, New Jersey 07656

Transferred to Digital Printing, 2011
Printed and bound in the United Kingdom

Library of Congress Cataloging–in–Publication Data

Advanced software applications in Japan / Edward Feigenbaum ... [et
    al.].
              p.   cm. –– (Advanced computing and telecommunications series)
        Consists of 4 works: Knowledge based systems in Japan, 1993;
    Database use and technology in Japan, 1993; Machine translation in
    Japan, 1992; Advanced computing in Japan, 1990.
        Includes bibliographical references.
        ISBN 0–8155–1360–7 (hardcover)
        1. Application software––Japan. I. Feigenbaum, Edward A.
    II. Series.
    QA76.76.A65A33   1994
    338.4'700633'0952––dc20   94–23430
                                                                   CIP

Foreword

This book is based on four reports prepared through the Japanese Technology Evaluation Center (JTEC), sponsored by the National Science Foundation (NSF) and administered by Loyola College in Maryland. The book describes research and development efforts in Japan in the area of advanced software applications.

Over the past decade, the United States' competitive position in world markets for high-technology products appears to have eroded substantially. As U.S. technological leadership is challenged, many government and private organizations seek to set policies that will help maintain U.S. competitive strengths. To do this effectively requires an understanding of the relative position of the United States and its competitors. Indeed, whether our goal is competition or cooperation, we must improve our access to scientific and technical information in other countries.

Although many U.S. organizations support substantial data gathering and analysis directed at other nations, the government and privately sponsored studies that are in the public domain tend to be "input" studies. That is, they measure expenditures, personnel data, and facilities but do not assess the quality or quantity of the outputs obtained. Studies of the outputs of the research and development process are more difficult to perform since they require a subjective analysis by individuals who are experts in the relevant technical fields.

The National Science Foundation staff includes professionals with expertise in a wide range of technologies. These individuals have the technical expertise to assemble panels of experts who can perform competent, unbiased, scientific and technical reviews of research and development activities. Further, a principal activity of the Foundation is the review and selection for funding of research proposals. Thus the Foundation has both experience and credibility in this process. The JTEC activity builds on this capability.

Specific technologies, such as displays, telecommunications, or biotechnology, are selected for study by individuals in government agencies that are able to contribute to the funding of the study. A typical assessment is sponsored by two or more agencies. In cooperation with the sponsoring agencies, NSF selects a panel of experts who will conduct the study. Administrative oversight of the panel is provided by Loyola College in Maryland, which operates JTEC under an NSF grant.

Panelists are selected for their expertise in specific areas of technology and their broad knowledge of research and development in both the United States and in Japan. Of great importance is the panelists' ability to produce a comprehensive, informed and unbiased report. Most panelists have travelled previously to Japan or have professional associations with their expert counterparts in Japan. Nonetheless, as part of the assessment, the panel as a whole travels to Japan to spend at least one week visiting research and development sites and meeting with researchers. These trips have proven to be highly informative, and the panelists have been given broad access to both researchers and facilities. Upon completion of its trip, the panel conducts a one–day workshop to present its findings. Following the workshop, the panel completes its written report.

The methodology developed and applied to the study of research and development in Japan has now been shown to be equally relevant to Europe and to other leading industrial nations. In general, the United States can benefit from a better understanding of cutting–edge research that is being conducted outside its borders. Improved awareness of international developments can significantly enhance the scope and effectiveness of international collaboration and thus benefit all our international partners in joint research and development efforts.

Paul J. Herer
National Science Foundation
Washington, DC

Japanese Technology Evaluation Center
(International Technology Research Institute)

The Japanese Technology Evaluation Center (JTEC) at Loyola College in Maryland is operated for the Federal Government to provide assessments of Japanese research and development (R&D) in selected technologies. The National Science Foundation (NSF) is the lead support agency. Paul Herer, Senior Advisor for Planning and Technology Evaluation, is NSF Program Director for the project. Other sponsors of JTEC include the National Aeronautics and Space Administration (NASA), the Department of Commerce (DOC), the Department of Energy (DOE), the Office of Naval Research (ONR), the Advanced Research Projects Agency (ARPA), the U.S. Air Force, and the U.S. Army.

JTEC assessments contribute to more balanced technology transfer between Japan and the United States. The Japanese excel at acquisition and perfection of foreign technologies, whereas the U.S. has relatively little experience with this process. As the Japanese become leaders in research in targeted technologies, it is essential that the United States have access to the results. JTEC provides the important first step in this process by alerting U.S. researchers to Japanese accomplishments. JTEC findings can also be helpful in formulating governmental research and trade policies.

The assessments are performed by panels of about six U.S. technical experts. Panel members are leading authorities in the field, technically active, and knowledgeable about both Japanese and U.S. research programs. Each panelist spends about one month of effort reviewing literature and writing his/her chapter of the report on a part–time basis over a twelve–month period. All recent panels have conducted extensive tours of Japanese laboratories. To provide a balanced perspective, panelists are selected from industry, academia, and government.

The focus of the assessments is on the status and long–term direction of Japanese R&D efforts relative to those of the United States. Other important aspects include the evolution of the technology and the identification of key researchers, R&D organizations, and funding sources. The panel findings are presented to workshops where invited participants critique the preliminary results.

The Loyola College JTEC staff helps select topics to be assessed, recruits experts as panelists, organizes and coordinates panel activities, provides literature support, organizes tours of Japanese labs, assists in the preparation of workshop presentations and in the preparation of reports, and provides general administrative support. Mr. Cecil Uyehara of

Uyehara International Associates provided literature support and advance work for Parts I, II and III. Dr. Alan Engel and Ms. Kaori Niida of International Science and Technology Associates provided literature support and advance work for Part IV.

The Publisher wishes to thank Duane Shelton, Director of the International Technology Research Institute (ITRI) for his cooperation in making this book possible.

Preface

This book is divided into four parts, each part representing specific advanced software applications in Japan.

Part I (1993) examines Japanese expert systems applications and advanced knowledge-based (KB) systems R&D, and compares progress and trends with similar developments in the United States. It includes an executive summary, an introductory chapter, and chapters on: applications; tools and infrastructure; advanced research; national projects; integration with conventional data processing systems; and business perspectives. Site reports on the visits made to Japanese corporate, government and university facilities are included as appendices. The panel observed some contrasts between U.S. and Japanese KB research and applications: (1) Japanese computer manufacturers play a dominant role in the technology and business of expert systems. These large companies have mastered this technology as a core competence, and tend to use systems engineers rather than knowledge engineers to build systems. Consequently, integration with conventional information technology is handled routinely and smoothly. (2) Japanese companies have more experience in applications of KB systems technology to heavy industry, particularly in steel and construction. (3) Products based on the use of fuzzy control logic have had a big impact in Japanese consumer products. (4) Japanese companies are continuing their substantial investments in KB systems technology and business. (5) Compared to the U.S., the quantity of Japanese university research is considerably smaller, but the quality of the best work is as high.

Part II (1992) discusses database use and technology in Japan. Database research in industry is very much oriented toward support of development and new technology. It relies for its conceptual input greatly on publications from the U.S. and Europe. The researchers are well–read and often well–connected with foreign academic sources. They provide an important path for technology transfer.

An important driving mechanism in database development is the Japanese capability in the area of developing electronic products. High quality image acquisition, transmission, storage, display, and digitized voice data are emphasized. Database management systems are being expanded to provide support for such "multimedia." While fundamental database management systems are not being advanced, the incorporation of multimedia support will change their character greatly. It can be expected that purchasers of systems with multimedia requirements will, with Japanese image–processing hardware, acquire Japanese database software. This field is likely to grow rapidly. Computer–aided–design, computer–aided education, and other application areas that are critically dependent on graphics will be the initial users of this technology.

Part III (1992) provides an overview of the state of the art of machine translation (MT) in Japan and a comparison between Japanese and Western technology in this area. Machine translation is viewed in Japan as an important strategic technology that is expected to play a key role in Japan's increasing participation in the world economy. MT is seen in Japan as important both for assimilating information into Japanese as well as for disseminating Japanese information throughout the world as part of the export process. As a result, several of Japan's largest industrial companies are developing MT systems. Many are already marketing their systems commercially. There is also an active MT and natural language processing research community at some of the major universities and government/industrial consortia.

Part IV (1990) assesses Japanese technology in advanced computing. The summaries show that while Japan is ahead in some areas of advanced computing, these results do not yet show the effect of additional recent research and development as well as capital expenditures. The supporting data on R&D spending and on capital expenditures needed to maintain the short–term marketshare are provided. The Japanese competitive position should remain strong over the next five years. The competitive position of the U.S. with respect to Japan will depend, in part, on whether the U.S. is willing to match this rate of investment. The information in Part IV was originally prepared in 1990, and certain portions are now out–of–date. However, it is included in this book as it provides substantial background information.

Japan has been and remains relatively weak in software, but effective in software engineering. There is a serious shortage of talented software people who can be hired to work in the large high technology Japanese companies. Part of this stems from the financial community which offers higher salaries, so the best young people choose careers there. Some of this loss of personnel is mitigated by the effective software factories whose employees have a lower educational level than the graduates from the major universities. However, there is nothing in Japan yet to compare to the strong community of creative and talented software people in the United States.

Notice

Contents and Subject Index

PART II
DATABASE USE AND TECHNOLOGY IN JAPAN

PART III
MACHINE TRANSLATION IN JAPAN

PART IV
ADVANCED COMPUTING IN JAPAN

Part I

Knowledge–Based Systems in Japan

Edward Feigenbaum, Chairman
Peter E. Friedland
Bruce B. Johnson
H. Penny Nii
Herbert Schorr
Howard Shrobe

Robert S. Engelmore, Editor

Executive Summary

Expert Systems (ES), also called Knowledge-Based Systems (KBS) or simply Knowledge Systems (KS), are computer programs that use expertise to assist people in performing a wide variety of functions, including diagnosis, planning, scheduling and design. ESs are distinguished from conventional computer programs in two essential ways (Barr, Cohen et al. 1989):

1)   Expert systems reason with domain-specific knowledge that is symbolic as well as numerical;

2)   Expert systems use domain-specific methods that are heuristic (i.e., plausible) as well as algorithmic (i.e., certain).

Expert systems have become the most successful commercial applications of Artificial Intelligence (AI) research, first in the United States, and then in Europe and Asia. Thousands of systems are now in routine use world-wide, and span the full spectrum of activities in business, industry and government. Economic gain has been realized along many dimensions: speed-up of professional (and semi-professional) work; internal cost savings on operations; improved quality and consistency of decision making; increased revenue from new products and services; captured organizational know-how; improvements in the way a company does its business; crisis management; and stimulation of innovation.

From a business perspective, the expert systems industry in the U.S. consists of many small companies, or divisions of larger companies, which are selling both expert system development software and support services for assisting users in using that software or developing expert systems. Typical annual revenues for a small ES company or division of a larger company are in the range of $5 to $20 million a year per company. The aggregate total of such sales worldwide is in the range of several hundred million dollars per year.

The technology of expert systems has had a far greater impact than even the expert systems business. Expert system technology has become widespread and deeply embedded. As expert system techniques have matured into a standard information technology, the most important recent trend is the increasing integration of this technology with conventional information processing, such as data processing or management information systems.

Study Objectives

The primary objectives of this JTEC panel were to investigate Japanese expert systems development from both technological and business perspectives and to compare progress and trends with similar developments in the United States. More specifically, there were five dimensions to the study, namely, to investigate:

1) Business sector applications of expert systems
2) Infrastructure and tools for expert system development
3) Advanced knowledge-based systems in industry
4) Advanced knowledge-based systems research in universities
5) National projects, including:
   ICOT - the laboratory of the Japanese Fifth Generation Computer
        Project
   EDR - the Electronic Dictionary Research Project
   LIFE - the Laboratory for International Fuzzy Engineering

The JTEC panel visited 19 sites during its one-week visit in Japan (March 23-27, 1992), and conferred with other Japanese computer scientists and business executives both before and after the official visits. The panel visited four major computer manufacturers, eight companies that are applying expert systems to their operations, three universities, three national projects, and the editors of *Nikkei AI*, a publication that conducts an annual survey of expert systems applications in Japan.

Conclusions

The panel drew a number of conclusions from these visits, which are discussed in Chapter 8. A comparison of expert systems activities in Japan and the U.S., drawn from those conclusions, is presented in Tables E.1 and E.2.

Although there are many similarities in both the research and applications activities in Japan and the U.S., the panel observed some noteworthy contrasts:

o Japanese computer manufacturers (JCMs) play a dominant role in the technology and business of expert systems. The JCMs have mastered and absorbed expert system technology as a core competence. They tend to use systems engineers rather than knowledge engineers to build systems. Consequently, integration with conventional information technology poses no special problem for them, and is handled routinely and smoothly, without friction. These large computer companies also build many application systems for their customers; smaller firms specializing in AI software play only a minor role in applications building, compared to the United States.

o The majority of the Japanese expert systems tools are developed, sold, and applied by the JCMs. They have the resources to conduct research, develop new products, and persist in the business. In the U.S. most of the expert systems tools are developed and marketed by a handful of small companies. The Japanese can continue to invest in the research and development of new tools (which they are doing) and are in a better position to survive lean times. In contrast, American vendors must work with short-term objectives and lean cash reserves.

o Japan has more experience than the United States in applications of knowledge-based systems technology to heavy industry, particularly the steel and construction industries. In certain application tasks, such as closed-loop control, expert systems have been assimilated into the suite of techniques available to the systems engineers, and do not require the special attention sometimes afforded new technologies.

o The Japanese are ahead of the United States in the integration of problem solving techniques, due to a combination of factors. These include substantial Japanese investments experimenting with a wide range of technologies and in-house development of expert systems tools by Japanese computer manufacturers and other large organizations. These factors provide the understanding necessary for full integration of software with other data processing components. Another factor is the avoidance of artificial partitions between various methodologies.

o Products based on the use of fuzzy control logic have had a big impact on consumer products, including camcorders, automobile transmissions and cruise controls, television, air conditioners, washer/dryers, and many others.

o The panel saw continued strong efforts by Japanese computer companies and industry-specific companies (e.g., Nippon Steel) to advance their KBS technology and business. This situation contrasts with that in the U.S., where there is a declining investment in knowledge-based systems technology; lack of venture capital; downsizing of computer company efforts; and few new product announcements. It is a familiar story, and one worthy of concern, as this trend may lead to Japanese superiority in this area relatively soon.

o Although the quality of research at a few top-level universities in Japan is in the same range as at top-level U.S. universities and research institutes, the quantity of Japanese research (in terms of number of projects and/or number of publications) is considerably smaller by nearly an order of magnitude.

Table E.1
Comparison of Applications of ES in U.S. and Japan

	Current State	Trend
Quality of the best	O	⇒
Quantity relative to GDP	O	⇑
Support Structure	+	⇒
Tools	O	⇑
Consumer Products	+	⇑
Integration	+	*

Table E.2
Comparison of KB Research in U.S. and Japan

	Quantity		Quality	
	Current State	Trend	Current State	Trend
Adv. KBS Research in Industry				
Basic Research	–	⇒	–	⇒
Applied R & D	O	⇑	+	⇒
Adv. KBS Research in Universities	–	⇑	–	⇑
National Initiatives				
Parallel Symbolic Computation	+	⇓	+	⇒
Very Large Knowledge Bases	+	⇓	O	⇒
Fuzzy Logic Systems	+	⇑	+	⇒

Legend:
+	Japan now ahead
O	Japan and U.S. now about even
-	Japan now behind
⇑	Japan gaining ground
*	Japan trend is constant or gaining
⇒	Japan and U.S. progressing equally
⇓	Japan losing ground

1. Introduction

Robert S. Engelmore
Edward Feigenbaum

EXPERT SYSTEMS AND ARTIFICIAL INTELLIGENCE

Expert Systems are computer programs that are derived from a branch of computer science research called *Artificial Intelligence* (AI). AI's scientific goal is to understand intelligence by building computer programs that exhibit intelligent behavior. It is concerned with the concepts and methods of symbolic inference, or reasoning, by a computer, and how the knowledge used to make those inferences will be represented inside the machine.

Of course, the term *intelligence* covers many cognitive skills, including the ability to solve problems, learn, and understand language; AI addresses all of those. But most progress to date in AI has been made in the area of problem solving -- concepts and methods for building programs that *reason* about problems rather than calculate a solution.

AI programs that achieve expert-level competence in solving problems in task areas by bringing to bear a body of knowledge about specific tasks are called *knowledge-based* or *expert systems*. Often, the term expert systems is reserved for programs whose knowledge base contains the knowledge used by human experts, in contrast to knowledge gathered from textbooks or non-experts. More often than not, the two terms, expert systems (ES) and knowledge-based systems (KBS), are used synonymously. Taken together, they represent the most widespread type of AI application.

The area of human intellectual endeavor to be captured in an expert system is called the *task domain.*   *Task* refers to some goal-oriented, problem-solving activity. *Domain* refers to the area within which the task is being performed. Typical tasks are diagnosis, planning, scheduling, configuration and design. An example of a task domain is aircraft crew scheduling, discussed in Chapter 2.

Building an expert system is known as *knowledge engineering* and its practitioners are called *knowledge engineers.* The knowledge engineer must make sure that the computer has all the knowledge needed to solve a problem. The knowledge engineer must choose one or more forms in which to represent the required knowledge as symbol patterns in the memory of the computer -- that is, he (or she) must choose a *knowledge representation.* He must also ensure that the computer can use the knowledge efficiently by selecting from a handful of *reasoning methods.* The practice of knowledge engineering is described later. We first describe the components of expert systems.

The Building Blocks of Expert Systems

Every expert system consists of two principal parts: the knowledge base; and the reasoning, or inference, engine.

The *knowledge base* of expert systems contains both factual and heuristic knowledge. *Factual knowledge* is that knowledge of the task domain that is widely shared, typically found in textbooks or journals, and commonly agreed upon by those knowledgeable in the particular field.

Heuristic knowledge is the less rigorous, more experiential, more judgmental knowledge of performance. In contrast to factual knowledge, heuristic knowledge is rarely discussed, and is largely individualistic. It is the knowledge of good practice, good judgment, and plausible reasoning in the field. It is the knowledge that underlies the "art of good guessing."

Knowledge representation formalizes and organizes the knowledge. One widely used representation is the *production rule*, or simply *rule.* A rule consists of an IF part and a THEN part (also called a *condition* and an *action*). The IF part lists a set of conditions in some logical combination. The piece of knowledge represented by the production rule is relevant to the line of reasoning being developed if the IF part of the rule is satisfied; consequently, the THEN part can be concluded, or its problem-solving action taken. Expert systems whose knowledge is represented in rule form are called *rule-based systems.*

Another widely used representation, called the *unit* (also known as *frame, schema,* or *list structure*) is based upon a more passive view of knowledge. The unit is an assemblage of associated symbolic knowledge about an entity to be represented.

Typically, a unit consists of a list of properties of the entity and associated values for those properties.

Since every task domain consists of many entities that stand in various relations, the properties can also be used to specify relations, and the values of these properties are the names of other units that are linked according to the relations. One unit can also represent knowledge that is a "special case" of another unit, or some units can be "parts of" another unit.

The *problem-solving model,* or *paradigm*, organizes and controls the steps taken to solve the problem.   One common but powerful paradigm involves chaining of IF-THEN rules to form a line of reasoning. If the chaining starts from a set of conditions and moves toward some conclusion, the method is called *forward chaining*. If the conclusion is known (for example, a goal to be achieved) but the path to that conclusion is not known, then reasoning backwards is called for, and the method is *backward chaining*. These problem-solving methods are built into program modules called *inference engines* or *inference procedures* that manipulate and use knowledge in the knowledge base to form a line of reasoning.

The *knowledge base* an expert uses is what he learned at school, from colleagues, and from years of experience. Presumably the more experience he has, the larger his store of knowledge. Knowledge allows him to interpret the information in his databases to advantage in diagnosis, design, and analysis.

Though an expert system consists primarily of a knowledge base and an inference engine, a couple of other features are worth mentioning: reasoning with uncertainty, and explanation of the line of reasoning.

Knowledge is almost always incomplete and uncertain. To deal with uncertain knowledge, a rule may have associated with it a *confidence factor* or a weight. The set of methods for using uncertain knowledge in combination with uncertain data in the reasoning process is called *reasoning with uncertainty*. An important subclass of methods for reasoning with uncertainty is called "fuzzy logic," and the systems that use them are known as "fuzzy systems."

Because an expert system uses uncertain or heuristic knowledge (as we humans do) its credibility is often in question (as is the case with humans). When an answer to a problem is questionable, we tend to want to know the rationale. If the rationale seems plausible, we tend to believe the answer. So it is with expert systems. Most expert systems have the ability to answer questions of the form: "Why is the answer X?" Explanations can be generated by tracing the line of reasoning used by the inference engine (Feigenbaum, McCorduck et al. 1988).

The most important ingredient in any expert system is knowledge. The power of expert systems resides in the specific, high-quality knowledge they contain about task domains. AI researchers will continue to explore and add to the current repertoire of knowledge representation and reasoning methods. But in knowledge resides the power. Because of the importance of knowledge in expert systems and because the current knowledge acquisition method is slow and tedious, much of the future of expert systems depends on breaking the knowledge acquisition bottleneck and in codifying and representing a large knowledge infrastructure.

Knowledge Engineering

Knowledge engineering is the art of designing and building expert systems, and knowledge engineers are its practitioners. Gerald M. Weinberg said of programming in *The Psychology of Programming*: "'Programming,' -- like 'loving,' -- is a single word that encompasses an infinitude of activities" (Weinberg 1971). Knowledge engineering is the same, perhaps more so. We stated earlier that knowledge engineering is an applied part of the science of artificial intelligence which, in turn, is a part of computer science. Theoretically, then, a knowledge engineer is a computer scientist who knows how to design and implement programs that incorporate artificial intelligence techniques. The nature of knowledge engineering is changing, however, and a new breed of knowledge engineers is emerging. We'll discuss the evolving nature of knowledge engineering later.

Today there are two ways to build an expert system. They can be built from scratch, or built using a piece of development software known as a "tool" or a "shell." Before we discuss these tools, let's briefly discuss what knowledge engineers do. Though different styles and methods of knowledge engineering exist, the basic approach is the same: a knowledge engineer interviews and observes a human expert or a group of experts and learns what the experts know, and how they reason with their knowledge. The engineer then translates the knowledge into a computer-usable language, and designs an inference engine, a reasoning structure, that uses the knowledge appropriately. He also determines how to integrate the use of uncertain knowledge in the reasoning process, and what kinds of explanation would be useful to the end user.

Next, the inference engine and facilities for representing knowledge and for explaining are programmed, and the domain knowledge is entered into the program piece by piece. It may be that the inference engine is not just right; the form of knowledge representation is awkward for the kind of knowledge needed for the task; and the expert might decide the pieces of knowledge are wrong. All these are discovered and modified as the expert system gradually gains competence.

The discovery and cumulation of techniques of machine reasoning and knowledge representation is generally the work of artificial intelligence research. The discovery and cumulation of knowledge of a task domain is the province of domain experts. Domain knowledge consists of both formal, textbook knowledge, and experiential knowledge -- the *expertise* of the experts.

Tools, Shells, and Skeletons

Compared to the wide variation in domain knowledge, only a small number of AI methods are known that are useful in expert systems. That is, currently there are only a handful of ways in which to represent knowledge, or to make inferences, or to generate explanations. Thus, systems can be built that contain these useful methods without any domain-specific knowledge. Such systems are known as *skeletal systems, shells*, or simply *AI tools*.

Building expert systems by using shells offers significant advantages. A system can be built to perform a unique task by entering into a shell all the necessary knowledge about a task domain. The inference engine that applies the knowledge to the task at hand is built into the shell. If the program is not very complicated and if an expert has had some training in the use of a shell, the expert can enter the knowledge himself.

Many commercial shells are available today, ranging in size from shells on PCs, to shells on workstations, to shells on large mainframe computers. They range in price from hundreds to tens of thousands of dollars, and range in complexity from simple, forward-chained, rule-based systems requiring two days of training to those so complex that only highly trained knowledge engineers can use them to advantage. They range from general-purpose shells to shells custom-tailored to a class of tasks, such as financial planning or real-time process control.

Although shells simplify programming, in general they don't help with knowledge acquisition. *Knowledge acquisition* refers to the task of endowing expert systems with knowledge, a task currently performed by knowledge engineers. The choice of reasoning method, or a shell, is important, but it isn't as important as the accumulation of high-quality knowledge. The power of an expert system lies in its store of knowledge about the task domain -- the more knowledge a system is given, the more competent it becomes.

Bricks and Mortar

The fundamental working hypothesis of AI is that intelligent behavior can be precisely described as symbol manipulation and can be modeled with the symbol processing capabilities of the computer.

In the late 1950s, special programming languages were invented that facilitate symbol manipulation. The most prominent is called LISP (LISt Processing). Because of its simple elegance and flexibility, most AI research programs are written in LISP, but commercial applications have moved away from LISP.

In the early 1970s another AI programming language was invented in France. It is called PROLOG (PROgramming in LOGic). LISP has its roots in one area of mathematics (lambda calculus), PROLOG in another (first-order predicate calculus).

PROLOG consists of English-like statements which are facts (assertions), rules (of inference), and questions. Here is an inference rule: "If object-x is part-of object-y then a component-of object-y is object-x."

Programs written in PROLOG have behavior similar to rule-based systems written in LISP. PROLOG, however, did not immediately become a language of choice for AI programmers. In the early 1980s it was given impetus with the announcement by the Japanese that they would use a logic programming language for the Fifth Generation Computing Systems (FGCS) Project. A variety of logic-based programming languages have since arisen, and the term *prolog* has become generic.

THE APPLICATIONS OF EXPERT SYSTEMS

The spectrum of applications of expert systems technology to industrial and commercial problems is so wide as to defy easy characterization. The applications find their way into most areas of knowledge work. They are as varied as helping salespersons sell modular factory-built homes to helping NASA plan the maintenance of a space shuttle in preparation for its next flight.

Applications tend to cluster into seven major classes.

Diagnosis and Troubleshooting of Devices and Systems of All Kinds

This class comprises systems that deduce faults and suggest corrective actions for a malfunctioning device or process. Medical diagnosis was one of the first knowledge areas to which ES technology was applied (for example, see Shortliffe 1976), but diagnosis of engineered systems quickly surpassed medical diagnosis. There are probably more diagnostic applications of ES than any other type. The diagnostic problem can be stated in the abstract as: given the evidence presenting itself, what is the underlying problem/reason/cause?

Planning and Scheduling

Systems that fall into this class analyze a set of one or more potentially complex and interacting goals in order to determine a set of actions to achieve those goals, and/or provide a detailed temporal ordering of those actions, taking into account personnel, materiel, and other constraints.   This class has great commercial potential, which has been recognized. Examples involve airline scheduling of flights, personnel, and gates; manufacturing job-shop scheduling; and manufacturing process planning.

Configuration of Manufactured Objects from Subassemblies

Configuration, whereby a solution to a problem is synthesized from a given set of elements related by a set of constraints, is historically one of the most important of expert system applications. Configuration applications were pioneered by computer companies as a means of facilitating the manufacture of semi-custom minicomputers (McDermott 1981). The technique has found its way into use in many different industries, for example, modular home building, manufacturing, and other problems involving complex engineering design and manufacturing.

Financial Decision Making

The financial services industry has been a vigorous user of expert system techniques. Advisory programs have been created to assist bankers in determining whether to make loans to businesses and individuals. Insurance companies have used expert systems to assess the risk presented by the customer and to determine a price for the insurance. A typical application in the financial markets is in foreign exchange trading.

Knowledge Publishing

This is a relatively new, but also potentially explosive area. The primary function of the expert system is to deliver knowledge that is relevant to the user's problem, in the context of the user's problem. The two most widely distributed expert systems in the world are in this category. The first is an advisor which counsels a user on appropriate grammatical usage in a text.   The second is a tax advisor that accompanies a tax preparation program and advises the user on tax strategy, tactics, and individual tax policy.

Process Monitoring and Control

Systems falling in this class analyze real-time data from physical devices with the goal of noticing anomalies, predicting trends, and controlling for both optimality and failure correction. Examples of real-time systems that actively monitor processes can be found in the steel making and oil refining industries.

Design and Manufacturing

These systems assist in the design of physical devices and processes, ranging from high-level conceptual design of abstract entities all the way to factory floor configuration of manufacturing processes.

BENEFITS TO END USERS

Primarily, the benefits of ESs to end users include:

o A speed-up of human professional or semi-professional work -- typically by a factor of ten and sometimes by a factor of a hundred or more.

o Within companies, major internal cost savings. For small systems, savings are sometimes in the tens or hundreds of thousands of dollars; but for large systems, often in the tens of millions of dollars and as high as hundreds of millions of dollars. These cost savings are a result of quality improvement, a major motivation for employing expert system technology.

o Improved quality of decision making. In some cases, the quality or correctness of decisions evaluated after the fact show a ten-fold improvement.

o Preservation of scarce expertise. ESs are used to preserve scarce know-how in organizations, to capture the expertise of individuals who are retiring, and to preserve corporate know-how so that it can be widely distributed to other factories, offices or plants of the company.

o Introduction of new products. A good example of a new product is a pathology advisor sold to clinical pathologists in hospitals to assist in the diagnosis of diseased tissue.

THE EXPERT SYSTEMS BUSINESS

The industry, particularly in the United States, consists of many small companies, or divisions of larger companies, which are selling both expert system development software and support services for assisting with the usage of that software or development of expert systems. Typical annual revenues for a small company or division of a larger company range from $5 million to $20 million annually. The aggregate total of such sales world-wide is in the range of several hundred million dollars per year.

Selling consulting services is a vigorous part of the expert system business. In the United States, consulting is done by major consulting firms, such as Anderson Consulting or SRI International. These major firms compete with many small firms. In Japan, the consulting is done primarily by the computer manufacturers themselves. There is no longer a specialized expert systems hardware business. Expert systems are built for mainframes and for workstations (often UNIX-based).

It's fair to say that the technology of expert systems has had a far greater impact than the expert systems business. Expert system technology is widespread and deeply imbedded.

Current Business Trends

As expert system techniques matured into a standard information technology in the 1980s, the increasing integration of expert system technology with conventional information technology -- data processing or management information systems -- grew in importance. Conventional technology is mostly the world of IBM mainframes and IBM operating systems. More recently, this world has grown to include distributed networks of engineering workstations. However, it's also the world of a wide variety of personal computers, particularly those running the MS DOS operating system.

Early in its history, commercial expert systems tools were written primarily in LISP and PROLOG, but more recently the trend has been to conventional languages such as C. Commercial companies dedicated to one language or the other (e.g., Symbolics, Lisp Machines Inc., Quintus Prolog) have gone into bankruptcy or have been bought out by other companies.[1]

Finally, the connection of expert systems to the databases that are managed by conventional information technology methods and groups is essential and is now a standard feature of virtually all expert systems.

ADVANCED RESEARCH IN KNOWLEDGE-BASED SYSTEMS: INVENTING THE NEXT GENERATION

The basic categories of research in knowledge-based systems include: knowledge representation, knowledge use (or problem-solving), and knowledge acquisition (i.e., machine learning and discovery).

---

[1] Interestingly, this trend away from LISP and PROLOG is being reversed in some commercial computing systems. Apple Computer's new personal digital assistant, the Newton, has an operating system (Dylan) written in LISP, and one of the most popular systems for computer-aided design (AUTOCAD) is written in LISP dialect.

Knowledge Representation

In knowledge representation, the key topics are concepts, languages, and standards for knowledge representation. There are many issues involved in scaling up expert systems: defining the problems encountered in the pursuit of large knowledge bases; developing the infrastructure for building and sharing large knowledge bases; and actually accumulating a large body of knowledge, for example, common sense knowledge or engineering and technical knowledge.

Knowledge Use

Knowledge use, or problem-solving, research efforts involve the development of new methods for different kinds of reasoning, such as analogical reasoning, reasoning based on probability theory and decision theory, and reasoning from case examples.

The first generation of expert systems was characterized by knowledge bases that were narrow and, hence, performance that was brittle. When the boundary of a system's knowledge was traversed, the system's behavior went from extremely competent to incompetent very quickly. To overcome such brittleness, researchers are now focusing on reasoning from models, principles and causes. Thus, the knowledge-based system will not have to know everything about an area, as it were, but can reason with a broader base of knowledge by using the models, the principles, and the causation.

Knowledge Acquisition

The quest for a large knowledge base boils down to the problem of access to distributed knowledge bases involving multiple expert systems and developers. The effort to develop the infrastructure needed to obtain access is a research area called knowledge sharing. The goal of the knowledge sharing research is to overcome the isolation of first-generation expert systems, which rarely interchanged any knowledge. Hence, the knowledge bases that were built for expert systems in the 1980s did not accumulate.

Other Areas of Investigation

A major issue of expert systems research involves methods for reasoning with uncertain data and uncertain knowledge. One of the most widely adopted methods is called "fuzzy logic" or "fuzzy reasoning," especially in Japan, where fuzzy reasoning is the object of much research attention and much scrutiny on the part of American researchers.

Very lately, there has come on the scene the research topic of neural networks -- networks of distributed components operating in parallel to make classification decisions.   The links between neural networks technology and expert system technology are being explored.

Finally, research is underway to explore the use of new parallel computing methods in the implementation of expert systems and advanced knowledge-based systems. The new wave of computing is multi-processor technology. The question is, what will be the impact of such high-performance parallel computing activities on expert system techniques?

DESIGN OF THE JTEC STUDY GROUP ON KNOWLEDGE-BASED SYSTEMS AND THE SELECTION OF JAPANESE SITES.

Sponsors of this JTEC study defined the dimensions of the study as follows:

1)   Business sector applications of expert systems
2)   Advanced knowledge-based systems in industry
3)   Advanced knowledge-based systems research in universities
4)   Government laboratories, ICOT, the laboratory of the Japanese Fifth Generation Computer Project
5)   EDR -- research and development on electronic dictionaries (lexical knowledge base) for natural language processing

Finally, we were asked to observe the fuzzy systems work being done in Japan, any neural network applications that affect expert system development, and the new national project known as Real World Computing.

Half of this study effort has been aimed at applications of expert systems in the business sector. Knowledge-based system research in industry comprises fifteen percent of the effort, and knowledge-based system research in universities another fifteen percent. Two national laboratories (ICOT and EDR) each account for five percent of the total. The remaining ten percent focuses on miscellaneous topics.

During the week of our visit, the JTEC team visited 19 Japanese sites. Applications of expert systems to business sector problems and the industrial knowledge-based system research together accounted for 12 of the 19 visits.   University knowledge-based systems research accounted for three, ICOT and EDR accounted for two, and other visits two.

We chose the industrial sites to be visited based on the following criteria:

1)   Computer manufacturing companies that were known to be very active in KBS applications and research

2)   Non-computer companies at which there was at least one well-known expert system application
3)   Selected companies from certain industry groups that were known to be active and highly competent in building expert systems applications (for example, the steel, construction, electric power and communications industries)

Visits to university professors were selected on the basis of the panel members' personal knowledge of the leaders in academic knowledge-based system research in Japan. As it happens, these leadership positions were held by professors at the major universities: University of Tokyo, Kyoto University, and Osaka University.

Finally, we scheduled a special visit with the editor and the staff of *Nikkei AI Newsletter* to check facts that we believed we had accumulated and impressions that we had. *Nikkei AI* is the leading Japanese news publication in the field of knowledge-based systems applications and research.

2. Applications of Knowledge–Based Systems In Japan

Edward Feigenbaum
Peter E. Friedland
Bruce B. Johnson
Howard Shrobe

INTRODUCTION

A major purpose of this JTEC study was to survey the use of knowledge-based (KB) systems in Japanese industry. Our goal was to determine the breadth (how many) and depth (how important to the company) of KB systems as well as to analyze the methods and tools used to develop the systems. This chapter will first survey general trends of expert systems (ES) development and use within Japanese companies, based on annual surveys by the publication *Nikkei AI*. We will then illustrate some of the best of Japanese industrial utilization of KB systems technology through three case studies which we believe have had a great impact upon the business of the industrial user. Next, the breadth of applications that we observed will be presented, with descriptions of application types and type-specific features. Finally, we compare and contrast our view of KB systems utilization in Japanese industry with that in the United States, attempting to note any strong trends and predict the short-term future growth of KB systems in Japan.

TRENDS IN AI APPLICATIONS IN JAPAN

Each year, *Nikkei AI* publishes a survey of expert systems in Japan. For the *Nikkei AI* Winter 1992 Special Issue (Nikkei AI 1992), questionnaires were sent to 2200 companies, of which 295 responded.[1] Figure 2.1 shows that there has been a steady, approximately linear growth in the number of systems, both fielded and under development since 1987.[2] The rate of increase in the number of companies that are developing or using the technology has slowed in recent years. Although we are aware of no comparable study for companies in the U.S., we would expect a similar growth pattern.

The number of fielded systems reported in the 1992 survey was analyzed according to the type of application, as shown in Figure 2.2, along with a comparison to previous years. Diagnostic systems have traditionally been the most popular type of ESs. They were first developed 20 years ago (starting with MYCIN; Shortliffe 1976), and now have a well-understood methodology for their construction. The recent upswing in the diagnostic systems is due to two factors: (1) the entry of new ES-user companies; and (2) the application of diagnostic techniques in new areas, such as "help desk" and management analysis.

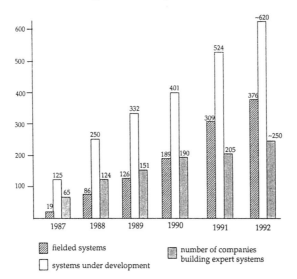

Figure 2.1. Growth of ESs in Japan (Source: Nikkei AI 1992)

---

[1] Neither *Nikkei AI* nor the JTEC panel know if the non-respondents have fielded systems or not. We must assume that some percentage of non-respondents have developed and/or fielded knowledge-based systems. Therefore, the figures quoted in the following discussion must represent minima.

[2] The JTEC panel's best guess of the number of fielded systems in Japan is somewhere between 1,000 and 2,000 (including PC-based applications), depending on assumptions about non-respondents to the *Nikkei AI* surveys.

The percentage of ES applications in the planning and design areas is declining, although the absolute number of systems in these areas is increasing because the total number of systems is increasing at a faster rate.   Figure 2.2 shows that diagnosis still represents the largest class of applications, although planning (including scheduling) is growing rapidly in importance.   Design and control applications are also high enough in numbers to be accorded mention as separate categories.   Three examples from our own review of Japanese ESs in scheduling, design and control (all of which have had a high impact on the organizations that use them) are discussed in the next section.   Based on our knowledge of activity in the United States, we would expect a similar mix of U.S. application types.

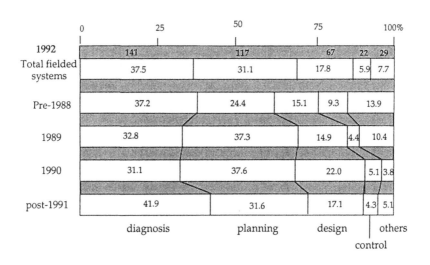

Figure 2.2. Types of ES Applications (Source: Nikkei AI 1992)

The *Nikkei AI* survey also looked at ES development from the point of view of organizational structure, i.e., who actually builds the systems. Here we see some contrast with the situation in the United States. In Japan, most ESs are built by an organization's MIS group or by its R&D division. Relatively few expert systems are contracted out to external companies. In the U.S., we suspect that a much larger percentage of ESs are built by the numerous companies that specialize in building custom systems (again, no U.S. domestic survey has actually been done).   The larger Japanese companies appear to have a tighter coupling among their R&D, product development and operations divisions, so that internal development and deployment of new technology is more easily achieved.

Comparing the results shown in Figure 2.3 with previous years, the *Nikkei AI* article comments that there has been an increase in the information systems division as ES builders. There has also been an increase in outsourcing, and a decrease in the laboratories as ES builders. *Nikkei AI's* editors observe that the category of end users developing their own systems is still small, but is expected to increase as the use of domain-specific tools increases. They also see the movement of application development from the laboratories to the information systems divisions as an indication that ES technology is now in the mainstream.

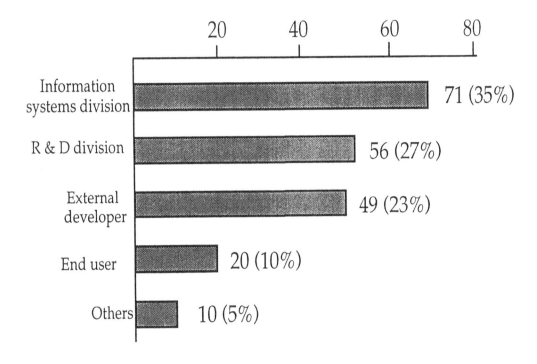

Figure 2.3. Locus of Development of ESs
(Source: Nikkei AI 1991)

Some other general conclusions from the *Nikkei AI* survey, for which we found support in our own visits, include:

o   a growing interest and involvement in related technologies, e.g., fuzzy logic, neural networks, object-oriented databases;

o   a steady move away from specialized computers (e.g., LISP machines) toward UNIX-based workstations;

o   a recognition of the value of KB systems in improving individual decision
        making, working procedures, and timeliness;

o   a recognition, by some companies, of operational problems such as
        obsolescence, maintenance and completeness of the KB. (One would expect
        similar problems with database systems.)

CASE STUDIES OF HIGH-IMPACT SYSTEMS

The impact of a new technology like KB systems can be measured both by the depth
and the breadth of its impact. Later in this chapter we discuss the breadth of KB
systems applications that we observed in Japan. This section provides insight into
the depth of KB systems impact by describing three examples of systems which
appear to have made significant changes in the way in which organizations conduct
their daily business. In all cases, KB technology was used to augment and replace
traditional computational technology for reasons of speed, reliability, and quality of
solutions.

Case 1: Modular House Configuration (Sekisui Heim)

The Company. Sekisui Heim is a housing division of Sekisui Chemical Company.
Begun in 1947, Sekisui Chemical was the first to develop plastic molds in Japan. Its
current annual revenue base is $1.35 billion, 50 percent of which comes from Sekisui
Heim.

In 1971, Sekisui Chemical created the Heim division to build modular houses. Unlike
prefabricated houses, modular houses are semi-custom houses designed and
constructed out of modules. Sekisui Heim promises to have a house ready for
occupancy in two months from the time a customer signs a contract with a design
on hand. Of the two months, 40 days are allocated for on-site work -- from ground
breaking to completion -- with a five-man crew. More than 80 percent of the house
is built in a factory. Sekisui has six highly automated factories, each of which can
complete enough components for a house every 40 minutes. The six factories are
distributed throughout Japan to meet the special needs of the respective regions.
Sekisui Heim, currently the fourth largest house builder in Japan, builds about 20,000
houses per year.

The Problem. A class of houses is designed by the Sekisui architects. Instances of
the house can be constructed out of modules called *units.* The units come in six
sizes (1.2 m and 2.4 m widths, and 3.6 m, 4.5 m, and 5.4 m lengths) that are designed
to be transportable on trucks.   The units can be subdivided into smaller
compartments, placed side by side to form a larger compartment, or stacked to form
multiple stories.

Within the constraints imposed for a particular house class (e.g., a particular roof design may be required for a particular class), the customer can design a house to suit his or her desires and needs. A room can be of any size as long as it can be configured from the units; the exterior walls can be made from a variety of different materials such as stucco, hardwood, and cement; the openings between rooms can be of many different sizes; and so on.

The most popular class of houses is called Parfait, of which more than 45,000 units have been sold. It is a contemporary looking two-story house with a flat roof. For a house with a floor space of 1600 square feet, the average cost is about $69,000 -- a unit cost of less than $45/sq. ft.

After the house has been designed, all the necessary parts must be identified and delivered to the factory floor in a timely manner. An average house requires about 5000 unique parts. Sekisui has 300,000 different parts in stock. Prior to the installation of an expert system (to be described in the next section), every time a new house design was introduced, there was an error rate in parts selection of about 30 percent for the first six months. As time went on the error rate decreased to about 5 percent. The high initial error rate made the introduction of new products highly problematic, and the steady-state error rate of 5 percent cut into profits. Some kind of computer-based help was needed to make Heim a viable business.

In 1984 Sekisui heard about expert systems and made a strategic decision to invest in the technology. Since the company was not familiar with the technology, it bought a 70 percent share in a small start-up company, named ISAC (International Sekisui AI Corporation). ISAC was started by the developer of a PROLOG language called K-PROLOG, currently the best-selling PROLOG in Japan. ISAC does about 40 percent of its business with Sekisui, building applications for both for the housing division and for other parts of Sekisui Chemical.

Sekisui Heim formulated a long-range plan for the development of computer programs for its business. Three kinds of capabilities were envisioned which were to be integrated into a tool kit to help with the complete process from design to production of modular houses:

1)   An intelligent CAD tool to help with the development of new designs

2)   A room layout consultant and other consultation systems to help in sales

3)   Production control and other expert systems to help with the actual manufacture of units

The first expert system to be put in routine use, HAPPS, identifies and selects the necessary parts for a given house design and schedules the delivery of the parts to the right place on the factory floor at the right time.   Sekisui Heim has also developed an expert system for sales personnel to help customers with room layouts, but it is experiencing limited acceptance by the sales force.

The HAPPS System. HAPPS is an expert system that selects and schedules the delivery to the factory floor of the correct parts for steel frame houses. There are two other versions for wood frame and high-rise houses, called TAPPS and MAPPS.

Once the house design is finalized by the customer, it is passed on to the factory. There, various types of information about the house are entered into the system. The interface uses a number of menu-driven windows that display the 'legal' options available for different parts of the house. Figure 2.4 shows the different options for stairs. The display shows the layout of the rooms and available options as icons, making the specification easy and clear.

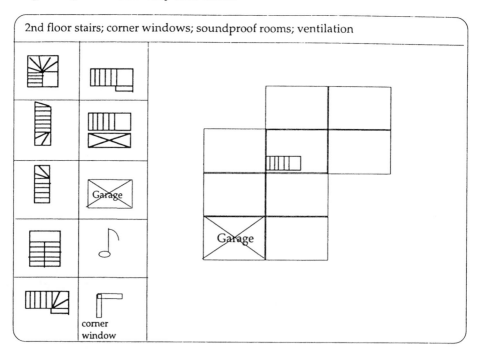

Figure 2.4. User Interface For Selecting Some Design Options

The necessary information for parts selection is gathered in the following order:

1)   House class name, house name, name code, address, etc.
2)   Sizes of the various units and their arrangements
3)   Eaves for first and second floor: type and color, position of gutter pipes

4) Entry way and stairs: the shape and location of the entry way, the shape and position of the stairways, step-down location, if any; type of windows, rooms to be soundproofed, etc.
5) Interface between units (such as doorways) and corridors
6) Other information, such as the order in which the units are to be manufactured

The input information basically describes the compositional relationships among the rooms composed of modules. For example, "an object of type x is located in unit y on floor z." From the specifications of the final product, HAPPS must determine all the parts needed to create the product. This process is called *parts explosion.*

In order to do the parts explosion, rules of the form, "If parts x and y are joined using z method, then use part s," are applied to all the objects specified in the design. The rule base is searched using K-PROLOG's pattern match and backtracking facilities.

The heart of the parts explosion process is the object hierarchy describing the parts and their interrelationships. Figure 2.5 shows the major classes and their position in the class hierarchy. Table 2.1 explains the individual classes.

HAPPS was developed on the Sun workstation. The compiled production version is downloaded and runs on the Hitachi Engineering Workstation 2050.

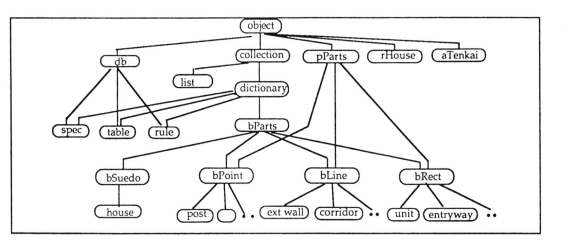

Figure 2.5. Parts Class Structure in HAPPS

Table 2.1
Explanation of the Classes

object	belongs to systems class; contains basic methods for all the classes
collection	belongs to systems class; contains basic methods for the collective class
dictionary	belongs to systems class; dictionary type collective class
list	belongs to systems class; list type collective class
db	attribute determination and rules used during the arrangement expressed as data
spec	output code for each part expressed as data and stored as instances
table	rules to determine attributes of parts in table form stored as instances
rule	rules to determine attributes of parts in IF-THEN rule form stored as instances
bParts	form of data used for each part (dictionary); method (links between parts and attribute management)
bSeudo	class of potential parts, hold the basic house information which are referenced during attribute determination
bPoint	class of parts that are represented as a dot on diagrams. Contains methods for creating deleting, locating the parts.
bLine	class of parts that are represented as a line on diagrams. Contains methods for creating, deleting, locating the parts.
bRec	class of parts that are represented as planes on diagrams. Contains methods for creating, deleting, locating the parts.
pParts	contains methods for debugging; used mostly during parts explosion.
rHouse	data base that manages the position of each part in order to find the positional relationship between the parts quickly
aTenkai	agenda used to control parts explosion

HAPPS was originally developed using K-PROLOG. However, the maintenance (including additions and modifications of rules and data) of the PROLOG system became a real problem when new product introduction increased to four times per year. To overcome this problem ISAC developed an object-oriented PROLOG called MethodLog, and HAPPS has been implemented in this language. In object-oriented systems, the data description and the procedures associated with the data are encapsulated into entities called *objects.* The proximity of all the relevant information about a piece of data facilitates maintenance.

The size of HAPPS is about 14,000 lines of PROLOG and 6,000 lines of C code (used primarily for writing the interface and data base access functions). It took a team consisting of four domain experts, two knowledge engineers, and 14 programmers two years to develop HAPPS.

The Payoff. The decision to build HAPPS, TAPPS, and MAPPS was a strategic decision for Sekisui Heim. It enabled the company to put itself in a profit-making position and to expand its product lines. The expert systems reduce the cost of making modular houses, improve the quality of products and services, and reduce the error rate. The steady-state five percent error in parts selection has been reduced to near zero.

The three systems cost approximately ¥450 million ($3.5 million at approximately ¥128/$) to build. The cost figure was calculated using the following formula: ¥1.5 million x manpower x months. Sekisui claims that the savings has been ¥1 billion ($8 million) annually.

Case 2: Aircraft Crew Scheduling (JAL)

The Company. Our next example comes from Japan Airlines (JAL), Japan's official international airline, which developed a KB system for crew scheduling (Onodera and Mori 1991). JAL maintains a fleet of over 100 wide-body aircraft: Boeing 747, 747-400, 767, and McDonnell-Douglas DC-10. They have a staff of about 2200 flight crew members (pilots, co-pilots, and flight engineers). The airline must produce a monthly crew allocation schedule taking into account a wide variety of constraints. These include crew training (for aircraft and route qualification), restrictions on maximum number of takeoffs and landings, vacation and meeting needs, crew turnaround times at various destinations, and many other needs and preferences. The schedule for a given month needs to be produced by the 25th of the preceding month to give adequate warning to crew and maintenance personnel.

The Problem. Before the development of the KB scheduling system, called COSMOS/AI, about 25 human schedulers were involved in solving the crew allocation problem. The hardest schedule (for JAL 747s) took 20 days to prepare (with a great deal of overtime). Moreover, the schedulers needed about a year to become expert in the problem. A related, very important issue was maintenance of scheduling knowledge, that is, updating information on planes, crews, government regulations, etc. In the summer of 1986, JAL decided to investigate various automated approaches for improving its solution to the crew scheduling problem. The airline developed two automated approaches to the problem, one a traditional operations research-based scheduling system (in cooperation with Hitachi), and the other a knowledge-based systems approach (with NEC).

The System. Testing of both systems began in the summer of 1988. The KB system was easily the system of choice for two major reasons: first, it produced better schedules because it was far better able to represent complex, yet informal constraints on crew preferences and other related factors. Second, it was much easier to maintain.

Technically, the JAL scheduling system uses straightforward heuristic scheduling methods. It builds crew pattern blocks that include pre-flight rest time, flight time, mandatory time at the destination, and a return flight. These blocks are then placed on the flight schedule, along with other time allocations like crew testing, vacations, and training, in order of most-constrained allocations first. When a problem occurs, time allocations are shuffled, moving the least constrained blocks first. The most complicated problems (the 747s) take two to three hours for a single scheduling run. Constraining factors which must be considered in producing the schedule are shown in Figure 2.6. The human experts still make final adjustments to the schedule.

The Payoff. The KB system became fully operational in February, 1990. It has reduced the number of human schedulers from 25 to 19 in a time when JAL operations increased by five to ten percent. Moreover, these 19 schedulers are now also assisting in other crew management tasks, reducing the actual scheduling manpower effectively to the equivalent of 14. The aforementioned 747 schedule now takes a maximum of 15 days to produce, with no overtime required, compared with 20 or more days, including overtime, to do the job previously. Training time has been reduced to two months. Overall, scheduling productivity has approximately doubled.

Two nice features of the JAL system are an excellent human interface and full integration with a mainframe-based corporate database that provides constant updates to the KB system. An example of the system's clear output, showing allocation of crew members over a 30-day period, is shown in Figure 2.7. The scheduling system itself is distributed among workstations specialized to the different aircraft types, although the workstations themselves share information on crews trained on multiple aircraft types. The system cost about ¥500 million ($3.9 million at ¥128/$) to build and paid for itself in direct cost savings in about 18 months. JAL views the harder-to-measure savings in increased crew satisfaction and ease of maintenance as equally important.

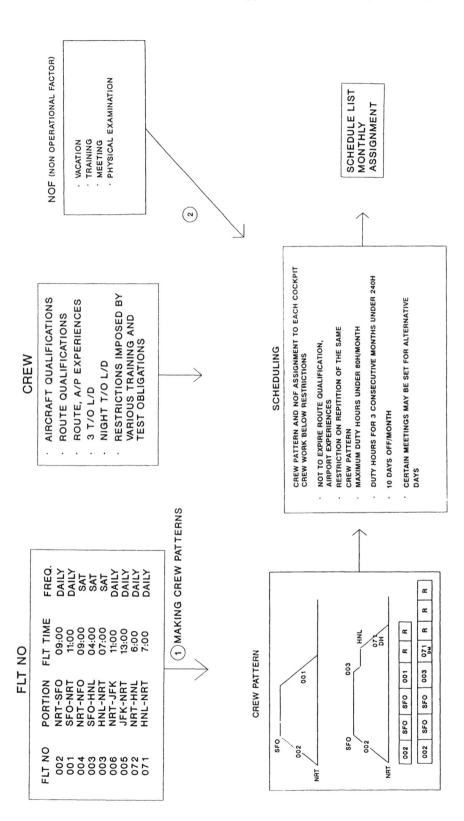

Figure 2.6. Sources of Knowledge and Constraints Used for JAL Crew Scheduling

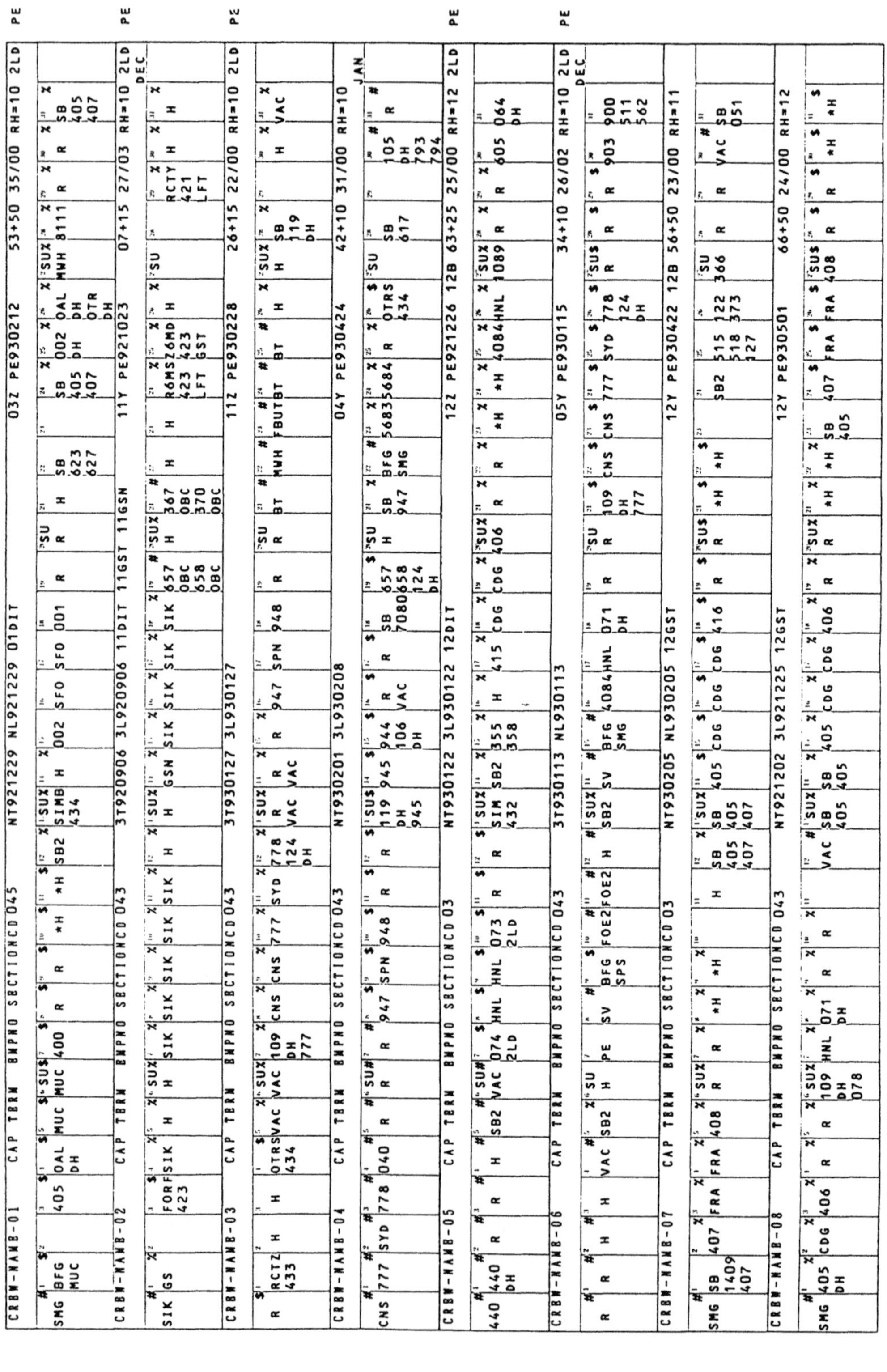

Figure 2.7.   Example of Output, Showing Crew Assignments For Each Day of the Month.

Case 3: Blast Furnace Control (NKK)

The Company. As early as 1986, NKK Steel Company's Fukuyama Works developed an expert system to predict abnormal conditions within its blast furnace. A blast furnace is a complex, distributed, non-linear process. Conventional mathematical modeling techniques have never been able to predict future dynamic states of the furnace with enough accuracy to support automated control. The system became operational in 1987. NKK and other Japanese steel companies have since developed other knowledge-based blast furnace control systems.

The Problem. Because the blast furnace feeds all other processes in the steel mill, any instability in the operation of the furnace is compounded by the impact on other processes further down the production line. Avoiding unstable operation of the furnace requires characterizing the current state of the furnace and projecting the conditions which will occur over the next several hours while there is still time to make adjustments.   Training a skilled blast furnace operator takes many years. Fewer young people want this type of career. Codifying the skill of experienced furnace operators reduces the training requirements.

Several factors contribute to the complexity of modeling a blast furnace. Material within it coexists in all three phases -- solid, liquid and gas. The large size of the furnace leads to long lag times (six to eight hours) before a change in raw-material charging takes effect. The device is inherently three-dimensional — there are no symmetries to simplify the geometric modeling. Moreover, the flow of material inside the furnace is itself a complex process. The thermal state of the furnace cannot be measured directly, but must be inferred from various sensor measurements.   The challenge for the furnace controller is to minimize the uncertainty in the operating temperature. The smaller the uncertainty, the lower the overall temperature needed to produce the pig iron (see Fig. 2.8), resulting in very large fuel savings.

The System. An expert system has been developed which successfully models the current state, predicts future trends with sufficient accuracy to make control decisions, and actually makes the control decisions.   These decisions can be implemented automatically or the operator can take manual control while still operating through the expert system's interfaces.

The system as a whole consists of three components: (1) a process computer gathers input data from various sensors in the furnace, maintains a process database and generates furnace control information; (2) the "AI processor" provides the knowledge and reasoning for assessing and interpreting the sensor data, hypothesizing the internal state of the furnace, and determining appropriate control actions; and (3) a distributed digital controller uses the furnace control data from the process computer to control the actual blast furnace. A schematic of the system is shown in Figure 2.9. The system is implemented in LISP with FORTRAN used for data preprocessing. The knowledge in the AI processor is contained in 400 rules, 350 frames, and 200 LISP procedures; fuzzy theory is employed in its inference engine. The FORTRAN preprocessor contains 20,000 procedural steps. The system has a cycle time of 20 minutes, compared to the furnace time constant of six to eight hours. Fuzzy set membership is used to relate the temperatures inferred from the instruments to actual temperatures. The membership functions are revised from time to time to tune the performance of the system.

At any time, the operator can select either manual mode or automatic mode. The system continues to make inferences about the state of the furnace even in manual mode. Thus, the operator may manually change a set-point and the system will evaluate the influence of that action and make further inferences.

The Payoff. The blast furnace control application is noteworthy for many reasons. The problem had not been solved previously by other techniques. It was developed by systems engineers, not knowledge engineers. It is in daily operation now at two plants and will soon be installed in two more. The company reports an estimated annual savings of $6 million, a reduction in staff of four people, and an improvement in the quality of the furnace output because of reduced fluctuations in furnace temperature.

The benefits of the expert system, however, have not been separately established. It is considered an integral part of a new furnace control system that was installed the last time the blast furnace was shut down for relining. The JTEC team found that this was a common characteristic of expert systems used as closed loop controllers, viz. benefits are not traced to the component level. This suggests that expert systems have taken their place among the suite of techniques available to the controls engineer and do not require the special attention sometimes afforded new technologies.

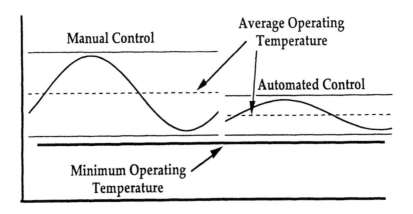

Figure 2.8. Fuel Cost Savings

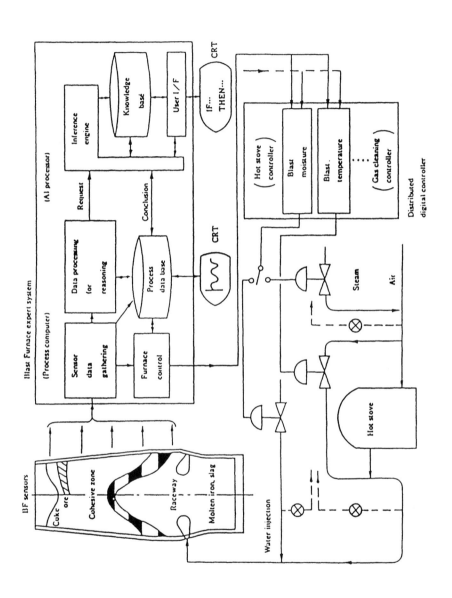

Figure 2.9. Blast Furnace Expert System

TYPES OF APPLICATIONS

As in the United States, applications of KB systems in Japan have evolved from mainly stand-alone systems for diagnostics to a wide variety of problem-solving domains. At the companies the JTEC team visited, we saw or were given evidence of many hundreds of diverse applications. With a few miscellaneous exceptions, all of these systems fall into one of the seven classes listed in Chapter 1.

The remainder of this section will discuss techniques employed for some of these classes of application and give a flavor for their prominence and diversity in Japan.

Diagnosis and Troubleshooting

Definition. Diagnostic systems comprise a broad range of applications that deduce faults and suggest corrective actions for a malfunctioning system or process. Numerous examples can be found in physical (electronic, mechanical, hydraulic, etc.) and biological domains, as well as in abstract domains such as organizations and software.

The functions of a diagnostic system typically include:

o   Collection of measurement data from instruments and/or the user
o   Characterization of the state of the system
o   If the system is in an abnormal state, an attempt to classify the problem
o   Use of a shallow knowledge, heuristic or statistical process to attempt to classify the problem
o   Use of a deep knowledge, casual or first principles model to predict which failures could cause observed symptoms
o   Suggested confirmation of tests or measurements
o   Refinement of diagnosis using the additional information
o   Presentation of diagnosis to human operator and, if desired, explanation of the line of reasoning
o   Suggested corrective or reparative actions
o   Receipt of confirming or corrective feedback and refinement of knowledge base for future use (learning)
o   Report of erroneous diagnoses or prescriptions to the knowledge base maintainer for manual corrections

Most diagnostic systems automate only a subset of these functions, leaving the other functions to humans or other types of information systems. It is common, for example, for a process control computer to capture measurement data over time and reduce these raw data to metrics. These metrics are then used by that part of the diagnostic system that is implemented with knowledge processing techniques. The capability of learning from past experience is rarely found.

Diagnostic systems or classification systems made up a high proportion of the earliest knowledge systems. While the emphasis has now shifted toward planning and scheduling systems which often produce greater benefits, diagnostic systems still comprise 35-40 percent of the total number of fielded systems (Nikkei AI 1992). It is likely that diagnostic systems will continue to represent a substantial proportion of knowledge system applications because tool vendors have produced a number of task-specific shells for diagnostic applications. This will make the development task easier and will broaden the base of people capable of developing diagnostic applications.

Applications. Electromechanical systems are probably the most common domain of diagnostic applications.   The JTEC team learned about major applications in electrical distribution system fault isolation, nuclear power plant diagnosis, telephone cross bar switch diagnosis and subway air conditioning diagnosis. Each of these are large systems with substantial benefits. One application at Nippon Steel handles 500 different kinds of electromechanical equipment comprising 25,000 component types (Minami and Hirata 1991).

Japanese steel producers have developed a number of diagnostic expert systems. One important application is the determination of the current state and trends in blast furnaces (see Case 3 earlier in this chapter). While not a complete diagnostic system, the characterization of "state" is the first step in a diagnostic system.

Several applications in the domain of computer systems were mentioned by the Japanese computer manufacturers. These included determining the best means to recover from system failures, and offering advice on software debugging.

In construction, determining the cause of concrete cracking has been automated (Obayashi Corp.). Applications in medical diagnosis and finance were mentioned, but not detailed.

The benefits from diagnostic applications include reduced down time, safe recovery from failures, and accumulation or preservation of knowledge. In the latter case, it was specifically mentioned that the more educated young Japanese do not want to make their careers in certain operational jobs. Capturing knowledge of experienced workers today is essential to future operations using less educated labor. In one case, "the cross bar switch diagnostician," the application avoids the necessity of training replacement personnel for this obsolete equipment.

A number of task-specific shells have been developed for diagnostic applications. These are identified and described in Chapter 3. Research and development in support of diagnostic tasks has resulted in the many task-specific shells reported in that chapter. This work is continuing with emphasis on new forms of diagnostic reasoning.

One particularly interesting research effort is a Toshiba project to diagnose unanticipated faults. A conventional heuristic expert system receives data about the system and diagnoses anticipated faults in a conventional way (using shallow knowledge that directly associates symptoms with likely faults). When it is unable to identify the problem, the knowledge system defers to a model-based reasoning subsystem which attempts to reason from first principles. That subsystem in turn utilizes a qualitative, fuzzy simulator to try out hypotheses and further reason from the simulated results.

Planning and Scheduling

A strong emphasis on this class of systems was apparent at many of the sites we visited. Using corporate estimates, somewhere between 30-50 percent of fielded KB systems in Japan focus on planning or scheduling, with a significant recent trend toward more applications. This may be because such systems are used routinely -- factory and airline schedules are created every day, week, or month -- and success is relatively easy to measure in terms of better schedules (the work-in-progress time or resources used to accomplish some tasks is less) or quicker production of schedules. Examples include:

o   Crew scheduling time at JAL was reduced from 20 to 15 days
o   Scheduling time for a Toshiba paper mill was reduced from three days to two hours
o   A Fujitsu printed circuit board assembly and test planner reduced the scheduling task by a man-year each calendar year
o   For an unspecified Hitachi task, scheduling was reduced from 17 hours to a few minutes

All of the systems we were able to examine in detail used straightforward heuristic scheduling methods. As in the JAL application described above, constraints were described in some formal manner and used to guide an initial placement of tasks, with the most constrained tasks usually scheduled first. Then a variety of straightforward backtracking methods (sometimes called schedule shuffling) were used until a complete and correct schedule was found. In most cases, a complete and correct schedule was good enough; there was little emphasis on optimization of schedules.

While several sites mentioned a need for reactive re-scheduling methods, we did not observe a currently operational system with those capabilities. However, the elevator-group control system described below may be considered an example of a highly reactive scheduling system. Within the United States, iterative improvement methods like simulated annealing are now being used to effectuate "anytime" re-scheduling. These methods very quickly produce a complete, but possibly poor, schedule, and improve the schedule until available time runs out, always maintaining a correct schedule when interrupted.

Configuration of Manufactured Objects from Subassemblies

The JTEC team saw very little application of ESs to configuration-type problems such as those that occur in design or manufacturing. The most prominent examples were the systems developed at Sekisui Heim for modular housing, discussed above, and a system developed at NTT for design of private telecommunication networks. Fujitsu is planning expert systems for computer integrated manufacturing (CIM), but did not elaborate. NEC has investigated rule-based and algorithmic approaches to LSI design and developed EXLOG, a system for synthesizing customized LSI circuits and gate arrays (Iwamoto, Fujita et al. 1991).

Process Monitoring and Control

The most significant example of a knowledge-based system for control was the one installed in 1987 at the NKK blast furnace, as described above. Since that time the steel and construction industries in Japan have been very active in developing knowledge-based control systems. These systems are characterized by their high degree of integration with conventional information processing systems and the widespread use of fuzzy control methods.

A second excellent example of a control system is one developed by Mitsubishi Electric for controlling a group of elevators. The AI-2100 Elevator-Group Control System, as it is called, uses a fuzzy rule base, divided into off-line and on-line types. Off-line rules are used as a sort of default set, independent of hall calls (i.e., the signals generated when passengers waiting in the halls push the up or down buttons). Off-line rules, for example, determine the number of elevators that should be near the ground floor, near the top, or near the middle of the building, depending on the time of day. On-line rules are invoked in response to hall calls, and aim to prevent bunching of cars in the same locations, thereby minimizing the average waiting time for passengers. Results of an extended simulation of a group of four elevators servicing a 15-story building revealed that the average waiting time was reduced by about 15 percent over a conventional elevator control system. The percentage of waits over 60 seconds dropped by almost a factor of two (Ujihara and Tsuji 1988). Since the degree of irritation felt by waiting passengers increases nonlinearly with waiting time, the reduction in psychological waiting time is quite significant. An optional feature of the system is a learning function, which allows the control system to adapt to changing traffic patterns and predict future conditions.

Examples from the construction industry of process monitoring and control KBSs are Obayashi Corporation's systems for automatic direction control of a shield tunneling machine and the swing cable control system (see site reports in Appendix E for more details).

Software Engineering

Applications of knowledge-based techniques to software engineering were one of the areas this JTEC panel was asked to cover. Improving the process of developing software is potentially one of the most highly leveraged applications for new technology.

Several Japanese companies indicated that 5-10 percent of their applications were in the development, testing or management of software. However, the panel's site visits were not structured to explore software engineering applications in any depth. We did not visit any software factories and we saw only three brief demonstrations of software-related applications. This in itself is an interesting outcome since several of the industrial research laboratories we visited had titles such as Software Engineering Research. Most research in those laboratories is focused upon new forms of software, as opposed to the use of knowledge-based techniques to support the development of conventional procedural software.

Applications. The examples the JTEC team saw included the generation of procedural programs from a state/event matrix and from a problem model. Both of these applications utilize transformation technology to transform a declarative specification into procedural code. Both operate at the individual program level, rather than the system level. With respect to the state of the art in the United States, there is nothing novel in either of these applications.

Another example was NEC's application of case-based reasoning to the retrieval of software quality improvement ideas. The case base has been developed over many years, which in itself is a unique contribution. Historically, the case base, which is company confidential, has been published in a book that is updated annually. However, the book has now become too large to be effective and an electronic case library has been established. The library indexes 130 attributes, and there are some clever techniques to minimize the number of index items which the user confronts. The JTEC team did not view this application as a convincing example of case-based reasoning, as there was no repair logic in the application. However, the main goal of the project was reformulation of the corporate knowledge to permit effective machine access, and the goal appears to have been successfully achieved.

At the University of Tokyo, Professor Ohsuga mentioned the possibility that knowledge-processing technology can be used to support conversion of declarative programs to procedural programs. The actual example we saw was the very small-scale program generator mentioned above.

Comparative Assessment with the U.S. None of the applications this JTEC team saw or heard about represent innovations beyond U.S. applications. The use of knowledge-based techniques for supporting the development of conventional software does not appear to be a priority task in the companies we visited.

COMPANY-SPECIFIC APPLICATIONS

This section is a survey of some of the applications that were described to the panel, either by oral presentation or in answers to our questionnaire. Most of this material is abstracted from the site visit reports in Appendix E. The companies that we visited that are not listed below, namely Japan Air Lines and Sekisui Chemical, basically had one major application each, and that application has already been discussed.

Fujitsu

Fujitsu Laboratories reports that it has built about 240 systems for internal use. The company also has knowledge of about 250 systems built by its customers, but cannot categorize any of them in terms of operationality. Fujitsu estimates that about 20 percent of the projects started get as far as a complete prototype, and of those, 20 percent get to an operational system status. A best overall guess is that five percent of the reported systems are in routine use. The current success rate in fielding expert systems is better than five percent. Because of the experience base it now has, Fujitsu is better able to select problems which are solvable by this technology, and the success rate is now somewhere between 75 and 95 percent.

Planning/Scheduling. The largest percentage of systems developed for internal use are for planning or scheduling. The most successful is PSS, a production support system for planning assembly and test of printed circuit boards. The application is relatively small, built on ESHELL, and runs on a mainframe. The system, which is in daily use, saves about one person-year per year by speeding up the planning time. A workstation version is under development.

Fujitsu stresses integration of KBS and conventional systems. It now has ES tools written in COBOL (YPS/KR) and in FORTRAN (FORTRAN/KR), to support such integration (see Chapter 3).

At Fujitsu, 60-75 percent of the development cost of a system goes into the graphic user interface (GUI). Better GUIs are needed. That need has stimulated work on a GUI called GUIDEPOWER.

In addition to the need for better GUIs, Fujitsu also pointed to other problems with the existing technology. Knowledge changes rapidly in the real world (e.g., in banking), and hence the maintenance of the KB is too costly using existing techniques. A more automated means of knowledge acquisition/revision is needed. Another problem is the relative paucity of development tools, such as for testing a system. Our Fujitsu hosts expressed the view that the ES and CASE worlds are not well matched -- in general, expert systems are best suited to ill-structured problems, whereas CASE tools are better suited to well-structured problems.

Finally, Fujitsu worked with NKK on the blast furnace system described earlier. It is one of the largest applications with which Fujitsu has been associated.

Hitachi

Hitachi has developed 500 to 600 systems for customers. It has sold on the order of 4,000 copies of its ES/KERNEL Systems, half of that number in the last two years, to approximately 1,000 customers. About 50 systems each are in field test mode, are completed prototypes, or are under development.

Construction. One of Hitachi's most successful applications is a tunnel construction planning system, developed for Okamura Corp. (Harada, Igarashi et al. 1990). Use of this ES has cut planning time in half, reduced variations in the plans due to personal factors, facilitated the preparation of alternative plans, and given inexperienced engineers the capability to draft detailed construction plans. The system (which combines KBS, relational databases, CAD and a reporting system) has been used on at least 20 projects to date.

Process Scheduling. Another highly successful system is for process scheduling in chemical plants. Use of the system has resulted in reducing the costs of raw materials and labor by billions of yen annually.

Initially, most of Hitachi's business applications were in banking and financial diagnostic systems, but more recently, industrial clients have requested scheduling systems. The largest application market now is in the insurance industry. Within the domain of planning and scheduling, job shop scheduling is the biggest market, accounting for 40-50 percent of the business, followed by process scheduling. Planning and scheduling applications got started three years ago. A Hitachi engineer worked with a customer to figure out how to do a planning application on ES/KERNEL after the customer had failed using a competitor's shell. Initially, the scheduling job took 17 hours, but eventually was reduced to five minutes of workstation time. The system has saved ¥7 billion. Hitachi is familiar enough with scheduling problems to divide them into four classes, each with its own solution technique. Until now, Hitachi has done most of the planning applications for customers, but is beginning to introduce courses so that customers can learn to do this task themselves.

Toshiba

Approximately 500 expert systems have been developed at Toshiba for both internal and external use, with about 10 percent in routine use. Design and planning/scheduling are the major growth application areas. Within design, the principal tasks are LSI and PCB design.

Paper Production. The most successful expert system is a paper production scheduling system for the Tomakomai mill of Ohji Paper Co., Ltd. The system uses 25 kinds of pulp, which are combined in 10 papermaking machines to produce 200 different paper products. There are hundreds of constraints to be satisfied. The system employs a top-down hierarchical scheduling strategy, starting with scheduling product groups, then individual products, and then line balancing. This application has reduced the time required to produce a monthly schedule from three days to two hours.

Microwave Circuit Design. Toshiba also reported data on a microwave circuit design system, called FIRE, built with an internally developed tool called Debut. FIRE captures the design process for highly parametric design problems. The system runs on a workstation, is C-based, and interfaces with microwave circuit simulators and a mechanical CAD system. The primary benefits of the system are speed-up of problem solving and accumulation of design knowledge.

A fault diagnosis system developed for Kyushu Electric Company is representative, and is in routine use by Kyushu operators. The system diagnoses faults and restores operation to an electric power system. The fault diagnosis system has 900 rules; the fault restoration system has 600 rules. The system was built using TDES-3, a real-time application shell that uses rules and frames for knowledge representation. The development team consisted mostly of Toshiba personnel, with domain experts supplied by Kyushu.

Toshiba also reported on a diagnostic system for a subway station facility, called SMART-7, which was built for the Tokyo Eidan 7th line. The system was built with a diagnostic knowledge acquisition support tool called DiKAST. SMART-7 is implemented as a support module that detects malfunctions in the air conditioning facilities. The system contains 1600 frames, and runs on a workstation. It was built by three system engineers in three months.

Electric Subassembly. Another expert system is used for placing electronic components on printed circuit boards. The knowledge base consists of about 70 rules and 8500 functions, and was built on top of the ASIREX tool. The ES is integrated with a PCB CAD tool called BoardMATE, a commercial product developed by Toshiba. The system took three years to develop, with an estimated labor cost of three man-years. The system has sped up problem solving by a factor of 10.

DSS. A small knowledge system (110 rules, 32K lines of C code) that Toshiba sells is MARKETS-I, a decision support system to determine the suitability of opening a convenience store at a particular site. Estimation accuracy is improved with the use of this system.

Banking. ESCORT is a banking operations advisor system that is used in Mitsui Bank. It plans the most appropriate procedure to get the computer banking system back on line following an accident. The system has about 250 rules and 900 frames, and was built using a LISP-based expert system shell called ExPearls. The GUI was written in C. The system runs on the AS3000 workstation.

Software Engineering. In the area of software engineering, Toshiba has developed an automatic programming system for sequence control. This system generates a control program for a steel plant from high-level specifications. It analyzes and refines the specification, generates code, and retrieves program modules. This is a fairly large system: 2,900 frames, 320 rules, and a library of 190 program modules. It was written in LISP, using an internally developed frame-based knowledge representation language with object oriented facilities. Twenty person-years went into its development, over a four-year span. The system has resulted in cost reduction and an improvement in the quality of the sequence control program designs. Test and verification are performed manually.

Reasoning Methodologies. One of the most advanced applications that was described to JTEC combines model-based and heuristic reasoning. The system is used for control of a manufacturing or processing plant (Suzuki, Sueda et al. 1990). The shallow reasoner uses knowledge in the form of a heuristic control sequence (see Fig. 2.10). When unforeseen events occur, for which the shallow knowledge is inadequate, the system can resort to deep knowledge, in the form of a model of the plant, to reason about an appropriate control sequence. The deep knowledge includes the structure of the plant, the function of the plant devices, causal relations among plant components and principles of operation. The system combines several advanced technologies: model-based reasoning, knowledge compilation, and qualitative reasoning.

The following approach is used: If the shallow knowledge is insufficient, go to the deep model. In the deep model, (1) use the causal model to deduce the abnormality; (2) find the operations that would bring the plant to a desired state; (3) find the conditions under which an operation should be performed; (4) simulate to test the hypotheses (the simulator uses qualitative reasoning and fuzzy control techniques). The knowledge estimator checks to see if the simulation indicates any unforeseen side effects. If the answer is yes, then the system determines what supplementary operations should be performed.   If the simulation result is satisfactory, the knowledge is stored in rule form for future use.   This process is called knowledge compilation.

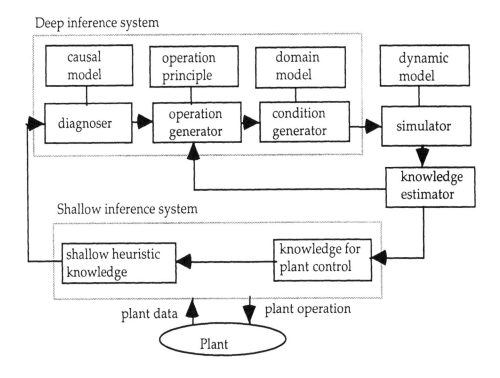

Figure 2.10. A Plant Control System Using Deep and Shallow Knowledge

The techniques of model-based reasoning and knowledge compilation have also been employed in an innovative system, called CAD-PC/AI, for automatically generating sequence control programs for programmable controllers. (For further details see Mizutani, Nakayama et al. 1992).

Assessment. Toshiba systems do not now use multiple sources of expertise, but they are trying to do so in their newer systems.   Many ESs are implemented with a combination of a shell/tool plus a programming language such as C or LISP.   The company has several training courses, ranging from a one-day basic course, to a two- to three-week application development course, to a multi-week advanced topics course.   About 10 percent of research funds go into training.   An important element of Toshiba methodology is to use task-specific shells, such as PROKAST or DiKAST.

ESs selected for implementation are chosen by a systems engineer or researcher. This technology is used only when conventional DP doesn't work. The prespecified selection criteria are performance and practical value. An economic justification is also sought. Usually the same people are used in all phases of application selection, development, insertion into the operational activity, maintenance and redesign.

Toshiba's largest project to date is a 5,000 rule system for diagnosis and control of an electrical power generator.

NEC

NEC has developed about 1,000 ES applications, of which 10 percent are in routine operation. The major task areas are diagnosis, scheduling, design, and software development aids. NEC's biggest success is the crew scheduling system, COSMOS/AI, developed with Japan Air Lines, discussed previously. Other applications include a software debugging advisor; FUSION, an LSI logic design tool; and a system called SOFTEX for synthesizing C/C++ programs from specifications (represented as state transition tables and/or flowcharts). SOFTEX is a 300-rule system built with EXCORE (see Chapter 3), developed by professional programmers and domain experts. The system is still about six months to one year from routine use. In order to make the system appeal to programmers, it has been necessary to incorporate in SOFTEX the functionality to enable customization, so that the generated program can fit each programmer's style.

Assessment. NEC admits to some unsuccessful projects, and attributes the lack of success to a number of reasons, including the knowledge acquisition bottleneck, the difficulty of integration with existing systems, and knowledge base maintenance. Unfortunately, these problems tended to get detected late rather than early.

Future ES applications at NEC are expected to employ technologies such as model-based diagnosis, case-based reasoning for scheduling and for software synthesis, and combining ES methods with algorithmic methods (model-based reasoning is one example).

NTT

NTT currently has 36 expert systems under development. Half of these systems perform diagnosis on various components of a communications system. Their most successful ES performs failure diagnosis and support of crossbar switching equipment. A task that typically takes four hours has been reduced to five minutes using the system. However, the main motivations for developing the system were the planned phase-out of crossbars and the need to avoid training new people on an obsolete device. Thus, the expert system's main value is in capturing and preserving expertise.

Nippon Steel

Nippon Steel has developed 100-130 expert systems for internal use (very few for external use). About 30 percent of these are now in routine use. Although most of the current applications are diagnostic/troubleshooting systems, the fastest growing area is in planning and scheduling.

Diagnostic/Process Control. Nippon Steel selected three representative applications to present to the JTEC panel, two of them diagnostic and one for process control. The first is a system for process diagnosis, used in the Oita works. The system is used in three factories for troubleshooting electrical and mechanical equipment, and has resulted in a reduction of production costs, development costs, and/or plant operators. The knowledge base contains about 160,000 knowledge fragments (comparable to about 50,000 rules). The system was developed with Nippon Steel's own shell, called ESTO, written in C++, and runs on networked Sun workstations. About 20 man-years went into its development, over a two-year period. The economic payback of this system is estimated to be about $2 million annually. The reliability of Sun hardware has been a problem in keeping the systems in use.

The second representative system provides supervision of blast furnace control. This is a large system, with 5,000-6,000 production rules. It was built on top of Hitachi's commercial tool EUREKA plus a neuro simulator tool called AMI, which was developed internally, and runs on a minicomputer. AMI was used to build a neural network for preprocessing (pattern matching) the raw data before it is input to the expert system. The principal paybacks have been improvements in decision making and in quality of product. About 14 man-years were expended in development, over two years. A major problem has been maintenance of the KB, which is not easily understood by people who had not built it.

Design. The third system is a design expert system for designing shaped beams. This is a large system, containing 3000 production rules and 500,000 lines of code, in LISP, FORTRAN and C. The system was built using ART (from Inference Corp.) and runs on networked Sun workstations. Twenty technical people (4 domain experts, 16 knowledge engineers) developed the system over an 18 month period. The principal payback is in reduction of the design cycle time by 85 percent and an increase in design accuracy of 30 percent. The estimated economic return is $200,000 annually. The system is felt to be too expensive, requiring a copy of ART at each new site.

Assessment. When developing systems that use multiple sources of knowledge (experts) the people at Nippon Steel have adopted a structured development method, much the same as used in conventional software development, which they feel is necessary to avoid unnecessary confusion. For diagnostic systems, they use their in-house tool, ESTO, which is designed to accommodate incomplete and inconsistent knowledge from multiple knowledge sources.

Nearly all systems are integrated with other systems, e.g., data processing, and Nippon Steel is working to establish an inter-factory LAN to facilitate this integration. Of 28 systems developed within the past two years, 60 percent can be characterized as using a combination of a rule-based inference engine plus added code written in a conventional language, typically C. A few systems integrate rule-based, fuzzy and neural network methods. Commercial tools were found to be inadequate in the way they permit access to external functions written in conventional languages, which motivated Nippon Steel to develop its own tools. Problems with current technology include slow execution speed for large-scale systems, high cost in time and effort of knowledge maintenance, lack of transparency of the inference process, tedious integration with existing software, and the general problem of knowledge acquisition.

The company cited many reasons for selecting an expert system application, among which are to acquire know-how, to capture and distribute expertise, to improve revenues and to reduce costs.

Most of the systems that have been developed are small (under 100 rules). It was found that the time to develop large projects increases more than linearly with the number of rules. The in-house consultants advise developers to keep their knowledge bases to within 300 rules, and if more are needed to segment the KB into modules each of which is within 300 rules.

Looking ahead several years, Nippon Steel envisions new expert systems that perform planning and scheduling over multiple factories or production lines. Future diagnostic and process control systems will employ model-based and case-based methods for more in-depth problem description and for recovery following diagnosis, with a capability for closed-loop control. Future planning/scheduling systems will be fully automatic and able to plan with multiple objectives. Future tools (infrastructure) will require knowledge engineers, be task-specific within a general problem solving paradigm, use a standard knowledge representation, and have a better user interface.

NKK

NKK has 25 ESs in routine operation, and five more in the field testing stage. Of the 37 systems that have been built or are in some stage of development, 16 combine the functions of advising, process control and diagnosis; 20 combine the functions of advising, planning/scheduling, and management integration aid. The two major applications are the blast furnace expert system discussed earlier in this chapter and a steelmaking scheduling system (Tsunozaki, Takekoshi et al. 1987; Takekoshi, Aoki et al. 1989).

All of the fully developed systems are integrated with conventional systems, and also use some high-level language (LISP, FORTRAN, PL-1) in addition to the ES shell (ESHELL for the blast furnace, KT for the planning/scheduling systems).

Rather than emphasize training in knowledge engineering and expert system development, NKK has chosen to train its systems engineers in systems analysis and modeling, which are more important skills for total system development. Expert systems techniques in themselves are of relatively small significance, in NKK's view. On the other hand, the company has developed expert system design tools, used in the Engineering and Construction Division, which embody a methodology for developing ESs. These tools, called NX-7 and NX-8, run on Xerox LISP machines and Sun workstations, and have been applied in developing ESs for operations support of refuse incinerators.

NKK often introduces an ES at the same time as it refurbishes its entire computer system (which itself may be just a part of a larger renewal project), making it difficult to evaluate the impact of the introduction of the ES. However, ESs are introduced only when conventional programming techniques fail to solve the problem at hand.

Regarding future development, NKK sees more use of in-the-loop control, moving from mainframes to engineering workstations and providing intelligent assistance on more advanced tasks of engineering and management. The company sees several problems with current technology: AI tools that are difficult to learn and use; relatively high difficulty in system maintenance; inadequate processing speed; the need to obtain knowledge automatically from data, and the need to solve problems (e.g., scheduling) by using previous cases.

Mitsubishi Electric

The JTEC team visited the Industrial Electronics and Systems Lab (IESL), a small group especially focused on power industry (electrical) problems. Thus we saw a very small part of the total ES activity at Mitsubishi Electric.

Mitsubishi Electric's single most successful application has been the ES for elevator group control, discussed earlier. Another success story is a fuzzy logic control system for metal machining, which became part of an electron-beam cutting machine that began selling three or four years ago.

Diagnosis. IESL has built three systems for internal use for finance, diagnosis, and planning (all are prototypes). The diagnosis system employs qualitative process modeling to determine problems with a boiler system. It started out as a 200-rule system, but when implemented with DASH is only 70-80 rules (some component knowledge is reusable). The system is fielded at Kansai Electric Power but is not in routine use yet. It reduces the time to make a diagnosis from three to four minutes down to one minute.

Energy Management. IESL is most interested in ES for energy management of electric power distribution networks. It envisions the technology used for diagnosis, restorative operation, reliability assessment, dispatching control, and operations planning. There are currently three energy management systems (EMS) (one from Mitsubishi Electric) in practical use in Japan. The Mitsubishi one is in use at the Kansai power distribution center. The KB is relatively small -- about 200 rules. There are six more systems in field test.

Assessment. Mitsubishi finds that Japanese power companies are very eager to use ES technology. They were led to believe that U.S. power companies were not interested in the technology, even though the Electric Power Research Institute (EPRI) appears interested.

IESL has a lot of experience in network diagnostic problems, so it does not have much failure in this area. In general, where an ES is built as an integral part of a larger system, the failure rate is very low. Mitsubishi considered integration from the very beginning and thus did not experience problems of integrating stand-alone ESs after they were built.

We were given a breakdown of types of ES applications in the power industry world-wide: diagnosis, 25 percent; operations, 25 percent; monitoring, 15 percent; control, 15 percent; planning 10 percent; others (simulators, maintenance, design, system analysis), 10 percent.

Tokyo Electric Power Company (TEPCO)

TEPCO has developed 30 systems, of which 11 are in routine use. The application domains for these 11 include design, consultation, control, prediction, planning and scheduling, fault location, hot-line service, and computer operations. Three systems are in field test, 14 in the prototyping, and two in the feasibility stage.

Forecasting. The most successful system is the daily maximum load forecasting system. Measures of success have been user satisfaction, a reduction in the absolute forecasting error rate from 2.2 percent to 1.5 percent, and a four-fold speedup in forecast generation. The system is actually quite small, with only about 100 rules, and was built using Toshiba's TDES3 tool. It runs on a Toshiba minicomputer and also on Toshiba workstations (Sun workstation compatible). The forecasting system is one component of, and integrated with, a much larger load forecasting system called ELDAC. The system was developed at a cost of approximately $2 million over a period of about 20 months. Two researchers and two experts at TEPCO designed the system and three system engineers from Toshiba built it. It is now used routinely by load dispatchers. Although the ROI is difficult to estimate, the use of the system precludes the need for a standby generator at a power station.

Assessment. About 50 percent of TEPCO's ES projects advance from the prototype stage to an operational system. The company's AI Technology Department is actively pursuing fuzzy logic, neural networks, genetic algorithms and computer graphics in addition to expert systems. Our TEPCO hosts made it clear that to them "AI" means not only Artificial Intelligence but also Advanced Information Technology.

Obayashi Corporation

Obayashi has built 25 expert systems for internal use and one for external use. Of these, six are in routine operation and nine more are at the field testing stage. Most of the systems (14) are classified as advisory systems.

Direction Control. Obayashi's most successful system is an automatic direction control system for shield tunneling (a method of tunnel construction first used in England in the 19th century). This system controls the direction of drilling, which must be accurate to within five centimeters per one kilometer of tunnel length. The non-linearity of the problem precludes the use of a mathematical model. The ES is now in use in some (not all) of Obayashi's drilling operations. The system is built on top of two shells, called AI-DNA and AI-RNA, sold by AdIn, a Japanese AI company. The system uses fuzzy control in its problem solving, is stand-alone, uses the C language, contains about 10,000 lines of code, and runs on a personal computer. It was designed and built by two civil engineers, two mechanical engineers, and one systems engineer (plus programmers), and is maintained by the domain expert and two technicians. Development time was one year, including the testing period. The primary payback has been improvement in the quality of direction control, and in a three to one reduction in personnel required for this task.

Assessment. Obayashi representatives report that 70 percent of ES projects that are started get as far as a prototype, and 30 percent actually get to an operational system. Using existing tools, they can envision building systems up to the size of a few thousand rules. Future systems planned by the corporation include other automatic control systems and intelligent CAD. The primary perceived problems with present technology are: knowledge acquisition; constructing design systems; incorporating model-based and case-based reasoning; and machine learning.

OBSERVATIONS AND CONCLUSIONS

It should first be noted that this JTEC panel's sample set for KB systems applications in Japan was strongly skewed to the side of success for the technology. We picked the places known to be prominent in the development and use of knowledge-based methods for problem-solving. By and large, that is what we saw: many fielded success stories, many more systems under development, and strong management support. If we had visited a random list of industries, we are certain the relative importance of KB systems technology would have been much less. With that as a caveat, we were still impressed by the depth and breadth of KB systems usage that was exhibited. In particular, the four large computer companies -- Fujitsu, Hitachi, Toshiba, and NEC -- have made major corporate commitments to KB systems technology, both as a tool for solving in-house problems and as a market for external sales. The effort at those four companies collectively seemed to be as large as the biggest U.S. corporate commitments (DEC and IBM).

We were also impressed by the number of high impact applications that we found. In addition to the ones detailed above, almost every site we visited seemed to have at least one KB system that had made a significant change in an important aspect of the company's business.

From a technology standpoint, the JTEC team saw very little that differed from first-generation KB systems applications in the U.S. As discussed above, there is relatively little use evident in Japan of the most advanced AI technologies such as model-based reasoning, machine learning, iterative improvement scheduling methods, etc. The one exception to this point is the widespread proliferation of fuzzy methods within KB system applications. As in the U.S., the emphasis is moving toward integrated application of first-generation KB systems. Almost all the significant work we saw interfaced with real devices, databases and/or conventional software systems.

3. Tools and Infrastructure for Knowledge–Based Systems

H. Penny Nii

INTRODUCTION

In this chapter we focus on tools for building expert systems, and on the associated R&D infrastructure. The types of tools currently on the market are indicative of the current technology available to the end user community, while tools under development can provide clues about the kinds of applications one can expect in the future. The level of activity of tool development also indicates the value being placed on the future of this technology. We get at this, in part, by profiling some key ES development tools and leading-edge players in the market.

EXPERT SYSTEMS BUILDING TOOLS: DEFINITIONS

An expert system tool, or shell, is a software development environment containing the basic components of expert systems. Associated with a shell is a prescribed method for building applications by configuring and instantiating these components. Some of the generic components of a shell are shown in Figure 3.1 and described below. The core components of expert systems are the knowledge base and the reasoning engine.

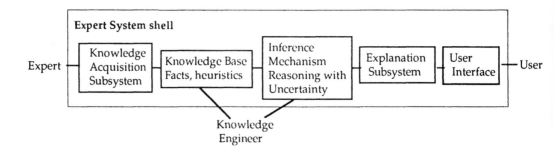

Figure 3.1. Basic Components of Expert System Tools

(1) **Knowledge base:** A store of factual and heuristic knowledge. An ES tool provides one or more knowledge representation schemes for expressing knowledge about the application domain. Some tools use both frames (objects) and IF-THEN rules. In PROLOG the knowledge is represented as logical statements.

(2) **Reasoning engine:** Inference mechanisms for manipulating the symbolic information and knowledge in the knowledge base to form a line of reasoning in solving a problem. The inference mechanism can range from simple *modus ponens* backward chaining of IF-THEN rules to case-based reasoning.

(3) **Knowledge acquisition subsystem:** A subsystem to help experts build knowledge bases. Collecting knowledge needed to solve problems and build the knowledge base continues to be the biggest bottleneck in building expert systems.

(4) **Explanation subsystem:** A subsystem that explains the system's actions. The explanation can range from how the final or intermediate solutions were arrived at to justifying the need for additional data.

(5) **User interface:** The means of communication with the user. The user interface is generally not a part of the ES technology, and was not given much attention in the past. However, it is now widely accepted that the user interface can make a critical difference in the perceived utility of a system regardless of the system's performance.

The following subsections survey Japanese ES tools that are on the market, observe current trends in tool development, and comment on the recent integration of fuzzy logic and neural networks into these tools. Finally, we describe in more detail one of the latest Japanese tools, ES/KERNEL2.

ES Building Tools on the Market

Traditionally, ES tools have been categorized by their hardware platform: PC- or Macintosh-based, workstation-based, or mainframe-based. (For example, see Harmon 1992a).

Recently, new types of tools have come on the market that are characterized according to tasks (e.g., diagnosis, planning) and problem-solving approaches (e.g., case-based reasoning or model based reasoning). These second generation tools encode the problem-solving know-how gained through building applications in different areas using the first generation tools. The emergence of such tools reflects the market condition in which vertical tools are perceived to be easier to use and easier to sell. A problem-specific, or task-specific, tool contains knowledge representation schemes and reasoning methods found useful for a particular class of applications and a task ontology associated with the problem class.

Table 3.1 lists most of the commercial tools developed in Japan. They are broadly categorized as general purpose, task-specific, solution-specific, and development methodology tools (i.e., tools for training implementors in the methodology for developing expert systems). There are also more general-purpose tools on the market than the list might indicate. A general purpose tool such as ES/KERNEL represents a class of tools, with a version of the tool for different types of hardware platforms -- ES/KERNEL/W for workstations; ES/KERNEL/H for mainframes and super-computers; ES/KERNEL/P for the personal computers; and ES/KERNEL/D for on-line data processing.

In addition to the tools developed by the Japanese, foreign-made tools, primarily American, make up about 30 percent of the tools used in fielded expert systems in Japan. This JTEC panel is not aware of any Japanese tools being sold in the U.S. Components of the next version of ES/KERNEL -- ES/KERNEL2 -- are being developed in Europe and will be marketed there. Figure 3.2 shows the relative popularity of the more common tools in use. The four most popular tools are those developed by domestic computer manufacturers, Hitachi, Fujitsu, and NEC. According to *Nikkei AI*, these tools are popular primarily because they can be used on hardware the customers already have. Tools that run on multiple platforms (mainframe, workstations, and PCs), such as ES/KERNEL and ESHELL, have been particularly popular. The decision to use American and small-vendor tools are generally made based on their features and capabilities rather than the platforms on which they run.

Table 3.1
Commercial ES Building Tools Developed in Japan

TOOL	COMPANY	REMARKS
General Purpose		
ESHELL	Fujitsu	LISP-based (UtilLisp), primarily a mainframe tool
ES/KERNEL	Hitachi	Being provided on UNIX workstations in C
EXCORE	NEC	
BRAINS	TIS	
XPT-II	CSK	
KBMS	NTT	
ASIREX	Toshiba	Second generation tool in C on workstation
Task-/Domain-specific		
APSHELL/DIAG	Fujitsu	Diagnostic
APSHELL/GUIDE	Fujitsu	Consultation
APSHELL/SCHEDES	Fujitsu	Scheduling
EUREKA	Hitachi	Real-time process control
ES/PROMOTE/DIAG	Hitachi	Diagnostic, built on top of ES/KERNEL
ES/PROMOTE/PLAN	Hitachi	Planning and scheduling
HPGS	Hitachi	Scheduling
DiKAST	Toshiba	Diagnostic with knowledge acquisition facility
PROKAST	Toshiba	Scheduling with knowledge acquisition facility
Debut	Toshiba	Parametric design
PLANBOX	NEC	Planning
FTX	IHI	Diagnostic
ESTO	Nippon Steel	Diagnostic
GENZO	Shimadzu	Diagnostic, classification, interpretation
GENZO-II	Shimadzu	Design and planning
GENZO-QAE	Shimadzu	Q/A systems
MEL-DASH	Mitsubishi	Electric Network Diagnostic
Solution-specific		
ES/TOOL/RI	Hitachi	Rule induction (under development)
EXCEEDS 3	Hitachi	Qualitative reasoning (under development)
Development Methodology		
ES/GUIDE	Hitachi	Text-based explanation of development methodology
ES/SDEM	Fujitsu	
TUPPS-ES	Toshiba	
ES/METHOD	NEC	
SOLOMON	Mitsubishi	
Others		
FORTRAN/KR	Fujitsu	FORTRAN-based, mainframe and workstation tool
YPS/KR	Fujitsu	COBOL-based, mainframe tool
KwSHELL	Fujitsu	General Purpose and Knowledge Acquisition tool

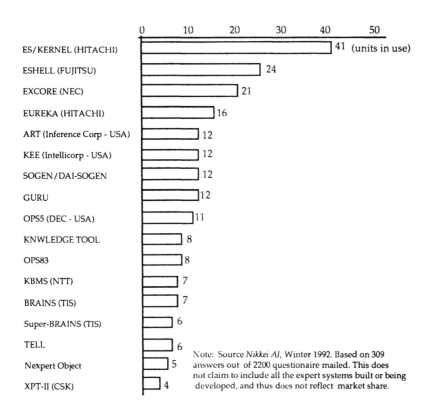

Figure 3.2. Expert System Tools in Use in Japan

In its 1991 annual survey of fielded expert systems, *Nikkei AI* reported 48 applications developed with ES/KERNEL and 47 with ESHELL. Up until 1991, ESHELL was the dominant tool. In 1992, ES/KERNEL had overtaken ESHELL by a wide margin (Figure 3.2). ESHELL is considered to contain more advanced AI techniques, but ES/KERNEL is considered more practical and easier to use. Sales of these tools are affected by the platform on which they run and the base language used to write the system. The ESHELL family -- ESHELL (mainframe), ESHELL/X (mainframe and workstation), ESHELL/FM (personal computer), ESHELL/SB (minicomputer) -- are written in UTiLisp (University of Tokyo Interactive Lisp, quite archaic by present standards). ES/KERNEL runs on UNIX workstations and is written in C. The rising popularity of workstation tools and the drop in the sales of mainframe tools correlate with the general trend in the United States. The move to workstations in the U.S. is ironic since the tools were originally developed on workstations. Of course, today's workstation environment is quite different from the earlier days.

Market Trends

As will be seen, the trends in the type of ES building tools that have been, and will be, on the market are generally the same for both Japan and the U.S. In contrast, machine learning tools are receiving much more attention in Europe than in either Japan or the U.S. Up to now, the basic technology base of both the Japanese and American tools originated in U.S. laboratories; the tools of the two countries have have more in common than not. The following is a description of some of the trends the JTEC team observed that relate to tool technology.

Specialization of tools. Most first generation, general-purpose tools were built and marketed by the information systems divisions of large computer companies. The same groups are also developing second-generation, task-specific tools. These specialized tools are also beginning to be developed and sold by engineers servicing the end-user community. For example, the fourth most widely used tool, EUREKA, was built by the Heavy Industry Division of Hitachi as a tool to build real-time process control systems. MEL-DASH (Komai, Matsumoto et al. 1991), a special tool for diagnosing electrical network faults, is being built by a group at Mitsubishi Electric's Industrial Systems Laboratory specializing in the electric power industry.

There are two underlying impetuses for developing task-specific tools. First, with a task-specific tool, the knowledge acquisition subsystem can be tailored to the particular class of problems for which the tool is intended, making knowledge acquisition easier for the application developer. The reasoning engine can also be customized to the task, making the system more efficient. The developers of MEL-DASH claim that specialization also allows them to build tools with a reusable library of software components and verification tools. Second, a task-specific tool geared to a particular end-user group's needs and ways of doing things is a good way to encourage use of the technology. Table 3.2, for example, shows Fujitsu's strategy for expanding the market for ES technology by providing tools for divisions that service end users.

Table 3.2 also shows another way in which Fujitsu is trying to expand the ES user base. YPS/KR and FORTRAN/KR are tools targeted to the COBOL and FORTRAN user communities. FORTRAN/KR claims to provide modeling facilities such as objects, rules and a high performance inference engine with fuzzy data, for integration in the FORTRAN programming environment. The representation of knowledge for design and control makes it easy to build intelligent and complex systems using FORTRAN programming in areas such as design, scientific computation and process control (Fujitsu America Inc. 1990). FORTRAN/KR runs on Fujitsu mainframe computers and Sun workstations.

Table 3.2
Fujitsu's Strategy for Expanding ES Usage

Up to 1989	1990	1991 and Beyond
Establish AI technology Expand to advanced users	Expand to end user and to production	Total problem solution
Expansion of AI applications (performance evaluation/ network diagnostic)	Expansion into end user divisions (provide application shells) APSHELL/DIAG APSHELL/GUIDE APSHELL/SCHEDES	Problem solution by knowledge process applications Enhancement of various applications
Expand ESHELL family (ESHELL/X, FM, SB) Expand AI languages (LISP, PROLOG)	Provide knowledge-ware, an advanced ES tool Expand into production areas (YPS/KR, FORTRAN/KR) Neural Network	Basis for total problem solution by -human interface -problem description -knowledge base management system

(Source: Fujitsu Limited)

The decision to invest in the building of a task-specific tool is based on the demand for application systems in that area. Historically, diagnosis was the most popular application area for the first few years after the introduction of expert systems. Thus, diagnostic problem-solving is a well understood task area. More recently, both Fujitsu and Hitachi claim that scheduling and planning systems have become popular, and there are demands for specialized tools in these areas. Toshiba claims that design systems, especially in the area of LSI routing, are also increasingly in demand.

An interesting phenomenon is the popularity of Hitachi's EUREKA, a tool for developing real-time control systems. It outsells domain shells in all other task areas, even though the number of real-time control systems being built is much smaller than other types of applications. Table 3.3 shows the actual numbers of applications developed by the top five companies using ES technology. There is a surge in 1991 in the use of control programs that go hand in hand with the increase in the use of neural networks. (The use of neural networks in conjunction with expert systems is described later in this chapter.)

Table 3.3
ES Development History of Top 5 ES-User Companies:
Number of Applications by Year

	1987	1988	1989	1990	1991	Total
Scheduling	2	7	15	5	2	31
Control	5	10	7	9	20	51
Diagnosis	5	6	2	15	11	39
Fuzzy	2	3	4	9	12	30
Neuro	0	0	2	6	25	33
TOTAL	14	26	30	44	70	184

(Source: A tutorial by Riichiro Mizoguchi, The First Congress on Expert Systems)

The popularity of EUREKA parallels the rising popularity in the United States of G2, a real-time control system tool developed by GENSYM. (However, the use of neural networks in control systems is still rare in the United States.)

Table 3.3 also shows that companies that successfully deploy expert systems are repeat users.

In addition to the tools sold by ES tool vendors, large companies are developing their own tools for specific task areas, which reflect what they have learned through their experiences. Company-specific processes and proprietary knowledge can be built into a tool and disseminated within the organization. Or, as at the Shimadzu Corp., the software system can be sold as part of, or a supplement to, a product line. Shimadzu Corp. produces general analysis and medical diagnostic devices. To build diagnostic and usage guidance software systems, the company developed GENZO-I, an analysis tool useful for diagnostic, classification, and interpretation tasks. GENZO-II, a hybrid tool using frames and rules, is used for synthesis problems such as planning and design (Hasegawa et al. 1991; Takata et al. 1991).

Workstation tools. Early developers of expert systems used American tools and LISP workstations to develop their applications. For example, Nippon Life Insurance developed its underwriting advisory system using KEE (KEE is a trademark of Intellicorp, Inc.) on the Symbolics workstation. Most early ES tools developed by the Japanese were for mainframes. It may be that the Japanese were forced to develop mainframe tools because there were none available at the time. Until recently, the ESHELL line, a mainframe-based tool, was the best-selling line.

In the United States, a shift towards open, client-server architectures began to have a noticeable effect on the tools market beginning in early 1990, when there was a dramatic increase in the sale of tools on UNIX-based workstations. Sales jumped from around 3500 units in both 1988 and 1989 to 6900 units in 1990 (Harmon 1992b). Although there is no comparable figure for Japan in terms of the actual number of tools sold, *Nikkei AI,* in its 1991 survey, noted an increase in the percentage of UNIX workstations used as the ES platform, and an accompanying decrease in the use of mainframe systems (see Fig. 3.3). Hitachi representatives believe that the sudden popularity of Hitachi's ES/KERNEL can be attributed to the increased popularity of UNIX workstations in Japan. Of the more than 4,000 units of ES/KERNEL sold since 1987, 2,000 were sold in the last two years.

Embedded systems and system integration. In the early exploratory period, expert systems were stand-alone systems solving isolated problems. As customer confidence grew in the ability of ES technology to deliver solutions, expert systems were incorporated in larger systems. Knowledge representation and reasoning tools were augmented with tools to access databases, to interface with existing programs, and to operate in a mainframe environment. In many cases, especially with mainframe-oriented tools, the expert system component became a part of larger systems. Today, embeddability — the ability to operate within many different environments and in concert with a variety of other software — is a crucial aspect of expert systems and their development tools.

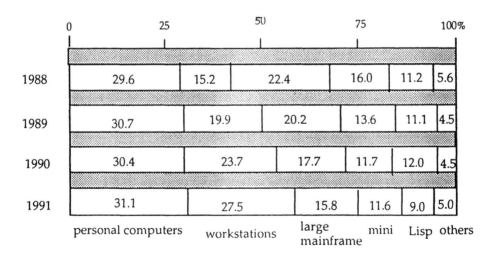

Figure 3.3.   Changes in the Hardware Types Used for ES Development
Note: "Others" Include PROLOG Machines. (Source: Nikkei AI 1991)

At the outset, computer companies were active in building ES applications. System engineers trained in the use of ES technology regarded expert system technology as merely another software methodology. Thus, from the beginning they addressed the problems of system integration and development methodology. Fujitsu's ESHELL, until recently the number one seller, was based on a blackboard architecture which facilitated integration. Fujitsu software engineers were also able to adapt, for better or for worse, the waterfall model of software development to ES development. Hitachi's ES/GUIDE, which contains a step-by-step guide to ES development, draws heavily on the spiral model of software development process combined with the waterfall model to handle the documentation process. All this indicates that the Japanese have already made substantial investment, and have a broad experience base, in the *process* of ES development. Combined with their early experience in building expert systems on mainframe computers and in integrating expert systems with other systems, Japanese software engineers seem well prepared for building large expert systems and conventional systems containing expert system components.

Novel Features: Fuzzy Logic and Neural Networks

Most ES tools contain similar features. Knowledge is generally represented as IF-THEN rules, and in newer tools knowledge can also be represented as frames. The reasoning methods include forward chaining and backward chaining. And, most tools have facilities for generating explanations of the application programs' reasoning. Japanese ES tools are technically indistinguishable from U.S. tools, except in three areas: the user interface, which is to be expected; the extensive use of fuzzy logic (or multi-valued logic) to express inexactness; and connections to neural networks.

In the most general sense, *fuzzy logic*, invented by Lotfi Zadeh (Zadeh 1965), is a multi-valued logic to express different degrees of certainty or uncertainty of assertions. Since expert systems contain heuristic knowledge, they must have a way of dealing with the problem of expressing and reasoning with uncertain data and inexact knowledge. Among the Japanese, fuzzy logic is an extremely popular solution for this problem. It is most popular among control engineers. The first significant use of fuzzy logic was in a Hitachi-built expert system that controlled the brakes on passenger trains (Yasunobu and Miyamoto 1985). Recently, fuzzy control has been used in consumer products -- for example, fuzzy rice cookers, fuzzy washing machines, fuzzy camcorders. Mitsubishi's fuzzy elevator system, described in Chapter 2, reduces the waiting time at floors.

A *neural network* is typically used as a pre-processor to process signal data for process control and manufacturing systems. The neural net converts signals into symbolic information that can be reasoned by expert systems. The SAFIA system shown in Figure 3.4 is an example of a typical process control program with a neural network front-end. Nippon Steel's SAFIA, built with Hitachi's EUREKA and Nippon Steel's own neuro-simulator AMI, controls the operation of the blast furnace. Typically, such expert systems are integrated with other types of software -- for example, a database management system, a user interface, and/or a statistical analysis package -- to create integrated control systems.

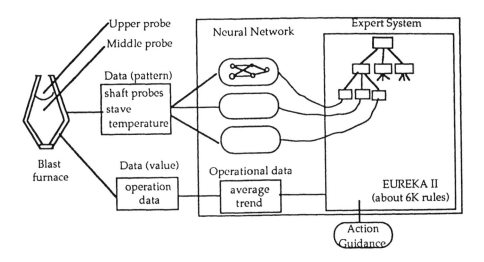

Figure 3.4. SAFIA Blast Furnace Control System – Nippon Steel

PROFILE OF A TOOL: ES/KERNEL2

ES/KERNEL2, the new version of the current best-selling tool, is geared to the development of large-scale applications (Hitachi Ltd. undated brochure). It gives the application developers choice in the use of reasoning methods: rule-based reasoning, object-oriented reasoning, and assumption-based reasoning can all be used within a single expert system. Associated with each reasoning method is a knowledge representation scheme best suited to it. For example, for object-oriented reasoning, knowledge is represented as frames, slots, and methods (see Fig. 3.5). ES/KERNEL2 also provides some advanced capabilities such as ATMS (Assumption-based Truth Maintenance System) and case-based reasoning (under development). Fuzzy logic has been available in ES/KERNEL and will be a part of ES/KERNEL2.

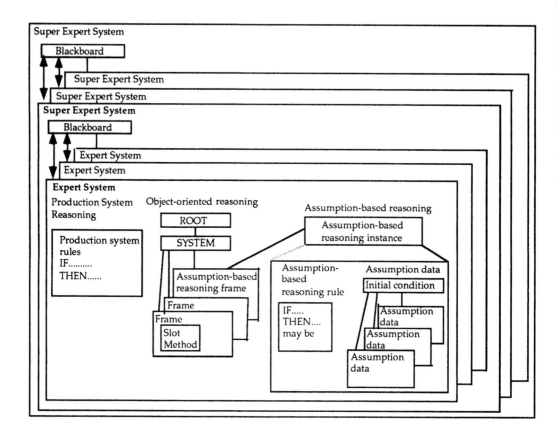

Figure 3.5. ES/KERNEL2, A Tool For Building Multi-Layered,
Cooperative Expert Systems

For large-scale tasks, many expert systems can be connected to perform multi-layered cooperative reasoning. The tool provides a means, in the form of a blackboard data structure, for one expert system to communicate with another. The cooperating expert systems form what are called super expert systems which in turn can cooperate with each other to solve still larger problems.

The reasoning control and knowledge representation components shown in Figure 3.5 sit within a sophisticated development environment (Figure 3.6).   The development environment follows the general structure of ES tools, as shown in Figure 3.1.

Seminal characteristics of ES/KERNEL2 include:

o   In place of a knowledge acquisition system intended for experts' use ES/KERNEL2 provides other tools, such as a knowledge editor, to help knowledge engineers enter and modify the knowledge base.

o   It provides graphic, as well as a multi-media, tools for building the end-user interface. These functionalities are built with X-windows.

o   The interface to external databases is designed to allow general-purpose database software to be entered into the system as frames and used in the reasoning process. Conversely, the results of the reasoning process can be stored in the database.

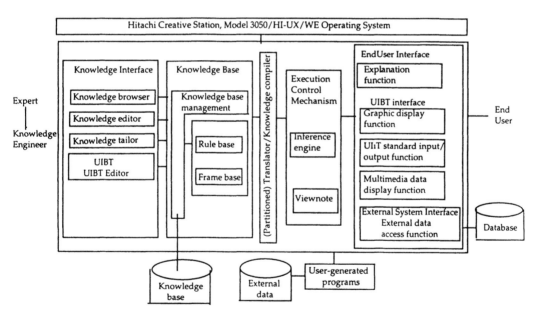

Figure 3.6. ES/KERNEL2 Development Environment
(Source: Hitachi Ltd. undated brochure)

One objective of the ES/KERNEL environment is ease of use. For example, knowledge can be expressed in English or Japanese. If the user wants to know language specifications or grammar while editing, an explanation of a particular term and usage examples can be displayed. Reportedly, more than 50 percent of an ES developer's time is spent developing the end-user graphic interface. ES/KERNEL2 provides a variety of graphic templates and edit functions for the development of the interface.

Another objective is efficiency. A translator converts knowledge into an easy-to-process intermediate language during development, and for the production version a compiler converts the developed knowledge into a format executable at high speed. An extended RETE algorithm matches rules and objects to speed up production system inference. Other features, such as incremental compilation and knowledge partitioning, also save development time.

PROFILE OF A TOOL VENDOR: HITACHI

Hitachi Laboratory was one of the early exploratory users of ES technology. The Nuclear Research Laboratory sent two scientists to the United States to study the technology in 1981. Hitachi was the first to use fuzzy logic in a major application, the control of braking systems in passenger trains (Yasunobu and Miyamoto 1985). In 1982 the Information Systems Division also became interested in expert systems. Hitachi system engineers began to build many expert systems for internal use as well as for customer use. To date, there are about 100 systems developed for internal use, and more than 300 systems for Hitachi customers (for example, see Hitachi 1991 brochure, in English).

Hitachi has a broad range of ES products on the market: (1) the popular general purpose ES/KERNEL series; (2) task-specific tools in the areas of diagnostic and planning and scheduling applications; (3) the knowledge acquisition tool ES/TOOL/W-RI which can generate rules inductively from examples; (4) user interface-building tools (UIBT); and (5) an ES building support tool that guides the builder in an ES development methodology based on the spiral model.

In addition, Hitachi possesses the EUREKA series tools developed by the Heavy Industry Division for building real-time process control applications. Within this series is a more specialized tool called APOS for building advanced plant operation systems. APOS is built on top of EUREKA. Interestingly, ES/KERNEL2 also claims to be a good tool for building real-time control systems. It has been used successfully to build an expert system to control the operations of another blast furnace (Tano, Masui et al. 1988).

Hitachi claims that the demand for scheduling applications is overtaking the demand for diagnostic and banking/financial applications. Within the task domain of planning and scheduling, job shop scheduling is currently the biggest market, accounting for 40 to 50 percent of the scheduling business, followed by process scheduling. Demand for this class of applications began about three years ago. Based on its experience in building applications in this area, Hitachi has classified scheduling problems into four classes, and has developed techniques to solve each one. The company built and now markets a planning/scheduling tool called ES/PROMOTE/PLAN.

Hitachi was the first company to offer an ES tool written in C, and the first to offer one for UNIX workstations. ES/KERNEL/W, a workstation version of ES/KERNEL, is currently the best-selling tool, with more than 4000 copies sold in the last two years to 1,000 different customers. Notably, fuzzy logic is available as a part of ES/KERNEL.

At Hitachi, research is rapidly converted into products. One product under development, EXCEEDS 3, is for qualitative reasoning. Hitachi is also working on making ATMS (Assumption-based Truth Maintenance System) and case-based reasoning available in ES/KERNEL2.

Hitachi Europe, a small division of about 15 people, is helping in the development of ES/KERNEL2, which will be marketed by Hewlett-Packard in Europe as ObjectIQ. Hitachi Europe has also been working with a British firm, LOGICA, and the University of Edinburgh to develop an alternative to rule-based techniques for building scheduling systems. Called WHISPA, the program is able to generate schedules that perform one to two orders of magnitude faster in test cases. WHISPA has since been renamed ES/PROMOTE2/W-PLAN, and was released in August 1992.

INFRASTRUCTURE: INDUSTRIAL RESEARCH AND TECHNOLOGY TRANSFER

Most of the companies the JTEC team visited are large enough to have their own research laboratories. Like their counterparts in the U.S., industrial laboratories of large companies in Japan engage in basic research and advanced development in a variety of areas. One example is Toshiba Electric, where the research and development infrastructure is similar to other computer companies active in selling ES tools and developing ES applications.

Toshiba Corporation Profile

Toshiba has five research laboratories that conduct long-range (five to ten years) research in areas ranging from computer hardware, to manufacturing, to software. In addition, Toshiba has eight development laboratories that look ahead three to five years. In 1991, with annual net sales of $22.9 billion, the company spent 8.2 percent of that on research, close to double the ratio in 1981, when it spent 4.8 percent of sales on research (see Fig. 3.7).

Toshiba's Systems and Software Engineering Laboratory (SSEL) was set up in 1987 with a charter to conduct research and basic development in systems and software areas and to develop corporate strategies in these areas. SSEL was also chartered to support operational divisions. SSEL has four divisions: (1) AI and human interface; (2) systems, covering distributed, neural network, and fuzzy systems; (3) software engineering; and (4) the systems and software development department, the mission of which is technology transfer. Although there are some good basic research activities -- for example, research on the use of multiple cases in case-based reasoning (Tanaka, Hattori et al. 1992) -- SSEL's primary strength lies in applied research.

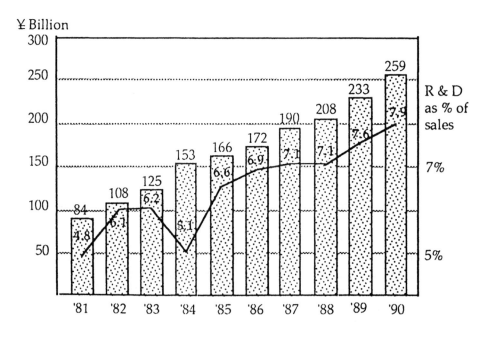

Figure 3.7. Toshiba Corporation R&D Expenditures of Non-Consolidated Base
(Source: Toshiba)

By applied research we mean the building of novel or complex application systems that use and extend the latest techniques from diverse areas. It is at once a technology transfer task as well as technology integration, refinement, and improvement task. Examples of advanced systems that are being built by SSEL include: model-based plant control systems, described in Chapter 2, which use advanced techniques, such as model-based reasoning, qualitative simulation, and knowledge compilation, in addition to the rule-based technique (Suzuki, Sueda et al. 1990) (research funded by ICOT); and model-based automatic programming systems (Nakayama, Mizutani et al. 1990). In addition to building advanced application systems, SSEL has developed prototype ES shells such as DiKAST (a diagnostic ES shell) and PROKAST (a scheduling ES shell). Both are knowledge acquisition, as well as problem-solving, tools integrating the results of SSEL's research in knowledge acquisition (Araki and Kojima 1991).

Infrastructure for Technology Transfer

As mentioned earlier, the best-selling Japanese tools were first developed by, and continue to be developed by, Japanese computer manufacturers. In the U.S., in contrast IBM's TIRS has done poorly in the market. DEC uses ES technology extensively inside the company, and makes money in training and consulting with other companies on the uses of the technology, but it does not have its own tool. U.S. tools are developed and marketed by a dozen or so small companies rather than major hardware companies. The Japanese can continue to invest in the research and development of new tools (which they are doing) and are in a better position to survive lean times. In contrast, American vendors must work with short-term objectives and lean cash reserves.

On the research front, the U.S. fares somewhat better. As is the case with Toshiba in particular, industrial research in Japan is generally a mix of some basic research and advanced development, as in the United States. However, basic research activities of Japanese companies are on a relatively small scale compared to some U.S. companies such as IBM, Bell Labs, and Xerox PARC.

On the other hand, Japanese applied research is very extensive and closely integrated with the development and sales arms of the companies. In all the computer companies many, if not all, of the tool prototypes were first developed and tested in research laboratories. The first explorations of ES technology occurred in the research laboratories of Fujitsu, Hitachi, and NEC. Similar exploration also occurred in other large industrial laboratories such as those of Canon, Nippon Steel, and NTT. The first applications were joint efforts of researchers, system developers, and customers. Thus, the researchers serve as technology explorers and technology transfer agents, both in the computer companies and in the user companies.

OBSERVATIONS AND CONCLUSIONS

In general, Japanese tool vendors are optimistic about ES technology. Hitachi appears optimistic about ES as a business. Although "AI fever" has receded, there is now a better understanding of the strengths and shortcomings of the technology. There are fewer exploratory users and more users demanding practical systems. There is also a steady increase in business.

The majority of Japanese ES tools are developed, sold, and applied by computer companies. They have the resources to conduct research, develop new products, and persist in the business.

Because of the close relationship between industrial research, system development, and sales personnel in Japanese companies, solutions to customer problems are identified cooperatively, and then quickly find their way into ES tools.

Many Japanese tools under development are at about the same level of sophistication as American tools. Although many new ideas originate in U.S. research laboratories, Japanese are quick to develop the technology and transfer it into products.

The predominant application areas have been equipment diagnosis, planning and scheduling, design, and process control. As in the United States, the Japanese companies are developing task- or domain-specific tools for diagnostic, planning/scheduling, and real-time control problems.   These tools are often combined with knowledge acquisition aids.

As in the United States, Japanese computer manufacturers are moving towards open, client server architectures.   The impact on the tools business is an increased demand in workstation tools, especially UNIX-based tools written in C. Concurrently, there is a slowdown in the demand for mainframe tools.

All the major Japanese computer companies conduct research in knowledge-based systems.   Most of the research is in applying or integrating new techniques to customer problems.   The industrial research laboratories serve as technology transfer agents for both imported and internally developed techniques and methodologies. At the same time, as in consumer products, Japanese companies are spending research money on improving and refining ideas and products.

On the negative side, the Japanese suffer from a proliferation of tools that reflects their computing industry: (1) there are several large computer manufacturers whose hardware products are incompatible; (2) customer loyalty keeps end users from shopping around; (3) customers tend to desire custom systems; and (4) there does not appear to be any movement towards standardization. However, with the move toward open systems architectures, these patterns may be significantly altered, and one or two dominant players may appear. Hitachi, with its UNIX workstation tool, is beginning to show signs of being one of them.

4. Advanced Knowledge–Based Systems Research

Edward Feigenbaum
Peter E. Friedland

UNIVERSITY RESEARCH

Although the best research in Japan compares favorably with that in the United States, the base of fundamental research in artificial intelligence in Japan is far less broad and deep. A reasonable way to measure this is by publication in the proceedings of the premier conference in the field, the International Joint Conference on Artificial Intelligence (IJCAI). IJCAI itself is truly international, alternating among Europe, Asia, and the United States every two years with reviewers spread broadly among all countries. It is extremely difficult for submissions to win acceptance; normal acceptance rates are 17-20 percent after rigorous peer review. The proceedings are universally regarded as one of the very few archival publication venues in the field.

An analysis of the most recent three IJCAIs (Australia in 1991, Detroit in 1989, and Italy in 1987) reveals the following results. There were 37 Japanese single or co-authored publications over that time span, compared to 387 American publications. Of those publications, 18 came from academia (nine from Osaka University, six from Kyoto University, and one each from Kyushu University, the University of Tokyo, and the Tokyo Institute of Technology). The remaining 19 publications came from government laboratories (five from ICOT and four from ETL) and industry (five from NTT, three from NEC, and one each from Hitachi and Toshiba). It should be noted that the industrial papers were heavily clustered in the fields of robotics (particularly machine vision) and natural language, both beyond the scope of this report. A complete analysis of U.S. publications was not undertaken, but roughly 75 percent were from academia, encompassing at least 50 different sites. Over the same time period, Germany produced 50 IJCAI publications, Canada, 48, the UK, 39, France 35, and Italy 23.

While in Japan, the JTEC team visited both Kyoto and Osaka Universities, as well as a relatively new center for research at the University of Tokyo. Based on the above statistics, the panel believes this provided reasonable insight into the overall Japanese academic AI research establishment.

Kyoto University

Our host at Kyoto University was Associate Professor Toyoaki Nishida, who runs an excellent small research group. Prof. Nishida is probably the most highly respected Japanese member of the qualitative physics research community, which entails work in symbolic reasoning about the behavior of physical devices and processes when formal mathematical models are either unknown or computationally intractable. His colleagues are mainly American; citations in his publications lean heavily on Prof. Ken Forbus at Northwestern, Dr. Johan deKleer at Xerox-PARC, and Prof. Elisha Sacks at Princeton. The only major Japanese collaborator who came up during discussions was Professor Tomiyama of the University of Tokyo. Prof. Nishida's own archival publications are in IJCAI and AAAI Proceedings.

Prof. Nishida's particular specialty is fundamental work on the mix of qualitative and quantitative modeling of dynamic systems. He represents systems in the form of differential equations and then symbolically represent change in those systems in the form of flow diagrams in a phase space. He has developed a flow grammar to allow representation of a variety of complex processes and a simplification method to allow prediction of some forms of device and process behavior under change (IJCAI-91 and AAAI-87 papers). He also believes that large systems can be decomposed into smaller, more understandable systems. His goal is to build what he calls a "knowledgeable community," a library of component modules that can be combined to express the behavior of large systems.

The visit to Professor Nishida's laboratory confirmed several important observations on the structure of traditional academic research in Japan also made by some previous JTEC panels. A research unit, sometimes referred to in Japanese as a *koza*, normally consists of one professor, one associate professor, and two assistant professors. There are a very small number of doctoral students (most students go into industry and may submit theses much later). Also, it is very difficult to pick out the best students and fund them (almost no students were supported as research assistants). That led to a situation in which Prof. Nishida did most of his own research with only an occasional Ph.D. student or two. In addition, the research group atmosphere at Japanese universities makes it very difficult to conduct interdisciplinary research. Several mechanisms being employed to correct these problems at other sites are discussed below.

Osaka University

Our visit to Osaka University was hosted by Professor Riichiro Mizoguchi. Prof. Mizoguchi is perhaps the best known example of an entrepreneurial American-style laboratory chief in Japanese AI research. He supervises eight doctoral students, a large number by Japanese standards. He often has foreign visitors in his laboratory. He has raised substantial sums of industrial co-funding for his laboratory. Being a full professor gives Mizoguchi considerably more flexibility than Assoc. Prof. Nishida at Kyoto, and he has used that flexibility to create a research setting much more American than Japanese.

Professor Mizoguchi's laboratory is conducting research in four areas of knowledge-based systems work. The first is in the role of deep knowledge in next-generation expert systems. His focus is on knowledge compilation -- the automatic generation of shallow knowledge (like experiential diagnosis rules) from deep knowledge (i.e., structure-function models of complex devices). His group is building and testing a system called KCII in the domain of automobile diagnosis.

The second area of research is knowledge acquisition. Prof. Mizoguchi's goal is to build an interviewing system capable of automatically constructing an expert system for a particular task with no intervention of a knowledge engineer. A system called MULTIS (Multi-task Interview System) has been built which attempts to relate a proposed problem-solving task to prior tasks in a case library.

The third area of research is large-scale, re-usable and shareable knowledge bases. Prof. Mizoguchi's laboratory is conducting fundamental work into building ontologies for both tasks and domains. To date, the work seems mainly theoretical, although Prof. Mizoguchi authored a report for the Advanced Software Technology and Mechatronics Research Institute of Kyoto detailing both a theoretical and empirical research plan for the area. He told us that Prof. Okuno of Tokyo University was the other Japanese researcher with an ongoing program in the area.

The final area of research discussed was intelligent tutoring systems. Prof. Mizoguchi's laboratory has designed a formal student modeling language (SMDL), based on PROLOG, but with a four-valued logic (true, false, unknown, and fail). Several prototype applications have been built, but none seemed to be in the formal testing stage at the time of our visit.

RCAST (University of Tokyo)

The Research Center for Advanced Science and Technology (RCAST) was founded in 1987 at the University of Tokyo. It was intended to break through the "stale" situation of the old university and serve as a pilot institution leading the reform of Japanese Universities. In particular, RCAST's charter calls for an emphasis on:

1)   Interdisciplinary studies
2)   International cooperation
3)   Mobility and flexibility of staff and research areas
4)   Openness to the public and to other organizations

All of these foci are regarded as weaknesses of the Japanese University system with its strong emphasis on rigid boundaries between research groups, each under a single senior professor.

RCAST has five focus areas for interdisciplinary studies:

1)   Advanced materials
2)   Advanced devices
3)   Advanced systems
4)   Knowledge processing and transfer
5)   Socio-technological systems

The group the JTEC team visited is in the fourth of these areas and is headed by Professor Setsuo Ohsuga and Associate Professor Koichi Hori. Professor Ohsuga, a former president of the Japanese AI society, is the director of RCAST. The lab has 18 graduate students, five of whom are non-Japanese, and five research staff members, two of whom are foreign visiting scholars. Much of the work in this lab is conducted in conjunction with industry consortia. The lab appeared rich in computer equipment: in addition to a dozen or more UNIX workstations of both U.S. and Japanese make, there were several Symbolics LISP machines and an ICOT PSI machine, although the latter seemed not to be in use. We were told that the lab's programming work has intentionally been switched to C from LISP and PROLOG to ease technology transfer to and from industry. This emphasis on industry collaboration and the relatively large presence of foreign students and researchers is one of the more interesting features of the lab and is consistent with the RCAST charter to break out of traditional Japanese university patterns.

Professor Ohsuga's research interests have centered on knowledge representation for many years. The current work is particularly focused on knowledge representation for intelligent computer aided design applications across a variety of domains. The lab's research covers the following areas:

1)   Knowledge representation
2)   The integration of knowledge bases and databases
3)   Intelligent CAD systems:
    a) Knowledge-based design systems for feedback control of industrial plants
    b) Design systems for aircraft wings
    c) Chemical knowledge information processing systems
4)   CASE; emphasis on specification development and conceptual modeling
5)   Articulation problems

This last area is the special concern of Professor Hori and deals with the problem of transforming vague conceptualizations into representations that can be manipulated by a knowledge-based system.

The central tool of Professor Ohsuga's group is a representation and reasoning tool called KAUS (Knowledge Acquisition and Utilization System), which has been under development since the mid-1980s. KAUS is a logic-based system and is an implementation of a logical system called Multi-Level Logic (MLL) developed by Professor Ohsuga. This is a many-sorted first-order logic, in which data structures are the terms of the logic. Data structures are formally developed from axiomatic set theory. KAUS has a meta level for control of the base level reasoner. One component of this involves the use of procedural attachments (in much the same spirit as Weyhrauch's FOL). Certain predicates, called procedural type atoms (PTAs), are treated specially by the logic; an expression involving such a predicate is evaluated by fetching a procedure associated with the PTA and applying that procedure to the arguments. The returned result is treated as the logical value of the expression. One particularly useful PTA is EXEC, which calls the UNIX EXEC routine on its arguments; this makes any procedure accessible through UNIX a part of KAUS. This mechanism is used to access conventional database systems, which essentially transforms any normal database into a deductive database.

KAUS is used in most of the research projects conducted in the lab. One project of note has been a collaboration with chemists around Japan. The goal is to develop a chemical compound design system. Early work in the group resulted in a system called Chemilog, which was an extended PROLOG system including representations and pattern matching for chemical structures. The insights of that work were re-implemented in KAUS by building a structure matching procedure for graph structures; the matcher was general enough to serve not only for chemistry but also for a variety of other engineering disciplines.

The following is a list of ongoing research projects in the lab:

o   Problem model design/transformation-based program development
o   Knowledge discovery and management in integrated use of knowledge
          bases and databases
o   A method for acquiring problem decomposition strategy from traces
o   Framework for connecting several knowledge-based systems under a
          distributed environment
o   Primitive based representation of adjectives and figurative language
          understanding
o   Structured connectionist studies in natural language processing
o   Interactive music generation system
o   Study of the development of neural networks in the context of artificial life
o   An approach to aid large-scale design problems by computer
o   Aiding FEM preprocessing with knowledge engineering
o   Supporting the development of intelligent CAD systems on KAUS
o   A method to assist the acquisition and expression of subjective concepts and
          its application to design problems
o   A study of computer aided thinking - mapping text objects in metric spaces

AIST, Nara and JAIST, Hokuriku

An additional item of potential importance to the field of knowledge-based systems research was briefly mentioned during our visit to Prof. Nishida's laboratory. This is the creation of two new graduate schools, called AIST and JAIST, Hokuriku with campuses in Nara and Ishikawa, respectively. Each graduate school will have 20 computer science research groups (each with the traditional four professors for computer science), of which three will conduct AI work. Prof. Nishida will leave Kyoto University to head the Knowledge-Based Systems Group at AIST, Nara. There will be an equivalently sized biological sciences faculty at Nara. JAIST, Hokuriku will consist of a graduate school for information science and one for material sciences. Each graduate school will admit about 125 M.S. candidates and 37 Ph.D. candidates per year. This certainly seems like a conscious effort to promote long-term U.S.-style graduate research and study, with computer science (including KB systems) recognized as a fundamentally important discipline. It will be interesting to track the progress of these two graduate schools.

As stated above, it appears that current Japanese basic research efforts in AI could be characterized as good quality, but small in number. The total IJCAI output of the entire community for the last three meetings was less than CMU or Stanford over the same period. RCAST was the first attempt to significantly expand the scope, and JAIST is a much more ambitious attempt to do the same.

INDUSTRIAL RESEARCH

Work in knowledge-based systems in Japanese industrial laboratories appears to be tightly coupled with application or product development. Japanese computer manufacturing companies and certain high tech companies carry out some knowledge-based systems research. Other types of companies do virtually none. The JTEC team observed a thin layer of excellent industrial research at Fujitsu, Hitachi, Toshiba, NEC, and NTT. From other publications, we know that there is excellent knowledge-based system work at IBM Japan and Sony. Perhaps the most extensive and the deepest of the basic research activities at companies was seen at Hitachi's Advanced Research Laboratory (under the direction of Dr. Hiroshi Motoda), at NEC, and at NTT.

The JTEC panel surveyed topics covered by industrial researchers of knowledge-based systems in Japan by looking at three years' worth of volumes of working papers of the special interest group on knowledge-based systems of the Japan Society for Artificial Intelligence. We looked at titles and abstracts only. Most of the work appeared to be follow-up studies to work that had entered the literature in the United States or Europe. The interest among Japanese researchers was very broad, touching many of the issues and research topics of current interest in the United States:

o   Automatic knowledge reformulation (Hitachi)
o   Imagistic reasoning (Hitachi)
o   Natural language understanding (Hitachi)
o   Personal learning machine (Hitachi)
o   Development of massive memory (4GB) workstation (Hitachi)
o   Machine learning (NEC)

NEC

As to research on large knowledge bases, NEC demonstrated systems containing extensive data on DNA and protein sequences, and on protein secondary structure. The systems are used for searching for common patterns in the sequence information. In other areas of AI, NEC has a well-documented body of research on model-based diagnosis, genetic information processing, learning (using a technique called Minimum Description Length), learning theory, inductive learning, knowledge acquisition for classification problems and for consultation systems, natural language understanding, and case-based reasoning. The company believes that the important aspects of second generation ES tools are the incorporation of machine learning, model-based reasoning, cooperative problem solving, and facilities for extracting knowledge from large databases.

NEC has also developed a language, called PRIME (PRimary Inference Mechanism with Environment), for describing a semantic model of a domain. The model can be used for deep-level inference. The inference process can then be compiled into a shallow knowledge base.

Fujitsu

Fujitsu Laboratories is conducting research in constraint satisfaction and optimization (Maruyama, Minoda et al. 1991), object-oriented knowledge bases for engineering, and machine learning. Mr. Maruyama presented a novel approach to solving constraint satisfaction and optimization problems, which he considers more effective than integer programming. The object-oriented work is aimed toward flexible management of design data, intelligent CAD support (including management of design constraints and constraint-based animation), and advanced methods for management of engineering information. Machine learning research has focused on applying computational learning theory toward inductive inference of decision trees in the presence of noisy data.

NTT

AI research at NTT is conducted in three major areas: common-sense reasoning (in a restricted sense); machine translation; and VLSI design. The work on common-sense AI focuses on making quantitative judgments in very large KBs. For example, how long numerically is a long river? The research also includes judging ambiguity in words -- a long vacation vs. a long pencil. The machine translation work is based on a belief in the great importance of specialized knowledge. Currently the system has 15,000 sentence structure descriptions. The VLSI design research is aimed at automatic synthesis techniques from high level descriptions of circuits (see Rich 1992).

5. National AI Research Projects

Edward Feigenbaum
Peter E. Friedland
Howard Shrobe

INTRODUCTION

The sponsors of this JTEC study requested that the panel investigate AI-related research activities and achievements at major national laboratories. To that end, the panel visited the Electronic Dictionary Research Project; ICOT, which is the laboratory of the Japanese Fifth Generation Computer Systems (FGCS) Project; and LIFE, which is the Laboratory for International Fuzzy Engineering. The panel also looked into a new national project, called Real World Computing, which is a successor to the FGCS project.

ELECTRONIC DICTIONARY RESEARCH (EDR) PROJECT

History and Goals

EDR was spun out from ICOT in 1986 with a nine-year charter to develop a large-scale, practical electronic dictionary system that could be used in support of a variety of natural language tasks, such as translation between English and Japanese, natural language understanding and generation, speech processing, and so forth.

EDR was established as a consortium in collaboration with eight member corporations, each of which supports a local EDR research group. About 70 percent of EDR funding comes from the Japan Key Technology Center (a government agency established by MPT and MITI); roughly 30 percent comes from the member companies. EDR was established with a nine year budget of approximately $100 million. This money pays for staff of about 70 members at both EDR headquarters and eight laboratories located at the member companies. About 50 of them are at the laboratories, and they are experienced in both lexicography and computer science. EDR places orders with publishing companies for various types of raw data for electronic dictionaries. The number of workers at these publishers at one time reached the maximum of 300, but it is currently less than 100.

The EDR conception of an electronic dictionary is quite distinct from the conventional online dictionaries that are now common. These latter systems are designed as online reference books for use by humans. Typically, they contain the exact textual contents of a conventional printed dictionary stored on magnetic disk or CD-ROM. Usage is analogous to a conventional dictionary, except that the electronic version may have hypertext-like features for more rapid and convenient browsing.

EDR's primary goal, in part, is to capture: "all the information a computer requires for a thorough understanding of natural language" (JEDRI, 1990). This includes: the meanings (concepts) of words; the knowledge needed for the computer to understand the concepts; and the information needed to support morphological analysis and generation, syntactic analysis and generation, and semantic analysis. In addition, information about word co-occurrences and listings of equivalent words in other languages are necessary. In short, the system is intended to be a very large but shallow knowledge base about words and their meanings.

The goals for the EDR research are to produce a set of electronic dictionaries with broad coverage of linguistic knowledge. This information is intended to be neutral in that it should not be biased towards any particular natural language processing theory or application; extensive in its coverage of common general purpose words and of words from a corpus of technical literature; and comprehensive it its ability to support all stages of linguistic processing, such as morphological, syntactic and semantic processing, the selection of natural wording, and the selection of equivalent words in other languages.

Accomplishments

Component Dictionaries. EDR is well on the way to completing a set of component dictionaries which collectively form the EDR product. These include word dictionaries for English and Japanese, the Concept Dictionary, co-occurrence dictionaries for English and Japanese and two bilingual dictionaries: English to

Japanese and Japanese to English. Each of these is extremely large scale, as follows:

Word Dictionaries
    General Vocabulary:
        English   200,000 Words
        Japanese   200,000 Words

    Technical Terminology
        English   100,000 Words
        Japanese   100,000 Words

Concept Dictionary   400,000 Concepts
        Classification
        Descriptions

Co-Occurrence Dictionaries
        English   300,000 Words
        Japanese   300,000 Words

Bilingual Dictionaries
        English-Japanese   300,000 Words
        Japanese-English   300,000 Words

The several component dictionaries serve distinct roles. All semantic information is captured in the Concept Dictionary, which is surface-language independent. The Concept Dictionary is a very large semantic network capturing pragmatically useful concept descriptions. (We will return to this later). The word dictionaries capture surface syntactic information (e.g., pronunciation, inflection) peculiar to each surface language.   Each word entry consists of the "headword" itself, grammatical information, and a pointer to the appropriate concept in the Concept Dictionary. The co-occurrence dictionaries capture information on appropriate word combinations. Each entry consists of a pair of words coupled by a co-occurrence relation (there are several types of co-occurrence relations). Strength of a co-occurrence relation is shown by the certainty factor, whose value ranges from 0 to 255. Zero means that the words cannot be used together. This information is used to determine that "he drives a car" is allowable, that "he drives a unicycle" isn't and that "he rides a unicycle" is. This can be used to determine the appropriate translation of a word. For example, the Japanese word *naosu* corresponds to several English words, e.g., "modify," "correct," "update," and "mend." However if the object of *naosu* is "error," then the appropriate English equivalent is "correct." Finally, the bilingual dictionaries provide surface information on the choice of equivalent words in the target language as well as information on correspondence through entries in the concept dictionary.

From the point of view of KBS, the Concept Dictionary is the most interesting component of the EDR project. As mentioned above, this is a very large semantic network capturing roughly 400,000 word meanings. What is most impressive about this is the sheer breadth of coverage. Other than the Cyc project at MCC, there is simply no other project anywhere in the world which has attempted to catalogue so much knowledge.

The Concept Dictionary has taken the approach of trying to capture pragmatically useful definitions of concepts. This differs from much of the work in the U.S., which attempts to capture the set of necessary and sufficient conditions for a concept to obtain (e.g., KL-One and its descendants). During our visit we asked how the researchers knew they had a good definition, particularly for abstract notions like "love." Their answer was, in effect, 'we're not philosophers, we capture as much as we can.'

EDR describes the concept dictionary as a "hyper-semantic network." By which is meant that a chunk of the semantic network may be treated as a single node that enters into relationships with other nodes. Entries in the Concept Dictionary (for binding relations) are triples of two concepts (nodes) joined by a relationship (arc). For example, "<eat> - agent --> <bird>" which says birds can be the agents of an eating action (i.e., birds eat). The relationship can be annotated with a certainty factor; a 0 certainty factor plays the role of negation. For restrictive relations the entry consists of a pair of a concept and an attribute (with an optional certainty factor); e.g., "walking" is represented by "<walk> -- progress /1 -->."

The "hyper" part of this hyper-semantic network is the ability of any piece of network to be aggregated and treated as a single node. For example, "I believe birds eat" is represented by building the network for "birds eat," then treating this as a node which enters into an object relationship with "believe." Quantification is indicated by use of the "SOME" and "ALL" attributes; the scope of the quantification is indicated by nesting of boxes.

EDR has identified a set of relations which seem to be sufficient; these are shown below. In our discussions, the EDR people seemed to be relatively convinced that they had reached closure with the current set.

Relation Labels

Relation	Description
Agent	Subject of action
Object	Object affected by action or change
Manner	Way of action or change
Implement	Tool/means of action

Material	Material or component
Time	Time event occurs
Time-from	Time event begins
Time-to	Time event ends
Duration	Duration of event
Location	Objective place of action
Place	Place where event occurs
Source	Initial position of subject or object of event
Goal	Final position of subject or object of event
Scene	Objective range of action
Condition	Conditional relation of event/fact
Co-occurrence	Simultaneous relation of event/fact
Sequence	Sequential relation of event/fact
Quantity	Quantity
Number	Number

Semantic Relation Labels

Part of	Part-whole
Equal	Equivalence relation
Similar	Synonymous relation
Kind of	Super concept relation

This framework for representation is similar to semantic network formalisms used in the U.S.; it is most similar to those which are developed for language understanding tasks (e.g., Quillian's work in the late 1960s; OWL; SNePS; and Conceptual Dependency). However, the EDR framework seems to be a bit richer and more mature than most of this research -- particularly so, since this particular thread of research seems to have waned in the U.S.

EDR has tried to develop a systematic approach to the construction of the Concept Dictionary. This involves a layering of the inheritance lattice of concepts as well as a layering of the network structures which define concepts.

Use of Hierarchies. As in most knowledge representation work, the use of Kind Of (IsA) hierarchies plays an important role, capturing commonalities and thereby compressing storage. In the EDR Concept Dictionary a top-level division is made between "Object" and "Non-Object" concepts; the second category is further divided into "Event" and "Feature." Under this top-level classification, EDR has tried to structure the inheritance hierarchy into three layers. In the upper section, "Event" is broken into "Movement," "Action," and "Change," which are further refined into "Physical-Movement" and "Movement-Of-Information."

The refinement of these concepts is governed by the way they bind with the subdivision of the "Object" concept. A concept is further divided if the sub-concepts can enter into different relations with subconcepts of the "Object" hierarchy. The middle section of the hierarchy is formed by multiple inheritance from concepts in the first layer. Again, concepts are subdivided to the degree necessary to correspond to distinct relationships with the subconcepts of "Object."

The third section consists of individual concepts. The subdivision of the "Object" hierarchy is constructed in the same manner, guided by the distinctions made in the "Non-Object" part of the network. The second layer is built by multiple inheritance from the first layer and bottoms out at concepts that need no further division to distinguish the binding relationships with parts of the Non-Object network (e.g., bird). The third layer consists specifically of instances of concepts in the second section (e.g., Swallow Robin).

Network Structures and Methods. The definition section of the network has six layers:

o   Section A contains concepts corresponding to entries in the word dictionaries; these "define themselves".
o   Section B contains semantic relations (part-of, kind-of, etc.) relating the concepts in Section A.
o   Section C contains concept descriptions describing the relations between defined concepts. These consist of non-semantic relations between entries of Section A (e.g., <a bird flies>[<to fly in space> - agent -> <bird>]).
o   Section D contains semantic relations between entries of Sections A and C. (For example, "carouse" might be a concept in section A, "to drink liquor" a description in section C in the form <drink> -object-> <liquor> and the kind-of link is in section D).
o   Section E contains compound concepts formed from two or more concepts from entries in section C.
o   Section F contains semantic relations between A, C, and E.

EDR's minimal goal is to finish sections A through C; they believe that this is achievable within their time-scale and will also be pragmatically useful.

EDR has adopted a pragmatic, example-driven approach to construction of the whole dictionary system. Although they have constructed computer tools to help in the process, people are very much in the loop. The work began with the selection and description of the dictionary contents of 170,000 vocabulary items in each language. Each of these is entered as a "Headword" in the word dictionary. Next, the corresponding word in the other language is determined and entered in the word dictionary if not present. A bilingual correspondence entry is then made in the bilingual dictionaries.

A corpus of 20 million sentences was collected from newspapers, encyclopedias, textbooks and reference books and a keyword in context (KWIC) database was created indicating each occurrence of each word in the corpus. Each word is checked to see whether it is already present in the word dictionaries; if not it is entered. Automated tools perform morphological analysis; the results are output on a worksheet for human correction or approval. For each morpheme, the appropriate concept is selected from the list of those associated with the word. Syntactic and semantic analysis is performed by computer on the results of the morphological analysis and output on worksheets. The results are verified by individuals. The relations between the concepts are determined and filled out on worksheets. Once corrected and approved, the morphological information is added to the word dictionaries. The parse trees and extracted concept relations, once approved, are stored away in the EDR Corpus. Co-occurrence information is extracted from the parse trees and entered into the co-occurrence dictionary. Concept information extracted in this process is compared to the existing concept hierarchy and descriptions. New descriptions are entered into the Concept Dictionary.

Milestones. In January 1991, EDR published the first edition of the dictionary interface. By December 1991, EDR had begun to organize an external evaluation group. In November 1992, the preliminary versions of the Word and Concept Dictionaries were distributed to twelve universities and research institutes, including two American universities, for evaluation. In March of 1993, EDR was scheduled to release for commercial use the second edition of the Word Dictionaries, the first edition of the Concept Dictionary, the first edition of the Bilingual Dictionaries and the first edition of the Co-occurrence Dictionaries. The second edition of the Dictionary Interface was also scheduled for release at this time. EDR plans to offer the dictionaries in commercial form world-wide; the commercial terms are planned to be uniform across national borders, although price has not yet been set. Discussions concerning academic access to the EDR dictionaries in the U.S. are ongoing.

Evaluation

Strengths and Weaknesses. During our visit to EDR, we asked several times what facilities were provided for consistency maintenance or automatic indexing. Our EDR hosts answered that there were a variety of ad hoc tools developed in house, but that they had no overall approach to these problems. They told us that it was very likely that a concept might appear more than once in the dictionary because there weren't really very good tools for detecting duplications. In general, their approach has been to write simple tools that can identify potential problems and then to rely on humans to resolve the problems. Although they seemed quite apologetic about the weakness of their tools, they also seemed reasonably secure that success can be achieved by the steady application of reasonable effort to the problem. The chief indicator of this is a feeling that closure is being reached, that most words and concepts currently encountered are found in the dictionary. In short, there is a feeling that as the mass of the dictionary grows, the mass itself helps to manage the problem.

In contrast, research in the U.S. has placed a much stronger emphasis on strong theories and tools which automatically index a concept within the semantic network, check it for consistency, identify duplication, etc. For example, a significant sector of the knowledge representation community in the U.S. has spent the last several years investigating how to limit the expressiveness of representation languages in order to guarantee that indexing services can be performed by tractable computations (the clearest examples are in the KL-One family of languages). However, no effort in the U.S. has managed to deal with "largeness" as an issue. With the exception of Cyc, knowledge bases in the U.S. are typically much smaller than the EDR dictionary system. Also, the theoretical frameworks often preclude even expressing a variety of information which practitioners find necessary.

Comparison with U.S. Research. In the U.S., we know of only three efforts which approach the scale of the EDR effort. The Cyc project is attempting to build a very large system that captures a significant segment of common sense "consensus reality." At present the number of named terms in the Cyc system is still significantly smaller than the EDR Concept Dictionary, although the knowledge associated with each term is much deeper. A second project is the "lexicon collaborative" at the University of Arizona, which is attempting to build a realistic scale lexicon for English natural language processing. To our knowledge this work is not yet as extensive as EDR's. Finally, NIH has sponsored the construction of a medical information representation system. A large part of the information in this system comes from previously existing medical abstract indexing terms, etc. This system is intended to be quite large scale, but specialized to medical information.

In short, we might characterize the large knowledge base community in the U.S. as long on theories about knowledge representation and use of deep knowledge but short on pragmatism: the number of surface terms in its knowledge bases is relatively small. EDR, on the other hand, has no particular theory of knowledge representation, but has built a practical knowledge base with several hundred thousand concepts.

The JTEC team found EDR's pragmatic approach refreshing and exciting. Although U.S. researchers have spent significantly more time on theoretical formulations, they have not yet succeeded in building any general knowledge base of significant size. EDR's pragmatic approach (and ability to enlist a large number of lexicographers in a single national project) has allowed it to amass a significant corpus of concepts with significant coverage of the terms of natural language. The organizing ideas of the EDR dictionary are not particularly innovative; they have been in play since Quillian (mid 1960s) and Schank (late 1970s). While stronger theoretical work and better tools are both necessary and desirable, there is no substitute for breadth of coverage and the hard work necessary to achieve it. EDR has accomplished this breadth and this is an essentially unique achievement. EDR's work is among the most exciting in Japan (or anywhere else).

Next Steps: The Knowledge Archives Project

Background and Organization. Dr. Yokoi, general manager of EDR, mentioned at the time of our visit to EDR that he has been working with others to prepare a plan for a new effort to be called the Knowledge Archives Project. At the time of our visit, the only information he had available was extremely preliminary and vague. We have since been sent a more complete draft entitled, *A Plan for the Knowledge Archives Project*, March 1992 with the following affiliations: The Economics Research Institute (ERI); Japan Society for the Promotion of Machine Industry (JPSMI); and Systems Research and Development Institute of Japan (SR&DI). An introductory note says that the project is called NOAH (kNOwledge ArcHives). "The knowledge archives," it states, "is the Noah's ark which will overcome the chaos of the turn of the century and build a new foundation for the 21st century" (ERI 1992).

The goal of the Knowledge Archives Project is to amass very large knowledge bases to serve as the "common base of knowledge for international and interdisciplinary exchange in research and technology communities." This will be achieved primarily through the use of textual knowledge sources (i.e., documents), being (semi-)automatically processed into very large scale semantic networks.

Achieving the goal will require the development of a variety of new technologies. As the draft plan states:

> The technology in which the acquisition and collection of vast amounts of knowledge are automated (supported); the technology in which knowledge bases are self-organized so that substantial amounts of knowledge can be stored systematically; the technology which supports the creation of new knowledge by using vast amounts of existing knowledge and by developing appropriate and applicable knowledge bases which fulfill the need for various knowledge usage; and the technology which translates and transmits knowledge to promote the interchange and common use of knowledge. In addition, development of a basic knowledge base which can be shared by all applications will be necessary. (ERI 1992)

The proposal is explicitly multi-disciplinary.   There is a strong emphasis on multi-media technologies, the use of advanced databases (deductive and object oriented, such as the Quixote system at ICOT), and the use of natural language processing technology (such as that developed at EDR). An even more interesting aspect of the proposal is that there is a call for collaboration with researchers in the humanities and social sciences as well as those working in the media industry.

The proposal calls for a new national project to last for eight years beginning in the Japanese fiscal year 1993 and running through fiscal year 2000. There are three phases to the proposed project: (1) A basic research stage (1993-1994); (2) initial prototype development (1995-1997); and (3) final prototype (1998-2000). The output of the project is not imagined as a completed system, but rather as a usable system and a sound starting point for continuing research. The basic organization will comprise one research center and eight to ten research sites. Staffing will consist of transferred employees from research institutes and participating corporations.

Research Themes. A variety of research themes are associated with the archive project, including:

1) Knowledge-grasping semantics. It is important to be able to understand meanings, to have computers interact with users at levels deeper than syntax. This theme is stated several times throughout the report and is often mentioned in the context of "reorganizing information processing systems from the application side." However, the proposal also notes that "AI has limited the range of objects and tried to search for their meaning in depth. Now it is important to deal with objects in a broader range but deal with the meaning in a shallow range" (ERI 1992).

2) The importance of being very large. "Handling of small amounts of slightly complicated knowledge would not be enough. Computers have to be capable of dealing with very large-scale knowledge and massive information." Largeness in and of itself is also inadequate. "Totally new technologies are required to automatically acquire and store massive knowledge as efficiently as possible. The technologies are exactly what the Knowledge Archive Project has to tackle" (ERI 1992). Reference is also made to memory-based (case-based) reasoning, and neural network technologies also may be relevant.

3) Necessity for diverse knowledge representation media. Humans represent knowledge in a variety of ways: textually, graphically, through images, sounds, etc. "Representation media for humans will play the leading role in knowledge representation, and those for computers will be considered as media for 'computer interface.' Knowledge and software will no longer be represented and programmed for computers, but will be represented and programmed for the combination of humans and computers" (ERI 1992).

4) Necessity for research based on the ecology of knowledge. "Knowledge is varied, diversified and comes in many forms. Knowledge is made visible as

one document represented by a representation media. The key technology of knowledge processing for the Knowledge Archives automatically generates, edits, transforms, stores, retrieves, and transmits these documents as efficiently as possible" (ERI 1992).

5)   Necessity for a shared environment for the reuse of knowledge. "The first step is to standardize knowledge representation media [Editor's note: It's significant that media is plural] and make them commonly usable. Logic and logic programming have to be considered as the basis of knowledge representation languages, that is the medium for computers" (ERI 1992). The mechanism for storing large bodies of knowledge and retrieving knowledge on request form a key part of this agenda. Next generation databases (as opposed to current AI KBs) are seen as the best initial technology for this goal.

6)   Progress of separate technologies. The goal of the NOAH project requires the use of a variety of technologies which the authors think have matured enough to enable an effort to begin. However, it will be a key goal to integrate these technologies and to foster their further development. The technologies identified are: natural language processing, knowledge engineering, multimedia, and software engineering.

7)   The accumulation of information and the progress of related technologies. Although Japan has lagged the west in online text processing (because of its particular language and alphabet problems), it is now the case that a vast amount of information is becoming available in electronic form. Much of this information is now online and accessible through networks. The publishing industry, libraries and others traditionally involved in the management of large amounts of information are seen as prospective users of the fruits of the project and also as prospective collaborators in its development.

8)   Fruitful results of various projects. The Fifth Generation Computer Project has produced new constraint logic programming languages which are seen as potential knowledge representation languages. The Parallel Inference Machines (PIMs) (or some follow-on) are expected to function as high performance database machines. EDR is seen as having produced robust natural language processing technology and "has made natural language the kernel language of knowledge representation media" (ERI 1992). The EDR's dictionary is cited as a very large knowledge base of lexical knowledge. Finally, the various machine translation projects around Japan are cited as other examples of natural language processing technology.

What Will Be Done. Although attention is paid to the notion that human knowledge has many representation media, the proposal singles out for special attention two media of importance: natural language, in particular, modern Japanese as the media to be used by humans, and the system knowledge representation language that will be used internally with the Knowledge Archives system.

Documents are seen as the natural unit of knowledge acquisition. Knowledge documents written in the system knowledge representation language form the knowledge base of the Knowledge Archives. Words, sentences, texts, and stories are examples of the various levels of aggregation which make up knowledge objects. Knowledge objects are mutually related to one another in a semantic network which enables them to be defined and to have attached attributes. Both surface structure and semantic objects are stored in the Knowledge Archives. Surface representations are retained because the semantic objects are not required to capture all the meanings of the surface documents.

Relationships connect knowledge objects. These include: links between surface structure objects, e.g., syntactic relationships and inclusion relationships; semantic links, e.g., case frame links between words, causality links between sentences; correspondence links between surface and semantic objects; equality and similarity links, etc. Corresponding to each type of link will be a variety of inference rules that allow deductions to be drawn from the information. Also, it is a goal to develop mechanisms for learning and self-organization.

Initially, much of the work will be done manually or in a semi-automated fashion. However, it is hoped that the system can take on an increasingly large part of the processing. To make the task tractable in the initial phases, documents will not be processed as they are but rather, summary documents will be prepared. These will be analyzed by the computer and attached to the complete document with synonym links.

The envisioned sources of documents for processing are at the moment quite broad, encompassing collaboration with humanities research groups such as the Opera Project (chairman, Seigou Matsuoka), newspaper articles, scientific and technical literature (primarily information processing), patents, legal documents, manuals, and more.

Summary and Analysis. Much of the archives proposal seems vague, although the general spirit is clear. It should be noted that the proposal is the initial edition of the plan. EDR is currently working on more concrete details for it. Using the technologies developed by EDR, machine translation projects, and to a lesser degree ICOT, the project will attempt to build a very large-scale knowledge base. Documents, particularly textual documents, will form the core knowledge source with natural language processing technology converting natural language text into internal form. At least initially, the work will be at best semi-automated, but as the technologies get better the degree of automation will increase. The knowledge base will support a variety of knowledge storage, retrieval and transformation tasks. Largeness is seen as the core opportunity and challenge in the effort. Cyc is the U.S. project most similar to the one proposed here, although it is important to note the difference in perspective (Lenat and Guha 1990). In Cyc, it is the job of human knowledge engineers to develop an ontology and to enter the knowledge into it. In the Knowledge Archives Project, the source of knowledge is to be existing textual material and the ontology should (at least somewhat) emerge from the self-organization of the knowledge base.

The proposal explicitly mentions the intention of collaborating with researchers outside Japan and of encouraging the formation of similar efforts in other countries. The proposal has not yet been approved, but its progress should be followed.

ICOT

History and Goals

ICOT was founded as the central research laboratory of the Fifth Generation Computer Systems project in 1982. It is now celebrating the end of its planned 10-year lifetime and in 1992 entered an 11th year. Since the JTEC panel's visit, we have learned unofficially that ICOT's life will be extended for a total of three more years with a reduced staffing level.

ICOT has concentrated on the development of languages and hardware for parallel logic programming. Because of the centrality of parallel processing in its research, we will necessarily spend significant time reporting on it. However, our interest in ICOT is in its effect on knowledge-based systems research and practice in Japan. We will try to maintain a focus on this aspect of the ICOT research.

The Fifth Generation Computer Systems project was motivated by the observation that "Current computers are extremely weak in basic functions for processing speech, text, graphics, picture images, and other non-numeric data, and for artificial intelligence type processing such as inference, association, and learning" (ICOT 1982). To address these shortcomings, the Fifth Generation project was commissioned to build the prototypes for a new (the fifth) generation of hardware and software. Early ICOT documents (1982) identify the following requirements:

1)   To realize basic mechanisms for inference, association, and learning in hardware and make them the core functions of the fifth generation computers.
2)   To prepare basic artificial intelligence software to fully utilize the above functions.

3)   To take advantage of pattern recognition and artificial intelligence research achievements, and realize man-machine interfaces that are natural to man.
4)   To realize support systems for resolving the "software crisis" and enhancing software production.

A fifth-generation computer system in this early ICOT vision is distinguished by the centrality of problem solving and inference; knowledge-base management; and intelligent interfaces.

Such a system obviously requires enormous computing power. In ICOT's view, it also required a new type of computing power, one more symbolic and inferential in character than conventional systems. Also, the system was explicitly assumed to rely on very large knowledge bases and to provide specialized capabilities for knowledge and database management. Finally, fifth-generation systems were assumed to interact with people in a more human manner, using natural language in both printed and spoken form.

The early ICOT documents call for a three-tier system. At its base is a tier for knowledge-base systems, which includes parallel database management hardware and knowledge base management software. This system was envisioned as "a database machine with 100 to 1000 GB capacity" able "to retrieve the knowledge bases required for answering a question within a few seconds" (ICOT 1982).

> The intention of software for the knowledge base management function will be to establish knowledge information processing technology where the targets will be development of knowledge representation systems, knowledge base design and maintenance support systems, large-scale knowledge base systems, knowledge acquisition experimental systems, and distributed knowledge management systems....One particularly important aim will be semi-automated knowledge acquisition, that is, systems will be equipped with a certain level of learning functions. (ICOT 1982)

Built on top of this are a problem-solving and inference tier, including hardware for parallel inference, abstract datatyping and dataflow machines. This tier includes software for a fifth-generation kernel language (see below), cooperative problem solving mechanisms and parallel inference mechanisms.

The final tier is the intelligent man-machine interface system. This was supposed to include dedicated special purpose hardware for speech and other signal processing tasks and software for natural language, speech graphics and image processing:

The intelligent interface function will have to be capable of handling communication with the computer in natural language, speech, graphics, and picture images so that information can be exchanged in ways natural to man. Ultimately the system will cover a basic vocabulary (excluding specialist terms) of up to 100,000 words and up to 2,000 grammatical rules, with a 99 percent accuracy in syntactic analysis.

The object speech inputs will be continuous speech in Japanese standard pronunciation by multiple speakers, and the aims here will be a vocabulary of 50,000 words, a 95 percent recognition rate for individual words, and recognition of processing within three times the real time of speech.

The system should be capable of storing roughly 10,000 pieces of graphic and image information and utilizing them for knowledge information processing. (ICOT 1982)

These three tiers were then supposed to support a very sophisticated program development environment to raise the level of software productivity and to support experimentation in new programming models. Also, the basic three tiers were supposed to support a very basic application system. Those listed in the 1982 document include: machine translation, consultation systems, and intelligent programming systems (including automated program synthesis and verification).

It was decided early on that the ICOT systems would be logic programming systems that would build on, but significantly extend, PROLOG. Also, it was decided that the logic programming language would be a kernel language that would be used for a broad spectrum of software, ranging from the implementation of the system itself up through the application layers.

In practice, ICOT's central focus became the development of a logic programming kernel language and hardware tailored to the efficient execution of this language. The system's performance target was to be from 100 MegaLIPS (logical inferences per second -- simple PROLOG procedure calls) to 1 GigaLIPS. As a reference point, ICOT documents estimate that 1 Logical Inference takes about 100 instructions on a conventional machine; a 1 MLIPS machine would therefore be roughly equivalent to a 100 MIPS processor, although this comparison may confuse more than it reveals. The rather reasonable assumption was made that achieving such high performance would require parallel processing: " the essential research and development will concentrate...on high-level parallel architectures to support the symbol processing that is the key to inference" (ICOT 1982). Furthermore, the assumption was made that achieving the desired performance target would require about 1,000 processing elements per system, given reasonable assumptions on the performance of a single such processing element.

ICOT's development plans were segmented into three phases. The goal for the initial phase was to develop a personal sequential inference machine (PSI), that is, a workstation tailored to efficient execution of a sequential logic programming language. This phase was also supposed to develop the system software for a high capability programming environment for fifth-generation software. The initial considerations of parallel systems were also to begin during this stage.

In the second phase, a refined personal sequential inference would be developed, the model for parallel programming would be settled upon and initial exploratory parallel architectures would be prototyped.

The third phase would build the Parallel Inference Machines (PIM). This would include not only the hardware effort, but a parallel operating system and a second-generation kernel language appropriate for parallel processing (Fig. 5.1).

Accomplishments - Hardware

During the first three-year phase of the project, the personal sequential inference machine (PSI-1) was built and a reasonably rich programming environment was developed for it.

To put this effort in context, we compare it to the U.S. project which it most resembles: the MIT LISP Machine. The MIT project had begun in the late 1970s and had just reached commercialization at the time of ICOT's inception. Like the MIT machine, PSI was a microprogrammed processor designed to support a symbolic processing language. The symbolic processing language played the role of a broad spectrum kernel language for the machine, spanning the range from low-level operating system details up to application software. The hardware and its microcode were designed to execute the kernel language with high efficiency. The machine was a reasonably high performance workstation with good graphics, networking and a sophisticated programming environment.

What made PSI different was the choice of language family. Unlike more conventional machines oriented toward numeric processing, or the MIT machine, which was oriented towards LISP, the language chosen for PSI was PROLOG. The primary appeal of PROLOG-like languages to ICOT was the analogy between the basic operations of PROLOG and simple rule-like logical inferencing. A procedure in such a language can be viewed as simply reducing a goal to its subgoals. Given

Development of ICOT Systems

	Sequential	Parallel
'82 -84 Initial Stage $55.3 M	Languages: KL0 & ESP Machines: PSI-I and SIMPOS 35K LIPS for KL0	Languages: GHC & KL1
'85 -88 Inter- mediate Stage $147 M	Machines: PSI-I I 330K LIPS for KL0	Machines: Multi-PSI 5M LIPS / 64 PEs for KL1 Parallel OS, PIMOS and small applications
'89 -92 Final Stage $139 M ————— **$341.3 M**	Machines: PSI-III (PSI-UX) 1.4 M LIPS for KL0	Machines: PIMs 1000 PEs (in 5 systems) 200M LIPS / 512 PEs for KL1

Figure 5.1. ICOT Accomplishments in Sequential and Parallel Systems

the emphasis on inference as a key component of the FGCS vision, the choice seemed quite natural. However, the choice of a logic programming framework for the kernel language was a radical one since there had been essentially no experience anywhere with using logic programming as a framework for the implementation of core system functions.

PSI-1 achieved a performance of about 35K LIPS, comparable to DEC-10 PROLOG, the PROLOG performance of the Symbolics 3600 (one of the follow-ons to the MIT LISP Machine) or Quintus's PROLOG implementation for Sun-3 class machines. This was fast enough to allow the development of a rich operating system and programming environment, but still quite slow compared to the Phase 3 goals (1000 processors achieving 1 GLIPS implies at least 1 MLIPS per processor). Two extended PROLOG-like languages (ESP and KL0) were developed for PSI-1. ESP (Extended Self-Contained PROLOG) included a variety of features such as coroutining constructs, non-local cuts, etc., necessary to support system programming tasks as well as more advanced logic programming. SIMPOS, the operating system for the PSI machines, was written in ESP.

Several hundred PSI machines were built and installed at ICOT and related facilities, and the machine was also sold commercially. However, even compared to specialized LISP hardware in the U.S., the PSI machines were impractically expensive. Dr. Chikayama at ICOT told us during our visit that the PSI (and subsequent) machines had many features whose purpose was to support experimentation and whose cost/benefit tradeoff had not been evaluated as part of the design. In his view, the machines were inherently non-commercial.

Phase 1. During Phase 1, it was decided to explore an "And-Parallel" approach to parallel logic programming. To simplify, this means that the subgoals of a clause are explored in parallel with shared variable bindings being the means of communication. The process solving one subgoal can communicate with a process solving a sibling subgoal by binding a shared variable to a concrete value. It was also observed that subgoals would have to spread out across the network of processors constituting the parallel machine and that it would require careful control to avoid the buildup of communication bottlenecks. By the end of Phase 1, the form of the parallel kernel language was clarified: it was to be a flat guarded horn clause (FGHC) language. A previous JTEC study, *JTEC Panel Report on Advanced Computing in Japan* (Denicoff 1987), has already reported on this so we will be very brief in explaining the concept. A flat guarded horn clause consists of three parts: 1) head, 2) guard, and 3) body. The head plays exactly the same role as the head of a PROLOG clause: it identifies a set of goals for which the clause is suitable (i.e., those goals which unify with the head). The guard and body collectively play the role of the body of a PROLOG clause, i.e., they are a set of subgoals whose truth implies the truth of the head. However, the body of the clause is not executed until all variables in the guard are applied and all literals in the guard are satisfied. In the case where two or more clauses have heads that unify with the same goal, only the body of that clause whose guard is first satisfied will execute (hence the name guarded horn clause).   "Flat" means that the guard can only contain built-in predicates, rather than those which are evaluated by further chaining. This greatly simplifies the mechanisms, without significantly reducing their expressive power.

The execution of an FGHC program is summarized in four rules:

1)   Relevance: Those clauses the heads of which unify with a goal are potentially executable.
2)   Synchronization: Until the caller has sufficiently instantiated the variable to allow the guard part of the clause to execute, execution of the guard is suspended.
3)   Selection: If there are more than one potentially executable clauses for a goal, that clause the guard of which succeeds first will execute its body and the bodies of all other competing clauses will never execute.
4)   Parallelism; the subgoals in the body are executed in parallel.

Figure 5.2 shows a set of FGHC for a prime sieve algorithm and how the clauses begin to elaborate a parallel process structure.   One should notice that this interpretation model does not lead to an automatic search mechanism as in PROLOG.   In PROLOG all relevant clauses are explored, and the order of exploration is specified by the programming model. In FGHC only a single relevant clause is explored; ICOT has had to conduct research on how to recapture search capabilities within the FGHC framework.

Phase 2. The second three-year phase saw the development of the PSI-2 machine, which provided a significant speedup over PSI-1. Towards the end of Phase 2, a parallel machine (the Multi-PSI) was constructed to allow experimentation with the FGHC paradigm. This consisted of an 8 x 8 mesh of PSI-2 processors, running the ICOT Flat Guarded Horn Clause language KL1 (not to be confused with the knowledge representation language KL-ONE developed at Bolt Beranek and Newman). Multi-PSI supported the development of the ICOT parallel operating system PIMOS and some initial small-scale parallel application development. PIMOS is a parallel operating system written in KL1; it provides parallel garbage collection algorithms, algorithms to control task distribution and communication, a parallel file system, etc.

Phase 3. Phase three has centered around the refinement of the KL1 model and the development of massively parallel hardware systems to execute it. KL1 has been refined into a three-level language. KL1-b is the machine level language underlying the other layers. KL1-c is the core language used to write most software; it extends the basic FGHC paradigm with a variety of useful features such as a macro language.

Example of KL1

prime (Max, Ps) <- true I generator (2, Max, Ns), sifter(Ns,Ps).

generator (N0, Max, Ns) <--N0 =< Max I
  Ns0 = [N0INs1], N1 := N0 + 1, generator(N1, Max, Ns1).
generator (N0, Max, Ns0) <-- N0 > Max I Ns0 = [].

sifter ([PIXs1], Zs0) <-- true I
  Zs0 = [P I Zs1], filter(P, Xs1, Ys1), sifter(Ys, Zs1).
sifter ([], Zs0) <-- true I Zs0 = [].

filter (P, [XIXs1],Ys0) <-- (X mod P) =/= 0 I
  Ys0 = [XIYs1], filter (P, Xs1, Ys1).
filter (P, [XIXs1],Ys0) <-- (X mod P) == 0 I
  filter (P, Xs1, Ys0).
filter (P, [], Ys0) <-- true I Ys0 = [].

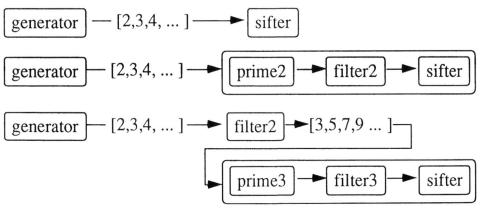

Figure 5.2. Prime Sieve Algorithm Using Guarded Horn Clauses

KL1-p includes the "pragmas" for controlling the implementation of the parallelism. There are three main pragmas. The first of these is a meta-level execution control construct named "shoen" which allows the programmer to treat a group of processes (i.e., a goal and its subgoals) as a unit of execution control. A shoen is created by calling a special routine with the code and its arguments; this creates a new shoen executing the code and all generated subgoals. These subgoals are, however, running in parallel. A failure encountered by any sub-process of a shoen is isolated to that shoen. Each shoen has a message stream and a report stream by which it communicates with the operating system; shoens may be nested but the OS treats the shoen as a single element. Suspending a shoen results in the suspension of all its children, etc. Fine-grain process management is handled by the shoen, freeing the OS from this responsibility.

The second pragma allows the programmer to specify the priority of a goal (and the process it spawns). Each shoen has a minimum and maximum priority for the goals belonging to it. The priority of a goal is specified relative to these.

The third pragma allows the programmer to specify the processor placement for a body goal. This may be a specific processor or a logical grouping of processors. All three of these pragmas are meta-execution control mechanisms which themselves execute at runtime; KL1-p thus allows dynamic determination of the appropriate priority, grouping and placement of processes.

During our visit, Dr. Chikayama mentioned that some of the current software is written in higher level languages embedded in KL1, particularly languages which establish an object orientation. Two such languages have been designed: A'UM and AYA. Objects are modeled as processes communicating with one another through message streams. The local state of an object is carried along in the cyclical call chain from dispatching routine, to service subroutine, back to dispatching routine. Synchronization among processes is achieved through the binding of variables in the list structure modeling the message stream.

Parallel Machines. There are five distinct parallel inference machines (PIMs) being developed to execute KL1, each being built by a commercial hardware vendor associated with ICOT. The PIMs vary in processor design and communication network. The abstract model of all PIMs consists of a loosely coupled network connecting clusters of tightly coupled processors. Each cluster is, in effect, a shared memory multiprocessor; the processors in the cluster share a memory bus and implement a cache coherency protocol. Three of the PIMs are massively parallel machines: PIM/p, PIM/m and PIM/c. PIM/k and PIM/i are research machines designed to study specific intracluster issues such as caching and bus communication. Multi-PSI is a medium scale machine built by connecting 64 PSIs in a mesh architecture. PIM/m and Multi-PSI do not use a cluster architecture (but may be considered as degenerate cases having one processing element per cluster).

The main features of the PIM communication systems are shown in Table 5.1. Relevant features about the processing elements' implementation technology are shown in Table 5.2.

Table 5.1
Main Features of Communication Systems

	Topology	# Clusters	# PE	Memory\Cluster
PIM/p	hypercube x 2	64	512	256 MB
PIM/m	mesh	256	256	80 MB
PIM/c	crossbar	32	256	160 MB
PIM/k		4	16	1 GB
PIM/1		2	16	320 MB
MultiPSI	mesh	64	64	80 MB

	# PEs/Cluster	#Network Interfaces/Cluster	Transfer Rate
PIM/p	8	8	33 MB/sec x 2
PIM/m	1	1	8 MB/sec
PIM/c	8	1	40 MB/sec
PIM/k	16		
PIM/1	8	1	
MultiPSI	1	1	10 MB/sec

It should be noted that cycle times for processing elements are relatively modest. Commercial RISC chips have had cycle times lower than these for several years (the lower the cycle time, the faster the instruction rate). Newly emerging processor chips (such as the DEC ALPHA) have cycle times as low as five nsec. Even granting that special architecture features of the PIM processor chips may lead to a significant speedup (a factor of three, at most), these chips are disappointing compared to the commercial state of the art. The networks used to interconnect the systems have respectable throughput, comparable to that of commercially available systems such as the CM-5. In certain of the PIMs each processor (or processor cluster) can have a set of disk drives; this may allow more balance between processing power and I/O bandwidth for database applications, but there is as yet no data to either confirm or refute this.

Table 5.2
Processing Elements' Implementation Technology

	Instruction Set	Cycle Time	Fabrication Technology	Line Width
PIM/p	RISC	60 nsec	standard cell	0.96 micron
PIM/m	CISC (ucode)	65 nsec	standard cell	0.8 micron
PIM/c	CISC (ucode)	50 nsec	gate array	0.8 micron
PIM/k	RISC	100 nsec	custom	1.2 micron
PIM/i	RISC	100 nsec	standard cell	1.2 micron
MultiPSI	CISC (ucode)	200 nsec	gate array	2.0 micron

Accomplishments - Software

ICOT's software efforts have been layered (see Figure 5.3). So far, we have discussed the bottom-most layer, that concerned with the operating system and language runtime system for parallel logic programming. On this foundation, ICOT has pursued research into databases and knowledge base support, constraint logic programming, parallel theorem proving, and natural language understanding.

In the area of databases, ICOT has developed a parallel database system called Kappa-P. This is a nested relational database system based on an earlier ICOT system called Kappa. Kappa-P is a parallel version of Kappa, re-implemented in KL1. It also adopts a distributed database framework to take advantage of the ability of the PIM machines to attach disk drives to many of the processing elements. Quixote is a knowledge representation language built on top of Kappa-P. It is a constraint logic programming language with object-orientation features such as object-identity, complex objects described by the decomposition into attributes and values, encapsulation, type hierarchy and methods. ICOT also describes Quixote as a deductive object oriented database (DOOD). Quixote and Kappa-P have been used to build a molecular biological database and a legal reasoning system ("TRIAL").

Organization of
ICOT Technology

Experimental Application Systems

Parallel VLSI-CAD   **Legal Reasoning**

Genetic Sequence Matching

Others?

**Knowledge Procesing
Software**

Natural Language

Parallel Theorem Provers

Constraint Logic
Programming

Basic Software

Parallel OS, PIMOS
KL1 Programming Env.

Parallel KBMS/DBMS
Kappa-P + Quixote

**Parallel Inference Machine
1000 PEs in Total**

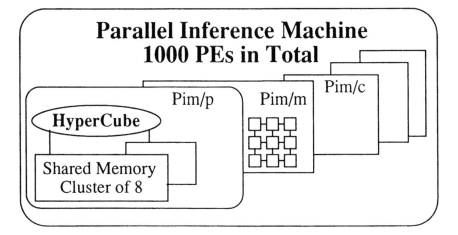

Pim/c

Pim/m

Pim/p

HyperCube

Shared Memory
Cluster of 8

Figure 5.3. ICOT's Layered Approach to Software Development

ICOT has been one of the world-class centers for research into constraint logic programming. All such languages share the idea of merging into a logic programming context constraint solvers for specific non-logical theories (such as linear equations or linear inequalities). Two languages of this type developed at ICOT are CAL (Constraint Avec Logique) which is a sequential constraint logic programming language which includes algebraic, Boolean, set and linear constraint solvers. A second language, GDCC (Guarded Definite Clauses with Constraints), is a parallel constraint logic programming language with algebraic, Boolean, linear and integer parallel constraint solvers.

Another area explored is automatic theorem proving. ICOT has developed a parallel theorem prover called MGTP (Model Generation Theorem Prover). This is written in KL1 and runs on the PIMs. MGTP has obtained a more than 100-fold speedup on a 128 processing element PIM/m for a class of problems known as condensed detachment problems. MGTP is based on the model generation proving methods first developed in the SATCHMO system. However, the ICOT version uses the unification hardware of the PIMs to speed this up for certain common cases. MGTP has been used as a utility in a demonstration legal reasoning system. It has also been used to explore non-monotonic and abductive reasoning. Finally, MGTP has been employed in some program synthesis explorations, including the synthesis of parallel programs.

Natural language processing has been a final area of higher level support software developed at ICOT. There have been several areas of work: 1) a language knowledge base consisting of a Japanese syntax and dictionary; 2) a language tool box containing morphological and syntax analyzers, sentence generator, concordance system, etc.; and 3) a discourse system which rides on top of the first two. These are combined in a parallel, cooperative language understanding system using type inference. The dictionary has about 150,000 entries of which 40,000 are proper names (to facilitate analysis of newspaper articles).

On top of these tools a variety of demonstration application systems have been developed. The following were shown running on the PIM machines at the 10th anniversary FGCS conference are listed here:

o   A diagnostic and control expert system based on a plant model
o   Experimental adaptive model-based diagnostic system
o   Case-based circuit design support system
o   Co-HLEX: experimental parallel hierarchical recursive layout system
o   Parallel cell placement experimental system
o   High level synthesis system: RODIN
o   Co-Lodex: a cooperative logic design expert system
o   Parallel LSI router
o   Parallel logic simulator

o   Protein sequence analysis program
o   Model generation theorem prover
o   Parallel database management system: Kappa-P
o   Knowledge representation language: Quixote
o   A parallel legal reasoning system: HELIC-II
o   Experimental motif extraction system
o   Mendels Zone: a concurrent program development system
o   Parallel constraint logic programming system: GDCC
o   Experimental system for argument text generation: Dulcinea
o   A parallel cooperative natural language processing system: Laputa
o   An experimental discourse structure analyzer

KL1 Development

When asked what they regarded as their legacy -- the core achievement of the 10-year ICOT program -- both Dr. Fuchi and Dr. Chikayama said that it was KL1, as opposed to the PIM hardware, the higher level software or the application demos.

Three key developments in KL1 are worth noting.

First, the language itself is an interesting parallel programming language. KL1 bridges the abstraction gap between parallel hardware and knowledge-based application programs. It is a language designed to support symbolic (as opposed to strictly numeric) parallel processing. It is an extended logic programming language which includes features needed for realistic programming (such as arrays). However, it should also be pointed out that like many other logic programming languages, KL1 will seem awkward to some and impoverished to others.

Second is the development of a body of optimization technology for such languages. Dr. Chikayama noted that efficient implementation of a language such as KL1 required a whole new body of compiler optimization technology. ICOT has developed such a body of techniques. Because there are several architecturally distinct PIMs (and the Multi-PSI), ICOT has been forced to develop a flexible implementation strategy for KL1. KL1 is compiled into an intermediate language, KL1-B. KL1-B is the abstract language implemented by each hardware system; it is a hardware model of a coupled multiprocessor in which some processors are linked in tightly coupled clusters. To build a KL1 implementation, the architect must transform the abstract KL1-B specification into a physical realization. This is done semi-automatically.

The third achievement is noticing where hardware can play a significant role in supporting the language implementation. Part of the architecture of the PIM (and PSI) processors is a tag-checking component which provides support for the dynamic type checking and garbage collection needed to support a symbolic computing language. This small amount of additional hardware provides a high degree of leverage for the language implementation without necessarily slowing down the processor or introducing undue complexity to the implementation. Such features, which might also support LISP and other more dynamic languages, may eventually find their way into commercial processors.

At the time of the JTEC team's visit to ICOT in March 1992, the first of the PIMs (PIM/m) was running PIMOS and KL1 reliably. This machine was still awaiting the arrival of modules providing additional processors. The second and third PIMs were being installed and had begun to execute KL1 code and parts of the OS. Multi-PSI was also available for experimentation. At the time of the 10th anniversary Fifth Generation Conference in June 1992, the remainder of the PIMs were running and were demonstrated.

Evaluation

The early ICOT documents suggested a push towards very advanced and very large-scale knowledge-based systems. Actually, the core ICOT efforts went off in a different direction. The central perspective of ICOT has been to develop parallel symbolic programming (in particular, parallel logic programming) by developing a new language and by developing experimental hardware to support the language.

The demo applications for the PIM machines seem comparatively routine. Even though each of these programs demonstrates the power of parallelism and each embeds some advance in parallel programming, when viewed as knowledge-based systems, these systems bring little new to bear. For example, the multi-sequence matching program has a new approach to simulated annealing which uniquely capitalizes on the available parallelism; however, it knows essentially nothing about genetics and proteins. This doesn't make the program useless or uninteresting; it is solving a task for which crunch seems to dominate over knowledge. However, from our perspective of studying advances in knowledge-based systems technology, the program is disappointing. The VLSI routing program is subject to the same critique. Of the programs demonstrated, the legal reasoning system is the only one which might be fairly termed a knowledge-based system. Here, parallelism was used to accelerate both case retrieval and logical argumentation. Nevertheless, for all the computational power being brought to bear, the system did not seem to establish a new plateau of capability.

The early ICOT documents discuss the management of very large knowledge bases, of large-scale natural language understanding and image understanding. Also, the early documents have a strong emphasis on knowledge acquisition and learning. Each of these directions seems to have been either dropped, relegated to secondary status, absorbed into the work on parallelism, or transferred to other research initiatives (such as EDR).

In summary, in answer to the question, "has ICOT directly accelerated the development of knowledge-based technology in Japan so far?," the answer would have to be "no."

However, there are other questions which are also relevant:

1) Has ICOT indirectly affected the state of knowledge-based technology in Japan?
2) Is the ICOT work likely to produce a platform that will ultimately accelerate knowledge-based technology in Japan?
3) Has ICOT's work advanced the state of parallel processing technology in Japan (or elsewhere)?

The answer to question 1 is almost certainly "yes." Our hosts at virtually every site we visited said that ICOT's work had little direct relevance to them. The reasons most frequently cited were: the high cost of the ICOT hardware, the choice of PROLOG as a language, and the concentration on parallelism. However, nearly as often our hosts cited the indirect effect of ICOT: the establishment of a national project with a focus on fifth-generation technology had attracted a great deal of attention for artificial intelligence and knowledge-based technology. Our hosts at several sites commented on the fact that this had attracted better people into the field and lent an aura of respectability to what previously had been regarded as esoteric. One professor told us that AI now gets the best students, and that this had not been true before the inception of ICOT and the fifth-generation project.

Question 2 is considerably more difficult to answer. ICOT's work has built an elegant framework for parallel symbolic computing. Most AI experts agree that without parallelism there will ultimately be a barrier to further progress due to the lack of computing power. However, this barrier does not seem imminent. Workstations with more than 100 MIPS of uniprocessor performance are scheduled for commercial introduction this year. With the exception of those sub-disciplines with a heavy signal processing component (e.g., vision, speech, robotics) we are more hampered by lack of large-scale knowledge bases than we are by lack of parallelism. It is, however, quite possible that in the near future this will be reversed and we will be in need of parallel processing technology to support very large-scale knowledge-based systems. We will then be in dire need of programming methodology and techniques to capitalize on parallel hardware. Should this occur, ICOT's work might provide Japanese researchers with a significant advantage.

This, however, depends on the answer to question 3: "Has the ICOT research significantly impacted parallel computing technology?" There are arguments to be made on both sides of this question. On the positive side, we can argue that KL1 is an interesting symbolic computing language. Furthermore, it is a parallel symbolic computing language, and virtually no interesting work has been done elsewhere for expressing parallel symbolic computation. Another positive point is that ICOT will have the test bed of the several PIM machines with which to continue experimentation. This is an unusual opportunity; no other site has access to several distinct implementations of the same virtual parallel machine. It is not unreasonable to expect significant insights to emerge from this experimentation. Finally, we can add that ICOT has confronted a set of interesting technical questions about load distribution, communication and garbage collection in a parallel environment.

On the negative side we may cite several arguments as well. ICOT built for itself a relatively closed world. In both the sequential and parallel phases of its research, there has been a new language developed which is only available on the ICOT hardware. Furthermore, the ICOT hardware has been experimental and not cost-effective for practical applications. This has prevented the ICOT technology from having any impact on, or enrichment from, the practical considerations of the industrial and business worlds.

Earlier we pointed to similarities between the ICOT PSI systems and the MIT LISP machine and its commercial successors. It is noteworthy that only a few hundred PSI machines were sold commercially, while there were several thousand LISP machines sold, some of which continue to be used in important commercial applications such as American Express's Authorizer's Assistant. The one commercial use we saw of the PSI machines was at Japan Air Lines, where PSI-2 machines were employed. (Ironically, they were re-microcoded to LISP machines.) Furthermore, the MIT LISP machine acted as a catalyst, providing a powerful LISP engine until better implementation techniques for LISP were developed for stock hardware. As knowledge-based technology has become more routinized in both the U.S. and Japan, commercial KBS tools have been recoded in C. In the U.S., the AI research community continues to use LISP as a vehicle for the rapid development of research insights; there seems to be little such use of the ICOT-based technology in Japan.

The PIM hardware seems destined for the same fate. The processing elements in the PIMs have cycle times no better than 60 ns; even assuming that the features which provide direct support for KL1 offer a speedup factor of three, this leaves the uniprocessor performance lagging behind the best of today's conventional microprocessors. Both HP and DEC have announced the imminent introduction of uniprocessors of between 100 and 200 MIPS. The interconnection networks in the PIMs do not seem to constitute an advance over those explored in other parallel systems. Finally, the PIMs are essentially integer machines; they do not have floating-point hardware. While the interconnection networks of the PIMs have reasonable performance, this performance is comparable to that of commercial parallel machines in the U.S., such as the CM-5.

It is interesting to compare the PIMs to Thinking Machines' CM-5. This is a massively parallel machine, a descendant of the MIT Connection Machine project.

The CM-5 is the third commercial machine in this line of development. It can support a thousand SPARC chips (and presumably other faster microprocessors as they arise) using an innovative interconnection scheme called Fat Trees. Although the Connection Machine project and ICOT started at about the same time, the CM-5 is commercially available and has found a market within which it is cost-effective. One reason for this is that it has quite good floating point performance. It appears that the only established market for massive parallelism is in scientific computing, leaving the PIMs with a disadvantage that will be difficult to overcome.

Our hosts at ICOT were not unaware of these problems. Dr. Chikayama mentioned a project to build a KL1 system for commercially available processors. This would decouple the language from the experimental hardware and make it more generally available. This greater availability could in turn allow a greater number of researchers whose interests are in large knowledge-based systems to begin to explore the use of the KL1 paradigm. Given their implementation strategy, this should not be an overwhelming task. One of the PIM hardware designers has also designed another parallel system (the AP-1000, which is a mesh connected system of about 1000 SPARC chips). This might be a likely target for such an effort.

In contrast to the Connection Machine efforts (and virtually all other parallel system efforts), which have increasingly focused on massively parallel scientific computation, the ICOT effort has continued to focus on symbolic computing. In contrast to the MIT LISP Machine efforts, which didn't achieve enough commercial viability to afford a push forward into parallelism, ICOT has had sustained long term government funding which has allowed it to persevere. Thus, it has remained the only research institution in Japan with a focus on massively parallel symbolic computing.

FUZZY LOGIC RESEARCH AND LIFE

History and Goals

In 1989, MITI decided to found a research institute to consolidate and propagate research in fuzzy logic. This institute, called LIFE (Laboratory for International Fuzzy Engineering), began operations in early 1990 under the leadership of Professor Toshiro Terano of Hosei University. It had three main foci to its program: decision support, which included work in both human-mediated and fully automatic control systems; intelligent robotics, which included work in speech and image understanding as well as robot planning; and fuzzy computing, which aimed to produce the computing hardware and software necessary to fully implement fuzzy systems. The institute was designed to be fully international in character, with long-term visitors from many countries and a relatively small permanent research staff. As a means of ensuring rapid technology transfer to Japanese industry (a hallmark of MITI institutes) LIFE's board of directors is made up of the presidents of most major Japanese computing companies.

A watershed in the history of LIFE occurred in November 1991, with the hosting of the International Fuzzy Engineering Symposium. The Proceedings of this meeting encompass over 1,100 pages of refereed papers that span the range of worldwide research in all areas of the field. The meeting also led to a serious reassessment of the role of LIFE. Simply put, Professor Terano and his senior staff decided that the development of fuzzy control systems had become a separate, self-sustaining field with its own professional society and meetings. Moreover, fuzzy control didn't have much to do with the original "Holy Grail" of providing help for developing truly human-friendly computer systems. Therefore, further work at LIFE was not to include the engineering of fuzzy control systems. This development has an interesting parallel in the expert systems community in the United States. To a large degree, expert systems work has become a field in itself, quite apart from the artificial intelligence research community. There are attempts (like the sponsorship of the Innovative Applications of AI conferences by the American Association of Artificial Intelligence) to prevent such a split, but the overall trend seems to be toward separate meetings and societies.

About Fuzzy Logic

Fuzzy logic, invented by Professor Lotfi Zadeh of UC-Berkeley in the mid-1960s, provides a representation scheme and a calculus for dealing with vague or uncertain concepts. It provides for the facile manipulation of such terms as "large," "warm," and "fast," which can simultaneously be seen to belong partially to two or more different, contradictory sets of values. Zadeh originally devised the technique as a means for solving problems in the soft sciences, particularly those that involved interactions between humans, and/or between humans and machines. Within the United States, with some exceptions, the technique has remained mainly of basic research interest.

The situation in Japan is quite different. Professor Terano, inspired by Zadeh's work, introduced the idea to the Japanese research community in about 1972. Perhaps because of a Japanese cultural view of the vagueness of human nature (all concepts belonging partially to contradictory sets), there was almost immediate enthusiasm for the idea. This led to active research and a host of commercial applications, almost entirely in the area of physical systems control. The currently fielded applications range from large-scale electro-mechanical processes, like subway systems and elevators, to mass market consumer applications like camcorder focus or smooth operation of automobile cruise controls. It is interesting to note that the actual applications of fuzzy logic are far afield from Zadeh's original notion of help for the soft sciences. We estimate that there are well over 200 fuzzy control systems in fully fielded use, and there are more than 2,000 engineers in the Japanese Fuzzy Control Society.

Current and Future Activities

Terano and his colleagues now view fuzzy control as but the first way station on the road to human-friendly systems. The evolution is fuzzy control, to fuzzy expert systems, to intelligent robots, to integrated AI systems. The 1992 LIFE research plan shows work in two main areas: communication and machine intelligence. Under communication, LIFE is conducting research in fuzzy computing (including natural language and linguistic modeling applications) and intelligent interfaces (to both humans and robots). Under machine intelligence, LIFE is pursuing work in fuzzy associative memory (software only), image understanding, and intelligent robots (the scope of which was left vague in our discussions). A total of about 30 full-time researchers are involved in all of these efforts.

REAL WORLD COMPUTING (RWC) PROJECT

Begun in April 1992, this 10-year project is the successor to the Fifth Generation Computer System Project. It is, however, in no way a continuation of the FGCS project (which is continuing in reduced form at ICOT for another three years). The FGCS Project was conceived as a research effort exploring the necessary infrastructure for knowledge-based systems; the computing systems developed at ICOT are called knowledge information processing systems. Knowledge-based systems are not part of the RWC concept.

The RWC project was planned by MITI's Electrotechnical Laboratory and will be executed by a central institute (located near ETL in Tsukuba) along with several so-called distributed institutes in companies or even foreign countries.

Unlike the FGCS project, which had a core theme of KBS and then developed subprojects in support of this theme (i.e., logic programming, natural language processing, parallel machines, KBS demo applications), the RWC project seems to be the result of a consensus-building process that has led to an eclectic mix of project goals. The three discernible themes are: 1) optical computers, 2) neural networks (this theme also stresses parallel computing, but it is not clear whether it stretches to cover conventional parallelism), and 3) ease of use. The third theme is still quite broad and fuzzy; it covers many topics and approaches, including: natural language understanding, speech understanding, soft logic (the next generation beyond fuzzy logic), probabilistic and statistical structure of logic, image understanding, multimedia and advanced user interfaces.

RWC stresses graphical user interfaces (GUIs) that are flexible, helpful, highly interactive, etc. Inference methods for flexible information retrieval and machine learning -- particularly in the context of forming associations between database items -- are also important. Many of these themes are also mentioned in the Knowledge Archives proposal being developed at EDR (discussed earlier in this chapter).

So far, the RWC goals are stated broadly and vaguely. The project planners are waiting for proposals for actual work to arrive. The real shape of the project will be determined by the work that is funded.

6. INTEGRATION OF ES WITH CONVENTIONAL DATA PROCESSING SYSTEMS

Bruce B. Johnson

INTRODUCTION

Most early industrial applications of expert systems were self contained. They typically used a general purpose expert system shell, ran on a single computer, and did not interface with other types of processing. Several years ago, a general movement toward integration with conventional data management systems began. Shells were redesigned to run within conventional architectures and to interface with relational databases.

Many of the expert systems we saw or discussed, and virtually all of the high-valued systems, were interfaced to data management systems as their input and output mechanism. The trend is the same in the U.S.

However, the Japanese have moved well beyond interfacing with data management systems into several other types of integration, which we discuss in this chapter.

INTEGRATION WITH PHYSICAL SYSTEMS

Many high-valued expert system applications are interfaced with physical systems. These applications often reside in the feedback path as part of the control logic of a dynamic system. Positioning the expert system in the feedback path greatly simplifies knowledge acquisition owing to the adaptive nature of closed loop systems. The expert system doesn't have to be as precise.

The JTEC panel saw two distinct control situations in Japan: low frequency systems and high frequency systems, where low and high are defined in relation to the execution speed of the expert system.

The blast furnace controller developed at NKK (see Chapter 2) is an excellent example of a low frequency application. The time constant of the blast furnace is six to eight hours. The controller utilizing conventional expert system techniques executes in a few minutes and is cycled every 20 minutes. At this rate, there are no dynamic stability problems.

Other applications, such as the control of a tunneling machine or a group of elevators, had much smaller time constants. In these cases, simple fuzzy logic or a fuzzy expert system was utilized. The fuzzy logic has several advantages:

1)   It produces a smoother control function and smoother system performance, and therefore does not have to cycle as often. This obviates the expert system performance problem.

2)   Fuzzy rules may perform the same function as five to ten conventional rules. This allows the inferencing to operate faster. It also reduces the size of the knowledge base, which simplifies both original knowledge acquisition and knowledge base maintenance.

3)   Depending upon whom you ask, dynamic system stability with a fuzzy expert system controller may or may not be an issue. It appears that there may be a theoretical problem in proving system stability, but stability has not been a practical problem.

Expert systems integrated with physical systems generally have been initiated in Japan by engineers in the operations area of the organization. This has two advantages: user-instigated systems are much more likely to succeed than systems originated by a technology group, such as AI researchers; and users are more likely to identify high-valued problems.

At the same time, it is often more difficult to associate a quantified value with the expert system. The engineers are more concerned with the total system than with any component. Benefits and value are likely to be attributed to the larger system and may not be broken down into individual components.

INTEGRATION OF PROBLEM-SOLVING TECHNIQUES

Still another form of integration is the combining of two or more problem-solving techniques such as expert systems, fuzzy logic, neural nets, model-based reasoning, qualitative physics, simulators, case-based reasoning, and parallel computing. Most of these combinations are still in the prototyping and experimental stages. Nevertheless, they are indicative of the depth to which the technology is being explored in Japan.

Specific examples include:

1) Fuzzy logic and neural networks: AdIn, a small Japanese ES company, has developed a prototype system that uses fuzzy membership functions within a neural network framework as a means of accelerating the learning process and improving problem solving performance.   The application is the interpretation of images.

2) Deep and shallow reasoning: a two-level expert system built by Toshiba (Chapter 2) is intended to diagnose unforeseen failures in a physical system. This system uses a shallow knowledge diagnostic system to handle foreseen failures, backed up by a deep knowledge system to tackle unforeseen problems. The deep knowledge system employs model-based reasoning and also employs a fuzzy simulator.

3) Model-based reasoning and parallel computing: NEC showed us a prototype model-based diagnostic system operating on a parallel processor.

4) Case-based and rule-based reasoning: a system developed at Toshiba which uses a recursive application of case-based reasoning; case-pieces are used to repair the mismatches in the primary case.

5) CAD and knowledge acquisition: Toshiba has developed a knowledge acquisition tool in which a design process for highly stylized objects is acquired by monitoring a CAD system.

FUTURE VISIONS

The Japanese envision much larger scale integration for the future. The concept of mechatronics, the large-scale integration of mechanical systems and informatics, is especially interesting. One example, computer integrated construction (CIC) at Obayashi, was illustrated by a video during the JTEC team's visit. CIC would automate the construction of structures such as buildings. The scope of automation includes design, logistics, and actual construction. Techniques such as planning and scheduling, robotics, and control will be required.

ANALYSIS

The Japanese are ahead of the U.S. in the integration of problem-solving techniques. The JTEC panel discerned at least three reasons for this trend.

Tools Investment

The Japanese have made substantial investments in experimenting with a wide range of technologies, sponsored in part by ICOT. As a result, a large number of industrial researchers have experience with multiple techniques. This enables them to see the logical combinations of techniques to use for a new problem.

Access to Products

Several Japanese companies have developed their own tool sets. This activity gives them the knowledge and access to software at a level which allows deep integration of the software, rather than simple data transfer interfaces.

Artificial Barriers

The U.S. has created artificial barriers between various methodologies due to the rise of many small technology companies. Most companies that are developing applications have relied upon shells developed by these small technology companies. The effect has been to create both technological and commercial barriers to the integration of techniques. This has limited progress in the U.S. to shallow integration.

7. Business Perspective

Herbert Schorr

HISTORY AND TRENDS

The pursuit of expert systems by Japanese companies has initially been technology-driven. That is, many companies pursued expert systems because it looked like a technology that they shouldn't miss (technology push), rather than the solution to a real business need (demand pull). The Japanese focused primarily on knowledge-based systems initially and often chose a diagnostic problem as a first application. Despite its limited usefulness, this is a well understood entry point into AI and into the methodology of knowledge-based system (KBS) development. Learning the technology has been accomplished largely by on-the-job training rather than by hiring people with formal training in AI or KBS.

When knowledge-based systems was a new area of information processing, it was not clear at first where the high payoff applications would be found. The search for such applications was similar to "wildcatting" in the oil industry, with an occasional big strike and many dry holes. Overall, there was a low initial success rate in finding and deploying applications, ranging from five to 40 percent for the four computer companies that the JTEC team visited. However, with several years of experience in selecting applications, the process has become much more reliable Fujitsu, for example, reported that its current success rate is between 75 and 90 percent in bringing a new application to operational status; the initial success rate was about 5 percent.

Several important business trends came across in our interviews:

1)   Japanese computer manufacturers now produce task-specific shells especially for diagnostics and planning. These new shells are intended to allow end users to write their own applications more easily than general-purpose shells allow (see Chapter 3 for more details). Although task specific shells have been developed and marketed in the U.S. for financial planning and risk assessment (among others), the trend is more pronounced in Japan.

2)   The need to integrate KBS applications with conventional data processing systems has led to a complete rewrite of shell products in C. This same trend has been in evidence in the U.S. for at least five years.

3)   There is a steady migration from mainframes to PCs and engineering workstations for running KBS applications (though both often access mainframe databases). A parallel trend exists in the U.S.

4)   The technology of knowledge-based systems has been assimilated within Japanese companies (in contrast to the U.S., where an outside consultant is often used to write such an application), and is part of the tool kit used to solve complex system problems. In fact, in many applications, the KBS is just part of an overall system, as in the NKK blast furnace. In companies where this in-house capability has been developed, we believe they are in a good position to gain competitive advantage. For example, the steel industry seems to be systematically using the technology throughout (NKK and Nippon Steel each have about 25 applications in routine use and more under development) and this, to our knowledge, surpasses anything being done in the steel industry in the U.S.

BUSINESS ADVANTAGES OF KBS TECHNOLOGY

Knowledge-based systems have wide applicability; we saw many examples in Japan with a high return on investment. In addition, many of the applications provide nonquantifiable improvements in individual decision making, timeliness and product quality. They can be categorized as follows (see Appendix E, Site Reports, for a description of the applications cited):

1)   Complex logic
      - SMART 7 - subway station facility diagnosis (Toshiba)
      - Kyushu Electric Utility fault diagnostic and restoration system (Toshiba)

2)   Solving an ill-formed problem (reasoning with uncertainty)
        - Blast furnace control (NKK)

3)   Situations in which rules change frequently
        - Crew scheduling (JAL)
        - Modular housing configuration (Sekisui)

4)   Need for use of heuristic knowledge
        - Design of shield tunneling system (Okamura)
        - FIRE - microwave circuit design (Toshiba)
        - PCB placement (Toshiba)
        - Design of expert system (Nippon Steel)

5)   Human-like Results
        - Crew scheduling (JAL)

6)   Planning
        - Paper production planning (Ohji)
        - Planning/scheduling (NKK)

Although Japanese computer manufacturers (JCMs) are the major developers of applications and tools (see below), other companies are also vigorously applying KBS technology throughout their business -- notably, the steelmaking and electric power companies. Of the 295 respondents to the 1992 *Nikkei AI* survey, 128 have KBSs that are currently in operational use or in development.

BUSINESS IMPACT ON THE JAPANESE COMPUTER MANUFACTURERS (JCMs)

In contrast to the U.S., most AI product development and consulting is done by the JCMs rather than small firms or specialized consulting firms. (This is, of course, the usual case in Japan, but is even more extreme in the case of KB systems. The large software-only houses have very little presence.) Table 7.1 shows the number of shells shipped since KB systems were first commercialized, approximately 10 years ago.

If we assume that the average workstation costs $40,000 (actually ranging from $16,000 to $80,000) and that a shell costs between $30,000 and $35,000, then the total cost to a customer is $75,000. Multiplying by the number of shells shipped gives an overall revenue estimate for hardware and software.

Table 7.1
Total KBS Shells Shipped

NEC	1000
Toshiba	400
Hitachi	4000
Fujitsu	3000

Revenues from consulting or system building, which were not available to us, are not included here and may possibly be the major revenue component. The estimates given in Table 7.2 for hardware and software revenues are probably too high, because a shell might be bought to run on an existing workstation. Also, the shell numbers include internal shipments (one-third of the total in Toshiba's case). Overall, the business appears to be between $3 and $20 million per annum per JCM (again, not counting revenues from consulting or system building for external clients).

Table 7.2
Estimated Revenue From KBS Shell Sales
($ in millions)

	Ten Year Revenue	Average Annual Revenue
NEC	$75	$7.5
Toshiba	$30	$3
Hitachi	$300	$30
Fujitsu	$225	$22.5

Observations on Business and Technology

We observed that there are many internal applications, that is, applications built by the JCMs for themselves. The return on investment (ROI) was not made available, but there was a clear need and usage. Areas of application included intelligent aids for engineering, production planning, configuration, and marketing.

The main platforms are engineering workstations and PCs, using the client/server model. Symbolic processors are not being used at all, and mainframes are in declining usage.

As to parallel processing, no one we spoke with sees a commercial role for PIM (from ICOT); they believe other approaches, such as those taken by Connection Machine and Intel Paragon, are more promising. However, the disinterest in the PIM may relate more to the language issue (PROLOG) than to the computer architecture.

Task-specific shells for diagnosis and planning are just coming out, and the hope is that they will have a wide market since they are intended to be used by end-users, not system engineers.

Sales are small compared to the expectations of several years ago. Presently, sales growth is flat and growth in the number of applications is also flat (exception: Hitachi).

No Japanese company the JTEC panel visited had written an application that is being resold. This parallels U.S. experience, where generic products for the financial and insurance industry, offered by several start-up companies, did not succeed. However, some PC-based products such as Tax Cut are selling in the United States. In Japan, application products that rely heavily on AI are not selling well. For instance, only 20 copies of ICAD and 10 copies of Concept Modeler have been sold; in the United States hundreds of ICAD systems have been sold. Poor sales of these systems may be due to a language problem (no *kanji* version), and/or to the fact that there is no version that originated in Japan, and/or to the lack of an effective marketing channel.

BUSINESS IMPACT ON NON-JCM COMPANIES

As stated previously, many Japanese companies that are not computer manufacturers have successfully deployed KBSs that are in day-to-day use and yielding a high ROI. Although most Japanese companies are reluctant to discuss ROI quantitatively, we gathered from some that they often require a two-year return of their investment in a system, and an investment of $500,000 or more would be considered large. On the other hand, they are quick to point out that there are other measures of success besides ROI: shorter turnaround, improved throughput, higher reliability, better individual decision making, etc.

Although several of the JCMs reported that the KBS business had flattened out, Mr. Yamanaka at Hitachi was optimistic about future growth for his company, and drew a rough sketch of estimated growth in four sectors: industrial, government, financial and retail (see Figure 7.1). The earliest major source of revenue for Hitachi has been in the financial area, but future growth will be relatively slow. Industrial applications are now starting to take off and will soon be the dominant source of revenues. Applications in the public sector will also grow at a healthy rate, but are starting from a low base. The retail sector is not expected to be investing in this technology in any significant way in the near future.

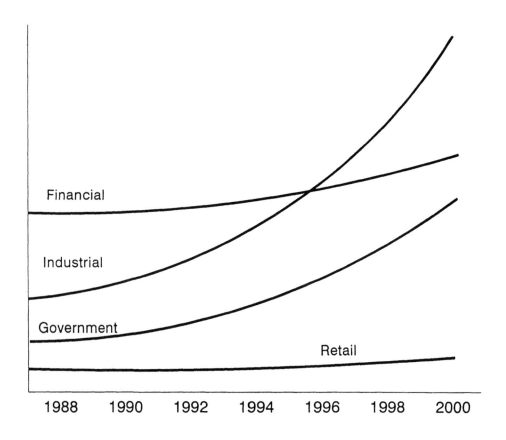

Figure 7.1.   Forecast by Hitachi of Growth of Knowledge-Based Systems in Four Sectors
(Source: Hitachi, Private Communication)

Despite Hitachi's optimistic forecast of future growth in the deployment of KBSs, we found few signs of a multiplier effect in those companies where a successful application has been deployed. For example, JAL, with an excellent deployed application, is moving very cautiously towards implementing other applications. KBSs provide the highest benefit in very specific applications. Unfortunately, there is an inverse relation between specificity and size of market. Applications seem not to be transferable to other companies or easily even within companies. Contrast this with an airline reservation system, where thousands of clerks can use it as well as travel agents and other airlines. The lack of exponential growth may well mean that the cost of wildcatting may be too high. This cost is due to the limitations of first-generation tools which we heard about over and over again in Japan, as well as the lack of skills and AI knowledge.

COMPARISON WITH CONVENTIONAL DATA PROCESSING

Anyone who has any experience with a conventional database understands that either organizing a database or writing new applications on top of an existing database is neither easy nor cheap.

Moreover, once the main applications that drove the installation of a database system are installed, there is often a demand to build additional applications for a small group of users. The ability to do this is limited by programmer productivity and ROI of users. Hence, why are database systems easily accepted and knowledge base systems having such a hard time? Some of the differences between the two technologies are summarized in Table 7.3. We add the following observations:

1)   The data intended for database systems are relatively easily acquired, having previously existed on paper. Knowledge acquisition, on the other hand, is often the major bottleneck in developing a KBS.

2)   The algorithms to manipulate the data are known: payroll, billing, accounts receivable, inventory cash analysis. The operations on a knowledge base are usually known (e.g., simple backward-chaining search through a rule base), but often not codified.

3)   The utility of computerizing a database application is easily discerned in advance (ROI can be developed ahead of time). The same is usually true for knowledge-based applications, although the estimate may be more approximate due to lack of experience with this relatively new technology. The ROI on actual deployed knowledge-based systems, however, has been very good.

4)   Once the separation of the data in a database from the program is made, it is easy to imagine other reports of value that could be obtained (e.g., tracking fast-selling items, receivables aging, customer profiles), so that developing a corporate database is a worthwhile endeavor.   Although knowledge bases are also separated from the inference engines that use them, a knowledge base typically is not reusable.   This problem is the subject of much research in the U.S. and in Japan (e.g., Professor Mizoguchi's work at Kyoto University).

5)   Initial database applications (e.g., airline reservation systems) are useful to many employees. By contrast, there are usually few users of a KBS. (The same can be said of many database applications after the main ones have been done.) Hence, one sees an emphasis in the database world on query languages so that end-users can write their own applications and generate their own reports.   A similar trend has not yet taken hold in the KB applications world, though task-specific shells are an attempt to provide a similar capability.

Table 7.3
Databases Versus Knowledge Bases

DATABASE	KNOWLEDGE BASE
data known	knowledge needs to be acquired
algorithms known (e.g., payroll)	often, heuristic need to be codified, though sometimes they exist in manuals
ROI predictable	application usefulness often unknown (new technology) deployed application ROI very good
reusable for other reports	little or no reusability
widespread usefulness to many people	useful to small number of people
attempts at query languages for end-users to create their own reports	task specific shells

PROBLEMS WITH CURRENT GENERATION KBS TECHNOLOGY

The JTEC panel's questionnaire asked about perceived obstacles to the introduction or proliferation of ESs in the organizations we surveyed. The following problems were reported, primarily by the JCMs, but also by many of the other companies:

Knowledge Acquisition

Several problems associated with knowledge acquisition were reported:

1)   Domain knowledge is hard to extract from domain-knowledgeable people.

2)   There are not enough tools available.

3)   There has been little success so far with domain shells. These shells are designed to allow domain experts to construct their own KBSs. *Nikkei AI* said that customers told them they found the products either too general (and therefore hard to use) or too specific (and still needing programming experts to customize).

Knowledge Maintenance

Knowledge changes often in the real world, hence the KBS needs constant updating. JAL, for example, uses two to three electronic data processing (EDP) people full time to change their crew scheduling program. Union rule changes, regulation changes, sickness, etc., all contribute to the need to reschedule frequently. The same problem would also arise if the applications were done with conventional data processing techniques, but it does tend to show that the use of KBS technology does not save on software maintenance.

Lack of Transferability

NKK found it hard to transfer a KBS application from one steel mill to another. They found that a few lines of a rule-based program were not difficult to understand, but the intent of the overall program was. Hence, they found that although the KB was locally understandable, the global knowledge was hard to discern.

Little Reuse of Knowledge

Every KBS application needs to be done *ab initio*. This is a well-known limitation of first-generation knowledge-based systems.

No CASE Methodology

There are no well established standards for creating a KBS. Techniques for testing a KBS to determine its scope of applicability are also not well established.

Expected Programmer Productivity

NKK commented that it found little evidence of an increase in programmer productivity over writing conventional data processing programs. Also the Nth application was not easier to do than the first. The main problem here may be that expectations raised by KBS technology were not met.

High Cost of Producing User Interface

Fujitsu found that 60 to 70 percent of the development cost of a KBS was spent on coding the user interface; other companies reported similar numbers.

Poor Performance

KBSs, particularly those with large knowledge bases, were found to run very slowly and to consume substantial computing resources. This affected the choice of applications. Real-time applications were mostly avoided, but so were others where resource consumption was a problem.

Programmer Education

Customers had little familiarity with LISP, in which most of the initial KBSs were written. Now that KBS products are being rewritten in C (and, in addition, Fujitsu has made available both FORTRAN/KR and COBOL/KR, which add rule capability to both of these languages), the language problem is going away. However, we also saw a reluctance to send EDP people to customer courses run by the computer companies. Companies often put great reliance on learning by trial and error. Unfortunately, many customers were unsuccessful in their attempts to build their first systems, and were turned off by AI.

ARE KNOWLEDGE-BASED SYSTEMS A BUSINESS?

One of the reasons knowledge systems are justified is that the functionality being computerized is complex. But one of the reasons that applications become complex is that their requirements are constantly changing (e.g., underwriting policies, tax laws, pricing policies). Although KBSs may in some cases be easier to change than conventional code, the cost of such changes can ruin the economics of an application. Furthermore, due to high functionality, the number of users of any KBS application seem to be small, and any costs must be retrieved from the benefits to this small number of users.

KBSs are not, in general, a complete solution, but must be combined with other technologies to solve almost any real problem. The KBS approach is more of a technique and a skill than a solution. Thus when we try to assess the value of a KBS, we are often looking at too small a grain size to speak of the cost-benefit of an application.   The NKK representatives made this point very explicitly.   When choosing techniques to solve a problem, such as choosing between C or LISP, or between linear programming and a KBS, one cannot normally attribute the costs or benefits to the technology employed. These attributes belong to the application (which probably uses many techniques).

There are business opportunities in selling shells, selling very broadly applicable and relatively static applications, and selling services for the development of high-valued solutions. The overall market, however, does not appear to be very large when measured against databases, spreadsheets, etc. This situation is the same in Japan as it is in the United States.

Knowledge-based systems at their present technology level are more likely to be a core competence -- a technique applied when appropriate, commingled with many of the more conventional data processing techniques, and applied to the internal processes of a business or as an embedded component of a product. Clearly, we need a next generation of technology to fully realize the enormous potential of AI; then we will probably see an exponential type of business growth. However, given the investment practices of the United States vs. Japan, the latter (both the JCMs and the companies using the technology) would appear to be in a better position to realize the benefits of new research results.

CONCLUSIONS

As in the United States, many applications with a positive ROI have been deployed in Japan in which KBSs are used as a part of solving a problem. Generally speaking, KBS as a business has not been successful (there are no success stories comparable to ORACLE, SYBASE, and INGRES products in the database world).   KBS applications tend to be complex and/or of narrow applicability, and to require continuous updating. Also, in contrast to conventional data processing, where economically justifiable applications are easy to find, selecting a KBS application is often a hit or miss process. For all these reasons, KBS technology has not done well as a business in either country.

Most successful new technologies grow initially at an exponential rate. While this was the case for KBS technology in Japan in the early days, we appear to be seeing slower growth there now. Even after a successful application, we often did not see the use of the technology multiplying within a company.

In order to have the potential for rapid growth, we heard in Japan that the technology needs to be improved in the following ways:

1)   Easier knowledge acquisition
2)   Reuse of the KB
3)   Ability to fully and directly express more of the model of the domain
4)   Need for a mature CASE-like methodology
5)   Easier development of the user interface

With these improvements, the cost and skill requirements of developing a new application could be brought down so that more attempts would be made to explore new areas of applicability (cutting the cost of wildcatting). This should realize the enormous potential of KBS technology.

Because so much of the technology has been mastered by and emanates from Japanese computer manufacturers, integration with conventional computing techniques is the norm and is handled easily. The JCMs' efforts, while downsized in some companies, continue to move ahead strongly -- witness the rewriting of shells from LISP to C, the attempt to develop task specific shells, and the move to workstations and PCs from mainframes. There is evidence that commercially the U.S. is investing at a lower rate compared to its previous rate -- owing to lack of venture capital and downsizing of computer company efforts, resulting in fewer new product announcements. This may repeat the familiar story of U.S. companies halting investment where the returns are poor, while the Japanese continue to invest. The Japanese may in this way develop commercial superiority.

8. Conclusions

Edward Feigenbaum

BUSINESS SECTOR APPLICATIONS OF EXPERT SYSTEMS IN JAPAN

On the basis of our site visits, plus additional data gathered by *Nikkei AI*, we can draw a number of conclusions about the state-of-the-art of expert system applications within the business sector in Japan.

The technology of expert systems has now been mastered by the Japanese. Since the early 1980s, when they first entered this field, they have completely caught up with the United States. They can apply the technology to any problem within the state of the art. Their best applications are equal to the best elsewhere in the world. Their use of the technology is not niched, but is widespread across many business categories.

Japanese computer manufacturers (JCMs) play a dominant role in the technology and business of expert systems. The JCMs have mastered and absorbed expert system technology as a core competence. They tend to use systems engineers rather than knowledge engineers to build systems. Consequently, integration with conventional information technology poses no special problem for them, and is handled routinely and smoothly, without friction. These large computer companies also build many application systems for their customers; small firms play only a minor role in applications building, in contrast with the United States.

Within the computer manufacturing companies, there is a close coupling between activities in the research laboratories, the system development groups, and the sales departments. The development and sales groups work closely together to develop custom systems for clients. The results are fed back to the research lab to provide requirements for the next generation of ES tools.

Viewed as a technology (rather than as a business), the field of expert systems is doing well in Japan, as it is in the U.S. As in the U.S., the experimentation phase is over, and the phase of mature applications is in progress. Following a normal learning curve, the ratio of successful deployments of expert systems to projects initiated has risen sharply, from about 5 percent in the early years to about 75 percent in recent years. Japanese appliers of the technology make eclectic use of AI techniques. Most of these techniques originated in the U.S. or Europe. As in the U.S., expert systems technology is often just a component of a bigger system -- expert systems are just another tool in the software toolkit. The Japanese do not attempt to analyze payoff at the component level, but look at the system level. Thus they do not measure the return on investment of these embedded expert systems. However, there are many applications in which the expert system is the main technology.

Viewed as a business, the expert systems field in Japan did not take off in any exceptional way compared to the U.S. or Europe. Although the overall level of activity is significant and important, there is no evidence of exponential growth. Components of the business consist of expert system tools, consulting, and packaged knowledge systems. Hitachi's expert system business seems the most viable. Other major players, such as Fujitsu and CSK, have had limited business success.

With respect to ES tools, Japanese tools are similar in sophistication to those sold and used in the U.S. Techniques and methodology developed in the U.S. have been, and continue to be, made into products quickly.

Japan has more experience than the U.S. in applications of KBS technology to heavy industry, particularly the steel and construction industries.

Aside from a few exceptions, the Japanese and U.S. ES tool markets follow similar trends: vertical, problem-specific tools; a move towards open systems and workstations; and an emphasis on integration of ESs with other computational techniques.

The number of fielded applications in Japan is somewhere between 1,000 and 2,000, including PC-based applications. The number of U.S. applications is probably several times that of Japan.

Fuzzy control systems (not counted in the above tally) have had a big impact in consumer products (e.g., camcorders, automobile transmissions and cruise controls, television, air conditioners, and dozens of others).

The JTEC panel saw continued strong efforts by Japanese computer companies and industry-specific companies (e.g., Nippon Steel) to advance their KBS technology and business. This situation contrasts with that in the U.S., where we see a declining investment in knowledge-based systems technology: lack of venture capital, downsizing of computer company efforts, few new product announcements. It is a familiar story, and one for concern, as this trend may lead to Japanese superiority in this area relatively soon.

KNOWLEDGE-BASED SYSTEMS RESEARCH IN JAPAN

Our conclusions in this area are summarized as follows:

A survey of three years of working papers of the Special Interest Group on Knowledge-Based Systems of the Japan Society for AI shows a wide range of research topics, touching on most of the subjects of current interest in the U.S.

The quality of research at a few top-level universities in Japan is in the same range as at top-level U.S. universities and research institutes. However, in the remainder of the Japanese university system the quality of research is not equal to that at first or second tier U.S. research centers. The quantity of research (in terms of number of projects and/or number of publications) is considerably smaller compared to the U.S.

LIFE is the world leader in applying fuzzy logic concepts to classic AI core problems.

Japanese industrial laboratories appear to be doing advanced development that is tightly coupled to application or product development. JCMs and some other Japanese high technology companies are carrying out some knowledge-based systems research, but most non-computer companies do none. We saw, essentially, a thin layer of excellent work at Hitachi, Toshiba, NEC, Fujitsu and NTT, and (on previous visits) at IBM Japan and Sony. The most basic and deepest work is at Hitachi's Advanced Research Laboratory, which is conducting advanced research in model-based reasoning and machine learning.

ICOT RESEARCH PROGRAM PROGRESS

Using massive parallelism, ICOT appears about to achieve its stated goal of 100 million logical instructions per second (LIPS) of theoretical peak performance. The Fifth Generation Project achieved its goal of training a new generation of computer technologists.

ICOT's experiments in parallelism have made an important contribution to parallel computing. ICOT is one of only a few sites in the world that is studying massively parallel *symbolic* computing.

ICOT created the funding and motivation to spur significant interest worldwide in AI, KBS and advanced computing paradigms.

The logic-based language, KL1, has been shown to work well as a programming language for parallel computing; together with the operating system PIMOS, KL1 does a good job of automatic load distribution. However, KL1 and PIMOS are unlikely to gain adherents outside the logic programming community. ICOT's logic programming research is world class, probably the best in the world.

On the negative side, ICOT has made little progress in the applications dimension. ICOT has had little impact on knowledge-based systems technology. The choice of PROLOG and logic programming has isolated ICOT from industry. The ICOT machines are research-only designs. Their high cost has prevented distribution outside of ICOT, and consequently has isolated ICOT from the industrial and commercial communities.

A successor project, called the Real World Computing (RWC) Project, was initiated in April 1992. It does not include knowledge-based systems within its scope.

EDR PROGRAM PROGRESS

EDR will likely produce a practical scale, machine-usable dictionary for Japanese and English.

The scale of EDR accomplishments is very impressive and should be taken as a model for similar research programs elsewhere.

A follow-on project, the Knowledge Archives Project, may be funded, and should be closely tracked.

EDR has not significantly improved the underlying technology for maintaining large knowledge bases. EDR has also not significantly added to our theoretical understanding of knowledge base organization.

EDR demonstrates that a funded national-scale project with a pragmatic focus can make a significant contribution.

Appendices

APPENDIX A.   PROFESSIONAL EXPERIENCE OF PANEL MEMBERS

Edward Feigenbaum, Panel Chair

Edward Feigenbaum is Professor of Computer Science at Stanford University and Co-Scientific Director of the Heuristic Programming Project at Stanford. He is one of the pioneers of artificial intelligence. His research has involved knowledge-based systems concepts, the invention of expert systems technology, and many applications of expert systems to engineering and business problems. He has served as Chairman of Stanford's Computer Science Department, and as Director of Stanford's Computer Center. Professor Feigenbaum is a co-founder of three start-up firms in applied artificial intelligence. He is co-editor of the encyclopedia, *The Handbook of Artificial Intelligence,* and is co-author of several books, including *The Fifth Generation* and *The Rise of the Expert Company.* He is an elected member of the National Academy of Engineering and the American Academy of Arts and Science and a Fellow of the American Association for Artificial Intelligence (AAAI). Dr. Feigenbaum received his BA, MS and PhD degrees from Carnegie Mellon University.

Robert S. Engelmore

Robert Engelmore is Senior Research Scientist and Executive Director of the Heuristic Programming Project (HPP) in the Computer Science Department at Stanford University, a position he has held since 1985. His primary professional interest is in applications of artificial intelligence methods to scientific, industrial, and military domains. In addition to his research pursuits at Stanford, Dr. Engelmore was Editor-in-Chief of *AI Magazine*, a quarterly publication of the American Association for Artificial Intelligence, from 1981 through 1991. He is co-editor of the book *Blackboard Systems* (Addison-Wesley, 1988). Dr. Engelmore has served as Program Manager for agency-sponsored research in artificial intelligence at the Defense Advanced Research Projects Agency, and was a founder of Teknowledge, Inc. He is also a consultant to industry and government on applications of knowledge systems technology. He has been active in the field of artificial intelligence since 1970. He is a Fellow of the AAAI.

Peter E. Friedland

Peter Friedland received AB (Chemistry) and BSE (Electrical Engineering) degrees in 1974 from Princeton University and a PhD in Computer Science from Stanford University in 1979, conducting research on the application of artificial intelligence to the design of experiments in molecular biology. He acted as Research Director of the MOLGEN project at Stanford, 1979-1986, continuing research into planning, knowledge representation, and learning within the biological domain. In 1980 he co-founded two companies, IntelliCorp and Teknowledge, to commercialize the emerging field of knowledge-based or expert systems. In January 1987, Dr. Friedland joined NASA Ames Research Center as Chief of the Artificial Intelligence Research Branch with responsibilities for creating a fundamental research capability in artificial intelligence within NASA, as well as managing an extensive collaborative program with industry and academia. In addition, Dr. Friedland co-manages (with Dr. M. Montemerlo) the NASA-wide AI program. He is a Fellow of the AAAI.

Bruce B. Johnson

Bruce Johnson is a partner in Andersen Consulting. He is the founder and current director of Andersen's Center for Strategic Technology Research (CSTaR). CSTaR conducts programs of research in business process design, decision technology, corporate knowledge management, groupware, managing the information explosion, and advanced software engineering. He also coordinates Andersen's research in other institutions. He helped found the Institute for the Learning Sciences at Northwestern University and serves as chairman of the Requirements Advisory Board of MCC in Austin, Texas, among others. Prior to forming CSTaR, he initiated Andersen's practice in artificial intelligence and worked as a systems engineering manager for NASA in Houston, Texas. Dr. Johnson is a member of the IEEE Software Industrial Advisory Board. He consults with commercial clients of Andersen Consulting and with research clients, such as the U.S. government. Dr. Johnson received his BS in Civil Engineering, an ME in Structural Engineering, and PhD in Structural Mechanics and Computer Science from Texas A&M University.

H. Penny Nii

Penny Nii is a Senior Research Scientist at the Knowledge Systems Laboratory (KSL) at Stanford University. She was the project leader of the KASE (Knowledge- Assisted Software Engineering) project, which developed a knowledge-based CASE tool for software system designers and analysts. She also developed AGE, one of the first expert system shells, which was licensed to Fujitsu and is marketed as ESHELL. Before joining KSL in 1975, she developed the HASP signal understanding program at Systems Control Inc. between 1972 and 1975. She worked in IBM's Federal Systems Division, T.J. Watson Research Center, and the IBM World Trade Asia Corporation. She is co-author, with Edward Feigenbaum and Pamela McCorduck, of *The Rise of the Expert Company* (Times Books, 1988) and *The First Artificial Intelligence Coloring Book*. Ms. Nii received a BS in Mathematics from Tufts University and an MS in Computer Science from Stanford University.

Herbert Schorr

Since 1988 Herbert Schorr has been Executive Director of the Information Sciences Institute of the University of Southern California. He is a graduate of the City University of New York and received his PhD in Electrical Engineering from Princeton University in 1963. He joined IBM after a year each at Cambridge University as a post-doctoral fellow and Columbia University as Assistant Professor. Dr. Schorr's career at IBM included development, research, and corporate planning assignments. Specific positions he has held include: Vice President, Product and Service Planning, Advanced Systems Development Division; Vice President, Systems Research Division; and ES Director, Advanced Systems, Enterprise Systems. In his last position at IBM he had product, marketing, and development responsibilities for AI within IBM, and similar responsibilities for image-enhanced systems.

Howard Shrobe

Howard Shrobe is a Principal Research Scientist at the MIT Artificial Intelligence Laboratory and was Technical Director of Symbolics Inc. His work has spanned the areas of VLSI design, computer architecture, and artificial intelligence. He received his MS and PhD degrees from the Artificial Intelligence Laboratory at MIT where he was a co-founder of the Programmer's Apprentice project. In 1979 he joined the staff of the MIT AI Lab as a Principal Research Scientist and in that role was one of the main designers of the Scheme-81 microprocessor (a LISP interpreter on a chip) and the DPL/Daedalus Integrated Circuit Design. He also helped found the Hardware Troubleshooting Project at the MIT AI Lab and is currently conducting research on designing and understanding mechanisms. At Symbolics, Dr. Shrobe was one of the architects of the Ivory microprocessor and of the NS CAD system used to design it. Since that time he has led the effort to develop Joshua, an AI programming language which introduced the notion of a Protocol of Inference. Dr. Shrobe is co-author (with David Barstow and Eric Sandewall) of *Interactive Programming Environment* and editor of *Exploring Artificial Intelligence: Surveys from the National Conferences on Artificial Intelligence*. He is a Fellow of the AAAI.

APPENDIX B.   PROFESSIONAL EXPERIENCE OF OTHER TEAM MEMBERS

Y. T. Chien

Dr. Y.T. Chien serves as the Division Director for Information, Robotics, and Intelligent Systems in the Directorate for Computer and Information Science and Engineering at the National Science Foundation. Dr. Chien received his MS and PhD degrees in Electrical Engineering from Purdue University. From 1967 to 1982, he was on the faculty of the Electrical Engineering and Computer Science Department, University of Connecticut. During that period, he served as Chair of the Department for four years (1976-80) and later became Assistant Dean of Engineering for Computer Research (1980-82). Prior to joining National Science Foundation he spent two years as a researcher and Group Leader at the Artificial Intelligence Center, Naval Research Laboratory, Washington, D.C. He is author (or co-author) of three books: *Fundamentals of Computing* (John Wiley); *Interactive Pattern Recognition* (Marcel Dekker); *Knowledge-based Systems, Tutorial* (IEEE Computer Society Press). He is a member of the Association for Computing Machinery (ACM) and American Association for Artificial Intelligence (AAAI) and a Fellow of the Institute of Electrical and Electronics Engineers (IEEE).

Robert Duane Shelton

Dr. Shelton received his degrees in electrical engineering from Texas Tech, MIT, and the University of Houston. He has been a professor at the University of Houston, Texas Tech, and the University of Louisville, where he was Chairman of the Applied Math and Computer Science Department. He has also worked as an engineer at Texas Instruments, at NASA on the Apollo Space communications system, and at the National Science Foundation as a science policy analyst. He has served as principal investigator on over 25 grants and contracts, totalling over $2 million. He is presently professor and Chairman of the Electrical Engineering Department of Loyola College in Maryland. He is also Director of the International Technology Research Institute (ITRI) at Loyola College, which conducts JTEC and WTEC studies for the National Science Foundation and other agencies, as well as assessments of foreign transportation technologies for the U.S. Federal Highway Administration under a program called the Transportation Technology Evaluation Center (TTEC).

Cecil H. Uyehara

Cecil Uyehara, President of Uyehara International Associates, is a consultant in the Washington, D.C. area on U.S.-Japanese relations (science and technology). He served in the U.S. government for almost 25 years, with the Air Force (weapons systems planning), the Office of Management and Budget (military assistance) and the Agency for International Development (AID). He has published on Japanese politics, scientific advice and public policy, and Japanese calligraphy. He organized the first U.S. Congressional hearings on Japanese science and technology, lectures at the U.S. Foreign Service Institute on Japanese science and technology and served as consultant to the *Yomiuri Shimbun* and the Library of Congress on Japanese calligraphy. He graduated from Keio University (BA), the University of Minnesota (MA) both in political economy, and received awards/grants from the Ford Foundation, American Philosophical Society, University of Minnesota (Shevlin Fellowship) and the National Institute of Public Affairs. Mr. Uyehara serves as Senior Consultant for Japan Operations for JTEC/WTEC, and in that capacity performed advance work and literature support for this JTEC study.

APPENDIX C.   QUESTIONNAIRE

The questionnaire shown below was sent in advance to all the organizations visited in this study, except for *Nikkei AI*. Section A focuses on industrial applications, and hence is relevant to the twelve industrial sites only. Section B contains questions about advanced research and was potentially relevant to all the recipients. The questions in Sections C and E were directed specifically to ICOT personnel. Section D was prepared specifically for the EDR project.

The questionnaire is quite long and detailed (particularly Section A), and we were not sure if any of our hosts would take the time to prepare written answers to the questions or merely use them as talking points at the meetings. We were surprised and delighted at the level of effort expended by most of the organizations in preparing written answers. In particular, Section A was completed by all twelve industrial sites. Section B was addressed by a few industrial sites, and served as a guide for discussion at the universities and national projects. ICOT did not prepare written responses to Section C and E, but the topics were discussed during the visit; the same situation applies to the EDR project.

A   INDUSTRIAL APPLICATIONS

The following questions are for organizations that have developed and are using expert systems.

1. Approximately how many expert systems has your company developed, or is developing?
    a.   for internal use?
    b.   for external use by customers?

2. Please categorize the above according to development status (give approximate percentages):
    a.   in routine operation
    b.   now in field test
    c.   in prototype stage
    d.   prototype still in development

3. Please state approximately how many applications you have in each of the following task areas:
    a.   design
    b.   advisory, or "help" systems
    c.   process control
    d.   planning and/or scheduling

     e.   diagnosis and/or troubleshooting
     f.   regulatory compliance
     g.   management or business integration aids
     h.   areas of manufacturing not included in any of the above categories
     i.   sales
     j.   finance
     k.   software development and management
     l.   intelligent interfaces to existing software systems

4.   What is the current most successful expert system that your company developed for its own use or for a customer? How do you measure its success?

5.   For each task area where you have one or more applications, select a representative system (including the most successful described above), and provide the following information:

     a.   what is the specific task?
     b.   how large is the knowledge base (number of frames, number of rules, lines of code, as appropriate)?
     c.   was a commercial development tool or framework used to build the application? If so, which one? If not, was an internally developed tool used?
     d.   is the application a stand-alone system, or is it integrated with conventional data processing systems?
     e.   what programming language was used (if any)?
     f.   what kind of hardware platform (personal computer, workstation, minicomputer, mainframe, client-server system, distributed or parallel system)?
     g.   what was the size and composition of the team that designed and built the system?
     h.   how long was the development time?
     i.   what was the development cost?
     j.   who developed the system (domain experts, professional programmers, professional knowledge engineers)?
     k.   who are the users?
     l.   who maintains the system, and how large is the maintenance team?
     m.   what kind of payback has been realized from this application (e.g., cost reduction, quality improvement, speed of problem solving or decision making)?
     n.   in economic terms, what has been the return per year?
     o.   what was the payback time, i.e., the number of months or years to pay back development costs?

p.   does this application cooperate with or depend on other expert systems (i.e., do they contribute to each other's operation in some way) and if so is there a synergy between the applications?

q.   what problems were encountered, if any, in integrating the system into the corporate environment, and how were these problems addressed?

6.   Has your company implemented any applications that require multiple sources of expertise? If so, was the expertise combined in a single system or through the coordination of multiple systems?

7.   Do you have any applications written partly using AI tools and partly using standard high level languages (COBOL, FORTRAN, PL/1, etc.)?

8.   How fully integrated with your operating system are your AI tools? E.g., can you call any access methods, procedural higher level language routines, library subroutines from your AI tool (and vice versa)?

9.   What training programs for expert system development work are in place in your company?

10.   Has your company developed a methodology for developing expert systems? If so, what is the methodology?

11.   In your company, how are expert systems
a.   selected (i.e., what criteria are used)?
b.   developed (i.e., by data processing group, by a knowledge engineering group, by outside contractor)?
c.   inserted into the company's operational activity?
d.   maintained?
e.   integrated with conventional data processing activities?

12.   Are there systematic review and redesign cycles for expert system projects?

13.   What percentage of projects that are started get as far as completing a prototype system?

14.   What percentage of projects get from the prototype stage to an operational system?

15.   Have there been any expert system projects that were unsuccessful? If so, what were the reasons for the lack of success? Was the problem caught early or late in the development cycle?

16.   Given your existing AI tools, how large a project would your organization undertake (e.g., in terms of number of rules or number of person-years devoted to the project)?

17.   What new expert system applications are planned by your company?

18.   What will be the progress of expert systems in your company? For example, will process control applications use in-the-loop control?

19.   What are the main problems with present technology?   What kinds of applications that are hard to build now would you like to see made easier? Do you see any need for advanced techniques (e.g., model-based reasoning, machine learning) in current or planned expert system applications? Do you see resistance to the use of those technologies?

20.   What other advanced computing technologies does your company use (not necessarily expert systems)?

B.   ADVANCED KNOWLEDGE-BASED SYSTEMS RESEARCH

1.   Are any efforts being made (besides EDR) to build the technology for large knowledge bases? Are there experiments in large knowledge bases? Is there a software or communication infrastructure that has been developed?

2.   What is the research being done experimentally or theoretically on model-based reasoning? Modeling of devices and reasoning about their behavior? Are any languages or systems being developed to assist with this work?

3.   What are the major projects in machine learning (using knowledge-based techniques, not neural networks)?

4.   Have you developed any new techniques to handle problems of reasoning with uncertain knowledge?

5.   If you think of advanced knowledge-based systems research as involved in "inventing the second generation" of knowledge-based systems, then what are the most important dimensions of this "second generation?" That is, what is it most important for the researchers to invent?

6.   What do you think are the important features that should be included in second generation development tools or frameworks?

7.   What is the interest among computer science and engineering students in knowledge-based systems research? How many Ph.D. students do you have working with you, or are working on knowledge-based systems in your department?

8.   Are you working on any advanced truth maintenance systems?

9.   Are you applying knowledge-based systems to natural language understanding? To problems of education, at any level?

10.   Are you doing any work in case-based reasoning research? What efforts in Japan in CBR are most worth studying?

11.   Are you working on general problems of knowledge representation, for example by inventing new concepts of KR, or new languages for KR, or new systems for KR?

12.   What are your sources of support for the research? From Ministry of Education? From other government agencies? Does any support come from companies?

C.   ICOT

1.   What do you consider to be the major technical successes on the Personal Sequential Inference (PSI) machine?   How successful was the effort to commercialize the PSI machine?

2.   What is the current work of the various ICOT laboratories?

3.   What performance is expected from the Parallel Inference Machine (PIM) to be completed in 1992?

4.   Briefly described, what is the current PIM architecture -- that is,
      a.   what are the activities at a node?
      b.   how is the communication between nodes handled?
      c.   what are the high-level parallel algorithms that organize the logical problem solving?

5.   What is the current state of the operating system for the PIM?

6.   What is the current state of ICOT's PROLOG work?

7.   What applications are being done at ICOT?   Are there expert system applications? What organizations outside of ICOT are using ICOT-developed technology to build expert system applications? What is the best application done with ICOT-developed technology?

8.   What are the major advances that have been made by ICOT in the Natural Language Understanding area?

9.   Can you quantify the role that ICOT has played in spreading knowledge of AI and logic programming among Japanese company engineers and managers?

10.   Assuming that there will be a second period of government funding for ICOT, what are the plans? How long? How many people at ICOT? What research will be undertaken? What level of government funding has been promised?

11.   Of all the things that ICOT has done in ten years, what stands out as the most satisfying to the Director and the staff? What was the most disappointing experience of the ten-year period?

12.   Several Japanese companies (and a few American companies) also explored novel architectures for LISP. Was there any relationship between this work and the work at ICOT? If so, how did the efforts influence one another?

13.   PROLOG and other logic-programming formalisms have not captured the same attention in the U.S. AI community as they have in Japan. Are you satisfied with your choice of logic-programming as the basic framework? Do you think that you should have adopted more of the functional programming style of the LISP-like languages?

14.   While PSI and PIM were being developed, the RISC revolution took place. To what extent did this affect your work? Would you have adopted more of a RISC-like architecture if your work had started later?

D.   ELECTRONIC DICTIONARY RESEARCH PROJECT

1.   What is the current state of the EDR project? In particular, what is the current state of completion of the semantic dictionary?

2.   Please give us some current details about implementation. What language is being used to handle representation? What set of concept primitives are you using?

3.   As the knowledge base gets larger and larger, what problems of scale-up are you encountering, and how are you handling them?

4.   Are the dictionaries (including semantic dictionary) in trial use in any of the companies? How is the use done?

5.   Are you going to use ICOT's PIM for running the dictionaries for natural language understanding projects?

6.   How big is the current staff of EDR? What are the plans for EDR? Will it grow? Shrink? What new projects will it undertake?

E.   REAL WORLD COMPUTING PROGRAM

1.   What research efforts will RWCP undertake in the area of AI or, more specifically, in the area of knowledge-based systems?

2.   For these AI-related or KBS-related projects, how much government funding is planned? Over what length of time? What companies are involved? Will there be a project institute? What is ETL's role in RWCP?

4.   Will these AI-related research projects focus on particular application domains (perhaps as testbeds), and if so what are they?

5.   What role will parallel computing play in these AI-related projects? What kind of parallel computing is envisioned?

APPENDIX D.   SITES VISITED BY JTEC TEAM

The following organizations were visited:

Universities

Kyoto University, Department of Information Science
Osaka University, Institute of Scientific and Industrial Research
University of Tokyo, Research Center for Advanced Science and Technology

National Projects

ICOT
Japan Electronic Dictionary Research Project
Laboratory for International Fuzzy Engineering Research

Companies

Fujitsu Laboratories Ltd.
Hitachi Systems Development Laboratory Ltd.
Japan Air Lines
Mitsubishi Electric Corporation
NEC C&C Systems Research Laboratories
Nippon Steel Computer Systems Laboratory
NKK
NTT Knowledge Systems Laboratory
Obayashi Corporation
Sekisui Chemical Co. Ltd.
Tokyo Electric Power Co.
Toshiba Systems and Software Engineering Laboratory

Publications

Nikkei AI

APPENDIX E.   SITE REPORTS

Full accounts of the JTEC team's visits to three universities and three national projects are contained in Chapters 4 and 5, respectively, and are not repeated here in full. Addresses for these organizations can be found at the end of the following site reports (page 196).

Site: **Fujitsu Laboratories Ltd.**
                            1015 Kamikodanaka
                            Nakahara-ku
                            Kawasaki 211, Japan

Date Visited: March 23, 1992

JTEC Attendees:

Feigenbaum
Nii
Schorr
Engelmore
Shelton
Kahaner

Hosts:

Dr. Shigeru Sato   Managing Director
Mr. Tomoharu Mohri   Deputy Mgr., Knowledge Processing Laboratory
Mr. Jun'ichi Tanahashi   General Mgr., Adv. Inf. Sys. Div.
Mr. Hiromu Hayashi   General Mgr., Processor Div.
Yasubumi Sakakibara   Fundamental Informatics Section
Fumihiro Maruyama   Knowledge Processing Laboratory

From Fujitsu Ltd:
Susumu Murakami   Mgr., 2nd Section, CAE Dept., Eng. Support Div.
Jun-ichi Komoda   Section Manager, Knowledge Based Systems
Hitohide Usami   Section Manager, AI Development & Support
                                  Section, SE Information Development Dept.

Fujitsu, the second largest computer company in the world, has been marketing AI tools, especially ESHELL, since 1984. They also have several products, e.g., for machine translation, and hardware for neuro-computing. ESHELL, which used to be the best selling ES tool in Japan, is now trailing behind Hitachi's ES/KERNEL. ESHELL began as a tool on mainframes using UTLISP. The market is shifting to products on UNIX-based workstations written in C. Fujitsu is trying to recapture the market with FORTRAN-based and COBOL-based tools, but its commitment to mainframes may be bucking the trend (not only in the ES area).

There are three groups involved with KBS:
>   The Research Laboratory (Sato et al.)
>   Product Development (Komoda, Murakami)
>   Systems Engineering/Knowledge Engineering, which makes the contacts with
>   clients (Usami)

The meeting began with a number of interesting comments, from director of the laboratory, Dr. Sato, whose association with KBS technology goes back to the late 1970s:

o   The growth of AI has not been as big as expected, as measured in total sales, but is nonetheless growing. The technology does, however, contribute to the sale of Fujitsu hardware.

o   There has been a rapid downsizing (in both the physical and economic senses). Consequently other technologies have gained in priority over AI, and manpower has shifted over to these newer technologies, such as multimedia and distributed networking.

o   The principal barrier to growth is technological. They have difficulty in constructing knowledge systems for complex customer applications.

o   ICOT is perceived as having had both positive and negative effects:

-       Positive: increased the level of basic research in computer science; developed parallel computing architectures, and increased the number of researchers.

-       Negative: emphasis on PROLOG was good for research, but bad for products; development of PIM machines did not benefit Fujitsu, which is now using 1024 SPARC chips in its AP1000 with a peak capacity of 8.53 GFlops (intended usage is in ultra high-speed scientific calculations).

o   Knowledge acquisition is the primary technical barrier, and is the only interesting research topic in ES, but the problem may be too hard.

Our hosts at Fujitsu did a very good job in filling out Part A of the questionnaire. Highlights:

o   They have shipped more than 3,000 ES shells, and have sold approximately 20 KBSs.

o   They have about 240 systems that they use internally, and know of about 250 systems built by their customers, but could not categorize any of them in terms of operationality. Later in the questionnaire, however, they stated that about 20 percent of the projects started get as far as a completed prototype; and of those, 20 percent get to an operational system status. A best overall guess is that five percent of the reported systems are in routine use. The current success rate in fielding expert systems is better than five percent. Because of the experience base they now have, the success rate is somewhere between 75 and 95 percent. They are better able to select problems which are solvable by this technology.

o   The largest percentage of systems developed for internal use are for planning or scheduling. Their most successful system is PSS, a production support system for planning assembly and test of printed circuit boards. It's a relatively small system, built on ESHELL, and runs on a mainframe. The system, which is in daily use, saves about one person per year by speeding up the planning time. A workstation version is under development.

o   Fujitsu stresses integration of AI and conventional systems. The company now has ES tools written in COBOL (YPS/KR) and in FORTRAN (FORTRAN/KR), to support integration.

o   60 to 75 percent of the development costs of a system goes into the interface. Better graphical user interfaces (GUIs) are needed. That need has stimulated work on a GUI called GUIDEPOWER.

o   Fujitsu worked with NKK on the blast furnace system, which is the largest application the company has been associated with.

Mr. Maruyama presented a novel approach to solving constraint satisfaction and optimization problems which purports to be better than integer programming (Maruyama, Minoda et al. 1991). He works at the Knowledge Processing Laboratory, which has a staff of about 40.

ADDITIONAL COMMENTS ON QUESTIONNAIRE:

Question 8:   ESHELL cannot keep up with real time. FORTRAN and C are the procedural languages used.

Question 15: Fujitsu gave up development half way through one project due to manpower and budget shortages.

Question 16: Existing tools are useful up to 2,000 rules, several thousand objects, though NKK used 4,000 rules in ESHELL for its blast furnace application.

Question 19 (main problems seen with existing technology):

1)   GUI, as mentioned above.
2)   Knowledge changes very fast in the real world (e.g., banking), hence the maintenance cost is too high.
3)   There are few development tools, e.g., testing tools.
4)   AI does not apply well to CASE.

Site: **Hitachi Systems Development Laboratory, Ltd.**
                               1099 Ohzenji
                               Asao-ku
                               Kawasaki-shi 215, Japan

Date Visited: March 23, 1992

JTEC Attendees:

Feigenbaum
Nii
Schorr
Engelmore
Shelton
Kahaner

Hosts:

Dr. Koichiro Ishihara	Senior Chief Researcher
Dr. Motohisa Funabashi	Chief Researcher
Toshiro Yamanaka	Sr. Engineer, Expert Systems Group, Information Systems Development
Dr. Hiroshi Motoda	Chief Research Scientist, Advanced Research Laboratory
Hiroshi Isobe	Dept. Mgr.
Shoichi Masui	Sr. Researcher
Singi Domen	General Mgr.
Dr. Keith Collyer	Sr. AI Engineer, Hitachi Europe Ltd.
Satoshi Okuide	Sr. Engineer, Information Systems Development (Kansai region)

The JTEC team's hosts from Hitachi did not fill out the application section of the questionnaire in advance, but Mr. Yamanaka filled it out partially after the meeting and sent usa facsimile copy. Hitachi has developed 500 to 600 systems for customers. The company has sold on the order of 4,000 copies of its ES/KERNEL systems, half of that number in the last two years, to approximately 1,000 customers. Approximately 50 systems are in each of the categories of field test, completed prototype, or under development.

Hitachi was the first Japanese computer company to provide ES tools on a workstation, in C. The ES/KERNEL tool is now the largest selling tool in Japan. ES/KERNEL is actually a series of tools, characterized either by the platform on which it runs or the task for which it is specialized. Hitachi's latest tool is

ES/KERNEL2. Of Hitachi's task-specific shells, ES/PROMOTE/W-DIAG is a diagnosis ES tool, built on ES/KERNEL and running on a workstation. ES/PROMOTE/PLAN is for planning and scheduling, and was built from scratch. ES/TOOL/W-RI is a rule induction tool, under development. It is a policy within Hitachi to build applications on top of Hitachi tools.

Hitachi is quick to add features to its tools. For example, fuzzy logic is a part of the shell. ATMS and case-based reasoning will be in the ES/KERNEL2 to be released soon. Hitachi's time-to-market for new methodology may well be shorter than any organization in the U.S.

Hitachi also sells, both internally and externally, a guide to building expert systems, called ES/GUIDE. It advocates a spiral model of system development combined with the waterfall model (used primarily for documentation).

In addition to the tools developed by the ES group, the Heavy Industry Division is selling a real-time process control shell (EUREKA-II) and an advanced plant operation system called APOS, which is built on top of EUREKA. These shells are often used by the Heavy Industry Division people to build applications for their customers. They have sold more than 2000 copies of EUREKA.

Hitachi does not have a central group responsible for ES development within or outside Hitachi. Each section is expected to know about and use ES technology as appropriate.

Mr. Okuide reported on the construction planning system that Hitachi developed for Okamura for shield tunneling. The system combines AI, relational databases, CAD and a reporting system.

Initially, the market was in banking and financial diagnostic systems, but this is being overtaken by industrial companies doing scheduling. Our Hitachi hosts also said that the largest application market now is in the insurance industry. Within the domain of planning and scheduling, job shop scheduling is the biggest market, accounting for 40 to 50 percent of the business, followed by process scheduling. This class of applications got started three years ago; a Hitachi engineer worked with a customer to figure out how to do their planning application on ES KERNEL after the customer had failed using a competitor's shell. Initially, the scheduling job took 17 hours, but eventually it was reduced to five minutes of workstation time. The system has saved ¥7 billion. Hitachi's people are familiar enough with scheduling problems so that they are able to divide them into four classes and have techniques to solve them. However, they still cannot do railroad schedules since that requires solving the bypass problem (putting locals on side tracks so that express trains can pass them). Up until now they have done most of the planning applications for customers, but now they are beginning to introduce courses so that customers can learn to do this themselves.

In a private communication, a Hitachi representative indicated that spending $500,000 for an application (as was done at Okamura Construction) was at the high end of what Hitachi's customers were prepared to spend on an application.

Our Hitachi hosts expressed optimism about the future for ESs. However, they find their customers want/require consulting services and, in general, this requirement limits their deployment of ESs.

With respect to advanced KBS research, Hitachi is working on acquiring knowledge directly from text, and on a product for multi-layered cooperative reasoning. It has a product under development (EXCEED3) for qualitative reasoning (!), and one for rule induction, a fuzzy reasoning version of ES/KERNEL. As second generation tools, Hitachi envisions task/domain-specific tools such as the ones mentioned above (ES/PROMOTE/W-DIAG, ES/PROMOTE/PLAN, ES/TOOL/W-RI). The company is working on an advanced ATMS add-on to ES/KERNEL, a case-based machine translation system (at SDL), and a CBR in ES/KERNEL2. Most research funding is internal, with some cooperative work with customers.

Dr. Motoda, who is regarded as one of the foremost researchers in AI in Japan, reported on his work on knowledge reformulation and concept formation using "imagistic" reasoning (also called "frustration-based learning"). There is no apparent line of technology transfer between Motoda's lab and the ES sales/support group.

Hitachi has a small division in Europe (Hitachi Europe Limited, about 15 people), maintaining technical awareness of Western developments, and providing development support for ObjectIQ (the western version of ES/KERNEL2-W). ObjectIQ is about to be released, and will be marketed in Europe by Hewlett-Packard.

Scheduling projects are Hitachi's new field of endeavor, and it is Hitachi's most important customer need. Hitachi's people feel that rule-based systems are not good enough and they need better technology. To this end, Hitachi Europe Limited (HEL) is working with LOGICA on WHISPA. This product uses standard scheduling technology which is categorized as local decision job shop scheduling. At the time of our visit, Hitachi expected a product in mid 1992. Test cases have demonstrated one to two orders of magnitude speed-up in generating schedules. Forty to fifty percent of Hitachi's customers want it. HEL is also working on a research project, called TOSCA, with Austin Tate at the University of Edinburgh. TOSCA uses blackboard technology in its research phase for flexibility in research prototyping. Areas to be incorporated in TOSCA are:

1)   Strategic (corporate) knowledge
2)   Informed decision making
3)   Improved capacity planning

TOSCA will be the next generation tool, and Hitachi will not release it until it gets customer feedback from WHISPA.

Site: **Japan Air Lines**
                                   c/o JAL Creative Systems
                                   12-38 Shibaura 4-chome
                                   Minato-ku
                                   Tokyo 108, Japan

Date Visited: March 27, 1992

JTEC Attendees:

Friedland
Nii
Schorr
Chien

Hosts:

Mr. Sanshiro Shirahashi   Director, Administration, Flight Operations
Mr. Akira Mori   Manager, 3rd Systems Division, JAL Creative
                                       Systems
Mr. Yasunari Imamura   Asst. Manager

PRESENTATIONS

Mr. Mori, who championed the introduction of the flight crew scheduling system at
JAL, discussed the history and development of that system, its architecture, user
interface, etc.

SUMMARY OF QUESTIONNAIRE

Japan Air Lines (JAL) has two ESs in routing operations, both for planning and
scheduling. The more important of the two is COSMOS/AI, for flight crew
scheduling (see discussion below). The system was built by NEC on NEC's
EXCORE tool, contains 45,000 frames, 220,000 lines of LISP code and 80,000 lines of
C code. The system was developed over a period of 2.5 years and cost
approximately $4 million. It was turned over to JAL for regular use in 1990. The
primary benefits have been in cost reduction and quality improvement, but no
quantitative results were given, except an estimate of six to seven years to pay back
development costs. No personnel were laid off; with COSMOS/AI, JAL is able to
schedule more planes with the same staff.

DISCUSSION

JAL has about 100 aircraft in their fleet (767, 747, 747-400, and DC-10s), and employs about 2,200 people as flight crew (pilots and flight engineers, etc.). Total cost of the system was ¥5 billion; the system has not quite paid for itself yet. Constraints on crew include training, government rules, union rules, and other customs.

Before the ES, 25 personnel were involved in flight crew scheduling. It took about six months to become expert in scheduling, assuming prior background in the constraints (about another six months to gain that knowledge). This has been reduced to two months total by the expert system.

The database on all flight information resides on an IBM 3090 mainframe. Data are updated by downloading from the host machine once a day at 3:00 a.m. JAL wrote a 3090 program which gathers changes, e.g., vacation days, etc.

The scheduling system runs on several UNIX workstations networked to the IBM system. An AI processor (NEC LISP machine) is attached to the workstations that process 747 schedules (busiest by far).

The basic function of the system is to make a schedule for the following month. This is due out on the 25th of each month.

The system uses the EXCORE frame-based tool -- LISP-based.

JAL does not yet have the capability to do reactive re-scheduling during the month of an operating schedule, but is working on it.

Formerly the 747 schedule took 20 days to prepare. This normally included considerable overtime. By using the ES, that time is reduced to 15 non-overtime days. Also, scheduling personnel have been reduced by about five (during a period when the flight load went up considerably).

JAL also claims that schedules are now better with fewer mistakes (actually claiming no mistakes at all after a monthly schedule has been accepted).

A toy prototype convinced management to proceed with the system. Acquisition of the knowledge was the hardest part.

The system became operational in February 1990.

The system is basically a heuristic one. Most constrained blocks (patterns of flight, stay in destination, return flight, required rest) are assigned first. Then blocks are shuffled (starting with least constrained) when problems are found.

The system takes two to three hours to produce the complete schedule for the most complicated runs.

Currently optimization is not important (any correct schedule is good enough).

JAL began development in September 1987. NEC did the first prototype, but system work is now in-house.

An operations research approach was also tried.   This was rejected as "too mechanical." The users did not like it because "human" constraints were ignored.

The system cannot completely finish a schedule. A human scheduling expert still makes final adjustments. After the schedule is finished by the humans, it is checked by ES to see that no constraints are violated (i.e., no mistakes).

Biggest virtue of the system is its maintainability. It is easy to add new rules about new planes, crews, etc. Two to three people are employed continually updating the scheduling KB.

JAL is also working on an aircraft cargo routing system (traveling salesman type problem), and on a career path system for flight crew members (i.e., tracking career milestones, etc.).

Although the system has not yet paid for itself, without it JAL may have needed more human schedulers, since JAL flights, crews, and planes have increased 20 percent, 10 percent, and 5 percent, respectively.

JAL management is very happy with AI (in the opinion of the group that we interviewed) and very proud of COSMOS/AI.

A paper on this system was presented at the First World Congress on Expert Systems in December 1991 (Onodera and Mori 1991). An earlier paper was presented at the 28th AGIFORS Symposium (Mori 1988).

Site: **Mitsubishi Electric Corporation (MELCO)**
                               Industrial Electronics and Systems Laboratory
                               8-1-1 Tsukaguchi Honmachi
                               Amagasaki-shi
                               Hyogo 661, Japan

Date Visited: March 26, 1992

JTEC Attendees:

Friedland
Feigenbaum
Nii
Chien

Hosts:

Dr. Toshiaki Sakaguchi   Manager, Advanced Systems Group, Industrial
                                   Electronics & Systems Laboratory
Dr. Ikuyuki Hirata   Manager, Strategic Planning Department, Central
                                   Research Laboratory
Dr. Toyo Fukuda   Manager, Advanced Systems Group, Industrial
                                   Electronics & Systems Laboratory
Mr. Shinta Fukui   Asst. Mgr., Computer Control Systems
                                   Engineering Sect., Power Systems Dept.
Dr. Keinosuke Matsumoto   Senior Researcher, Advanced Systems Group,
                                   Industrial Electronics & Systems Laboratory
Mr. Ichige   Senior Researcher, Planning Division

ORGANIZATIONAL DATA

Mitsubishi Electric Corporation has four R&D laboratories in the Osaka area: Central Research; Manufacturing Development; Materials & Electronic Devices; and Industrial Electronics & Systems. There are approximately 1,000 scientific and technical personnel within those laboratories. The corporation as a whole has 13 R&D laboratories throughout the country. One of the highlighted accomplishments in its 1991 corporate profile is the development of the MELCOM PSI, a sequential inference machine for AI applications, and MELCOM PSI II, a large-scale integrated version.

There are about 10 AI researchers at the Central Research Lab, and another 20-30 in the Industrial Systems Laboratory.

DISCUSSION

We met with people in the Industrial Electronics and Systems Lab (IESL), a group especially focussed on power industry (electrical) problems.   (Dr. Hirato of the Strategic Planning Department of the Central Research Lab was present but with minimal participation.) Therefore, we saw what is going on in a small section (one of a dozen research labs that Mitsubishi Electric runs) of a very large company.

Our hosts were most interested in ES for energy management systems (EMS) as applied to electric power distribution networks.   MELCO sees uses for this technology in diagnosis, restorative operation, reliability assessment, dispatching control, and operations planning. There are currently three EMS systems (one from Mitsubishi) in practical use in Japan. The Mitsubishi one is in use at the Kansai power distribution center -- a system with about 200 rules. There are six more systems in field test.

Mitsubishi finds that Japanese power companies are very eager to use ES technology.   They were led to believe that U.S. power companies were less interested in the technology even though EPRI appears interested.

IESL has a lot of experience in network diagnostic problems -- an industry survey shows about 50 percent of ESs in the diagnostic area -- thus does not have many failures in this area. In general, where an ES is built as an integral part of a larger system, the failure rate is very low. Mitsubishi considered integration from the very beginning, and thus did not experience problems of integrating stand-alone ESs after they were built.

MELCO has developed a domain-specific tool for network diagnosis, called DASH (Komai 1991 #594). It looks quite sophisticated, using both frames and rules. The tool is built to reuse knowledge (a library of network models), to be maintainable by the end-users, and to be verifiable (verification assumes correct models in the library). One application which was rewritten in DASH reduced the number of rules from 200 to 70-80 by using rules classes categorized by network types. In this area, the important needs for the future are an ability to reason fast with more than 1,000 network nodes and easier/faster knowledge acquisition.

Our hosts discussed the usual issues of system integration and realtime operation.

DETAILS

Our hosts stated that every ES building event has to start from scratch. No domain knowledge is saved in libraries; no task knowledge is saved. Their DASH tool is aimed at both problems.   For the former, they are preparing domain specific libraries, e.g., relating to power networks. Structural components in the network are expressed as objects in an object-oriented programming system; functional specifications, however, are represented as state transitions in a transition network. They chose not to use message passing and methods attached to the objects (as is normal in object-oriented programming) because they found it difficult to express causal relations in this representation. We were given a demo of the system.

A system developer spoke on real ESs for energy management applications. There aren't any in practical use yet. The architecture is to put the ES on a workstation and connect it by a network to the computer that runs the EMS. That computer runs a huge program and is overloaded, so the ES needs its own platform.

This ES for diagnosis is a 200 rule system, but when implemented with DASH it is only 70-80 rules (some component knowledge is reusable). The system is fielded at Kansai Electric Power but is not in routine use yet. It speeds up the diagnosis from three to four minutes down to one minute.

MELCO's most successful ES is one that controls group elevator scheduling. This is an on-line real-time scheduling system that helps determine which elevator should stop where to pick up passengers. The typical application has four to five elevators in a 20 story building. The rules employ fuzzy logic. The system was first used two years ago in Kobe -- there are many installations now. The ES has been awarded many prizes, e.g., the Electric Industries Association award. MELCO has also developed a fuzzy logic control system for metal machining which became part of an electron beam cutting machine the company began selling three to four years ago.

Power industry ES applications world-wide in 1991:

Diagnosis	25%
Operations	25%
Monitoring and control each	15%
Planning	10%

Others: education/simulator; maintenance; design; system analysis

Dr. Sakaguchi's wishes for the "second generation:"

1)   Most of all, reusability of knowledge.
2)   Greater ease of maintenance. The power companies tell them that plant people must be able to maintain the system by themselves.
3)   Ease of verification of the system. At present it is tedious.

MELCO is also doing work on optical neuro-computers, but we didn't get into details.

MELCO's best AI systems are the elevator control application described above and the metal machining system.

The company did some work on an expert system for onboard use in control of the power system for the Japanese Experimental Module, to be attached to Space Station Freedom, but funding was cut before final development.

They also have an expert system for diagnosis of a "large rotating machine."

Several years ago a "knowledge media station" -- combination of AI and hypermedia -- was built to demonstrate the value of the PSI machine.

Current AI work is done on UNIX workstations using C, C++, and OPS83.

MELCO representatives expressed the view that ICOT was successful politically, but not technically. They see parallel computation important for simulation, not for AI. ICOT has had no influence on their operations yet. However they feel that it won a political victory in terms of showing the world that Japanese are spending money on basic research.

Note: The four MELCO laboratories at the Osaka location produced a brochure; in it are some interesting and diverse applications (including the fuzzy elevator control system), indicating that ES technology appears to be known in different parts of the company and is used routinely where appropriate.

Site: **NEC R&D Center**
                               1-1 Miyazaki 4-chome
                               Miyamae-ku Kawasaki
                               Kanagawa 216, Japan

Date Visited: March 24, 1992

JTEC Attendees:

Johnson
Schorr
Nii
Engelmore
Shelton

Hosts:

Tatsuo Ishiguro	Vice President, Research and Development Group
Dr. Masahiro Yamamoto	General Manager, C&C Systems Research Laboratories
Dr. Masanobu Watanabe	Research Mgr., Basic Technologies Research Lab
Takeshi Yoshimura	Mgr., Basic Technologies Research Lab
Yoshiyuki Koseki	Mgr., Research, Basic Technologies Research Lab
Akihiko Konagaya	Mgr., Research, Computer System Research Lab

ORGANIZATIONAL DATA

NEC's net sales, as reported in its 1991 brochure, were $26.2 billion. The company has 118,000 employees. The new corporate philosophy emphasizes computers & communications (C&C). C&C operations accounted for 47 percent of net sales in 1991. In July 1991 the company reorganized into 10 operating groups. We met with members of the C&C Systems Research Laboratories, which is a component of the Research and Development Group. The R&D group accounts for one percent of annual sales, and employs 1,600 people. (Corporate-wide R&D accounts for 10 percent of sales and employs about 10,000 people.)

The C&C Systems Research Laboratories encompasses many individual laboratories devoted to networks, systems, terminals, and basic technologies. Each of these individual laboratories develops ES applications and/or tools.

PRESENTATIONS

We discussed the answers to the questionnaire, after which we toured the laboratory and were given demonstrations of five systems: genetic information processing, parallel object-oriented language A'Um-90, Adaptive Model-Based Diagnostic System, Software Synthesis Expert System, and Corporate-wide Case-Based System.

SUMMARY OF QUESTIONNAIRE

NEC has developed about 1,000 ES applications, of which 10 percent are in routine operation. The major task areas are diagnosis, scheduling, design, and software development aids. The company's biggest success has been the crew scheduling system, COSMOS, developed with Japan Air Lines (Onodera and Mori 1991). This is a large ES (45,000 frames, 7,000 rules, 300,000 lines of code), built on the EXCORE tool. It runs on ten engineering workstations (EWS4800, which has up to 320 megabytes of memory) and four LISP machines (LIME), and is integrated with the host data processing system. The system was turned over to JAL in 1990, where it is now routinely used by JAL schedulers. Before the system was installed, one month of scheduling required two or more days of effort (with overtime) by 24 people. A monthly schedule can now be generated in 15 days by 19 people. Other applications that were reported include a software debugging advisor; FUSION, an LSI logic design tool; and a system called SOFTEX for synthesizing C/C++ programs from specifications (represented as state transition tables and/or flowcharts). SOFTEX is a 300-rule system built with EXCORE, developed by professional programmers and domain experts. The system is still about six months to one year from routine use. In order to make the system appeal to programmers, it was necessary to incorporate in SOFTEX the functionality to enable customization, so that the generated program fits each programmer's style. Their primary general purpose ES building tool is EXCORE, although many systems also use C, LISP, and sometimes even COBOL. EXCORE itself exists in both LISP (EXCORE/CL) and C versions (EXCORE/KWB). NEC has developed a methodology (EXMETHOD) for building ESs, based on the use of EXCORE, that provides guidelines for knowledge representation and acquisition. Training programs are in place that run in duration from five days to one month.

NEC admits to some unsuccessful projects, and attributes the lack of success to a number of reasons, including the knowledge acquisition bottleneck, the difficulty of integration with existing systems, and knowledge base maintenance.   These problems tend to get detected late rather than early.

With respect to building large KBSs, the limiting factors are: speed of inheritance; KB management and the amount of memory implied by that; and the need for faster hardware (500 MIPS range).

Future ESs at NEC are expected to employ technologies such as model-based diagnosis, case-based reasoning for scheduling and for software synthesis, and combining ES methods with algorithmic methods (model-based reasoning is an example).

As examples of research in large knowledge bases, NEC demonstrated systems containing extensive data on DNA and protein sequences, and on protein secondary structure. The systems are used for searching for common patterns in the sequence information. NEC has a well-documented body of research in model-based diagnosis, genetic information processing, learning (using a technique called Minimum Description Length), learning theory, inductive learning, knowledge acquisition for classification problems and for consultation systems, natural language understanding, and case-based reasoning. The company believes that the important aspects of second generation ES tools are the incorporation of machine learning, model-based reasoning, cooperative problem solving, and facilities for extracting knowledge from large databases.

NEC also has developed a language, called PRIME (PRimary Inference Mechanism with Environment), for describing a semantic model of a domain. The model can be used for deep level inference. The inference process can then be compiled into a shallow knowledge base.

DISCUSSION

NEC has built two task-specific shells on top of EXCORE: DIAGBOX, for diagnosis; and PLANBOX for planning. These shells were released in January 1992. EXCORE itself has sold about 1000 copies. Its price is about ¥500,000. The system runs on the NEC workstation, on a mainframe, and, just recently, on a personal computer.

NEC uses system engineers, not knowledge engineers, to develop applications.

NEC feels that it is important that KBS technology is "harmonized" with conventional software technology.

The sale of expert systems is not rising as rapidly as had been expected, and in fact is flat now during the current recession in Japan.

NEC's systems for *kanji* character recognition and for speaker independent machine translation were also mentioned. The latter was demonstrated at Telecom 91, and translates among four languages: Japanese, English, French and Spanish. NEC's machine translation system has been discussed in a previous JTEC report (Rich 1992).

The model-based diagnosis system mentioned above has been used for diagnosing a packet-switched network. The knowledge base contains structural and behavioral models of the device to be diagnosed. Given input/output pairs, the system identifies the faulty component. A minimum entropy technique is used to select the most effective test to perform as the diagnosis proceeds. A single fault is assumed. The Minimum Description Length (MDL) technique is employed here, and in the genetic processing applications mentioned above. MDL is a means to finding an optimum trade-off between overfitting (which implies very long descriptions to cover all examples) and underfitting (which causes a high error rate). The use of MDL seems to be popular at NEC.

Regarding sales, scheduling is increasing; diagnostics are dipping slightly now, but our hosts believe that area will soon resume modest growth. Five years ago their customers needed extensive help in developing ESs but now they don't. Internally, they feel they have many design tasks in NEC that will benefit from the use of ES; they appear to be using it vigorously internally.

Regarding ICOT's influence, today it is a small percentage of the AI'ers in Japan, but this was not so in the beginning. NEC did not build a PIM but is building a parallel processor made up of microprocessors; their architecture is similar to CM-5.

OBSERVATIONS

The heart of our visit was the demonstration of five applications. Our hosts offered little or no explanation of the problem solving approach apart from the demonstrations, which leaves a number of questions unanswered. Interestingly, the demonstrations tended to employ the older expert system techniques -- no fuzzy logic or neural nets. Yet the applications were quite advanced with respect to the general state of the art.

Regarding SOFTEX, given that engineers in the telecommunications industry think in terms of state transitions, the input specification can be considered to be high level. However, the transformations to procedural code are fairly straightforward because the structure of the specification and the structure of the resulting program appear to be isomorphic, i.e., each specification corresponds to a single program. The larger system is presumably structured in a way that enables this program-by-program approach. While this was a nicely packaged and clearly presented demonstration, we did not see anything that is pressing the state-of-the-art. After our visit, our hosts explained that there was insufficient time to describe the entire system and they had not yet disclosed the technology in the SOFTEX shell. NEC has in fact synthesized other programs beyond the state transition model software that was demonstrated to us and has published a paper describing the system (Yamanouchi 1992).

One of NEC's demos was a corporate-wide case-based system. This was an application in support of software quality improvement. For many years, NEC has collected examples of quality problems and improvements submitted from the organization. The traditional book form of distribution has become useless as it has grown large. What we saw was a simple retrieval example with emphasis upon the design of an index. There was no "repair" function. This application was more of a cultural statement than an interesting application of technology.

The payoff of ES applications wasn't (or couldn't be) quantified. NEC's people found the usual oft-stated limitations of the technology. They found it a very useful tool for internal use by the company. Their applications improved quality by allowing more trials by improving the speed of iteration. They also had some applications with a big ROI. They had no applications they were able to sell in multiples to customers.

The Basic Technologies Laboratory is in charge of VLSI CAD tools, knowledge-based systems, databases, and software architectures. The group does basic research as well as applications to support field personnel. (The term "basic" appears to mean something different in the Japanese labs from we generally mean. Perhaps the difference is not between the Japanese and the U.S., but between company labs and universities.)

Note that although diagnostic programs are fielded, most Japanese do not consider them as being in routine use since "the need for diagnostics do not arise very often." (Is the zero defect policy actually working?)

We saw a demonstration of a distributed, model-based diagnostic program running on a 16-processor ICOT machine. Overall, NEC's research program is similar to what one would find at an average AI lab in the United States.

Site: **Nippon Steel Corporation**
                               Electronics Research Laboratories
                               6-10-1 Fuchinobe
                               Sagamihara
                               Kanagawa 229, Japan

Date Visited: March 26, 1992

JTEC Attendees:

Johnson
Schorr
Shrobe
Engelmore

Hosts:

Dr. Hiroshi Iwasaki   Director
Nobukuni Nakano   General Mgr., Computer Systems Lab
Yoshiteru Iwata   Mgr. Software Technology Center
Yutaka Miyabe   Sr. Researcher, Computer Systems Lab
Osamu Dairiki   Sr. Researcher, Software Engineering Group
                                     Leader, Knowledge Engineering Group
                                     Leader, Computer Systems Lab

ORGANIZATIONAL DATA

We visited Nippon Steel's Electronics Research Laboratory (ERL). Unlike NKK, where we visited an actual steel mill, this visit was really to one part of a large software house, doing advanced development and providing its own ES tools. Nippon Steel has approximately 1,000 research scientists in four research laboratories, of which about 235 are in ERL. ERL itself has five laboratories and one center. We interacted with members of the Computer Systems Laboratory (CSL), which has about 50 people. Subjects covered by CSL include:

o   Image processing
o   Graphics
o   Picture communication
o   Knowledge engineering
     -    tools for hybrid KBSs (i.e., integration with neural networks)
     -    practical platforms
o   Software engineering
o   Parallel processing

PRESENTATIONS

During our visit we discussed the answers to the questionnaire and saw several demonstrations of KBSs and other advanced software that is being developed at CSL.

SUMMARY OF QUESTIONNAIRE

Nippon Steel has developed 100 to 130 expert systems for internal use (very few for external use). About 30 percent of these are in routine use. Although most of the current applications are diagnostic/troubleshooting systems, the fastest growing area is in planning and scheduling.

Our hosts selected three representative applications, two of them diagnostic and one for process control. The first is a system for process diagnosis, used in the Oita works. The system is used in three factories for troubleshooting electrical and mechanical equipment, and has resulted in a reduction of production costs, development costs, and/or plant operators. The knowledge base contains about 160,000 knowledge "fragments" (comparable to about 50,000 rules). The system was developed with Nippon Steel's own shell called ESTO, written in C++, and runs on networked Sun workstations. About 20 man-years went into its development, over a two year period. The economic payback of this system is estimated to be about $2 million annually. The reliability of Sun hardware has been a problem in keeping the systems in use.

The second representative system provides supervision of blast furnace control. This is a large system, with 5,000 to 6,000 production rules. It was built on top of Hitachi's commercial EUREKA plus a "neuro simulator" tool called AMI developed internally, and runs on a minicomputer. AMI was used to build a neural network for preprocessing (pattern matching) the raw data before it is input to the expert system. Improvements in decision making and in quality of product have been the principal paybacks. About 14 man-years were expended in development, over two years. Maintenance of the KB has been a major problem, one not easily understood by people who were not involved in its construction.

The third system is a design expert system for designing shaped beams. This is a large system, containing 3,000 production rules and 500,000 lines of code, in LISP, FORTRAN and C. The system was built using ART (from Inference Corp.) and runs on networked Sun workstations. Twenty technical people (4 domain experts, 16 knowledge engineers) developed the system over an 18 month period. Principal payback is in reduction of the design cycle time by 85 percent and an increase in design accuracy of 30 percent. The estimated economic return is $200,000 annually. The system is felt to be too expensive, requiring a copy of ART at each new site.

When developing systems that use multiple sources of knowledge (experts) Nippon Steel has adopted a structured development method, much the same as used in conventional software development, which is intended "to avoid unnecessary confusion." For diagnostic systems, Nippon Steel uses its in-house tool, ESTO, which is designed to accommodate incomplete and inconsistent knowledge from multiple knowledge sources.

Of 28 systems developed within the past two years, 60 percent can be characterized as using a combination of a rule-based inference engine plus added code written in a conventional language, typically C. A few systems integrate rule-based, fuzzy and neural network methods. Commercial tools were found to be inadequate in the way they permit access to external functions written in conventional languages, which motivated Nippon Steel to develop its own tools.

Our hosts reported that they do not have a structured training program, and as a result they have seen the development of many poorly organized expert systems.

The company cited many reasons for selecting an expert system application, among which are to acquire know-how, to capture and distribute expertise, to improve revenues and to reduce costs.

Nearly all systems are integrated with other systems, e.g., data processing, and they are working to establish an inter-factory LAN to facilitate this integration.

Although most projects reach the prototype stage (28 out of 30 in recent past), it is difficult to estimate how many actually get to successful operational status. Mr. Dairiki estimates that only 10 percent (Mr. Miyabe estimates 20 percent) really reach successful status on an ROI basis.

Most of the systems that have been developed are small (under 100 rules). It was found that the time to develop large projects increases more than linearly with the number of rules. The in-house consultants advise developers to keep their knowledge bases to within 300 rules, and if more are needed to segment the KB into modules each of which is within 300 rules.

Problems with current technology include slow execution speed for large-scale systems, high cost in time and effort of knowledge maintenance, lack of transparency of the inference process, tedious integration with existing software, and the general problem of knowledge acquisition.

Looking ahead several years, Nippon Steel envisions new expert systems that perform planning and scheduling over multiple factories or production lines. Future diagnostic and process control systems will employ model-based and case-based methods for more in-depth problem description and for recovery following diagnosis, with a capability for closed-loop control. Future planning/scheduling systems will be fully automatic and able to plan with multiple objectives. Future tools (infrastructure) will reduce or eliminate the need for knowledge engineers, will be task-specific within a general problem solving paradigm, will use a standard knowledge representation, and will have a better user interface.

DISCUSSION

A corporate goal is to increase productivity by the application of knowledge engineering.

Nearly all ESs are integrated into larger systems, e.g., in control applications. There are approximately 2,000 systems engineers at Nippon Steel. The company is one of the ten largest systems integrators in Japan. The ERL brochure shows nine systems built by CSL.

LISP and PROLOG aren't used very much due partly to their heavy resource consumption. Another reason is a result of the lack of programmers in Japan who have a command of these languages.

OBSERVATIONS

This is a very eclectic group, mixing rule-based, fuzzy and neural network methods in their applications as they believe they are needed.

Comments about both steel companies (Nippon Steel and NKK): They have lots of applications, most of them small-scale diagnostic systems. The systems are developed by systems engineers out in the steel works. One might postulate that there is a different business model at work here than in the U.S. The large Japanese companies investigate new technologies by building an internal competence rather than hiring an outside firm.

The company will not invest in an application unless it can retrieve its investment in two years.

The bulk of their applications appear to be small diagnostic ESs, though some are larger. As at NKK, they are developed by (plant) engineers, not researchers.

The group we visited at Nippon Steel was actually part of a computer group, and not directly involved with steelmaking. However, they have helped the steel people build some applications and were quite knowledgeable about those applications.

This laboratory is more like a U.S. software research group than anyplace else we visited. Applications are built primarily by people connected directly with the application, with the help of the knowledge engineering group. They have built a diagnostic shell of their own, based on a maximum entropy type of formalism (Minami and Hirata 1991).

They had a very large supply of high performance engineering workstations (top of the line Suns and SGIs). We saw one demo of a deformation solid modeler ("computer clay"). In many ways this group is reminiscent of a corporate computer science lab like Schlumberger's; their charter is to do advanced information processing including AI, graphics, etc.

Mr. Dairiki was very candid. He said that the reason for the low failure rate of projects is that they redefine the goals of a project that's not going so well; maybe its goal becomes familiarizing themselves with the technology. In selecting projects they want to get a payback in two years. Many successful projects don't actually get used; they met the need but the need wasn't vital enough. He thinks they need to do a better job of requirements analysis, etc.

As at NKK, a real project at Nippon Steel is developed with heavy contribution by people from the field. In the diagnostic system listed as representative, 20 foremen and 3 software engineers developed the application.

How do people get started on an AI project? They don't get formal training. Usually they buy the "best shell at that time" and take the training course (some of them) and plow through the manuals. Then they jump into building a system largely through on-the-job training. This sometimes leads to FORTRAN written as rules, but the systems work.

Two applications were mandated, those listed as "given policy" in the answer to question 11. These were done to maintain a "high tech aura", e.g., to answer a system that NKK had publicized.

Sometimes projects aren't stopped soon enough because they don't realize that they don't understand the problem they're attacking.

Overall, this group was very impressive. Since expert system development is a field activity, this group can concentrate on building tools that will leverage these activities. They have already done some of this with their diagnostic shell. It might be that this model of research and development gets at the important questions more effectively than the U.S. model of development in industry and research in universities.

Site: **NKK Kawasaki facility**
                                   c/o NKK Corporation
                                   1-1-2 Marunouchi
                                   Chiyoda-ku
                                   Tokyo 100, Japan

Date Visited: March 26, 1992

JTEC Attendees:

Johnson
Schorr
Shrobe
Engelmore

Hosts:

Isamu Komine   Asst. General Mgr., Planning & Coordination
                                        Dept., R & D Div.
Toshio Okawa   Manager, Control Engineering Team, Electronics
                                        Research Ctr.
Taichi Aoki   Asst. Manager, Process Control Dept., Fukuyama
                                        Works
Shuichi Yamamoto   Process Control Dept., Keihin Works

PRESENTATIONS

We visited the Keihin Works located on a man-made island (Ohgishima) in Tokyo
Bay.

Most of the time was devoted to NKK's primary application, which is a diagnosis and
control system that is used for stabilizing the output of blast furnaces. We saw a
video of this application, discussed it with Mr. Komine et al., and then went to a blast
furnace control room to see the system in actual operation. The system solves the
following problems:

o   prediction of abnormal conditions, such as a too rapid descent of the charge
        ("slip") or the permeable passage of gas through the charge ("channeling");
o   thermal control, i.e., keeping the bottom of the furnace at the proper
        temperature;
o   burden distribution, i.e., keeping the material in the furnace distributed in an
        axially symmetric way.

The furnace responds very slowly to changes in input, so one needs a good understanding of the device; one can't rely on immediate feedback from sensors.

The KB is structured into many knowledge sources, each of which has only a few rules.

The system was developed and is maintained by a group of systems engineers, who are domain experts. There are no knowledge engineers at NKK.

SUMMARY OF QUESTIONNAIRE RESPONSE

NKK has 25 ESs in routine operation, and five more in the field testing stage. Of the 37 systems that have been built or are in some stage of development, 16 combine the functions of advising, process control and diagnosis; 20 combine the functions of advising, planning/scheduling, and management integration aid. The blast furnace expert systems are described in Chapter 2.

All of the fully developed systems are integrated with conventional systems, and also use some high-level language (LISP, FORTRAN, PL-1) in addition to the ES shell (ESHELL for the blast furnace, KT for the planning/scheduling systems).

Rather than emphasize training in knowledge engineering and expert system development, NKK has chosen to train its systems engineers in systems analysis and modelling, which are more important skills for total system development. Expert systems techniques in themselves are of relatively small significance, in NKK's view. On the other hand, the company has developed expert system design tools, used in its Engineering and Construction Division, which embody a methodology for developing ESs. These tools, called NX-7 and NX-8, run on Xerox LISP machines and Sun workstations, and have been applied in developing ESs for operations support of refuse incinerators.

NKK often introduces an ES at the same time as it refurbishes its entire computer system (which itself may be just a part of a larger renewal project), making it difficult to evaluate the impact of the introduction of the ES. However, ESs are introduced only when conventional programming techniques fail to solve the problem at hand.

Regarding future development, our NKK hosts envision more use of in-the-loop control, moving from mainframes to engineering workstations, and providing intelligent assistance on more advanced tasks of engineering and management. They see several problems with current technology: AI tools that are difficult to learn and use; relatively high difficulty in system maintenance; inadequate processing speed; need to obtain knowledge automatically from data and to solve problems (e.g., scheduling) by using previous cases.

DISCUSSION

The developers of all of NKK's ESs are out in the various departments. They have extensive knowledge of the application domain, but were not skilled in AI or ES when they started the projects. Learning at first proceeded by trial and error; some engineers were sent to training courses. There is now a well established methodology for ES development at NKK. Expectations for this technology may now be too high.

Our hosts expressed the view that the newer techniques of fuzzy control or neural networks were too limited for most of the control applications at NKK. They also stated that the Fifth Generation Project had no influence on their operations. They have a few links with AI departments at Japanese universities. Mr. Okawa, for example, is interested in model-based reasoning and maintains such a link for this purpose.

OBSERVATIONS

A blast furnace is a complex, distributed, non-linear process. Conventional mathematical modeling techniques have never been able to predict future states of the furnace with enough accuracy to support automated control. As early as 1986, NKK Steel had developed an expert system to predict abnormal conditions within the furnace. NKK and other Japanese steel companies have since developed blast furnace control systems.

Because the blast furnace feeds all other processes in the steel mill, any instability in the operation of the furnace is compounded by the impact on other processes. Avoiding unstable operation of the furnace requires characterizing the current state of the furnace and projecting the conditions which will occur over the next several hours while there is still time to make adjustments.

An expert system has been developed which successfully models the current state, predicts future trends with sufficient accuracy to make control decisions, and actually makes the control decisions. These decisions can be implemented automatically or the operator can take manual control while still operating through the expert system's interfaces. The system continues to make inferences in manual mode, evaluating the influences of manual operations, then making further inferences.

NKK's Keihin Works system is integrated in the process control computer. It is implemented in LISP with FORTRAN used for data processing. The system has 400 rules, 350 frames, and 20,000 steps.

The benefits of the expert system have not been separately established. It is considered an integral part of a new furnace control system that was installed the last time the blast furnace was shut down for relining. We found that this was a common characteristic of expert systems used as closed loop controllers, viz. benefits are not traced to the component level. This suggests that expert systems have taken their place among the suite of techniques available to the controls engineer and do not require the special attention sometimes afforded new technologies.

Expert systems are not, in general, a complete solution, but must be combined with other technologies to solve almost any real problem. ES is more of a technique and a skill than a solution. We are looking at too small a grain size to speak of a business or of cost/benefit of an application. NKK representatives made this point very explicitly.

Most of NKK's applications were done by the steelmaking division; however, the last five on their list were done by the construction division in cooperation with the R&D lab.

Thus, for the most part, engineers in each department develop ESs. They are already domain experts; they know the factory and the business and only need to learn AI. This they do by trial and error, but with very few errors. Very few of NKK's engineers have attended IBM or Fujitsu training courses.

In designing this application, NKK needed to integrate with the conventional data processing of the steel works, so AI had to couple with high level languages. Development and maintenance of ES was done by the same group of system engineers. They can't quantify the AI development cost since AI is usually used as part of a larger project. They did not see any increase in their software productivity using AI. They also didn't find that ES transferred very well from one steel plant to another. Maintenance by engineers who didn't develop the system is very hard. Hence, they only apply AI where conventional methodology does not work well.

Our hosts stated that they found little methodology for writing ESs. NKK people found little management resistance in employing AI. They initially had great expectations for AI. These are now lower, and they can now select the proper subject area for employing AI.

They feel fuzzy logic is very limited and neural networks are similar to fuzzy in this respect, i.e., neural nets have too limited an input/output relationship. It is good for pattern recognition, which is only part of control technology. Hence, what's done by both neural networks and fuzzy logic can easily be done by other methods. "Sometimes NN [neural network] or Fuzzy techniques are used to make an organization appear 'high tech'."

There is no AI group per se at NKK. Applications there have been developed by engineers trained in control theory or industrial engineering or whatever. Although they seem pretty sophisticated about AI (they have interest in model-based reasoning, fuzzy, neural nets, etc.) none of the people have had any formal AI training.

Our NKK hosts said that they have had very few project failures because they determine as part of the feasibility study whether to go ahead. They also said that in their view a good system analysis is the key; anybody experienced in doing a good system analysis can then decide what part of the system should be an expert system, and could probably build it. When they use the term "engineer," they typically mean somebody who can do that kind of analysis.

Blast furnace operators take a long time to become skilled (five to ten years). Furthermore some of the conditions treated, like slip and channeling, happen very rapidly, and thus are difficult to control by hand.

One of our hosts said that they are considering introducing more expert systems "because industry is trying to improve the working environment of laborers." One of our hosts remarked to us that "AI tools are getting easier to use."

Site: **NTT Yokosuka Laboratories**
                               1-2356 Take Yokosuka-shi
                               Kanagawa-ken 238-03, Japan

Date Visited: March 23, 1992

JTEC Attendees:

Friedland
Johnson
Shrobe
Chien

Hosts:

Dr. Tsukasa Kawaoka   Executive Mgr., Knowledge Systems Laboratory
                                  NTT Network Information Systems Laboratories
Mr. Daiji Nanba   Senior Research Engineer, Supervisor
Mr. Toshiyuki Iida   Senior Research Engineer, Supervisor
Mr. Fumio Hattori   Senior Research Engineer, Supervisor
Dr. Satoru Ikehara   Senior Research Engineer, Supervisor
Mr. Francis Bond

ORGANIZATIONAL DATA

NTT's Knowledge Systems Laboratory has about 100 researchers -- 80 scientists and 20 engineers (perhaps "technicians" was meant rather than engineers). There are about 200 other personnel in the company doing actual application building.

PRESENTATIONS

The meeting consisted of two parts. The first part was a question and answer session on NTT operations, the company's expert system development tool "KBMS," and answers to the questionnaire. The second part consisted of a series of demonstrations of expert systems in the areas of private network design, intelligent tutoring, machine translation and a data entry system for service orders.

SUMMARY OF QUESTIONNAIRE

NTT has currently 36 expert systems under development. Half of these systems perform diagnosis on various components of a communications system. The company's most successful ES performs failure diagnosis and support of crossbar switching equipment. A task that typically takes four hours has been reduced to five minutes using the system. However, the main motivation for developing the system is that they are going to phase out the rest of the crossbars and no longer want to train people on it. With the expert system they don't need experts.

There is also research in three major areas: common sense AI (but note a quite specific definition of this as limited to reasoning quantitatively about ambiguous concepts and modifiers), machine translation, and VLSI design (high level description going to synthesis methods).

The work on common sense AI focuses on making quantitative judgments in very large KBs -- e.g., how long numerically a "long" river is. This also includes judging ambiguity in words, e.g., a long vacation vs. a long pencil. The machine translation work is based on belief in the great importance of specialized knowledge. Currently the system has 15,000 sentence structure descriptions.

NTT has developed a company-proprietary process for ES development.

OBSERVATIONS

Our overall impression was one of considerable vitality and high morale. NTT did a meticulous job in filling out our questionnaire for both applications of KB systems and more basic KB research. Major questions the answers which remain ambiguous are precise quantitative payoffs of currently fielded systems and whether the research work described adequately explains the activities of a 100 person laboratory.

Diagnosis is the biggest area, by far, of application development. The biggest ES "win" for NTT has been a crossbar diagnosis system. This is fully automatic and integrated with trouble-reporting systems. Dr. Kawaoka stated that "the battle for expert systems has been won at NTT."

The JTEC team saw demos of four systems: design of local switching networks, verification of service orders, machine translation, and an intelligent tutoring system. This latter work seemed fairly simple and not at all state-of-the-art. The switching network design system used straightforward heuristic methods (as opposed to a combination with linear programming methods), the service order verification work was nicely tied to an optical character recognition system, the machine translation work was impressive.

A 100-person AI lab is very large by any standards, and represents a huge corporate commitment. Moreover, these are not the same people who build the applications.

The technology was generally mid-1980s vintage.

None of the applications are simple "advisors."

NTT's perspective appears to be that all knowledge is heuristic and is mined from experts, rather than having a more formal problem formulation (such as model-based reasoning) or a more automated knowledge acquisition technique (such as case-based reasoning). It was surprising that there is no ongoing research in model-based diagnosis, given the corporate emphasis on diagnosis.

NTT's analysis of the benefits did not seem to rely heavily on cost/benefit justification but rather upon incremental quality/service improvements. In fact this is a possible hypothesis for the JTEC study: a high percentage of Japanese expert system initiatives reach the operational stage because the Japanese value incremental quality and service improvements which may not have the easily quantifiable cost/benefits expected by U.S. businesses. Expert system technology seems well suited to solving problems which produce these "soft" benefits.

Computer-based Instruction: Individual frames are represented with crude computer graphics or with analog audio or video. No DVI is employed. The application relies upon manual indexing to establish goals and subgoals and to map the frames of training material to the subgoals. No case-based indexing is used. It was not clear to us how the user model interacts with the selection of subgoals. Forms oriented data entry is the norm. This is not state of the art, namely graphical course maps which allow direct manipulation and which rely upon an underlying object-oriented design, which the NTT application apparently does not employ. In general this application lacks the features which will capture the imagination and provide motivation to students. This may not be very important in Japan, given the work hard/study hard ethic. It would be a fatal flaw in the U.S. The JTEC team did not see any indication that this application has been installed.

Service Order Entry system: This application inputs manually encoded information, uses a scanner and optical character recognition (OCR) to encode the information, and supports manual verification through on-screen comparison of the image with the encoded information. Next the order is checked for consistency. Finally, the system sends a transaction in some form to the service order transaction processing systems. This is a basic application which is installed in a large number of locations. It operates on PCs with a scanner and OCR box attached.

Network design system: This is a synthesis problem, but was primarily solved through heuristic methods.

Crossbar switch diagnostic application: NTT has developed its own Knowledge-base Management System (KBMS). They call it a second generation KBMS. KBMS is marketed separately. The system is comparable to KEE.

NTT is developing a Japanese to English translation system which is impressive. It is not clear that the particular approach will scale up, however.

The expert systems we saw were pretty typical of what you would see anywhere. They seemed to be at the same state of the art as in the U.S. Overall, the quality of the engineering work was very good.

The number our hosts gave for percentage of applications that progress from prototype to deployment is a staggering 95 percent! They staff the average project more heavily than we typically do in the U.S. — about 10 people seemed average. Finally, they said that quality control was a primary source of system suggestions; again quite different from the U.S.

Site: Obayashi Corporation
                                Mitsuwa Ogawa-machi Bldg. 3F
                                3-7 Kanda Ogawa-machi
                                Chiyoda-ku
                                Tokyo 101, Japan

Date Visited: March 25, 1992

JTEC Attendees:

Johnson
Shrobe
Schorr
Engelmore

Hosts:

Shinshirou Matsuoka   Sr. Manager, Center of Information Systems
Michio Nakao   Deputy Manager, System Development Dept.
                                No. 2, Center of Information Systems

ORGANIZATIONAL DATA

The Obayashi Corporation is one of the world's major general construction contractors, among the top five in Japan. As of December 1990, there were approximately 12,000 employees, including 161 research scientists and technicians and 140 systems engineers. Revenues for 1990 were close to $10 billion. The corporation has over a dozen overseas subsidiaries, including three in the United States (Obayashi America, James E. Roberts - Obayashi, and Obayashi Hawaii).

PRESENTATIONS

After opening remarks by Mr. Matsuoka, Mr. Nakao discussed two expert systems at Obayashi. The first is an automatic drilling control system for shield tunneling (a method of construction first used in England in the 19th century. This system controls the direction of drilling, which must be accurate to within five centimeters per one kilometer of tunnel length. The non-linearity of the problem precluded the use of a mathematical model. The system employs fuzzy control to solve the problem. The system is now in use in some (not all) of Obayashi's drilling operations.

The second system is a swing control system for a cable crane, which is used to transport casting concrete for dam construction. Controlling the swing of the basket as it is accelerated, moved and decelerated to its final position is a non-linear control problem that was solved by using rules obtained from skilled crane operators. The system is being implemented directly in C, and will be integrated with a programmable controller using fuzzy control techniques.   There are approximately 2,000 rules now, with more expected after the testing phase. Expected payback is a fourfold reduction in personnel.

We were also shown an interesting video on a "Super Construction Factory" planned for the 21st century, in which high-rise buildings are built almost entirely by specialized robots. The realization of this vision would require extensive research in advanced robotics and robot planning.

SUMMARY OF QUESTIONNAIRE RESPONSE

Obayashi has built 25 expert systems for internal use, and one for external use. Of these, six are in routine operation and nine more are at the field testing stage. Most of the systems (14) were characterized as advisory systems. The automatic direction control system for shield tunneling was built on top of two shells, called AI-DNA and AI-RNA, sold by AdIn, a Japanese AI company. The system is stand-alone, uses the C language, contains about 10,000 lines of code, and runs on a personal computer. The system was designed and built by two civil engineers, two mechanical engineers, and one systems engineer (plus programmers), and is maintained by the domain expert and two technicians. Development time was one year, including the testing period. The primary payback has been in improvement in the quality of direction control, and in the reduction of personnel required for this task, from three to one.

Obayashi reports that 70 percent of ES projects that are started get as far as a prototype, and 30 percent actually get to an operational system. Using existing tools they can envision building systems up to the size of a few thousand rules. Future systems planned by the corporation include other automatic control systems and intelligent CAD.   The primary perceived problems with present technology are knowledge acquisition, constructing design systems, the need to incorporate model-based and case-based reasoning, and the need for machine learning.

OBSERVATIONS

The automated building construction concept (CIC: Computer Integrated Construction) and the highly automated tunneling systems were very impressive in concept. To the extent Japan succeeds in fulfilling this vision of CIC, another U.S. industry may be at risk.

Obayashi started with AI ten years ago. Our hosts stated that they want to use CADAM and AUTO CAD, but these products need to be made Japanese language capable. Hence, since they have no access to these products, they feel they are three to four years behind U.S. construction companies. This is based on written reports that Mr. Matsuoka has read of a scheduling ES used by Bechtel International, a pipe laying application by Stone and Webster, and structural design and visualization systems that Skidmore, Owens uses. Moreover, he believes that Europe is also ahead of Japan because ESPRIT has started on standardization of models (STEP) and in Japan they are just starting to discuss that issue. Mr. Matsuoka also feels that Japan may be three to four years behind in user interface technology.

AI, the dream, still exists in Japan. However, interest in AI and ES is decreasing in Japan, though many down-to-earth applications are occurring. Many companies use ES in special areas only and that activity is increasing. Initially, there were a high number of prototypes, but the research budget for AI prototypes has been reduced. Production systems are increasing; people now know what works and what doesn't.

Of Obayashi's own applications, many prototypes in the planning stage don't make it to use. Why? It is hard to make an indispensable system. Obayashi's people find that they can use AI in automatic control applications. They are using neural network learning to set up the parameters of a fuzzy control system.

Why does Obayashi use ESs?

1)   Lack of skilled personnel/engineers
2)   Cost savings
3)   Environment
4)   Logistics
5)   Energy

Number (1) is the main driver.

Obayashi often undertakes projects to learn the technology.

Site: **Sekisui Chemical**
                               Umeda Center Building
                               2-4-12 Nakazaki-nishi
                               Kita-ku
                               Osaka 530, Japan

Date Visited: March 26, 1992

JTEC Attendees:

Feigenbaum
Friedland
Nii
Chien

Hosts:

Shuhei Kawai   Director and General Mgr., Information Systems
Norimasa Imazeki   Executive Director, ISAC, Inc.
Ichiro Terajima   Manager, ISAC, Inc.
Nobukuni Kino   ISAC, Inc.
Shigeki Kimura   ISAC, Inc.

ORGANIZATIONAL DATA

Sekisui Chemical, which developed the first plastic mold in 1947, has expanded into the fields of housing, building materials, industrial and agricultural equipment, and packing and home building materials. Sekisui's annual revenue is $1.35 billion, and it has 6,200 employees.

Sekisui Chemical has a housing division that sells modular housing, i.e., semicustom housing that is made 80 percent in the factory. This housing division is the fourth or fifth biggest seller of houses in the country (they sell 20,000 homes per year). This constitutes about 50 percent of the company's business. The rest of the company makes plastics (PVC, etc.). This division, called Sekisui Heim, competes with another company, Sekisui House, in which Sekisui has a 21 percent ownership position. Sekisui Heim has annual sales of $488 million.

DISCUSSION

The leader of the Sekisui team meeting us was Mr. Kawai. He is Director of the company's Information Processing Department. When Mr. Kawai was director of

Sekisui's housing division, he was experiencing a problem of a five percent error rate in parts selection, resulting in project delays. He heard Ed Feigenbaum's talk and decided to try ES. The company started by buying 70 percent of a small company now named ISAC (International Sekisui AI Corporation). ISAC does contract work for Sekisui and also sells software, e.g., K-PROLOG, the best selling PROLOG in Japan, and METHODLOG, an object-oriented frame system on top of PROLOG. They are now getting into relational databases with a multi-media interface, and other software products. Two members of the JTEC team visited their offices in Tokyo on the Saturday after the JTEC visit week and saw demonstrations of most of their expert system applications.

Sekisui's main system involves semi-custom configuration (actually they think of it as a parts-picking application). They have to make a specific material list for a house, and those materials have to be delivered to workstations on the factory floor. There are 300,000 different parts in the inventory, of which only several tens of thousands participate in any particular house building. The house itself, as designed by the customer working with the sales office, has to be transformed into a set of parts lists (so many 2 by 4s, so many wall modules, so many bolts, so many plumbing pipes of length L, etc.) The entire process is a rule-driven and constrained process, where the rule book is provided by the Sekisui Design Center, which designs the major classes of houses that are possible (e.g., the Parfait line, the Gloire line, and the Avante line). It is a huge rule book. When a new class of house is introduced, there are many errors made (much inefficiency) until the staff learns the new system very well. Now they simply convert the rule book to a knowledge representation and the expert system immediately performs flawlessly.

Sekisui has a version called HAPPS for its steel frame houses, another for wood frame houses (TAPPS), and a third for high rise houses (MAPPS) -- see Chapter 2 for additional details. HAPPS, TAPPS, and MAPPS are used to figure out which parts from an inventory of about 300,000 parts are needed for each particular house and where they go in the assembly process. About 5,000 different parts are needed for any particular home.

Sekisui has spent ¥450 million building the systems, and the payback is ¥1 billion ($8 million at approximately ¥128/$) per year!

The systems are written in K-PROLOG and METHODLOG, but run in C on UNIX workstations.

In addition there is a system called APEX that interfaces with the customer to aid in the design of the house. APEX has a CAD system and list of all the different sales options (degrees of freedom of customer choice). The customer designs (with the help of the sales person) by playing what-if games at the workstation. The APEX can even give the customer roughly estimated costs of any specific design, as well as a 2.5 D rendering of what the house will look like when finished (in addition to the floor plans of course). APEX is designed to help salesmen work with the customer to design a modular home. It has been in use for two years, for 10-20 percent of sales. There has been some resistance by sales force -- the problem is apparently with the user interface. We saw this system, much enhanced in drawing and rendering capability, being run on a portable workstation (essentially a very large laptop) and there is a version of this in color.

After a house has been ordered, Sekisui has 2 months to completion including 40 construction days (80 percent completion in the factory). The house must be finished at the site.

Opinion of Mr. Kino, founder of ISAC, AI fever is over in Japan, but ES is now accepted as a legitimate technology/methodology just like FORTRAN or COBOL. There is increasing awareness of what ES can/cannot do; steady increases in orders are expected.

These systems are motivated by the cost of training people and by past mistakes in part selection. Manual methods took 3 years to train experts and result in about a five percent error rate. Now a few days training is enough. Knowledge acquisition for this system came mainly from Sekisui's housing design books. This is a "big win" system -- it saves about ¥1 billion/year. That number seems a little low given that Sekisui does about ¥350 billion/year in housing sales. This is perhaps in the top five of ES applications in terms of impact in the world. Another motivation was lots of problems every time they sold a new type of house. Development began in 1986. Operational use began in 1989.

ISAC has sold about 800 copies of K-PROLOG, about 20 copies of METHODLOG -- an object oriented PROLOG built originally for internal use.

SEEDS/STREAM is an application that provides design support for chemical adhesives. This sounds very much like the 3M application. The system outputs ratios of chemicals in final process for synthesizing adhesives.

Sekisui also has a scheduling system for scheduling use of plastic extruders in its factory. There is the need to re-schedule 2-3 times per week. This system supports human experts and is in use in 8 factories. First operational three to four years ago. It took over a year to develop the system. The result was a reduction in the size of the scheduling team from four to two people per factory and a reduction in scheduling time from four hours to ten minutes.

We asked our hosts why they have developed no process control applications. The answer: that is simply not a main part of Sekisui's business.

Our hosts commented on their lessons learned:

o   An object oriented approach is a good one
o   User interfaces are very important

Comments on Sekisui's future plans: the company is interested in case-based reasoning and constraint-based scheduling for more complex problems.

Sekisui has added 37 new employees in information systems this year and has been teaching them UNIX and C. This is a way of getting new ideas (including ES) into the mainline (and mainframe) information systems world.

See Chapter 2 for further details.

Site: **Tokyo Electric Power Company (TEPCO)**
                                1-3 Uchisaiwai-cho
                                Chiyoda-ku 1-chome
                                Tokyo 100, Japan

Date Visited: March 27, 1992

JTEC Attendees:

Feigenbaum
Johnson
Shrobe
Engelmore

Hosts:

Yoshiaki Ichihara	General Mgr., R&D Planning Dept., Engineering Research and Development Administration
Kiyoshi Goto	Manager, R&D Planning Dept., Engineering Research and Development Administration
Yoshiakira Akimoto	General Mgr., Artificial Intelligence Technology, Computer & Communication Research Ctr.
Hideo Tanaka	Manager, Artificial Intelligence Technology, Computer & Communication Research Ctr.
Jun Hagihara	Senior Researcher, Artificial Intelligence Technology, Computer & Communication Research Center
Hiromi Ogi	Senior Researcher, Artificial Intelligence Technology, Computer & Communication Research Center
Hiroko Miyamoto	Research Engineer, Artificial Intelligence Technology, Computer & Communication Research Center
Tetsuo Matsuta	Research Engineer, Artificial Intelligence Technology Computer & Communication Research Center

ORGANIZATIONAL DATA

TEPCO is the largest privately owned electric utility in the world, and is one of ten electric power companies in Japan. Total revenues for the fiscal year ending March 1991 were ¥4.4 trillion. TEPCO's generating capacity is over 46 billion watts, and it services over 22 million customers. There are approximately 40,000 employees.

Our hosts were from within two departments of the Engineering Research & Development Administration (approximately 400 people, with an annual budget of about ¥68 billion):   the R&D Planning Department and the AI Technology Department within the Computer & Communication Research Center (C&CRC). There are approximately 100 people in the C&CRC. The AI Technology Department employs 14 technical staff.

PRESENTATIONS

Our hosts prepared a very thorough response to the questionnaire. They distributed a report on AI applications within TEPCO, plus a table listing all their application systems -- a total of 30 -- including the purpose of the system, stage of development, AI tool or language used, and size of the KB (see Table TEPCO.1). We were also given copies of about 17 technical papers that have been published and presented at various conferences, symposia and workshops.

The R&D strategy of the AI Technology Dept. has three thrusts:

1)   "maybe technology" -- research in new areas for solving more difficult problems, e.g., machine learning;
2)   "can be technology" -- feasibility studies through prototyping;
3)   "should be technology" -- building practical applications in cooperation with other departments.

The department is actively pursuing fuzzy logic, neural networks, genetic algorithms and computer graphics in addition to expert systems. Our hosts made it clear that at TEPCO "AI" means not only Artificial Intelligence but also Advanced Information Technology.

Most of the technical discussion focussed on one particular application, a system for forecasting maximum daily load on the power system.

SUMMARY OF QUESTIONNAIRE RESPONSES

TEPCO has developed 30 systems, of which 11 are in routine use. The application domains for these 11 include design, consultation, control, prediction, planning and scheduling, fault location, hot-line service, and computer operations. Three systems are in field test, 14 in the prototyping, and two in the feasibility stage. The most successful system is the daily maximum load forecasting system. Measures of success have been user satisfaction, a reduction in the absolute forecasting error rate from 2.2 percent to 1.5 percent, and a four-fold speedup in forecast generation. The system is actually quite small, with only about 100 rules, and was built using

Toshiba's TDES3 tool. It runs on a Toshiba minicomputer and also on Toshiba workstations (Sun workstation compatible). The forecasting system is one component of and integrated with a much larger load forecasting system called ELDAC. The system was developed at a cost of approximately $2 million over a period of about 20 months. Two researchers and two experts at TEPCO designed the system, and three system engineers from Toshiba built it. It is now used routinely by load dispatchers. Although the ROI is difficult to estimate, the use of the system precludes the need for a standby generator at a power station.

About 50 percent of TEPCO's ES projects get from the prototype stage to an operational system.

OBSERVATIONS

TEPCO's AI group is not formally trained. Some of the people were transferred in, e.g., the young woman engineer, Ms. Hiroko Miyamoto, who built the AI part of the load forecasting system. They have a 14 person group in the lab.

The systems they have built are typically small, in the range of 100 to 300 rules. Applications are usually built by the people who need them (at least by the organization that needs them), with help from the lab if needed.

Table TEPCO.1
Expert System Applications at Tokyo Electric Power Company

No.	Application System	Development	Purpose	Stage	Hardware Platform	AItool or Language	KB Size
Design							
1	Knowledge-based Layout Design System	Research Center	To design equipment layout at a trunk substation	In use	Mainframe	List FORTRAN	1900 rules
2	Distribution line design system	Research Center	For more efficient design of low-voltage line	Prototype	LISP machine	LISP KEE	____
3	Sequence circuit verification system	Research Center	To verify some protective relaying circuit	Prototype	Mainframe Workstation	LISP	____
4	System for generating cross sections of a stratum	Research Center	To get appropriate cross section from stratum database	In use	Personal Computer	LISP	____
5.	Advanced CAD system for distribution substation construction	Research Center	For more integrated business from construction to management	Prototype	Personal Computer	LISP C	____
Advisory or Help System							
6	Customer consultation system	Research Center	To answer customers' questionnaire on electric business	In use	Office Workstation	C	____
7	Advanced Video Instructor (ADVISOR)	Research Center	To train how to inspect equipment through multi-media information	Prototype	Workstation	LISP OPS5	20 rules
8	Simulation-based Pedagogical Learning Environment (SIMPLE)	Research Center	To train power system analysis by visual simulation	Prototype	LISP Machine	LISP Flavors	____
9	Advanced CAI system for electric work	Research Center	To support little-experienced engineers of electric work	Prototype	Personal Computer	OPS83	150 rules
Control							
10	Control system for self-propelled tunneling robot	Research Center	For more flexible tunnelling by fuzzy control	In use	Personal Computer	BASIC	100 rules
11	Rule-based control for fuel cell plant	Research Center	For more robust control of chemical power plant	Feasibility Study	Personal Computer	FORTRAN	80 rules
12	Rule-based distributed voltage control for power system	Research Center	For more flexible control of voltage/reactive power	Feasibility Study	Personal Computer	BASIC C	12 rules
Planning/Scheduling							
13	Daily maximum load forecasting	Research Center	To forecast the highest demand of the day and the next day	In use	Workstation	C TDES3	100 rules
14	Power system outage scheduling system	Research Center	To give adjusting information for operators	Prototype	LISP Machine	LISP KEE Flavors	50 rules 300 frames
15	ES for generating switching sequences at a large substation	Research Center	For more efficient generation of switching sequences	Field test	Workstation	LISP KDL	600 rules 600 frames

Table TEPCO.1 (Continued)

No.	Application System	Development	Purpose	Stage	Hardware Platform	AItool or Language	KB Size
16	Power generation scheduling system	Power System Operation Dept.	To determine an operation schedule of generation units under several constraints	Prototype	Mainframe	PROLOG	50 frames
17	Power system operation planning system	Power System Operation Dept.	For more reliable operation of trunk power system	In use	Mini-computer Workstation	LISP MIPS	100 rules
18	Thermal power unit maintenance scheduling system	Thermal Power Dept.	To get more efficient schedule of generation units inspection	In use	Mainframe	LISP Super-BRAINS	209 rules 87 frames
19	Start-up scheduling and operation support system for fossil power plants	Research Center	To reduced the start-up time without shortening the lifetime of a generation unit	Prototype	Mainframe	LISP FORTRAN	600 rules
Diagnosis/Trouble shooting							
20	Supervisory system for a large substation	Research Center	To monitor whole equipments at a substation and find abnormalities or faults	Field test	Workstation	Super-BRAINS (Cversion)	1300 rules 1500 frames
21	Transient stability expert system	Research Center	To evaluate transient stability of a power system	Prototype	Workstation	FORTRAN	—
22	Trunk power system restoration system	Research Center	To isolate a faulted section and restore sound system	Prototype	LISP Machine	LISP KEE	10 rules 500 frames
23	Guidance system for trunk power system restorative control	Research Center	To give operators an appropriate restorative operation and procedures	Prototype	Workstation	OPS83 FORTRAN	200 rules
24	Diagnosis system for thermal power plant	Research Center	To diagnose whole plant equipments	Prototype	Workstation	LISP PROLOG	2000 rules 1500 frames
25	Fault location system for transmission lines	Transmission Dept.	To isolate a faulted line from the power system	In use	Personal Computer	PROLOG	100 rules
26	Maintenance system for electric equipments in intelligent building	Research Center	To manage electric equipments in an intelligent building	Prototype	Personal Computer	PROLOG	721 frames
Sales							
27	TEPCO hot-line service system	Research Center	For quick allocation of service vehicles to customers	In use	Personal Computer	OPS83	50 rules
28	Computer mapping system for customers	Research Center	To search a customer's address and its location from map database	Field test	Workstation	C	—
Software development/Management							
29	Job control language generating system	Information System Dept.	To get Job Control sequences more easily	In use	Mainframe	Super-BRAIN	240 rules
30	computer operation scheduling system	Information System Dept.	To get batch job control sequences more easily	In use	Mainframe LISP machine	LISP KEE	1000 frames

Site: **Toshiba Corporation**
                             70 Yanagi-cho
                             Saiwai-ku
                             Kawasaki-shi 210, Japan

Date Visited: March 24, 1992

JTEC Attendees:

Johnson
Schorr
Nii
Engelmore
Shelton

Hosts:

Dr. Seiichi Nishijima   Director, Systems & Software Engineering Lab.
Takeshi Kohno   Sr. Mgr., 1st Research Dept., SSEL
Toshikazu Tanaka   Res. Scientist, AI Technology Group, SSEL
Dr. Ken-ichi Mori   Technology Executive, Information Systems &
                               Automation Systems Group

ORGANIZATIONAL DATA

Toshiba's 1990 reported net sales were $22.9 billion. The number of employees totalled 72,000 (these data do not include subsidiary groups). Information/communication systems and electronic devices comprise 57 percent of sales. R&D expenditures were 7.9 percent of sales. Between 1989 and 1990 Toshiba's sales in information and communication systems went from 28 percent to 57 percent. The corporation is therefore paying at lot of attention to computer-related products and technologies. We visited the Systems & Software Engineering Laboratory (SSEL), founded in 1987, and one of several corporate laboratories within the Toshiba R&D organization. SSEL has three research departments and a technology transfer department. The three research departments are: (1) AI and human interfaces, (2) distributed, fuzzy, and neural net systems, and (3) software engineering. The three divisions use the results of the research of other departments; for example, fuzzy logic is a part of the next generation ES tool.

PRESENTATIONS

We were given an overview of Toshiba's AI activities by Mr. Nishijima, followed by more detailed presentations: Mr. Kohno talked about Toshiba's ES tools; Mr. Tanaka discussed a design system that uses case-based reasoning; Mr. Kohno presented a model-based expert system for flexible plant control, a joint project with ICOT.

SUMMARY OF QUESTIONNAIRE RESPONSES

Toshiba's responses were the most extensive of any organization's.

Approximately 500 expert systems have been developed for both internal and external use, of which about 10 percent are in routine operation.   Design and Planning/Scheduling are the major growth application areas.   Within design, the principal tasks are large scale integration (semiconductors) and printed circuit board design.

The most successful expert system is a paper production scheduling system for the Tomakomai Mill of Ohji Paper Co., Ltd.   The system uses 25 kinds of pulp, which are combined in 10 paper making machines to produce 200 different paper products. There are hundreds of constraints to be satisfied.   The system employs a top-down hierarchical scheduling strategy, starting with scheduling product groups, then individual products, and then line balancing.   The time required to produce a monthly schedule was reduced from three days to two hours.

Toshiba also reported data on a microwave circuit design system, called FIRE, built with an internally developed tool called Debut.   FIRE captures the design process for highly parametric design problems.   The system runs on Toshiba's AS4000 workstation, is C-based, and interfaces with microwave circuit simulators and a mechanical CAD system.   The primary benefits of the system are speed-up of problem solving and accumulation of design knowledge.

A representative fault diagnosis system has been developed for Kyushu Electric Company, and is in routine use by Kyushu operators.   The system diagnoses faults and restores operation to an electric power system.   The fault diagnosis system has 900 rules; the fault restoration system has 600 rules.   The system was built using TDES-3, a real-time application shell that uses rules and frames for knowledge representation. The development team consisted mostly of Toshiba employees, with domain experts supplied by Kyushu.

Our hosts also reported on a diagnostic system for a subway station facility, called SMART-7, which was built for the Tokyo Eidan 7th line.   The system was built with a diagnostic knowledge acquisition support tool called DiKAST. SMART-7 is implemented as a support module that detects malfunctions in the air conditioning facilities. The system contains 1,600 frames, and runs on a AS4000 workstation. It was built by three system engineers in three months.

Another expert system is used for placing electronic components on printed circuit boards. The knowledge base consists of about 70 rules and 8,500 functions, and was built on top of the ASIREX tool. The ES is integrated with a PCB CAD tool called BOARDMATE, a commercial product developed by Toshiba. The system took three years to develop, with an estimated labor cost of three person-years. The system has resulted in a factor of ten speed-up in problem solving.

A small knowledge system (110 rules, 32,000 lines of C code) that Toshiba sells is MARKETS-I, a decision support system to determine the suitability of opening a convenience store at a particular site. Estimation accuracy is improved with the use of this system.

ESCORT is a banking operations advisor system that is used at Mitsui Bank. It plans the most appropriate procedure to get the computer banking system back in operation following an accident. The system has about 250 rules and 900 frames, and was built using a LISP-based expert system shell called EXPEARLS. The GUI was written in C. The system runs on the AS3000 workstation.

In the area of software engineering, Toshiba has developed an automatic programming system for sequence control. This system generates a control program for a steel plant from high-level specifications. It analyzes and refines the spec, generates code, and retrieves program modules. This is a fairly large system: 2,900 frames, 320 rules, and a library of 190 program modules. It was written in LISP, using an internally developed frame-based knowledge representation language with object oriented facilities. Twenty person-years went into its development, over a four year span. The system has resulted in cost reduction and an improvement in the quality of the sequence control program designs. Test and verification are performed manually.

Toshiba's systems do not now use multiple sources of expertise, but the company is trying to do so in its newer systems. Many ESs are implemented with a combination of a shell/tool plus a programming language such as C or LISP. Toshiba has several training courses, ranging from a one-day basic course, to a two- to three-week application development course, to a multi-week advanced topics course. About 10 percent of research funds go into training. An important element of Toshiba's methodology is to use task-specific shells, such as PROKAST or DiKAST.

ESs selected for implementation are chosen by a systems engineer or researcher. This technology is used only when conventional data processing doesn't work. The pre-specified selection criteria are performance and practical value. Toshiba also looks for an economic justification. Usually the same people are used in all phases of application selection, development, insertion into the operational activity, maintenance and redesign.

Toshiba's largest project to date is a 5,000 rule system for diagnosis and control of an electrical power generator.

Our hosts characterized their progress as steady.

DISCUSSION

Toshiba has developed several sophisticated shells for particular types of problems. These are oriented toward enabling the end-user organization to develop its own detailed knowledge bases.

Toshiba's first generation shell is MYEXPERT, a rule-based tool that runs on J-3100 personal computer and is commercially available.

Toshiba's second generation shells include:

o   ASIREX: a general purpose production system, with frames, in C. It runs on an AS4000 workstation, and is commercially available.

o   TDES3: a real time system, using Schema, LISP, and C. It runs on an AS4000.

o   EXPEARLS: a built-in type shell in-office system, with frames, LISP. It runs on an AS4000.

Toshiba's domain shells (developed on ASIREX) include:

o   DiKAST: a diagnosis shell (for classification problems). It contains a problem solver (DIPROS), an interview-based knowledge acquisition facility, a knowledge analyzer and a knowledge debugger.

o   PROKAST: like above, but for scheduling.

o   DEBUT: for parametric design; it can preserve and reuse a designer's knowledge.

Another tool is KASE (Knowledge Acquisition Support Environment), which supports knowledge acquisition so that ESs can be developed by domain experts without the involvement of knowledge engineers. KASE has been used for diagnosing defects in color picture tubes and in casting parts, for support of repairing hard disk drives, and for fault diagnosis of a traffic signal system.

With respect to advanced KBS activity, Toshiba is seriously exploring model-based and case-based reasoning, machine learning, natural language understanding, and advanced assumption-based truth maintenance systems (ATMSs). We received twelve technical papers from our hosts on a wide variety of subjects and systems, all in English.

OBSERVATIONS

R&D

Toshiba's pipeline of R&D through applications seems well balanced.

A new development, which uses recursive case-based reasoning (to two levels), deserves further study (Tanaka 1992). The idea is to use other cases, rather than rules, to modify a case that doesn't quite fit.

The model-based plant control system designed to handle unforeseen problems was particularly interesting. A conventional, heuristic, shallow reasoning layer handles anticipated problems. It defers to the deeper, model-based layer when unable to handle a problem. The deep reasoning layer has a fuzzy, qualitative physics simulator.

Toshiba is the only organization that is paying much attention to a formal problem solving framework into which the heuristics fit. Others are mostly following a straight heuristic "interview the expert" approach.

Although several software development types of applications were counted in the statistics, we did not see any examples. It is possible that, at Toshiba, software engineering research is focused upon only the newer types of software.

Applications

In general, Toshiba appears to be very advanced in the application of knowledge-based systems. The range of application types (problem solving situations) is quite broad. The proportion of applications reaching operational status is high.

The range of techniques and technologies being integrated at Toshiba is quite broad (fuzzy expert systems, CBR with neural nets, simulators, conventional order processing systems, etc.). Toshiba has clearly moved beyond the introductory stage in that few if any of their applications are stand-alone systems.

Toshiba's strategy: train engineers and provide them with tools.

The JTEC team was impressed by the use of "soft" justifications for systems efforts. Toshiba does not seem to be encumbered by the ROI/MBA mentality that pervades U.S. thinking. Continuous process or product quality improvement, for example, is sufficient justification.

Our hosts view was that the most important features in the next generation tools are: task specific tools, knowledge acquisition tools, cooperative problem solving, and advanced reasoning, such as case-based and qualitative reasoning.

In general, Toshiba has organized its research activities into five to ten year projects which are conducted in corporate research labs, 3-5 year projects in the development labs, and the more immediate problems in the business group. (This type of organization seems to be common -- for example, at Mitsubishi.)   For software the path is more direct.   The Systems and Software Engineering Lab (SSEL), although under the corporate lab for organizational purposes, does research and basic development (such as prototyping of tools) and supports the work of operational groups.   It also does corporate planning for system and software technologies.

Although a relative newcomer, Toshiba seemed the most balanced and best organized of the computer manufacturers we visited (NEC, Fujitsu, Hitachi) with respect to their approach to ES technology development and the ES business.

Toshiba's second generation shells, recently introduced, run on SPARC workstations. The company's ASIREX shell costs ¥4 million, and its workstations run from ¥1.8 million to ¥10 million in the maximum memory configuration.

Toshiba's ES business is steady, but below expectations.   The number of people using ES is increasing. Toshiba's strategy is to have its software engineers study AI technology and use it internally.

Toshiba gave very little business data. The company reports a 17 percent hit rate on getting from start of an ES project to deployment. Applications are moving to planning from diagnostics. According to our hosts, LISP machines are finished. Toshiba appears to have many good internal applications.

ADDRESSES FOR OTHER SITES VISITED

Kyoto University
Department of Information Science
Sakyo-ku
Kyoto 606, Japan

Osaka University
Institute of Scientific &
  Industrial Research
8-1 Mihogaoka Ibaraki
Osaka 567, Japan

University of Tokyo
RCAST
4-6-1 Komaba, Meguro-ku
Tokyo 153, Japan

Japan Electronic Dictionary Research Institute
Mita Kokusai Building Annex
1-4-28 Mita, Minato-ku
Tokyo 108, Japan

ICOT
Mita Kokusai Building, 21F
1-4-28 Mita, Minato-ku
Tokyo 108, Japan

Laboratory for International Fuzzy Engineering Research
89-1 Yamashita-cho
Naka-ku
Yokohama-shi 231, Japan

Information on the JTEC team's visits to the above sites is contained in the body of
this report, primarily in Chapters 4 and 5.

APPENDIX F.   BIBLIOGRAPHY

Araki, D. and S. Kojima 1991. "KASE Project toward effective diagnosis system development." *Proc. of the Banff Knowledge Acquisition for Knowledge-based Systems Workshop.*

Denicoff, M. (ed.) 1987. *JTEC Panel Report on Advanced Computing in Japan.* Available from the National Technical Information Service (NTIS) of the U.S. Department of Commerce as NTIS report # PB88-153572/XAB.

DOC 1991. "Fuzzy Logic: A Key Technology for Future Competitiveness." Office of Computers and Business Equipment, International Trade Administration, U.S. Department of Commerce, November, 1991.

Economic Research Institute (ERI) 1992. "A Plan for the Knowledge Archives Project," March 1992 (unpublished). Available from the Japan Society for the Promotion of Machine Industry: Kikai-Shinko Bldg. B1, 3-5-8 Shiba-koen, Minato-ku, Tokyo 105, Japan.

Feigenbaum, E. A., P. McCorduck et al. 1988. *The Rise of the Expert Company*, New York, Times Books.

Filman, R.E. and R.W. Weyhrauch 1976. "An FOL Primer." Stanford University. AI Laboratory Memo 288.

Fujitsu America Inc. 1990. "Object-Oriented Knowledge-Based System FORTRAN/KR." October 1990.

Harada, M., Z. Igarashi et al. 1990. "Development of Expert System-Supported Construction Planning for a Shield-Tunneling Method." *Innovative Applications of Artificial Intelligence 2.* Menlo Park, CA, AAAI Press. 66-79.

Harmon, Paul (ed.) 1992a. *Intelligent Software Strategies.* Vol. VII, No. 7, 1992.

Harmon, Paul (ed.) 1992b. *Intelligent Software Strategies.* Vol. VIII, No. 2, 1992.

Harrison, M.A. (ed.) 1990. *JTEC Panel Report on Advanced Computing in Japan.* Loyola College, Baltimore, MD. Available from the National Technical Information Service (NTIS) of the U.S. Department of Commerce as NTIS report # PB90-215765.

Hasegawa, S. et al. 1991. "Knowledge Arrangement Support Tool GENZO-QAE." *Shimadzu Technical Review* 48(3).

Hitachi, Ltd. 1991. "Hitachi Expert Systems at Work." Brochure, Hitachi Ltd., Tokyo 140, Japan.

Hitachi, Ltd. Undated. "Hitachi Knowledge Systems Expert Building Tools ES/KERNEL2 Series." Brochure.

ICOT 1982. "Outline of Research and Development Plans for Fifth Generation Computer Systems" May 1982.

Iwamoto, M., S. Fujita et al. 1991. "Combining Rule-based and Algorithmic Approaches in LSI Design." *World Congress on Expert Systems 1991*: 1302-1309.

Japan Electronic Dictionary Research Institute, Ltd. (JEDRI) 1990. "An Overview of the EDR Electronic Dictionaries." TR-024. April 1990. Page 1.

Komai, K., K. Matsumoto et al. 1991. "MEL-DASH: A Diagnostic Application-specific Expert Systems Shell for Network Fault Diagnosis." *Third Symposium on Expert Systems Application to Power Systems, April 1-5, 1991, Tokyo-Kobe.*

Lenat, D.B. and R.V. Guha 1990. *Building Large Knowledge-Based Systems: Representation and Inference in the Cyc Project*, Addison-Wesley Publishing Co., Inc., Reading, MA, 1990.

Maruyama, F., Y. Minoda et al. 1991. "Solving Combinatorial Constraint Satisfaction and Optimization Problems Using Sufficient Conditions for Constraint Violation." *Proc. of Int'l Symp. on AI.*

McDermott, J. 1981. "R1: The Formative Years." *AI Magazine* 2(2):21-29.

Minami, E. and T. Hirata 1991. "An Expert System for Large Scale Fault Diagnosis in Steel Manufacturing." *Proc. World Congress on Expert Systems 1991.* 1311-1318.

Mizutani, H., Y. Nakayama et al. 1992. "Automatic Programming for Sequence Control." *Innovative Applications of Artificial Intelligence 4.* Menlo Park, CA, AAAI Press. 315-331.

Mori, A. 1988. "Cockpit Crew Scheduling System by AI." *28th AGIFORS Symposium.*

Nakayama, Y., H. Mizutani et al. 1990. "Model-Based Automatic Programming for Plant Control." *Proc. of the 6th Conference on Artificial Intelligence Applications.*

Nikkei AI 1991. "Special Edition: General Review of Expert Systems in Use." *Nikkei AI.* Special Issue, Winter 1991.

Nikkei AI 1992. "Special Edition: General Review of Expert Systems in Use." *Nikkei AI.* Special Issue, Winter 1992.

Onodera, K. and A. Mori 1991. "Cockpit Crew Scheduling and Supporting System." *Proc. World Congress on Expert Systems.*

Rich, Elaine (ed.) 1992. *JTEC Panel Report on Machine Translation in Japan.* Loyola College, Baltimore, MD. Available from the National Technical Information Service (NTIS) of the U.S. Department of Commerce as NTIS report # PB92-100239.

Shortliffe, E.H. 1976. *Computer-Based Medical Consultation: MYCIN.* New York, American Elsevier.

Suzuki, J., N. Sueda et al. 1990. "Plant Control Expert System Coping with Unforeseen Events: Model-based Reasoning Using Fuzzy Qualitative Reasoning." *Proceedings of the 3rd International Conference on Industrial and Engineering Applications of AI and Expert Systems,* July 1990.

Takata, N. et al. 1991. "Genco: Expert System Building Support Tools." *Shimadzu Technical Review* 48(3).

Takekoshi, A., T. Aoki et al. 1989. "Application of Knowledge Engineering for Iron and Steel Making Works." *NKK Technical Review* 56.

Tanaka, T., M. Hattori et al. 1992. "Use of Multiple Cases in Cased-Based Design." *Proceedings of the 8th IEEE Conference on Artificial Intelligence Applications.*

Tano, S., S. Masui et al. 1988. "EUREKA-II: A Programming Tool for Knowledge-based Real-time Control Systems." *Hitachi Review* 37(5).

Tsunozaki, Y., A. Takekoshi et al. 1987. "An Expert System for Blast Furnace Control at Fukuyama Works." *Nippon Kokan Technical Report Overseas* 51.

Ujihara, H. and S. Tsuji 1988. "The Revolutionary AI-2100 Elevator-Group Control System and the New Intelligent Option Series" *Mitsubishi Electric ADVANCE* 5-8.

Weinberg, G.M. 1971. *The Psychology of Computer Programming.* New York, Van Nostrand Reinhold.

Yamanouchi, T. et al. 1992. "Software Synthesis Shell SOFTEX/S" In *Proceedings of the Seventh Knowledge-Based Software Engineering Conference*, McLean, Virginia, September 20-23, 1992, IEEE Computer Society Press.

Yasunobu, S. and S. Miyamoto 1985. "Automatic Train Operation by Predictive Fuzzy Control." *Industrial Applications of Fuzzy Control*. Amsterdam, North-Holland. 1-18.

Zadeh, L. 1965. "Fuzzy Sets." *Information and Control*. 8:338-353.

APPENDIX G.   GLOSSARY

AI   Artificial Intelligence

ATMS   Assumption-based Truth Maintenance System

CBR   Case-Based Reasoning

ES   Expert System(s)

FGCS   Fifth Generation Computing Systems project

FOL   First Order Logic

GUI   Graphic User Interface

KBS   Knowledge-Based System(s)

KE   Knowledge Engineer

KR   Knowledge Representation

LISP   Programming language; name derived from "List Processing"

MDL   Minimum Description Length

MGTP   Model Generation Theorem Prover

OWL   A knowledge engineering language for frame-based representation
              (implemented in LISP)

PIM   Parallel Inference Machine

PROLOG   Programming language; name derived from "Programming in Logic"

PSI   Personal Sequential Inference

PTA   Procedural Type Atoms

RETE   The standard implementation technique for forward chaining pattern
              matching (developed by C. Forgy)

SNePS   The semantic network processing system developed by S.C. Shapiro

UIBT   User Interface Building Tools

Part II

Database Use and Technology in Japan

Gio Wiederhold, Chairman
David Beech
Charles Bourne
Nick Farmer
Sushil Jajodia
David Kahaner
Toshi Minoura
Diane Smith
John Miles Smith

Executive Summary

This report presents the findings of a group of database experts, sponsored by JTEC, based on an intensive study trip to Japan during March 1991. Academic, industrial, and governmental sites were visited. The primary findings are that Japan is supporting its academic research establishment poorly, that industry is making progress in key areas, and that both academic and industrial researchers are well aware of current domestic and foreign technology. Information sharing between industry and academia is effectively supported by governmental sponsorship of joint planning and review activities, and enhances technology transfer. In two key areas, multimedia and object-oriented databases, we can expect to see future export of Japanese database products, typically integrated into larger systems.

Support for academic research is relatively modest. Nevertheless, the senior faculty are well-known and respected, and communicate frequently and in depth with each other, with government agencies, and with industry. In 1988 there were a total of 1,717 Ph.D.'s in engineering and 881 in science. It appears that only about 30 of these were academic Ph.D.'s in the basic computer sciences.

Industrial research is well supported. Support services are marvellous in terms of hardware, and researchers are encouraged to publish. Industrial Ph.D.'s, given as recognition for publications (following the British model), are common. The number of industrially grounded Ph.D.'s is roughly equal to the number of academic ones.

The Japanese government, overall, seems to have less influence on database research directions than is perceived by outsiders. The funding supports some laboratories and projects, but academic researchers have considerable flexibility in choosing the directions for government-sponsored research. The level of government funding for industrial laboratories is relatively low and does not influence market-driven priorities. However, these projects do require regular meetings of academic, government, and industrial researchers, increasing mutual awareness and understanding. Similar information sharing results from review panels of NIH and, sometimes, NSF, where proposal reviewers learn much from each other. The presence, in Japan, of industry participants on these panels, broadens their relevance and enhances technology transfer.

Technology transfer is enhanced by governmental requirements and support of review boards joining academia and industry.

The database research we saw in industry is very much oriented toward support of development and new technology. It relies for its conceptual input greatly on publications from the U.S. and Europe. The researchers are well-read and often well-connected with foreign academic sources. They provide an important path for technology transfer.

An important driving mechanism in database development is the Japanese capability in the area of developing electronic products. High quality image acquisition, transmission, storage, display, and digitized voice data are emphasized. Database management systems are being expanded to provide support for such "multimedia." While fundamental database management systems are not being advanced, the incorporation of multimedia support will change their character greatly. We can expect that purchasers of systems with multimedia requirements will, with Japanese image-processing hardware, acquire Japanese database software. This field is likely to grow rapidly. Computer-aided-design, computer-aided-education, and other application areas that are critically dependent on graphics will be the initial users of this technology.

We expect that multimedia technology will provide an important path for the introduction of Japanese database software into European and U.S. markets.

Japanese hardware for computer systems is roughly equivalent to U.S. systems, except again in the areas of multimedia support and optical mass storage, where the Japanese have a substantial advantage. Parallel architecture and database accelerator schemes are of active interest.

Hardware support for database systems is provided equally well by Japanese and foreign companies. Sony is an important supplier of workstations, but U.S. companies such as SUN Microsystems are also well represented. Japanese mainframe-based database systems are similar to their U.S. counterparts, but this market shows less growth and is less fluid.

Relevant research on topics such as database accelerators is being pursued. This work can be seen as a specialization of research into parallel computation, which is pursued by computer researchers everywhere with equal intensity. The payoff is likely to come as demands on database computation increase.

The JTEC study also surveyed the industry that maintains databases and sells information retrieved from these databases. In this area Japanese databases provide useful services internally, but are not in a position to export their services. There is substantial use in Japan of Western databases, both via U.S. and European vendors and via Japanese resellers. Some internal developments are oriented towards providing image data as well. Providing such services on an international scale awaits high capacity communication lines and acceptance of standards. In this area the relative situation seems stable.

While Japan is not viewed today as a world-level player in the database area, the infrastructure is in place for Japan to make important contributions in areas where there is high growth potential and linkage with consumer hardware.

Qualitative Comparisons Between the U.S. and Japan

The panel has prepared a qualitative comparison of the present status and trends in database systems research in the U.S. and Japan. For the purposes of this comparison, the subject matter covered by the panel was divided into seven subtopics: mainframes, hardware-pc, workstations-servers, storage, database content, database management systems, and new database technologies. Figures 1 through 7 represent the panel's findings in each of these subareas.

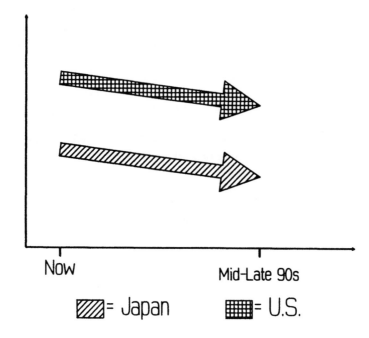

Figure 1. Mainframes

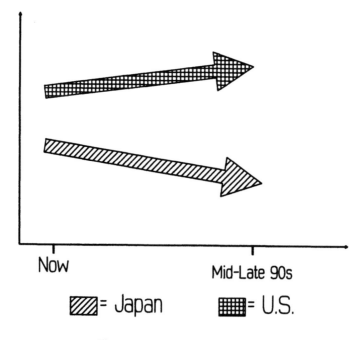

Figure 2. Hardware - PC

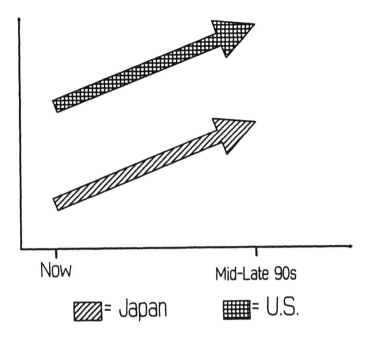

Figure 3. Workstations - Servers

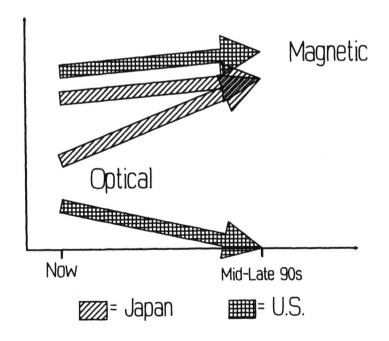

Figure 4. Storage

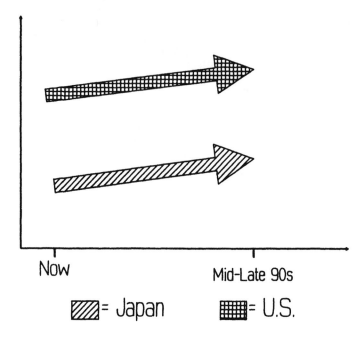

Figure 5. Database Content

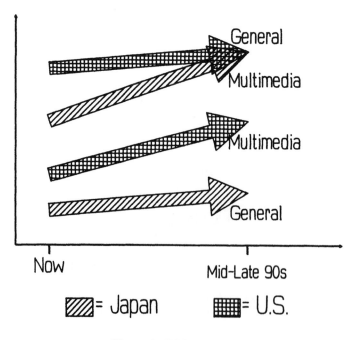

Figure 6. DBMSs

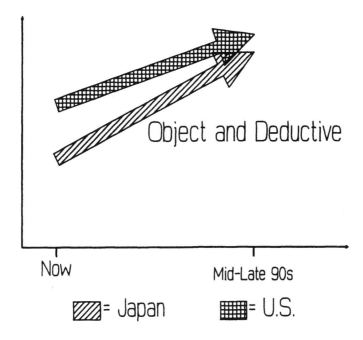

Figure 7. New DB Technologies

1. Introduction

This report presents the findings of a study group composed of eleven database specialists who visited Japan from March 23 to March 29, 1991. The group included representatives from the database systems industries, database service industries, academia, and government. This was their first visit to Japan for several of the participants, while others had interacted with colleagues in Japan for many years. Short biographies of the participants are given in Appendix A.

Thirty-one sites were visited by teams with from two to six participants. The entire study group team was together for an initial visit to the Ministry of International Trade and Industry (MITI), and for planning and wrap-up sessions. The sites were diverse, and included major Japanese companies, some small specialized companies, government laboratories, and universities. They are listed with the names of the principal contacts in Appendix B.

Short site reports from the individual visits are in Appendix C. We had many pleasant social interactions as well, but are omitting them from this report. This omission should not diminish their importance, nor the appreciation we have towards our hosts.

1.1 Coverage

It is obvious that in the short timeframe of the study, complete coverage could not be achieved. We apologize to those Japanese colleagues we have missed, either because of scheduling problems or lack of awareness. We have tried to keep this report factual so that the effects of selection bias are minimized; generalities based on our observations are in the concluding section.

1.2 Motivation

It is important for U.S. researchers, technologists, marketing specialists, and negotiators to understand Japan. It is an important country that is playing a critical role in business and world affairs. This importance extends to the area of our expertise, computing and databases. We all rely on Japanese hardware in our computer systems, and it is likely that we will deal increasingly with Japanese data and software as well. We should not view this as a threat or, in a defeatist sense, as a loss. Instead, it appears that we can best envisage a world in which our systems are composed of a wide variety of components, organized and accessible in a manner that will serve all of our needs best.

Japan presents a social homogeneity which distinguishes it from the variety found in the U.S., Europe, or other regions of similar size in the world. But within this social structure, we find individuals and companies with a wide range of approaches, outlooks, methods, and aspirations. Specific, novel, and interesting examples cannot be viewed as a general prototype or a trend, but merely as a potential seed for new possibilities. It is important to note that this is not a report on databases for Japan, Inc., but rather a collection of reports that illustrate a range of research and application interests.

Readers of this report may be tempted to extrapolate our findings to other areas of computer science or even science in general. We do not believe that such extrapolations are necessarily valid.

1.3 Overview

The remainder of this report is organized into several sections. We begin with a short section on the Japanese database research and development establishment to place the remainder in context.

The bulk of this report consists of small summaries of individual topics stressing the state of the art, but also indicating likely changes. The state of the industry that uses databases to disseminate information is the topic of Section III.

A subsequent section focuses on integration, since the capability of future database and information systems depends on the smooth meshing of its components.

We list the contributing authors in the various sections, but the responsibility for errors and omissions rests with the chair of the study, since many editorial changes were introduced.

2. Database Research Infrastructure

As is the case in other countries, the Japanese government uses databases to administer a variety of governmental activities. However, not all of the relevant databases are inside government offices. It does appear that the Japanese government has, through various measures, done more than most other governments to further database use and technology. The effort has not been massive, but has had subtle, yet important effects on the structure supporting technological progress in the database and in other related areas.

2.1 Role of the Japanese Government in Database Activities

Authors: Sushil Jajodia and David Kahaner

After an overview of the relevant overall structure we will cover in more detail the ministries and their offices involved in database activities.

2.1.1 The Japanese Government's Structure and Use of Databases

The Government of Japan (GOJ) is organized around the prime minister who heads the government. He is assisted by a cabinet composed of ministers (education, justice, foreign affairs, etc.). Each of the ministries has its own budget, and to some extent each provides support for database activities. In 1987, at an Inter-ministerial Council, a plan was formulated to promote GOJ databases; every ministry and agency is expected to improve their databases in accordance with this plan. Furthermore, in 1989 the Cabinet first decided to promote the open system interconnection (OSI) model in accordance with the international standard. As a result of these actions, databases have become an important aspect of many parts of the Japanese government.

Two ministries are significantly involved in database use, the Ministry of International Trade and Industry (MITI), and the Ministry of Education (MONBUSHO). Both MITI and MONBUSHO support significant database activities through grants for research and development, tax incentives, loans, and other mechanisms. The ministries have subunits that also provide support. Like NSF, MONBUSHO supports the national universities and provides research grants to academic researchers. For example, Japan's National Institute for Education Research, its National Education Center, and its National Women's Education Center are funded to produce various new types of databases. MONBUSHO also administers the National Center for Science Information System (NACSIS). MITI runs the highly automated Patent Information Organization (JAPIO). The Ministry of Post and Telecommunications (MPT) also provides support for database activities, by supervising the compilation of an online database directory and studying how the new digital communication capabilities provided by ISDN can be used to improve database distribution.

Another important part of the Japanese government is the Science and Technology Agency (STA), which reports directly to the prime minister's office. STA, in addition to having research programs, also supports the Japan Information Center of Science and Technology (JICST) with its extensive databases.

The GOJ also has a legislative arm, the Diet, which supports the National Diet Library (NDL), which is similar to the Library of Congress. At the NDL, all publications (including informal grey literature) published in Japan are deposited, except for classified military documents and other materials withheld from the public. The NDL has developed a database of its catalogue, and provides it on tapes and CD-ROMs, and via an online system to public libraries.

The discussion below is organized around the GOJ units. It is not meant to be a complete synopsis of GOJ database science activities, but only describes those aspects of significant interest to the JTEC database team.

2.1.2   MITI

The Ministry of International Trade and Industry supports several activities that affect database use and technology.

(a) Database Promotion Center.   Japan is aware that it is behind the U.S. in the use and development of databases, particularly for science, and there is a strong effort being made to improve the position of the Japanese database industry. The Japan Database Promotion Center (DPC), established in 1984, has as its goals the promotion of database construction; research and development of the basic technologies related to databases; establishment of efficient clearing services; education propagation and training associated with databases; and international information exchange informing other countries about Japanese databases.

Japanese online databases in science and technology were first developed by JICST and JAPIO in the mid-1970s. Business databases were established a few years earlier. This sequence is about ten years behind corresponding efforts in the U.S. The delay was due in part to the lag in computer technology for handling the Japanese language and in part to the reluctance of the Japanese to sell intangibles, in this case information, as a product. The Japan Database Industry Association (DINA), established in 1979, now has over 100 members and is quite active. Furthermore, since the early 1980s both the information industry and the GOJ have attempted to promote database development and use. Since 1983, MITI has published an annual database directory that provides a comprehensive list of both Japanese and foreign databases that can be accessed in Japan. The 1989 directory, in Japanese, is about 3,000 pages long and lists over 3,000 databases. An English introductory version to Japanese original databases is about 100 pages long.

The DPC is a non-profit organization supervised by MITI dealing with databases. It is founded by private companies and keeps track of various database statistics such as the following: "MITI's survey reports that the Japanese database service industry's sales reached ¥106.3 billion in 1988 ... In their *Outlook of the Information Industry for the year 2000*, submitted in 1987, estimated sales were placed at ¥144.5 trillion for the entire information industry in the 2000's, and at ¥3.4 trillion for information provision services including database services. If we estimate the sales of database services in the early 2000's ery roughly on the basis of ¥106.3 billion of 1988 with a tentative growth rate of 30%, it could be expected to reach ¥2.5 trillion." In addition to the database directory, DPC also publishes an annual *Database in Japan 19xx*, which should be referred to for additional statistical data.

Information is of growing importance to Japan's economy. The "Information Society" is a standard phrase used to describe the near term social environment. MITI has formulated the following sequence of policies to develop and improve databases:

o Promote important database production.

o Encourage international cooperation regarding databases.

o Adjust tax policy to encourage database-producing corporations.

o Support system development to increase database operational efficiency.

o Create a database directory.

o Support research into the production and organization of databases.

o Produce public databases and encourage movement of GOJ data to the private sector.

The DPC provides financial support for private organizations for database research and construction. For example, the Sharp Corporation has been funded to study a concept called Set Theory DataBase (STDB) for document retrieval.

MITI has the additional role of sponsoring certain national projects. The Institute for New Generation Computer Technology (ICOT) is a national project with an object oriented database as a subproject (see below). Another is the Interoperable Database System Project (INTAP), which endeavors to establish an open system architecture in Japan. It appeared to the JTEC visitors that the project has been mostly passive. It focuses on validation of conformance with OSI standards. Dr. Akio Tojo (Managing Director of the Information Technology Promotion Agency) considers this project to be one of the most successful MITI R&D projects in the IT area. MITI also supports the International Multimedia Association, which became a non-profit organization supervised by MITI in April 1991 and is expected to establish international relationships with relevant organizations. Finally we were told that MITI itself planned no new international projects in the database area.

(b) Japan Patent Information Organization.   Data relating to patents has been processed by the Japan Patent Information Organization (JAPIO) since 1985. It currently has about 250 staff members. In addition to printed documents (or "Gazettes") there is a computerized information service built around large databases. Computer equipment includes six Hitachi mainframes (M682H, M680H, M680D x 2, M662K), 420 gigabytes (GB) of magnetic disks, and 3,100 GB of optical disks. The full texts of all Japanese patents are electronically filed and total entries in the database exceed 31 million. All the database data are in Japanese except for the foreign documents bibliographic database and English abstracts of Japanese unexamined patents. The latter have been available through the Orbit online service since 1976. JAPIO itself offers an online service called Patent OnLine Information System (PATOLIS) which has issued about 4,000 issued passwords. Three basic services are offered:

o Retrieval, using a special interactive terminal. Search keys corresponding to patent classification, applicant, keyword, and so forth, can be combined using the logical operators AND, OR, and NOT.

o File history in response to patent number specification.

o Correspondence search for foreign patents.

Western users can access the database via a leased line or through commercial services such as VENUS-P. Because most of the data is in Japanese, it is not surprising that all but a few of the passwords are issued to users in Japan, although in 1989 there were far more passwords issued in Europe than in the U.S. For more detailed patent information, JAPIO also offers a batch retrieval service which extends the keys allowed in PATOLIS. JAPIO also supplies the full text of patents and patent publications on optical disks.

(c) Sigma Project.   The Sigma project was initiated by MITI in 1985 as a five-year project to improve software quality and productivity in a standard operating system environment. No new database management systems (DBMSs) were to be developed. The policy was to utilize commercially available RDBMSs on Unix workstations, with the manipulation of Kanji an important criterion. The project fostered the use of existing RDBMSs on Unix systems, and one such system (UNIFY) has sold more than 25,000 copies in Japan.

(d) ICOT.   The Institute for New Generation Computer Technology was established in 1982 by MITI to provide a focus for original research in new technologies, specifically artificial intelligence (AI) and knowledge bases having persistent databases as a component. Its cornerstone was a ten-year project called "Fifth Generation," which focused on the construction of a logic-based parallel inference computer. Within this project ICOT developed two deductive databases, PHI [Hani:91] and CRL. Prof. Nishio and several other professors from the Obase consortium participate in an ICOT working group on deductive object-oriented database technology. Theoretical results have been obtained about query evaluation algorithms. A Deductive Object-Oriented Database (OODB) language, QUIXOTE, is also being developed.

One of the most important functions of ICOT is that it enables young database researchers to come together outside of their parent companies. Several working groups have been formed and meet periodically.

2.1.3   Science and Technology Agency

The Science and Technology Agency (STA) of the prime minister's office has a budget of approximately $3.8 billion. Two activities are worthy of note in the context of databases.

(a) JICST.   The Japan Information Center of Science and Technology (JICST) is the country's central body for distributing science and technology information. (A related organization is NACSIS, described under MONBUSHO in Sect. 2.1.4.) JICST's databases store scientific and technological literature, factual and other data, that are made available to any user on a fee-for-service basis. The information is collected from more than 15,000 journals of which more than 8,000 are from outside of Japan. The database has almost 8,000,000 citations and abstracts, of which about half are domestic. Also included are technical reports, conference proceedings, research projects carried out at public research institutes, and government reports that are often difficult to obtain through other means. Financing is via government support and user fees; JICST's 1991 budget is about ¥15 billion. JICST has a main office in Tokyo, a library in Tsukuba Science City, and branch offices in a dozen Japanese cities, Paris, and Washington, D.C. JICST has a staff of about 325. Further information about JICST is provided in Section 5.

JICST is not a database research organization in the sense of developing new concepts. However, in addition to providing an online service, JICST does engage in applied research in machine translation, expert system technology for abstracting and indexing full text Japanese databases, fuzzy information retrieval techniques, friendly user interfaces, and development of a chemical substance molecular weight database for organic compounds, inorganic substances, metallic materials and high polymers.

JICST also has been active in promoting a National Information Policy in Japan. In the future, JICST will:

o Investigate the problems of using databases that result from overdiversification of dissemination modes.
o Enhance bibliographic database coverage to include more of the grey literature.
o Promote the construction and dissemination of factual databases.
o Encourage standardization.
o Develop full text databases.
o Promote networking between information processing and information dissemination centers.
o Extend dissemination systems to include multimedia and user friendly services.
o Promote the construction of English language databases.

(b) **Other STA Projects.**   Two other projects were discussed with the JTEC team. The first project was the "Research on the Development of Knowledge Base System to aid Chemists in Designing Chemical Substances and Chemical Reactions." This project was funded at a level of approximately ¥100 million over five years, and included six universities, fourteen government research labs, and one industrial organization (NTT). The work involved software and systems developed at different places, with the core database system (SYNDES) from Tsukuba University. Three or four of these systems are to be demonstrated in October 1991 in Tokyo. We were told by Prof. S. Kito (Aichi Inst. Tech.) that the system developed in Kyoto was the largest. Since the total amount is quite modest (averaging less than $8,000 per year per institution), it is obvious that the main effect of STA funding was to support cooperation, integration, and technology transfer rather than fundamental research.

The other project was the "Development of a Self-Organizing Information Base to Aid Researchers in Creative Research." This project has the goal of creating an intelligent large hypertext database system. The first phase of this project began in April 1991 and will last three years; the second phase will last an additional two or three years. Project members include JICST; Ryukoku, Tsukuba, Kobe, and Hokkaido universities; and ETL, NTT, FujiXerox; and other industrial partners. STA provides funding at the level of $100K-150K per university per year. ETL administers the projects for each university.

2.1.4   MONBUSHO

The Ministry of Education, in addition to its general role of supporting the national universities, supports some specific database activities.

(a) **NACSIS.**   The National Center for Science Information Systems (NACSIS) is a national inter-university research institute. It is the nucleus organization for scholarly information transfer, providing the services of shared cataloging, compilation, processing, and dissemination of information including (but not limited to) scientific and technical fields. The significant differences between NACSIS and JICST are:

- o Most of JICST's users are from industry (see Section 5.2); NACSIS mainly serves the academic research community.
- o JICST is limited to scientific and technical information; NACSISOB incorporates the social sciences and humanities.
- o JICST does its own abstracting; NACSIS primarily collects, purchases or leases data.

NACSIS has a full-time staff of almost ninety, about one-third of the size of JICST. It was a branch laboratory of Tokyo University until 1986, but has been independent since then. NASCIS projects a very energetic and forward-looking image. In fact, while most of the staff are in the Operations or Administrative departments, almost two dozen members of the Research Department hold university titles (including seven professors) and some have joint appointments. More information on NACSIS, and its system SIS, can be found in Section 5.2.

(b) **Grant-in-Aid.**   With the growth of large databases it will be necessary to learn how to mine them for nuggets of useful information or knowledge. Using the knowledge inherent in the data, very large knowledge bases can be built up. A new program has begun this year on Knowledge Discovery in Databases. This general area will probably become one of the most important new research topics in Japan.

(c) **Academic Groups.**   University researchers supported by MONBUSHO are engaged in a variety of database projects. The projects are typically quite small.

Japanese university researchers face some serious difficulties. The number of graduate students interested in database research is declining. To begin with, the total number of graduate students in computer science is very small, and many of these are entering such "popular" areas as artificial intelligence.

About half of the graduate students are from outside Japan (mainly from the People's Republic of China), and almost all of these students leave Japan once they finish their education. This differs, of course, greatly from the U.S., which is better able to integrate productive individuals into its social fabric.

Japanese students are less motivated to continue on to academic graduate programs since industry relies on its own training programs. Moreover, capable industrial researchers can obtain a Ph.D. degree by showing that their publications are worthy of such a degree.

Although the Japanese government is committing more resources to build research infrastructure in Japanese universities, some fundamental problems are yet to be resolved.

(d) **Professional Societies.**   There are two professional societies that promote database research: the Information Processing Society of Japan (IPSJ) established in 1970, and the Institute of Electronics, Information, and Communication Engineers (IEICE), established in 1971. There are two special interest groups within them that focus on databases: the Special Interest Group on Database Systems (SIGDBS) associated with IPSJ, and the Special Interest Group on Data Engineering (SIGDE) within IEICE. The IEICE is roughly equivalent to the IEEE in the U.S., while the IPSJ parallels the ACM. Each society has its own journals. Each holds annual conferences and workshops on various aspects of databases.

Two new professional societies, Japan Society for Software Science and Technology and Japan Society for Artificial Intelligence, were founded recently. Journals published by these societies also have a growing number of articles related to databases [Nish:91].

There is now a Japanese-printed English language publication: the monthly *IEICE Transactions*. It has non-Japanese associate editors. The journal covers

1 Fundamentals of electronics, communication and computer sciences,
2 Communications,
3 Electronics, and
4 Information and systems.

(Prior to 1992 these journals were issued bound together, but they will now be distinct.) This Japan-originated English publication is not well-known now outside of Japan. *IEICE Transactions* also contains English abstracts of Japanese-language papers published in the *IEICE Computer* and the *IEICE Information Processing* journals. These two journals cover the IEICE areas of Information and Systems. The volume of abstract material is modest and might be a candidate for reprinting in selected IEEE Computer Society newsletters, such as the *IEEE CS Data Engineering Bulletin*. *IEICE Transactions* also lists the English titles of the unrefereed workshop reports from the forty-seven technical groups of the IEICE.

2.2   Funding Sources

Tenured Japanese university researchers receive some support from the Japanese government directly. However, most research support for significant efforts comes from industry, which means that university researchers must show that technology transfer can take place effectively. Thus, there is a great deal of emphasis on prototyping.

2.3   International Collaboration

Japanese university researchers seem to collaborate freely with U.S. and European university researchers. Many Japanese industries provide study leaves, typically for one year, for their promising researchers. Several researchers we met have spent an extended period of time at U.S. universities. Most international conference series are now being held occasionally in Japan, increasing the potential for greater cooperation in the future.

The problems of language differences fall mainly on Japanese researchers. Their ability to read English is a significant benefit to them.

2.4   U.S. Influence and Faddism

While the basic research efforts are very interesting, we did not hear or see any novel research direction or idea in the database area that was developed by Japanese university researchers. Most of these efforts seem to follow in the footsteps of U.S. researchers.

When a new idea reaches a certain level of visibility it is easily picked up by multiple Japanese researchers at that time. Since their base research funding is not tied to commitments made in formal research proposals, they can redirect their attention rapidly. This flexibility can be advantageous, but can also lead to faddism and abandonment of long-term, basic research directions. In this sense academic and industrial research show some similarities, and probably some empathy as well.

2.5   Conclusions

There is no doubt that Japanese university researchers are very productive and maintain high levels of research activity. This is especially impressive since their overall number is small, and the amount of support they receive in the form of research funding and from graduate students is quite small. Although government is taking steps to improve the situation, it is likely that the shortage of graduate students will continue to exist. Unless this most fundamental problem is solved, the enormous potential for graduate research at Japanese universities cannot be fully realized.

3. Technology Topics

In this section we report on database technology as found in Japan, focusing on nine topics:

1 Object Databases
2 Knowledge Bases
3 Multimedia Databases
4 Interoperable Databases
5 Database Hardware
6 Database Applications
7 Database Security
8 Database Tools
9 Database Management Systems

We stress areas of great activity, and report only briefly on topics where activity is less.

3.1 Object Databases

Author: David Beech

There is considerable activity in Japan in the field of object databases. Indeed, there is a worldwide sense that objects are likely to be at the heart of the next generation of database technology. This may well be a self-fulfilling prophecy, since anything can be described as an object, and the technical sense of the term is still negotiable in the object database world. Even in Japan, the land of consensus, there is no commonly agreed-upon definition of what an object database is — consensus takes time.

It is therefore necessary for us first to identify the main contending emphases to establish a framework to which the Japanese work can be related. We will then survey ongoing work in industry, in the universities, and in a consortium that has both industrial and academic participation, before summarizing our findings.

3.1.1 What is an Object Database?

There are perhaps three major trends in the development of object database systems — to concentrate (a) on multimedia objects, (b) on complex, structured objects, or (c) on programming language objects. There is considerable overlap between these approaches conceptually, but the differences in emphasis can produce very different systems.

(a) Multimedia Objects. The simplest use of object concepts occurs in the storage and retrieval of multimedia information. The binary representation of a voice message, a color image, or a video recording is intuitively thought of as an *object* due to its individuality and its synthetic nature — it is as though it springs into life when created, and it is highly unlikely that it is the same as any other object unless there has been explicit copying. In everyday life, it is too unwieldy a model, except to a handful of mathematicians, to consider all such multimedia phenomena to be instances of a pre-existing domain of immutable *values*.

Yet in a database system, there is no conceptual dividing line between a short bit string and a long one. For example, a string of 2 gigabytes offers a domain of $2^{(2^{34})}$ possible values. Thus a relational database system could treat images as values, and its storage management could be adjusted to give efficient support to these vastly enlarged domains. Since there is some perceived marketing value in claiming object support, one is likely to encounter such claims made about relational or other systems capable of handling such "binary large objects" (BLOBs).

The positive side of this use of the term "object" for a BLOB is that it is a first step in the direction of a more general conceptual model that would fully justify the terminology.

If a relational system is extended, not just with a type LONG, but with types VOICE, IMAGE, and VIDEO, say, and these types have appropriately defined functions and can be given more specialized subtypes, then such a system would begin to share the rich model of other object systems, although perhaps offering only limited extensibility.

When this perspective on multimedia objects is allied to the market potential for their support by databases in the office — and the home — of the future, it should be clear that this is an important and ultimately reputable use of the terminology of object databases. Multimedia capability is already becoming an important emphasis in practical systems, as described in section 3.3 of this report.

(b) Complex Objects.   Many applications still store their data in files rather than in databases, because their data structures often are not a good match with those supported effectively by database systems (such as rows in relational tables). The data may be in large aggregates composed of many interconnected simple structures. An aggregate of information often corresponds to an object in the user's mind, such as an aircraft wing, an architectural drawing, or a programming system, and these are usually referred to as *complex objects*.

There is considerable demand for more convenient and efficient database support for complex objects in such fields as computer-aided design, manufacturing, and software engineering, since a database system provides more functionality than a file system in controlling multi-user access and in automating recovery from system failures.

Programming languages are strong in providing complexity within a single structure, but usually rely on the programmer to *navigate* within and between structures rather than providing higher-level aggregation. This can lead to unacceptable performance in a database system if the navigation requires location of data in disk blocks instead of in internal memory. Systems that try to overcome this problem provide various forms of paging, indexing, physical clustering, and caching.

Although there is some work in complex objects underway in Japan, we did not find a strong emphasis on it.

(c) Programming Language Objects.   Currently much programming and system design is said to be *object-oriented*. As applied to database systems, "oriented" is little more than a noise word, especially in the Orient where it is hard to know which way to turn to become oriented. In the programming language world, the term tends to be associated with the more interpretive object languages, such as SMALLTALK-80 and CLOS (the Common Lisp Object System). We shall not use the phrase unless we wish to give it this connotation. There is an older tradition, still very much alive, of compiled object languages that originated with SIMULA-67 and has led to such languages as C++ and EIFFEL. Most object database systems that emphasize programming language objects currently concentrate on a C++ interface.

The common characteristics of object languages are their type (or class) systems that classify objects according to their interfaces (the attributes of the objects; and the operations that may be performed on the objects). The types may be placed in a hierarchy where more specialized subtypes inherit the interfaces of their supertypes, adding their own extensions to the interface. The implementation of the type is encapsulated within the type definition, so that systems may be constructed in a modular fashion.

In object database systems emphasizing programming language objects, users are permitted to define new types, including the functions that operate on them, so that such systems can be extended and can embody user-defined semantics for their types. Such systems clearly have a general model that makes them suitable for handling the various multimedia objects discussed above, provided that the storage management of large objects is suitably optimized. They are also capable of providing the basic underlying structures for complex objects, and of addressing such performance issues as physical clustering.

There are two main approaches to interfacing object languages and object databases. The first is driven from the programming language end, and aims to provide a "seamless" interface so that a minimal language extension will handle persistent objects similarly to transient ones. This usually means that the database system supports only a single language, at least initially. The other approach is driven from the database end, and aims to provide a language-neutral database system using a type or class system very similar to those of several programming languages. The language interfaces may then take various forms, such as embedded database language statements, function calls, or a seamless syntax that can map to these.

3.1.2   Industrial Projects in Object Database Systems

Although there are not yet any Japanese object database products, whereas in the U.S. there are several, we found a number of substantial prototype systems in Japan and extensive research activity that generally showed a good blend of theoretical and practical considerations. Japanese researchers are well-informed in this area and appear to find it congenial territory, which helps contribute to rising standards in both the content and presentation of their database literature.

Three industrial object database prototype systems were described to us: MANDRILL (Hitachi), JASMINE (Fujitsu), and ODIN (NEC).

Mandrill.   The MANDRILL system [Yama:89] at Hitachi's Systems Development Laboratory at Kawasaki aims to improve database productivity, applicability, and performance. The wide range of applications includes not only Computer-Aided-Design (CAD), Manufacturing(CAM), and Software-Engineering (CASE), but also Office Information Systems (OIS), Management Information Systems (MIS) and Geographic Information Systems (GIS). Many of the points of the Object-oriented Database System Manifesto (presented by Atkinson, et al. in Kyoto, 1989) are being addressed. A preliminary version 1 of MANDRILL was built in 1988/89, with the version 2 prototype scheduled for completion in 1991, and application studies in C planned for 1992.

The approach at Hitachi has been to build an object layer over an existing DataBase Management System (DBMS) and its file system interfaces, with the intention of supporting multimedia information as well as conventional data. The central part, MANDRILL/CORE, first provides a logical media layer to establish system-independence from the underlying database and file systems, and then builds its object layer over it. Applications access the object layer via statements of the MANDRILL/QUEST database language embedded in programming languages.

The QUEST language is somewhat like SQL, the current standard database query language based on IBM's research, although no attempt has been made at a close integration or compatible extension. QUEST commands are treated as system-defined methods (functions) that can be applied to objects. Users may also define their own methods. The object model has the usual class hierarchy. In addition, attributes of a class may be tagged as inverses of other attributes or as referring to parts of an aggregate object. A complex object defined by means of attributes with **has_parts** tags may be processed as a whole, being retrievable, for example, by a single **complexselect** statement. Database integrity is supported by offering user-defined triggers, and authorization controls are applied at the granularity of the object instance. MANDRILL version 2 is a completely different successor system not presented to us in detail. It is a pure object-oriented database system with a database programming language called MANDRILL/POP (persistent object-oriented programming language).

Jasmine.   The JASMINE system [Aosh:90] is being developed by Fujitsu Laboratories Ltd., a Fujitsu subsidiary in Kawasaki. It is an object database system that supports set-oriented queries containing path expressions. Constraints and demons (triggers) may be defined, and the system may be extended by new nodes, attributes, and links defined procedurally in JASMINE/C. Both textual and image data are supported in the window interface, with hypermedia applications in mind.

The data model has classes with single inheritance, and attributes which may either be **property** (stored) or **procedural** (computed by methods written in JASMINE/C). Classes are either **immediate** (value) or **referential** (objects with identifiers). Inverse functions are supported for properties linking referential objects. Each member of a persistent object may also be annotated, like a slot in a frame-based AI language.

The prototype system described to us has been built on XDE, an extended relational storage manager supporting nested relations but lacking concurrency and recovery in its first version. Reservations were also expressed about its performance in navigating between objects. For knowledge-base applications especially, a facility called MEMORY KB provides an in-memory equivalent for storing and manipulating transient objects linked by memory pointers.

JASMINE may thus be characterized as an object database system offering a seamless C-based language interface, where the seamlessness applies to similar ways of referencing and using persistent and transient data. However, it is not seamless C — in both cases the objects are defined by the JASMINE/C class extensions where the language is in competition with similar extensions in C++. JASMINE/C also makes database-inspired extensions emphasizing associative retrieval by adding set-oriented operations with predicates much as in relational languages, and AI-inspired extensions to support demons. The OODB JASMINE project seems to be on a par with similar research prototypes produced in other parts of the world. It is used for multimedia projects as described in Section 3.3.3 and has been supported as part of the National Interoperable Database System Project (see Sections 3.3.2 and 3.4.2).

Odin.   At the NEC Systems Research Laboratories, also in Kawasaki, the ODIN object database system [Hiro:91] is under development. This has emphasized the "seamless C++" approach, and the prototype has itself been written in C++ to run on an NEC Unix workstation. Applications written in ODIN/C++ are preprocessed by referencing and updating the class definitions in the database schema to produce pure C++ with ODIN method calls.

The class hierarchy permits multiple inheritance, and each class has a set of all its associated instances. The class concept is carried through the whole design, such that a database is a set of classes, and a set object is an instance of the set class.

View classes may be defined by selecting objects from a given class, by joining corresponding objects from two or more classes, or by grouping objects from a class into subsets. The original instance variables and methods may be restricted in the view, and users can overload the update operations with their own methods.

The implementation of the system has a physical structure virtualization layer, and pays particular attention to the storage of large variable-length multimedia objects, to object and page buffering, and to transaction control.

3.1.3 Multimedia Databases

In addition to the interest in multimedia applications of general-purpose object databases described above, we encountered two other projects focusing specifically on multimedia support. One, the IMAZONE image database system at Ricoh, is a product headed in an object direction. The other was an evaluation study of an object database management system for multimedia usage carried out by NTT Data.

IMAZONE.   We mention IMAZONE [Kuni:90] [Shir:91] [Iiza:91] here because its developers see it as potentially capable of making effective use of an object database system. Presently the object database concepts in its design are implemented on G-BASE (exported as RICOHBASE to avoid confusion with a different G-BASE system in the U.S.), which is a relational system extended with structural links. It is based on the work carried out by the laboratory director who was at the University of Texas. It effectively supports multimedia data, as described in Section 3.3.3.

NTT Study.   A different perspective is provided by an evaluation [Suzu:91] carried out by NTT Data Services, who are system integrators rather than DBMS vendors. In evaluating the GEMSTONE object database product from the U.S. for multimedia support, NTT was convinced of the value of a strong type system, a class hierarchy with multiple inheritance, and user-defined methods, for handling the ever-growing variety of media data types and subtypes, as well as the complexity of hypermedia objects. However, NTT saw the need for better concurrency and transaction management of such extended media as optical disks, and for network management, whether methods run on clients or servers. Their conclusion was that object database systems still need much practical improvement for effective multimedia application.

3.1.4 University Projects

A brief review of object database research that the team encountered in universities follows. It illustrates our general finding that Japan has done considerable state of the art work in the conceptual modeling of object databases often allied to some prototyping or broad consideration of implementation issues.

Kobe and Kyoto Sangyo.   The widest range of object database modeling and prototyping activities appeared to be at Kobe University and Kyoto Sangyo University. We will consider them together because of substantial amount of joint work conducted by the two universities. At the conceptual level, papers have been published during the past three years on schema design [Tana:89a], object views [Tana:88b], complex objects [Tana:88c], natural joins [Tana:90b], and versions ("alternative objects") [Chan:89].

Extensions to relational systems have included a BLOB approach to storing and retrieving POSTSCRIPT text and graphics objects in the database [Tana:88a], and an SQL-Navigator which dynamically attaches methods to objects to support a hypertext style of navigation [Sana:90]. Recent work has been on TEXTLINK which supports hypertext on an object database system.

This is an illustration of the trend we observed, to move from a good general understanding of the object database field to specific applications in the hypermedia world.

Kyushu.   New work is being started at Kyushu University in the design and implementation of object-oriented persistent programming languages for multimedia databases. A planned series of languages take their names from the various stages in the life-cycle of the yellowtail tuna, for which in Japanese there are apparently as many words as eskimos have for snow. The distinctive feature of this project [Maki:91] is that it has begun by examining performance aspects of object heap management using alternative virtual memory approaches on the MACH operating system.

Library and Information Science.   The Library and Information Science University in the Tsukuba science city specializes in information management. Preliminary work over the past six years has led to a project to develop a system named OMEGA (Object-oriented Multimedia Database Environment for General Application) [Masu:90a]. Current emphasis is on the part-of relationship, and on referencing and synchronization issues that arise in dealing with complex objects.

Hokkaido.   Although current activity at Hokkaido University is largely in the multimedia area, this was preceded by more general object database investigations.

In particular, their object data model ODM [Moza:89] brings together object ideas from SMALLTALK-80 and set-oriented ideas from the relational database model. The concept of a relation as a set of tuples is generalized to that of the "u-set" (uniform set) of objects. The uniformity of a u-set resides in the fact that all of its elements must be conformable to the base class of the u-set, i.e., must satisfy its interface. The u-set is itself defined as an object class with appropriate methods, both for the usual set operations and for the relational operations: project, Cartesian product, and join, on the instance variables of objects regarded as tuples.

3.1.5   Obase Consortium

A novel development is the formation of the Obase Consortium, which will operate from September 1990 through August 1993. Membership is as follows:

- Senri International Information Institute (Osaka)
- Universities
  - Himeji Dokkyo
  - Kobe
  - Kyoto Sangyo
  - Osaka
- Industries
  - Fujitsu
  - Fuji Xerox Information Systems
  - Hitachi
  - Kobe Computer Services
  - Kobelco Systems
  - Matsushita Electric
  - Toyo Information Systems

The objectives are to investigate current ODBMSs and applications, to develop a new Object-Database Management System (OBASE) together with ODB design tools, and to carry out related research. The emphasis in the current, preliminary applications study appears to be on hypertext, video, and all forms of document management.

Specifics about the Obase Consortium were provided by Prof. S. Nishio (Osaka University). Each industrial partner funds Obase at a level of about $150,000 over three years. The project began by investigating the advantages and disadvantages of conventional OODBMSs, and then moved on to the development of some specific applications. Currently the Obase researchers are using the VERSANT OODBMS to implement these applications, which include a fuzzy retrieval system for a movie database and a LATEX document OODB.

3.1.6 Summary

The main conclusions regarding object databases follow:

- There is not yet any commercially available Japanese object database management system.

- There is substantial current, well-informed object database research, especially in theory and concepts, as well as in relatively straightforward prototyping. Deeper investigation of efficient implementation is less in evidence, except in the treatment of binary large objects.

- It is unlikely that a Japanese general-purpose object database management system is imminent as a product, not only for technical reasons, but also because the strategic questions related to how to design such a system to become an industry standard rather than one among many proprietary systems have not yet been decided. Open object database standards, now in an early state of discussion, may change this expectation.

- There is a strong emphasis on the applicability of object database technology to the management of multi/hypermedia information, which is likely to lead to the early appearance of more specialized object database management systems for integrated media support.

This last point makes it likely that object databases, supporting multimedia on Japanese image and voice hardware, will be one of the early export items for the Japanese software industry.

3.2   Knowledge Bases

Author: Gio Wiederhold

We define knowledge bases as the combination of processable knowledge, stored as rules, logic, or frames, which can be applied to data, either in conventional databases, in in-memory databases, or as ground rules. It is a technology with great potential, since the application of knowledge to factual information permits effective use of even limited computer represented knowledge. As the factual data are updated to reflect changing situations, the knowledge can be reused.

3.2.1   Past Research

A major focus of the initial plans for the Fifth Generation Project was the development of knowledge-base technology. For the knowledge base a PROLOG-based schema was foreseen. The factual data would be processed, when needed, by powerful, parallel database machines. While the Fifth Generation Project initiated much research activity, we found no actual systems or prototypes that followed the original architecture. Its progress is well documented in ICOT publications. While knowledge-base technology is now well-understood, the lack of a database infrastructure, using common standards, limits its applicability.

3.2.2   Current Research

However, research on knowledge bases is progressing in academia, often based on in-memory storage models. This approach is similar to current directions in the U.S. While previously memory-based systems were not considered adequately scalable, it is obvious that the rapid growth of workstations (now they typically have more memory than the upper limit of the last generation of mainframe computers) makes this direction valid. In-memory databases do require continuous backup to assure persistence. Where knowledge changes slowly and the focus is on queries, simple backup techniques suffice in practice.

While Japanese researchers are well aware of knowledge representation technologies, we did not find any large-scale efforts to establish large collections of knowledge as, for instance, the MCC CYC project [Lenat]. This may be an omission on our part, since we focused only on knowledge bases that involve database storage. Databases are likely to be employed in such efforts, but are not an essential feature.

Neural Nets.   Several recent research efforts consider neural nets. Here knowledge is not managed explicitly, but is captured automatically from example sets, for which answers, typically classification parameters, are given. The results are stored as discrimination values in internal nodes, and can then be used to classify new examples.

Neural net knowledge can then be exploitable to classify images, ranging from Kanji calligraphy to faces [Kuni:90]. This research area is relatively new and immature. Japanese researchers in this area are well aware of the state of the art, and appear to be experimenting widely with the current technology. If this technology can be usefully applied in future database systems, then the background knowledge available in Japan is adequate to implement these techniques. These methods could then complement multimedia technology.

3.3   Multimedia Database Systems

Authors: John Miles Smith and Diane Smith

Computer systems are now able to handle multimedia information such as audio, video, images and text. A huge commercial market is expected to develop in multimedia systems in the next decade. Success in this market requires the integration of consumer electronics and computer systems, and is likely to be an area of intense interest both in the U.S. and in Japan. Multimedia database systems, which manage repositories of multimedia information, are a central component of multimedia applications.

After a description of the background of multimedia database systems, the impact of the three major Japanese technology drivers (national projects, commercial products, and academic research) are reviewed. Subsequently, each key technical area is considered, and the results of Japanese projects visited by the team are described for each area. General comparisons are made with the state of the technology in the U.S. The final section draws some conclusions about Japanese research in multimedia databases.

It should be noted that the opinions and recommendations in this section are based on a sample of organizations visited by the study team. The study focused on organizations that are active in database research and development. However, due to the interdisciplinary nature of the multimedia area and due to emerging commercial competition, it is possible that some organizations doing important work were not visited, and that for some organizations visited, the study team was not informed about some proprietary work.

3.3.1   Background

Until recently, computer systems focused on the manipulation of alphanumeric data. However, much of the information processed by human beings is in the form of audio, video, images and text. Higher computer speeds and larger storage capacities are required to process these information media than are required to process alphanumeric data. Computer systems have now passed the threshold where these information media can be processed cost-effectively. As computer systems and communication networks continue to improve, higher volumes of media information can be supported and increasingly sophisticated processing operations can be performed at high speed.

The result is that new classes of computer applications can be developed for the home, education, entertainment and technical industries. For example, computers can be used to access encyclopedias of information containing text, images, video and audio recordings. Family photograph albums can be captured on computer storage and retrieved and displayed on the computer screen. Movies can be downloaded from commercial databases and played back through the computer. Videoconferencing can be held via computer interface, and sections of the conference (video, audio, and presentation material) can be stored for later review and editing. Geographic information, previously available in the form of paper maps, can be retrieved from computer storage and analyzed in powerful and flexible ways.

Multimedia computer systems can handle several information media. Typically, they support I/O devices such as microphones, scanners, videocameras, FAXmodems, and color monitors. For all of these devices, the multimedia computer systems can capture, process, and playback information. With conventional storage systems such as books and videotapes, the information is connected in a single linear sequence. However, when multimedia information is captured in computer storage, it can be linked together and retrieved in any and multiple meaningful sequences. This allows users to search for information in whatever way is most effective for the purpose at hand. Computer systems which allow multiple links for storing and searching multimedia information are often referred to as *hypermedia* systems.

Multimedia systems are expected to be a huge growth market for the computer industry over the next decade. In addition, they will have a profound impact on existing markets for consumer electronics. Televisions, telephones, audio systems, VCRs, videocameras, still cameras, copiers, and FAX machines may all become extensions of integrated computer systems, and not stand-alone products. Japan's electronics industry is well aware of the opportunities provided by multimedia computer systems. Both the United States and Japan are positioned to acquire a share in this market. The United States is ahead but is losing ground in the computer industry, while Japan is well ahead in consumer electronics. In the 1990s the battle will be joined to successfully integrate these two technologies.

Multimedia database systems are a key component of multimedia computer systems. They will provide the services to store and retrieve multimedia and hypermedia information, and support the sharing of this information across user groups. There is a substantial technology gap that must be bridged to provide these services effectively for multimedia data. For example, an image requires approximately three orders of magnitude more space for storage than an alphanumeric string. At the same time, matching image segments against a retrieval pattern is a much more time-consuming operation for an image than a string. Finally, the index structures required for speeding access to information are quite different for certain kinds of multimedia data (e.g., maps). Solving these technical problems is critical to realizing the potential of multimedia computer systems.

As a result, the status and direction of Japanese multimedia database projects is an important factor in formulating U.S. strategy in multimedia computer systems.

3.3.2   Technology Drivers

From the study, three drivers emerged that are generating new technology development in the multimedia database area:

1 A Japanese national project called the "Interoperable Database System" (IN-DBS) project [Tojo:91, Tojo:85];
2 The commercialization of existing multimedia system technology in niche application areas; and
3 Some innovative academic research projects involving multimedia data.

The effects of these three drivers are different but synergistic. The first has drawn attention to the opportunities in multimedia databases, triggered investigation into various development problems, and increased the level of expertise in Japanese industry. The second has created practical extensions of existing database technology, and greater understanding of the performance and capacity problems to be solved. The third is creating more fundamental advances in multimedia database technology with the potential for use in future products.

The National Research and Development Project on Interoperable Database Systems started in 1986 and has just come to the end of its six-year program. The project was supported by the Agency of Industrial Science and Technology of MITI and executed by the Electrotechnical Laboratory (ETL) and sixteen participating companies. The project was started with the goal of developing technology in four areas:

1 The integration of distributed heterogeneous database systems;
2 The reliability of database systems;
3 The architecture of computer networks to support heterogeneous database systems;
4 The support of multimedia information in database systems.

The specific subgoals for the multimedia area include:

1 Network protocols for handling multimedia data;
2 Conversion algorithms for mapping between different information formats;
3 Data compression and feature extraction; and
4 Transformation of bit-mapped documents into structured objects.

Based on information obtained during the study, it appears that the multimedia work concentrated on the last two subgoals. A common project theme was to store maps (e.g., municipal, plant, and telephone service network) in a database, to build feature-recognition and feature-matching algorithms, and to provide real-time scrolling and zooming via a graphical user interface. This theme was apparent in projects discussed at ETL, NTT, Mitsubishi, and Toshiba, and [Tojo:91] indicates that Hitachi also has a similar project. All these projects appear to have been influenced directly, or indirectly, by the Interoperable Database System program.

From the point of view of commercial products, the most important multimedia data types are text, image and drawing. Virtually all office documents can be captured and processed using these three data types. Several Japanese companies offer document management products with a database system component. For example, Ricoh has the IMAZONE image database construction tool that runs on top of its RICOHBASE database system. Hitachi's "Document Filing System" uses a special-purpose database to support semantic matching. Toshiba has a product set called the "Total Office Productivity Support System" that includes a document management tool OA-FILING that operates in conjunction with its RDB/V database system.

From a database system perspective, Ricoh's RICOHBASE is the most advanced product. RICOHBASE is an extended-relational database that has been specially designed to manage images, and IMAZONE provides tools to help C programmers build image database applications.

Ricoh's manufacturing capability in optical and electronic products provides an important motivational focus to its research laboratory. We present their technological approach in Sect. 3.3.3.

Of the academic projects involved in the study, two stood out as making significant contributions in the multimedia database area:

- Dr. Tanaka's group at the Un. of Hokkaido [Tana:89, Tana:91],
- Dr. Fujiwara and Dr. Kitagawa's group at the Un. of Tsukuba [Jian:89,Luan:89].

The Hokkaido group is driven to create new multimedia technology. For example, storage of video information, content-based search for video segments, efficient representations and content-based searching for bit-mapped documents, and object-oriented graphical generators for multimedia applications. In contrast, the Tsukuba group is motivated by two information systems considerations. The first is to develop database systems for chemical/material substance information (the databases are actually published on CD-ROM). The second is to develop new database system architectures that can more effectively manage multimedia data. These efforts are investigating innovative approaches to fundamental problems in multimedia database systems.

To nurture multimedia activities in Japan and to foster cooperation with overseas activities, MITI is supporting the founding of an "International Multimedia Association." The goals are technology interchange, expanding the base of expertise, and popularizing the benefits of the technology. At this stage, national, multinational and foreign companies are being sought as founding members of the association. According to the brochure describing admission to the association, U.S. companies IBM, Apple, Intel and Microsoft are expected to participate. It would appear that MITI is looking to the International Multimedia Association to help guide the next steps in Japan's commercialization of multimedia technology.

3.3.3   Technology Survey

To fully achieve the promise of multimedia database systems, technology must be developed and deployed in five technical areas:

1 Base technologies;
2 Database system architecture;
3 Content-based retrieval;
4 Hypermedia storage and retrieval; and
5 Application generation tools.

These five areas will be covered in this section. For each area, the technology will be briefly described and motivated. Then Japanese projects in the area will be summarized.

Base Technologies.   The term *base technologies* refers to underlying capabilities in information capture, playback, storage, and transmission that are prerequisite to the commercial exploitation of multimedia systems. These nondatabase base technologies were not explicitly covered by this study and will be treated only briefly here.

Japan's technological capability in the audio, video, and imaging areas of consumer electronics is well-known. While basic research is probably on a par with that in the US, Japan is leading the commercialization of these technologies with high-definition TV, electronic still cameras, FAX and photocopiers, and digital audio systems. Due to the large information content of multimedia data, very high capacity storage devices are required. For example, a reasonable color image requires 1 megabyte (MB) or more of storage. Only forty such images can be stored on the 40 MB hard disk drive found in a typical PC. As a result, optical disk technology must be used, which provides about 5000 MB per optical platter with current products. Similarly, the transmission of multimedia data requires very high-speed communication networks. Japan has been commercially operating a limited ISDN (Integrated Services Digital Network) since the middle 1980s; this will soon expand across the country. Japan is a leader in both the base technologies and their commercial exploitation.

Database System Architecture.   Database system architectures must be extended to handle multimedia data. One approach is to extend relational database systems (RDB) so that multimedia data can be stored and retrieved along with regular alphanumeric data. In general, extended relationall database systems (ERDB) work well for multimedia data items that are always accessed as a whole (e.g., as a single image or as a single video segment). However, they do not work well for data items with a complex internal structure that must be accessed on a component-by-component basis (e.g., a structured document or a CAD model). For this purpose, object-oriented database systems (OODB) have been developed, and are becoming commercially available in the U.S. A disadvantage of commercial OODBs is that they do not provide the high performance we expect when querying data items with a uniform structure (e.g., business transaction records). It is an active research issue to combine the advantages of ERDB and OODB into a single database system.

Most of the commercial products and National IN-DBS Project efforts use a combination of an RDB and a file system to manage multimedia data. Multimedia data items are represented as files. Pointers to these files are stored in fields in the relational tables to connect relational data with associated multimedia data. The file manager may use an optical disk jukebox for data storage. The advantage of this approach is that it requires no modification to the relational database. The disadvantage is that applications become responsible for ensuring that the relational and file data are mutually consistent during normal operation, and for ensuring the recoverability of mutually consistent states in the event of a failure.

Ricoh's commercial product IMAZONE [Rico:90] is an image database construction tool being built by Ricoh at their Software Division in Bunkyo-ku, Tokyo.

The emphasis is on support of complex graphical objects, variety of media, and high volume. IMAZONE uses an ERDB that can store multimedia data items directly in fields of the relation. However, the size of each such field was limited to 64 Kbytes at the time of the JTEC panel's visit. 2 Gbytes were supported from the end of 1991. In that case larger data items must be stored in a separate file system and then connected back to the ERDB by an ID number. Since IMAZONE supports linkage of records, that connection can be relatively transparent to the user. The file system can support an optical jukebox. Some vendors in the U.S. now allow very large field sizes in their ERDBs, and provide for mapping of these fields directly onto an optical jukebox.

From the discussion with the RICOHBASE group, it is clear that this group has faced and solved many of the practical performance and capacity problems associated with multimedia databases in the context of office documents.

Two research projects visited by the study team are developing ERDBs for multimedia data. At Hitachi Research, an experimental multimedia database system called MANDRILL [Yama:89] is being developed based on object-oriented extensions to SQL. At IBM Japan, the first version of an experimental database system called MODES [Kosa:87] has been implemented, and work is underway on a second version. The first version of MODES extends an RDB in three ways:

1 By introducing a field type that is a pointer to an external file,

2 By allowing the selection of storage devices (in particular, optical devices) for these files, and

3 By defining virtual input/output systems which are able to handle these file types.

The second version is developing a *card* user interface paradigm for the storage, retrieval and display of multimedia data.

Two other research projects are pursuing OODBs for multimedia data management. At ETL, an open database system called AXIS [Koji:88, Koji:91] is under investigation as part of the National IN-DBS Project. AXIS seeks to provide extensibility so that a system kernel can be extended to meet the needs of particular applications. The specifications of extensions to the system are stored in a system database that is accessible to application developers.

Multimedia systems being produced at ETL and private research laboratories may not be considered real innovations. Such products are already being used in some simple applications. Also, these projects have certainly awakened interest in multimedia technology.

At the University of Library and Information Science, OMEGA [Masu:91] is under development. The current effort is to prototype processors for the data definition language and the query language. The main emphasis is on integrating a number of semantic constructs and operations into an object oriented data model.

Content-Based Retrieval.   No matter what database system is being used for multimedia data, a key challenge is to develop algorithms and data structures for data items so that they can be retrieved based on the semantic content of that data item. For example, to retrieve all images that contain a human face, or to retrieve all documents that contain a certain phrase. Content-based retrieval requires efficient algorithms to match a given *pattern* against a similar *pattern* in the multimedia data item. Content-based retrieval allows retrieval conditions to be determined at the time of retrieval. In contrast, attribute-based retrieval requires that the attributes be known at the time the database is created, and that their values be given at the time an item is stored.

Several companies (ETL, NTT, Mitsubishi and Toshiba) are investigating feature extraction from a variety of map information including municipal maps, manufacturing plant layout, and utility networks. Mitsubishi, for example, is interested in finding areas in a plant layout where the topology is similar to another area in the layout. Maeda and his colleagues [Maed:88] have been working on algorithms for a simplified version of this problem involving the layout of rooms in a house. They abstract the room topology in a house to adjacency relationships. They then search a "realty" database to find houses with a layout similar to that of a given house by matching on their adjacency relationships. In another example, Toshiba has developed a geographic information system using optical disks. The database consists of image data for base maps with vector and alphanumeric data overlays. In [Okaz:90], techniques are described for obtaining a seamless base map from a conventional atlas and for distributing image data to multiple optical disks for concurrent retrieval.

A group at ETL has been pursuing content-based retrieval using a more abstract collection of images, namely trademark symbols. In [Kato:91], a *graphical feature vector* has been developed that abstracts a trademark symbol into five distinct analytic features. Trademarks are compared for similarity by differencing their vectors. The group has demonstrated that subjective similarity of symbols correlates well with small vector differences.

At Hokkaido University, Tanaka and his research group have been working on content-based retrieval of video information. Their initial work focused on the detection of *cuts* in a video segment. A cut is where one scene ends and another begins. They have developed algorithms to reliably detect cuts. Recently, they have extended their work to search a videotape for specific content. Prof. Tanaka showed a video of a car race, in which the same cars showed up from a variety of angles and in various contexts at different stages of the race. In a convincing demonstration, Prof. Tanaka was able to retrieve all of the video frames which included a specific selected car. Work of similar quality in the U.S. is largely sponsored by the intelligence communities. Although reported in the open literature, this work seems not to have had much commercial impact, perhaps because of the high cost of the hardware.

3.3.4 Character Recognition

In a project called the "Transmedia Machine," Tanaka [Tana:89] has developed techniques for implementing text processing on the content of scanned images of text documents. The usual approach today is to employ optical character recognition (OCR) to regenerate the original text from the image. However, OCR is often difficult, particularly when multiple fonts or different character sets are used. For many text editing operations, it is not necessary to recognize individual characters. It is sufficient to recognize just the line and character boundaries, and treat characters and lines as rectangular sub-images. Characters can then be made to flow as line length and spacing are changed, and as characters are inserted and deleted. Hitachi is developing a Kanji full-text search machine [Fuji:91].

Text-processing in Japanese is complicated by the absence of spaces to indicate word boundaries. The same Kanji symbol can initiate a one-, two-, or three-symbol word. The hardware is further described in Section 3.5.1. Emphasis is on development of a very high-speed machine that can quickly scan very large text databases.

Hypermedia.   As described before, hypermedia refers to the linking of multimedia data objects together so that information can be retrieved by following the links. For example, the service manual for repairing a car could be stored as a collection of information (text, diagrams, video) linked together based on symptoms and diagnostic results. The same piece of information may appear along several different links. Hypermedia systems must provide a graphical interface that allows the user to navigate (or browse) along the links to find the required data. In some cases the required data may be a composite of several linked items stored in the database. This may require automatic layout algorithms to compose the data items into an efficient form for human examination. For example, if a car repair step includes some text instructions with two diagrams, then all three items must be arranged on the user's monitor in such a way that important information is not obscured.

Ishikawa [Ishi:90] has used Fujitsu's experimental object-oriented database system JAS-MINE (see Section 3.1.2) to build a prototype hypermedia system that serves as a visitor's guide to Kyoto. JASMINE's object hierarchy is extended with special classes to contain multimedia information. Links between information are represented by object attributes. Users can directly navigate between objects, or use a query language for retrieving objects based on their classes and attributes. Key features of JASMINE are exploited for hypermedia information management. For example, the version control subsystem is used to keep track of different versions and configurations of visitor guidebooks, and triggers are used to notify users of changes to stored information.

Hitachi is starting a new project called "Personal Information Base." The general idea is to overlay a multimedia database with a semantic network of concepts. The user interface takes advantage of human memory characteristics to retrieve information by navigating the conceptual structures. A prototype browser and editor has been developed.

Dr. Kambayashi at Kyoto University has investigated an automatic layout problem associated with the presentation of map data. With a geographical information system, a user can select information from a database and request that it be displayed in the form of a map. Since the content and form of the map can be defined dynamically, the positioning of information on the map is determined at the time of map generation. A classical example is the positioning of names close to the map objects they describe without obscuring other critical information. Kambayashi describes practical methods for solving this latter problem in real-time.

Based on the rather fragmentary data gathered during the visit, the U.S. has research and commercial leadership in the hypermedia area. With the exception of Kambayashi's project, Japanese research of hypermedia is superficial. A number of U.S. projects have explored this area in much more depth.

However, work on hypertext and image-processing, as seen at NEC, provides an important infrastructure upon which hypermedia systems development can proceed rapidly.

Application Generation Tools.   A multimedia (or hypermedia) database system only provides services for information storage and retrieval. To be useful for a particular purpose, an application program must be written that calls on those services on behalf of the user. For example, an application will typically allow a user to enter data from some input device (e.g., a keyboard or scanner), check the consistency of that data, retrieve data using certain predefined queries and parameters, organize and aggregate data into certain output formats, and transmit or print the result. In many situations it is desirable for a user who is not a professional programmer to create or modify his or her own application. For this purpose, application generation tools are used. These tools normally provide a *skeleton* for a certain class of application. The user then *fleshes out* this skeleton to include the specific details required for the application on hand. Application generation tools are commercially available for relational database systems, and others have been developed for certain specialized multimedia applications, such as document processing. Application generation tools for general-purpose multimedia database systems are still in the research and development stages.

The multimedia application generation tool seen during the visit was the INTELLIGENT-PAD system created by Tanaka [Tana:91]. INTELLIGENTPAD falls into the same software category as Apple's HYPERCARD and Xerox's NOTECARDS. They all provide an object-oriented programming system with a strong visual representation for objects. However, INTELLIGENT-PAD goes beyond the other tools by allowing object construction via direct manipulation of the visual representation. Each object is represented as a *pad*, that is, a stack of sheets. Database properties are handled through the persistence of the underlying pad data. New pads are created by pasting one pad on top of another. This provides an elegant and surprisingly powerful programming paradigm. A prototype implementation of INTELLIGENTPAD has been built by Tanaka's research group at Hokkaido University.

While still in the experimental stage, INTELLIGENTPAD is a creative and promising research result, and stands on a par with other U.S. work in this area. INTELLIGENTPAD is an exception in that it presents novel advanced programming and system abstractions. The overall U.S. lead in software owes much to research into such novel paradigms.

3.3.5   Conclusions

The style of Japanese research in the multimedia database area contrasts strongly with that of U.S. research. Japanese research tends to be pragmatic. It is focused on creating a concrete target application that stresses the capabilities of current systems. Research results tend to be incremental improvements to current system software, together with insights into the target application. U.S. research tends to be more profound. It is focused on creating new system concepts that can be applied to many target applications. Research results include more fundamental advances in system software technology.

At the database system level, Japanese researchers rely on the U.S. to provide the major software technologies. There are academic projects aimed at architectural advances, but in reality they are largely just variations on U.S. research themes. At the content-based retrieval level, there is good stand-alone research in progress, but the results are generally not integrated back into an overall database system architecture. There is a noticeable lack of research in Japan in multimedia database tools and application generators. The Japanese researchers are more concerned with building applications directly than with understanding the general methodologies involved.

From the examples mentioned above, it is clear that Japanese groups are covering a wide spectrum of media types in their research on content-based retrieval. Their techniques are being investigated in isolated but important applications. It will be some years before these techniques are fully integrated into the architecture of a database system that can handle the full spectrum of media types. The U.S. is ahead in most aspects of research into content-based retrieval, as well as in some aspects of commercialization – particularly in the areas of geographical information systems and CAD/CAM database systems. As might be expected, Kanji text retrieval is an area where Japan is ahead. The most innovative work is underway at the universities (e.g., Tanaka's group). However, this work is under-funded and it will be difficult for researchers to keep pace with relatively well-funded groups such as MIT's "Media Lab."

The principal Japanese advantage in the multimedia database area is at the hardware component level — their capability to design and manufacture high quality displays, storage devices, and audio/video systems. This capability is supported by a strong vertical integration going all the way up to application products. The lack of standards in new technology is overcome by joint product planning teams. This setting, combined with the Japanese focus on concrete applications, positions them to commercialize packaged hardware solutions based on available system software technology in the multimedia area. At some point in the future, software technology may become the roadblock to continued progress. At that point Japan is likely to invest more research effort in creating the fundamental software technology needed. In the interim, Japan can rely on the rest of the world.

Japanese industrial research takes a conservative approach in the multimedia database area. On the whole, it is following the direction of the "Interoperable Database System" National Project. The more widely publicized "Fifth Generation Project" has had little or no influence on Japanese industry in this area. Innovative research is underway at the universities (e.g., Hokkaido and Tsukuba). However, this research has significantly less funding than key multimedia research centers in the U.S. (e.g., MIT's Media Lab), and the researchers will find it difficult to keep pace except in specialized niche areas.

The Japanese choice of target application areas throws some light on where they see early commercial opportunities for multimedia databases. The applications seen by the study team include:

      Industrial Plan Maps (Mitsubishi)
      Utility Service Maps (NTT)
      Urban Maps (Toshiba)
      Museum Holdings Database (National Museum of Ethnology)
      Fashion Industry Database (NTT Data Systems)
      Japanese Document Reader (Toshiba)
      Chemical Substances (University of Tsukuba)

In some areas, such as chemical substances data management and Kanji document processing, the Japanese work is on the leading edge. In other areas such as mapping applications, Western companies have leadership capabilities and the Japanese are in catch-up mode. Since the field is not yet mature, the eventual results of the research, development, and marketing investment are unclear. Even less clear is the eventual allocation of market-share, since the market is in its infancy.

3.4   Interoperable Databases

Author: Toshi Minoura

We expect that most database activity of the future will involve multiple computers. When computing activities are distributed, issues of joint operation must be addressed.

3.4.1   Current State

Most of the current distributed applications in Japan, such as banking systems, are processed by centralized computer systems. Only a few distributed database systems are deployed. However, the Japanese understand the importance of interoperation among computers of different sizes and from different vendors in the "information-based society" they envision.

3.4.2   Interoperability and Standards

The most notable move toward the vision of an information-based society is the National Research and Development Program on Interoperable Database Systems (Interoperability Program), managed through INTAP (Interoperability Technology Association for Information Processing). INTAP is an industry consortium created to perform research and development focused on open network systems architecture.

The Interoperability Program was started by MITI in 1986 with a total projected budget of $100 million. It is expected to end in March 1992. The official goal of the program was "to establish fundamental technology indispensable for realizing multimedia reliable distributed database systems on interoperable computer network systems."

The projects supported by the program were divided into four major areas:

1 Database systems architecture (discussed earlier under the acronym IN-DBS),
2 Multimedia technology,
3 Distributed systems technology, and
4 Open network systems architecture.

Open systems permit multiple participants to use and contribute software. Without that concept there is much dependence by a user on a single vendor. As such, the concept changes drastically the entry cost for new, innovative companies in the software and hardware arena.

The major participants in this MITI program are ETL, Fujitsu, Hitachi, Matsushita, Mitsubishi, NEC, Oki, Sharp, Sumitomo and Toshiba. Furthermore, NTT, IBM Japan, and Nihon Unisys participated in the interoperability experiments among heterogeneous computer systems. Fuji Xerox and DEC Japan are also members of INTAP.

Tojo summarized the results of this project as follows [Tojo91]: "*Although it is true that there may still exist a number of problems not resolved completely, it is also true that most of the key issues of interoperability are being attacked in the project. It is expected that the result of the project will broadly accelerate the development and use of real open interoperable information systems* ".

In other words, the project has not yet produced a coherent set of technologies as aimed in the official goal. Real-time interoperation is not yet a practice. However, there are some important results.

Implementation and Documentation.   Based on the ISO OSI reference model [ISO:84], the INTAP participants have produced detailed implementation standards for the protocols from layer 1 to layer 7. There are 3,830 pages of these standards. The networks supported include ISDN, FDDI, and CSMA/CD LAN. The application level (layer 7) protocols include FTAM (File Transfer, Access and Management), MOTIS (Message Oriented Text Interchange Systems), ODA/ODIF (Open Document Architecture/Interchange Format), distributed transaction processing, and RDA (Remote Database Access).

The implementation protocols are tested at Interoperable Networking Events (INEs) '88, '90, and '91. The successful experiments of FTAM involved BULL (France), DEC (Great Britain), ICL (Great Britain), and Olivetti (Italy) in addition to the member companies of INTAP. They have established the INTAP Conformance Test Center (ICTC) to certify OSI products implemented by various vendors. About twenty OSI products from various vendors have been certified so far. To provide the environment for interoperability tests of OSI products, INTAPnet was established in 1989.

The Japanese are actively participating in international standard setting in this field. Their primary stage is Asia-Oceania Workshop (AOW), with participation by China, Australia, Korea, and Japan. They intend to cooperate fully with EWOS and NIST OIW. A key player of the Japanese standardization activity, Fujitsu, is participating also in the RDA standardization activity on the U.S. side, the SQL Access Group.

This program can be regarded as another example of Japanese government projects whose actual goals are to disseminate information (education) and to provide some seed money for research activities at private companies.

Distributed Databases.   The Japanese have not yet built homogeneous distributed database systems that perform distributed query processing. (This omission may be due to the observation that, from a commercial point of view, such systems are generally not viable.) We encountered no efforts to build federated systems. A project on federated heterogeneous database systems started at ETL (Interim Report, 1989) seems to have fizzled out.

Hitachi has installed its relational systems at about 170 sites. Among them are about thirty distributed systems with an average of two to three nodes. Mostly ISO standards are followed, and OSI RDA support is being developed. However, some customers want compatibility with DB2, the principal IBM product for relational databases.

Fujitsu was the first company in Japan that developed a relational database system. Fujitsu seems to move directly to heterogeneous systems based on the OSI RDA standard.

Currently, Oki does not sell distributed database systems. Its product group is extending its relational system REAM, incorporating the RDA standard for remote data access. The system may be ported to non-Oki platforms. ORACLE has been ported to Oki minicomputers.

3.4.3   Conclusion

Distribution of databases, while less applied in Japan than in the U.S., is being built on a solid foundation of standards, especially the RDA standard favored in Europe, rather than the direct use of SQL, as used for current implementations. Since RDA is based on SQL, the transition will not be difficult, but any incompatibility can hurt. For autonomous federated systems, an important compound of broad-based information systems, the RDA standard is especially relevant. Unless RDA is provided and supported in U.S. systems, as promoted by the RDA-SQL-ACCESS consortium, this style of distribution will assure early system compatibility of Japanese software with the European market. Such a direction could cause isolation of more narrowly-SQL-based U.S. vendors.

3.5   Database Hardware

Author: Nick Farmer

In Japan, as in other parts of the world, most databases are accessed using conventional computers. While there are a large number of small databases on personal computers, most significant databases have, in the past, been loaded on a large central mainframe, using a variety of different database management systems.

There appears to be considerable dissatisfaction with the current environment. In a survey by Hayashi in 1985, users noted significant dissatisfaction with the performance of all types of database management systems running on conventional computers.

	Problems	No.	Rank
1.	Poor flexibility with changes to the data structure	65	1
2.	Inadequate efficiency for processing	63	2
3.	Poor capability to manage a large quantity of data	36	3
4.	Limitation of program development	29	4
5.	Poor fittable functions to each application	27	5
6.	Too expensive to install the DBMS	27	5
7.	Too expensive to operate the DBMS	19	7
8.	Others	12	8
9.	Poor expandability of the system	6	9
10.	Bugs in the DBMS	4	10

Some of these reasons motivate research and development activities for special purpose hardware devices, with the goal of improving the performance of database management systems. Use of hardware support also provides a more stable interface than more flexible software and operating systems conventions, especially where standards are absent.

3.5.1   Research and Development

These research and development activities are being carried out by a number of Japanese universities and by most Japanese computer manufacturers. Of special note are the activities at the following institutions and corporations:

Organizations Involved in Research on Database Hardware Technology	
Universities	Computer Manufacturers
University of Hiroshima	Fujitsu
Hokkaido University	Hitachi
Tohoku University	Matsushita
Tsukuba University	Mitsubishi
	NTT
	Ricoh
	Toshiba

Most of the research and development activities discussed in this chapter were carried out between 1984 and 1990. Since the most active area of database interest during this time was associated with the relational model, this is also where most of the hardware-related activities were focused. The simplicity of the relational model favors hardware oriented approaches.

In addition to the relational model, there has been some interest in full-text searching of both Japanese and English language material. No activities were mentioned relative to special purpose hardware for the object database model probably because this model is not yet sufficiently stable enough to support special-purpose hardware implementations.

Areas of potential interest relative to special-purpose hardware include:

- Special purpose VLSI components
- Vector processors
- Intelligent disks
- Parallel processing
- Pipelined operations

While a specific project may be focused on one of these areas, projects often span multiple areas. For instance, intelligent disks may also use parallel logic, and vector processing may take advantage of pipelined operations. Nevertheless, the discussion that follows will be structured along the lines of the five principal areas listed above.

3.5.2 Special Purpose VLSI Components

Most of the interest in special purpose VLSI components for database access has focused on three areas:

- Key search in the relational model
- Character match for full-text searching
- Sorting

Professor Tanaka of Hokkaido University has done extensive work on special-purpose VLSI devices for database machines. He has proposed a special-purpose sort module that can handle sorting of variable length character strings in a pipelined fashion, that can begin to output the sorted list immediately after the last input character has been received.

Fujisawa and his colleagues at Hitachi have worked on a system to search Japanese text files [Fuji:91]. They use a two-stage search process, with a bit-map surrogate search followed by a condensed text search. They can scan text at approximately 100 million bits per second if the surrogate hit ratio is less than or equal to 15 percent. Their goal is to be able to process 25,000 documents per hardware unit, for document sizes up to 20,000 bytes per document, with retrieval times of approximately five seconds, for queries that have 1,000 or fewer terms.

3.5.3 Vector Processors

Most examples of the use of vector processors have been restricted to numerically intensive computing. Vectorizing algorithms are better understood in this area, and the applications requiring vector processors are more prevalent. However, some of the same basic techniques used for numerically intensive computing can be carried over to special-purpose character-oriented vector processors.

In areas where vector processors have been used to support database processing, they have typically been connected to conventional processors running a relational database management system. This allows the vendor of the database management system to be able to selectively use the vector processor in those areas where the vector processor has the greatest advantage. It does not require the application system to be aware of the vectorizing algorithms. It also takes advantage of the file updating capability of the native database management system.

Torii and his colleagues at Hitachi have developed an integrated database processor (IDP) that exploits the parallelism inherent in a relational system by dynamically rearranging the pointer structures into a vectorized format. The integrated database processor is connected to a conventional computer running the Hitachi RDB1 relational database management system. The query analyzer in RDB1 determines whether or not each query is suitable for the vector processor. Performance improvements of between two and thirty have been observed when combining the specialized vector processor with a standard RDB1 configuration.

3.5.4   Intelligent Disks and Accelerators

One of the characteristics of applications based on a database management system is that it is often necessary to transfer large amounts of data from secondary storage to primary storage, and perform a significant level of computation on that data, with the objective of selecting a very small percentage of the retrieved data to pass along to the application. This tends to stress all of the major architectural components of conventional computers: input and output devices, channels, memory, and processors. In order to reduce the load on the other system components, special-purpose "intelligent" disks have been constructed that allow some of the processing to be moved much closer to the data on secondary storage.

Various implementations have placed special-purpose processor components at different levels. Some have been placed at the disk controller level, some at the disk device itself, and some at the individual track on the disk. Implementations have been oriented towards both full-text retrieval and relational database applications. Full-text retrieval applications have used special-purpose character string-matching devices. Relational database applications have focused primarily on the select and join operators.

Inoue and his colleagues at NTT Communications have developed a special relational database processor called RINDA that performs key database operations such as search and sort at very high speeds. RINDA consists of one or more content search processors (CSP) and relational operational accelerator processors (ROP) connected between the channel of the host computer and the disk controller.

RINDA is controlled by the conventional database management systems DEIMS-5, running on a conventional processor. Studies have shown that RINDA dramatically reduces retrieval time through the use of parallel retrieval from multiple disks and multiple track read mechanisms. For certain queries RINDA performance has been found to be 10 to 100 times better than a conventional database management system alone.

Kitajima and his colleagues at Hitachi have emphasized disk caching techniques to increase online transaction processing throughput. They have experienced improvements ranging from 1.6 at a 50% cache hit ratio, to 3.0 at an 80% cache hit ratio. They have also investigated a data filter within a disk controller to reduce the channel load. This device has shown a throughput improvement factor of between 2 and 100 in an early prototype.

3.5.5   Parallel Processing

One obvious way to improve the performance of database applications, especially when the database is large, is to partition the database function into several independent operations and perform the operations in parallel. Equally obvious is the fact that the success of this approach is heavily dependent on the effectiveness of the partitioning algorithm. Most past research into partitioning algorithms has been directed towards numerically intensive computing applications, and not much has been done on database-related applications.

Most research into partitioning algorithms for database applications has focused on the join operator for the relational model. Some database applications, text searching of document database for example, allow a simple partitioning by document or range of documents.

Most research in the past has been oriented towards coarse-grain parallel systems with only a few processors. However, there is some current interest in massively parallel systems. Professor Tanaka at Hokkaido University has proposed a multiport disk cache system that will support several thousand processors.

3.5.6 Pipelined Operations

In addition to the performance gains from using special purpose hardware such as VLSI components, vector processors, and intelligent disks, additional gains can be realized by segmenting the problem into separate operations and running the operations in parallel, as described in the previous section. Within each parallel system it is possible to gain even more performance by structuring the system in a way that allows multiple operations to be processed in an overlapped fashion. That is, the total processing can be treated as a "pipeline," with information flowing in one end in "raw" form, with the information processed in several distinct steps so that a final fully-processed data object can flow out one end of a pipe while raw data is still flowing in the other end. The components of a database system that have been treated in this fashion include character string matching, join operations, and sorting.

3.5.7 Jukebox

Sony Corporation and Ricoh are building jukeboxes to hold sets of their optical platters and increase total system storage capacities. The availability of consumer products that handle multiple platters enables rapid development of reliable devices in this arena. The availability of jukeboxes reduces pressure to increase the capacity of individual platters, and permits the establishment of standards that represent state-of-the-art technology.

3.5.8 Conclusion

The preceding sections have covered the specific areas where special-purpose hardware has been used to address the performance-related aspects of database management systems. In general, the areas of activity in Japan over the last five years are similar to those pursued in the U.S. and in Europe. The results of the research and development activities, while of a substantial nature, have not yielded any breakthroughs.

The area of hardware support for text processing is a promising innovation. As discussed in the section on object databases, many modern DBMSs provide large fields (Binary Large Objects or BLOBs), but lack extensions for operating on them. BLOBs are useful for storing text fields, but with that facility comes the need to process text. Either extended indexing or fast text searching must be provided before textual BLOBs can be used effectively.

There are very few commercial database products built around special purpose processing hardware, either in Japan or elsewhere. The improving price-performance ratio of conventional computer systems, especially the newer Reduced Instruction Set Computers (RISC), reduce the potential of special-purpose hardware and make it more difficult to recover the significant investment required to develop and produce special-purpose hardware systems.

Japanese industry is in a good position to take advantage of these options, if such hardware developments can be effectively integrated. Japan is a major vendor of storage hardware and large capacity optical units. Together with Japanese capability in image and sound products, there is an excellent structure in place to build vertically integrated multimedia systems.

3.6   Security

Author: Sushil Jajodia

During our visit, we investigated the information security efforts at various sites in Japan. We also received a copy of the Security Guidelines (in English) from Mr. Hideo Setoya, who is the manager of the Information Processing Systems Development Division at MITI. (Since our visit Mr. Setoya moved to another bureau. His successor is Mr. Satoru Ishida.)

Our overall conclusion is that the Japanese are in the very early stages of considering the security aspects of database systems. Their Security Guidelines mainly involve physical and procedural security. Little security work is being supported by the Japanese government. Some work is being done by the Japanese Electronics Industry Association (JEIA), which has a security committee headed by Mr. Koichi Mori.

Lack of interest in security appears to be influenced by two factors:

1 Japanese culture appears to be such that product vendors are trusted to develop correct products.

2 Computers in Japan are not as highly networked as in the West. As a result, the Japanese have not, to our knowledge, suffered major virus attacks or intrusions from unauthorized users.

However, Japanese companies are keenly aware of the information security evaluation and requirements activities in the U.S. and in Europe. For example, Japanese companies such as Hitachi and Fujitsu are working with the United Kingdom's Communications-Electronics Security Group (CESG) so that their companies' products can be evaluated for use in the United Kingdom. Japanese companies also provided detailed comments on the Information Technology Security Evaluation Criteria (ITSEC) published by the European Community (EC).

In the U.S. the major driver for database security is the Department of Defense, which mandates requirements. Industry adapts slowly, but cannot ignore the requirements. The Self-Defense Forces of Japan do not seem to issue such mandates or purchase systems that are vertically integrated, so that these concerns become internal to the suppliers.

Concerns for personal privacy seem negligible in Japan, especially in comparison with Western Europe. Some public databases (see Section 5) seem to provide information which is close to that planned for the Lotus MARKETPLACE product, which was cancelled due to public uproar as a perceived invasion of privacy.

3.7   Database Tools

Author: Toshi Minoura

In addition to the basic DBMS, most users need software that effectively utilizes the information obtained from the databases. High-level tools of this type are referred to as fourth-generation languages, or 4GLs.

In Japan, most software is custom-made, and the use of software tools is not yet common. However, leading computer companies like Fujitsu and Hitachi provide a set of state-of-the-art software tools for their own machines. Package software that can be used on platforms from different vendors has mostly U.S. origins. For example, the most popular 4GL used in Japan is the Japanese version of ACCELL, which runs on Unix-based workstations provided by several Japanese vendors.

To give an idea of the software packages and tools available for the machines produced by Japanese computer manufacturers, we list those provided by Fujitsu for their mainframes.

1 EPG II (Executive Planning Guide).
2 C-NAP II/NA (Needs Analysis), SA (Systems Analysis), DA (Data Analysis).
3 YAC II (Yet Another Control chart), YPS (YAC II Programming System), YPS/APG (YPS Application Program Generator). These are COBOL program generators.
4 ADAM/IRD (Application Development And Management / Information Resource Dictionary).
5 CASET (Computer Aided Software Engineering Tools). An extensive set of CASE tools, including data dictionary support, data structure and form generators, and prototype test support.
6 BAGLES (Business Application Generator's Library for Extensive Support).

Hitachi also provides a similar line-up within its Software Engineering Workbench (SEWB). The PAD (Program Analysis Diagram) system automatically generates COBOL programs from structure diagrams.

Fujitsu provided the following list of application development tools for its workstations.

1 (Knowledge system HCI Server, interface generator).
2 KR (Knowledge Representation and inference).
3 NOAH (New Object-oriented And knowledge media management system for intelligent applications with Human interface). A commercial version of JASMINE.
4 IP (Intelligent Pad). A simple hypermedia system.

As standards for databases and their interfaces become established, the market for generic database tools will increase. Here is an opportunity for established U.S. vendors to serve a growing market. It will of course be necessary to invest in adaptation of these tools to the language and system requirements of the Japanese community.

3.8   Database Management Systems (DBMSs)

Authors: Sushil Jajodia, Toshi Minoura, Gio Wiederhold

As indicated in earlier sections, most databases in current use in Japan operate on U.S. (DB2, IMS, ORACLE, etc.) or German (ADABAS) database management system platforms. Very similar database systems are available on Japanese computers which do not provide compatible operating systems, such as the Hitachi (RDB1), Oki (REAM), and NTT (DEIMS-5) relational database management systems.

These systems are not perceived as being very satisfactory, as shown in [Hayashi:85], summarized in the table introducing Section 3.5. These problems strongly mirror dissatisfaction experienced everywhere among database users. Japanese database system software does not seem to differ inherently in quality from that seen elsewhere. However, comparisons are difficult since systems are in different stages of maturity.

3.8.1   Database Management Systems of Japanese Origin

In this section we describe the current state of affairs with respect to development of database management systems in Japan. Since Japanese industry is very strong in the area of electronic products, it is not surprising that hardware plays an important role in the development of DBMSs. Performance is an overriding consideration for the users of DBMSs. For this reason the Japanese have put their strength to work and are building database accelerators to enhance overall database performance, as described in Section 3.5.4. Projects representative of this enhanced performance follow.

Two notable efforts, one by Hitachi Ltd. and the other by NTT also are described. Hitachi is currently working on XDM/DF (eXtensible Data Manager), a distributed database management system. It provides many advanced distributed database features, including location transparency, unified access interface, and a two-phase commitment protocol.

We also describe the system integration efforts of NTT Data Systems, an independent service company that focuses on consulting and system integration. Every major organization today has systems purchased from several different vendors. These systems must be linked into a unified system, although components may be loosely coupled.

RDB1/DP (Hitachi Ltd.)   . RDB1/DP is Hitachi's commercial relational DBMS. To improve overall performance, RDB1 (Hitachi's commercial relational DBMS), uses a new pipelined vector processor called IDP [Tori:87].

RINDA (NTT).   RINDA is a relational database processor for speeding up two common relational operations – search and sort – efficiently. This makes RINDA especially suitable for performing nonindexed queries. In conventional database management systems, nonindexed queries consume much CPU time and I/O time and are often not feasible. The two common approaches create bottlenecks. If a search is performed on all rows of a relation, the amount of data that must be transferred becomes large and much CPU time is consumed. If on the other hand tuples are sorted on selected columns, the processing cost for sorting is high – on the order of $(n \log n)$ – and a large amount of memory is required.

RINDA removes both bottlenecks by providing specialized hardware that can perform an order n time sort on a large internal memory and on-the-fly search on disk storage.

A key property of RINDA is that it can be easily introduced into the existing systems without any modification of existing applications [Inou:89].

SDC (Kitsuragawa, University of Tokyo).   Kitsuregawa and members of his group at the University of Tokyo are working on a high-performance, parallel relational database server called the Super Database Computer (SDC), for a join-intensive environment. The basic architecture of SDC is shared-nothing providing high performance where search results are independent [Kits:90].

XDM (Hitachi Ltd.).   The XDM (eXtensible Data Manager) is Hitachi's large mainframe DB/DC system which supports both relational and structured databases. It provides many advanced distributed database features including location transparency, unified access interface, and two phase commitment protocol.

3.8.2   Other DBMSs Mentioned in This Report

A Deductive Object-Oriented Database language, QUIXOTE

The core database system (SYNDES) from Tsukuba, which uses QUIXOTE

The JASMINE system being developed by Fujitsu Laboratories Ltd.

The IMAZONE image database construction tools for RICOHBASE

RICOHBASE, an extended relational DBMS supporting linked connections

OMEGA, Object-oriented Multimedia DB developed at the UNLib Tsukuba

The Hitachi RDB1 relational and XDM/DF distributable database management system

REAM, by Oki, an RDBMS being enhanced with RDA

3.8.3   Adaptation to the Japanese Market

To reach the Japanese market, foreign products have to be adapted at least to handle Japanese character sets. In earlier foreign products little consideration was given to handling non-ASCII or non-EBCDIC character representations. The absence of a single standard for Japanese characters hinders foreign developers as well. The simpler conventions do not provide for the following complications found in practical Japanese text:

- o integration of Roman numbers and terms
- o vertical and horizontal orientation
- o font changes concomitant with changes in orientation
- o complications induced by the combination of the first two points
- o layout problems induced by mixed orientations

Some Japanese companies have invested greatly in making these adaptations.

Oracle and NTT Data.   NTT Data uses various database products in building large, vertically integrated applications. They have a copy of the source code of the U.S.developed ORACLE system, and have modified it to meet the needs of the turn-key systems that they build. Recently Oracle Corporation has established an office in Japan to serve their Japanese customers directly with their own, now internationalized products.

ADABAS and Software a.g., Far East.   A similar level of adaptation was made by an entrepreneur to the product of a German company, Software a.g.: ADABAS. This product has achieved an important niche in the Japanese market. It has focused on the IBM and compatible mainframe market, where many other offerings were not suited to adaptation. Ongoing cooperation with the source company and its U.S. offshoot have motivated further internationalization.

For several important areas, such as Japanese textual retrieval for JICST, adaptations to ADABAS have been made available as well. This has created new market opportunities not covered by other DBMS products. Modules, such as report generators specifically oriented toward the Far East market, are also available.

3.9   Summary

The DBMS market is yet far from settled. While RDBMS approaches are well-known, many applications use older and less general software. Where this software has been adapted to the Japanese market it will be at least as hard to replace as in the U.S., where the application codes are yet often older.

However, the demands for new applications and advanced facilities are high, so that there remain many opportunities in this market, which seems to be equally open to all participants.

4. DBMS Product Infrastructure

Author: Diane Smith and John Smith

This section presents the market context within which database technology is deployed, as products and services. It describes the channels used by American companies and the roles these channels play in the Japanese marketplace and in Japanese global marketing strategy. The market factors that have shaped database products in both the U.S. and Japan are identified. The section concludes with a discussion of Japan's response to these drivers.

4.1 DBMS Technology Channels

To facilitate comparison between U.S. and Japanese products and services, we characterize the DBMS marketplace by three channels: off-the-shelf (OTS), original equipment manufacturer (OEM), and systems integration (SI). While this is not the only possible characterization, it does permit us to highlight the differences between the two countries.

"Off-the-shelf" products are sold through the most familiar channel in the U.S. marketplace. Database products distributed through this channel include DBMSs and database tools. Both hardware vendors and independent software vendors sell a wide variety of such products: DBMSs based on the CODASYL, relational, and object data models; DBMSs that operate on mainframes, mini-computers, workstations, personal computers, and database servers.

In the OEM mode, products are marketed to third party, value-added resellers (VARs). VARs typically build applications on top of DBMS products and resell them as "turn-key" systems. While this mode of of marketing a product is frequently thought of as part of the OTS channel, it is distinguished here because this channel is just emerging within Japan, and is worth separate comment.

In systems integration, existing hardware, software and communication products are integrated, frequently with custom software, to produce large customized systems that automate business, engineering, and manufacturing processes. In SI typically, services in addition to products are sold: integration, documentation, installation, and maintenance services as well as the production of custom software.

4.2 DBMS Market Drivers

The Japanese market appears to differ markedly from the U.S. market with respect to DBMS products. In the U.S., there is a strong demand for both OTS products and for open systems. This is particularly true in the commercial marketplace. In the 1970s, this led to the emergence of both hardware and third party independent software vendor-supported DBMS products. In the 1980s, with the widespread acceptance of the relational model as a de facto standard for DBMS interfaces, there was an explosion of DBMS products. In the 1990s, these products are expected to be available on a wide variety of hardware platforms and to be compliant with OS and communications standards.

The demand for standardization of software product interfaces increased in the 1980s and has continued into the 1990s. The relational query language SQL was released as an ANSI standard in 1984. Major efforts are being made to develop application data model standards and interchange standards such as RDA to support computing in networked environments.

In Japan, the emphasis in large corporate software acquisitions has been on buying total system solutions. These large hardware/software systems are typically custom systems developed in partnership by the customer and the vendor, with the vendor not only supplying the system, but installing it, operating it, and maintaining it.

In summary, one can characterize the major U.S. drivers of database technology as being the development of off-the-shelf products and open systems, while in Japan, the drivers appear to be the requirement for total, custom systems. This difference in market drivers in the U.S. and Japan has produced differing patterns as to how the various distribution channels are perceived and used.

4.3   Japanese Positioning

To better understand how database products are positioned with respect to the OTS, OEM, and SI channels in Japan, we first distinguish the different classes of companies that produce these products within Japan. The class of companies most visible outside of Japan is that of the full-product line hardware vendors. These are typically part of very large Japanese corporations. Members of this class that we visited are Hitachi, Mitsubishi, Toshiba, and NTT. IBM Japan also falls into this class although it is not, per se, a Japanese company.

A second class consists of manufacturers of office products and hardware peripherals such as faxes, scanners and printers. Ricoh, visited by the JTEC team, is typical of this class. The final class is that of independent software vendors. The only member of this class visited by JTEC was the Japanese associate of a German company, Software a.g.

4.3.1   Japanese OTS Database Products

Japanese computer hardware companies produce a variety of off-the-shelf database products. Their software offerings are typically products that run on large mainframes and are based on proprietary operating systems. For example, Toshiba produces both a CODASYL-based DBMS and a relational DBMS for its mainframe computer. These products are well supported — they are upgraded on a regular basis to include the same types of features as U.S. DBMS software products. For example, the Hitachi XDM/RD (Relational Database) now supports distributed data.

The Japanese computer companies also offer an interesting range of database hardware products. Hitachi, for example, produces intelligent disks, search engines, and hardware accelerators. Toshiba offers a similar set of products, a number of which use specialized chips produced by Toshiba.

In discussions with Toshiba we explored the rationale for developing specialized hardware, since U.S. companies have not found it profitable to develop a wide range of similar offerings. A number of these products are bundled with either mainframe or peripheral systems. Toshiba views these products as adding to the quality of the overall system in terms of either reliability or performance and therefore are not considered optional. Furthermore, Toshiba is unconcerned about the need to upgrade the specialized chips as technology advances, since this type of consideration is built into its normal engineering and manufacturing processes.

The products discussed at the site visits and described in the brochures made available to us are summarized in Section 3.9.

4.3.2   The OEM Channel in Japan

The OEM channel is used in two different ways in Japan. Hardware vendors use independent software vendor DBMS products to fill out the software product lines for their hardware offerings. For example, Toshiba uses ORACLE on its UNIX-based workstation offering. It also uses a tool package developed by McDonnell-Douglas as part of its software product line.

The second use of the OEM channel is to produce turn-key systems. This is atypical in Japan, although it is standard practice in the U.S., where they represent a major marketplace opportunity. The particular example we saw of a company producing a product for the OEM market was Ricoh. Ricoh has developed a software integration platform called IMAZONE. It integrates the use of Ricoh's scanners, faxes, optical storage devices, and printers for use in building imaging and document management systems. It provides a set of tools (e.g., an image editor; image storage and retrieval software; and a relational DBMS (RICOHBASE)) specially tuned to handle images and graphical data.

Several Japanese value-added resellers (VARs) are using IMAZONE to build turn-key systems. One is building a technical manual management system. A second is building a grading system to support the Japanese "cram" schools. This system will direct assignments faxed in by students to the instructors who will grade them. The instructors will view the assignments in electronic form, use an editor to mark them with grade, corrections and comments, and return them to the students via fax. Electronic copies of the transactions will be stored and managed by the system.

Although it was not on the official visit list, Murata, a small Japanese company that has been succeeding as a VAR, was visited informally by Toshi Minoura. Murata has built a CIM system using the ORACLE DBMS product. This is one of the few examples we saw of this channel being used as it is in the U.S.

4.3.3   System Integration

Because the emphasis in Japan has been on the acquisition of total and custom solutions, systems integration is the most important channel in Japan. To meet this demand, the large Japanese hardware vendors have developed strong, vertically integrated hardware, software and service offerings. These include mainframes and peripherals, operating systems, DBMSs and tools, text and image subsystems, and a service organization that can design, implement, document, test, install and maintain large systems.

Typically, a company like Mitsubishi will specialize in selected vertical markets (e.g., utilities and railroads). To support these markets, the company will develop as part of its product offerings whatever technology is needed. At Mitsubishi, we saw the prototyping of a scanner-based system for the input of utility floor plans. An image recognition system specific to the symbols used on floor plans was being tested. The system being developed links real-time sensors on a plant floor to a display showing the floor plan, and to data representing the interrelationships of equipment on the floor so that problems can be recognized and diagnosed.

The research activities supported by these companies frequently tie in directly to their targeted markets.

4.4   The Japanese Response to the Global Database Market

As the Japanese anticipate expanding their markets, they are responding to the factors they see driving the U.S. and global marketplaces. The U.S. market drivers, open systems and OTS software, also are strong factors in the European and global marketplaces.

The response from the Japanese government to the global market drivers has been twofold. MITI, through INTAP, has initiated a major program on interoperability and is providing significant support of international standards.

Japanese companies have also made a visible and significant commitment to standards support. Each company we visited supports representation on the international standards committees. In addition, they keep in close touch with technology developments worldwide by sending staff members abroad and by interacting with Japanese university faculty that maintain close contact with the international database research community.

Japanese university database faculty are particularly aggressive in interacting with the international research community. This is in part because many of them feel that there is not enough interest in their research by Japanese companies. However, this works to the advantage of the Japanese companies because faculty members become a very efficient means of culling external results and introducing them into Japan, through student training and research publications made available at Japanese language conferences. This and the fact that many Japanese professionals can read English provide efficiency in propagating international technology.

4.5   Observations

While the information we gathered with respect to the Japanese database technology marketplace is purely anecdotal, it set the context for understanding differences between Japan and the U.S. with respect to developing and deploying database technology.

In the U.S., the OEM market is entrepreneurial. The two examples we found in Japan follow this pattern. While the group we visited at Ricoh is part of a relatively large company, it differed from the groups we visited at other large companies in several ways. To begin with, the group is headed by a woman, Dr. Kunii. At no other site did we meet with a woman in a professional leadership role. Not only was the group headed by a woman, but one of the chief technical leads was a female Ph.D. We saw at least one other woman on the staff, a programmer from Ireland.

Dr. Kunii received her Ph.D. from the University of Texas. Members of her staff, both junior and senior, described their work environment as being open, in the American style. They were proud of their creativity and in what they had accomplished. They credited Dr. Kunii with creating their environment, and with the success of the group. There is a shortage of trained scientific workers foreseen in Japan. Since Japan does not easily accept foreigners, we can expect that Dr. Kunii's example presages changes for the future. How these changes will affect the fabric of Japanese society is a question outside the scope of our report.

The requirement for total and customized solutions established in Japan is emerging as a global market driver. U.S. companies are repositioning to meet this demand. Defense contractors have decades of experience in performing systems integration. Typically, they put together teams of companies to deliver the components and services needed to pursue a given opportunity. However, the U.S. defense marketplace is very different from the commercial marketplace. The procurement process is standardized and slow; ideally, selection is made on the basis of technical adequacy and low bid. Continuity is often broken. Requirements are often obsolete and inflexible.

This contrasts with the Japanese commercial marketplace, where procurement is based on long-term strategic relationships and involves deep application knowledge restricted to a limited number of application areas. As discussed in Section 4.3.3, Japanese firms are strongly vertically integrated, and hence are able to supply total solutions without negotiating complex teaming arrangements. They have built up foreign experience and reputation in the Middle East and Asia within their target markets.

Large U.S. firms such as IBM, DEC, and UNISYS are now emphasizing this marketplace. Smaller software companies selling specific applications are offering integration services. We can expect intense competition between the U.S. and Japan over systems integration business in the near term.

5. Database Use Industry

Authors: Charles P. Bourne and Nick Farmer

In addition to database technology we consider the industry that sells information from databases. Funding sources for the government-sponsored services were identified in Section 2 of this report, and include STA (JICST) and MONBUSHO (NACSIS). This industry is mature, and typically uses software that differs from the software provided by generalized DBMS providers, although there are important exceptions, as noted earlier for ADABAS, as adapted by Software a.g., Far East. This industry focuses on effective search services, and on acquisition and maintenance of large information files.

5.1 Database Search Services

In contrast with the computer database searching in the 1960s and 1970s, which was predominantly a mainframe batch searching activity, most of the computer-based search systems in operation throughout the world today are operating now in an interactive online mode. This panel concentrated its attention on interactive mainframe systems, which is the focus of this chapter. New computer architectures, as networked workstations, have not yet impacted the suppliers, whose focus is the maintenance and storage of large databases.

5.1.1 Points of Comparison

In reviewing the Japanese database search services we considered the following attributes as the basis for comparison.

Size of the Service. Thousands of online search systems are in operation today throughout the world. Most of them are strictly inhouse systems that are in operation to serve the needs of individual organizations (e.g., a corporate management information system). Others have been developed to serve larger but limited constituencies (e.g., regional or national law enforcement networks, airline reservations systems). A relatively small number of online systems have been established to operate on a worldwide basis to provide information (often for a fee) to almost any interested user (e.g., the NLM Medline service). Some services have been developed for end-user or consumer markets to serve customer populations with over 100,000 subscribers. We have reviewed the Japanese online services in this context, and have not found any that have yet operated on the scope and scale of activities that are seen with several U.S. services. They would have to go through a development and learning process before they could do that — but they are able to do so.

Content. Online search systems are in operation throughout the world today that collectively address a great variety of types of information to be stored and searched. Online search service is provided throughout the U.S. on a regular production basis with at least the types of file content shown in Table 5.1 (although not usually all provided from the same search service). North American and European online services are extremely competitive with each other, and because of that, have been fairly proactive in developing new system features as enhancements or improvements to their search systems (e.g., multi-file search software, word proximity searching, online search aids, improved document delivery service, improved customer service). The online services in Japan, which are oriented toward Japanese-language databases, generally do not compete directly with North American and European online services. Furthermore, since many of the Japanese systems are government supported and directed towards a particular market segment, e.g., industry or academia, there is little competition within Japan. This lack of competition has resulted in a somewhat slower pace relative to adoption of new system features.

252

Types of File Content	Description (Examples)
bibliographic files	indexing and abstracting records (Biological Abstracts, Chemical Abstracts); catalog records (Catalog of the Library of Congress)
fulltext	full character representation of news publications, journals, newsletters, and other material (New York Times, Washington Post, New England J. of Medicine, Associated Press newswire)
biographic information	information about people (Amer. Men and Women of Science, Who's Who)
directories	organization descriptions (Moody's Corporate Profiles, Encyclopedia of Associations)
financial data	company financial reports (SEC Online), stock and commodity price, financial time series
demographic information	information about populations (1990 U.S. Census data)
images	scanned bit-representations of image data (U.S. trademarks and patent drawings)
chemical structure	representations of chemical structures (Chemical Abstracts Services Registry, Beilstein)
scientific numerical data	physical properties, measurements of various substances, spectrographic or other measured data about various substances

Table 5.1   File content of searchable databases

Operational Support.   The level and extent of computer system support in place at some of the major online services in North America and Europe seems to be far above that provided by almost all of the online services in Japan. Examples of such activities are shown in Table 5.2.

Type of Support	Description (Examples)
search service for multiple files per search	There is concurrent availability of more than 100 files for users to choose from on several U.S. search services.
	Most Japanese search services provide only a few databases.
current file updates	Many U.S. public search services provide daily or even hourly updates to their search files (Official Airline Guide, some news files).
	Few Japanese online services have updates as frequently as daily.
large files	No public online search service in Japan operates with the file sizes and storage requirements experienced by several U.S. online search services.
extensive file maintenance	Several U.S. online search services perform massive file maintenance activities on a regular production basis (many file updates and reloads for multiple files on a single system, with a combined storage size of over 500 Gbytes).
	No large-scale support activities such as these were seen with any of the Japanese online search services.
full-time availability	A 7-day/week, 24-hour/day (public utility equivalent) service with over 99% real availability is a service objective that many U.S. search services approach.
	Few Japanese online services approach this level of computer system support.

Table 5.2   Support levels for database searching

None of the Japanese online systems seemed to be operating with the power and sophistication of computer support activity provided by the U.S. search services.

Database Search Service as an Export Industry.   A small number of the Japanese online services make their online services available to users outside of Japan. Examples are listed in Table 5.3. The actual use of the services outside of Japan is rather small.

Service	Acronym	Host Organization
JICST Online Information System Service	JOIS	JICST of STA
NACSIS Information Retrieval Service	NACSIS-IR	NACSIS of MONBUSHO
Japan Economic Journal	NIKKEI	Nihon Keizai Shimbum, Inc.
COMLINE Business/Industry Monitors	COMLINE	COMLINE Int'l Corp.

Table 5.3   Japanese services available internationally

The STN Service, an international cooperative of online search services that provides service worldwide, includes a Japanese participant (JICST), but this special case, is not an example of a Japanese search service trying to independently reach and serve a global market. Japanese online search services are not a significant export activity at this time.

5.2   Databases as Export Products

This segment of the report will consider databases as a product for distribution inside and outside of Japan.

As pointed out in reports by the Database Promotion Center in Japan [DPC:90], a large and growing number of databases are produced in Japan. However, in contrast with hundreds of North American and European organizations that produce English-language databases and expect to realize some revenue from the use of those databases, few Japanese organizations have prepared databases as a proprietary product to be sold or licensed (particularly outside Japan) as a revenue-generating product for use on computer systems other than those of the originator. A key reason for this is undoubtedly that databases in Japanese have a very limited international market, and few English-language databases are produced in Japan. Specific examples of the few English-language databases produced in Japan and made available to search services outside of Japan are shown in Table 5.4. These are in addition to those listed in Table 5.3. These files are not used extensively outside of Japan.

Supplier Initial Year	Database	Volume Content
Asahi-Shimbum 1986	Asahi-Shimbum Online News fulltext records	> 10 000
COMLINE International Corp. 1986	COMLINE Business Analysis fulltext records	2 000
1986	COMLINE Industrial Monitor daily updates	40 000
	COMLINE Japan Daily daily update Areas: Biotechnology, Chemicals, Computers, Electronics, Industry Automation, Telecommunications, Transportation	
1986	Tokyo Financial Wire citations, daily updates	20 000
Japan Info. Center of Science & Technology (JICST) 1985	JICST File on Science, Technology and Medicine in Japan citations and abstracts	1 000 000
	Japanese Government & Public Research in Progress descriptions of research projects covering 600 Japanese institutions	30 000
Japan National Diet Library 1977	Japan MARC catalog records	700 000
Japan Patent Info. Org. 1955	JAPIO Japanese patents abstracts and drawings	31 000 000
Japanese Standards Assoc.	Kikaku Net citations to Japanese and foreign standards	213 000
JIJI Press Ltd. 1980	JIJI Press Ticker Service JIJI Press wire service fulltext records	
	JIJI Securities Data Service (JSD) Tokyo Stock Exchange Stocks current information	≈ 1 600
Kyodo News Int'l Inc. 1984	Japan Economic Newswire (Tokyo) English-language fulltext newswire stories reported by Kyodo News Service	> 140 000

Table 5.4 to be continued

Supplier Initial Year	Database	Volume Content

Nihon Keizai Shimbum Inc.
(NIKKEI)   1980
	Japan Economic Journal
	    fulltext records
	NEEDS (separate time-series files)
	    Areas: demographics, commodity prices,
	    business/finance, retail point-of-sale data	

1964	NIKKEI Financial File
	    financial time series
	NIKKEI Stock and Bond Price File
	    Stocks traded in Japan
	    twice-daily update
	NIKKEI Telecom II Japan
	    Financial News and Data
	    fulltext coverage of Japanese
	    business/financial community
		1,200

Nomura Research Inst. 1965	NRI/E Japan Economic and Business DB time series for the Japanese economy	5 600
QUICK Corp. 1971	QUICK Information System economic information	
Sumika Technical Info. Service 1983	Japan High Technology Monitor citations	30 000
Teikoku Databank, Ltd.	Teikoku Databank profiles of Japanese companies	45 000

Table 5.4   English language accessible databases

JICST, supported by the prime minister's office through STA, provides various online services such as bibliographic databases and factual databases through the JICST Online Information System, JOIS and JOIS-F respectively, in Japanese. JOIS and JOIS-F run on Hitachi mainframes.

Services are provided to branch offices through a network of 14.4, 19.2, and 64 Kbps lines and then to users through 300-2400 bps lines. Overseas users can also use these systems to access some of the databases but must do so via the Japanese language. In addition, JICST participates in the Scientific and Technical Information Network (STN), which is a worldwide integrated computer network system for scientific and technical information.

Table 5.5 gives details of the various services and their usage.

	JOIS		JOIS-F	STN
Type of Service	Bibliographic DB		Factual DB	Bib. and Fac. DB
When Started	1976		1988	1987 (in Japan)
Number DB	15		7	96
Number Items	23M		0.6M	67M
Used Hours/Month	12 000		30	3 000 (Japan)
Number Queries/Month	88 000		250	26 000 (Japan)
Number of users	('90)	('86)	('90)	('90)
	8 700	4 600	900	2 500 (Japan)
Company	74%	76%	85%	79%
University	9	11	5	11
Government	5	5	4	5
Institute	3	3	2	3
Hospital	3	3	-	-
Other	6	2	4	2

JOIS: JICST Online Information System (Japanese)
JOIS-F: JICST-Factual Database System (Japanese)
STN: Scientific and Technological Network International:
     USA-Germany-Japan (English)

Table 5.5   JICST database parameters

The Science Information System (SIS) of MONBUSHO has NACSIS at its center. SIS electronically links university libraries, computer centers, and national research institutes (such as the National Lab for High Energy Physics), and provides various online database services. The communication hardware part of this service is the Science Information Network (SIN), which is a privately operated packet switching network employing packet multiplexers installed throughout Japan at major research areas. This network will serve as the main communication facility for the Inter-University Computer Network of Japan (an N-1 network). Plans are to permit fulltext, graphics, voice and image communications. NACSIS's computer system includes Hitachi mainframes (M-684H, M-682H) with special database accelerator hardware, and large magnetic, optical and semiconductor disks. A 10 Mbps Ethernet is used internally for R&D, and to provide workstation access to the main system. To provide electronic mail service, an NEC ACOS 1000 mainframe and disks are provided, along with two 48 Kbps lines to SIN and some lower speed lines to public telephone networks. From SIN a 9.6 Kbps line connects to the British Library, and a 14.4 Kbps line connects to NSF and the Library of Congress, both in Washington, D.C.

A substantial set of services is associated with cataloging, aiming eventually at having only one catalog of all scholarly material in Japanese universities. Basic software is XDM-RDB enhanced to allow multi-valued entries. Currently almost 500 concurrent terminals can be supported, with an average interval of about 45 seconds between commands per user (thinking time). Most Japanese workstations can be used as cataloging terminals as well as IBM 5500-series terminals. A special full-screen interface has been provided to allow the input and display of Japanese characters.

For retrieval, about thirty databases can be queried including standard databases such as MathSci, COMPENDEX Plus, and the Harvard Business Review. The NACSIS databases include reported synopses or research projects conducted through research grants-in-aid by the Ministry of Education (Japanese and English), dissertation index (Japanese), academic conference papers (Japanese and English), a union catalog of Japanese and foreign books and serials, and a database directory (Japanese). The NACSIS databases include about three million pieces of data from Japanese university library catalogs. Hitachi provides an enhanced version of the U.S. system ORION, on which many applications have been written to adapt the user interface. Typically, several dozen users will be concurrently on the system.

NACSIS focuses on service, but it has a number of research activities, as well. There is substantial interest in advanced hardware such as optical media, and in parallel systems such as an N-cube; new database models such as nested-relation; quality control methods for database construction; human interfaces; and formal description languages for communication protocols based on temporal logic. However, the staff is concerned that performance not be degraded by the use of new techniques.

While we were at NACSIS, we were given a demonstration of the query system, which generated about two dozen references to object databases from Japanese authors. Although several members of the JTEC database team had queried other databases available in the U.S., accessing the NACSIS system would have been very helpful in deciding which sites to visit. We encourage future teams to use this service, which is available via the NSF. At the same time the team had the opportunity to discuss impediments to its use in the U.S. Although the NSF staff is exceptionally cooperative and helpful, because the facility uses specialized hardware, it is difficult for remote researchers to use. This is an important item for potential improvement.

Some files about Japanese activity are produced by organizations outside of Japan. Articles in Japanese scientific and technical journals have been routinely covered for years by the major international indexing and abstracting services outside of Japan (e.g., Biological Abstracts, Chemical Abstracts, Engineering Index, Index Medicus, and Mathematical Reviews). Furthermore, several databases have recently been produced by Western organizations to specifically cover Japanese activities for Western users (e.g., Japan Technology, JAPI).

One of the major reasons for the low number of databases produced by the Japanese for export is simply that the international information industry operates largely with English-language information, and English is not the primary language of the Japanese database producers. In comparison with many other countries where the database is originally produced in English, any Japanese database must undergo a Japanese-to-English translation effort before it can be made available as a significant export product. North American and European database producers would be similarly disadvantaged if the international information industry happened to serve primarily a Japanese-speaking customer base.

Given the extra effort and cost that is required for Japanese organizations to produce English-language databases, it does not seem likely that the Japanese information industry will produce English-language databases that would be direct competitors to existing U.S. databases. This would be particularly true for any databases that provide worldwide coverage of a particular subject area (e.g., Medline, Biological Abstracts, Mathematical Reviews), but it might be less true for niche databases with an audience that is accustomed to paying higher prices for information (e.g., Pacific Rim business information). There are several efforts to develop an effective Japanese-to-English machine translation capability, but current systems do not seem to be operating yet with a cost and performance level that is likely to have a significant impact in the immediate future.

Japanese database producers have little experience to date in providing databases and their updates to multiple computer services worldwide, and in providing the accompanying marketing, training and customer support services to the recipients of those databases. In contrast with some U.S. database producers (e.g., NTIS, NLM) who provide their databases and current updates to more than twenty organizations worldwide, very few Japanese database producers have the experience of providing their databases, updates, and associated support to more than two or three other organizations.

In summary, the Japanese database industry is in a position to develop and improve the information products that are relevant to activity in Japan (e.g., Japanese newswires, Japanese organization directories, Japanese stock prices and time series data, and other source publications), but does not appear to be in a position to provide significant direct competition with the U.S. database industry in topical areas.

5.3   Database Technology

Currently available Japanese databases represent a range of technical complexity with respect to record structure and file organization that is quite familiar to U.S. database producers and search services. Files and record structures associated with library catalog files (Japan MARC vs. LC MARC), bibliographic files (JICST-E vs. Engineering Index), company directory files (Teikoku vs. Dun's), and newswire services (Kyodo vs. UPI) are of the same degree of technical complexity for databases produced in both countries.

However, the U.S. producers and services have, on a case-by-case basis, pushed a relatively plain database technology to establish more complex structures and capabilities in the file and record formats to increase utility and advantage for the user. These organizations have, in a sense, pushed the operational envelopes of the search system capabilities by changing file and record structures, not by changing the computer hardware requirements. Examples of expanded file features in operation today in the U.S. include:

- expansion of the number of separately searchable fields in a record (say, over 200)
- expansion of the number of records that can be searched at one time in a single file (say, over 20 million records per file)
- expansion of the number of separate files that can be searched at one time by the user (say, over 200)
- searching and consolidation of master/subordinate records (say, sections within a handbook, questions within a questionnaire, Congressional Hearings records subordinate to a specific Bill).

In no case did we see Japanese databases that matched the large and more complex U.S. databases of the type listed above. We have no reason to believe that they could not handle these problems. We mention it only to note that U.S. institutions have already faced and passed a number of technical and application obstacles that the Japanese probably have not faced yet. In that regard, the U.S. could be considered to be further ahead with database technology.

Image Management.   There is one area of database technology where the Japanese should receive special recognition, namely high quality image storage and retrieval. Team members visited the National Ethnology Museum to observe a system used there to store high-quality three-dimensional color images of museum artifacts, along with associated descriptive information. A file of over 50,000 such images had already been assembled (at 7 MB/image, this represented a total storage volume of 350,000 MB), and a retrieval capability implemented for an inhouse system to search, retrieve, and display specific color images on the basis of their indexed attributes. The system was built by the IBM Tokyo Research Laboratory. A dial-up capability was planned for researchers at remote locations.

Another color-image storage and retrieval system was demonstrated by NTT Data Communication Systems Corp. in Tokyo for operational use by the Textile Rationalization Agency. Both of these image retrieval systems were developed by Japanese R&D organizations, but neither of them have received any extensive operational use to date.

Additional Japanese image storage and retrieval systems were seen at Ricoh, IBM Japan, and other institutions as part of office information systems in development. Several other systems were mentioned by our hosts during our visits to various Japanese organizations.

Several U.S. search systems also provide operational online search, retrieval, and display of scanned images (e.g., U.S. trademarks) or generated images (e.g., chemical structures), but this aspect is still not seen on a large scale in the U.S.

Multimedia storage and retrieval systems appear to be an area where the Japanese organizations are as advanced as those in the U.S.

5.4   Summary Assessment

For database search services, the Japanese organizations at this time are judged to be:

- behind the U.S. in terms of size and extent of offerings, technical features, and performance
- not a significant challenge to the U.S. online search service industry
- not catching up in database services.

For database content as an export product, the Japanese organizations at this time are judged to be:

- far behind the U.S. in producing databases as an export product
- short on experience in producing/supporting databases for use by large numbers of search services
- facing an inherent and continuing disadvantage in competing to produce English-language products
- not a significant challenge to the U.S. database industry
- not catching up in database content production.

Japanese online database service organizations at this time are judged to be:
- familiar and experienced with mainstream technology
- less familiar and experienced with large and complex files and retrieval situations that tend to stretch the bounds of normal database practice
- probably as current as U.S. organizations with regard to image or multimedia retrieval systems
- catching up with technology

6. Summary

In this section we integrate the findings of the preceding chapters and focus on areas where Japanese efforts have been intense, and are likely to have effects that transcend Japan in a significant way.

6.1 Multimedia Databases

In terms of infrastructure technology, the most significant advances we saw were in multimedia technology. By building database systems that exploit the Japanese strength in electronic devices, such as high-capacity optical and magneto-optical storage, document and image scanners, and image presentation on standard video, high-definition video, and computer-driven monochrome and colorfax equipment, unique advances are being made. These capabilities are not yet well integrated into networks and standards are lagging. The Japanese ISDN network is poised for a major expansion in bandwidth (from 256 KB to 4 GB). The availability of such links will further motivate this direction and cause pressure for integration of advanced multimedia, especially image technology, into databases.

Today there is significant dependence in Japan on foreign database management system technology. Most of the vendors of these database management systems are planning to provide support for the management of large, variable-sized data elements, as needed for multimedia database management. It will depend on the effectiveness of these extensions whether established DBMSs will be used for the multimedia services of the future. Otherwise it will be necessary for the developers of multimedia systems to develop their own DBMSs. The availability of standards such as SQL and ADA, makes entry of new DBMSs that satisfy these standards feasible. Even if they are less mature, having multimedia capability can be a decisive factor in the market.

Intermediary solutions do exist. Conventional DBMSs can reference images in distinct files for images and the large objects, and these can be accessed indirectly. However, such solutions are more complex to manage and are likely to be intermediate solutions. Furthermore, if pattern matching or associative access to image and voice data becomes a reality, then the indirect approach will no longer be feasible.

It is becoming understood that eventually access to multimedia databases will be required. Associative access means finding an image that 'looks like this image' or that contains features 'like these'. Speech files can be interpreted for voice print identification as well as contents. Research into this problem is in the early stages, both in the U.S. and in Japan, so that its relative success cannot now be assessed. Japanese efforts have focused on neural-net technology, which is likely to be quite effective for the simpler matching problems, but may not deal well with feature-based searching. The availability of excellent technology in Japanese laboratories reduces their entry cost for researchers interested in this field. If this research direction either catches the interest of Japanese industrial research, or if academic research in this field finds support, rapid progress is possible.

6.2 Government and Database Research and Development

The influence of governmental initiatives seems to be pervasive, but much less deep than other reports on Japanese technology indicate. It may also be less deep than governmental officials hope and surmise.

As indicated in Section 2, the Japanese academic establishment receives relatively little research project and student support from the Japanese government; support for industrial research laboratories is also minor. There are of course substantial government-funded research laboratories, for which governmental support is critical.

But overall, the direct government influence on technology directions seems minor. However, there is a very strong indirect effect. The participants meet regularly in committees and workshops. This communication benefits rapid dissemination of Japanese research, and even more importantly, of evaluated foreign research.

The dependence on foreign research does cause some faddism, since novel and superficial ideas are easier to disseminate in discussion groups than deep results. However, weak ideas are rapidly recognized when put to the test in industrial research laboratories. When the ideas are government sponsored, they may live longer, but are unlikely to confuse the primary direction of Japanese industry.

Acknowledgments

This study was supported by the National Science Foundation, the Department of Energy, and the Department of Commerce. Individuals were also partly supported by their institutions. Operational management of this study rested with the JTEC office at Loyola College in Maryland. Duane Shelton accompanied us in Japan. Important contributions were made by Geoff Holdridge, specifically the graphics for the qualitative comparison (see Executive Summary). Without the assistance of all supporters, institutional and personal, this report could not have been created. Most of the arrangements for our visit were made by Cecil Uyehara under contract with Loyola College. His knowledge, insight, and participation in the study visit considerably enhanced this report.

We also must convey a warm appreciation to our Japanese hosts. They handled our questions cooperatively and with concern, often providing needed background information. At many sites, informative formal presentations had been prepared at considerable effort. There were also occasions with wonderful food and beautiful scenery. Even though the press of time was always upon us, we also were able to appreciate the country and its inhabitants.

We thank our Japanese hosts for their useful comments during the review process of this report.

Appendices

A. Participants' Biographies

David Beech

Affiliation: Oracle Corporation, 500 Oracle Parkway, Redwood Shores, CA 94065

Telephone: 415-506-6420 Fax: 415-506-7200

Email: dbeech@oracle.com

David Beech is Senior Architect and Manager of Object Systems for Oracle Corporation. He joined Oracle in 1988 after eight years with Hewlett-Packard Laboratories, where he initiated work in object databases in 1982, which evolved into the Iris project, for which he designed and implemented the Object SQL language. Prior to this, he was with IBM from 1963 to 1980 and was a member of the original design team for the DB2 relational database system from 1976 to 1979. Earlier work was in programming languages, where he was PL/I Language Manager for IBM and was a major contributor to the design, implementation, formal specification and standardization of the language. He has also pursued interests in user interfaces, and was chairman of the IFIP Working Group 2.7 on Computer System User Interfaces from 1982-1989. He has published numerous technical papers, and has chaired and organized international conferences. He received his M.A. in Mathematics from the University of Cambridge, and initially taught mathematics for five years.

Charles Bourne

Affiliation: DIALOG Information Services, 3460 Hillview Avenue, Palo Alto, CA 94304

Telephone: 415-858-3775 Fax: 415-858-3847

Charles Bourne is Vice President of DIALOG Information Services, where he has been in a product development/product manager capacity since 1976. From 1971-76 he was simultaneously Professor-in-Residence, School of Library and Information Studies, and Director, Institute of Library Research, both at the University of California-Berkeley. He has worked on the development of a great variety of computer-based information systems. He has served on advisory boards to several professional publications. He was a consulting correspondent to the National Academy of Science Committee on Scientific and Technical Information, a UNESCO consultant to Indonesia and Tanzania, a U.S. National Academy of Sciences consultant to Ghana, and a member of the U.S.-Egyptian Task Force on Technical Information. He is presently a member of the Library of Congress Network Advisory Committee. He received his B.S.E.E. from the University of California-Berkeley, and his M.S.I.E. from Stanford University. He has been President of the American Society for Information Science and a member of the Board of Directors of the National Information Standards Organization.

Nick Farmer

Affiliation: Chemical Abstracts Service, 2540 Olentangy River Road, Columbus, Ohio 43210

Telephone: 614-447-3714 Fax: 614-447-3713

Email: naf20@cas.org

Nick A. Farmer is Director of Information Systems at the American Chemical Society's Chemical Abstracts Service. He is responsible for all aspects of computer systems, including research, technology, development and operations. Farmer joined Chemical Abstracts Service in 1970 as a senior programmer and subsequently served as advanced development manager, development projects manager, and senior research and development engineer before being named Assistant Director of Research and Development in 1982, and Director of Research and Development in 1984. He was appointed Director of Information Systems in 1986. In addition to his responsibilities at Chemical Abstracts Service, Farmer is a member of the Board of Directors of Hampden Data Services, a software development company located in the United Kingdom. Farmer received the B.S. and M.S. degrees in electrical engineering from the University of Maryland.

Sushil Jajodia

Affiliation: George Mason University, ISSE Department, Science and Technology II, Room 459, Fairfax, VA 22030-4444

Telephone: 703-993-1653 Fax: 703-993-1521

Email: jajodia@gmuvax2.gmu.edu

Sushil Jajodia is Professor, Information Systems and Systems Engineering at the George Mason University. He joined GMU after serving as Director of the Database and Expert Systems Program within the Division of Information, Robotics, and Intelligent Systems at the National Science Foundation. Previously he was the head of the Database and Distributed Systems Section in the Computer Science and Systems Branch at the Naval Research Laboratory, Washington, D.C., and Associate Professor of Computer Science and Director of Graduate Studies at the University of Missouri, Columbia. His research interests include information systems security, database management and distributed systems, and parallel computing. He has published more than sixty technical papers in refereed journals and conference proceedings and has co-edited three books. He has served in different capacities for various journals and conferences. He is on the editorial board of the IEEE Transactions on Knowledge and Data Engineering. He is a senior member of IEEE Computer Society and a member of the Association for Computing Machinery. Jajodia received his Ph.D. from the University of Oregon, Eugene.

David Kahaner

Affiliation: Office of Naval Research, Asia, APO San Francisco, 96503-0007

Telephone: 81 3 3401-8978 Fax: 81 3 3403-9670

Email: kahaner@xroads.cc.u-tokyo.ac.jp

David K. Kahaner joined the Office of Naval Research, Asia in November 1989. He obtained his Ph.D. in applied mathematics from Stevens Institute of Technology in 1968. From 1978 until 1989 Dr. Kahaner was a group leader in the Center for Computing and Applied Mathematics at the National Institute of Standards and Technology, formerly the National Bureau of Standards. He is currently on leave of absence from that position. He was responsible for scientific software and library development on both large and small computers. From 1968 until 1979 he was in the Computing Division at Los Alamos National Laboratory. Dr. Kahaner is the author of two books and more than fifty research papers. He also edits a column on scientific applications of computers for the Society of Industrial and Applied Mathematics. He has had sabbatical appointments at the University of Michigan, Vienna, Turin, and the ETH in Zurich. His major research interests are in the development of algorithms and associated software. His programs for solution of differential equations, evaluation of integrals, random numbers, and others are used in many scientific computing laboratories. Since joining ONR's Tokyo office, Dr. Kahaner has written more than thirty reports on computing activities in Japan, which are circulated to hundreds of readers worldwide.

Toshi Minoura

Affiliation: Oregon State University, Dept. of Computer Science, Corvallis, Oregon 97331.

Telephone: 503-737-5574 Fax: 503-737-3014

Email: minoura@cs.orst.edu

Toshimi Minoura is Associate Professor of Computer Science at Oregon State University. He has conducted research on deadlock problems, true-copy token schemes, multi-version concurrency control, and reliable storage subsystems. He also supervised an application development using a 4GL system for the U.S. Environmental Protection Agency. He is currently working on an action-base system for manufacturing control, which is an active object system using transition rules. He was co-recipient of the 1988 Asahi Newspaper Invention Award for his contribution to a rule-based process control system. This technology is widely used to fully automate large power plants in Japan. Dr. Minoura received the B.S. and M.S. degrees from Tokyo University in 1968 and 1979 and the Ph.D. degree from Stanford University in 1980, all in Electrical Engineering.

Diane Smith

Affiliation: Xerox Advance Information Technology, 4 Cambridge Center, Cambridge, MA 02142.

Telephone: 617-499-4404 Fax: 617-499-4409

Email: dsmith@xait.xerox.com,

Dr. Diane Smith is the Director of Technology for Xerox Advanced Information Technology (XAIT). She is responsible for setting technology directions, the execution of projects, and technology transfer activities. She has held this position since 1979 when XAIT was a division of Computer Corporation of America (CCA). In 1988, she transitioned the CCA Advanced Information Technology (both staff and technology) into the corporate structure of Xerox. She has participated in the development of technology in the areas of object management, database design tools and methodologies. Her group developed an object-oriented data management program incorporating advances in spatial data handling, inferencing, and interoperability. She led the development of a database design workbench supporting requirements analysis, and conceptual, logical and physical design. Her product group is currently developing a workflow manager which supports the definition and execution of long-term processes using and developing complex objects. Prior to joining CCA, she taught in the Department of Computer Science at the University of Utah.

John Smith

Affiliation: Digital Equipment Corporation, 55 Northeastern Blvd., Nashua, NH 03062

Email: jmsmith@databs.dec.com,

Dr. John Miles Smith joined Digital Equipment in 1988 and is manager of the Database Tools group. He is responsible for defining the end-user and application development toolset layered on Digital's Database Management Systems. His technology interests include multimedia document management, engineering data management and the user environment. He was previously at Computer Corporation of America as Vice President of the Research and Systems Division. After joining CCA in 1979, he was responsible for the acquisition and execution of contract R&D projects in the areas of Distributed Database Systems, Heterogeneous Database Integration, CAD/CAM Data Management, Highly-Available Database Systems, and Expert Database Systems. He was on the faculty of the University of Utah from 1972 to 1978. He and his wife, Diane, built a research program in database technology with notable contributions in query processing, database design methodologies, data models, and database machines.

Gio Wiederhold

Affiliation: Stanford University, Dept. of Computer Science, Stanford, CA 94305-2140.
Telephone: 415-725-8363 Fax: 415-725-7411
Email: gio@cs.stanford.edu

Gio Wiederhold is a professor of Computer Science and Medicine (Research) at Stanford University. He worked in industry from 1958 until 1976, when he left industry to obtain a Ph.D. at the University of California in San Francisco. Since that time he has been on the Stanford faculty. He is active in the application and development of knowledge-based techniques to database management. He is the Editor-in-Chief for ACM's Transactions of Database Systems and Associate Editor of Springer-Verlag's M.D. Computing magazine. Wiederhold has written more than 200 publications in computing and medicine, including a widely used McGraw-Hill textbook on Database Design, and a 1987 book, File Organization for Database Design. A textbook on Medical Informatics, with Ted Shortliffe, was published in 1991. He has been chairman and program chairman of several conferences. He consults for many governmental and commercial enterprises, including the United Nations Development Program, the U.S. Department of Health and Human Services, various U.S. defense agencies, Silicon Valley innovators and companies in Japan and Europe. From 1991 to 1993 he is on research leave at DARPA, managing their programs in knowledge and databases.

B. Sites Visited and Contacts

6.2.1   Government

Ministry of International Trade and Industry (MITI)
Information Systems Development Division
Machinery and Information Industries Bureau
Address: 1-3-1 Kasumigaseki, Chiyoda-ku, Tokyo 100
Telephone: 3-3580-3922
People Visited: Mr. Hideo Setoya

Institute for New Generation Computer Technology (ICOT)
Address: Mita Kokusai Bldg, 1-1-28 Mita, Minato-ku, Tokyo 108
Telephone: 3-3456-3195
People Visited:
Dr. Kazuhiro Fuchi, Director, Research Center
Takashi Kurozumi, Deputy Director, Research Center
Kazumasa Yokota, Chief, Third Research Laboratory
Dr. Shumichi Uchida, Manager, Research Department

Information Technology Promotion Agency
Address: Shuwa-Shibakoen 3 - chome Bldg., 3-1-38, Shibakoen, Minato-ku, Tokyo 105
Telephone: +81-3-3433-2350 Fax: +81-3-3437-5386
People Visited: Dr. Akio Tojo, Managing Director

Japan Information Center of Science and Technology (JICST)
Address: 2-5-2 Nagatocho, Chiyoda-ku, Tokyo 100
Telephone: 3-581-6411
People Visited: Ms. Hisako Uchida

6.2.2   Industry

Fujitsu at INTAP
Address: 24 Daikyocho, Sjinjuku-ku, Tokyo 160
Telephone: 3-3358-2721
People Visited:
Mr. Shozo Tanaka, Senior Manager
Mr. Fumiaki Tsuboi, Manager, 1st Engineering Department
Mr. Yoshio Izumida, Section Manager, Artificial Intelligence Laboratory
Mr. Hiroshi Ishikawa, Researcher, Knowledge-Based Engineering Section

Hitachi
Address: 1099 Ohzenji, Asu-ku, Kawasaki 215
Telephone: 044-966-9111
People Visited:
Takashige Kubo, Deputy General Manager, Systems Development Laboratory
Seiichi Yoshizumi, Department Manager, 3rd Research Department, SDL

Hiromichi Fujisawa, Senior Researcher, Central Research Lab
Shunichi Torii, Senior Researcher, Advanced Processor Research Department, CRL
Kazuhiro Satoh, Senior Researcher, 3rd Research Department, SDL
Shigeru Yoneda, Senior Researcher, R/D Planning Office, SDL
Hiroyuki Kitajima, Senior Researcher, 3rd Research Department, SDL
Hidefumi Kondo, Senior Researcher, 5th Department, SDL
Kazuo Masai, Senior Engineer, Software Development Center

IBM Japan

Address: Tokyo Research Laboratory 5-19, Sanbancho, Chiyoda-ku, Tokyo 102
Telephone: +81-3-3288-8280
People Visited:
Dr. Jung-Kook Hong, Manager, Applied Image Processing Systems
Mr. Kohichi Kajitani, Researcher
Dr. Norihisa Suzuki, Director

Kozo Keikaku Engineering

Address: 4-38-13, Honcho Nakano-ku, Tokyo
Telephone: 3382-6581
People Visited:
Hiroshi Ando, Senior Researcher
Terumi Hanmyo, Chief of Research and Development Department

Mitsubishi Electric Corp.

Address: 5-1-1 Ofuna, Kamakura, Kanagawa 247
People Visited:
Mr. Junichi Shibayama
Mr. Satoshi Tanaka
Mr. Koji Wakimoto

NEC

Address: Ugarashi Bldg, 2-11-5 Shibaura, Minato-ku, Tokyo 108
Telephone: 3-5467-1080
People Visited:
Kiichi Fujino, Vice President, C & C Software Development Group
Masao Matsumoto, Associate Chief Engineer, C & C Software Development Group
Kunihiro Sugawara, Assistant General Manager, EDP Systems Engineering Division
Isao Kamoi, Engineering Manager, Database Development Department
Ryuichi Ogawa, Supervisor, Applied Information Technology Research Laboratory
Kyoji Kawagoe, Research Manager, Terminal Systems Research Laboratory
Yoichi Miyashita, Engineering Manager, Software Architecture Department
Shuji Nakata, Systems Manager, 2nd Systems Department
Kunitoshi Tsuruoka, Research Manager, Basic Technologies Research Laboratory

NTT Processing Laboratories

Address: 1-1-7 Uchisaiwaicho, Chiyoda-ku, Tokyo 100

Telephone: 0468-59-2694
People Visited:
Dr. Masato Haihara, Director
Mr. Masaharu Araki, R&D Public Relations

NTT Data Services

Address: 1-26-5 Toranomon, Minato-ku, Tokyo 105
Telephone: 3-3580-4535
People Visited:
Yutoki Sasaki, International Affairs
Tsutomu Shibata
Akikazu Ida
Kouichi Suzuki
Dr. Y. Tachibana, Senior Vice president

Oki Electric Industry Co. Ltd.

Address: 4-11-22 Shibaura, Minato-ku, Tokyo 108
Telephone: 3-3456-3219
People Visited:
Mr. Yunosuke Haga, General Manager, Systems Laboratory
Mr. Suguru Kawakami, Computer Systems R & D Division
Dr. Atsushi Ohori, Senior Researcher, Kansai Laboratory
Dr. Nobuyoshi Miyazaki, Senior Researcher, Manager, Systems Laboratory

Ricoh

Address: Tomin-Nissei-Kasugacho Bldg., 1-1-17 Koishikawa, Bunkyo-ku, Tokyo 112
Telephone: 3-3815-7261
People Visited: Dr. Hideko Kunii, General Manager, Software Division

Software AG, Far East

Address: 1-6-1 Nishi Shinjuku, Shinjuku-ku, Tokyo 160
Telephone: 3-3340-2467
People Visited: Mr. Y. Ishii, President

Toshiba

Address: 1 Komukai Toshibacho, Kawasaki 215
Telephone: 44-549-2078
People Visited: Dr. Kazuo Narita

Universities

Hokkaido University

Address: 8 Nishi, 13 Kita-Ku, Sapporo 060
Telephone: 011-716-2111
People Visited: Professor Yuzuru Tanaka

Kobe University
Address: Rokkodai Nada, Kobe 657
Telephone: 78-881-1212
People Visited:
Professor Katsumi Tanaka and Professor Shojiro Nishio

Kyoto University
Address: Sakyoku, Kyoto
People Visited: Professor Yahiko Kambayashi

Ryukoku University
Address: Seta, Otsu 520-21
Telephone: 0775-43-5111
People Visited: Professor Toshiyuki Sakai

Tokyo University
Address: 7-3-1 Hongo, Bunkyo-ku, Tokyo 113
Telephone: 3-3816-1783
People Visited: Professor T.L. Kunii

Aichi Institute of Technology, Toyota, Nagoya
Address: 1247 Yachigusa, Yagusa-cho, Toyota, Aichi
Telephone: 0565-48-8121
People Visited: Professor S. Kito

Tsukuba University
Address: Tennodai, Tsukuba, Ibaraki 305
Telephone: 0298-53-5532
People Visited: Professor H. Kitagawa and Professor Y. Fujiwara

University of Library and Information Science
Address: 1-2 Kasuga, Tsukuba, Ibaraki 305
Telephone: 0298-52-0511
People Visited: Prof. Yoshifumi Masunaga

Kyushu University
Address: 6-10-1 Hakozaki, Fukuoka 812
Telephone: 92-641-1101
People Visited:
Dr. Toshihisa Takagi, Associate Professor
Mr. Susumu Goto, Ph.D. Student
Dr. Hirofumi Amano, Research Associate
Dr. Mohammed E. El-Sharkawi, Research Associate

6.2.3   Research Laboratories

Interactive Interface Systems Laboratory at ETL
   Address: 1-1-4 Umezono, Tsukuba Science City, Ibaraki 305
   Telephone: 0298-54-5413
   People Visited:
   Dr. Akio Tojo
   Dr. Toshikazu Kato

Research Center for Advanced Science and Technology (RCAST)
   Address: 4-6-1 Komaba, Meguro-ku, Tokyo 153
   Telephone: 3-481-4483
   People Visited:
   Setsuo Osuga, Professor
   Koichi Hori, Associate Professor
   Hirayuki Yamanouchi, Research Assistant

6.2.4   Inter-University Research Institutes

National Museum of Ethnology
   Address: 10-1 Banpaku, Senri, Suita, Osaka 565
   People Visited: Dr. Shigeharu Sugita

National Center for Science Information Systems (NACSIS)
   Address 3-29-1, Otsuka, Bunkyo-ku, Tokyo
   Telephone: 3-3942-2351
   People Visited:
   Prof. Akira Miyazawa
   Prof. Hisao Yamada, Director, R&D Department
   Prof. Teruo Koyama
   Prof. Masamitsu Negishi
   Prof. Kimio Ohno, General Coordinator
   Prof. Hiromichi Hashizume

C. Trip Reports

MONDAY, MARCH 25, 1991

Site Visited:	Oki Electric Industry Co. Ltd.
	Tokyo

People Visited: Yunosuke Haga
                       General Manager
                       Systems Laboratory
                       Research & Development Group

                       Suguru Kawakami
                       Computer Systems R&D Division

                       Dr. Atsushi Ohori
                       Senior Researcher
                       Kansai Laboratory

                       Dr. Nobuyoshi Miyazaki
                       Senior Researcher, Manager
                       Knowledge Information Processing Department
                       Systems Laboratory

JTEC Participants: Jajodia, J. Smith, Farmer, Minoura, Shelton

Notes taken by: Jajodia

Oki Electric is involved in many activities related to information systems worldwide. Only three groups were represented at the meeting; a fourth group (CAD Department) sent written responses to a questionnaire that was sent by JTEC in advance. These groups represent only a small part of Oki's overall activities in databases.

The principal database product is REAM, a relational DBMS that runs on proprietary Oki Operating System and UNIX on Oki minicomputers and workstations. A distributed, open version is under development that would be ported to non-Oki platforms.

ORACLE has been ported to run on Oki minicomputers.

Dr. Ohori heads a research group in the Kansai Laboratory which is located in Osaka. Currently the group consists of Dr. Ohori and one other member. The group is investigating theoretical aspects of integrating databases and programming languages. Dr. Ohori finished his Ph.D. in 1989 at the University of Pennsylvania under the direction of Professor Peter Buneman. Dr. Ohori is continuing his collaboration with Professor Buneman. In addition, he is also collaborating with Professor Joachim Schmidt of the University of Hamburg. Dr. Miyazaki and his group in the Systems Laboratory participate in ICOT projects PHI [Hani:91] [Miya:89] and QUIXOTE [Mori:90].

Site Visited:	Hitachi, Systems Development Laboratory Kawasaki
People Visited:	Takashige Kubo Deputy General Manager Systems Development Laboratory (SDL) Seiichi Yoshizumi Department Manager 3rd Research Department, SDL Hiromichi Fujisawa Senior Researcher Central Research Lab (CRL) and Software Development Center Shunichi Torii Senior Researcher Advanced Processor Research Department, CRL Kazuhiro Satoh Senior Researcher 3rd Research Department, SDL Shigeru Yoneda Senior Researcher R&D Planning Office, SDL Hiroyuki Kitajima Senior Researcher 3rd Research Department, SDL Hidefumi Kondo Senior Researcher 5th Department, SDL Kazuo Masai Senior Engineer Software Development Center
JTEC Participants:	D. Smith, Bourne, Kahaner, Wiederhold, Beech, Uyehara
Notes taken by:	Beech

We visited Hitachi's Systems Development Laboratory near Kawasaki and were welcomed by Mr. Takashige Kubo.   We were treated to a number of substantial presentations describing major projects there and in related parts of the company.   Since 1978 the SDL has been the focus for software R&D, with the Central Research Laboratory focusing primarily on hardware, and an Advanced Research Laboratory pursuing a 10- to 20-year vision.

One major theme was hardware assistance for DBMS performance.

Work on intelligent disk system technologies was presented by Hiroyuki Kitajima, with emphasis on disk caching to increase OLTP traffic (showing a factor of 1.6 improvement at a 5% hit ratio, rising to 3.0 at 80%--in new product), and a data filtering disk controller to reduce channel load (prototype showing factors in range 2 to 100 as queries become more complex).

Mr. Shunichi Torii from the Central Research Laboratory described an integrated database processor which was applying vectorization hardware to database indexing and sorting (with improvement by a factor of 4 on a vectorized quicksort).

Mr. Hiromichi Fujisawa, also from the Central Research Laboratory, described an index-free full-text search machine for large Japanese text databases. Recognition is complicated by the fact that Japanese text does not have a delimiter between words, but using hardware multi-string searching with two-stage surrogate (surrogate bit map search, condensed text search), scanning at 100 megabits/sec is achieved if the surrogate hit rate is 15%. The goal is to carry 25,000 documents per unit, averaging 20 Kbytes per document, with retrieval time of five seconds for a query with a maximum of 1,000 terms.

XDM is the large mainframe DB/DC system to which much of the R&D is directed. Mr. Kazuo Masai summarized advanced features of the product, including two-phase commit and their subsystem recovery strategy. The relational part of the system has 170 installations, of which 20-40 run "distributed" (2-3 nodes). Support for the OSI Remote Data Access standard is being developed.

Mr. Kazuhiro Satoh covered two aspects of research on next-generation database systems. One was concerned with fuzzy queries, which allowed use of predicates such as "is low" or "about 80", and used fuzzy functions that were dynamically updated in the data dictionary. The other project was the Object DBMS named MANDRILL, whose goal is improve database productivity, applicability, and performance. The range of applications was seen as very wide, including not only CAD/CAM/CASE, but also OIS, MIS and GIS. Many of the points of the object-oriented manifesto (presented by Atkinson et al. in Kyoto, 1989) were addressed. A preliminary version 1 was built in 1988/89, with the version 2 prototype scheduled for completion in 1991, and application studies in C planned for 1992.

Beyond this, Hitachi also participates in four longer-term ICOT projects. Mr. Hidefumi Kondo described some preliminary work on subsumption in the knowledge-base system QUIXOTE.

In general discussion moderated by Mr. Seiichi Yoshizumi, we were able to explore a number of wider issues.

There is a small amount of government funding of industrial projects, at the level of 1-2% in SDL, and 4-5% in CRL.

There are 20-30 visiting international researchers in the CRL, and it is intended to start such a program in the SDL.

External publication is encouraged, and the Hitachi journal is in the public domain.

Customer requirements are influenced by compatability with IBM; e.g., they are beginning to consider the requirement for a Repository.

Secure systems are in general felt to be of less concern at the moment in Japan than in Europe or the United States.

Software quality is important, but it did not appear that any formal methodology or any unusually intensive testing were employed.

Optical storage is being applied to file systems, but not yet to their DBMS.

TUESDAY, MARCH 26, 1991

Site Visited:	NTT Communications and Information Processing Laboratory Tokyo
People Visited:	Masato Haihara Director Information Processing Systems Laboratory
	Takeshi Tanaka Research Group Leader Advanced Information Systems Laboratory
	Hideki Fukuoka Research Group Leader Information Processing Systems Laboratory
	Katsumi Teranaka Research Group Leader Base Systems Architecture Laboratory
	Masaharu Araki R&D Public Relations
JTEC Participants:	J. Smith, Jajodia, Shelton
Notes taken by:	J. Smith

The group was welcomed by Mr. Masato Haihara, who described the overall charter of the Laboratory. He will be the point of contact for future communications regarding this visit. The Communications and Information Processing Laboratory is one of 11 NTT R&D laboratories. The priorities of these laboratories are:

1. Improved user services to NTT customers,
2. Next-generation technologies for communication networks, and
3. Basic research towards future communication systems.

The group received presentations and demonstrations on three projects: RINDA, MAP VISION and FEAL.

RINDA is a relational database system hardware accelerator for non-indexed queries. Improvements in processing time of 10-100 times are claimed over conventional software techniques. The demonstration involved a relational database system running on an NTT DIPS computer, with a RINDA accelerator that could be switched in or out to compare query performance against conventional software. Comparisons were shown for a complex selection (40 times faster), a join (25 times faster) and a substring match (200 times faster). RINDA supports on-the-fly disk search, and an "order N" search in random-access memory.

MAP VISION is a map retrieval system built over a relational database system. It combines attribute data with graphical data stored using the database's "long column" feature. The user interface provides zooming of the graphical data with attribute overlays. The data input system includes image scanning with automatic recognition for features such as houses, roads and contour lines. The geographical representation is divided into areas based on a rectangular mesh. The database structure uses many relations with very long tuples.

FEAL is a fast data encipherment process for secure communications. FEAL has been embedded in several products including fax, digital phones, and an image/video transmission system. The first two products use a software version of FEAL, while the last product uses an LSI chip version. Performance of 100 times better than DES is claimed. For example, FEAL can encrypt a 10,000 byte message in about three seconds, whereas DES can only handle a 100 byte message in the same amount of time. Decryption occurs at the same speeds.

Site Visited:	Institute for New Generation Computer Technology (ICOT) Tokyo
People Visited:	Dr. Kazuhiro Fuchi Director Research Center
	Takashi Kurozumi Deputy Director Research Center
	Kazumasa Yokota Chief Third Research Laboratory
	Dr. Shumichi Uchida Manager Research Department
JTEC Participants:	J. Smith, Jajodia, Shelton
Notes taken by:	Jajodia

Our meeting began with a presentation from Dr. Uchida giving an overview of various research activities on databases and knowledge bases at ICOT. Following his talk, we heard a presentation from Mr. Yokota, who described his work on QUIXOTE. This led to a general discussion of the various activities of ICOT. We were also given a brief tour of ICOT facilities.

The ICOT project began in 1982, to last for a period of 10 years. ICOT researchers hope that MITI will allow the project to continue with the level of funding about half of the original project. If approved, the next phase will emphasize developing hardware and applications.

The research at ICOT has two general directions:

1. Extend the relational model in the direction of deductive and object-oriented databases (DOOD), and
2. Build highly parallel machines on which DOOD can run efficiently.

ICOT is currently engaged in research on the following topics:

1. Database
    -- Sequential Nested Relational DBMS (KAPPA-II)
    -- Parallel Nested Relational DBMS (KAPPA-P)
2. Knowledge Base
    -- Knowledge Base Language (QUIXOTE), located on KAPPA
3. Applications
    -- Molecular Biological Databases (in QUIXOTE and KAPPA)
    -- Legal Precedent Databases (in QUIXOTE)
    -- Electronic Dictionary Databases (in KAPPA)
    -- Natural Language Processing Systems (in QUIXOTE)

ICOT publishes a journal entitled *ICOT Journal*, which is distributed to 600 overseas locations. ICOT has generated about 1,500 technical reports and memoranda. These are sent to about 30 organizations regularly and are available to others upon request. ICOT also actively organizes conferences and symposia where results are presented.

ICOT has invited 65 overseas researchers for short visits between 1982 and 1990. The number of visitors and their countries are as follows: 20 (U.S.A.), 15 (U.K.), 4 (France), 7 (F.R.G.), 5 (Canada), 5 (Israel), 4 (Sweden), 2 (Italy), 1 (Australia), 1 (Austria), 1 (Holland). Recently, ICOT has also accepted some researchers from the U.S. and France for visits up to six months to a year.

Site Visited:	Kozo Keikaku Engineering Tokyo
People Visited:	Hiroshi Ando Senior Researcher
	Terumi Hanmyo Chief of R&D Department
JTEC Participants:	Farmer, Minoura
Notes taken by:	Farmer

Kozo Keikaku Engineering (KKE) was established in 1959 to provide architectural and engineering services to a variety of government and industrial clients in Japan. In addition to their traditional services, for the last 10-15 years they have expanded, and now provide computer related services. KKE licenses a variety of software packages in the fields of architectural design, structural analysis and design, and engineering services. The company also has an office in San Francisco.

KKE was selected as a site to visit because of its software-related activities. Approximately half of its 400 staff members are software engineers. KKE has made a significant investment in computing hardware and software. They have a Fujitsu mainframe, several midrange systems, approximately 80 engineering workstations, over 200 personal computers, and many terminals. They currently rent time on a supercomputer and plan to purchase one in 1992.

KKE's experience with using database systems is fairly limited. They use DB-3 on their personal computers and UNIFY on some of their UNIX-based engineering workstations and midrange systems. They have some databases on CD-ROM that are not very frequently used. They do not use any external database services. They do not distribute any engineering databases.

Mr. Ando made an interesting observation about why there is not more use of databases at KKE. He noted that libraries are not common in Japan, and that most Japanese are accustomed to having their own information. Therefore they tend not to use shared information sources. He also indicated that paper-based information services are very comfortable for Japanese users.

KKE does not yet use multimedia products, but does make extensive use of computer graphics. They are starting to look at object oriented programming, but have not yet become interested in object oriented databases. Mr. Ando noted that the MITI/INTAP project will likely be important to KKE in the future.

While KKE is not very active in the database area, they are active in software in general. They develop a lot of software internally augmenting it with externally developed packages, especially from the US and Europe. Mr. Ando felt that Japan does a good job in developing hardware but that Japanese software is not yet up to world standards.   Software maintenance is a problem for KKE, especially for porting their software products to new hardware platforms.

Site Visited:	IBM Japan, Tokyo Research Laboratory
	Tokyo

People Visited:	Dr. Jung-Kook Hong
	Manager
	Applied Image Processing Systems
	Tokyo Scientific Center

Kohichi Kajitani
Researcher

Dr. Norihisa Suzuki
Director

JTEC Participants:	Farmer, Bourne, Minoura

Notes taken by:	Minoura

We first met Dr. Hong, who showed us the Color Image Database System (CIDB) developed by his group. The goal of the project was to integrate image processing and database technologies, particularly to retrieve stored images by specifying their graphical features. Various image compression techniques such as Huffman coding, modified Huffman coding, and run-length coding were also tested.

CIDB uses SQL/DS on VM to store ordinary data such as character strings and numbers, and image data separately as CMS files. The window manager used is a proprietary one. The system was developed in C, ASSEMBLER, and PL/1. Database recovery and concurrency control mechanisms are not applied to image data stored as separate files.

The system runs on PS/55, which is the IBM Japanese PC, connected to a mainframe. The connection is provided by a synchronous link SRPI 3270 PC with a data rate of 16 Kb/sec. Image data may be stored in WORM optical disks connected to a mainframe. IBM introduced such WORM devices in 1990.

The demonstrated system stored information for resort facilities owned by IBM Japan. Retrieved information for each resort facility was displayed in a form that included a picture of that facility.

The development of the system was started in 1985 in cooperation with the Ethnology Department at the Osaka National Museum. CIDB is currently a product of IBM Japan.

Mr. Kajitani then demonstrated a hypermedia system called "SMART DB." SMART DB seems to correspond with MODES2, reported by Kosaka et al. [Kosa:87].

MODES2 can be best understood as integration of Apple's HYPERCARD system, the DAPLE data model, and a window system. DAPLE functions are assumed to provide HYPERCARD links for navigation. Cards connected by links can be displayed simultaneously, if requested, in multiple windows. A collection of cards to be browsed can be selected by a form-based query. Data to be displayed in one displayed card may actually come from different cards. The view mechanism of the underlying relational system supports this feature. Functional links are used only for navigation, and synchronized browsing is not supported.

The SMART DB is built on a relational database system and a window system, both of which are custom-made products.

Finally, we discussed general matters with Dr. Suzuki. The major research areas for IBM Tokyo Research Laboratory are those related to Japanese markets, including Japanese document processing and machine translation (English/Chinese and English/Korean as well as English/Japanese).

He told us that he could not discuss current research topics. However, he offered us some interesting comments and observations on general matters.

We could not determine the relative strength of interaction of this laboratory with other IBM laboratories or with MITI.

Japanese database research is concentrated in the areas of knowledge DBs, OODBs, and multimedia DB applications, and not much work can be found on concurrency control, recovery, or security. Database machines being developed by Japanese companies may be important. Hitachi and Mitsubishi are involved in this area. They developed embedded processors for hashing, vector processing, and sorting.

WEDNESDAY, MARCH 27, 1991

Site Visited:	Tsukuba University Institute for Information Sciences and Electronics (IISE) Tsukuba
People Visited:	Dr. Yuzura Fujiwara Professor
	Dr. Hiroyuki Kitagawa Associate Professor
JTEC Participants:	J. Smith, Minoura, D. Smith, Jajodia
Notes taken by:	D. Smith

The Database Research Group in the Institute for Information Sciences and Electronics (IISE) at Tsukuba University is a very active group with a large number of ongoing projects. Prof. Fujiwara's work is driven by application areas. He has developed a number of scientific and engineering databases: CORES-organic syntheses in chemistry, CAPDAS-polymers, a semiconductor database, and a superconductor database, as well as a multilingual dictionary called CD-WORD. These are available to the public through MITI. They are on CD-ROMs that can be accessed on NEC and IBM-compatible PCs.

Of particular interest to the group is their work on integrating database management and knowledge management. They want to support learning and analogical reasoning over the database. In this context, "learning" means identifying a new pattern of chemical reactions from existing data and rules. "Analogical reasoning" means inferring a probable truth by analogy with previously stored similar data.

Professor Fujiwara is developing a chemical structure database system called CHARM. His group was dissatisfied with the ability of relational DBMSs to handle complex chemical structures as well as learning and analogical reasoning. They have modelled chemical graphs using a functional data model. They are constructing a prototype DBMS using Ricoh's extended relational DBMS (RICOHBASE) as a storage manager. ADTs are being used as attribute domains. Research is being done on optimization strategies.

Professor Kitagawa has been working for a number of years on nested relations. He is involved in the IISE extensible database system project, MODUS, which is an attempt to build a multiple data model DBMS. Nested relations are used as an implementations mechanism.

Professor Kitagawa is working under Professor Fujiwara on a design object version server called DOVER. The goal of this project is to study the role of generic objects in version management. The system will provide visual browsing facilities.

Site Visited:	Information Technology Promotion Agency
	Tokyo

People Visited:	Dr. Akio Tojo
	Managing Director

JTEC Participants:	Minoura, Smith

Notes taken by:	Minoura

Dr. Tojo was director of the Computer Science Division at Electrotechnical Laboratory and was instrumental in the planning and execution of the National Research and Development Program on Interoperable Database System (interoperability project) started in December 1985 [Tojo:91]. Before he became the director of the Computer Science Division, he worked in the area of pattern recognition.

IPA is a non-profit organization with a broad mandate to promote information processing technology. Most of its operating funds come from the Japanese government. MITI related ex-government officials are often assigned to its top positions.

The major subject of our discussions was the interoperability project. Details are reported in Section 1.3.

Site Visited:	Interactive Interface Systems Laboratory
	ETL
	Tsukuba Science City
People Visited:	Dr. Toshikazu Kato
JTEC Participants:	J. Smith, Minoura, Shelton
Notes taken by:	Minoura

Dr. Kato demonstrated two multimedia systems: TRADEMARK and ART MUSEUM. The development of both of these systems are supported by the national research and development project on interoperable database systems. The details of these systems can be found in references [Kato:88, Kato:91].

The TRADEMARK system is intended to be used by the Japanese patent office. When the patent office receives an application for the registration of a new trademark, it is compared with already registered ones. If the new one is too similar to any existing one, its application is rejected. This process is laborious if manually performed.

The TRADEMARK system performs this retrieval by query-by-visual-example (QVE), which operates as follows. A proposed trademark or its sketch is read by a camera and its graphic feature (GF) vector is computed. The GF vector of the new trademark is compared with those of the existing trademarks. Then, the trademarks similar to the new one in terms of the distances of their GF vectors are retrieved.

The current system uses a "handcrafted database system", which they intend to replace with Sybase. The system is more a pattern-recognition system than a database (or knowledge-base) system.

Another system briefly demonstrated was the ART MUSEUM system. This system retrieves pictures, given adjectives that characterize the pictures, such as clear, bright, and clean. The retrieval is performed based on the GF vector, which was automatically computed from the distribution of RGB intensity values in each picture.

Site Visited: University of Library and Information Science
                           Tsukuba Science City

People Visited: Yoshifumi Masunaga
                           Professor

JTEC Participants: D. Smith, Jajodia

Notes taken by: Jajodia

We met Prof. Masunaga in his office at the University of Library and Information Science. Since he was the Chairperson of the Executive Committee for the Second International Symposium on Database Systems for Advanced Applications (DASFAA'91) which was only a few days away, he was very busy trying to contact those authors who had not yet registered for the conference. In spite of his hectic schedule, he was kind enough to take some time from his busy schedule and meet with us.

The University of Library and Information Science (ULIS) is located in Tsukuba Science City, the so-called "Brain City" of Japan. Located roughly 60 km from Tokyo, Tsukuba Science City has two national universities (Tsukuba University and ULIS), and 58 governmental and semi-governmental research and development institutions.

ULIS was established in 1979 as the only Japanese university dedicated to the study of library and information science. ULIS offers a four-year undergraduate program leading to the degree of Bachelor of Arts (*Gakugei Gakushi*) and a two-year graduate program leading to the degree of Master of Arts (*Gakujutsu Shushi*). The enrollment is limited to 150 students each year in the B.A. program and to 16 students per year in the M.A. program. In addition, 20 students may be admitted per year to the third year of the four-year B.A. program.

Almost all of the students seek outside employment upon completion of their B.A. program. The following table lists the placement of graduates for the year 1988:

National and Public Organizations	20
Private Universities and Schools	19
Software Companies and Information Services	37
Other Industries	49
Graduate Courses at ULIS	3
--	
Total	125

Site Visited:	NEC Shibaura
People Visited:	Kiichi Fujino Vice President C&C Software Development Group
	Masao Matsumoto Associate Chief Engineer C&C Software Development Group
	Kunihiro Sugawara Assistant General Manager EDP Systems Engineering Division
	Isao Kamoi Engineering Manager Database Development Department
	Ryuichi Ogawa Supervisor Applied Information Technology Research Laboratory
	Kyoji Kawagoe Research Manager Terminal Systems Research Laboratory
	Yoichi Miyashita Engineering Manager Software Architecture Department
	Shuji Nakata Systems Manager 2nd Systems Department
	Kunitoshi Tsuruoka Research Manager Basic Technologies Research Laboratory
JTEC Participants:	Kahaner, Farmer, Beech
Notes taken by:	Beech

Our meeting with NEC took place in Shibaura, and was hosted by Dr. Kiichi Fujino, vice-president of the C&C Software Development Group. He gave us an overview of the company, whose activities incorporate many aspects of the fields of electronics and consumer electrical goods, with 115,000 employees. Information processing is now the largest division, with 46% of the total sales of 3.444 billion yen. In addition to R&D carried out in-house, work is done by many subsidiaries--33 in software alone.

DBMSs are not the main software focus, since the OEM approach has been followed for the UNIX workstation market, with several U.S. vendors providing relational systems. RIQS II is the NEC mainframe product, geared originally in 1979 to the network model and COBOL support (repeating groups). More recent extensions were described by Isao Kamoi. These have added SQL DML, but the DDL is proprietary.

Kunitoshi Tsuruoka from the Systems Research Laboratories in Kawasaki presented the ODIN object database system. This has emphasized the "seamless C++" approach, and the prototype has itself been written in C++. The two distinctive features are the provision of "view classes", and the virtualization of physical structure.

Another research project was described by Ryuichi Ogawa from the C&C Information Technology Research Laboratories. This was concerned with the problems of synchronization and editing in the development of audio-visual hypermedia systems.

Masao Matsumoto approached database systems from another angle, stressing their desirability for support of an integrated CASE environment.

We were informed that NEC is participating in ICOT's FGCS project.

Site Visited: National Center for Science Information Systems (NACSIS)
                                 Tokyo

People Visited: Prof. Akira Miyazawa

                                 Prof. Hisao Yamada
                                 Director
                                 R&D Department

                                 Prof. Teruo Koyama

                                 Prof. Masamitsu Negishi

                                 Prof. Kimio Ohno
                                 General Coordinator

                                 Prof. Hiromichi Hashizume

JTEC Participants: Beech, Farmer, Kahaner

Notes taken by: Farmer

NACSIS is an inter-university research institute, whose purpose is to gather, organize, and provide scholarly information to Japanese universities, as well as to carry out research and development related to scholarly information and a science information system. NACSIS was officially formed in 1986, but its roots go back to 1973. NACSIS is funded by the Japanese Ministry of Education, Science and Culture.

NACSIS collects scientific databases and loads them into a retrieval system, and provides information services to the university community throughout Japan. NACSIS operates the Science Information Network, a packet switched network, with nodes throughout Japan, and with satellite links to the British Library in London and the National Science Foundation in Washington.

NACSIS operates a large computer system, with several large mainframes with over 700 gigabytes of disk space, mostly magnetic, but with some optical disks. NACSIS provides a cataloging service for university libraries, and an information retrieval service based on over 27 different databases.

The cataloging service uses the XDMRD database management system from Hitachi. NACSIS extended it to handle multivalue groups. This application supports over 500 concurrent users for the input of catalog information of materials acquired at university libraries. Performance of this service is a problem for NACSIS with over 45 seconds interaction time for the typical transaction (including thinking time for the operator), and a rapid growth of user libraries and the catalog database.

The information retrieval service uses the ORION information retrieval software from Hitachi. This software is similar to Information Dimensions Inc.'s BASIS, but has a different user interface in the Japanese language. This service generally has about 10-20 concurrent users, and performance is satisfactory.

In terms of research and development activities, NACSIS is interested in parallel searching, multimedia, and compound document handling. They are also generally interested in the electronic library paradigm. NACSIS is considering using a nested relational model for full-text retrieval, but it has not considered using a different information model for their catalogue service because of performance concerns.

Because NACSIS is funded by the Ministry of Education, Science and Culture, services are restricted to the university community. NACSIS would like to be able to provide services internationally, but currently can only do so in a limited way with the National Science Foundation and the British Library.

Site Visited: NTT Data Services
                             Tokyo

People Visited: Dr. Y. Tachibana
                             Senior Vice President

                             Yutaka Sasaki

                             Tsutomu Shibata

                             Akikazu Ida

                             Kouichi Suzuki

JTEC Participants: Wiederhold, Bourne, Uyehara

Notes taken by: Wiederhold

NTT Data Services is an independent service company that focuses on consulting and system integration. Their formation was the result of a consent decree as part of the privatization of NTT a few years ago. They serve many clients of the former NTT data communications division, with a focus on finance.

They have very modern facilities in several downtown Tokyo locations, but the company plans to move to a new suburban facility. They have 7,000 employees. We were received by Mr. Sasaki of their International Affairs department, saw some videotapes, and heard technical presentations by:

1.   Tsutomu Shibata (stock and bond information system to support trust officer's workstations);
2.   Akikazu Ida (fashion support system for textile board); and
3.   Kouichi Suzuki (Japanization of ORACLE, distribution, multimedia direction).

After the presentation, Mr. Sasaki accompanied us to a shorter meeting with Dr. Y. Tachibana, Senior Vice President responsible for their planning department.

They consider databases fundamental to their business. NTT Data is now acquiring tools and products for integration equally from NTT and other companies. For instance, a substantial investment was made in adapting ORACLE for the Japanese market. NTT Data acquired the source code to carry out Japanization of character formats. Lack of comments made the task more difficult. The resulting code grew to such a large size that another c-compiler had to be used. A new report generator was written--here conversion was not feasible.

They also buy research support for NTT, SRI International, and others. Other sources of research results are the open literature. They were well aware of relevant publications and textbooks, although influenced--as we all are--by faddishness in unrefereed or weak publications.

We would have liked to spend more time discussing their research and development directions, but had already exceeded our stay by one hour. They are obviously well positioned to introduce applications of database technology in Japan and elsewhere.

THURSDAY, MARCH 28, 1991

Site Visited:	Aichi Institute of Technology Nagoya
People Visited:	Professor Shigeharu Kito
JTEC Participants:	Wiederhold, Farmer, Kahaner
Notes taken by:	Wiederhold

Aichi Institute of Technology is a private college in Toyota located in the hills west of Nagoya, Japan's premier industrial city. Prof. Kito is in the department of industrial engineering and is performing advanced research in expert systems for catalyst design. He reported that after work at CMU (Carnegie Mellon University) was discontinued, he stands alone in this difficult field.

The expert system was developed under STA support on large NTT PCs (30 Mb memory), with their product 'KBMS' rule-based expert system. Twenty organizations (6 academic, 2 industrial, and several national research labs) participated in the STA project called "Research on the Development of Knowledge-based Systems to aid Chemists in Designing Chemical Substances and Chemical Reactions." Joint meetings were held, but cooperation focused on a few colleagues, such as Dr. Hattori from Nagoya University. A final report is due in June 1991, with a demonstration in Tokyo in 1992. If the STA budget permits, an English translation of the report would be prepared, which the researchers would welcome.

The PC-based KBMS approach was difficult. Eventually Dr. Kito moved to a direct implementation of a rule system with frame-based data structures using GOLD-HILL LISP. The system had about 200 rules used in several phases of the design process. There is no reagent database associated with the expert system.

Dr. Kito plans to extend this work beyond oxidizing catalysts. He is also investigating discrimination net techniques with researchers at Kansai University and neural net technology, as published in the literature. The learning phase of the neural net, 50,000 iterations over a set of 32 cases, was demonstrated to us on a SONY NEWS system with a subsequent discrimination of that set. Nine features were used.

A new STA initiative "Development of Self-Organizing Information Base to Aid Researchers in Creative Research" is likely to provide support.

Current new and further work is expected to be carried out on SUN, SONY NEWS, and Data General workstations, using a core system developed by Prof. Osuda at Tokyo University.

We discussed furthermore the lack of research-oriented support for students at Japanese universities. For instance, the student working on the neural net development is about to leave to go to another school closer to home. It is also difficult to follow industry. Dr. Kito said that NTT has many researchers working on neural nets, and is interested in rule extraction.

Site Visited:	Fujitsu at INTAP Tokyo
People Visited:	Shozo Tanaka Senior Manager
	Fumiaki Tsuboi Manager 1st Engineering Department
	Yoshio Izumida Section Manager Artificial Intelligence Laboratory
	Hiroshi Ishikawa Researcher Knowledge-based Engineering Section
JTEC Participants:	Beech, Minoura, Uyehara
Notes taken by:	Minoura and Beech

We visited Fujitsu researchers at Interoperability Technology Association for Information Processing (INTAP). Mr. Tsuboi, who is currently affiliated with INTAP, is also from Fujitsu and is expected to return there after the completion of INTAP's mission.

Fujitsu claims to be a total systems vendor. Its computer products include IBM-compatible super and mainframe computers, UNIX workstations, and personal computers running MS/DOS or OS2. Fujitsu is also a major supplier of communications and semiconductor products. The total sales of Fujitsu are $18 billion, with those of computers at $11 billion.

Fujitsu introduced a network DBMS called AIM in 1973. In the late 1970s, the group, led by Dr. Akifumi Makinouchi at Fujitsu, implemented the first RDBMS in Japan [Maki:81], which led to the Fujitsu RDBMS product AIM/RDB2.

Fujitsu does not sell DBMSs as software products. Instead it sells them as part of total systems. Two major areas of applications including DBMSs are banking systems and stock-market systems. The banking systems run at up to 300,000 transactions/hour, and stock-market systems at up to 7,000,000 transactions/day. DBMS applications of lesser importance include library systems, patent systems, and chemical compound systems. They believe that document and CAD/CAM databases may become important. About 900 people (300 from Fujitsu and 600 from outside software houses) are involved in the development of these applications.

A "total system" sold by Fujitsu includes mainframe hardware, systems software, terminals, communications hardware and software, applications software, and sometimes an SE. The SE sent to a customer site with the hardware is eventually called back after a few years' stint. The customer service at this level is extremely appreciated by some unsophisticated clients.

Computers within large corporations (with more than 3,000 employees) are already networked. The most pressing need for interoperability is felt by medium-size companies (with 300 to 3,000 employees) that are currently relying on stand-alone computers. The computers of these companies must be linked to those of their banks, suppliers, and customers. Mr. Tanaka believes that this will happen within the next 10 years. He also expects that Japanese government procurements will require open systems once necessary standards are established.

Fujitsu researchers are heavily involved in the international, standardization activities through OSI Asia-Oceanic Workshop (AOW). They are familiar with such U.S. standardization activities as SQL-Access Group, NIST PDAS and Express.

An interesting research project was described by Hiroshi Ishikawa from Fujitsu Laboratories Ltd., a subsidiary in Kawasaki. The title of his presentation was "An Object-Oriented Knowledge Base Approach to Next-Generation Hypermedia Systems." The JASMINE system is an object database system that supports set-oriented queries, including the use of path expressions. Constraints and triggers may be defined, and the system may be extended by new nodes, attributes, and links defined procedurally in JASMINE/C. Both textual and image data are supported in the window interface.

Site Visited:	Research Center for Advanced Science and Technology (RCAST)--University of Tokyo Tokyo
People Visited:	Setsuo Ohsuga Professor
	Koichi Hori Associate Professor
	Hiroyuki Yamanouchi Research Assistant
JTEC Participants:	Minoura, Beech
Notes taken by:	Beech

Professor Setsuo Ohsuga described the scope of his group as being the application of artificial intelligence to engineering problems, especially to all aspects of the design process. Examples of application areas that have been studied are the design of new chemical compounds, and the design of aircraft wings. The aim is to design a new computing system, guided by the principles that a knowledge base should be separated from the database, and that a key to success is to decompose a complex problem in such a way as to exploit parallelism.

Koichi Hori is applying cognitive science to the design of human interfaces to database systems. He demonstrated a prototype of a concept formation aid for database design. Nodes are clustered on the screen, subject to neighborhood relations, as a means of abstracting higher-level structure.

Theoretical investigation and implementation of a knowledge base system was the focus of Hiroyuki Yamanouchi's work. This involved multi-layer logic and analogical reasoning. The applications mentioned above had been pursued to a complexity of systems with about 100 transformation rules. The chemical compound example was demonstrated, where all one-step transformations are displayed, subject to constraints to avoid toxicity.

An important development for RCAST is the introduction in the forthcoming academic year of a new graduate school for interdisciplinary study beyond a Master's degree. This will span materials, devices, social sciences, and information processing. It is being funded by the Ministry of Science and Technology. Another new departure is that it is planned for industrial companies to provide financial support and send participants.

FRIDAY, MARCH 29, 1991

Site Visited:	Toshiba
People Visited:	Akira Miyoshi Senior Manager Technical Strategy Planning Computer Division
	Kazuo Narita Senior Manager International Visits and Liaisons Research Administration Staff
	Kazuo Yamamoto Manager 2nd Basic Software Section Advanced Computer Development Department Oume Works
	Katsunori Terada Oume Works
	Yojiro Morimoto Research Scientist Information Systems Laboratory Research and Development Center (RDC)
	Sakai Hiroshi RDC
JTEC Participants:	D. Smith, J. Smith
Notes taken by:	D. Smith

We were hosted by Mr. Akira Miyoshi, who is the contact person for Toshiba. Mr. Kazuo Narita acted as facilitator and interpreter.

Toshiba is a $19 billion corporation with over 160,000 employees. Forty-four percent of its business is split between heavy electrical and consumer products. The majority of its business is in information and communications technology and electronic devices (20% of the total is in DRAMs).

Toshiba covers the full spectrum of database-related activities: it produces commercial database software and hardware products, performs system integration for customers in a number of application areas, and has a large number of research and advanced development projects. There were people at the meeting representing each of these broad areas.

The commercial products are targeted primarily at the domestic Japanese market. Toshiba markets two DBMSs: a network model DBMS modeled after IDS I from GE that has been on the market for 20 years, and a relational product (RDB V) for their proprietary operating system (OS V) that has been on the market for four years. They fill out their product line, as needed, with third-party software.

Toshiba discussed their integration activities with respect to the GIS marketplace. They develop systems for municipal applications--the management of gas and water pipes. These systems are built on the UNIFY DBMS and use optical disk storage for their data repositories. The ORACLE DBMS is used as the basis for systems they provide to the nuclear power industry. They also produce sophisticated systems for a number of other markets including banking, hotels, airport and highway systems, hospital systems, and general administration systems.

In research and advanced development, Toshiba's interests lie in CSCW (computer-supported cooperative work), multimedia, VLSI CAD and AI. They are just starting up their CSCW and multimedia activities; they will use documents as their focus (e.g., how can a single document be effectively worked on by several people). In AI their emphasis is is on natural language processing: English to Japanese translation, Kana/Kanji processing and natural language query processing. Both of these interests will be combined to create an automatic conference room with video monitoring to count votes, document scanning and management, and language translation.

Site Visited:	Mitsubishi Electric Corp. Computer and Information Systems Laboratory Kanagawa
People Visited:	Hisao Koizumi Manager Department of Information Systems Research
	Dr. Tohei Nitta Manager Overseas R&D Planning
	Toru Kubo Manager Technical Contract Section
	Koji Wakimoto Image Processing Group
	Satoshi Tanaka Image Processing Group
	Mitsuhide Shima Image Processing Group
JTEC Participants:	D. Smith, J. Smith
Notes taken by:	J. Smith

We were hosted by Mr. Hisao Koizumi, who explained the position of the lab in the Mitsubishi R&D organization. The Computer and Information Systems Laboratory is one of six labs in the Ofuna Research Complex. Research fields at the lab include: large-scale parallel processors for processing scientific and technical data, software engineering for the development of high-quality engineering and business data processing software, encryption/decryption algorithms for prepaid card systems, parallel inference machines for AI applications, machine translation systems for high- quality translation from Japanese to English, and multimedia technology for maintenance and design databases. This last project is being conducted in the Image Processing Group, and was the main subject of the visit.

As part of the National Project on Interoperable Database Systems, Mitsubishi is developing technology for multimedia database systems. The application is geared towards databases containing industrial plant information. They are using a third-party database system extended with external image files. The two key problems are: 1) capturing raster images and converting them to vector form by automatic recognition of objects, and 2) image retrieval by pattern matching on similar graphical information.   They demonstrated a prototype system that solves a simplified version of the retrieval problem for the layout of rooms in a house. They abstract the room topology in a house to adjacency relationships. They can then search a "realty" database to find houses with a layout similar to a given house by matching on their adjacency relationships.

Site Visited: Kyushu University
                        Fukuoka

People Visited: Dr. Toshihisa Takagi
                        Associate Professor

                        Mr. Susumu Goto
                        Ph.D. Student

                        Dr. Hirofumi Amano
                        Research Associate

                        Dr. Mohammed E. El-Sharkawi
                        Research Associate

JTEC Participants: Minoura, Beech

Notes taken by: Minoura

We first attended a presentation on the DEE (Deductive Engine for Engineering databases) made by Mr. Goto, who is working on his Ph.D. under Professor Takagi. The details of the talk can be found in [Taka:91].

The major objective of this project was to measure performance of integrated recursive query processing methods against a large set of facts obtained from a real application. The set of facts used in the experiment was obtained from pipe-and-instrumentation (P&I) diagrams of a petrochemical plant. The facts indicated the connectivity relationships among the devices in the plant, and they totalled 6,497.

Two major components of the DEE system are the rule transformer and the bottom-up evaluator. A recursive query is first transformed into a form that can be efficiently evaluated by the bottom-up evaluator, which uses the semi-naive evaluation method. According to the structure of the query, the rule transformer selects one of the following three methods for query transformation: the magic-set method, the NRSU method, and the KRS method. DEE allows negative literals in rule bodies.

We did not ask about comparison with a simple Prolog implementation. In this project, only the connectivity of components was addressed. They are proposing to use an object-oriented database and to unify it with their deductive engine to handle more complex aspects of CAD. However, they were at an early stage of this integration.

We were then shown videotape presentations of the projects conducted by the group led by Professor Kambayashi, who recently moved to Kyoto University. The video presentations were on the following three topics: 1) automatic placement of labels for the regions in a map, 2) a pseudo-natural language interface for a relational database system, and 3) version control for a CAD database.

One result addressed in the first presentation was the following. Assume that we want to place the label for a region at its center. The center of a region may be defined as the center of the smallest rectangle enclosing it or the largest rectangle enclosed by it. This topic is important for some applications.

ENLI (Example-Based Natural Language-Assisted Interface), developed by the second project, can be regarded as QBE where table templates and join conditions are replaced by English sentences, which can be edited to formulate a query. The system does not parse a query stated in a natural language.

Such topics as version history, cooperative design, and equivalence were discussed in the third presentation.

Finally, Dr. El-Sharkawi discussed the theoretical investigation in his thesis of object migrations between classes due to updates, where the updates may take the form of adding or dropping instance variables, or of modifying the values of existing instance variables. (In his model, a class has not only a set of instance variables and a set of methods, but also an associated predicate which may be falsified by a value update.) Various kinds of migration are classified, and the implications of an object changing its class are considered for the representation and querying of temporal databases and versioning systems.

Site Visited:	Faculty of Engineering
	Hokkaido University
	Sapporo
People Visited:	Dr. Yuzuru Tanaka
	Professor
	Electrical Engineering Department
	Dr. Akihiro Yamamoto
	Lecturer
	Electrical Engineering Department
JTEC Participants:	D. Smith, J. Smith
Notes taken by:	J. Smith

Prof. Tanaka greeted us in his laboratory and presented an historical overview of his research activities. His earlier work focused on multi-microprocessor computer system architectures, database dependency theory, and database machine design. The current activities of his research group focus on object-oriented databases, multimedia application building tools, and full-text databases.

Prof. Tanaka provided us with written answers to the issues raised in the JTEC questionnaire. As a university group, their main emphasis is on research, but they also disseminate their research results to the major industrial R&D labs through group meetings. The research is mainly funded by industry rather than by the Ministry of Education. Their current direction in data models is driven by their concept of dynamic, persistent media objects called "pads". Pads provide a new paradigm for the building of information management applications. Prof. Tanaka spent a year as a visiting scientist at the IBM T.J. Watson Research Center. He felt that, on the whole, software research in the U.S. is more receptive to novel ideas. Software research in Japan tends to expand on current research concepts, rather than to open up fundamentally new ground.

Prof. Tanaka's research team provided demonstrations of three current projects: IntelligentPad, Transmedia and Video Database.

IntelligentPad is based on the Controller/View/Model (CVM) concept--the controller determines user interactions with an object, the view determines the displayed appearance of the object, and the model determines the internal representation of the object. A pad is a CVM object. Pads can be composed to form more complex pads by graphically pasting one pad on another, and using a scripting language to define their interconnection. IntelligentPad can be viewed as an application generator for an object-oriented database system.

The Transmedia project is concerned with text processing on the content of scanned images of text documents. The usual approach today is to employ optical character recognition (OCR) to regenerate the original text from the image. However, OCR is often difficult, particularly when multiple fonts or different character sets are used. For many text editing operations, it is not necessary to recognize individual characters. It is sufficient to recognize just the line and character boundaries, and treat characters and lines as rectangular subimages. Characters can then be made to flow as line length and spacing are changed, and as characters are inserted and deleted.

The Video Database project is aimed at the content-based retrieval of video information. Initial work focused on the detection of "cuts" in a video segment. A cut is where one scene ends and another begins. They have developed algorithms to reliably detect cuts. Recently, they have extended their work to search a videotape for specific content. Prof. Tanaka showed a video of a car race, in which the same cars showed up from a variety of angles and in various contexts at different stages of the race. In a convincing demonstration, Prof. Tanaka was able to retrieve all of the video frames which included a specific selected car.

Editor's note: Site reports for Ricoh (software division), Japan Information Center for Science and Technology (JICST), Software AG (Far East), the National Museum of Ethnology, Kobe University, and Kyoto University are not included above because they were received after the publication deadline. See Appendix B (p. 66) for a complete list of sites visited by the panel.

Bibliography

[Ando:89]
Ando, A., Hayakawa, Y., Ito, M., and Tamura, N.
 Matsushita Electric Industrial Co., Ltd.
 "Retrieval System Using Stream-Data Processing"
 Data Engineering, December 14, 1989.

[Aosh:90]
Aoshima, M., Izumida, Y., Makinouchi, A., Suzuki, F., and Yamane Y.
 Fujitsu Labs, Kyushu University
 "The C-based Database Programming Language JASMINE/C"
 Proceedings of the 16th VLDB Conference, Brisbane, Australia, August 1990.
 Extends C with single-inheritance class hierarchies, functional data model,
 and persistence. Describes prototype implementation XDE, and NF2 storage
 manager.

[Chan:89]
Chang, T.S., and Tanaka, K.
 Kobe University
 "Alternative Objects in Object-Oriented Databases"
 *Proceedings of the International Symposium on Database Systems for Advanced
        Applications*, Seoul, Korea, 1989.
 Introduces notion of "alternative objects" as a kind of versioning in
 which the objects can behave in the same manner for all applicable
 messages.

[Cusu:90]
Cusumano, Michael A.
 Japan's Software Factories: A Challenge to U.S. Management
 Oxford University Press, 1990.
 Japanese implementations of DARPA's Software Works Initiative.

[DPC:91]
Database Promotion Center, Japan
 Directory of Japanese Databases in 1990
 Database Promotion Center, 1990, 185pp.

[DPC:90]
Database Promotion Center, Japan
Databases in Japan 1990
Database Promotion Center, 1990, 81pp.
Authoritative survey of public database services and contents;
brief mention of general DBMS technology (present situation of In-House
Database: pp.39-41).

[ElSh:90]
El-Sharkawi, M., and Kambayashi, Y.
Kyushu University
"Efficient Processing of Distributed Set Queries"
Parbase, March 1990.
Set expressions which can be reduced to cardinality comparisons
are much cheaper to execute.

[ElSh:90]
El-Sharkawi, M., and Kambayashi, Y.
Kyushu University
"The Architecture and Implementation of ENLI: Example-Based Natural
Language-Assisted Interface"
Parbase, March 1990.
A form of QBE.

[ElSh:91]
El-Sharkawi, Mohammed
Kyushu University
"Answering Queries in Temporal Object-Oriented Databases"
2nd Int. Symp. on Database Sys. for Adv. Appl., Tokyo, April 1991.

[Fuji:91]
Fujisawa, Hiromichi
"An Index-Free Full-Text Search Machine for Large Japanese Text Databases"
Received 1991.

Fuji:85]
Fujiwara, Y., et al.
Tsukuba University, Institute for Information Sciences and Electronics
"A Dynamic Thesaurus for Intelligent Access to Research Databases"
FID 44, Helsinki, August 1985.

[Fuji:90]
Fujiwara, Y., Luan, Y.Q., Yamaguchi, K., Ohbo, N., and Kitagawa, H.
"Representation and a Model of Chemical Information with Generic Hierarchy"
Information Processing Society of Japan (IPSJ) 30th Anniversary Conf., 1990.
CHESDAS proposal for handling isomeres and isotope-based compounds,
implemented on Ricoh G-BASE.

[Fuji:90]
Fujiwara, Y., Ohbo, N., Kitagawa, H., and Yamaguchi, K.
"The Information Base Systems for Materials Research"
CODATA 12, Columbus, Ohio, July 1990.
Sketch of model of OPM-IBS is a recursive labeled directed hypergraph;
problems with other models and standards.

[Fuji:90]
Fujiwara, Y., et al.
"Self Organizing Information System for Materials Design"
CAMSE 1, Tokyo, 1990.
System configuration of proposal in response to SAT thrust.

[Goto:91]
Goto, F., and Tanaka, Y.
"Introducing a Large Vocabulary into Prolog"
PRICAI 90.

[Hama:90]
Hamano, Hisato
ASCII Corp (Tokyo)
"Vertical Typesetting with TEX"
TUGBOAT, Vol.11, No.3, September 1990.
Description and background of pTEX public domain software. JIS standard
recognizes 6353 Kanji characters for levels 1 and 2. The minimum
requirement of the Ministry of Education is 1945 joyo Kanji characters.
Most books are written as V-text (vertically, right to left) but
mathematics and science texts are written as H-text (horizontally, down).
Some characters differ in H and V. Japanese has no spaces between words,
and linebreaks can occur anywhere (*Kin-soku* rule). There are
three standards for writing 2-byte Kanji codes and 1-byte English ASCII
codes: JIS-using lscape characters, Shift-JIS, and EUC (Extended Unix),
using the eighth bit. In V-text English words have their characters related.

[Hani:91]
Haniuda, H., Abiru, Y., and Miyazaki, N.
OKI and ICOT
"PHI: A Deductive Database System"
IEEE Pacific Rim Conf. on Communications, Computers and Signal
Processing, Victoria, BC, Canada, May 1991.
With performance evaluation on a large, artificial database.

[Hatt:80]
Hattori, T., Niwa, H., and Satsuma, A.
Nagoya University
"Performance of Promoted SnO2 Catalysts Designed by an Expert System
Approach for Oxidative Dehydrogenation of Ethylbenzene"
Applied Catalysis Letter, Vol.50, 1980, pp.L11-L15, Elseviers.

[Hatt:88]
Hattori, T., Kito, S., and Murakami, Y.
Nagoya University
"Integration of Catalyst Activity Pattern (INCAP); Artificial Intelligence
Approach in Catalyst Design"
Chemistry Letters, 1988, pp. 1269-1272, Chem. Soc. of Japan

[Haya:85]
Hayashi, Y.
Omron Tateisi Electronics Co.
"Operational Technology Problems on Practical Database Systems in Japan
and their Structural Analysis"
IEEE, 1985.

[Hiro:91]
Hirosawa, Yochihiro
NEC Corp, C and C Systems Research Laboratories
"Overview of ODIN"
Presentation materials, received April 1991.
c++ interface used registered classes, including view classes.
View methods are select, join, group. File class supports storage class.

[Hita:91]
Hitachi
"Knowledge-based Document Filing System"
Brochure, 1991.
Concept network to help user retrieve color documents. Also background
of laboratory.

[ICOL:90]
Institute for New Generation Computer Technology (ICOT) Librarian
"Publication List"
ICOT Report, November 1990.
List of available TRs and memoranda in English.

[ICOT:90]
ICOT
Outline of Fifth Generation Project
TR, 1990.
Intermediate stage report, plans for final, third stage.

[Ida:91]
Ida, Akikazu
NTT Data, Tokyo
"An Overview of Full Color Image Database System--SR-ret"
NTT Data, March 1991 presentation materials.
Full color, PC resolution image database with compression, to serve fashion
industry. Also article storage and facsimile distribution.

[Iiza:91]
Iizawa, A., and Shirota, Y.
Ricoh, Software Research Center, Tokyo
"Optical Disk-Based Multi-media Database"
TR, received March 1991.
Description of IMAZONE. Object extensions to Ricoh G-BASE to support
magneto-optical jukebox in three standard formats: TIFF (Tag Image File
Format), xwd (X-window dump format), SUN (raster), with display on VDT,
laserprinter, or FAX. Compressions, and image manipulation (copy, move
invert, mirror, rotate, expand and contract, skew, paint rectangle and
polygon). Also samples.

[Inou:89]
Inoue, U., Hayami, H., Fukuoka, H., and Suzuki, K.
NTT, Communications and Information Processing Laboratory, Kanagawa
"RINDA, A Relational Database Processor for Non-Indexed Queries"
DASFAA 1, April 1989, Seoul, Korea, pp.382-386.

[ISO:84]
ISO
"Information Processing Systems--Open Systems Interconnection-
Basic Reference Model"
IS7498, 1984.

[Ishi:90]
Ishikawa, H.
"An Object-Oriented Knowledge Base Approach to a Next Generation of
Hypermedia Systems"
Proc. 1990 COMPCON, Spring 1990.

[Issa:90]
Issam, H., Shiratori, N., and Noguchi, S.
Tohoku University
"A New Realization for Parallel Data Base Machines with Its Model"
SIG Notes, IPSJ, March 1990.

[Ishi:90]
Ishii, Takemoshi (Chair)
MITI, Industrial Electronics Div., Machinery and Information Industry Bureau
"Report of the Research Committee on the New Information Processing
Technology: Executive Summary"
TR, April 1990.
A new focus on intuitive versus logical processing. Issues of incompleteness
of information, changeability of information, combinatorial complexity,
strong connectivity, and parallelism. The required technologies are
'soft' (flexible) and massively parallel distributed processing with
optical technologies and pattern recognition. Basis for research into
Self-Organizing System. Comparison with U.S., EC and U.K. efforts.

[Ishi:90]
Ishikawa, Hiroshi
Fujitsu
"An Object-Oriented Knowledge Base Approach to a Next Generation
of Hypermedia System"
COMPCON 1990.

[Ishi:91]
Ishii, Yoshioki
Adabas
"DBMS Market Share in Japan"
Received March 1991.
Information related to Adabas Far East.

[Jian:89]
Jiang, S.J., et al.
"Abstract Data Types in Graphics Databases"
Proc. IFIP TC-2 Working Conference on Visual Database Systems, Tokyo, April
1989.

[Kaha:91]
Kahaner, David
"Japanese Database Activities"
Received April 1991.
The activities of the Japan Database Promotion Center.

[Kamb:90]
Kambayashi, Yahiko
Kyoto University
"Bibliography of work by Yahiko Kambayashi"
February 1990.

[Kamb:91]
Kambayashi, Yahiko
Kyoto University
"Studies on the Name Placement Problem of Geographical Database
Systems"
Report, March 1991.
Final report; mesh and top-down methods.

[Kamb:91]
Kambayashi, Yahiko (ed.)
Kyoto University
"Studies on Pseudonatural Language Interfaces for User-Friendly Database"
Kyoto University, Integrated Media Experimental Lab, Report March 1991.
Includes four reprints.

[Kato:88]
Kato et al.
"TRADEMARK: Multimedia Database with Abstracted Representation on
Knowledge   Base"
Proc. 2nd Int. Symp. on Interoperable Info. Systems, 1988.

[Kato:89]
Kato, K., Fujisawa, H., Ohyama, M., Kawaguchi, H.,
    Hatakeyama, A., Kaneoka, N., and Akizawa, M.
"An Index-Free Full-Text Search Machine for Large Japanese Text Bases"
IEEE Data Engineering, December 1989.

[KatM:89]
Kato, T., and Mizutori, T.
Electrotechnical Lab
"Multimedia Data Model for Advanced Image Information System"
Advanced Database Systems Symposium, Kyoto, 1989.

[Kato:90]
Kato, T., and Kurita, T.
Electrotechnical Lab
"Visual Interaction with Electronic Art Gallery"
Database and Expert Systems Applications, Tjoa and Wagner (Eds.), Springer-Verlag, 1990.

[Kato:91]
Kato et al.
"A Cognitive Approach to Visual Interaction"
Proc. Int. Conf. on Multimedia Info. Systems, January 1991.

[Kita:87]
Kitamura, T., Hayami, H., Nakamura, T., and Inoue, U.
NTT, Japan
"Relational Database Machine Architecture Based on an Attached Processor Approach"
Denki Tsushin Kenkyusho Kenkyu Jitsuyoka Hokoku, Vol.36, No.5, 1987, pp. 663ff.

[Kita:90]
Kitagawa, H., and Kunii, T. L.
Tsukuba University
"Nested Table Handling by Flat Table Operator"
HICSS 23, January 1990, IEEE CS, pp.288-297.
Nested relational model.

[Kito:80]
Kito, S., Hattori, T., and Murakami, Y.
Aichi Institute of Technology, Department of Industrial Engineering (Toyota, Japan)
"An Exploit Systems Approach to Computer-Aided Design of Multi-Component Catalysts"
Chemical Engineering Sc., Vol.45, No.8, pp. 2661-2667.
Rule-based system.

[Kito:90]
Kito, S., Hattori, T., and Murakami, Y.
Aichi Institute of Technology (Toyota, Japan)
"A Knowledge Representation for Use of Catalyst Activity Pattern"

[Kito:90]
Kito, S., Hattori, T., and Murakami, Y.
Aichi Institute of Technology (Toyota, Japan)
"Expert Systems Approach to Computer-Aided Design of Catalysts."

[Kits:90]
Kitsuregawa, M., and Ogawa, Y.
"Bucket Spreading Parallel Hash: A New, Robust, Parallel Hash
Join Method for Data Skew in the Super Database Computer (SDC),"
Proc. 16th VLDB Conf., 1990.

[Kobu:91]
Kobuchi, Youichi
Ryukoku University
"State Evaluation Functions and Lyapunov Functions for Neural Networks"
Neural Networks, to appear 1991.
Analysis of neural network learned nodes.

[Koji:88]
Kojima, I., et al.
"The Architecture of an Open Multimedia Database System"
Proc. 2nd Int. Symp. on Interoperable Information Systems, 1988.

[Koji:91]
Kojima, I., et al.
"Implementation of an Object-Oriented Query Language System with Remote
Procedure Call Interface"
1st Int. Workshop on Interoperability in Multidatabase Sys., Kyoto, 1991.

[Kona:89]
Konagaya, A., and Yokota, M.
NEC
"DNA Sequence Knowledge Base System (KNOA)"
Workshop on Future Trends in Logic Programming, 1989.
Homology search with gap insertion; the Genback, NBRF, DNA and Protein
databases, is in Prolog clauses on CHI machine, has 320 MB main memory.

[Kosa:87]
Kosaka, K., Kajitani, K., and Satoh, M.
IBM Japan
"An Experimental Mixed-Object Database System"
IEEE Office Automation Symp., April 1987.

[Kuha:91]
Kuhara, S., Satou, K., Furuichi, E., Takagi, T., and Takehara, H.
Kyushu University
"A Deductive Database System PACADE for the Three Dimensional Structure
of Protein"
24th Hawaii Int. Conf. on Sys. Sciences, 1991.

[Kuni:90]
Kunii, H. S.
"Graph Data Model and Its Data Language"
Springer-Verlag, 1990.

[Kuro:90]
Kurozumi, Takashi
ICOT
"An Introduction to the Fifth Generation Computer Systems Project"
ICOT Journal, No.29, 1990.
Only background and organizational growth.

[Luan:89]
Luan, Y.Q., et al.
"Functional Approach to Chemical Structure Databases"
Proc. DASFAA, Seoul, Korea, April 1989.

[Maed:88]
Maeda, A., Tanaka, S., Hirata, T., Futatsumata, T., and Shibayama, J.
Mitsubishi
"A Multimedia Database System Featuring Similarity Retrieval"
Proc. 2nd Int. Symp. on Interoperable Information Systems, 1988.

[Maki:91]
Makinouchi, M., and Aritsugi, M.
Kyushu University
"The Object-Oriented Persistent Programming Language for Multimedia Databases"
TR CSCE 91-C04, Dept. of CS and Comm. Eng., Kyushu University.
Discusses use of Mach virtual memory mapping for multimedia objects.

[Masa:91]
Masai, Kazuo
Hitachi
"Advanced Features of Integrated DB/DC System XDM"
Received March 1991. Presentation material reported at DASFAA 1.
Extensible data manager, together applications and various databases.

[Masu:91]
Masunaga, Yoshifumi
"Design of OMEGA: An Object-Oriented Multimedia Database Management System"
Journal of Information Processing, Vol.14, No.1, 1991.

[Masu:90]
Masunaga, Yoshifumi
 University of Library and Information Science, Tsukuba
 "Object Identity, Equality and Relational Concept"
 in *Deductive and Object-Oriented Databases*, Kim, Nicholas, and Nishio (eds.),
 Elsevier N-H, 1990.
 For real world data modeling, introduces three new kinds of object equality:
 trivial-equal, referential-equal, and arbitrary-equal.

[Masu:90]
Masunaga, Y., and Sasaki, T.
 University of Library and Information Science, Tsukuba
 "Design and Implementation of a Mathematica Formula Database for
 Computer Algebra System GAL"
 IPSJ 30th Anniversary Conf., 1990, pp.235-244.
 Specialized indexing to resolve problems; multiple hits are typical;
 database is less than 1000 in test.

[Mish:89]
Mishina, Y., and Kojima, K.
 Central Research Lab., Hitachi Ltd.
 "A String Matching Algorithm for Vector Processors"
 IEEE Data Engineering, December 1989.

[MITI:90]
MITI, Industrial Electronics Div., Machinery and Information Industry Bureau
 "Report of the Research Committee on the New Information Processing
Technology"   MITI Tokyo, March 1990.
 Basis for sixth generation project, calling for international cooperation.

[MITI:91]
MITI
 "Interoperable Database Systems"
 Received March 1991.
 INTAP overview.

[Miya:89]
Miyazaki, N., et al.
 OKI and ICOT
 "A Framework for Query Transformations in Deductive Databases"
 Journal of Information Processing, Vol.12, No.4, 1989.

[Miya:89]
Miyazaki, Nobuyoshi
Oki
"Horn Clause Transformation by Restrictor in Deductive Databases"
Journal of Information Processing, Vol.12, No.3, 1989.

[Miya:90]
Miyazaki, Nobuyoshi
Oki
"Selection Propagation in Deductive Databases"
Data and Knowledge Engineering, New-Holland, Vol.5, No.4, 1990.

[Miza:90]
Mizaguchi, S., Kurihara, S., Ohta, K., and Morita, H.
NTT Communications and Information Processing Lab
"Expansion of FEAL Cipher"
NTT Review, Vol.2, No.6, December 1990, pp.117-127.

[Mori:90]
Morita, Y., Haniuda, H., and Yokota, K.
Oki and ICOT
"Object Identity of QUIXOTE"
IPSJ SIG Reports 90-DBS80-12, November 1990.
Identity is also the property for users to a specific object; QUIXOTE
uses extended term representation as oids, which can include some
attributes of the object.

[Moza:89]
Mozaffari, M., and Tanaka, Y.
Hokkaido University
"ODM: An Object-Oriented Data Model"
in *New Generation Computing*, Vol.7, 1989, pp.3-35, OHMSHA and
Springer-Verlag.
Integrates object-oriented features (as in SMALLTALK-80) with extended
relational model (concept of 'uniform set'); generalization of relations;
operations have a selector, parameter list, and a selected method; messages
for objects include size, include distincts, subset, eq, union, intersect,
set difference, do, select, insert, delete; no implementation.

[NACS:91]
NACSIS
"National Center for Science Information System (NACSIS)"
Received March 1991.
Lots of databases, accessible in U.S. via National Science Foundation.

[Nami:89]
Namiuchi, M., Kiyoki, Y., and Liu, P.
Tsukuba University
"Implementation of a Parallel Processing Scheme for Deductive Databases and
Resource Allocation Strategies"
IEEE Data Engineering, July 1989.

[NCFI:90]
National Committee of FID of Japan
JICST and NACSIS
"The National Information Policy in Japan"
Tokyo, 1990, 9pp.
Overview of status and plans for effective distribution of scientific
and technical information, sponsored by Science and Technology Council
(Prime Minister, Minister of State for Science and Technology, Minister
of Education, etc.).

[NEC:91]
NEC
NEC Japan
"Characteristics of KBMS"
Received March 1991.
PC expert system, product summary.

[NTT:90]
NTT Data Communications System Corporation
NTT Data, Tokyo
"Creating Value for Business and Society"
NTT Data, 1990.
Corporate brochure, listing projects and clients.

[Negi:90]
Negishi, Masamitsu
NACSIS
"Research Activities in Japan and Japanese Articles Registered in
Western Databases"
in *Japanese Information in Science, Technology and Commerce*,
IOS Press, 1990.
The number of papers in four databases was investigated; three
databases appear to be heavily biased toward Western articles;
Japan now occupies the second position after the U.S. in many fields.

[Nish:91]
Nishio, Shojiro
 Department of Information and Computer Sc., Osaka University
 "Status Update on Database Technology in Japan"
 IEEE Pacific Rim Conference on Communication, Computer, and Signal Processing,
 Victoria, B.C., Canada, May 1991.
 Excellent review, includes activities of professional societies.

[Ogaw:89]
Ogawa, Y., and Kitsuregawa, M.
 Institute of Industrial Science, University of Tokyo
 "Bucket Spreading Strategy: A Novel Parallel Hash Join Method for the Super Database Computer"
 Data Engineering, December 14, 1989.

[Ohni:89]
Ohnishi, H., Kiyoki, Y., and Shinjo, Y.
 Institute of Information Sciences and Electronics, Tsukuba University
 "Resource Allocation Strategies in the Parallel Processing System SMASH"
 Data Engineering, December 14, 1989.

[Okaz:90]
Okazaki, A., et al.
 "Image Based Geographic Information System using Optical Disks"
 Proc. Image Communications and Workstations Conference, Society
 of Photo Optical Instrumentation Engineers, Santa Clara, CA, February 1990.

[Ooom:84]
Ooomote
 "Studies on High Performance Secondary Storage for Distributed System and its Application to Database Machine"
 Denshi Gijutsu Sogo Kenkyusho Kenkyu Hokoku, December 1984.

[Rico:80]
Ricoh
 Ricoh, Software Research Center, Tokyo
 "Introduction to RICOHBASE"
 Company brochure for American market of G-BASE, based on H. Kunii Graph-Data model. It handles both general queries and navigation via explicit links.

[Rico:90]
Ricoh
"Commercial Product Brochure"
Ricoh Corporation, Software Research Center.

[Rico:91]
Ricoh Corp.
Tokyo, Japan; Santa Clara, California
"The Interactive Three-dimensional Solid Modeling System: DESIGNBASE"
Ricoh Corp, received March 1991.
Brochure to introduce product to U.S. customers.

[Saba:6]
Saba, Shoichi (Chair)
International Multimedia Association (Tokyo)
"Guidance of Admission"
Brochure soliciting membership.

[Saka:87]
Sakai, Toshiyuki (ed.)
Kyoto University
"Sakai Lab"
Kyoto University Report, March 1987.
Overview of information processing activities 1957-87 and its IMES report.

[Saka:88]
Sakai, T., and Aichi, Y.
Kyoto University
"Multi-media System IMES"
Proposal, 1988.
Proposal from Sakai lab at Kyoto, basis for directions at Ryukoku University.

[Saka:91]
Sakai, Toshiyuki
Kyoto University
"Expectation of AI in 21C"
AI 87, Japan
Commemorative speech draws many relationships.

[Saka:91]
Sakai, Toshiyuki
 Ryukoku University
 "Introduction for Our Researchers"
 Ryukoku University, March 1991.
 Focuses on computer interactive systems.

[Sana:90]
Sanada, N., and Tanaka, K.
 Kobe University
 "Adding Methods to Relational Database Constructs"
 Received March 1991.
 Describes a prototype hypertext system named SQL-Navigator. Major features
 are (1) RDB constructs as objects, (2) predicate-based dynamic method
 attachment, and (3) realization of direct manipulation.

[Sato:91]
Satoh, K., Tasaka, M., Yamamoto, Y., and Namioka, M.
 Hitachi, Systems Development Laboratory
 "INDAS/ff, - a Fuzzy Information Retrieval Facility of the Intelligent
 Database System INDAS - Its Architecture, Query Processing, and Visual
 User Interface"
 4th IJSA World Congress, 1991.

[Sato:85]
Satoh, K., Tsuchida, M., Nakamura, F., and Oomachi, K.
 Hitachi, Systems Development Laboratory
 "Local and Global Query Optimization Mechanisms for Relational Databases"
 VLDB 85, Stockholm 1985, pp.405-417.
 Includes good overview.

[Shik:91]
Shikata, Tsutoma
 NTT Data, Tokyo
 "Investment Reseach Data Base System"
 NTT Data, March 1991, presentation material
 A system which mediates outside vendor financial database for use at
 trust officers' workstations. It uses IBM 9370 equipment to analyze
 and adjust stock and bond information, compute beta values. Uses SAS tools,
 summarization and graphs. Older information is summarized.
 All information is locally archived and backed-up, total current volume
 for one bank is 5 Gbytes.

[Shir:91]
Shirota, Y., Iizawa, A., and Kunii, H. S.
Ricoh, Software Research Center, Tokyo
"Image Database Construction Tools for RICOHBASE"
Proc. of the IEEE Pacific Rim Conf. on Communications, Computers, and Signal Processing, Victoria, B.C., Canada, May 1991, pp.277-283.

[Sood:85]
Sood, A., and Qureshi, A.
"Database Machines: Modern Trends and Applications"
NATO Advanced Study Institute on Relational Database Machine Architecture, Les Arcs, France, July 1985.

[Suzu:82]
Suzuki, K., Tanaka, T., and Hattori, F.
NTT Public (Yokohama, Japan)
"Implementation of a Distributed Database Management System for Very Large Real-Time Applications"
IEEE COMPCON 25, September 1982.
Plans for a hierarchical distributed architecture to support 50tps and 106 bytes: DEIMS-3.

[Suzu:89]
Suzuki, T., Takagi, T., and Ushijima, K.
Kyushu University
"Efficient Bottom-up Evaluation of Negative Closed Queries on Stratified Databases"
Advanced Database Sys. Symp., Kyoto, 1989.

[Suzu:91]
Suzuki, Kouichi
NTT Data, Tokyo
"Database R and D Activities in NTT Data Communication Corporation"
NTT Data, March 1991, presentation materials.

[Taka:91]
Takagi, T., Suzuki, T., Goto, S., and Ushijima, K.
Kyushu University
"Applicability of a Deductive Database for CAD Systems"
DE 7, April 1991.
Prototype evaluation to querying in petrochemical plant, written in PROLOG used magic sets, Naughton, and Kempert. The database derived from a drawing has about 1000 components, loaded into memory.
The alternatives are carefully evaluated on a simple case.

[Tana:80]
Tanaka, Y., Nozaka, Y., and Masuyama, A.
 Hokkaido University
 "Pipeline Searching and Sorting Modules as Components of a Data Flow
 Database Computer"
 Information Processing 80, S.H. Lavingto (ed.)
 North-Holland Publishing Co., IFIP, 1980.

[Tana:84]
Tanaka, Y.
 Hokkaido University
 "Bit-Sliced VLSI Algorithms for Search and Sort"
 VLDB 10, Singapore, August, 1984.

[TaYu:84]
Tanaka, Y.
 Hokkaido University
 "A Multiport Page-Memory Architecture and A Multiport Disk-Cache System"
 New Generation Computing, Vol.2, 1984, pp.241-260, OHMSHA, Ltd., Springer.

[TnYu:84]
Tanaka, Y.
 Hokkaido University
 "MPDC: Massive Parallel Architecture for Very Large Databases"
 5GCS Conference, 1984, edited by ICOT.

[TanY:84]
Tanaka, Yuzuru
 Hokkaido University
 "A Multiport Page-Memory Architecture and a Multiport Disk-Cache System"
 NGC, Vol.2, 1984, pp.241-260.

[Tana:85]
Tanaka, Yuzuru
 "MPDC: Massive Parallel Architecture for Very Large Databases"
 5GCS Conference, ICOT, 1985, pp.113-137.

[TanY:85]
Tanaka, Y.
 Hokkaido University
 "A VLSI Algorithm for Sorting Variable-Length Character Strings"
 New Generation Computing, Vol.3, 1985, pp.307-328 OHMSHA, Ltd., Springer.

[Tana:86]
Tanaka, Y.
"Massive Parallel Database Computer MPDC and Its Control Schemes for Massively Parallel Processing"
NATO OSI Series F24, Database Machines, Sood and Qureski (eds.), Springer, 1986.   File segmentation, object locking, dataflow control; a demonstration machine was built later.

[Tana:89]
Tanaka, Y., et al.
"Transmedia Machine"
Journal of Information Processing, Vol.12, No.2, 1989.

[Tana:91]
Tanaka, Y.
"A Synthetic Dynamic-Media System"
Proc. Int. Conf. on Multimedia Information Systems, Singapore, 1991.

[TanK:88]
Tanaka, K.
Kobe University
"Storing and Manipulating Multimedia Database Objects by Postscript and Relational Databases"
Proc. 2nd Int. Conf. on Interoperable Information, INTAP, Tokyo, 1988.
Applies embedding of Postscript in RDBMS to geographical database example.

[TaYI:88]
Tanaka, K., Yoshikawa, M., and Ishihara, K.
Kobe University; Kyoto Sangyo University
"Schema Visualization in Object-Oriented Databases"
IEEE DE 4, Los Angeles, 1988.
Introduces virtual classes and schemata to provide users with different views of an object-oriented database.

[TanY:88]
Tanaka, K., and Yoshihara, M.
Kobe University; Kyoto Sangyo University
"Towards Abstracting Complex Database Objects: Generalization, Reduction, and Unification of Set-type Objects" (extended abstract)
Proc. 2nd Int. Conf. Database Theory, Bruges, S-V Lecture Notes in CS, Vol.326, 1988.
Introduces notion of "element-based" generalization relationships between complex objects and two new abstraction operators: reduction and unification.

[TaYI:89]
Tanaka, K., Yoshikawa, M., and Ishihara, K.
Kobe University; Kyoto Sangyo University
"Schema Design, Views, and Incomplete Information in Object-Oriented Databases"
J. of Inf. Proc., Vol.12, No.3, 1989.
Considers issues listed in title plus update propagation, in a SMALLTALK-80 context.

[TSSM:89]
Tanaka, S., Shima, M., Shibayama, J., and Maeda, A.
Mitsubishi
"Retrieval Method for an Image Database based on Topological Structure"
SPIE Vol. 1153, App. of Dig. Im. Proc. XII, 1989.

[TanI:89]
Tanaka, Y., and Imataki, T.
Hokkaido University
"INTELLIGENTPAD: A Hypermedia System Allowing Functional Compositions of Active Media Objects through Direct Manipulations"
Information Processing 89, IFIP, North Holland 1989.
View pads for output, controller pads for input, and model pads.

[TaTM:89]
Tanaka, Y., Takahashi, K., and Mozaffari, M.
Hokkaido University
"Transmedia Machine"
J. of Inf. Proc., Vol.12, No.2, 1989.
NATO OSI Series F24, Database Machines, Sood and Qureski (eds.), Springer, 1986. Basic operations for text processes.

[Tana:90]
Tanaka, Yuzuru
"A Tool Kit System for the Synthesis and the Management of Active Media Objects"
Deductive and Object-Oriented Databases, Kim, Nicholas, and Nishio (eds.) Elsevier N-H, 1990.
Visual synthesis of database interface objects: INTELLIGENTPAD.
Pads are objects with a persistent physical presentation form, a value and a function (WP, graph drawing, ..). Pads can be combined by pasting, [Hend, CHI] on Trillium [Henderson, CHI '86].
Demo implementation in SMALLTALK.

[TanC:90]
Tanaka, K., and Chang, T.S.
Kobe University
"On Natural Joins in Object-Oriented Databases"
in *Deductive and Object-Oriented Databases*, Kim, Nicholas, and Nishio
(eds.), Elsevier N-H, 1990.
Introduces natural join operation for composing complex objects, and
discusses how to realize it by message passing.

[TanH:91]
Tanaka, Hidetoshi
Institute for New Generation Computer Technology
"Protein Funcation Database as a Deductive and Object-Oriented Database"
Received March 1991.
Plans to use QUIXOTE at ICOT with complex data and inference rules.

[Tana:91]
Tanaka, Yuzuru
Hokkaido University
"Vocabulary-Based Logic Programming"
Received March 1991.

[TanT:91]
Tanaka, Y., and Torii, H.
Hokkaido University
"Transmedia Machine and its Key Wordsearch and Image Texts"
Received March 1991.

[Tana:91]
Tanaka, Y.
Hokkaido
"Vocabulary Building for Database Queries"
Formal model addressing after language flexibility, access flexibility,
semantics.
Received March 1991.

[Tana:91]
Tanaka, Yuzuru
Hokkaido University
"Informative Space Model"
Received March 1991.
Semantic model based on morphism to compose information subspaces.

[Tojo:85]
Tojo, A., and Sato, T.
ETL
"Interoperable Database System: A New National R and D Project and its
Impact on Multimedia Information Processing Technology"
IEEE CS Workshop on CAPAIDM, November 1985.

[Tojo:91]
Tojo, Akio
ETL, Tsukuba, Japan
"National Research and Development Plan on Interoperable Database Systems"
Workshop on Interoperability in Multidatabase Systems (IMS'91), Kyoto,
Japan, April 1991.
MITI sponsored project (1986-1992) on database architecture, multimedia
technology, distributed system technology, and open systems carried out
by ETL, INTAP, and companies; references and implementation schedule. COSI.

[Tori:87]
Torii, S., Kojima, K., Yoshizumi, S., Sakata, A., Takamoto, Y.,
    Kawabe, S., Takahashi, M., and Ishizuka, T.
Hitachi Ltd.
"A Relational Database System Architecture Based on a Vector Processing
Method"
IEEE DE3, February 1987, Los Angeles, CA.

[Tori:88]
Torii, S., Kojima, K., Kanada, Y., Sakata, A., Yoshizumi, S., and Takahashi, M.
Hitachi Ltd.
"Accelerating Non-Numerical Processing by an Extended Vector Processor"
IEEE DE4, Los Angeles, February 1988.

[Tori:88]
Torii, S., et al.
"Accelerating non-numerical processing by an Extended Vector Processor"
DE4, 1988.

[Tosh:91]
Toshiba
"RDD/V"
Received March 1991.
SQL relational DBMS for Toshiba equipment.

[Tosh:91]
Toshiba Corp.
"Corporate Technology Management"
Received March 1991.
Research organization and funding--only 1.5% government.

[Tsut:90]
Tsutsumi, F., Takagi, T., and Ushijima, K.
Kyushu University
"An Effective Program Transformation of Logical Recursive Queries in Deductive Databases"
Far-East Workshop on Future Database Systems, 1990.

[Waki:90]
Wakimoto, K., Shima, M., Tanaka, S., and Maeda, A.
Mitsubishi
"An Intelligent User Interface to an Image Database Using a Figure Interpretation Method"
IEEE Conf. on Pattern Recognition 10, June 1990.

[Waki:91]
Wakimoto, K., Shima, M., Tanaka, S., Shibayama, J., and Maeda, A.
Mitsubishi
"Knowledge-Based Multimedia Information Retrieval Applied to Plant Diagrams"
IMS'91, Kyoto, April 1991.
Navigation by semantic zooming, panning, backtracking, and alternatives.

[Wied:91]
Wiederhold, G., Beech, D., and Minoura, T.
"Multi-media Database Development in Japan"
IEEE Data Engineering Bulletin, Vol.14, No.3, September 1991, pp.36-45.

[Yaji:91]
Yajima, K., Kitagawa, H., Yamaguchi, K., Ohbo, N., and Fujiwara, Y.
Tsukuba University
"Optimization of Queries Including ADT Functions"
DASFAA 91, Tokyo, April 1991.
Consider high cost of function evaluation during selection.

[Yama:89]
Yamamoto, Y., Namioka, M., Moki, K., and Satoh, K.
Hitachi, Systems Development Lab
"An Experimental Multimedia Database System: MANDRILL--Its Architecture
and Language"
DASFAA 1, Int. Symp. on Database Sys. for Adv. App., Seoul, Korea, April 1989.
Design overview for an object DBMS, with some high-level operations on
complex (i.e., interconnected) objects but no discussion of implementation
times such as caching and component sharing; nor is there any discussion of
multimedia aspects mentioned in title.

[Yama:90]
Yamazaki, M., Yobe, M., and Fujiwara, Y.
Matsushita (Kawasaki); Yokohama University; Tsukuba University
"The Image-based Database on Electronic Materials using CD-ROM"
CAMSE 1, Tokyo, August 1990.
IEIDA materials database prototype, uses MS-Windows.

[Yoko:91]
Yokota, K., Kawamura, M., and Tanaka, H.
ICOT, 3rd Research Lab.
"Overview of R and D Activities in Databases and Knowledgebases in ICOT"
Received March 1991.
From KAPPA and PHI (1985) to DOOD and QUIXOTE, also parallel computing,
PSI to PIM.

[Zhou:91]
Zhou, N.Z., Takagi, T., and Ushijima, K.
Kyushu University
"Improving the Efficiency of Prolog Programs by Using Matching Instead of
Unification"
IPSJ S36-FAI 8802
For restricted conditions a transformation can convert SLD to SSLD resolution,
giving much faster proofs.

Part III

Machine Translation in Japan

Jaime Carbonell, Chairman
Elaine Rich, Co–Chairman
David Johnson
Masaru Tomita
Muriel Vasconcellos
Yorick Wilks

Executive Summary

The goal of this report is to provide an overview of the state of the art of machine translation (MT) in Japan and to provide a comparison between Japanese and Western technology in this area. The term "machine translation", as used here, includes both the science and technology required for automating the translation of text from one human language to another (for example from Japanese to English or from French to Japanese).

Machine translation is viewed in Japan as an important strategic technology that is expected to play a key role in Japan's increasing participation in the world economy. MT is seen in Japan as important both for assimilating information into Japanese as well as for disseminating Japanese information throughout the world as part of the export process. As a result, several of Japan's largest industrial companies are developing MT systems. Many are already marketing their systems commercially. There is also an active MT and natural language processing research community at some of the major universities and government/industrial consortia.

Although MT products are already available, their incorporation into the everyday translation process is just beginning. The JTEC team visited two translation service bureaus that were using MT for about 20% of their volume, and there are others that are also starting to exploit MT. The volume of translation done using MT may grow quickly in the near term, since new networking services are making MT services more easily accessible. MT systems are also being used internally in many companies, including both the companies that have built the MT systems as well as their customers. The primary use for MT today is in translating technical documentation for products to be sold abroad. The volume is still relatively small but appears to be growing steadily. There is also an increasing use of MT systems embedded in other applications, such as database retrieval systems, electronic mail, and (in the prototype stage) speech-to-speech translation systems.

Most of the effort to develop MT in Japan has been devoted to systems that translate from English to Japanese (E/J) and from Japanese to English (J/E). But over the last several years, several of the systems have been extended to cover other languages, including the common European languages (such as German, French, and Spanish) and other Asian languages (such as Chinese and Korean).

Users reported varying degrees of success with MT. Although some users reported reduced productivity, many continue to rely on MT for such benefits as consistency of translated terms. Other users report productivity gains of up to 300%. Productivity gains of 30% appear average, with higher numbers for restricted application domains and lower ones for broader domains for which the system has not been finely tuned. Most uses of MT require some human pre- or postediting to produce acceptable quality translations.

Most of the MT systems now available in Japan are transfer-based systems. The majority of them exploit a case-frame representation of the source text as the basis of the transfer process. There is a gradual movement toward the use of deeper semantic representations, and some groups are beginning to look at interlingua-based systems. The Electronic Dictionary Research Project (EDR) is building a dictionary that will contain at least 400,000 concepts, as well as the associated Japanese and English words. When this dictionary is available, it will provide one important tool for building interlingua-based systems. All the commercial MT systems available today translate a single sentence at a time, although some exploit a small amount of information about the larger context.

The currently available commercial systems clearly reflect the significant investments that have been made by the Japanese. They have dictionaries ranging in size from 50,000 to 800,000 entries (the latter including specialized technical terms). Many have over 300,000 entries, but none are as rich or as detailed as the EDR dictionary.

There is a clear consensus among MT vendors in Japan that the dominant factor that influences MT acceptance is the accuracy and fluency (collectively termed "quality") of the resulting translations. Other factors, such as purchase price and friendly user interfaces, although important, are much less significant. The vendors are therefore concentrating most of their efforts on improving quality, primarily by enlarging their dictionaries and grammars, and, secondarily, by gradually moving toward systems that perform deeper levels of semantic analysis.

A comparison between the U.S. and Japan in terms of MT and related technologies shows that Japan is ahead of the U.S. in several important ways, including the commercial use of MT, the acceptance of MT among users, the development of knowledge sources such as dictionaries, and the use of optical character recogniton (OCR) as an input modality, as well as in funding levels for R&D in MT. The U.S. has led in funding for basic research in natural language processing (the scientific underpinning of MT), and continues to lead in technological diversity (the number of different approaches that are being considered), linguistic diversity (because of a greater interest in the U.S. in the European languages), and level of effort devoted to R&D in speech processing. In both the U.S. and Japan, total funding for MT (including R&D, commercialization, deployment, and day-to-day use) appears to be on a gradual but steady rise.

The Japanese have made, and continue to make, a very significant commitment to MT. This commitment is visible in several ways, including Japanese industrial and government funding levels, the Japanese view of MT as an international prestige technology, and, most recently, in the increasing, steady, day-to-day acceptance and use of MT in the Japanese marketplace. Overall, the Japanese commitment to MT is greater than the U.S. one, though the latter is by no means insignificant.

1. Introduction: Machine Translation in Japan and the U.S.

Jaime Carbonell

1.1 The State of the Art in Machine Translation

The goal of machine translation (MT) is to automate the process of translating natural languages: English to Japanese (E/J), Japanese to English (J/E), Russian to French (R/F), Spanish to English (S/E), and so forth. In the ideal case, the translation would be fully automated, highly accurate, stylistically perfect and applicable to any topic and any style of texts. In present day reality, MT is only partially capable of achieving these objectives, with trade-offs between degree of automation vs. accuracy, breadth of coverage and text type vs. stylistic appropriateness, etc. Research and development proceed inexorably forward, gradually improving the MT state-of-the-art. But for certain classes of applications, MT is already a viable commercial reality, as we see below.

Currently, there is one recognized European commercial MT system (METAL by Siemens), two to four major American commercial MT systems (SYSTRAN, LOGOS, etc.) and at least three times that many Japanese MT systems. (See Figure 1-2.) In general, all of these systems produce rough translations containing errors of content and style that are typically corrected by a human translator (the "posteditor"), who is fluent in both the source and target languages. In addition, some of them require that the input text be "pre-edited" by a person fluent in the source language, before the MT system is used. The primary economic benefit results when less human effort is required to produce and correct machine translations than to produce them from scratch --- at least in situations in which stylistic perfection is not absolutely required. Secondary benefits accrue from other sources, such as consistency across translations and the embedding of MT into an already automated text production process.

1.2 The Role of Machine Translation

There are two primary roles for machine translation:

1. Assimilation of information in multiple foreign languages into the native language.

2. Dissemination of text in the native language into multiple foreign languages for a variety of reasons, chiefly as product literature to promote exports.

Each of these two roles makes different demands on an MT system. Dissemination requires very accurate and stylistically sound translation, as the translated texts will usually be printed and disseminated widely, and, in the case of technical documentation, acceptance of the product or service in the foreign market will be determined in part by the quality and timeliness of the translated text. On the other hand, assimilation places less stringent requirements on stylistic quality and may impose relaxed accuracy requirements as well. Often texts are translated only to determine what they are about, which requires only the roughest of translations, and only the small percentage of those found potentially relevant require more accurate or complete translation. The information analyst (e.g., a scientist, a technology watcher, an economic monitor, etc.) can tolerate stylistically imperfect texts even for those texts that are fully translated, though accuracy may be at a premium.

Unlike accuracy and style, where the requirements for dissemination are far more stringent than for assimilation, when we look at the ability to exploit topic and style constraints, we see that assimilation presents the more difficult problem. Documents for multilingual dissemination, such as operating and assembly manuals for electronic equipment, share a common subject matter and a common writing style. In many cases, the same organization that is responsible for the translation has control over the production of the original documents and so can enforce stylistic rules that enhance the accuracy of MT. In contrast, the assimilation task must be flexible enough to accomodate documents on diverse topics and written in diverse styles. We describe the use of MT for both assimilation and dissemination in more detail in Section 6.1.

MT systems should be evaluated with respect to the user's primary objectives — either assimilation or dissemination. Within each category, the requirements for such factors as diversity, accuracy, volume, speed, etc., should be analyzed. Although most MT systems, especially Japanese ones, have not been developed to specialize in either primary function, current trends indicate that specialization to accommodate user demands may be a way of obtaining greater performance on the desired dimensions.

1.3 An Historical Sketch of Machine Translation

This section provides a brief sketch of the history of the development of MT systems. A summary of this discussion is shown in Figure 1-1. For additional background and historical perspective, see [Hutchins 86] and [Nagao 89]. We also return to this subject in Chapter 8, when we discuss the status of MT in Europe.

Work on machine translation started in the United States in the 1950s. Warren Weaver, a vice president of the Rockefeller Foundation, had been impressed by early projects undertaken in England by Booth, Britten, and Richens between 1946 and 1949, and in 1949 he wrote the "Weaver Memorandum", in which he proposed that there are language universals, that the basis of language is logical, and that the use of techniques from cryptanalysis to encode and decode the meaning of natural language would be the key to translating by computer [Weaver 55]. The first MT work in the U.S. was begun by E. Reifler at the University of Washington in 1950 and initially concentrated on German to English (G/E). A second G/E effort began at the University of Texas during the late 1950s. Other MT work in the U.S. during the 1950s focused primarily on Russian to English (R/E) translation, largely fueled by the Cold War and Sputnik and the perceived need for tracking Soviet technology. R/E MT was first demonstrated by Georgetown University in 1954. In 1956, larger efforts on R/E translation began both at the University of Washington and Georgetown University. During this period, the earliest small-scale Japanese MT systems also started.

By the 1960s the first European MT research had begun, most notably the GETA [Vauquois 84] project in Grenoble, France, led by Professor Bernard Vauquois. The efforts in Japan continued, although they remained small, but work in the United States increased. For example, work was revived at the University of Texas on the system that would be named METAL [Bennett 85] in the early 1970s. Development of the SYSTRAN system had also started by the end of this decade [Toma 76]. All these efforts encountered a series of scientific and technological difficulties. In particular, it proved difficult to produce semantically accurate translations by purely lexical and syntactic means. In fact, the philosopher-mathematician Bar-Hillel stated that lexical ambiguity could not be resolved without recourse to world knowledge, and without resolving ambiguity it was impossible to translate accurately. The state of the art in the 1960s did not permit semantic analysis, and therefore Bar-Hillel concluded that MT was not then possible. Perhaps more damaging to U.S.-based MT was the ALPAC report [ALPAC 66], produced under

YEARS	U.S.	EUROPE	JAPAN
1950s	Start Sizable MT Projects		Early MT Research
1960s	METAL GEORGETOWN ALPAC: MT drastically cut	Start MT GETA	Basic NLP R & D
1970s	SYSTRAN Basic NLP R & D	EUROTRA	Basic MT R & D
1980s	"grass roots" Restart MT R & D SYSTRAN	EUROTRA {METAL, SYSTRAN	MU System MT boom in industry labs
1990s	"Official" MT R & D SYSTRAN Multi–Lingual NLP	End EUROTRA Basic NLP R & D	MT Products R & D too: CICC, EDR, ATR, . . .

Figure 1-1: MT Historical Highlights

the auspices of the U.S. Academy of Sciences in 1966. ALPAC stated that MT was not economically feasible, among other reasons, because of the high cost of computers in the 1960s compared with the relatively low cost of human translators at that time — a situation now clearly reversed. In consequence, most but not all U.S. funding for MT research and development (R&D) evaporated in the 1960s. In this post-ALPAC climate it was left to the private sector to step into the breach. During this period, SYSTRAN, a private company, developed an R/E system that was installed for the U.S. Air Force [Toma 76].

The 1970s witnessed continued progress in France, the first widely used MT system in Canada (TAUM-METEO, developed at the University of Montreal for translating weather forecasts between English and French), and continued progress in the remaining U.S. MT efforts, most notably SYSTRAN and METAL. In spite of the hiatus in most U.S. MT R&D, research into the underlying science and technology of natural language processing (also called computational linguistics) continued unabated. In Japan, the pace of MT efforts quickened. Earlier efforts that had focused on basic work in natural language processing became the basis for substantial work on MT. See [Uemura 86] for a summary of some of these early efforts. Professor Makoto Nagao's laboratory at Kyoto University became a well-known center of MT work in Japan. The MU project [Nagao 86] got underway at Kyoto and elsewhere, with substantial government money and the goal of building a comprehensive MT system. (See Chapter

9 for details on this effort.) The research projects of the 1970s were to pave the way for the large Japanese MT R&D efforts of the 1980s and their commercialization in the 1990s. Fujitsu with its ATLAS-I project in 1978 represented one of the first industrial commitments to large-scale MT.

Company	System	MT Method
Bravice	MICROPAK	Syntactic Transfer
Catena	STAR	Syntactic Transfer
CSK	ARGO	Interlingual
EDR	EDR Electronic Dictionaries	Interlingual
Fujitsu	ATLAS-II	Interlingual
Hitachi	HICATS	Semantic Transfer
IBM, Japan	SHALT	Syntactic Transfer
JICST	JICST	Semantic Transfer
Matsushita	PAROLE	Syntactic Transfer
Mitsubishi	MELTRAN	Syntactic Transfer
NEC	PIVOT	Interlingual
Oki	PENSEE	Syntactic Transfer
Ricoh	RMT	Syntactic Transfer
Sanyo	SWP-7800	Syntactic Transfer
Sharp	DUET	Semantic Transfer
Toshiba	ASTRANSAC	Semantic Transfer

Figure 1-2: Japanese Industrial MT Systems

The 1980s witnessed an historically unparalleled set of initiatives in Japanese MT. In the early 1980s, the MU project was in full swing, supported by substantial government funding. MU focused on translating abstracts of scientific papers between Japanese and English. The MU system has subsequently served as the basis of the JICST translation system, which is in everyday large-scale government use for scientific abstract translation. In the same time period, virtually every large computer and electronics company in Japan endeavored to build its own MT system, most with substantial R&D teams (dozens of researchers) over many years, as summarized in Figure 1-2. (See Section 1.6 for an explanation of the entries in column 3 of this figure.) The majority of these efforts have produced working MT systems, mostly for translating Japanese to English and English to Japanese. Several new government-sponsored efforts were started in the late 1980s in Japan, most notably at the Center of the International Cooperation for Computerization (CICC), where the focus is on interlingua-based translation between Japanese and several Asian languages (see Section 9.9), and at EDR, which has undertaken a large effort aimed at building shared dictionaries and knowledge bases to support MT (see Section 9.6). Another new R&D effort is the work at ATR on a translating telephone. (See Section 9.10.)

Europe witnessed the EUROTRA phenomenon [Johnson 85] in the 1980s. This effort, spanning over a decade, was sponsored by the European Community (EC), and had the ambitious goal of translation between every EC language pair. Although not successful at this ambitious goal, EUROTRA energized European computational linguistics and MT activities. (See Section 8.3.) Also during this period, the

METAL system was acquired by Siemens/Nixdorf and moved to Europe.

In the late 1980s, MT research started again in earnest in the United States, emerging from the long shadow of ALPAC with the establishment of several substantial initiatives, including the Center for Machine Translation at Carnegie Mellon University, several MT efforts at IBM, the University of New Mexico, MCC, New York University, and the University of Southern California's Information Sciences Institute. Although representing greater technological and linguistic diversity, the U.S. and European MT efforts have not yet matched those of the Japanese in terms of sheer numbers, budget, longevity, and commercial maturity.

The 1990s have followed trends that were established in the late 1980s. These include increased MT R&D in Japan, and initial commercialization of MT systems in the Japanese market. A significant development in the Japanese MT sector is the emergence of MT in established translation services, such as Inter Group (which uses Fujitsu's ATLAS-II) and IBS (which uses Sharp's DUET system and NEC's PIVOT). MT services may be offered both with and without postediting, with even the former priced somewhat below the higher quality human translation. Some customers prefer MT, while other customers prefer human translation. (See Chapter 6 for a more detailed discussion of this phenomenon.) Other developments of the early 1990s were the cancellation of the EUROTRA project by the EC and the increasing pace of MT R&D in the United States.

1.4 The Japanese View of Machine Translation

The Japanese see MT as being very important. The following excerpt from a brochure handed out by Fujitsu at MT Summit III provides a good example of this attitude:

> Japan is well known as an exporter of manufactured goods, but perhaps less well known as an importer of knowledge and information. As far back as the 7th century AD, there was a steady flow of knowledge into Japan from China and the Korean peninsula. After a period of self-imposed isolation, the late 19th century—the so-called Meiji Restoration—saw the floodgates opened and knowledge and know-how poured in from Europe and the United States.

> Even now, news, information and data from overseas are beamed into Japan, translated into Japanese, and disseminated by the mass media and other communication channels. And conversely, as Japan's influence in the world becomes ever greater, there is more and more overseas demand for information originating in Japan. The latter means that, more than ever before, there is an enormous need for Japanese-to-English technical translation.

> Translation has always been demanding of manpower, money and time. Every year in Japan, about 100 million pages are translated at a cost of around 500 billion yen. A golden opportunity for translators? Maybe, but for a variety of reasons, including the boycotting of English during the Second World War, the number of Japanese with the necessary skills is severely limited.

> Fujitsu, itself demanding vast amounts of Japanese-to-English translation, has been trying to bridge the gap by developing the ATLAS machine translation system. Machine translation has been a goal of computer science since the late 1950s, but only recently, due to advances in artificial intelligence and computational linguistics, has it become even remotely practical.

Throughout this report, we provide evidence of the substantial investment that a large number of Japanese companies have been and are making in MT technology. We will also describe the results that these investments have already produced, and offer some hints of what the future may hold.

1.5 A Comparative Analysis of Japanese and U.S. Machine Translation

The state of the art in Japanese and U.S. MT can be analyzed comparatively from several perspectives, as illustrated in Figures 1-3 through 1-14. These figures represent rough composite estimates based on the knowledge the panel has about MT efforts, both here and in Japan.

Figure 1-3 shows that funding for MT R&D in Japan is substantially higher than in the U.S., although U.S. funding promises to increase gradually. New Japanese corporate funding is more focused on productivity and commercialization while maintaining an active and steady R&D effort level. Figure 1-4 indicates the expected increase in commercial MT in Japan in response to this trend. It also shows little growth in commercial MT in the U.S. during this period. (The gestation period for new MT systems is fairly long, so the favorable commercial effects of increased R&D may only be expected to be evident in the U.S. starting around the turn of the century.)

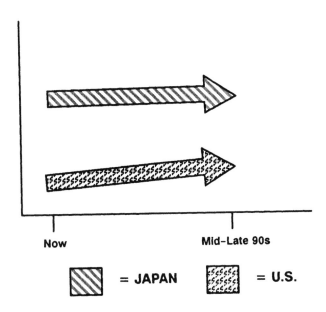

Now   Mid–Late 90s

= JAPAN   = U.S.

Figure 1-3: Funding for R&D in MT Technology

Improved accuracy (see Chapter 7) appears to be the single most important factor in determining how widely accepted MT will become. Both Japanese and U.S. efforts are expected to show steady improvement in accuracy, as shown in Figure 1-5. The largest differential will be in special-purpose (in terms of topic and style of texts) vs. general-purpose MT. Neither country enjoys a clear advantage in terms of accuracy. Special-topic MT gives greater accuracy now and promises more substantial improvements in the near-term future than general-purpose MT. The latter will also improve in accuracy, slowly but inexorably, extrapolating from present trends.

Figure 1-6 shows that in both Japanese and U.S. markets MT is gaining gradually in acceptance, with Japan having and maintaining a lead. As illustrated in Figure 1-7, the same situation and trends are

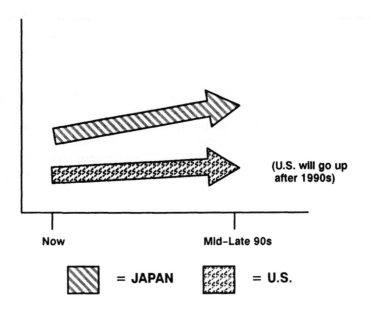

Figure 1-4: Commercial Use of MT

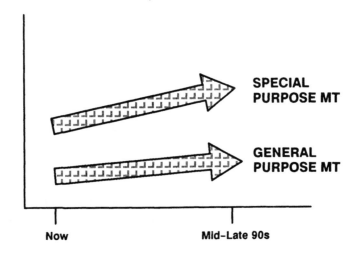

JAPAN AND U.S.

Figure 1-5: Accuracy of MT

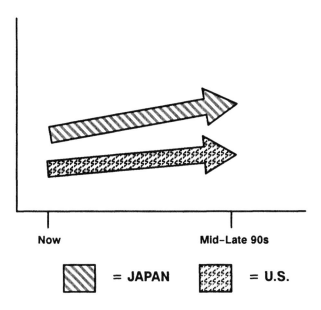

Figure 1-6: Acceptance of MT

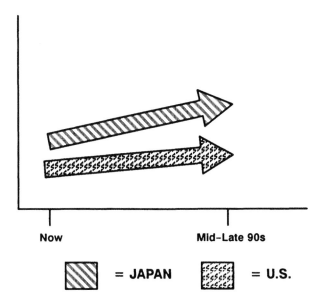

Figure 1-7: Integration of MT

present for the integration of MT systems into other text processing software: text editing, document production, printing, formatting, optical character reading (OCR), etc.

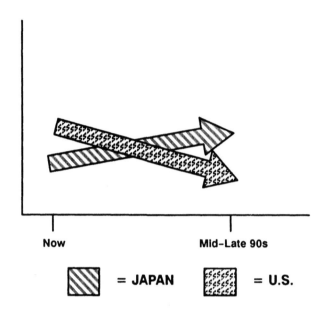

Now   **Mid–Late 90s**

▨ = JAPAN   ▦ = U.S.

Figure 1-8: Funding for Basic Research in Natural Language Processing

The basic science and technology underlying MT is natural language processing (also called computational linguistics), which is the study of computer processing of language, including: parsing algorithms, language generation algorithms, grammar formalisms, knowledge representation, computational lexicography, and inference techniques. Traditionally, the U.S. has been a bastion of scientific research in this area, but research funds in the U.S. have been decreasing. (See Figure 1-8.) In contrast, Japanese and European funding for the basic research underlying MT is increasing and will surpass U.S. funding levels, if they have not already done so. The U.S. research infrastructure risks being surpassed in the one dimension where it has traditionally led: computational linguistics, both the basic theory and computational methods.

Figures 1-9 and 1-10 indicate that the U.S. leads Japan in technological diversity (for better or worse) and in linguistic diversity. The former refers to the variety of technological approaches to MT, as discussed in the following section, and the latter refers to the number of languages between which MT systems are being developed. Present trends indicate that the U.S. will maintain its lead in technological diversity, but the gap will narrow in linguistic diversity as new Japanese projects, such as CICC (translation among several Asian languages), get underway, and Japanese commercial systems continue their trend toward expansion into European languages, as exemplified by Fujitsu's efforts in multilingual MT (German, French, and Spanish).

MT requires multiple knowledge sources, including lexical, grammatical, and semantic ones. (See

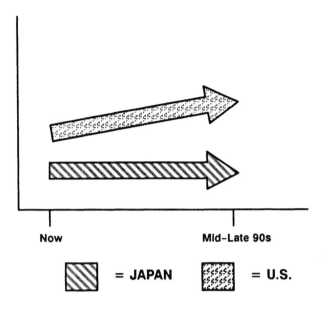

Figure 1-9: Technological Diversity

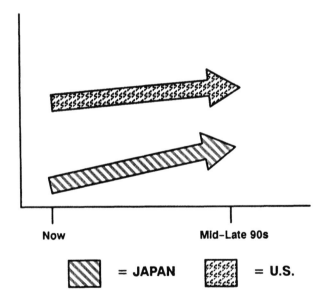

Figure 1-10: Linguistic Diversity

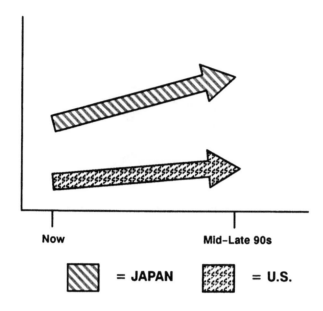

Figure 1-11: Private Knowledge Sources

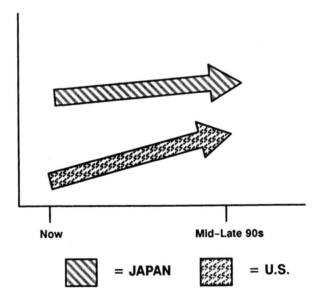

Figure 1-12: Shared Knowledge Sources

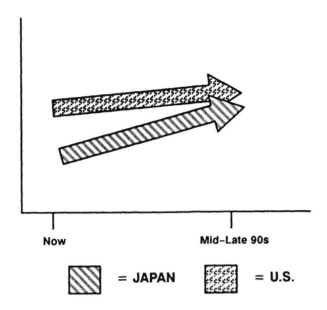

Figure 1-13: R & D in Speech Recognition and Speech-to-Speech MT

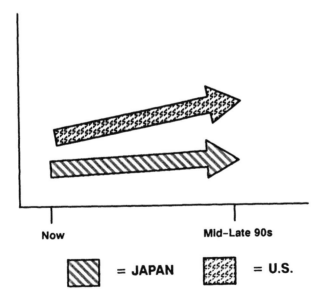

Figure 1-14: R & D in Other Natural Language Processing Technologies

Chapter 4 for a detailed discussion.) These knowledge sources are large and expensive to build and maintain. Therefore, they are valued resources in MT research and are even more important in successful MT system deployment. Figure 1-11 indicates a Japanese lead (and possibly widening gap) in private knowledge sources, i.e., those built and owned by the large computer and electronics firms that build and market MT systems. Although Japan also leads in shared knowledge bases (most notably EDR), the gap may narrow assuming continued funding from DARPA and other U.S. government agencies that are targeting some funds specifically at building shareable knowledge sources. (See Figure 1-12.)

The U.S. also maintains a lead in other related research areas. For example, Figure 1-13 shows that the U.S. leads in speech recognition technology, but both the U.S. and Japan are working on the early integration of speech technology into speech-to-speech MT. Specifically, in Japan this is going on at ATR and at some companies such as NEC. Figure 1-14 shows the status of related natural language processing (NLP) technologies such as automatic extraction of knowledge from text (e.g., to populate databases), NLP-based human-computer interfaces, routing and classification of texts for assimilation, etc. The U.S. has a narrow lead these areas that may widen if current trends continue.

1.6 Paradigms for Machine Translation

Historically, many different approaches to MT have been tried with varying degrees of intensity. Figure 1-15 captures all of the major paradigms for machine translation. The arrows represent transformations that may occur during the translation process. It should be clear from the figure that there are many paths from source to target texts.

Early MT efforts focused primarily on the bottom levels of the figure. Over the years there has been a steady trend upward toward systems that exploit deeper analyses of the source text as the basis for translation. More specifically, the first methods developed for MT were the direct methods; they attempted to map words, phrases, and entire clauses from the source to the target language, without performing any analysis of the source text beyond straightforward morphological processing. A common approach was to build huge numbers of specific direct transfer rules by hand. Because of the enormity of the task and the poor results that came from the necessarily incomplete rule sets, this approach was abandoned early. However, three modern variants of the direct approach are currently being investigated:

- Statistically-based approaches at IBM in the U.S.,

- Example-based (also called case-based or analogical) translation at Kyoto University and ATR in Japan. (See Section 9.2.), and,

- Direct-transfer translation, also at ATR. (See Section 9.3.)

All require large, bilingual, sentence-aligned corpora, but none requires millions of hand-built direct transfer rules. These projects are still in the early research stages, but show promise.

Moving up one step in the figure, we get to syntactic transfer systems. In these, the source text is "parsed" or analyzed into syntactic structures. These structures (known as "parse trees") are transformed into corresponding syntactic structures in the target language by applying a set of hand-coded transfer rules. The lexical items (at the leaves of the syntactic tree) are also transferred by a bilingual transfer dictionary. After transfer, a syntactic generator maps the lexically-bound target-language syntactic structures into the target language text. This paradigm is sometimes called "transfer-based MT" or

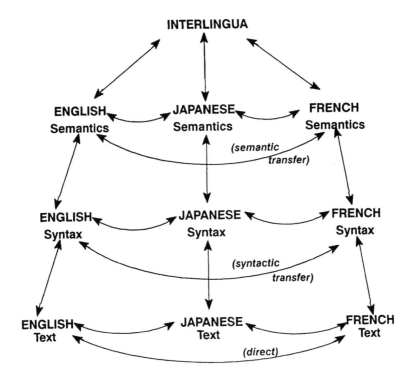

Figure 1-15: Interlingual vs. Transfer MT

"traditional transfer," and until recently has been the most popular paradigm for MT. Substantially fewer transfer rules are needed than were necessary in direct systems because the rules capture linguistic generalizations. However, there are problems with syntactic transfer:

- The lack of semantic analysis results in poor disambiguation and hence errors in the translation, and

- If a multilingual system is required among N languages, N^2 sets of transfer rules must be developed (one for each uni-directional language pair).

The first of these problems can be at least partially solved by moving upward again, toward a greater degree of semantic analysis. Almost all syntactic transfer systems in use today extract some semantic features and exploit them during translation. A further step has been the development of the "semantic transfer" paradigm, which is now widely used in Japan. Here the analysis is deeper, including syntactic and at least partial semantic analysis of the source text prior to starting the transfer phase. (This approach is shown in the upper horizontal arc in Figure 1-15.) The transfer occurs between corresponding semantic representations (typically case frames) from source to target, and then the generator maps these tranferred case frames into the target text. In principle, translation accuracy improves because some disambiguation occurs prior to transfer, and since semantic representations in different languages are more similar to each other than syntactic ones, the transfer component is smaller (although still N^2 for N languages).

If complete syntactic and semantic analysis is performed, then it is possible to produce a meaning representation, called an interlingua, independent of source or target language. The interlingua may contain just the meaning of the source text, or it may also contain a language-independent description of the linguistic form that was used in the source text so that effects such as focus can be recreated properly in the target. Once an interlingual representation is obtained, the text is generated into one or more target languages. No explicit transfer phase is necessary. In essence, the interlingua approach trades off more effort at analysis and generation for no effort at all in transfer.

There is considerable debate in the scientific community as to which is the best approach to MT. It is generally recognized that transfer (either syntactic or semantic) may be the easiest to build for a single language pair, whereas the interlingual approach may provide translations of better quality and/or provide the most extensible paradigm in a multilingual environment. Most everyone agrees that there are cases in which the ability to extract meaning is critical if high quality translations are going to be produced. People differ, however, on how hard it will be to do this in a practical way, and so there is disagreement on when (if ever) a true general-purpose interlingual system will be able to be built. Another reason for disagreement about the role of interlingual systems is that, in some researcher's eyes, using an interlingua necessarily means discarding surface linguistic facts from the source text, thereby reducing the fluency of the translation in some cases. Many proponents of the interlingual approach reply by saying that linguistic facts, as well as semantics, can be captured (in a linguistically neutral way) in the interlingua.

Despite the intensity of the "interlingua debate", it turns out that existing Japanese commercial MT systems can mostly be accounted for by the middle range of Figure 1-15. There are no direct systems and there are no "pure" interlingual systems, although some, such as NEC's PIVOT and Fujitsu's ATLAS-II, are closer to being purely interlingual than most others. This can be seen in Figure 1-2, with the following caveat: It is important to keep in mind that the transfer-interlingua dimension is a continuum rather than a discrete choice, so there are some borderline cases that are difficult to characterize precisely. For example, Ricoh's system uses slightly more semantics than most syntactic transfer systems but less than most semantic transfer systems. Similarly, commercial interlingua-based systems also exploit some transfer rules, even though that is not part of the "pure" interlingual paradigm. Throughout this report, we have attempted to describe the approach of each system in the terms that a particular system's designers use, even though we recognize that these terms are not always applied consistently.

Although there is debate about which point along this spectrum shows the most promise as a basis for MT systems (and, as we just mentioned, there is not even full agreement on exact terminology), there does seem to have been a gradual movement upwards over the years towards deeper analysis and interlingual systems. One example of this is the long-term, large-scale CICC project in which several of the major Japanese MT companies participate. (See Section 9.9 for a discussion of this effort.) Chapter 9 will elaborate on this trend and describe in more detail the research that is being done on interlingua-based systems.

In addition to the transfer-interlingua dimension, systems differ with respect to where the human intervention occurs. Postediting is the most typical situation: The MT system attempts its best translation and a human posteditor corrects the mistakes after careful comparison of source and target sentences to fix errors of both content and style. Pre-editing the source text to make it easier to translate is also sometimes used. Typical pre-editing operations include breaking up long sentences into shorter, more easily analyzed ones and replacing ambiguous passages and words with less ambiguous ones. Many Japanese systems (and some American ones such as Xerox's specialized use of SYSTRAN) combine both pre- and postediting in an attempt to do less of the latter.

Another possibility is "just-in-time editing" or "user query", where the MT system queries the author (or translator) interactively during the analysis to resolve ambiguity as needed.   Finally, research also addresses machine-aided translation (MAT) where the human translator is in control and the MAT system provides productivity tools such as on-line terminology banks and grammar checkers.   The latter approaches are being investigated more in the U.S. than in Japan, which partly accounts for the greater U.S. technological diversity discussed in the previous section.

1.7 Structure of the Report

The rest of this report is organized around a set of topics that together cover the most important aspects of the state of the art of MT in Japan. Chapter 2 describes in more detail the technical ideas that underlie MT systems. Chapter 3 describes the languages and the application domains that are receiving the most attention in Japanese MT work today. Chapter 4 discusses the knowledge sources (primarily dictionaries) that are used in Japanese MT systems. Chapter 5 outlines the life cycle of a typical MT system in Japan. Chapter 6 surveys the uses of MT in Japan and briefly discusses both a set of user sites and a set of vendor sites that were visited. Chapter 7 talks about the major factors (quality and productivity) that influence the acceptance of MT in Japan. Chapter 8 puts this analysis of MT in Japan in perspective by describing the status of MT efforts in the United States and in Europe. Chapter 9 moves away from a focus on deployed systems and describes the main thrusts that current MT research in Japan is taking. Finally, Chapter 10 offers a very brief analysis of the future of MT in Japan.

Following the main body of the report is a list of the references that were cited. Although we had access to literature in both English and Japanese, we have made a conscious effort to cite works in English (because of their much greater accessibility) whenever possible. (Of course, when fully accurate MT comes of age in the next century, such linguistic biases in citations should no longer be necessary.) Three appendices follow the list of references. The first summarizes the sites that are mentioned in the report. The second contains short biographies of the panel members. And the last is a list of abbreviations used throughout the report.

2. Technical Infrastructure

David Johnson

This chapter is concerned with providing a high-level overview of the basic technology underlying the linguistic processing characteristic of typical state-of-the-art, Japanese MT systems on the market today.

Figures 2-1, 2-2, and 2-3 contain schematic charts, taken almost verbatim from [Hutchins 86], of each of the three main kinds of MT systems (interlingual, transfer, and direct) shown in Figure 1-15. Note that "SL" means "source language" and "TL" means target language.

Since most of the MT systems on the market today are either syntactic or semantic transfer-based systems, this chapter describes the transfer-based approach. In chapter 9, we describe other approaches, including interlingual and example-based systems. Knowledge sources (lexicons, thesauri, etc.) are explored in Chapter 4.

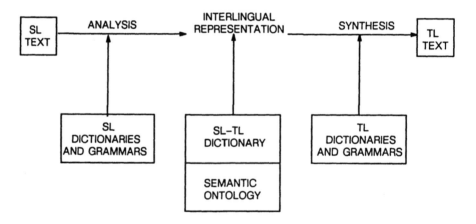

Figure 2-1: Interlingual MT System Architecture

We will first sketch the major stages involved in machine translation, and then examine the three key functions of a typical MT linguistic processor — analysis (parsing); transfer; and generation (synthesis) — effecting the overall translation from source sentence to target sentence. Detailed comparisons or evaluations of specific systems will not be made, although specific systems will be used as examples of the approaches we describe.

2.1 Overview of the Translation Process

The flow of control from input to output in NEC's PIVOT system, a typical, sophisticated, production-level MT system, is shown in Figure 2-4. In this system, there are eight stages: (1) text input, via keyboard, optical character recognition (OCR) or other means; (2) pre-translation, where words not registered in any source-language dictionary or other knowledge source are located and placed in a file; (3) and (4) registration by a human pre-editor of "unknown" words (note that, in fact, many such words will

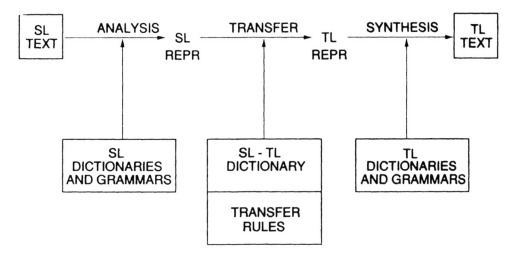

Figure 2-2: Transfer MT System Architecture

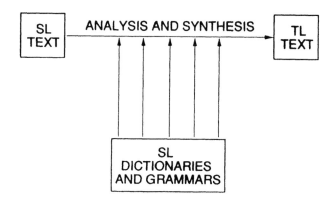

Figure 2-3: Direct MT System Architecture

not have translations, e.g., names, addresses, acronyms); (5) translation (by machine). This corresponds to the box "Machine Translation Process Software" in Figure 2-5 (taken from [Nagao 89]), which shows in more detail how the translation process typically works. Many systems omit (6) correction of analysis. It is followed by (7) translation, a repeat of (5), and (8) post-editing. As the stages listed in Figure 2-4 suggest, the time taken by the computerized translation process will generally comprise only a very small part of total translation time. Thus, speed of translation in (5) is not the crucial factor in the cost-effectiveness and user acceptability of a particular system. Instead, the key issue is the quality of this stage of translation, and it is in this arena that all MT systems fall down.

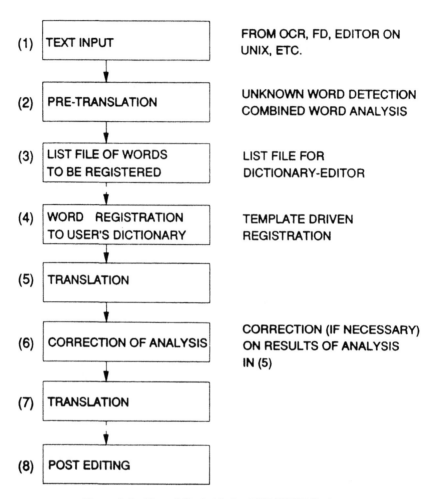

Figure 2-4: Flow of Control in the NEC PIVOT System

2.2 Translation Stages of the Linguistic Processor

Linguistic processing (Step 5 of Figure 2-4) generally proceeds through six basic stages: (1) morphological analysis of the source language; (2) syntactic analysis of the source language (parsing); (3) semantic analysis of the source language (semantic feature analysis); (4) transfer (mapping the internal representation of the source-language sentence into the internal representation of the target-language sentence); (5) syntactic generation of the target language sentence; and (6) morphological generation of the target language sentence.

Figure 2-6, which depicts the translation flow in Ricoh's MT system, is an example of a syntactic-transfer system that exploits some semantic feature information. This should be compared to the flow chart shown in Figure 2-7, for Hitachi's HICATS/J-E semantic-transfer system. Notice that both systems go through the same basic stages, i.e., they are not very different in terms of overall system organization.

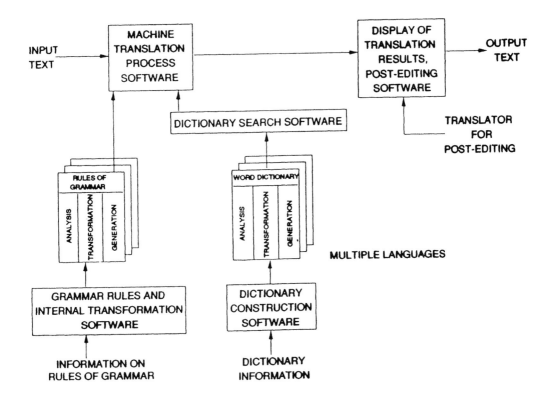

Figure 2-5: The Basic Software of a Machine Translation System

All of the systems described here are transfer-based, i.e., they are not direct nor are they true interlingual systems. But, as we noted in Section 1.6, the transfer-interlingua dimension is really a continuum, consequently, it is often difficult to characterize systems precisely according to one of the three types. In some transfer systems the level of transfer is syntactic; in others it is asserted to be semantic. It is not clear, however, what is at issue here, since some so-called semantic representations are often language-specific and not very detailed, while some so-called syntactic transfer systems can be highly abstract and fairly language neutral.

However, as a matter of design methodology, in the case of so-called semantic transfer, there is an explicit effort, on the one hand, to purge the output of analysis of obviously language-specific material such as specfic case markings and word order. On the other hand there is an effort to make use of a limited set of putatively universal semantically oriented labels such as "agent", "theme", recipient", and so on. This use of a common representation language --- unordered trees with explicit labeling of relations

INPUT   OUTPUT

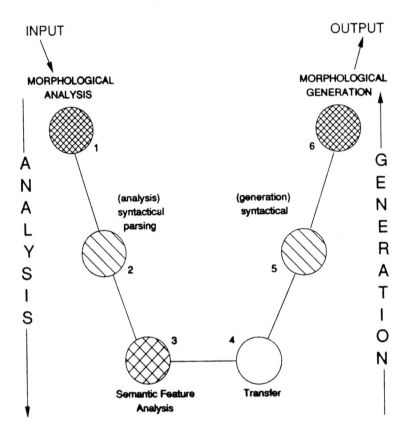

MORPHOLOGICAL   MORPHOLOGICAL
ANALYSIS   GENERATION

A   G
N   E
A   (analysis)   (generation)   N
L   syntactical   syntactical   E
Y   parsing   R
S   A
I   T
S   I
          Semantic Feature   Transfer   O
          Analysis   N

Figure 2-6: Flow of Control in the Ricoh MT System

like "agent" (dependency structures) — for source and target languages would seem to facilitate the minimization of superficial differences, and thus be a practical compromise between overly language-bound syntactic representations and a true interlingual representation.

2.3 Analysis

Two steps are essential to a thorough analysis of the source text — morphological analysis and lexical look up. Then the input string is parsed with respect to a formal grammar of the source language. The analysis grammar is often an augmented context-free phrase-structure grammar, but augmented transition networks (ATNs) are also commonly used.

The result of parsing is one or more phrase-structure trees that represent the syntactic constituent structure(s) of the source sentence. Constituent structure encodes the part-whole relations of words and phrases, as well as word order.

For example, the constituent structure of the English sentence, "He ate cake," is shown in Figure 2-8. The constituent structure for this sentence indicates that "he" is a Noun(N), which is, in turn, a Noun Phrase (NP). Together, the verb (V) "ate" and the noun phrase (NP) "cake" constitute the verb phrase (VP) "ate cake". The NP and VP together make a sentence (S).

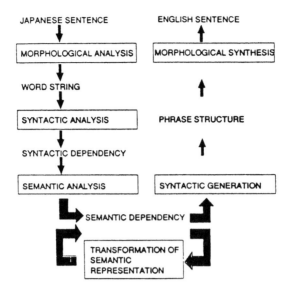

Figure 2-7: HICATS/J-E Translation Process

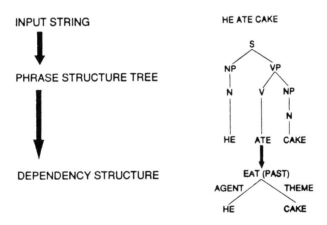

Figure 2-8: The Result of Parsing

Japanese sentences are organized as sets of phrases called *bunsetsu*. A *bunsetsu* is typically composed of a content expression and a function word that indicates the role of the content expression in the overall sentence. In some cases these function words behave the way prepositions do in English (except that function words come after their corresponding content expression). In other cases, the function words mark roles (such as subject and object) that are indicated in English by word order. A complete syntactic analysis of a Japanese sentence shows how the *bunsetsu* it contains relate to each other to form the overall analysis of the sentence.

The next stage of analysis is the conversion of phrase-structure trees to dependency structures. Dependency structures contain fewer nodes, in general, than corresponding phrase structure trees, since each governing node in a dependency structure is a lexical item --- the head of the phrase (i.e., phrasal nodes) are thrown away. The explicit representation of the linguistically crucial notion of phrasal head is one of the key advantages of dependency representations. This is an important advantage for natural language processing systems, because the head carries most of the linguistic information governing the properties of the phrase. This information can be associated with specific lexical entries, and, after lexical look up, will be uniformly located at the roots of dependency phrases and hence readily accessible to rules during processing. To illustrate, in Figure 2-8, the head of the clause is the verb "eat." The lexical entry for "eat" would, no doubt, specify that any phrase headed by "eat" takes an agent that is an animal and a patient that is edible.

The second advantage of dependency representations is the explicit representation of grammatical relations, often called *cases*. Explicit representation of grammatical cases such as agent and theme facilitates the matching of linguistic information contained in dictionary entries with requirements specified in rules. In contrast, constituent structure trees only implicitly represent grammatical relations in terms of the part-whole relation and linear order of constituents. Since grammatical relations are crucial for carrying out the transfer process, the explicit representation of such relations is a significant advantage. In the case of the simple example in Figure 2-8, the dependency structure of the English sentence is structurally the same as its correspondent in Japanese. Therefore, in this very simple case, transfer would only involve lexical substitutions.

```
(5700) NP POSTP
            --> PP(%NP,CASE=CASE(POSTP),
         TOPIC=TOPIC(POSTP),KOOU+KOOU(POSTP),
         PSMODS=PSMODS...POSTP)

(5840) VERB --> VP(sVERB,HINSISEI='YOU')

(5851) PP(~DAI,~NO,SF,CASE)
         VP(~NO,CASESO,CASE(PP),ISIN.CASESO,
           CASE(PP).NOTIN.CASES,
           <(@CASE(PP).EQ.'DIV"|
           @CASE(PP).ISIN.SF(PP)>)
           -->VP(-NAI,CASES=LISTIFY<CASE(PP)>...CASES,
               PRMODS=PP...PRMODS,N=N(PP)+N+4,
               <TOPIC(PP),+DAI>)
```

Figure 2-9: Example Analysis Rules from JETS

As mentioned above, analysis grammars are typically collections of context free phrase structure rules augmented with various features that impose conditions on the applicability of the rules. Three sample rules for Japanese, taken from IBM's JETS system are shown in Figure 2-9. The first rule (5700), for example, states that a noun phrase (NP) followed by a postposition (POSTP) makes a postpositional phrase (PP), provided that the conditions specified as features on the PP node are met.

Analysis grammars can become quite large --- ranging anywhere from several hundred to several thousand rules. Note, however, that it is difficult to judge the coverage of a grammar based on its rule size, since the coverage of an individual rule can vary dramatically. In many cases, rules can call program subroutines, and so are able to perform complicated manipulations.

The crucial unresolved problem in this stage of the translation process is ambiguity --- both lexical and syntactic. For instance, given the sentence, "He saw a dog with a rhinestone collar," a purely syntactic analysis cannot determine that the phrase "with a rhinestone collar" modifies "dog" rather than "saw." Compare, "He saw a dog with his telescope," where the opposite bracketing is appropriate. Quite often, an input string will result in a set of parse trees. Hopefully, the correct one will be among this set (although it might not be!). At this stage, the semantic features attached to words in the source language dictionaries will be used to block inappropriate structures. For instance, in the English examples above, the English dictionary might indicate the semantic information that "saw" is typically modified by a prepositional phrase "with ..." whose object is some sort of instrument for viewing. On the assumption that "telescope" but not "collar" is marked in the dictionary as "+ viewing instrument," the unwanted parse can be filtered out.

One can readily see from this simple example that the set of required semantic features could, for general English at least, be open ended. This is the main reason why attempts at filtering out all and only the bad parses have failed for the general (domain independent) case, but work somewhat better for specific domains. If one knows that an MT system is to be used for computer-related documents, for instance, and the word "disk" is used, one can be fairly certain that the meaning is the specialized term "computer disk" and not a record or simply a thin, circular object. However, even in specialized areas, the technique of using semantic features and compatibility testing to screen parses is faulty and certainly has limits. Overall, the problem of filtering sets of syntactically well-formed parses on the basis of semantic information seems to be the largest single obstacle to MT becoming an unequivocal technical success. Hence, this filtering problem is the motivating factor for exploring alternative approaches, such as the use of deep reasoning in interlingual systems (see Section 9.1) or the incorporation of probabilistic information based on specific corpora into conventional analysis procedures.

Figure 2-10, an example from IBM Japan's JETS system, illustrates the use of both inherent semantic features on nouns and selectional features on verbs, in conjunction with a scoring metric, to determine the most highly valued parse. Figure 2-11 illustrates in more detail the scoring mechanism used in JETS. MT systems differ in the number and kinds of features used, and they also vary according to whether they use syntactic-oriented case relations such as subject or direct object; semantically oriented case relations such agent or theme; or morphological cases such as, for Japanese, *ga* or *ni* (see Figure 2-10).

Figures 2-12 [Nagao 89], 2-13 [Nagao 85], and 2-14 [Nagao 89] give some indication of the variation in specific cases and relations used in various systems. However, regardless of the specific realization, the basic process is the same: (1) mark nouns listed in a dictionary with inherent semantic features such as "human" or "location" and (2) specify for each sense of every verb an *argument frame* or *case frame*, which shows what semantic features the various verbal arguments take, e.g., the agent of "know" must be a human; the agent of "eat" must be an animal; the intransitive "break" as in, "Glass breaks," takes a patient argument (realized as the subject), but the transitive "break" as in, "John broke the glass," takes both an agent argument and a patient argument.

There are two other types of grammar frameworks often used for parsing: transformational grammar, as exemplified by the MU/JICST system, and augmented transition networks, as exemplified by Toshiba's and CSK's systems. Figure 2-15 summarizes the major approaches to analysis.

Kare   ni heya wo deru   youni me de   aizushi ta
("he") ("room") ("leave") ("eye") ("make a sign")
("I made a sign to him with my eyes to leave the room")

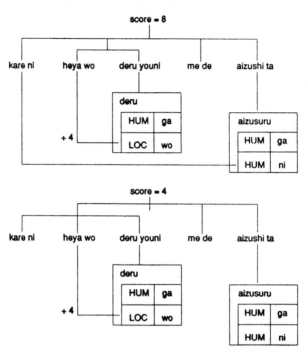

Figure 2-10: Using Selectional Restrictions and a Scoring Metric

	Sm = Sp	Sm ≠ Sp	Sm = Unknown or Sp = Unknown*
Cm = Cp	+4	+1	+2
Cm = Unknown+	+2	+0	+1
Otherwise	+0	+0	+0

Sm: Semantic feature of modifier
Sp: Semantic feature of predicate
Cm: Case particle of modifier
Cp: Case particle of predicate
+ Information not found in the lexicon
* Case article missing

Figure 2-11: The JETS Scoring Procedure

2.4 Transfer

The transfer stage consists, conceptually, of two subprocesses: (1) lexical transfer and (2) structural transfer. (These may be interleaved in practice.) Figure 2-16 illustrates lexical transfer for the simple Japanese sentence, *"Boku ga sakana o tabeta"* (I ate fish). The top of Figure 2-16 shows the mapping from the Japanese phrase-structure tree to the dependency structure, headed by the Japanese verb

(1) Subject	*The boy* walked home.
(2) Object	She found *the book*.
(3) Recipient	gave *to her*.
(4) Origin	received *from him*.
(5) Partner	to consult with ...
(6) Opponent	to protect from ...
(7) Time	in 1980 ...
(8) Time-from	from May of last year, ...
(9) Time-to	until next year, ...
(10) Duration	over a period of five minutes, ...
(11) Space	... is located at ...
(12) Space-from	to return from ...
(13) Space-to	to send to ...
(14) Space-through	to pass through ...
(15) Source	to translate from Japanese
(16) Goal	to translate into English
(17) Attribute	to be rich in ...
(18) Cause	to be due to ...
(19) Tool	... with a hammer ...
(20) Material	to be made out of ...
(21) Component	to consist of ...
(22) Manner	at a rate of ...
(23) Condition	to determine under the conditions of ...
(24) Purpose	adapted to ...
(25) Role	to use as ...
(26) Content	to be seen as ...
(27) Range	with regard to ...
(28) Topic	as for the topic of ...
(29) Viewpoint	from the perspective of ...
(30) Comparison	better than ...
(31) Accompaniment	together with ...
(32) Degree	an increase of 5%
(33) Predication	... is ...

Figure 2-12: The 33 Cases Used in the Analysis of Japanese in MU

1. AGenT	17. RANge
2. Causal-POtency	18. COmpaRison
3. EXPeriencer	19. TOOl
4. OBJect	20. PURpose
5. RECipient	21. Space-FRom
6. ORIgin	22. Space-AT
7. SOUrce	23. Space-TO
8. GOAl	24. Space-THrough
9. CONtent	25. Time-FRom
10. PARtner	26. Time-AT
11. OPPonent	27. Time-TO
12. BENificiary	28. DURation
13. ACCompaniment	29. CAUse
14. ROLe	30. CONdition
15. DEGree	31. RESult
16. MANner	21. ConCessive

Figure 2-13: The English Cases Used in MU

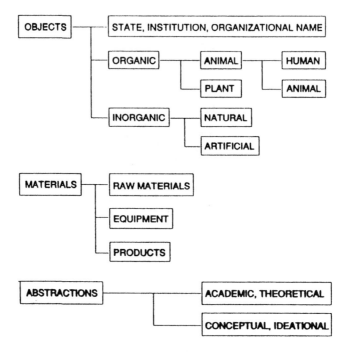

Figure 2-14: Example Semantic Primitives Used in MU

- Transformation Grammar
    - Subgrammars
    - Heuristic Rules
        - Ordered by reliability
    - Lexically triggered rules
- Augmented transition networks
- Augmented context-free phrase structure grammars
    - Syntactic/semantic features
    - GPSG, LFG
- PS ==> DS mapping
    - Semantic features
    - Parse scoring

Figure 2-15: Summary of Approaches to Analysis

tabeta (ate). The valence relations (superficial case relations) are encoded as features on the arguments; e.g., *boku* (I) is marked for *wa* (topic) and *ga* (subject), and *sakana* (fish) for *o* (direct object). Semantic interpretation maps the valence representation to a deep-case dependency structure in which *boku* (I) is marked as the agent and *sakana*(fish) as the theme of the clause.

The dictionary information needed to map superficial cases into deep semantic cases in this example is shown in Figure 2-17 (taken from [Nagao 86]). Next, lexical transfer replaces *tabe* with "eat", *boku* with "I", and *sakana* with "fish." Structural changes are not required in this atypically simple example.

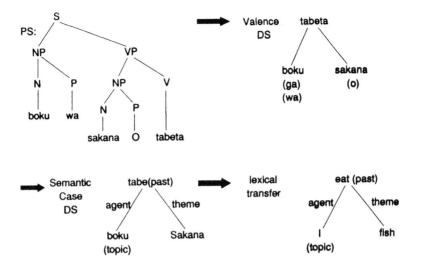

Figure 2-16: An Example of the Transfer Process

	Surface Case	Semantic Primitives of N	Deep Case
Eat	N-GA	Eatable Material	OBJECT
	N-GA	Animal	AGENT
	N-0	Thing	OBJECT

Figure 2-17: Example of a Dictionary Entry for "Eat"

J-Surface-Case	J-Deep-Case	E-Deep-Case	Default Preposition
ni	RECipient	REC,BENeficiary	to(REC--to,BEN--for)
	ORIgin	ORI	from
	PARticipant	PAR	with
	TIMe	Time-AT	in
	ROLe	ROL	as
	GOAl	GOA	to
	...	...	...

Figure 2-18: Default Rule for Assigning English Case to the Japanese Postposition *ni*

Lexical transfer can be a very difficult process, even without obviously tricky cases such as idioms and metaphors. For instance, Figure 2-18 shows the complexity inherent in translating the Japanese postposition *ni* into its English counterparts [Nagao 85]. As shown, the Japanese postposition *ni* can signal a variety of semantic relations that require different prepositions to be used in the corresponding English translations. The correct translation of particles requires a semantic analysis of sentences. That is to say, the complexity of translating even minor function words can be challenging.

Japanese Sentential Connective	Deep Case	English Sentential Connective
Renyo	tool	by -ing...
(-shi)te	tool	by -ing...
Renyo	cause	because...
(-shi)te	"	"
-tame	"	"
-node	"	"
-kara	"	"
-to	time	when...
-toki	"	"
-te	"	"
-tame	purpose	so-that-may
-noni	"	"
-you	"	"
-you	manner	as if
-kotonaku	"	without -ing...
-nagara	accompany	while -ing
-ba	circumstance	when...
...	...	...

Figure 2-19: Correspondence of Sentential Connectives between Japanese and English in the MU System

A similar problem arises in the translation of sentential connectives, as shown in Figure 2-19 (taken from [Nagao 86]). These tables do, however, encode in an accessible and easily maintainable format some of the basic linguistic knowledge necessary for transferring so-called function words such as postpositions/prepositions and sentence connectives. This sort of table-driven processing cleanly separates data from processing algorithms, and, although insufficent to encode all the knowledge needed for correct choices, represents a sensible beginning toward solving the general problem.

Structural transfer is a process by which the internal representation of the Japanese source sentence is restructured to provide a simple and sound basis for generating an appropriate English correspondent. Figure 2-20 shows an example of this process from Hitachi's HICATS-J/E system. The Japanese sentence, *"Kono sisutemu wa ouyouhan'i ga hiroi,"* means literally, "As for this system, application range

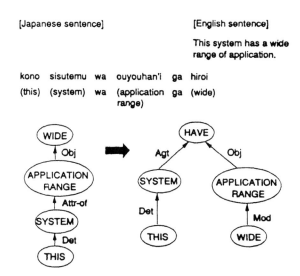

Figure 2-20: Transformation of Semantic Representations in HICATS

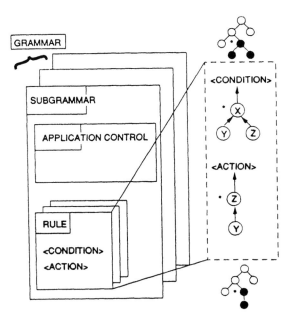

Figure 2-21: HICATS Grammar Description Language

is wide." The desired English correspondent is, "This system has a wide range of application." In Figure 2-20, a transfer rule — a tree transformation — restructures the Japanese internal structure (whose main predicate is "WIDE") into an English-oriented one (whose main predicate is "HAVE"). The English-oriented structure is then passed to the English generation grammar and results in the sentence, "This system has a wide range of application," as desired. HICATS uses a single grammar description language in which rules are organized into subgrammars and each rule is specified as a condition/action pair. (See Figure 2-21.) In addition, conditions controlling the application of rules can be specified, e.g., whether the rule is optional or obligatory. This high-level grammar organization seems fairly common, at least wherever transformational grammars are used.

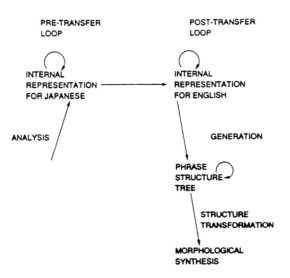

Figure 2-22: Transfer and Generation in MU

- Transformational Grammar (Tree Transduction)

- Stages
    - Pre-transfer: Structure Changing

    - Transfer Proper
        - Lexical Transfer
        - Structure Changing

    - Post-transfer: Structure Changing

- PS==>DS (Valence Representation)

- DS==>DS (Semantic Case Representation)

Figure 2-23: Summary of the Transfer Phase

Transfer grammars typically consist of a large group of transformational rules that restructure dependency trees. Transfer grammars can be very complicated. One aspect of this complexity is the triggering of subgrammars by specific lexical items. This data-driven organization, while flexible, makes it difficult to understand the processing flow, since changing the dictionary can have far-ranging effects on which rules are applied. It is also not atypical for the transfer component to have three stages involving structural transfer: (1) pre-transfer, (2) transfer proper, and (3) post-transfer (as shown for the MU system in Figure 2-22 [Nagao 85]). The distinction among these phases is somewhat arbitrary but provides a productive distinction in practice. The main stages and functions of the transfer stage are summarized in Figure 2-23.

2.5 Generation

As discussed, the final stage, generation (or synthesis), takes the output of transfer and ideally produces a well-formed sentence in the target language. In most systems, transfer output is converted to a phrase-structure tree, which includes the proper word order for the target language sentence.

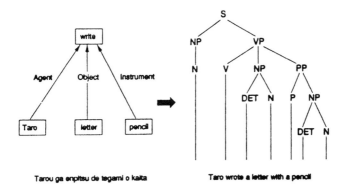

Figure 2-24: A Generation Example from HICATS

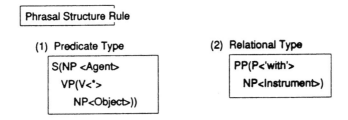

Figure 2-25: A Generation Rule from HICATS

This is illustrated in Figure 2-24. This transduction is carried out either by applying a set of transformational rules or a set of phrase-structure templates, such as those shown in Figure 2-25. For example, the predicate type rule in Figure 2-25 encodes the fact that a dependency pattern headed by a verb and containing an agent and object can be mapped into the constituent structure pattern (S NP (VP V NP)) such that the agent corresponds to the first NP and the object to the second one. The relational type rule, also shown in Figure 2-25, maps prepositions and their objects into PPs (prepositional phrases), where the objects are identified by their semantic relations (e.g., "instrument"). The two generation rules in Figure 2-25 encapsulate the linguistic knowledge needed to map the dependency structure shown on the left in Figure 2-24 into the constituent-structure tree shown on the right.

In many MT systems, the generation component is, compared to analysis and transfer components, relatively small; that is, much of the work needed to construct a target language sentence is done in the structure-changing part of the transfer process. Generation is basically viewed as a clean up stage, and as such will often consist of ad hoc routines rather than robust grammars that accurately reflect the linguistic facts of the target language. Hence these grammars are not bidirectional, that is, they cannot be used for both parsing and generation. Figure 2-26 summarizes the major techniques and grammatical frameworks used in generation.

- Transformational Grammar

- Augmented Transition Network

- Augmented Context Free Phrase Structure Grammar

- Ad-Hoc Program (not Grammar-Based)

- Typically:
    - Minor Component

    - No Independently Justified Grammar

Figure 2-26: Summary of Techniques Used in Generation

3. Languages and Application Domains

Muriel Vasconcellos

3.1 Current Range of Source and Target Languages

Reflecting the nation's political, economic, and social imperatives, Japan's machine translation activities have focused largely on English and Japanese. There are at least 20 MT systems in Japan whose developers are addressing the complex challenge posed by translation between these two languages. The extent to which the corresponding knowledge sources have been developed in English and Japanese varies in proportion to the history of system development. Several of the projects date back 8, 10, and 12 years. The present discussion refers to all systems---long-standing, new on the market, and research prototype---since what is of interest here are Japan's priorities and an appreciation of where investments are being made.

Figure 3-1 shows the respective language combinations being developed under the 20 MT initiatives for which the JTEC team had information.[1] Figure 3-2 shows the number of sites at which each combination is being developed, thus giving a rough indication of the relative importance of the different languages for Japan. The intent of both of these tables is to show the diversity that was observed. But it should be kept in mind that they do not accurately reflect the distribution of actual effort on the various language pairs, since some entries correspond to well-developed systems, while others represent small, experimental prototypes.

Of the sites visited by the JTEC team, 17 have already developed or are in the process of developing MT systems that translate from Japanese into English (J/E), from English into Japanese (E/J), or in both directions. In the majority of cases, initial efforts were concentrated on Japanese into English because of the far greater demand for that combination. At the same time, however, there has also been considerable motivation to develop English into Japanese. The difference, of course, is that in the case of J/E the target market is foreign with Japanese information being disseminated to wider audiences; with E/J it is national and information from overseas is being assimilated for the people's own use. Work on this combination is attractive for several reasons: (1) in Japan there is an important demand for information translated from English; (2) it is the "easier" of the two combinations to develop, since, by comparison, Japanese source analysis is a far more daunting challenge; and (3) posteditors are available in much larger numbers and are less expensive to hire and train. In fact, despite the greater demand for J/E, there are nearly as many offerings for E/J: from Japanese into English there are 17 systems, and from English into Japanese there are 15 (see Figure 3-2). Thirteen sites have systems in both directions. In addition, the JEIDA Report [JEIDA 89] mentions CBU's HANTRAN, for E/J, and Mitsubishi's MELTRAN, for J/E.

After years of concentration on English and Japanese, some of Japan's MT developers have recently ventured to add other languages. A major effort is being undertaken by the Center for the International Cooperation in Computerization (CICC), a MITI-organized international consortium that has the participation of seven industry giants, for developing an interlingua-based system in Japanese, Chinese,

---

[1] The information in this table is drawn primarily from the panel's visits to the sites mentioned. The exceptions to this are the lines corresponding to CBU's HANTRAN system and Mitsubishi's MELTRAN system, which are taken from [JEIDA 89].

Developer	J/E	E/J	Other
ATR	•	•	
Bravice	•	•	E/C, /K, K/E, E/F, /G, /I, /P, /S, F/E, S/E
Catena		•	F/J
CBU		•	
CICC			J/C/Indonesian/Malay/Thai (all pairs)
CSK	•	•	
Fujitsu	•	•	E/C, /K, /F, /G, /S, /Innuit, /Swahili, J/C, /K, /F, /G, /S
Hitachi	•	•	
IBM	•	•	E/C, /K
JICST	•		
Matsushita	•		J/C
Mitsubishi	•		
NEC	•	•	K/S/Thai (all pairs)
NTT	•		
Oki	•	•	J/C
Ricoh	•	•	
Sanyo	•	•	
Sharp	•	•	
Systran Corp.	•	•	
Toshiba	•	•	

Key: C=Chinese, E=English, F=French, G=German, I=Italian, J=Japanese,
K=Korean, P=Portuguese, S=Spanish.
E/J means English to Japanese.

Figure 3-1: Source and Target Language Combinations in Japanese MT Systems,
by Site

Thai, Malay, and Indonesian. This undertaking is described in greater detail in Section 9.9.

Efforts at adding new languages to existing interlingua-based systems are being pursued at Fujitsu and NEC.   Fujitsu is developing experimental versions of the ATLAS-II system that accept English or Japanese as source languages and can generate target text in German, French, Spanish, Chinese, Korean, Japanese, and English. There have also been experiments with Swahili and Innuit. NEC's PIVOT project has started research on Korean, Thai, and Spanish. ATLAS-II and PIVOT are likely to be headed for commercial markets in the West, and in fact ATLAS-II is already known in Europe and was recently launched in the United States.

Matsushita, collaborating with researchers in China, has started work on a Chinese target for the Japanese source component of PAROLE. Japanese-to-Chinese is also the subject of development

Target / Source	Chinese	English	French	German	Indonesian	Innuit	Italian	Japanese	Korean	Malay	Portugese	Spanish	Swahili	Thai
Chinese					1			1		1				1
English	4		2	2		1	1	15	4		1	3	1	1
French		1						1						
German														
Indonesian	1							1		1				1
Innuit														
Italian														
Japanese	4	17	1	1	1				3	1		2		2
Korean		2						1						
Malay	1				1			1						1
Portugese														
Spanish		2						1	1					1
Swahili														
Thai	1	1			1			2	1	1		1		

Figure 3-2: Source and Target Language Combinations, by Languages

efforts by Oki Electric, which is adding Chinese as a target language to PENSEE, under a project being carried out in conjunction with Nanjing University [Wang 90]. Catena's STAR system is being enhanced with a capability of translating French into Japanese [Aizawa 90].

The two other companies whose list of MT languages goes beyond English/Japanese have a history of MT involvement that began outside Japan, and their objectives do not necessarily parallel those of Japanese industry.   IBM   is developing English/Chinese and English/Korean for the translation of documentation to support the sale of U.S. products.   Bravice (which appears to have gone out of business in early 1991) informed the JTEC team that it had seven pairs of European languages in various stages of development for the personal computer (English into French, Spanish, Portuguese, Italian, and German; French into English; and Spanish into English), as well as a PC system translating from English into Chinese. In addition, Bravice subcontracted with Executive Communication Systems in Provo, Utah, for the development of a bidirectional English/Korean prototype, which was delivered through TRW's Federal Systems Group to the U.S. Signal Corps. Bravice had also started work on a Japanese/Korean translation capability.

3.2 Addition of New Source and Target Languages

A few of the companies that now have one direction only, either E/J or J/E, have immediate or future plans to add the other direction. In the near term, ATR and JICST plan to expand into English/Japanese. Fujitsu intends to upgrade the Japanese source component of ATLAS-II so that it will be sufficiently robust to stand alongside English as a multitarget source for its other languages.

In addition to the languages mentioned in the previous section, a few others are in the wings, mainly for the interlingua-based systems. ATLAS-II, which already has an impressive inventory, will be expanded to cover additional European languages. CICC, in turn, may eventually include English in its suite of Asian languages. CSK plans to expand its ARGO system into the languages of Western Europe and Southeast Asia.

Except as noted so far, it would appear that the typical transfer-based developer visited by JTEC, rather than adding new languages, would prefer to focus efforts on improving the accuracy of their J/E and/or E/J systems, expanding into new domains for existing combinations, building up knowledge sources, integrating into the electronic publication chain, and developing user-friendly interfaces, customized tools, and other nonlinguistic enhancements.

Clearly cost is an important factor in determining the rate at which systems are extended to new language combinations. There is good reason to expect that it will be relatively less costly to add new target languages to systems that have a well-developed source analysis module coupled with a robust set of transfer rules or an interlingua. It should be kept in mind, however, that with interlingual systems considerable effort is required in order to bring a source language up to full multitarget capability.

Several developers provided the JTEC team with information on the cost of adding new languages. Systran quoted a cost of US$100,000 to add a new target language to an existing multitarget source, regardless of the language. Dictionary-building is extra.[2] On the other hand, a new, fully operational multitarget source language may cost anywhere from 10 to 50 times as much—US$1,000,000 for an Indo-European language such as Czech or Norwegian, US$2,000,000 for a Roman alphabet non-Indo-European language such as Hungarian or Turkish, US$3,000,000 for a non-Roman alphabet non-Indo-European language for which existing work in Japanese could be utilized (e.g., Chinese or Korean), and US$5,000,000 for an entirely new project such as Arabic. A second estimate came from Bravice, where the company's president, Takehito Yamamoto, estimated that to add a new language combination if one of the languages is English takes about 250 person-months, and if both languages are new, at least 480 person-months. Matsushita indicated that to add a new source or target language to PAROLE would take about 20 person-years. Fujitsu reported that the addition of a new language takes three to five years at 5

---

[2]Figures supplied by Denis Gachot, president of Systran Translation Systems, Inc. According to Gachot, dictionary development costs US$3.00 for a stem entry and US$6.00 for a multiword expression. Entries of the latter kind represent about 20% of the total dictionary. For an application in a limited domain, the dictionary should have from 40,000 to 60,000 entries; for a general-purpose application it should have from 100,000 to 150,000 entries.

to 10 people per year plus additional resources for dictionary development.

3.3 Application Domains, Domain Adaptability

It is useful to distinguish between special-purpose and general-purpose MT systems. Special-purpose, or domain-specific, systems are designed to handle text in a limited subject area that has fairly predictable linguistic structures and vocabulary. Depending on the area covered in the domain, there may be very few ambiguities to resolve (i.e., few meanings and readings to make decisions about), and these decisions can be facilitated by the use of a knowledge base that gives a full range of attributes for the agents, objects, etc.,in the text. The lexicon need not be very large (up to 60,000 stem entries). Development costs are relatively low by MT standards. From the user's perspective, the output is fairly stable, requiring considerably less human intervention than a general "try-anything" application.

The general-purpose system is a much greater challenge for MT: there are many ambiguities, the MT dictionary must be rich with coding if it is to support the choices that are required, and it must have far more entries---at least 100,000 to 150,000. The MT product, because it is less predictable, requires greater human intervention.

Paralleling these contrasts, the domain-specific system is usually for the dissemination of information and therefore calls for high standards of quality. It is often used for translation from a single source to multiple target languages. The general-purpose system, on the other hand, may be used for the assimilation of information over a broad range of topics and can be useful even if quality standards are relaxed---as indeed they must be if the cost of human intervention is to be minimized. In such applications there may be several source languages translated into a single target.

There is a clear market for both domain-specific and general-purpose systems. Domain-specific systems can be used in many applications that are of significant technical and commercial interest. General-purpose systems are also important. They are more interesting commercially because they can attract a broad range of clients. As a result, many companies are working with this goal in mind. Sometimes general-purpose systems can be successfully customized for special applications as well. They are amenable to such downsizing when they have the capacity to process the syntactic and semantic information needed for eliciting context-sensitive translations---i.e., they are domain-adaptable.

In Japan, a number of systems began by being domain-specific, focusing for the most part on the area of computer manual translation, which is said to represent 80% of all MT use in the country. Often their developers were hardware manufacturers who saw MT first as a tool for helping them to reach overseas markets and second as a potential commercial product. Typically, a system begins as domain-specific and gradually progresses to be domain-adaptable and ultimately general-purpose. (See Chapter 5.) This was the case with CSK's ARGO (expanding from tightly-worded financial bulletins to economic texts and now branching out into political and social areas and biotechnology): Fujitsu's ATLAS-II (banking, pharmaceuticals, chemicals): Hitachi's HICATS (information processing, electronics, computers, civil engineering, construction, transportation, natural science, biology, machinery, chemicals, metals); NEC's PIVOT (aviation E/J, navigation J/E): Oki Electric's PENSEE (medicine, finance, electronic communication), and Toshiba's ASTRANSAC (general-purpose, with domains such as information science, electronics).

On the other hand, some systems have been designed and developed for more general-purpose translation from the start. The JICST system, for example, translates database abstracts in a variety of scientific and technical fields. Since this was its goal from the beginning, a substantial amount of work has gone into building up its technical lexicon. Some of the preceding systems are also being used for general purposes in translation bureaus. Another that was developed from the start as a general-purpose system is Sharp's DUET E/J. Perhaps the most challenged MT system in Japan is Catena's STAR at NHK (Japan's public television station), which is being used to write subtitles for excerpts from English-language news stories, which may be on any topic that is worthy of headlines. STAR is also being used on an experimental basis to monitor incoming newswire bulletins on a near-real time basis. It is not a coincidence that all the projects mentioned have been engaged in MT development for more than a decade.

The trend in Japan of starting with a specific application and working up to a general-purpose system contrasts somewhat with patterns in the West, where there seems to be more of a dichotomy between special- and general-purpose systems. However, commercial general-purpose systems are often domain-adapted for a specialized application---for example, SYSTRAN at Xerox Corporation---and perform sufficiently well to meet the needs of the user.

The range of language combinations and domains, many of which have been the subject of intensive dictionary work, show that Japan is moving ahead persistently on a broad front. This strategy, when followed appropriately, cannot fail to contribute to the performance of Japanese MT systems.

4. Knowledge Sources for Machine Translation

Yorick Wilks

4.1 Overview of Knowledge Sources

The knowledge sources needed to perform MT depend at least to a limited extent on the MT method used. For example, some current U.S. projects (such as the work at IBM on English to French MT [Brown 89]) make use of very large-scale statistical information from texts, while Japanese systems do not. Conversely, an experimental MT system at Kyoto University uses   large lists of sample sentences against which a sentence to be translated is matched [Sato 90], whereas currently no U.S. systems do this. Most MT systems, however, make use of at least some of the following kinds of knowledge sources:

- Morphology tables

- Grammar rules (including analysis, generation, and transfer rules)

- Lexicons

- Representations of world knowledge

Sometimes the first, second, or fourth of these knowledge sources may be absent. For instance, it is possible both to analyze and to represent the English language without the use of morphology tables, since it is inflected only to a small degree; for the analysis of a highly inflected language like Japanese, on the other hand, they are almost essential. Some analysis systems do not use an independent set of identifiable grammar rules, but these systems must somewhere contain syntactic information, such as the fact that in English an article precedes a noun. Although there is room for doubt as to whether certain items of linguistic knowledge belong in morphology or grammar (in Italian, for example, forms like pronouns may stand alone, but can also act as suffixes to verbs: e.g., *daglielo*), in Japanese and English this ambiguity of type is very unlikely. The fourth category is even more uncommon. Only some MT systems (usually those that owe some allegiance to artificial intelligence methods) claim to contain world knowledge representations.

The third form of knowledge (lexical) appears in virtually every MT system, however, except for the purely statistical type of system referred to earlier. Unfortunately, the distinction between lexical and world knowledge can also be tricky. In a German lexicon, for example, *Das Fraulein* is marked as neuter in gender but, in the real world, it must be marked feminine, since the word means "a young woman." We should deduce from this that a lexicon is a rag-bag of information, containing more than just semantic information about meanings.

Although there are many ways in which the development of these knowledge sources can take place, we will mention one example. Toshiba developed its knowledge sources in the chronological order shown in Figure 4-1. Because the role of knowledge sources within an MT system depends so heavily on the overall structure of the system, it is interesting to look also at Toshiba's overall translation procedure, which is shown in Figure 4-2. Without committing to a specific view of what "semantic transfer" means, we can infer that the bolder arrows represent the translation tasks to be performed, while the lighter arrows indicate Toshiba's view of where the knowledge forms they emphasize distribute across those tasks.

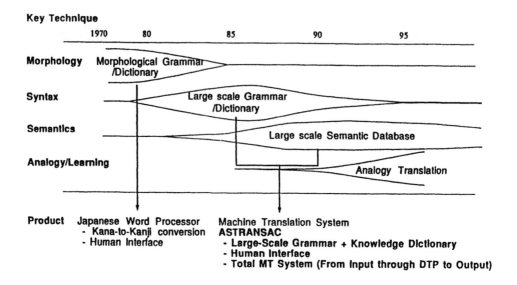

Figure 4-1: Toshiba's Development of Knowledge Sources

4.2 Use of Knowledge Sources in Specific Japanese MT Systems

Much of this chapter's content could be summed up by the tables shown in Figures 4-3 and 4-4, which list 22 systems by their major features, such as the type of MT system (direct, transfer, or interlingual[3]), the major language directions expressed as letter pairs (e.g. J/E for Japanese to English), the type of grammar (ATN's, case-frame, etc. - see Chapter 2), the number of rules (if available), the lexicon's size and type (also if available), and any kind of knowledge representation that is used.

One noticeable feature of the table is that only one MT system explicitly claims to use a knowledge representation: IBM Japan's SHALT2 uses the Framekit-based system. Also note that although the EDR Electronic Dictionaries have been included on the chart, they are not an MT system, but a very large scale set of lexical and conceptual tools, as described below.

What NTT (in the system type column) describes as J/J transfer means extensive, automatic, pre-editing to (a) remove character combinations known to cause problems for analysis programs and (b) insert segmentation boundaries into sentences to break them into sections, making analysis easier [Ikehara 91]. This process is also called source-to-source translation. Variations of these methods were found at other sites (e.g., Sharp and NHK), and although (b) originated in earlier MT practice, these methods constitute a practical heuristic that has almost certainly improved translation quality.

---

[3]In Chapter 1, these terms were defined. But we also presented there a caveat about their use, since this terminology has not been standardized. Here, as in Chapter 1, we use the developer's words to describe each system.

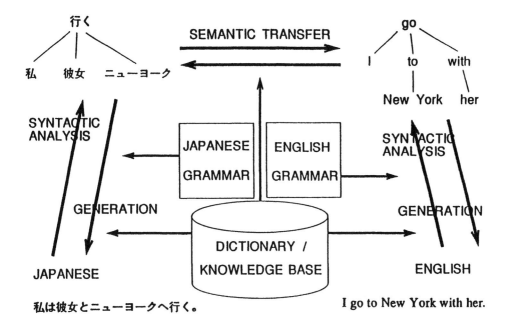

Figure 4-2: The Translation Process in the Toshiba System

4.3 Knowledge Sources and Linguistic Theory

Techniques such as source-to-source translation are interesting because they fall under the rubric of what Bar-Hillel (wrongly believed by many to be the arch-enemy of MT) described when he wrote that "MT research should restrict itself, in my opinion, to the development of what I called before 'bags of tricks' and follow the general linguistic research only to such a degree as is necessary without losing itself in Utopian ideas [Bar-Hillel 71]."

More than U.S. projects, and much more than European projects like EUROTRA, Japanese MT work has arrived at the same conclusion as Bar-Hillel. Very little Japanese work owes much to Western-style linguistic theory beyond some general use of "case frame" and some concepts taken from unification grammar. Instead, it has developed its own indigenous, Japanese tradition of linguistic description, as exemplified in the work at NTT.

If accurate, this observation is a reason to re-examine the Western notion of "knowledge sources." Given that the list at the beginning of this chapter took its categories directly from Western linguistics and does not tailor itself very well to Japanese MT work (if one agrees that the most successful Japanese systems are mainly driven by the information in their lexicons, as is SYSTRAN), then our very

Company	System Type	Grammar	Lexicon	Knowledge Representation
ATR	Semantic Transfer E/J	Lexically-Based Unification Grammar (JPSG) 130 Rules	Case-Roles Thesaurus	----
Bravice	Syntactic Transfer J/E & E/J	J/E 4K Rules E/J LFG/UNIFIC 8K Rules	J/E: 70K Basic 240K Technical E/J: 40K Basic	----
Catena STAR	Syntactic Transfer E/J	2,000 Context-Free Rules	20K Basic 55K Technical	----
The Translator	Syntactic Transfer E/J	3,000 Context-Free Rules	25K Basic 35K Technical	----
CICC	Interlingual (J,C,TH,IN,MAL)	----	50K Basic 25K Technical	----
CSK	Interlingual J/E & E/J	ATNS	50K	----
EDR (Not an MT system)	Implicitly Interlingual	----	J: 300K E: 300K	400K Concepts in Concept Dictionary
Fujitsu ATLAS-I	Syntactic Transfer J/E	----	----	----
ATLAS-II	Interlingual J/E	5K J Rules 5K E Rules 500 Transfer Rules	70K Each Way +300K Technical in subdictionary	----
Hitachi	Semantic Transfer J/E & E/J	Case-Based J/E: 5,000 Rules E/J: 3,000 Rules	J/E 50K E/J 50K	----
IBM SHALT	Syntactic Transfer E/J	Phrase Structure 200 E Rules 800 Transfer Rules 900 J Rules	E/J 90K	----
IBM SHALT2	Semantic Transfer E/J	----	LDOCE	Framekit-Based Representation

Figure 4-3: Knowledge Sources in Japanese Systems

assumptions of what knowledge sources actually drive MT should be reassessed.

For the sake of clarity, it may be profitable to return to the notion of a knowledge source, and to throw some additional light on it by contrasting it with MT without knowledge sources.

Earlier we mentioned that current work at IBM/Yorktown Heights performs English to French (E/F) MT without help from any of the knowledge sources we listed above. Even its definition of what constitutes a word is derived from frequent collocation measures of other "words," and therefore is not a priority. That

Company	System Type	Grammar	Lexicon	Knowledge Representation
JICST	Semantic Transfer J/E	1500 J Rules 500 Transfer Rules 450 E Rules	350K J 250K E	----
Matsushita	Syntactic Transfer J/E	800 J Rules 300 Transfer Rules	31K Each Direction	----
NEC	Interlingual J/E & E/J	Case-Frame Grammar	90K J/E, 70K E/J +600K Technical Lexicons	----
NTT	Syntactic Transfer J/E (J/J Transfer)	----	400K (Includes 300K Proper Nouns)	----
Oki	Syntactic Transfer J/E & E/J	Context-Free Rules 1K Rules Each Direction	J/E: 90K E/J: 60K	----
Ricoh	Syntactic Transfer E/J	2500 Rules 300 Transfer Rules	55K	----
Sanyo	Syntactic Transfer J/E & E/J	Context-Free Phrase-Structure 650 Rules Each Way	50K Each J/E & E/J	----
Sharp	Semantic Transfer J/E & E/J	Augmented Context-Free and Case Frames	J/E: 70K E/J: 79K	----
Systran Japan	Transfer J/E & E/J <->	Multi-Pass Phase-Finding	E/J 200K (Interpress) J/E 50K	----
Toshiba	Semantic Transfer J/E & E/J	ATN+Lexical Rules 100K Rules Each Way	50K General <200K Technical <200K Users	----

Figure 4-4: Knowledge Sources in Japanese Systems

system generates word strings that connect to form statistically "natural strings," frequently at the expense of their relation to anything in the source text. This is accomplished without any knowledge sources: that is, without any analytic, combinatory, or symbolic structures.

An interesting example at the other end of the spectrum is SYSTRAN [Toma 76]. Although SYSTRAN is primarily an American system and thus really outside the scope of this report, its J/E and E/J modules are still owned in Japan by Iona International Corporation. The contrast between SYSTRAN and the IBM E/F system is instructive here, partly because the systems' goals are to translate by symbolic and statistical methods, respectively, and partly because it is SYSTRAN's "sentence correct percentage" that IBM would have to beat to be successful although it is nowhere near doing so at the present time.

SYSTRAN has also been described at least in parody as utilizing no knowledge sources; it has been thought of by some as having, in effect, a mere sentence dictionary of source and target languages. Nor is this notion as absurd as linguists used to think: the number of English sentences under fifteen words long, for instance, is very large, but not infinite. So, based on the preceding definition, an MT system that did MT by such a method of direct one-to-one sentence pairing would definitely not have a knowledge source. But, although part of the success of the SYSTRAN Russian/English system installed at the U.S. Air Force's Foreign Technology Divison is certainly due to its 350,000-word lexicon of phrases, idioms, and semi-sentences [Wilks 91], SYSTRAN does not really conform to this parody of it [Toma 76]. Moreover, the new version of SYSTRAN, according to their president, is being re-engineerd with a more conventional modular structure and explicit knowledge sources.

One might say that while U.S. and European systems tend to fall toward the extremes of a spectrum (running from linguistically-motivated systems at one end to those with no knowledge sources at the other), Japanese systems tend to fall in between, and to have *sui generis* knowledge sources, as does SYSTRAN itself.

Another way of thinking about knowledge sources for MT is that they are never completely pure data in the way that linguistic theory sometimes supposes. That is to say that the role and content of a knowledge source cannot really be understood without some consideration of the processes that make use of it.

4.4 Lexicon Samples

Figure 4-5 shows an example from the ATR lexicon, and is for the verb *kudasai*. It is unusual in that it is a lexical entry for a strongly linguistically-motivated system; indeed, one can deduce from its structure that it is almost certainly intended to fit within an HPSG[4] grammar system. This confirms that such knowledge sources are not independent of the processes that apply to them.

It is important to emphasize once more the paramount role of lexicons in many Japanese systems, their substantial size (and the manpower required to construct them), and the wealth of specialized technical lexicons available in some of these systems. For example, Figure 4-6 shows the set of 13 technical lexicons available for the Fujitsu ATLAS system. These are in addition to the basic dictionary, which contains about 70,000 entries. The effort required to build an MT dictionary depends on several factors. We were given several different estimates for the rate at which system builders could add new terms to the dictionary, ranging from five entries/hour (Matsushita) to six person years to customize a dictionary for a new application (Hitachi).

As noted, SYSTRAN is a strongly lexically-dependent MT system. SYSTRAN's J/E and E/J modules have three types of dictionaries described by the company in [SYSTRAN 91] as:

- A "word boundary" dictionary for matching words and establishing word boundaries in Japanese text, where each word is not clearly bounded by spaces (as in English and other European languages).

- A "stem" dictionary containing source language words and their most frequently used target language equivalents. This dictionary also contains morphological, syntactic, and semantic information about each entry word.

---

[4]Head-Drive Phrase Structure Grammar [Pollard 87].

.3.4   依頼

人に動作をするように頼む場合のムード。直接依頼の「下さい」「てもらう」のみ登録されている。

直接依頼形式 直接相手に動作の依頼をする。

間接依頼形式 自分の実情を述べて、相手に間接的に動作の依頼をする。

- ～て / て下さい / てちょうだい

- ～てくれませんか / てもらえますか / てもらえませんか

- ～てほしい / てもらいたい / てほしいんだけど

- ～てくれるといいんだが / てくれるとありがたいんだけど

「下さい」の語彙記述の例

「下さい」は、動詞テ形（「送って下さい」）、または、サ変名詞（「御参加下さい」「お送り下さい」）を下位範疇化する補助動詞として記述されている。

```
([[PHON (:DLIST      kudasai
                 |?X07| )]
 [SYN [[SLASH [DLIST[IN ?X04[]]
                   [OUT ?X04]]]
      [HEAD [[POS  V]
            [GRFS [[SUBJ [[SYN [[SUBCAT (:LIST )]
                                [HEAD [[POS P]
                                      [FORM が]
                                      [COMPLEMENT +]]]]]
                         [SEM ?X02[]]]]]]
            [ASPECT +]
            [VASP [[CUNG +]
                  [HONE -]
                  [ACTV +]]]
            [SUBV +]]]
      [VN [DLIST[IN ?X05[]]
              [OUT ?X05]]]
      [MORPH [[CTYPE NONC]]]]]
 [SEM [[RELN 下さい -REQUEST]
      [AGEN ?X03[]]
      [RECP ?X02]]]
 [PRAG [[RESTR (:DLIST       [[RELN  RESPECT]
                             [AGEN ?X03]
                             [RECP ?X02]]
                            [[RELN  POLITE]
                             [AGEN ?X03]
                             [RECP ?X02]]
                           |?X01| )]
       [SPEAKER ?X03]
       [HEARER ?X02]]]
 [ORTH (:DLIST      下さい
              |?X06| )]]
([[SYN [[MORPH [[CFORM INFN]]]]]]) ; 連用形（「下さいますか」）
([[SYN [[MORPH [[CFORM IMPR]]]]]]); 命令形（通常の用法）
([[SYN [[SUBCAT (:LIST     ?X11[[SYN [[SUBCAT (:LIST    ?X10[[SYN [[SUBCAT (:LIST )]
                                                               [HEAD [[POS P]
                                                                     [FORM が]
                                                                     [COMPLEMENT +]]]]]
                                                         [SEM ?X06[]]]
                                                   )]
                                     [HEAD [[POS ADV]
                                           [GRFS [[SUBJ ?X10]]]]]]
                                [SEM ?X09[]]]
                          )]
                    [HEAD [[MODL [[EVID DIRC]]]
                          [GRFS [[SUBJ [[SEM ?X08]]]
                                [COMP ?X11]]]]]])
 [SEM [[RECP ?X08]
      [OBJE ?X09]]]
```

Figure 4-5: An Example Entry from the ATR Dictionary

Field	Number of Entries
Biology and Medicine	9,200 words
Industrial chemistry	14,400 words
Meteorology, Seismology, and Astronomy	13,500 words
Mechanical engineering	28,100 words
Civil engineering and Construction	14,400 words
Physics and Atomic Energy	15,000 words
Transportation	21,800 words
Plant	36,000 words
Automobile	18,000 words
Biochemistry	15,000 words
Information processing	26,000 words
Electircity and Electronics	17,100 words
Mathematics and Information	31,900 words

Figure 4-6: Technical Lexicons Available for the ATLAS System and Used to Supplement the Basic General-Purpose Lexicon

- A "limited semantics" (LS) dictionary of expressions, special collocations, and macro instructions for handling translation problems of low to medium complexity.

These are accessed within the main SYSTRAN framework, as shown in Figure 4-7. SYSTRAN's dictionary list for its newer multitarget systems is shown in Figure 4-8. The English-Japanese component (at 150,000 source items) is about three times the size of the corresponding J/E dictionary, which alone would account for its superior quality in the sample test conducted during the JTEC visit. This newer system is called multitarget because SYSTRAN has now fully integrated its earlier methodology of detaching and reusing chunks of older programs for new languages. SYSTRAN is now described as a transfer rather than a direct system. This is an interesting evolutionary, bottom-up approach to design development.

A sample of SYSTRAN's small J/E dictionary is shown in Figure 4-9. This dictionary is at an early stage of development but already displays the standard and successful SYSTRAN trend towards long source strings, within the now well-understood limits, in its approach to other languages.

Finally, the adventurous EDR dictionary project [EDR 90] (see Section 9.6) provides a formal,

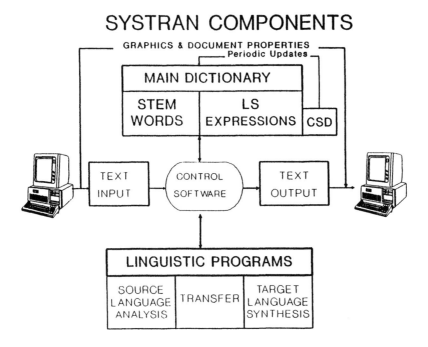

SYSTRAN COMPONENTS

Figure 4-7: The Use of Dictionaries in SYSTRAN

E-Multitarget	Source	Target
ENGLISH SOURCE	172,056	
English-French		200,166
English-German		129,916
English-Italian		149,387
English-Portugese		42,130
English-Spanish		103,337
English-Korean		6,412
English-Arabic	162,640	150,147
English-Dutch	97,994	79,075
English-Japanese	156,866	66,384
English-Russian	19,329	34,773

Figure 4-8: SYSTRAN Dictionary Size
(As of 6/30/89)

```
1NEW DICTIONARY RECORDS
1DC STEM/ID/EXPRESSION          POS  JAPANESE - ENGLISH    140    W T M MEANING      02-18-91  PAGE      1  D SYN AA GR CC WC    DATE
                               BPO                               N G I                                    P     RN AE 22 D2    LAST
                                                                   D                                      Q      T  DF 01 13  UPDATED
031  #ATAMA#WARI .BCPRT Q#DE                                     1 0 0 HEAD                                1 000 00 00   0  01-24-91
                                                                2 0 0 PER                                 0 000 00 00   0
                               N01 01-24-91 ASSIGN MNG TO 'ATAMAWARI DE'; ASK-7 (KE)
B1   #GEN#BA Q#DE                                               1 0 0 SITE                                 1 000 00 00   0  10-29-90
                                                                2 0 0 ON                                  0 000 00 30   0
                               N01 10-29-90 GENBA DE = 'ON SITE'; J3INTEC2-88  (LG)
41   #HAI#KA .AD Q#DE                                           1 0 0 DIRECTION                            1 000 20 00   0  09-21-83
                                                                2 0 0 UNDER                               0 000 00 30   0
                               N01 09-21-83 JFAC3C-235 (HA)
                               N02 09-21-83 SET TR= 'UNDER THE DIRECTION OF' (HA)
B2   #HURUI Q#TOKORO Q#DE Q#HA                                  1 0 0 $$$                                  0 000 00 20   0  10-10-90
                                                                2 0 0 LOOKING BACK INTO HISTORY           0 000 00 30   0
                                                                3 0 0 $$$                                  0 000 00 20   0
                                                                4 0 0 $$$                                  0 000 00 20   0
                               N01 10-10-90 ASSIGN MNG., TOKORO MULT MN PROJECT.  MMWDTOKO-132 (LG)
41   #I#MI Q#DE                                                 1 0 0 SENSE                                1 004 00 00   0  06-09-89
                                                                2 0 0 IN                                  0 000 00 30   0
                               N01 06-09-89 JABAF-42; JFIFTHC-22,46; JFIFTHB-7 (HA/LG)
0
41   #I#TAKU .POS=10 .AD/MODL                                   1 0 0 REQUEST                              1 004 00 00   0  04-08-83
     .IF .B2B .SQ#YORU                                          2 0 0 AT                                  1 000 00 30   0
     .OR .BCPRT Q#DE
                               N01 04-08-83 VOX79-4 (HA)
B4   #ITI #KOU.KUTI Q#DE #IEBA                                  1 0 0 $$$                                  0 000 00 20   0  10-11-89
                                                                2 0 0 $$$                                  0 000 00 20   0
                                                                3 0 0 $$$                                  0 000 00 20   0
                                                                4 0 0 PUT SIMPLY                           0 000 00 30   0
                               N01 10-11-89 BIT1 (MC)
41   #ITU#POU .BL+SSU .PW,CW .BR Q#DE .BR .SQ#HA                1 0 0 OTHER HAND                           1 000 20 00   0  03-17-87
                                                                2 0 0 ON                                  0 000 00 30   0
                               N01 03-17-87 TRANSLATE EXPRESSION 'ON THE OTHER HAND' (YD/HA)
418  #KAN#REN Q#DE .PW,CW .BMODL+BPQ=28 .PW,CW,B20,B30          1 0 0 RELATION                             1 000 00 00   0  02-22-84
     .Z-LMOD .PW,CW .Z-MODL                                           CDS-GENTO
                                                                2 0 0 IN                                  0 000 00 30   0
                               N01 02-22-84 RESET 16/26 TO 30/20 BETWEEN PW AND BPQ28 MODIFIER AND
0                              N02 02-22-84 SET ON SPHNCD GENTO (HA)
41   #KEI.KATATI Q#DE .PW,CW                                    1 0 0 WAY                                  1 004 00 00   0  01-07-91
     .IF .BANTEC+ANSUB .MID,0                                         1 FORM                               1 004 00 00   0
     .OR .ANTEC+N-LINKGVR .MID,1                                2 0 0 IN                                  0 000 00 30   0
     .OR .Z-MODL .AD .MID,1                                           1 IN                                 0 000 00 30   0
     .OR .B26 .POS=20 .PW,CW .MID,0
                               N01 10-29-90 ALLOW CONSISTENTLY ADVERBIAL FUNCTION OF KATATI DE (LG)
                               N02 10-29-90 CASE MARKER DE PROJECT.  (LG)
B18  #KIYOU#DOU .BR Q#DE .POS=50 .PW,CW .S-POS=30               1 0 D JOINTLY                              0 000 00 30   0  10-29-90
                                                                2 0 0 $$$                                  0 000 00 20   0
                               N01 10-29-90 KIYOUDOU IS ADV WHEN FLLWD BY DE.  DE IS MADE CSHKR
                               N02 10-29-90 IN HOMOR.  J3ENERGY-25 (LG)
41   #KOU#SEI .PSV .BOBJ .BCPRT                                 1 0 0 CONSIST                              3 004 00 01   0  09-08-83
     .IFNB Q#KARA                                               2 0 0 OF                                  0 000 00 30   0
     .OR Q#DE                                                   3 0 0 $$$                                  0 000 00 30   0
                               N01 09-08-83 XJEOBJ2-34 (HA)
                               N02 09-08-83 EXPAND TO INCL #KARA CPRT AS WELL AS Q#DE (HA)
41   #KUTI#UTUSI .N-LINKGVR .BCPRT                              1 0 0 MOUTH TO MOUTH                       0 000 00 00   0  04-08-83
0    .IFNB Q#NI                                                 2 0 0 $$$                                  0 000 00 20   0
     .OR Q#DE                                                   3 0 0 $$$                                  0 000 00 20   0
                               N01 04-08-83 SET TRANSLATE Q#NI/Q#DE WHEN PW IS NOT A PRED. NOM. (MO)
                               N02 04-08-83 SST01-136 (MO)
B2   #SE#KAI #KI#BO Q#DE                                        1 0 0 WORLDWIDE                            2 000 80 00   0  01-02-90
                                                                2 0 0 SCALE                               1 000 00 00   0
                                                                3 0 0 ON                                  0 000 00 30   0
                               N01 01-02-90 AGRMNT-2 (HA/MS)
41   #SIYU#DOU .BCPRT Q#DE                                      1 0 0 HAND                                 1 004 70 00   0  05-07-81
                                                                2 0 0 BY                                  0 000 00 30   0
                               N01 05-07-81 WIS4-27 (BO)
418  #SOBA .AD Q#DE .PW,CW .Z-LOCAT+S-PROX                      1 0 0 VICINITY                             1 000 20 00   0  09-21-83
```

Figure 4-9: A Sample from the SYSTRAN J/E Dictionary

conceptual description of at least 400,000 head items (roughly corresponding to word senses), with an interface to sense definitions in English and Japanese. A sample of the English interface is shown in Figure 4-10. The dictionaries are designed to be a knowledge source in the pure sense, free of implied process, although, in fact, their conceptual coding scheme will most likely appeal to a lexically-driven, interlingual MT system. This is an enormous enterprise; it is both manpower- and computation-intensive. It is not yet clear how much of the conceptual coding has been completed, even though both language interfaces are available.

Funds for the project have been provided both by the government and by major companies with MT activity [Fujitsu, NEC, Hitachi, etc.]. While these companies all plan to make use of the EDR dictionary's

[royal] 〈00C7405〉 very fine and costly
[royal] 〈0d48d2〉 a member of the royal family
[royal] 〈03F6944〉 of a person noble and refined in mind and character
[royal] 〈0d48d3〉 a small mast, sail, or yard, set above the topgallant
[royal] 〈0d48d4〉 a size of writing paper
[royal] 〈0d48d5〉 a size of printing paper
[royal] 〈0d48d6〉 any one of various coins in former times
[royal] 〈0ea551〉 to become holy and sacred／尊くおごそかなさまになる
[royal] 〈00F7FF4〉 of a condition of a thing, excellent／すぐれてよいさま
[royal] 〈0fa960〉 of a condition of a view, magnificent／眺めが壮大であるさま
[royal] 〈1086d6〉 precious things／得がたいもの
[royal] 〈03BD198〉 a facility built by a king or his family／国王や王族が設立した施設
[royal] 〈03CE55B〉 of a condition, excellent／すばらしいさま
[royal] 〈03CE649〉 of a condition, satisfactory／満足がいく状態であるさま
[royal] 〈03CF0DA〉 a state of being excellent and noble／優れて気高いさま
[royal] 〈03CF119〉 luxurious and magnificent／規模が大きく、りっぱで美しいさま
[royal] 〈03C2E5〉 a condition of someone having a noble position／身分が高く、尊いさま
[royal] 〈03CF6A7〉 a state of being solemn and respectable／おごそかで立派なさま
[royal antler] 〈26d6a3〉 the third tine above the base of a stag's antler
[royal blue] 〈03C6272〉 a vivid bright indigo named royal blue／ロイヤルブルーという，あざやかな明るい藍色
[royal blue] 〈03EE202〉 a colour named royal blue
[royal coachman] 〈026D6A5〉 a fishing fly named royal coachman
[royal coachman] 〈03C34FB〉 a fishing fly with a mosquite-shaped feather attached to it／羽毛で蚊の形に作ったつり針
[royal commission] 〈26d6a6〉 a group of people commissioned by the Crown
[royal commission] 〈26d6a7〉 the inquiry conducted by royal commission
[royal demesne] 〈26d6a8〉 the private property of the Crown
[royal fern] 〈026D6A9〉 a fern named royal fern
[royal fern] 〈03C0EBF〉 a fern named osmund／ゼンマイというシダ植物
[royal flush] 〈26d6aa〉 a straight flush in poker, named royal flush
[royal jelly] 〈026D6AB〉 a nutritious secretion of the pharyngeal glands of the honeybee, named royal jelly
[royal jelly] 〈03C6271〉 a nutritious secretion of the honeybee named royal jelly／ロイヤルゼリーという，ミツバチの栄養になる分泌物
[royal mast] 〈26d6ac〉 the mast next above the topgallant
[royal moth] 〈0d5293〉 a moth named saturniid
[royal moth] 〈03BCDB7〉 an insect named io moth／山繭蛾という昆虫
[royal palm] 〈26d6ae〉 a palm tree named royal palm
[royal poinciana] 〈26d6af〉 a tree named royal poinciana
[royal purple] 〈03C5BA7〉 a color named royal purple／青紫という色
[royal purple] 〈03EDB37〉 a dark reddish purple
[royal tennis] 〈26d1f2〉 court tennis
[royal tern] 〈26d6b2〉 a tern named royal tern
[royal water] 〈03C3172〉 a mixture of nitric acid and hydrochloric acid／濃塩酸と濃硝酸の混合液
[royalism] 〈03E99D8〉 the condition of adhering to monarchism
[royalist] 〈0d48d8〉 someone who supports a king or queen, as in a civil war, or who believes that a country should be ruled by a king or queen
[royalist] 〈0d48d9〉 typical of someone who supports a king or queen, as in a civil war, or who believes that a country should be ruled by a king or queen
[royalize] 〈0d48da〉 to make royal
[royalize] 〈0d48db〉 to assume royal power
[royally] 〈0d48dd〉 with the pomp and ceremony due a sovereign
[royally] 〈0d48dc〉 by the crown
[royally] 〈0d48de〉 with the utmost care and consideration
[royally] 〈0d48e0〉 on a large scale; gloriously
[royally] 〈0d48df〉 in a splendid manner; magnificently
[royalty] 〈00D48E2〉 people of the royal family
[royalty] 〈00D48E3〉 a payment made to an author or composer for each copy of his or her work sold, or to an inventer for each article sold
[royalty] 〈03F6436〉 the rank of a king or queen
[royalty] 〈0d48e4〉 a share of the product or profit kept by the grantor of especially an oil or mining lease
[royalty] 〈026BDB7〉 a payment made to the mineral content of a certain area of land
[royalty] 〈03C1A4A〉 a payment made as a fee for a copyright／著作権の使用料
[royalty] 〈03C1A4C〉 authority of the king／王の威光
[royalty] 〈03CEBCC〉 the rank of king or queen／王としての位
[royalty] 〈0d48e1〉 royal power and rank
[royalty] 〈03E99DC〉 the condition of having regal character or bearing
[royster] 〈00DB85E〉 to swagger
[rozzer] 〈03CB627〉 a person whose occupation is called policeman
[rozzer] 〈03F5E91〉 a person who belongs to the police
[rpm] 〈0d48e8〉 = r.p.m.
[rps] 〈0d48e9〉 = r.p.s.
[rpt] 〈00F0C4C〉 to announce something publically／（何かを）公表する
[rpt] 〈03F60F0〉 to repeat; an act of repeating
[rpt.] 〈03CF4EF〉 to announce something publically by a paper or orally／何かを書類や口頭で公表する
[rpt.] 〈00F0C4C〉 to announce something publically／（何かを）公表する

Figure 4-10: An Example of the English Interface to EDR's Concept Dictionary

final form, the intention is also to make the entire system available everywhere for a reasonable price.

EDR strives to be maximally cooperative with researchers world-wide, both in terms of joint effort on the project itself (where they already have a collaboration agreement with UMIST and UK and exchanges of technical information with a French team), and on subsequent use of the material for MT.

5. Life Cycle of Machine Translation Systems

Masaru Tomita

This chapter describes how MT systems are developed in Japan. During the JTEC visits, few of the sites provided specific information on the development of their MT systems. JTEC team members were also not given precise information about the amount of money spent on MT development in Japan. Therefore, what follows is based on informal conversations with their researchers and project leaders, with some speculation on our part.

As with most or all MT systems, the projects in Japan tend to have the following four stages:
- Research Prototype — a "toy" system to demonstrate feasibility of the approach and framework,

- Operational Prototype — for public demonstration and to validate the system,

- Practical System (Special-Purpose) — for actual day-to-day use,

- Commercial System (General-Purpose) — to generate revenue.

Of course, each project is different. Some systems do not evolve into commercial systems. Some projects have stepped back to prior stages to redesign or reimplement their systems. Some systems (as will be described in Chapter 6) are intended for different kinds of environments. What is described in this chapter is a generalization of all the projects.

5.1 Research Prototype

The first step in developing an MT system is to design its theoretical framework and build a small laboratory prototype system to demonstrate the feasibility of the framework. The number of researchers per system at this stage is very small. Usually a principal researcher coordinates the entire system design and a few other researchers assist in designing details or implementing a prototype system. The typical duration of this stage is one or two years.

In Japan, the results of this stage are typically published in the following technical journals and professional meetings:
- Domestic Journals
  - JOUHOU SHORI GAKKAISHI *(Journal of IPSJ: Information Processing Society of Japan)*
  - JOUHOU SHORI GAKKAI RONBUNSHI *(Transaction of IPSJ)*
  - DENKI TSUUSHIN GAKKAISHI *(Journal of IECEJ: The Institute of Electronics and Communication Engineers of Japan)*
- Domestic Meetings
  - SHIZENGENGO SHORI KENKYUUKAI (IPSJ Working Group in Natural Language Processing)
  - ZENKOKU TAIKAI (IPSJ semi-annual National meeting)
- International Journals
  - *Computational Linguistics*
  - *Machine Translation*

- International Meetings
    - COLING: International Conference on Computational Linguistics
    - ACL: Association of Computational Linguistics
    - MT Summits

It is worth noting that even private companies do not hesitate to publish their results at this stage (technical approaches, grammar formalism, dictionary configuration, theoretical framework, etc.). Possible explanations are:

- Prestige is one of the important factors. The more publication, the more recognition.

- Competitors do not like to adopt other approaches anyway. Each project wants to maintain originality. If some competitors adopt your approach, this means more prestige to you, and less prestige to them.

- The information does not help the competitors very much, after all. Many believe that the difficulties of MT lie in the development stage, not in the design stage. It is fun to design an MT system, but very hard to develop it into a fully operational environment.

The research prototype system is usually very primitive; it may have only a few hundred words in its dictionary, and may be very slow with little consideration for efficiency. It can translate only a small set of sample sentences, and does not work for most other sentences. The research prototype is clearly not sufficient for public demonstration.

MT projects at ICOT and ETL stop here; their objectives are to demonstrate specific theories of language and not to develop operational MT systems. Most academic projects at universities also stop here, with the exception of the MU project, which aimed at operational system development.

5.2 Operational Prototype

Once a research prototype has been implemented and its framework is proven feasible, the next stage is to develop an operational MT system based on the research prototype. A typical operational prototype has:

- broad grammar coverage to handle most input sentences,

- a dictionary with 10,000 - 100,000 entries, and

- modules to cope with practical problems such as idiomatic expressions, proper nouns, segmentation, punctuation, etc.

At this stage, the number of researchers increases to around 10 ~ 30. Development of the operational prototype takes place in two steps: first, developing an initial version of the system; and second, testing and debugging it. For the initial system development, three major tasks are necessary:

- Creating Dictionary Entries. It takes many people many months just to enter dictionary entries within the specifications defined during the research stage. This well-defined task is often considered tedious, and most projects find it convenient to subcontract the task to an outside software house.

- Writing Grammar Rules for Analysis, Transfer and Generation. The task of grammar-rule writing also may be tedious, but it is hard to give to outside subcontractors because:
    - The task of grammar-writing is not as well-defined as dictionary development.
    - The task is quite difficult to divide into smaller subtasks.
    - The task requires special skills. Grammar writers must be familiar not only with the

syntactic structures of the source and target languages, but also with the system's implementation.

- The task requires interaction with other members of the project. One of the important missions of the grammar writers at this stage is to give feedback to the designers of the grammar formalism and the system implementers.

- System Programming. The task of system implementation may be easier to distribute to several researchers. An MT system can be divided into modules such as the analysis module, the transfer module, the generation module, modules for morphological analysis and synthesis, a module to handle idioms, and a module to handle proper nouns. Each of the modules can be assigned to a single programmer; and some of them could be subcontracted.

When the dictionary entries and an initial version of the grammar rules have been completed, and when the system modules have been programmed, then the real enterprise, testing and debugging, begins. Usually each project has a large corpus of sentences to use to test its system. The typical debugging cycle is:

1. Running the system through (a part of) the corpus.

2. Evaluating translation output produced by the system.

3. Analyzing the cause of each error/mistranslation.

4. Notifying appropriate researchers responsible for the bugs.

5. Returning to step one after all bugs are fixed.

This cycle continues until the system's performance becomes satisfactory. This is a very difficult process because the cause of errors may be in the grammars, dictionaries, or system programs, as well as in the fundamental design or framework of the system. Different people are responsible for maintaining different parts of the system.

In this way, a research prototype evolves into an operational prototype system. At the end of this stage, the system is usually announced publicly, and demonstrations of the system are given at press conferences and at technical meetings, such as the MT Summits (Hakone - 1987, Munich - 1989, Washington D.C. - 1991), the EDR Symposium and Workshop (Tokyo - 1988, Kanagawa - 1990), and other conferences and trade shows.

ATR and CICC will stop here. The MU project also stopped here. However, the university's hope was that somebody else would pick up their operational prototype and develop it further to make it practical. In fact, the MU project was picked up by JICST and used as a basis for the JICST Machine Translation system.

5.3 Practical System (Special-Purpose)

After an operational prototype has been developed and public demonstrations have been given, the next step is to make the system usable in a day-to-day translation operation. The following three improvements are usually required:

- Specialized grammar and dictionary. The grammar rules and dictionary entries have to be adapted for the particular task domain.

- System Robustness. The system must endure under heavy daily operation. For example, it cannot afford to crash under any circumstance.

- Better User Interface. The system must be sufficiently user-friendly to be used by nonproject members.

- Peripheral Software. Pre- and postediting tools, user dictionary development tools, etc., must be developed.

Here are some examples of internal and external use of MT systems:
- Internal Use
    - IBM Japan (SHALT) --- Translating IBM manuals
    - JICST --- Translating scientific abstracts
- External Use
    - Fujitsu (ATLAS-II) --- Mazda Motor Corporation
    - NEC (PIVOT) --- Japan Convention Services, Inc.
    - HITACHI (HICATS/JE) --- Japan Patent Information Organization
    - etc.

At this stage, external use tends to be like a joint venture project; the users are usually very cooperative. Let us elaborate just one of the examples of external use --- Fujitsu's ATLAS-II at the Mazda Motor Corporation. Mazda started a joint venture after Fujitsu completed its operational prototype in 1985.
- First year (85/86) --- Feasibility study
    - Evaluation by Translation Service Department.
    - Preparation of Mazda's basic dictionaries and accumulation of pre-editing know-how.
    - Summary of evaluation and planning of system tuning.
- Second year (86/87) --- Trial and system tuning
    - System trial with service manuals.
    - Systematic maintenance of dictionaries.
    - Tuning of processing function for translation.
- Third year (87/88) --- Business use
    - Application to various overseas product manuals.
    - Gradual maintenance of dictionaries and accumulation of know-how for business use.
    - Preparation of expansion plan.
- Fourth year (88/89) --- Expansion of application
    - Expansion of application to technical documents.
    - Gradual integration into integrated document processing system.

5.4 Commercial System (General-Purpose)

If a system has proven useful in a specialized task domain, the next and final step is to make it general purpose, so that it can be used by many customers for multiple purposes. One of the biggest motivations for developing a general-purpose commercial system is to earn revenue directly from the system. There are three ways for a general purpose MT system to generate income:
- Sales as a software package (US$5,000 to US$30,000 per copy),
- Monthly lease (software and hardware), and

• Online service (charge for CPU time or by the word or page of text to be translated).

Unlike users at the prior stage, users at this stage are not necessarily cooperative; in fact, they are often critical and impatient. The number of people on the project at this stage is large — as many as 100 and many of them are customer-support personnel.

In the last two or three years, several translation service companies have started systematic use of MT systems.   (See Chapter 6.) Some users of these systems have said that the quality of MT-produced translation, even with human assistance in pre- or postediting, is lower than that of full human translation without MT. However, in some cases the service bureau will charge less (often around 30% less) for MT-produced translation, and some customers appear to be happy with lower-quality translation at lower cost. Other users demand higher quality translation.

5.5 Ongoing Use

Several factors determine the fate of an MT system once it has been put into production. For example, experience has shown that if a system is not operated by appropriately trained people then the results will be unsatisfactory, which will lead to the system being abandoned. The level of support provided by the manufacturer is also very important, particularly since some kinds of modifications to MT systems, such as expansion of the grammars, cannot be done by the users; they must be implemented by the developers.

6. The Uses of Machine Translation in Japan

Muriel Vasconcellos

6.1 Introduction

As might be expected, the large number of machine translation systems originating in Japan is matched by a broad variety of roles that have been found for the technology. The JTEC team was able to observe not only the full range of uses for MT that have been tried in other countries but also some variations and innovative applications that are being pioneered for the first time anywhere. Undoubtedly the heavy demand for translation between Japanese and English, the relative scarcity of highly qualified translators in these combinations, and the impressive linguistic distance between the two languages have stimulated the search for creative ways to enlist MT in the service of communication with the West.

Despite the many different MT modalities, domains, and translation purposes that are being tried, there is in fact a dearth of hard data about how Japan's more than 20 systems are actually being used. An authoritative summary of all the applications would be impossible. For this reason, the present chapter has been limited to a discussion of types of applications in the broad sense, with illustrative examples where appropriate. The rest of this section examines some of the general issues. Section 6.2 offers "case studies" drawn from the sites visited and other data available to the JTEC team, and Section 6.3 summarizes the reports of usage by the commercial vendors contacted during the course of the mission.

6.1.1 Modalities of Implementation

Based on form of input files

For any source language, the use of electronic files as input for MT makes a major difference in its overall cost-effectiveness by cutting down on human intervention at the front end. Since the input of Japanese is exceptionally complex, given the tedious problem of typing in kana and kanji, the savings to be realized are naturally even greater. It comes as no surprise, therefore, that the Japanese are exploring a variety of MT applications that take advantage of the fact that the input text has already been captured in machine-readable form.

The electronic files used for MT input in Japan come from a range of sources that include desktop publishing processes, public telecommunication networks, newswire services, and databases. Optical character recognition (OCR) has recently started to achieve sufficient accuracy to be considered a practical way to convert paper documents in high quality print into electronic ones, as discussed below.

As in the West, MT is often embedded in the publishing chain. Hardware manufacturers, the major users of MT in Japan, have introduced the technology into a process that starts at the point where specially trained writers draft their texts in-house and generate files that can be used both for publication directly in Japanese and for input to MT. Desktop publishing is the typical mode of operation for hardware manufacturers that have developed MT systems to translate their own product manuals. (See Section 6.1.3.)

For companies that do not have their own MT system, the translation of manuals is sometimes subcontracted to translation service bureaus that use MT. In a number of cases, the files are transmitted from the customer to the translation agency through a computer service network. At CSK, a major computer service company, customers' files are received on-line for machine translation into English by the firm's proprietary system, ARGO. (See Section 6.2.1.)

At the time of the JTEC visit, CSK was developing an international network that would permit ARGO to be accessed on-line in the United States. The general public can already tap into Fujitsu's ATLAS-II via NIFTY-Serve, the Japanese network modeled after CompuServe, and obtain a machine translation from Japanese into English. Any of NIFTY-Serve's 200,000 subscribers can exercise this option; the cost is ¥10 per minute of connect time and ¥1 for each word of English output. The customer can either submit a file or key in the text directly. NEC has followed suit with its PIVOT system, which since December 1990 has been available on PC-VAN, Japan's other major computer service network with a similar number of subscribers and 104 access points in Japan, and, in addition, through GEnie it has the equivalent of more than 550 access points in North America [Sakurai 91].

Internal electronic mail (email) can be a vehicle for MT input as well. At Oki Electric, for example, staff can access the company's PENSEE system as a menu option on their desktop terminals. Fujitsu also offers email access to its MT system, ATLAS-II.

At Nippon Hoso Kyokai (NHK), the nation's public television station, Associated Press wire reports are being monitored and translated on an experimental basis by Catena's STAR system. STAR keeps up with the incoming stream on a near real-time basis. In a reverse application, CSK uses ARGO to pick up data from the Japanese securities market and supply the corresponding English translation to the Nikkei Telecom network, which in turn links up with Reuters and is beamed to the world's 40 major financial centers.

Databases provide another form of ready electronic input. For this reason, plus a number of others, they are seen to be a natural application for MT. And in fact MT is already being exercised on the databases at the Japan Information Center of Science and Technology (JICST) and the Japan Patent Information Organization (JAPIO). The importance of translating databases is discussed in Section 6.1.2 below.

When electronic files are not available, several factors enter into deciding whether or not it is worthwhile to use labor-intensive means to create a machine-readable document. If the investment of time and manpower is justified, the question that remains is whether optical character recognition (OCR) can be of assistance. Both in Japan and elsewhere, OCR has been used for some time as a tool to facilitate the task of MT input. However, the technology is not the panacea that some had hoped it would be. Even with English, which presents fewer challenges than languages with accents and diacritics, not to mention those with non-Roman alphabets, OCRs still produce misread characters. For purposes of MT input, where "close doesn't count," the OCR-generated file needs to be reviewed for errors—a problem in Japan, where speakers and writers of English are at a premium. The relative usefulness of OCR for inputting English in Japan can be deduced from the fees charged for raw MT supplied by IBS, one of the translation bureaus visited: input using OCR is charged at ¥200 per page, versus ¥360 when manual input is required.[5] From these figures it may be assumed that OCR costs 44% less but by no means

---

[5]The figures of ¥200 and ¥360 are based on the fee schedule circulated by IBS at the time of the JTEC visit, according to which raw MT cost ¥290 per page with input in the form of an electronic file, ¥490 per page for OCR input, and ¥630 per page for manual input. At this writing, $US1 = ¥130.

obviates the need for human intervention.

OCR for the Japanese language, of course, is more challenging. Several companies (most notably Fuji Electric, Toshiba, and Sharp, among others) have developed products that read kana and kanji, but they still have limitations. There appears to be little use of OCR as a front end for Japanese to English MT systems, although the technology is poised to make rapid inroads.

Based on Degree of Human Intervention

For several reasons, human intervention becomes an extremely important issue in machine translation between Japanese and English. To begin with, the two languages are linguistically quite distant from one another,[6] which means that the challenge for the computer is greater than it is when translating among European languages. This inevitably leaves more work to be done by human beings either upstream, downstream, or midstream. The use of highly paid professional translators to work with MT quickly adds to the cost of the process. Moreover, for translation into English, such professionals are in relatively short supply in Japan. These are all disadvantages for MT acceptance, where the value of an application is measured in terms of cost, speed of turnaround, and ease of implementation---always in light of the purpose of the particular translation. It is clear that MT will meet with the greatest acceptance wherever human intervention can be minimized.

The manual aspects of text input have already been mentioned. In addition, when the source text is in Japanese, many MT applications rely on pre-editing to facilitate the linguistic task that confronts the machine. Given the distribution of available human resources in Japan, it is more practical and economical to hire non-translator native speakers of Japanese to massage the input than to induct Japanese speakers of (often shaky) English into the complexities of postediting. Sophisticated user-friendly interfaces for pre-editing have been or are being developed for a number of the systems that the JTEC team saw --- for example, ALT-J/E (NTT), ASTRANSAC (Toshiba), ATLAS-II (Fujitsu), DUET-E/J (Sharp), HICATS (Hitachi), PAROLE (Matsushita), STAR (Catena), and JICST (scheduled for 1991). Such interfaces speed up the translation task by providing ready criteria for simplification of the grammatical structure so that the input is more in line with the capabilities of the MT system itself.

Pre-editing does not necessarily eliminate the need for postediting. The degree of intervention required in the output depends on the purpose for which the translation is to be used. If postediting can be dispensed with---whether because the quality is good to begin with, or because problems have been solved in pre-editing upstream, or because the application does not require a high level of quality---then MT becomes much more economically attractive. As a general rule, postediting costs are higher than pre-editing, in part because postediting requires a highly trained bilingual translator who can compare the source and target texts, rather than two monolingual readers, as is the case for pre-editing.

The ultimate MT application is the one that uses raw MT directly and requires no human intervention whatsoever. Raw MT is currently being sold in Japan. As noted above, it can be purchased via NIFTY-Serve, which reports 50-60 accesses a day, and on PC-VAN, a new application. It is also available from the IBS translation service bureau, which at the time of the JTEC visit was selling raw DUET-E/J and is now selling raw ASTRANSAC via PC-VAN. In addition to the processing of input and output, for

---

[6]See [Becker 84] on translation between distant languages.

which a small fee is charged, pre-editing is offered for an additional ¥500 per page. These prices are at most less than half the cost of finished translation, but even so, clients usually prefer for IBS to do the postediting and provide them with a final product. The main obstacle to sales of raw translations is accuracy. More accurate raw translations would lead to much greater sales.

6.1.2 Translation for Assimilation: Domains and Applications

MT is considered to be well suited for applications in which the purpose of the translation is to gather information, convey the gist of a text, or perhaps answer specific questions that the end-user has in mind---in other words, applications for *assimilation*, in which large volumes of foreign text are scanned and translation quality is not a high priority. Often, with applications of this kind, quick turnaround is essential because the information has a limited shelf life, after which it is worthless or of little value. When human intervention can be minimized downstream as well, MT becomes very attractive because of its speed. If the input text is already machine-readable, MT becomes an especially attractive option.

In Japan, even more than elsewhere, attention has been focused on databases as prime candidates for information-only translation using MT. The fact that the files are already in electronic form sets the stage for an effective application, but other considerations are even more compelling: they contain valuable, sometimes critical, information that is not normally translated. Several factors militate against translating databases in the traditional way. To begin with, the task is immense, while human translators are costly and in short supply. Even if there were enough translators, there is no organized customer base to support such an effort. From the standpoint of the consumer, especially in the West where goals must be met in the near term, there has been little impetus so far for investing in the capture of information from such sources; consumers are unwilling to set a price for information before they know how valuable it will be to them. This is a classic problem in information science.

The situation can be remedied to a large degree, however, with the help of robust, general-purpose MT systems, which can be a powerful tool for screening information. As a first pass, MT can provide quick translations of titles and descriptors, alerting analysts to potential areas of interest [Bostad 90]. Once the analyst has spotted material of interest, MT can then provide additional information through translations of the corresponding abstracts. Often the unedited raw output is sufficient for the purpose. This tool is especially valuable in bridging the gap between Japanese and English, where linguistic differences hide all clues to the concepts that analysts may be seeking. This scanning function of MT can greatly reduce the need for high-cost human involvement.

It should be emphasized that the use of MT for database searching requires powerful general-purpose systems with very large and carefully refined knowledge sources---in other words, systems that have had the benefit of long-term investments of manpower to build up the "know-how" needed to produce translations in a wide variety of technical domains.

In Japan, the first database operation to enlist the aid of machine translation was the Japan Patent Information Organization (JAPIO), an auxiliary arm of MITI and the Japanese Patent Office which has been working with Hitachi's HICATS/JE since 1985 to facilitate the translation of patent titles and abstracts for distribution around the world. JAPIO's database---more than 10 million entries of domestic data and another 16 million entries of foreign data---is the backbone of its service, which offers information retrieval for the public in the areas of patents, utility models, designs, and trademarks. With the aid of HICATS, each year some 300,000 titles and 270,000 abstracts (averaging 4.4 sentences in length) are translated into English.

More recently the Japan Information Center of Science and Technology (JICST) launched a massive program using its own MT system to translate the content of its database into English. (See Section 6.2.6.)

Another database-type application is CSK's   use of ARGO to translate information on the Japanese securities market into English for use by Reuters. (See Section 6.2.1.)

MT is also being used in the J/E direction to feed the JAPINFO database supported by the European Commission in Luxembourg, which is available through the DataStar network and has about 300 regular users in nine countries including the United States. In this case, however, the input documents are in the form of hard copy and need to be keyed in manually in order to submit them to MT. (Section 6.2.5.)

A different and innovative application for information-only translation (i.e., not high enough quality for dissemination) is STAR's around-the-clock translation into Japanese of incoming Associated Press news bulletins. This service is primarily used to identify incoming stories that are of interest so that they may receive more careful translation. (See Section 6.2.7).

Despite the Japanese tradition of information-gathering and the current interest in databases, the JTEC team did not identify any MT application in Japan comparable to the use of SYSTRAN in the United States, which has been being used to monitor foreign technology for more than 20 years [Bostad 90], [Vasconcellos 91].[7]

6.1.3 Translation for Dissemination: Domains and Applications

In the case of translation for *dissemination*, quality is usually more important, so MT is typically more appropriate for well-defined domains. However, applications differ: one application may call on MT to deal with many topics, whereas another may limit translations to a single domain (a specialized subject area that has a sublanguage with a relatively small, unambiguous vocabulary and simple, predictable syntactic structures) while a third one may fall somewhere between these two extremes. The first type of application calls for *general-purpose* or "try-anything" systems similar to, and at least as robust as, those that handle translation for assimilation. At the other end of the scale, *specialized* systems for domain-specific applications may require less MT development and are not as costly to implement. Texts in specialized subject areas make good grist for MT because they tend to yield predictable, uniform results

---

[7]The prime example of an MT installation that produces information-only translations is the U.S. Air Force's Foreign Technology Division (FTD), Wright-Patterson AFB, Ohio. FTD provides translations to scientific and technical analysts whose job is to stay abreast of foreign developments and prevent technological surprise that could threaten the United States. SYSTRAN has been in continuous operation at this site since 1969, generating translations from Russian, and more recently German, French, and Spanish, into English at a rate of 50,000 to 60,000 pages a year.   In 1978, Russian/English output was deemed mature enough to be delivered to consumers with only partial postediting. In this semi-automated process, which involves intervention in about 20% of the text, a software module identifies known potential problem areas in the MT output and brings them to the attention of the posteditor. More recently, MT was made directly available to analysts through a gateway to the mainframe from their desktop PCs. They can use this connection to obtain raw MT with immediate turnaround. Since the texts have to be input by hand, the mode is best used for rapid translation of book titles, tables of contents, captions of tables and graphs, and isolated sentences and paragraphs. Despite this limitation, however, the system is tapped as often as 600 times a month [Bostad 90], and some of the analysts have indicated that they would be willing to accept raw MT for full-length documents, forsaking partial postediting, if the manual entry of the input could be done for them [Vasconcellos 91].

that sometimes require very little human intervention (e.g., METEO [Chandioux 89], [Grimaila 91][8]); they require relatively less development effort to bring them to a fully functional level; and they often produce higher accuracy translations.

In Japan, MT is being used to disseminate texts not only from Japanese into English but also from English into Japanese. By far the most common MT application is for internal J/E translation in hardware companies that sell their computer products overseas. Providing product documentation in English is crucial to their capturing markets in the United States, Europe, and other parts of the world. Indeed, most of the firms visited--- Fujitsu (ATLAS-II), Hitachi (HICATS), Matsushita (PAROLE), NEC (PIVOT), NTT (ALT-J/E),   Oki Electric (PENSEE), Ricoh (RMT),   Sanyo (SWP-7800), Sharp (DUET-E/J),   and Toshiba (ASTRANSAC)---gave this as their main reason for being involved in MT, or at least cited it as a major application and probably their original one. Hardware firms not visited that have developed MT systems are Canon (LAMB) and Mitsubishi (MELTRAN), both still in the research stage. Eight of these companies---Fujitsu, Hitachi, NEC, Oki, Ricoh, Sanyo, Sharp, and Toshiba---have gone on to develop a commercial product.

While the translation of product documentation certainly keeps the MT systems busy in Japan (said to represent 80% of all MT use), companies that have developed their own systems are using them increasingly for other in-house tasks as well. At the same time, translation service bureaus are finding that MT helps to shave costs, and they are using the technology as an aid to the production of translations of high quality in a broad range of applications, limited mainly by whether or not clients present their texts in machine-readable form.

Bravice's MICROPAK,   in addition to being used for product documentation, is said to be popular among researchers at universities and hospitals, who use it to produce English-language articles and reports for publication abroad.

At NHK, the use of MT to assist in creating Japanese subtitles for television introduces an entirely new type of MT application — one that is highly demanding. (See Section 6.2.7.)

6.2 User Sites Visited

Given the short duration of the JTEC mission, the team was only able to see a few of the MT user sites in Japan. Different members of the team were able to visit a total of seven sites where MT was in practical use. The circumstances varied and the sample was broad, but it in no way purports to be complete. The team is aware of a number of interesting applications that could not be included because of the shortness of the visit. This section summarizes highlights from the seven installations.

---

[8]One of the most successful cases of MT for dissemination is the translation of Canadian weather forecasts around the clock by METEO, which in the last 15 years has processed more than 100,000,000 words for the Canadian public [Chandioux 89]. This application involves repetitive text with a limited vocabulary, although the input comes in free syntax from a variety of sources. Very little intervention is needed in the machine output (about 4% [Grimaila 91]).

6.2.1 CSK

CSK Corporation, Japan's leading computer multiservice company, provides computer programming and software development services, and it also sells and leases computers. CSK's internal work in artificial intelligence provided synergy for the development of a Japanese/English MT system (TEE), which was placed in service in September 1986. Through this capability, in which CSK had the cooperation of Nihon Keizai Shimbun, Inc., vital data on the Japanese securities market is currently supplied to the Japan News Retrieval service via the Nikkei Telecom network, which, as mentioned earlier, links up with Reuters and from there is broadcast worldwide. In April 1988, CSK introduced ARGO, a newer system that produces faster and better translations in the areas of both finance and economics. The following year a prototype Japanese/English version was also introduced.

The input texts for ARGO are prepared by specialized writers. Both pre- and postediting are done, with emphasis on the latter. A native Japanese translator and a native English editor are integral parts of the CSK team that produces their daily output. CSK also offers Japanese/English MT service to at least 10 customers in Japan, for which ARGO processes some 37,500 pages a year.

The clients, most of them with texts in fields relating to securities and economics, have generally reported that ARGO has been useful for them. They are free to extend the source and target dictionaries but not to modify the grammar, which is done by CSK at least in part on the basis of their feedback. The developers are constantly seeking to improve the quality of translation.

CSK is in an expansion mode. In addition to its international network (Section 6.1.1), the company is developing a more convenient user interface, and it has plans to broaden its client base over the next five years by adding new domains, more languages, and large specialized dictionaries in support of these efforts.

6.2.2 DEC

Digital Equipment Corporation (DEC), a U.S. company with operations in Japan, uses MT software developed by another firm to translate its user documentation. A small percentage of DEC's total translation production from English into Japanese is done with the help of Toshiba's Translation Accelerator, ASTRANSAC.

This application began in March 1989. Currently ASTRANSAC supports the translation of about 100 pages of product documentation a month. It is also used occasionally for information purposes only or for first drafts. The experience to date with the product manuals is that MT has cut translation time by half and that costs are considerably reduced. Whereas the output of a traditional human translator is 5 pages a day, ASTRANSAC makes it possible to produce 11.4 pages a day. Cost savings are greatest when the input file contains SGML[9] markup tags and the codes are automatically ported into the target text. (See Section 9.11.) This feature eliminates the need to reintroduce the codes and reformat the text. The cost of traditional translation is ¥6,000 per page plus ¥3,000 for formatting, whereas with MT the total cost of the two steps together is ¥5,300 per page. Posteditors are paid between 50% and 70% of the regular translation fee, depending on the type of text.

---

[9]Standard Generalized Markup Language (ISO Standard 8879).

Translation quality leaves something to be desired, and postediting, in which technical writers get involved, is rather heavy. Pre-editing, with dictionary updating for unknown words, is also necessary. The pre-editing interface is deemed to be excellent, and the dictionary updating interface is user-friendly. Postediting is done on the company's own VAX equipment, although the Toshiba text editor is considered to be good.

Toshiba is responsive to DEC's requests for improvements and customer-specific adaptations.

6.2.3 IBM

Unlike DEC, IBM Japan opted to develop its own MT software to aid in the translation of product manuals from English into Japanese. The System for Human-Assisted Language Translation (SHALT) was placed in service at IBM's Japan Translation Center in July 1988, and from that date until the time of the JTEC visit it had been used to produce 60 manuals. SHALT also facilitates the translation of other computer-related documents, including memoranda to customers. Although no actual figures were supplied to the JTEC team, IBM has stated elsewhere that it is counting on productivity gains from the use of SHALT on the order of 150% to 300% [Smith 89].

SHALT does not rely on pre-editing in this application, but the user is expected to begin the process by running an interactive search for unknown words. Dictionary entries are prepared for all the missing words using interactive software. Once the target output is produced, postediting is undertaken using IBM's proprietary Translation Support System (TSS).   SHALT occupies an important place in the document production chain, in which every effort is made to automate the publication process.

A very different and much-improved English-to-Japanese system, SHALT2 (see Chapter 9), is already in the wings. SHALT2, in addition to producing translations of better quality, will have machine-learning capability and will be expanded into other domains and language combinations, including Korean and Chinese as target languages.

6.2.4 IBS

International Business Service (IBS), a translation service bureau that receives work from a wide range of sources, was using Sharp's DUET-E/J for translating from 10% to 20% of its volume from English into Japanese at the time of the JTEC visit. They had also used Bravice's MICROPAK and Oki's PENSEE, and and recently had acquired NEC's PIVOT system (J/E and E/J). In December 1990, IBS inaugurated MT service on PC-VAN, a major computer service network, using PIVOT in both directions. IBS is the official translation bureau for this service, and in the first six months of operations they have reached a volume of more than 2,000 pages a month [Kazunori, personal communication]. In their own words, they have now introduced MT into their translation business "in earnest" [Sakurai 91]. It is now understood to be their predominant mode of operation.

Through PC-VAN, clients can send their files to IBS via modem. Previously the company did not use MT for the J/E combination because of the problem of inputting Japanese text, but with this new network capability IBS has gained the possibility of working from Japanese to English. The charge for texts that are pre-edited but not postedited is ¥1,200 (both directions), or about half the charge for human translation from English to Japanese (¥2,100- ¥2,900 per page) and an even smaller fraction of the rate for human translation from Japanese to English (¥4,100-¥4,900).

Prior to the PC-VAN connection, input for MT was optically scanned. The OCR output was verified by a native English speaker using the WordStar or WordPerfect spelling checker.

Since as a translation service bureau IBS receives texts in a wide range of subject areas, productivity gains with MT are bound to be less impressive than figures reported for more homogenous and circumscribed applications. Nevertheless, the process is economical because the overall task can be divided into small steps, as in a production line, taking advantage of operators who are not as highly paid as translators wherever possible.

With DUET-E/J, from 40% to 60% of the English input was being pre-edited at the time of the JTEC visit, while the rest was considered adequate to submit directly to the computer. Pre-editing is done by a native speaker of Japanese using interactive software that assists in such areas as filling in ellipses, marking source words for their part of speech in the particular context, bracketing, expanding reduced relative clauses, and breaking up long sentences. Postediting, of course, must be done by Japanese native speakers, and sometimes two passes are required. The postedited MT output usually becomes input for the next step in the desktop publishing chain.

With PIVOT on PC-VAN, the upstream process has three steps: entry of not-found words (even though IBS's version of PIVOT has a lexicon of 600,000 entries), pre-editing, and correction of mistakes in syntactic analysis. Six rules are applied for pre-editing, which can be done by a monolingual person and takes only 0.6 minutes per sentence (average length 21 words). The most time-consuming task is analysis and correction of syntactic errors, which averages 5.1 minutes per sentence. Final rewriting of the output takes only 1.6 minutes per sentence [Sakurai 91]. Even though MT with PIVOT is currently taking on average 27% longer than traditional hand translation, IBS still considers it to be more economical because of the utilization of lower paid operators. They also like MT because jobs can be split up, terminology is uniform, and the work can be more easily managed with people working in teams. In any case, IBS hopes to improve the slowness of turnaround (caused largely by the fact that this is a general-purpose application with random input) through dictionary-building and adjustments in their manning structure.

The IBS application is interesting because of the new on-line capability, the fact that raw pre-edited MT is available for purchase, the wide variety of texts being handled, the regular use of OCR to capture input, and the number of different MT systems that have been tried.

6.2.5 Inter Group

This company has been offering a wide array of language services since 1966: technical translation, simultaneous interpretation for international meetings, translator and interpreter training, planning and support for meetings, and, more recently, MT pre-editing, postediting, dictionary-building, posteditor training for translators, and user support.

At the time of the JTEC visit, Inter Group was using Fujitsu's ATLAS-II for about 20% of their total translation volume. They also had a contract with JICST to pre-edit and postedit technical abstracts translated by the JICST MT system. So far, all the MT work done at Inter Group has been from Japanese to English. The company had a sizable roster of personnel engaged in various aspects of MT. More than 100 subcontractors were being used for postediting alone. In the company's biggest MT application, ATLAS-II has been used since 1987 to translate some 1,000 technical abstracts a month for the

JAPINFO project.   (See Section 6.1.2.)   The JICST system was also being used to translate technical abstracts. (See Section 6.2.6). Inter Group was using and providing translation support for the ATLAS-II on-line MT service on NIFTY-Serve. (See Section 6.1.1.)

Translations with ATLAS-II may be received and dispatched as electronic files, which resolves the problem of text input, although in the JAPINFO project, manual input is still required because the materials have been gathered from a broad range of hard-copy sources. With ATLAS-II, pre-editing is minimal; the emphasis is on postediting. With the JICST system, on the other hand, pre-editing is stressed rather than postediting.

MT has brought improvements in productivity for Inter Group. Calculation of all the steps in the process has shown that MT, when used on general applications, takes from 68% to 76% of the time required for traditional human translation (HT). On the basis of these figures, translators are paid 30% less for postediting than for HT. Thus, Inter Group is able to produce translations both faster and at a lower cost.

In 1987, shortly after MT Summit I, Fujitsu approached Inter Group and proposed that the company enter the business of training people to use MT. By the end of 1988, Inter Group had introduced MT postediting into the regular curriculum of its training institute, Inter School. The course is given twice a year for 18 weeks at four hours a week. At the time of the JTEC visit it already had 50 alumni, of whom 35 were working for the firm in the capacity for which they had been trained. In addition to training posteditors, Inter Group has been offering a consultation service for Fujitsu customers who are faced with MT for the first time. Four days of intensive introductory sessions are followed by three months of consultation during which the new user practices document input, pre-editing, postediting, and dictionary-building.

In yet another project, Inter Group serves as a subcontractor for the Electronic Dictionary Research (EDR) project.   Inter Group's job includes providing definitions for new words as they come up in the corpus. The definitions are largely adapted from commercial hard-cover dictionaries.

The company's future plans call for building specialized dictionaries for ATLAS users. The company sees text input as one of its major problems and looks forward to greater integration of MT into the total document production chain.

6.2.6 JICST

The Japan Information Center of Science and Technology (JICST) employs its own system to translate Japanese scientific abstracts for its English database, JICST-E. JICST provides information in Japan via the JICST On-Line Information Service (JOIS) and the Scientific and Technical Information Network (STN) [Ashizaki 89]. The initiative to translate the JICST database into English, prompted by the desire to promote worldwide distribution of Japanese scientific and technological information, dates from 1984. Since 1986, JICST has been developing its own practical MT operation based on the results of the MU project, which was supported by the Science and Technology Agency (STA) Promotion Coordination Fund, during the period 1982-1985. Total investments as of mid-1991 are estimated at ¥900 million.

Following three years of intensive dictionary development, beta-testing of JICST began in 1989, and full production got under way in July 1990. Since then, about 29,000 titles and 9,000 abstracts (including titles) have been translated using MT. This amounts to about 17% of all the records in JICST. The target for 1991 is 70,000 titles and 20,000 abstracts, representing 41% of all the records. The abstracts, while they may be from any scientific or technical domain, tend to be concentrated in the area of electrical engineering.

Pre-editing is relied on, and the system performs best on short sentences. Currently the turnaround using MT is approximately the same as for conventional manual translation. The computer takes about three days to translate 1,000 abstracts. A job this size also entails a week of pre-editing, two weeks of postediting, one week of proofreading, and two weeks of manual keyboarding to input the final translation. A new interactive pre-editing tool for flagging 10 types of problems in the input is being introduced, and attention is now focused on reducing the time spent on postediting. Pre-editing and postediting are farmed out to four different translation bureaus.

While savings from faster turnaround have yet to be demonstrated, the JICST MT system has already been shown to be less expensive, since its total cost amounts to only 59% of that for conventional translation. JICST does not feel, however, that the present MT system is appropriate for mass production. There are plans to increase the percentage of MT-produced abstracts in JICST-E, shorten the lag time, and reduce costs even further.

Plans for the immediate future include building the store of technical terminology to a level of 500,000 noun entries plus 12,000 verbs by the end of 1991.   Very soon JICST will be offering an on-line MT network service similar to that offered on NIFTY-Serve and PC-VAN. (See Sections 6.1.1, 6.2.4, and 6.2.5.) JICST plans to make raw MT available to the public to be used either for information scanning or for final translations to be postedited by professional translators. JICST also plans to develop E/J capability in order to provide Japanese translations in the national database of abstracts from foreign academic journals and scientific and medical reports.

6.2.7 NHK

Once every day, Japan's public broadcasting corporation, Nippon Hoso Kyokai (NHK), produces a program of news from around the world that is considered to be the core of its services [Aizawa 90]. "World News" is fed by video, audio, and wire reports arriving constantly in English, French, German, Italian, Russian, Korean, and Chinese. All this material must be edited and woven into a professional show for broadcast via satellite to the Japanese public. A team of some 50 interpreters and translators work in shifts around the clock to sort through incoming communiques and provide NHK's audiences with Japanese-language versions in the form of simultaneous interpretation or subtitles. As is the case with any news broadcasting, time is of the essence, so the work has to be done as quickly as possible. With news generated in the United States, the clock ticks even faster because of the time difference between Japan and the Americas.

Enter machine translation. In 1986, NHK and Catena-resource Institute, Inc. became partners in development of the English/Japanese STAR system, which is now being used to prepare subtitles for a daily 5-minute broadcast segment and to provide real-time raw translation of incoming Associated Press wire reports on an experimental basis. It should be kept in mind that news text is an inherently difficult challenge for MT because of its broad coverage. There is no limit to the subject areas to which news headlines can refer.

In the subtitle production system, the first step is for the operator/translator to listen to the news in English and transcribe it into a summarized, simplified form, which is then submitted for MT processing. This version of STAR produces output sentence by sentence. For each sentence, three different Japanese versions are generated in descending order of desirability based on a preferential weighting of possible outcomes (a switch can be set to display more or fewer versions). The weighting criteria include "comprehensibility," "complexity," and "rareness." Faced with the three options, the operator/translator chooses the best and does any further postediting that may be required. If the translation is correct but "awkward and charming," it may be left as the machine produced it. (A Japanese viewer has commented that the subtitles seem very good compared with raw MT but not as good as traditional human translation.)

The AP wire reports, on the other hand, are machine-translated using a batch version of STAR without any pre- or postediting. The purpose is to monitor the news; if an item is picked up for rebroadcasting, it then goes through the regular programming cycle, with translation provided as appropriate.

Strategies for improving system performance take their cue from the very different conditions in the application environment. With the subtitle production system, the focus is on finding ways to cut down on human intervention---to save time in this case, as well as money. The subtitles are a challenge for MT for several reasons. At the input end, the audio version of the program is transcribed in a painstaking process that involves capturing each word on the tape. After this step, there is considerable pre-editing. Postediting is also necessary, because NHK's responsibility for the information it provides to the public requires that there be no mistakes in meaning. And there are other constraints as well: the Japanese subtitle has to be brief; it has to be synchronized with the corresponding action on the screen; and it has to be as informative as the original English text. With the AP wire service news, on the other hand, translation quality is not so important, which makes it possible for the operation to be totally independent of human intervention from start to finish. Since the main goal of this application has already been met— that is, to attain sufficient speed so that the translation can keep up with the bulletins as they come in— NHK is free to concentrate on improving the translation engine itself.

There are three sources of NHK feedback for researchers. First, the operators flag the hard copy to call attention to errors in the dictionary or grammatical problems in the MT system, a large portion of which can be corrected by NHK R&D staff. Second, the R&D staff works directly with the developers, Catena-resource Institute. And third, troublesome areas are detected based on a review of the log and the time spent on human intervention for the different steps in the process. This information helps to set priorities for R&D and action to be taken.

The main challenge at the moment is to streamline human intervention in the subtitle production system, which, so far, has not been able to improve on the time taken for traditional translation. The current operation is very labor-intensive, with tasks not necessarily being performed by the most suitable personnel. NHK staff feel that improved deployment of human resources would make it possible to speed up the process and reduce the number of operators required.

6.3 MT Users: The Vendor Perspective

The previous section highlighted the user sites visited by members of the JTEC team. The team also heard about MT applications directly from MT vendors, who reported on ways in which their customers were using their systems. Many of these vendors are also users (as was pointed out in Section 6.1.3), so many of the commercial developers had gotten into the MT business in large part to satisfy their own translation needs. This information is summarized in the present section. Again, it does not purport to be exhaustive.

Bravice,[10] at the time of the JTEC visit, was claiming brisk sales of MICROPAK, its PC-based Japanese-English system. Some 4,800 units were said to be in the hands of users. This figure would undoubtedly make MICROPAK the MT system with the widest market penetration in the world.[11] Among the purchasers cited were Tokyo University (27 copies), Toshiba (30 copies) and Honda (30 copies). Company President Takehiko Yamamoto stated that 60% of the 4,800 units had been purchased for use in corporate settings and 40% for use in academic environments and hospitals for the preparation of technical papers in English. Honda harnesses its MICROPAK units into a network to facilitate product documentation. Use of MICROPAK normally entails pre-editing as well as postediting. Not all purchasers become active users—perhaps only 65%. Mr. Yamamoto emphasized that customization early on—i.e., the addition of 3,000 to 7,000 application-specific dictionary entries during the first months of operation—is an important factor in the client becoming a regular user. Feedback has been collected by the sales staff on an ongoing basis and incorporated into new releases.

Fujitsu was the first of the Japanese companies to become involved in MT. Its Automatic TransLAtion System (ATLAS), now in its second version, is a general-purpose system which has been tried on a wide variety of applications. The company reported that there were 200 users of ATLAS-I, 130 users of the mainframe version of ATLAS-II, and 150 users of ATLAS-II on workstations. Inter Group (Section 6.2.5) has been their service bureau. As mentioned earlier, ATLAS-II is available on-line to subscribers of NIFTY-Serve. Within Fujitsu, ATLAS-II has been used to produce 40 manuals for the company's own products. Mazda uses it for similar purposes and has incorporated it into a total document management system. They report that their productivity has increased by 30%. They are pleased with the role that MT has played in standardizing source texts and developing a lexicon of corporate terminology. On average, Fujitsu's users are experiencing a 50% reduction in costs, as well as shortened delivery times [Sato 89]. In customized applications, Fujitsu claims 80% accuracy, but this performance level declines somewhat on random general text [Valigra 91].

Hitachi, another early entrant into the MT arena, has developed HICATS, a general-purpose system. Three products are now on the market: J/E and E/J on mainframe, and J/E on workstation. The E/J workstation version was described as being nearly ready at the time of the JTEC visit. The mainframe versions have each been sold to about 100 customers and the J/E workstation version to another 100. One customer is Toin Corporation, a translation service bureau that uses HICATS to translate product documentation. Another customer for the J/E mainframe system is the Japan Patent Information Organization (JAPIO — See Section 6.1.1 above), which has built the dictionary to a level of 300,000 entries. A JAPIO evaluation performed on a corpus of 5,000 titles showed that 40% of them could be

---

[10]According to information received in early 1991, Bravice is no longer in business.

[11]However, no independent confirmation could be obtained for this sales figure, nor could we find reliable user testimony for it.

used directly without postediting, 26% required slight postediting, 32% required substantial revision, and 2% were not translated at all. So far, turnaround does not represent any improvement over human translation. This application is still in the beta-testing phase and is expected to be fully operational by the end of 1991. For its other applications, most of which are in specialized domains, Hitachi estimates that it takes six person-years to fine-tune a dictionary. Once this is done, HICATS handles 60% of the sentences correctly, which means that human intervention is greatly reduced and productivity is more than doubled. Some users were said to be disappointed in the quality of output and the effort required to build the dictionaries. An experiment showed that pre-editing speeds up the process slightly (on a given job, 25.8 minutes without pre-editing vs. 23.6 minutes with pre-editing) [Kaji 88].

NEC has been using its PIVOT system for internal documentation and launched it as a commercial product in July 1990 (J/E and E/J). In mid-1991 the company reported more than 120 users outside NEC [Kazunori, personal communication]. As noted earlier, PIVOT was introduced as an on-line service to subscribers of PC-VAN in early 1991. (See Section 6.2.4.) IBS is their service bureau for all these applications. In production mode, pre-editing is done by monolingual operators with a view to reducing the time spent by professional translators. The company expects that the future of the product will be strongly user-driven. Another service bureau that uses PIVOT is Subaru International, a company that provides translations, among other services.

Oki Electric's PENSEE (J/E and E/J) is used internally and is also a commercial product. It has several active users. One unit has been purchased by MCC in the United States. PENSEE is not currently being used by any translation bureaus. Osaka Gas Co., a partner, tests the system and aids in refining the dictionary. Pre-editing and postediting are required, but they are kept to a minimum. Users are encouraged to make entries in the dictionary (except verbs). As noted earlier, PENSEE is integrated into the company's internal electronic mail service.

Ricoh's RMT/EJ, a system designed for the general office environment, has been in beta-test on the Japanese market since March 1989, and the company was in the process of incorporating user feedback before introducing it as a commercial product. Pre- and postediting are recommended but not mandatory. Pre-editing includes interactive updating of the dictionary with new entries, plus the addition of new features to existing entries. The system also has interactive postediting software that permits efficient manipulation of the output and displays up to five possible translation results, alternate translations, and the original source word or phrase for any Japanese character generated in the target [Yamauchi 88]. Ricoh's J/E effort, still in the research stage, will be limited to special-purpose applications, since the company is skeptical about the capability of current MT to produce a robust general-purpose system that translates from Japanese to English.

Sanyo has a J/E product, SWP-7800, already on the market, and the JTEC team was told about research prototypes in both directions, which have since been announced as commercial products (under the name HEAVEN JE/EJ). With SWP-7800, pre-editing consisted mainly of spell-checking and text reformatting, while an interactive mode permitted selection of the target word from among several choices offered, as well as dictionary consultation. There were also facilities for postediting, and the user could update the dictionary in simple cases. There was no information available on user experience.

Sharp's DUET-E/J has been on the market since 1988. DUET-E/J II (the second generation of DUET) began to be marketed in 1990. The two systems together are reported to have an installed user base of

600 clients, mostly for the English/Japanese combination. About 45% of the applications are for general or "miscellaneous" purposes, while approximately 30% are for reports, 25% for manuals, and 2% for patents. This distribution differs somewhat from the needs of prospective users, who would like to use MT more for patents and contracts. Internally, DUET supports 90% of the company's translation needs. DUET has also been used by: (1) public agencies such as MITI (Policy Planning Information System Department) and the Australian Embassy in Tokyo; (2) manufacturers such as Nissan and Digital Equipment in Japan; and (3) printing companies and translation bureaus such as Nikkei Printing, Toppan Printing, Nagase Co., Ltd, and Subaru International. Several books were recently translated from English to Japanese using DUET to produce the first draft.

Toshiba states that they have about 80 customers who use their Translation Accelerator, ASTRANSAC[12], from English into Japanese, plus a few who work in the other direction. These are general-purpose systems, although most of their clients are makers of computers and other hardware. One customer is the Digital Equipment Corporation (see 6.2.2). Toshiba also has translation service bureaus and a trading company as users. Typically, ASTRANSAC is incorporated into the overall text production process, from input to desktop publishing, but it is also used on a personal basis. Four-fold increases in productivity have been reported with product documentation. The company emphasizes pre-editing for the J/E version and postediting for the E/J version. Dictionary updating is user-friendly. Toshiba's development team is anxious to respond to feedback from users, not only on the quality of translation but also with regard to facilities for the human interface. In a comparative test that considered each step in the translation process, a series of texts that were human-translated in 20 to 50 minutes were translated with the aid of ASTRANSAC in 8 to 27 minutes [Amano 89].

In 1987, ASTRANSAC was used in an experimental on-line satellite hookup between Japan and Switzerland as part of the 5th World Telecommunications Exhibition (Geneva, 20-27 October 1987). For purposes of this demonstration, the system was linked up to the input and output modules of an interactive dialogue system [Amano 88], so that conference participants could converse via keyboard with the Toshiba laboratory in Japan. The translations were considered to be of good quality. The main factor that impaired system performance was sloppy input, which could have been avoided in a more controlled environment.

6.4 The Broader Outlook

The fact that MT use is taking hold in Japan may be more important than measurable gains in productivity and cost (as described in the following chapter). It was seen, for example, that the IBS users of PIVOT, despite lower productivity, were satisfied with the reduced requirement for high-cost translators, unified terminology, and easier project management [Sakurai 91]. Moreover, IBS cited an advantage that might not occur to a Western manager --- namely, "teamwork is built" [Sakurai 91].

There seems to be a general sense that the steady growth of successful MT applications, with dissemination of these experiences, is the way to consolidate the technology. It is also recognized as the way to find out what MT can and cannot do --- for the Japanese are anxious to understand and deal with these realities.

---

[12]ASTRANSAC was preceded by TAURAS [Amano 89], an experimental model that is not being marketed.

7. Acceptance of MT: Quality and Productivity

Muriel Vasconcellos and Elaine Rich

It is extremely difficult to calculate the extent to which MT is in actual use in Japan. Not all the MT units that have been sold are currently in service. The JEIDA report estimates total sales at 4,000 units at the time of their survey [JEIDA 89], but goes on to add: "many are said to have been returned to the seller and some are not used and are idle." Bravice, for example, estimated the proportion of "sleeping" users at 35% of those who had purchased the system. Sharp, on the other hand, reported that they have sold 600 copies of the DUET E/J system, and so far none has been returned. A questionnaire sent to DUET's users showed that 82.6% of the total 600 units are in frequent use.

These numbers suggest that there is, at least in some cases, a difference between buying an MT system and using it effectively. This suggests that it is worthwhile to take a look at the expectations versus the reality of MT, and to see which factors have the greatest bearing on MT acceptance.

7.1 Productivity and Cost

Productivity is a function of many things, including quality of the machine-produced translations, throughput, and ease-of-use of the tools that are provided for such tasks as pre- and postediting and dictionary updating. But raw translation quality is by the far the most important of these because, as quality goes down, the amount of human intervention required goes up. This chapter explores the state of the art with respect to both quality and throughput and summarizes the overall measures of productivity obtained by the JTEC team. Several cases in which MT improved productivity were cited in the last chapter. With product documentation and other specialized applications, there have been reports of productivity gains ranging up to 400%, with concomitant improvements in turnaround and savings in cost. On the other hand, productivity gains of about 30% are typical of general-purpose applications. It is mostly in these latter areas that there have been some reports of user frustration and, in some cases, actual loss of productivity.

Increased productivity means faster turnaround. Winning the race to get products to market, especially the U.S. market, can be vital to corporate profits, and even survival. In many cases MT, by speeding up the translation of essential documentation, has definitely made it possible to accelerate product delivery, thereby achieving the goal for which it was developed.

Increased productivity also means lower translation costs. For a fully postedited product, the cost is typically between 65% and 75% of the cost of traditional human translation. While this is certainly a motivating factor, it does not appear to be the primary one in Japan, where there is general recognition of the fact that investments have to be made in order to get past the language barrier.

The up-front cost of MT systems is apparently not an issue. (Although it is worth noting that the software cost of MT systems is quite low. Almost all sell for under US$15,000.) At the JEIDA/JTEC meeting in Japan, the JEIDA members voiced a nearly unanimous lack of concern about the price of their product. On the contrary, they said, the average corporate purchaser of MT in Japan may be suspicious of a low-priced product.

7.2 Translation Quality

Both users and vendors of MT systems in Japan realize that the quality of the translations produced is overwhelmingly the most important factor in determining the usefulness of MT. As part of a survey for the JEIDA Report, 27 companies commented on their ideas and expectations about machine translation [JEIDA 89]. The sample had a heavy proportion of general companies that had not yet had direct contact with MT, but it also included translation bureaus and a few firms that are already using MT. By far the most frequent objection to MT was that the quality was poor. Only 17% of all respondents felt that MT was usable for rough translation (14% of the general companies, 25% of the translation bureaus, and 50% of the firms already using MT). Each group, of course, brings a different perspective. From the responses to these and other questions, it may be concluded that the general companies (mainly firms that do not yet use MT) want an MT system that does not require human intervention. In other words, they want a system that is fully automatic and that produces high-quality machine translation. They are apparently not interested in MT as a tool for translation support. Many professional translators, on the other hand, even when they are not yet using MT, already recognize its potential, and those who are using it (albeit a much smaller proportion of the sample surveyed) are more willing to accept the output. Of course, it should be kept in mind that the groups of respondents are to some extent self-selected: if they do not use MT, whether in general companies or translation bureaus, it may well be that they are predisposed against it, since they certainly have not lacked for opportunities to try it out.

1 Productivity in science itself
  is often measured in terms of
  papers produced, presented,
  and/or published.

科学自身のProductivit
yは、たびたび、生み出されて、提
出された論文について測定されて、
および／または、出版される。

2 Another frequently used measure
  of creativity is the number of
  patents applied for, granted,
  etc.

創造的の別の頻繁に使用された物差
しは、申し込まれた特許権の数であ
るとか、与えたなど。

3 According to The National
  Science Board, the U.S. share
  of the world scientific and
  technical articles in
  engineering and technology
  dropped 10% from 1981 to 1986.

国民科学ボードに従って、エンジニ
アリングと技術の世界科学および技
術記事のアメリカ合衆国分け前は、
1981から1986まで10％を
低下させた。

Figure 7-1: Example 1: One English to Japanese Translation

The opinions that the JTEC team heard during its visit echoed the JEIDA report in their emphasis on the importance of translation quality. When the JEIDA group itself met with the JTEC team, most of the JEIDA members stated that their own view was that quality is the most important factor in increasing user acceptance of MT. They also said that their own highest priority was to improve translation quality in their MT systems. This is not surprising, since some of the developers visited by JTEC mentioned explicitly that they had received complaints from their users about raw MT quality and/or the effort needed to customize the systems.

1	Productivity in science itself is often measured in terms of papers produced, presented, and/or published.	科学自体における生産力は、製造された新聞に関してしばしば測定されます（示される、かつ、または、公表される）．
2	Another frequently used measure of creativity is the number of patents applied for, granted, etc.	創造性の他の頻繁に使用された方法は、〔に〕適用できられる承諾された特許の数、などです．
3	According to The National Science Board, the U.S. share of the world scientific and technical articles in engineering and technology dropped 10% from 1981 to 1986.	The National Science Boardによれば、工学、及び、技術における世界の科学の、そして、技術的な品物の米国シェアは、1981年から1986年まで10％減少しました．

Figure 7-2: Example 2: A Second English to Japanese Translation of the Same Text

The pressing need for quality translation stems from two major concerns: poor quality implies increased human intervention in the best of cases, and in the worst of cases it means that the MT output is unintelligible and/or irreparable. Human intervention is costly, and the more it can be minimized or rationalized through the assignment of less skilled operators, the more the technology will show savings for its users in terms of both time and money. If the output is totally unusable, the technology has failed. Because of the linguistic distance between Japanese and English, the language pair to which most of these comments implicitly refer, these MT systems are especially vulnerable: a poor machine translation system can produce unintelligible output no matter how enthusiastic and forgiving the consumer is. Although some of the companies were reluctant to disclose the criteria they use for evaluating translation quality, one of them offered the following five-level scale:

1. Failure or error in syntactic analysis.

2. Intended meaning not conveyed because of inappropriate word choice.

3. Basically meaning conveyed, but with minor errors.

4. Literal translation: no grammatical mistakes but expressions lack refinement.

5. Naturally expressed correct translation.

Much depends on the application, of course. Specialized applications produce more reliable results and therefore require less postediting. For example, HICATS was found to handle 60% of its sentences correctly in one of its applications. In the case of IBS (Section 6.2.4), 40% to 60% of the DUET E/J output required pre-editing, but the rest of the input was considered adequate to submit directly.

One aspect of quality to which MT makes a positive contribution is the standardization of terminology. A number of users in Japan have reported that they are pleased with the role MT has played in this regard, and they have even remarked that the presence of MT has helped to improve consistency in original technical writing.

1

Productivity in science itself is often measured in terms of papers produced, presented, and/or published.

科学それ自体の生産性は、生産される、そして、／を贈られる、または、出版された新聞の点からしばしば測られる。

2

Another frequently used measure of creativity is the number of patents applied for, granted, etc.

創造性の別のしばしば中古の寸法は、かなえてやるその他られる願い出られる特許の数である。

3

According to the national science board, the U.S. share of the world scientific and technical articles in engineering and technology dropped 10% from 1981 to 1986.

合衆国は、世界科学のと技術的な品で1981から1986まで10%を降ちられるテクノロジーをそして設計することにおいて国立科学委員会によって分け合う。

4

The Japanese scientific position, measured by papers produced, has been rising 0.5% per year.

日本の科学の位置は、生産される新聞によって測られると、年について0.5%を上っている。

Figure 7-3: Example 3: A Third English to Japanese Translation of the Same Text

Before embarking on its site visits, the JTEC team selected one short passage in English and one in Japanese. At each of the sites where there were operational MT systems we asked our hosts to try our sample texts on their system, going in which ever direction(s) they supported. Almost all were willing to try. It is, of course, difficult to conduct a quantitative evaluation of the results of this informal experiment. For one thing, not all the systems came at the task equally well prepared. Some of the systems are intended to be general purpose and so should do well with a randomly selected text. Others are intended to be customized for particular domains; they in general did not have the necessary vocabulary to handle our examples without some tuning first. But Figures 7-1 through 7-6 show examples of the results we observed. As a basis for comparison, we asked a professional translator to translate the Japanese text into English. He produced two translations for each sentence, one fairly literal (labeled A) and one that he described as "natural" or "idiomatic" (labeled B). His translations were:

Sentence 1

A. High-tech industry grew rapidly, and one day, Japan suddenly appeared to have become a world super-nation.

B. Japan's high-tech industry grew quickly. Virtually overnight, it seemed, the nation had become an economic superpower.

```
[ 文番号:1 ]                      High-tech industry extends rapidly, and
ハイテク産業が急速に延び、あ      one day so that Japan is a universal major
る日突然、日本は世界の超経済      economic nation, it suddenly appears.
大国になってしまったように見
える
[ 文番号:2 ]
その結果、いや応なく世界のナ      Like it or not as a result, being expected
ンバー・ワンとしての指導力を      to give play one · number universal
発揮することを期待されて、と      guidance one's strength, a Japanese will
まどっている日本人も多いこと      be also a frequent thing.
だろう
[ 文番号:3 ]
                                      Now, Japan was struck with a trade problem
今や日本は貿易問題で欧米諸国      from Western countries, and followed and
からたたかれ、NIES諸国か      was given from NIES countries the height
らは追いあげられ、すでに流行      of "trade friction" with the feeling which
語となった感のある「貿易摩擦」    already turned into a cant.
のまっただ中におかれている
```

Figure 7-4: Example 4: One Japanese to English Translation

Sentence 2

A. As a result, whether they like it or not, Japanese people are expected to display leadership as No. 1 in the world, and there are probably many confused Japanese.

B. Like it or not, Japan is now expected to display the kind of leadership befitting its status as "No. 1" in the world. This new role undoubtedly leaves many Japanese people perplexed.

Sentence 3

A. Nowadays, Japan is being bashed by the European and American countries over trade problems, chased by the newly industrialized economies, and has become the center of trade friction, which has already acquired the atmosphere of an "in" expression.

B. Japan has become the whipping-boy of Europe and America in countless trade disputes, and the target of competitive pressures to catch up with it from the newly industrializing economies of East Asia. Japan finds itself in the midst of a veritable storm of "trade friction" — a phrase that has already become a household word throughout the land.

The translator also made the following note: The author appears to stretch the meaning of trade friction (written in kanji in a literal translation from English to Japanese) to include purely competitive pressures from SE Asia. Japanese often adopts English words and then modifies their meaning — a real pitfall for translators, machine and human alike, if they are not truly bilingual.

7.3 Throughput

Although it is difficult to compare throughput numbers across systems because of differences in both hardware platforms and kinds of texts, we include some representative throughput figures in Figure 7-7 to provide a rough idea of the order of magnitude of speeds at which current systems perform. All the numbers are given in words per hour. When we could, we included in parentheses after the speed the hardware platform on which the speed was obtained. These numbers came from two different sources.

```
SENTENCE NAME =       111
ハイテク産業が急速に伸び，ある日突然，日本は世界の超経済大国になって
ARTC NODE FOUND/SKIPPED(@S1192)
しまったように見える。
```

Japan is visible in order to high tech manufacturing improve rapidly, and in order to become super-economy large country in world suddenly some.

```
SENTENCE NAME =       112
その結果，いや応なく世界のナンバー・ワンとしての指導力を発揮すること

ARTC NODE FOUND/SKIPPED(@S1192)
を期待されて，とまどっている日本人も多いことだろう。
```

As a result, an abounding thing will also be the Japanese whom it has been at loss by expecting that there is and that there is not 応, and that it demonstrates the leadership as no. ワン of world.

During pre-editing, sentence 1 was divided up and was eventually translated as:

High-technology industry in Japan developed rapidly.

Then Japan became super-economy large country.

Figure 7-5: Example 5: A Second Japanese to English Translation of the Same Text

Those labeled (1) were taken from literature supplied by the vendors at MT Summit III in July 1991. Those labeled (2) were taken from [JEIDA 91].

It is important to keep in mind that these numbers reflect only the time required to run the texts through the MT system. As we have described elsewhere, the total time required to produce usable translations will be much larger, since other things, such as pre- and postediting are also required.

7.4 Customization

There is increasing awareness in Japan of the importance of user-friendly tools for customizing an MT system. Many developers rank this factor second only to quality in importance, and one of them felt it was even more essential in terms of gaining user acceptance. All MT applications require some fine-tuning, and users will have a sense of control over their systems when they can readily elicit usable translations that incorporate their own terminology and other preferences. Mainly, this means developing easy and efficient interfaces for pre-editing, postediting, and dictionary updating. But it can also involve interactive variations such as those described for Ricoh, as well as basic tools including corpus extraction, indexes of key words in context, etc.

1　ハイテク産業が急速に伸び、ある日
　　突然、日本は世界の超大国になって
　　しまったようにみえる。

2　その結果、いや応なく世界のナンバ
　　ーワンとしての指導力を発揮するこ
　　とを期待されて、とまどっている日
　　本人も多いことだろう。

As a result, the expected and
confused Japanese will be many
things of showing guide power
as ワン number in the world where
いや応 quacks.

3　いまや日本は貿易問題で欧米諸国か
　　らたたかれ、NIES諸国からは追いあ
　　げられ、すでに流行語となった感の
　　ある「貿易摩擦」のまっただ中にお
　　かれている。

On Japan of doing having まや
is beat from a European and
American various countries by a
trade question, it finishes
being chased from NIES various
countries and the "trade
friction" placing of it which
has a sense of becoming a
popularity word already is done
in まっ 's being free.

Figure 7-6: Example 6: A Third Japanese to English Translation of the Same
Text

Company	System	Languages	Speed (w/h)	Source
Catena	STAR	E/J	15,000	(1)
Catena	The Translator	E/J	10,000-20,000 (MAC IIcx)	(1)
Fujitsu	ATLAS-II	J/E	60,000 (FACOM M380)	(2)
Hitachi	HICATS	E/J	30,000-60,000 (HITACM-680)	(2)
Hitachi	HICATS	J/E	20,000-60,000 (HITACM-680)	(2)
Matsushita	PAROLE	J/E	30,000 (Solbourne)	(2)
Mitsubishi	MELTRAN	J/E	5,000-10,000 (MELCOM PSI/UX)	(1)
NEC	PIVOT	J/E	>30,000 (EWS4800)	(1)
NEC	PIVOT	E/J	>20,000 (EWS4800)	(1)
NTT	ALT-J/E	J/E	5,000 (VAX8800)	(2)
Oki	PENSEE	E/J and J/E	15,000	(1)
Ricoh	RMT-E/J	E/J	4,500	(2)
Sharp	DUET	E/J	12,000	(1)
Toshiba	ASTRANSAC	E/J and J/E	10,000-20,000	(2)

Figure 7-7: Throughput Rates for Selected MT Systems

7.5 Integration

MT brings greater savings in terms of both time and money when it is fully integrated into the publication chain. The two key factors in this regard are input of the source text and generation of MT output files that retain typesetting codes. The problems of text input were discussed in Section 6.1.1. Time is at least as important as cost. Manual keyboarding of MT source text can cut deeply into the advantages to be gained by using the technology. This problem is being solved to some extent with OCR, but even more important, the widespread use of word processing, coupled with the capacity to transmit electronic files via network, means that a steadily increasing proportion of input text is already going to be machine-readable. Up to now, OCR for such languages as Japanese, Chinese, and Arabic has posed a major challenge. The availability of OCR for Japanese will be especially important for U.S. efforts to access information in that language because of the difficulties that Westerners face in inputting kana and kanji. At the output end, many MT installations in Japan are already linked to desktop publication. The remaining challenge is to be able to capture all formatting codes, because this capability will greatly reduce time and effort spent.

7.6 Open Systems and Software Portability

Increasingly in the United States, software is built to be as independent of particular hardware platforms as possible. The idea of open systems, in which customers can buy pieces of hardware and software from multiple vendors and be assured that they will work together, has begun to dominate the computer industry. At least with respect to MT, this has not yet happened in Japan. Most of the commercial MT systems have been developed by hardware platform vendors. Their MT systems run only on their hardware. Thus users must have access to the appropriate hardware before they can run the MT system of their choice. The availability of some MT systems over commercial networks (as described in Section 6.2) reduces this problem somewhat from the user's point of view. Nevertheless, the close connection of the main MT systems to particular hardware platforms suggests that many of the vendors may be looking ahead to a time when MT will be widespread and will create a new demand for their hardware. We expect, however, that at least some of the MT vendors will make their MT software available on internationally standard operating systems, independent of hardware. The increasing acceptance of the UNIX family of operating systems, for example, makes this trend inevitable even in Japan.

8. MT Contrasts Between the U.S. and Europe

Yorick Wilks

Although this report focuses on state of the art of MT in Japan, it is useful to look briefly also at the MT picture in the United States and in Europe for a broader perspective. For a more detailed description of some of the efforts that are mentioned here, see [Hutchins 86].

To compare MT in Japan with that in the United States and Europe, one must distinguish between the true and mythical histories of the technology in these last two locations. The widely-believed mythical history, shown in Figure 8-1, states that MT began in the U.S. in the late fifties. Funding peaked when the ALPAC report recommended that federal funding be withdrawn [ALPAC 66]. Europe and Canada then continued their MT work and, since 1977 or so, have been joined by Japan, now the main contributor to MT research and development.

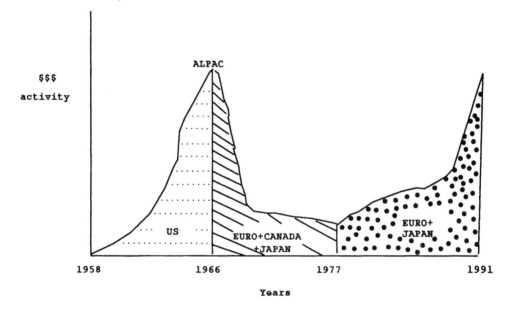

Figure 8-1: An Incorrect Model of the History of MT Development

But this picture is misleading in several ways (see Chapter 1). First, it ignores the substantial contribution made to the earliest MT development by the USSR and Western Europe. Second, it ignores the fact that some Europeans (particularly the British, who had developed several major systems in the sixties) also stopped government funding of MT as a result of the ALPAC report. That the French are widely believed to have made the major European MT effort is largely a result of their refusal to be influenced by U.S. trends, while the Canadian decision to start MT development in the mid-sixties was not so much a result of ignoring U.S. influence as Canada's enormous translation needs, imposed by legislation that equalized the federal status of English and French. Third, this picture ignores the fact that MT work got going in Japan almost as soon as it did in the U.S., although the Japanese effort did not

417

scale up seriously until the 1980s.

A final fallacy in the mythical history of MT is that U.S. work ceased shortly after the publication of the ALPAC report. In fact, U.S. defense funds continued (although at a lower level) to support MT work at Texas, Berkeley, and other sites. The use and development of the SYSTRAN system at the U.S. Air Force's Foreign Technology Division in Dayton, Ohio was begun during that period and continues to the present. MT has recently undergone a serious resurgence in the U.S., particularly with respect to work on interlingual systems.

Thus the true history of MT is better captured diagramatically in Figure 8-2.

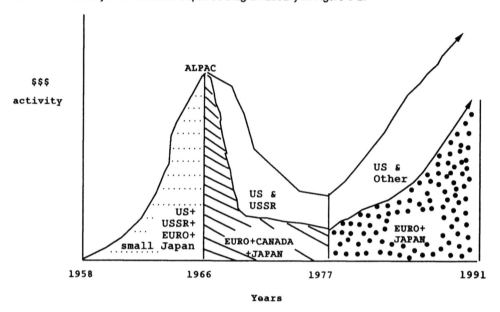

Figure 8-2: A Better Model of the History of MT Development

One mysterious aspect of MT history is the Westerner's nearly total ignorance of Soviet research, although there is a great deal of unclassified material on it, much of which is available in translation (e.g., [Melchuk 63]). Paradoxically, the USSR's greatest influence on MT has probably been exporting of researchers whose first spoken and research language is Russian (e.g., Raskin and Nirenburg in the U.S.; Perschke in the European Community).

While it is difficult to obtain precise figures for government-funded MT in the U.S., Japan, and Europe during the last 15 years (the approximate period of Japan's MT growth), rule-of-thumb figures would probably be US$20 million, US$200 million and US$70 million respectively. The European figure is largely accounted for by the EUROTRA project and the U.S. figure by support of the FTD work with SYSTRAN.

It would be a great mistake, however, to assume that those figures offer simple mapping of the MT quality R&D in the three zones. Even though this report is not devoted to the topic, an impressionistic verdict (based in part on the JTEC survey) is that the EUROTRA project has not yet produced a system beyond a very limited demonstration (see below), and the huge expense in Japan has produced a handful of systems that compare in breadth, speed, and quality with the best of SYSTRAN's language couples (but keep in mind that J/E and E/J are not among SYSTRAN'S best pairs).

Interestingly, EUROTRA's goal was explicitly to equal and then surpass SYSTRAN through research advances — precisely what it has not achieved.   This goal was imposed by the EC Information Science Directorate, which had also purchased SYSTRAN for trial use in the seventies, four years before EUROTRA funding began. SYSTRAN has been substantially extended in Luxembourg, and is now being used for rough internal translation of certain classes of memoranda. Its use is increasing.

If further correction were needed of the mythical view that Japanese (if not European) MT has already taken over the world scene, one could turn to Figure 8-3 (taken from [JEIDA 89]). The table lists uses of MT systems by organizations in the U.S., Europe, and Canada. Notice that only one of the systems listed (ATLAS) originated outside North America.

a) Utilization in Canada

Canadian government	TAUM-METEO
Canada GM	SYSTRAN

b) Utilization in the United States

U.S. government	SYSTRAN
NASA	SYSTRAN
U.S. Air Force	SYSTRAN
XEROX	SYSTRAN
Caterpillar	SMART
PAHO	PAHO

c) Utilization in Europe

CEC	SYSTRAN
	ATLAS-II
NATO	SYSTRAN
KFKS	SYSTRAN
Minitel	SYSTRAN

Figure 8-3: Origination of MT Systems Used in Europe and North America

8.1 Major MT Centers and Systems in the US

A partial list of MT R&D groups in the U.S. follows. It is a list subject to rapid change (e.g., the CMU, CRL, ISI, and IBM groups have only recently been strengthened by the new DARPA initiative in MT). The list also excludes smaller commercial MT groups such as Alps, Smart, Globalink, etc., as well as smaller university-based groups at Hunter College, Monmouth College etc.:

• Carnegie Mellon University's Center for Machine Translation.

• Computing Research Laboratory at New Mexico State/Tradux.

• Linguistic Research Center at the University of Texas at Austin (originators of METAL).

- IBM/Yorktown Heights. One group is pursuing the statistical approach, another a traditional one.
- Pan American Health Organization (PAHO).
- SYSTRAN development group.
- LOGOS development group.
- New York University (sublanguage translation).
- University of Southern California's Information Sciences Institute (ISI).
- MCC.

Other than CMU and CRL, none of the groups has more than ten people. Although the list is incomplete, it should be clear that levels of personnel and funding are considerably lower in the U.S. than in Japan. More details about system type, languages and materials treated, etc., can be seen from the table of four major U.S. MT products, shown in Figure 8-4.

	Languages	Type	Topics	Status	Organization
LOGOS	E,G,S,F	Transfer Some semantics	Manuals and general	Commercial U.S. owned	Logos Corp.
SYSTRAN (at FTD)	E,R	Direct	Technical literature	U.S. Govt.- funded	LATSEC, Inc.
SYSTRAN (multitarget)	E,F,S, etc.	Transfer Some semantics	Manuals and general	Commercial	SYSTRAN
METAL	E,G	Transfer Case-frame semantics	Manuals and general	Commercial	Siemens/ Nixdorf

Figure 8-4: Major US MT Products

However, we should not confuse progress and the state of the art only with dollars spent and researchers and/or developers employed. No comparison between Japanese and American or European work would be balanced unless we stressed the pivotal role of SYSTRAN [Toma 76]. At this time, SYSTRAN remains the international benchmark for MT, one that Japanese (or any new U.S. or European efforts) would have to improve upon demonstrably in order to have pulled ahead of the U.S. in MT. Conveniently, SYSTRAN is also a benchmark in that its levels of achievement are fairly well fixed, and have barely shifted upwards in terms of percentage of correctly translated sentences for its principal languages for many years [Wilks 91]. SYSTRAN proved not only that MT really works, in the sense of satisfying a substantial class of users but also that stamina (i.e., long-term commitment of funds and effort to MT) pays off. The Japanese have certainly taken this lesson to heart. The Europeans have done so to a lesser extent, as exemplified by their commitment to the EUROTRA program (see below).

8.2 Influences among MT Groups

Simply listing current MT groups in the U.S. leaves out many important effects at work: effects and relationships that are essential to understanding how international MT has become, as has all of science, engineering and commerce.

Many of the influences among MT groups are explicit, and are related to migrations and sabbaticals of researchers. Others are the effect of the close proximity of groups, or of the decay of one and the rise of another. Sometimes influences are connected to the movement of key personnel. Others are simply academic and intellectual. Still others are the result of commercial sale (e.g., Weidner to Bravice and Texas' METAL to Siemens/Nixdorf). These influences are summarized in Figure 8-5. Notice that both theoretical and software connections are intercontinental.

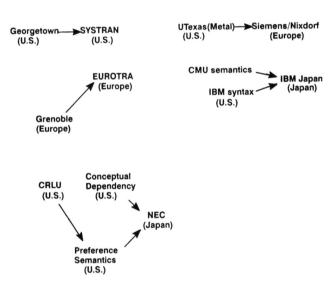

Figure 8-5: Influences on MT Efforts

These same connections can be illustrated by mapping major systems on a time line, as shown in Figure 8-6, which is a more detailed version of Figure 1-1. Here the systems are divided into three main system types: direct, transfer, and interlingual. Figure 8-6 shows that there is a gradual movement towards methods that exploit semantic analysis and this shift transcends continental boundaries.

Other factors also make it increasingly difficult to classify MT work as simply belonging to a particular continent or country. The following illustrates a trend away from such simple identifications:

- IBM Japan's new MT system (JETS) has had substantial research contributed by the United States.
- Systran's J/E and E/J systems are currently owned by a Japanese company (Iona), although that may change.
- SYSTRAN itself is closely tied to French business interests.
- Fujitsu's J/S system is under development at Fujitsu Espana in Barcelona.

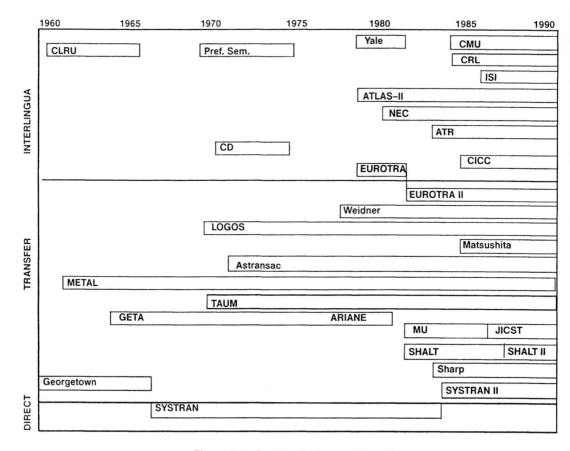

Figure 8-6: Past MT Systems: A Time Line

- This year, both Canon and Sharp have set up new MT R&D labs in the United Kingdom.

- The Texas METAL system is now owned by Germany (Siemens/Nixdorf), although development continues in both the U.S. and Germany.

8.3 Current European Systems

For more than a decade after 1966, GETA [Vauquois 84] at Grenoble was the best known European system, and since 1980, EUROTRA has occupied that position. They have both been supported by enormous quantities of government funds and were defensible in terms of the linguistic theories of their time, but have never worked very well.

EUROTRA [Johnson 85] was a bold initiative formally launched in 1982, financed by Directorate XIII of the CEC (the European Commission) in Luxembourg and by the Trade and Industry ministries of most of the European Community (EC) states. It was set up to meet the translation needs of the Commission and Community which, for some documents, required translation into all nine languages of the EC (implying the ability for 72 pair-wise translations). Some documents appear only in the six principal languages, and many central documents appear only in the three core languages (English, French, German) since there is an assumption that all "eurocrats" can read one of these. But even these latter two methods imply enormous volumes of translation, given that the EC is a larger entity than the U.S., both in population and

GNP.

The EUROTRA program for a multilingual MT system, to be constructed by multistate teams, was initially impressive. It has already cost over US$50 million, but has only a very small demonstration program to show for it at the present time (even though the formal funding is now coming to an end and is continuing only for programs to extend the lexicon). Its initial aim was to translate CEC documents within the Luxembourg bureaucracy, but this has now been scaled back to the mere treatment of examples.

The best features of the EUROTRA methodology were the separation of software methodology from linguistic specifications, and the separation of the work into modules concerned with particular languages (though not necessarily based on particular states). These features have been incorporated into other systems (e.g., at CMU and in ULTRA [Farwell 90] in the U.S., and in SWETRA, and SWISSTRA [Estival 90] in Europe.)

The initial design in the early 1980s was a compromise between those who wanted the system to be basically interlingual and semantics-driven, and those who wanted to preserve as much as possible of the GETA representational structure (multilevel dependency trees to encode semantic, syntactic, and morphological information). This compromise held until about 1984 when detailed implementation was due to begin.

Around that time, the whole design team was reconstructed, although the top-level project leadership was unchanged, and EUROTRA went through a series of changes motivated almost entirely by considerations of linguistic fashion. This led to the present situation in which EUROTRA is transfer-based, and the representation is a form of unification grammar, the system being entirely syntax-driven.

That EUROTRA has produced so little for so much investment is significant and instructive for efforts elsewhere. If it is a failure, it has been almost entirely a management failure. Its concentration on linguistic issues, at the expense of engineering and implementation ones, contrasts with Japanese and benchmark U.S. approaches. It ignored what one might call a golden rule for almost any prototype and product: to settle on a representation, stick to it, and develop it to its maximum capabilities.

The problems EUROTRA has experienced to date should not cause one to ignore other approaches in Europe, such as SUSY (at Saarbruecken), SWETRA and SWISSTRA, all of which have contributed to and benefited from EUROTRA, despite the recent cancellation of the EUROTRA effort.

One might end with the following remarkable example, shown in Figure 8-7, which in a way, sums up the MT relationship between the U.S. and Europe. The figure is the first part of a substantial public document released by the European Commission at a language trade fair in 1989. It describes the EC's investment in EUROTRA and, since such documents must appear in at least English and French, it adds on the right a translation provided by the SYSTRAN E/F version the EC has worked on for over 12 years, with the added header "TRADUCTION BRUTE SYSTRAN", indicating that it is raw SYSTRAN translation, although the document may have been postedited without removing that label. It is clear though, that somewhere in the EC, someone has a sense of humor...

COMMISSION
DES COMMUNAUTÉS
EUROPÉENNES

Direction Générale
Télécommunications, Industries de l'Information et Innovation

ORIGINAL

Contribution for DG XIII brochure
EUROTRA

EUROTRA is a Community research and development programme for the creation of a machine translation system of advanced design capable of dealing with all the official languages of the EC. It was adopted by Council Decision 82/752/EEC of 4 November 1982 and extended by Council Decision 86/591/EEC of 26 November 1986 to include Spanish and Portuguese following the accession of Spain and Portugal.

The programme is jointly financed by the Community and its member states. Its objective is the creation of a prototype system which would be operational for a limited subject field and for a limited number of

TRADUCTION BRUTE SYSTRAN

Contribution pour la brochure de DG XII
EUROTRA

Eurotra est un programme communautaire de recherches et de développement pour la création d'un système de traduction automatique de conception avancée capable de traiter de toutes les langues officielles de la CE. Il a été adopté par la décision 82/752/EEC du Conseil du 4 novembre 1982 et élargi par la décision 86/591/EEC du Conseil du 26 novembre 1986 pour comprendre espagnol et Portugais après l'adhésion de l'Espagne et du Portugal.

Le programme est conjointement financé par la Communauté et ses Etats membres. Son objectif est la création d'un système prototype qui serait opérationnel pour un domaine limité et pour un nombre limité de types de texte

Figure 8-7: An Example of EUROTRA Output

9. Research and Development

Elaine Rich

There is a strong and longstanding commitment in Japan both to MT research and to a technology transfer process that has been very successful in moving results from research labs into development organizations. A relatively early example of this was the government-sponsored project that led to the development of the MU system. This project required the close collaboration of four research organizations. Its structure was described in [Nagao 85] as follows:

> At Kyoto University, we have the responsibility of developing the software system for the core part of the machine translation process (grammar writing system and execution system); grammar systems for analysis, transfer and synthesis; detailed specification of what information is written in the word dictionaries (all the parts of speech in the analysis, transfer, and generation dictionaries), and the working manuals for constructing these dictionaries. The Electrotechnical Laboratories (ETL) are responsible for the machine translation text input and output, morphological analysis and synthesis, and the construction of the verb and adjective dictionaries based on the working manuals prepared at Kyoto. The Japan Information Center of Science and Technology (JICST) is in charge of the noun dictionary and the compiling of special technical terms in scientific and technical fields. The Research Information Processing System (RIPS) under the Agency of Engineering Technology is responsible for completing the machine translation system, including the man-machine interfaces to the system developed at Kyoto, which allow pre- and post-editing, access to grammar rules, and dictionary maintenance.

This research prototype has since been used as the basis for the production MT system currently in use by JICST.

As this example suggests, part of the reason that the Japanese have been so successful at making use of their MT research results may be the diversity of organizations within which the research is being done. Current R&D efforts are taking place within four kinds of institutions in Japan: academic, industrial, government, and consortium labs. Historically, the most visible academic lab has been the one at Kyoto University under the direction of Professor Makoto Nagao. Other labs also exist at Tokyo Institute of Technology, Osaka University, and Kyushu University, among others. All of the industrial sites that have previously developed production MT systems also have ongoing research and development projects (although some are primarily focused on development rather than on research). These include NEC, Fujitsu, Hitachi, IBM Japan, CSK, Oki, Sanyo, Toshiba, NHK/Catena, Sharp, and Bravice. In addition, Matsushita, Ricoh, and NTT have begun research efforts. Substantial MT efforts are underway at two government-supported labs, CICC and JICST, and two consortia, ATR and EDR, are doing work in MT or related technologies. In addition, there is a substantial amount of basic research in natural language processing at many of those same institutions, as well as at ICOT, ETL (Electrotechnical Laboratory), and many universities.

These efforts are focused on the following major areas:
- New overall approaches to translation, including:
    - Interlingua-based translation
    - Example-based translation
    - Transfer-based translation
- New grammatical frameworks
- New approaches to target text generation

- Development of dictionaries
- Treatment of discourse-level phenomena
- Better tools for users
- Extension of the Japanese and English systems to additional languages
- Speech-to-speech translation
- Embedding MT into larger information-processing systems

This chapter will describe the work in each of these areas in more detail.

9.1 Interlingua-Based Translation

Chapter 1 showed that MT systems could be described as falling along a continuum defined by when the transfer from the source to the target is performed. At one extreme would be systems that translate sentences directly (i.e., with no prior analysis to determine their internal structure). This overall approach is not used in any current system but it can be used as part of a more comprehensive MT architecture. At the other extreme are systems that map the source text into a complete meaning representation and then map that back out to target text, with no actual transfer between the two languages at all. In the middle are systems (including most of the ones now in existence) in which some analysis is performed. Next a transfer step maps the analyzed structure into a corresponding structure in the target language. Finally target generation takes the remaining steps toward constructing the final target text. Figure 1-15, repeated here as Figure 9-1, shows some of the major points along this spectrum.

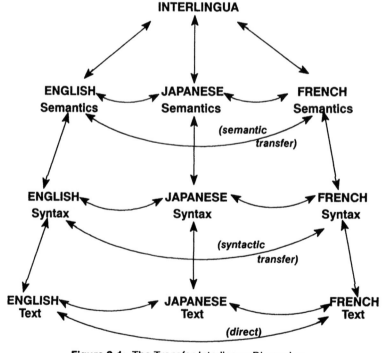

Figure 9-1: The Transfer-Interlingua Dimension

For a long time, almost all of the MT systems built in Japan could best be described as syntactic transfer systems. They followed the line of arrows shown second from the bottom in the figure; that is, they analyzed the source text into a syntactic form, then applied transfer rules, sometimes to transform the source syntactic form itself, and then, in any case, to derive a target form, which then served as the basis for generation. Some systems began to move higher up the diagram, including Fujitsu's ATLAS-II [Uchida 89a], NEC's PIVOT [Muraki 89, Ichiyama 89], and CSK's ARGO.   These systems build a partial semantic representation of the source sentences, and use that either as the basis for a transfer operation or as a form of interlingua. The semantic representations they use are based on the idea of a case-frame structure, in which each sentence is represented as a major predicate and a set of semantic roles, each of which is filled by some major constituent of the sentence. These constituents, in turn, are represented as structures that are built out of a set of semantic primitives that describe the entities that can exist in the domain of discourse. But, as shown in Figure 9-1, an explicit transfer step is still required because case frames remain quite close to the linguistic surface form. Almost all Japanese MT systems today exploit this basic approach, although they vary in several ways, including the depth of the semantic representation and the extent to which surface linguistic facts, such as word order, are extracted from the source text and used to guide target generation.

The idea of moving further toward interlingua-based systems has been advocated by some Japanese researchers for a long time (for example, see [Uchida 89b]). But other very influential figures (for example [Nagao 87]) argue that it is not yet practical to build deep, meaning-based systems, and there has been less work in this area in Japan than in the U.S. In the last several years, however, interest in moving further toward meaning-based systems has increased considerably in Japan. The main reasons for this are:

- Transfer rules must be written for every language *pair*. In contrast, the rules for mapping to and from the interlingua need only be specified for each language once. So, particularly for an MT system that is intended to handle several languages, the amount of development work should decrease as the need for transfer rules goes down.

- Since, in an interlingual system, each language can be specified almost entirely on its own with little consideration of the others, the various languages can be developed relatively independently. This means, in particular, that each language can be developed in its native country by native speakers.

- There appears to be a limit to how good a translation system can be if it has no representation of meaning. The problem is that many sentences are ambiguous. But often it is not possible just to pass the ambiguity on to the target text, since languages differ on the ambiguities they allow. In these cases, it is necessary to decide on the intended meaning of the source text in order to translate it correctly into the target. Sometimes this can be done without any actual representation of meaning (for example by using selectional restrictions as described in Section 2.3, or by using the example-based approach that will be described in Section 9.2), but in some cases it appears to be necessary to reason about the meaning of the sentence in its discourse context in order to choose the correct translation. To do this requires a meaning representation of the texts that can be used in conjunction with one or more knowledge bases that describe the domain(s) of the texts that are being translated.

Several efforts are moving in the direction of deeper, interlingua-based systems. The first is the work at EDR on building a widely available dictionary that maps from words (in English and Japanese) to a semantic conceptual structure. This dictionary is intended to be used as a basis for MT systems that make use of the conceptual structure as an interlingua. We will describe this effort in more detail in Section 9.6. There is already one major MT effort underway that uses the EDR dictionary and its conceptual structure. This is the multilingual (Japanese, Chinese, Thai, Malay, and Indonesian) system that is being built at CICC.   See Section 9.9 for a discussion of this effort.

Another important effort is the SHALT2 project at IBM Japan. SHALT2 is an E/J system (although extensions to other languages are planned; see Section 9.9), that is based on the earlier work at IBM on SHALT, a transfer-based system, as well as on collaborations with Carnegie Mellon University and their work on interlingua-based systems.

One idea that has come up in several places in Japan is to view each sentence as having more than one component, corresponding to the propositional content of the sentence as well as various other properties, including the speaker's attitude and intent in producing it. Then all the components need not be treated the same way; some can be translated using transfer rules, while others may be mapped to an interlingua (or relatively language-independent form). For example, the NADINE system at ATR (see Section 9.7), divides the meaning of a sentence into two parts, the propositional content and the illocutionary force.   The illocutionary force component is what distinguishes between questions, commands, and declarative statements. It is mapped into a language-independent interlingua, while the propositional content is translated using a transfer-based system that is driven by a set of rules associated with individual words in the lexicon [Hasegawa 90]. Another example of this basic approach is the MLMT (Multi-Level Machine Translation) method that has been developed for the ALT-J/E system at NTT [Ikehara 89, Ikehara 91].   In this approach, a Japanese sentence is first decomposed into an objective component and a subjective one (which includes the speaker's emotions and intentions). The objective part is translated using a transfer-based system. Then the subjective part is rearranged using a table-driven method and recombined with the objective component. A third example is the work at ETL [Ikeda 89], which divides each sentence into three parts, the propositional content and two kinds of attitude descriptors. But in this work, the representations of the three parts taken together are viewed as an interlingual representation of the sentence and all are translated through the interlingua.

Despite this increased interest in interlingua-based systems, however, there is still no clear consensus that that is the right way to go. For example, several relatively new projects, including ones at IBM (JETS), Matsushita, Sanyo, Ricoh [Yamauchi 88], and Toshiba, are based on the more traditional transfer approach.

9.2 Example-Based Translation

Interlingual MT systems are based on the idea that the *meaning*, rather than just the *form* of the source text can be used to drive the translation process. One interesting alternative is to go back to the idea of relying at least partially on the form and to appeal to a large database of previously translated forms to guide each new translation. The idea that one can solve a problem by appealing to a knowledge base of prior problems and their solutions is beginning to show promise in a large variety of computerized problem-solving contexts [Stanfill 86], so it is not surprising that it is being applied to MT. Work on example-based machine translation (EBMT) was pioneered at Kyoto University [Nagao 84, Sato 90] and is now being conducted at several industrial labs, including Hitachi and ATR.

A schematic representation of the process in the ATR system [Sumita 90] is shown in Figure 9-2. The idea here is to retain the traditional first step in MT, namely an analysis of the source text, as well as the traditional last step, generation into the target language. And the idea of an explicit transfer step that maps from the source to the target is also retained. But instead of basing the transfer step on a set of rules and dictionary entries, all of which were carefully crafted by the MT system builder, an example-based system, as its name implies, drives the transfer process by a database of translated examples. This database is augmented by a thesaurus that is used to enable the system to find examples that, although they do not exactly match the current text, are close to it in the sense that the words are related in the thesaurus and thus can be expected to be translated in analogous ways.

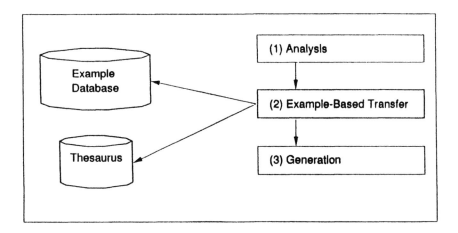

Figure 9-2: Example-Based Machine Translation

Japanese	English	Translation Pattern
yooka no gogo [8th, afternoon]	the afternoon of the 8th	B of A
kaigi no sankaryoo [conference, application fee]	the application fee for the conference ? the application fee of the conference	B for A
kyoto no kaigi [Kyoto, conference]	the conference in Kyoto ? the conference of Kyoto	B in A
issyuu no kyuuka [a week, holiday]	a week's holiday ? the holiday of a week	A's B
hoteru no yoyaku [hotel, reservation]	the hotel reservation ? the reservation of the hotel	AB
mitsu no hoteru [three, hotel]	three hotels ? hotels of three	AB

Figure 9-3: Examples for Use in EBMT

Figure 9-3 shows a simplified fragment [Sumita 90] of an EBMT database. It also illustrates the kind of problem that this approach is trying to solve. Japanese uses particles, such as *no*, to indicate many kinds of relationships among sentence constituents (as shown in the first column of the figure). English also has mechanisms for indicating those relationships (as shown in the third column). The problem is that there is not a one-to-one relationship between the Japanese method and the English, so the Japanese particle *no* can have several different translations into English, depending on the meanings of the constituents that it is connecting.

The traditional way to solve this problem is for the MT system builder to encode a set of rules that attempt to describe the circumstances under which each of the various translations should be used. In the EBMT approach, such rules are not necessary. Instead, examples of the various translations are collected from actual texts and stored in a database such as the one in the figure. When a new sentence is to be translated, it is compared against the examples. If there is an exact match, then it is clear what to do. But usually there is not a precise match. In fact, the key to the success of this approach is the ability of the system to find the right close match. This is done by using the thesaurus. So, for translating a Japanese phrase corresponding to [Tokyo,conference], the third example offers the best choice because Tokyo and Kyoto are both cities. To make this idea more precise, the EBMT system exploits the notion of *semantic distance*, which is defined by a formula that can be calculated for any (input,example) pair.

Experimental results [Sumita 91] on the *no* example show a correct translation rate, using a database of about 2000 examples, of 78%, as compared with an estimated success rate of 20%, which would be achieved if the single most common translation ("B of A") were used all the time.

In some ways, this work on example-based MT is moving in a very different direction than is the work on a meaning-based interlingua described in Section 9.1. But there is also a view, expressed to us, for example by Professor Hajime Narita of Osaka Univeristy, that EBMT can serve as a bridge technology until the necessary framework for genuine A.I.-based MT systems is developed. The increasing availability of machine-readable, bilingual corpora -- on which this technique depends -- means that this may be a useful approach.

9.3 Transfer-Driven Translation

A third interesting new approach to the design of an overall MT architecture is the idea of transfer-driven machine translation (TDMT), which is also being pursued at ATR. TDMT can be thought of as contrasting with the more traditional approach to MT, which is analysis-driven in the sense that the bulk of the effort in the system is devoted to producing an analysis of the source text that is as accurate and complete as possible given the level of description on which the system is based (be it syntactic constituent structure, semantic case frames, or a deep interlingua). This analysis is then used to drive the transfer (if necessary) and generation processes. In contrast, in the TDMT approach, as little analysis as possible is done, and then only as it is needed. So some sentences or phrases might be translated directly by matching them against stored patterns that are tied to the appropriate translation. If that does not work, then syntactic analysis is done, and again transfer occurs if it is clear what to do. If not, semantic analysis is done and transfer is tried again.

Several empirical observations underlie this approach. On the one hand, there are texts that cannot be translated correctly without recourse to the meaning of each sentence, as well as the discourse context provided by surrounding parts of the text. In these cases, a deep analysis is clearly required. But there are many other examples in which surface pattern matching works and is fast. In particular, in at least some domains, there may be a small set of distinct sentences that account for a very large percentage of the sentences or utterances that are encountered. If this happens, then it makes a lot of sense simply to store the translations of those sentences and look them up as they are needed. For example, in the telephone conference registration domain, the 10 most frequent utterances account for 22% of the total utterances out of corpus of 15,811 sentences accumulated at ATR. Not surprisingly, the top four utterances are *hai, moshimoshi, wakarimashita*, and *soudesuka*. It is likely that most texts (as opposed to the interactive dialogues studied at ATR) do not have quite this concentration of very common sentences, and as the size of the domain increases, the number of different sentences needed to cover a significant fraction of the corpus also will increase. Nevertheless, the idea that some very common sentences may be able to be translated with very little analysis seems powerful. It is particularly so in combination with some of the ideas that are being pursued in the EBMT work, including the fact that large bilingual corpora, which are necessary as the basis for any surface form-based translation system, are becoming available.

9.4 Grammars

Two traditional approaches to grammar development have provided the basis for most of the MT system development in Japan – case frames   and phrase structure   (possibly incorporating transformations) grammars. Most ongoing efforts continue to use these traditional frameworks, since there is a fairly widely held belief that these techniques provide the best available foundation for large sytems. But there is also some research on alternative approaches.

9.4.1 Constraint Dependency Grammars

One alternative approach is to view grammars as sets of constraints on how a sentence can be put together. Then constraint propagation can be used gradually to narrow the set of possible interpretations until, ideally, only one that satisfies all the constraints remains. This approach is being pursued by several different groups. For example, at ICOT it is   being implemented using a form of logic programming [Sugimura 88]. But as long as this process is internal to the parser, it may produce no noticeable change in system behavior from the point of view of an MT system user.

However, it is also possible to make this approach visible to the user and to enlist the user's aid during source sentence analysis. This is being explored in the JETS J/E system at IBM. A schematic example of their interactive parser, JAWB [Maruyama 90a, Maruyama 90b], is shown in Figure 9-4. The input to the constraint-based parser is a list of the phrases (*bunsetsu*) contained in the sentence. The grammar rules are viewed as providing a set of constraints on the way that the phrases can be combined to form the overall syntactic structure of a sentence. Each time a new sentence is encountered, the grammar rules fire, and their constraints are propagated. The result of this step is usually a set (sometimes very large) of possible interpretations for the sentence. The grammar rules themselves are usually inadequate for reducing the size of the set because syntactic knowledge alone cannot provide the basis for selecting among competing interpretations. Fortunately, it is not necessary to represent all of the interpretations explicitly. Instead, they are represented implicitly using the constraints. The approximate size of the set of candidate interpretations is displayed to the user, who can exploit additional knowledge about the meaning of the sentence and thus has the ability to add constraints that the grammar alone could not provide. To make it easy for nonlinguists to use this system, users are allowed the opportunity to add only one kind of constraint. The system displays the phrases it has found, and for each dependent phrase, the candidate phrases on which it might depend are shown. The system also displays its first choice for the dependency. The user can look at the alternatives and then choose one.

Since choices at several different points in the parse all interact to produce a large number of complete parses, it often happens that the user, by adding only a small number of additional constraints, can substantially reduce the total number of possible interpretations. The system allows the user to add a constraint and then see the result of propagating it through the existing constraint set. This enables the user to add constraints interactively, checking to make sure to avoid inadvertently ruling out the correct interpretation, until only a single consistent interpretation remains. Although this may appear to be solving the parsing problem by throwing it back on the user, it is important to keep in mind that the system is still doing all the bookkeeping and often all the user needs to do is to make a couple of decisions, each of which involves only a small number of alternatives. In one evaluation study, JAWB's best guesses were right only 47% of the time, but with user assistance the correct interpretation was found 99.8% of the time. (The remaining cases were ones where the initial constraints provided by the grammar ruled out the correct interpretation before it could be selected by the user.)

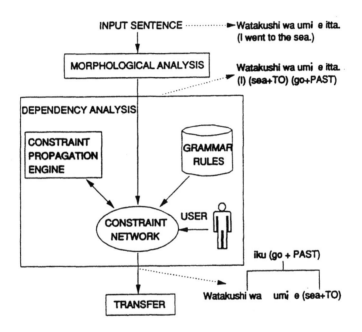

Figure 9-4: The Use of Constraint Dependency Grammar in JAWB

9.4.2 Alternative Grammatical Frameworks

The constraint dependency approach is novel both in how the grammar rules are represented and in the overall control regime that applies during the parsing process. Some other research efforts are directed at the more restricted issue of the grammar itself, without proposing a new control scheme.

The JTEC team did not see any work on totally new linguistic frameworks. But we did see work that uses frameworks other than the traditional ones described above. For example, ideas from the English Head-Driven Phrase Structure Grammar system (HPSG) [Pollard 87] and the Japanese JPSG [Gunji

87][13] form the linguistic basis for the syntactic analysis component [Kogure 89] of the speech-to-speech translation system being developed at ATR (see Section 9.10).

Another example of a newer syntactic framework being used for MT research is LFG [Bresnan 82, Kaplan 89], which is being used as a basis for research on the English/Japanese system at Bravice; on SHALT2 at IBM;   and for some of the experimental work at ATR [Kudo 90]. There is also a substantial amount of work in many of the labs that do basic research on natural language processing on the use of various unification-based systems as the basis for sentence analysis, and, to a lesser extent, sentence generation. Although this work is novel and interesting from a linguistic point of view, its results will probably not have a substantial impact on the performance of MT systems viewed from the outside (i.e., by looking just at translation results rather than at the mechanisms that produced them).

But a final category of grammatical research may have such an impact, and that is work on bidirectional grammars.   Such grammars allow a single linguistic description of a language to be used both for analysis (when the language is used as the source) and for generation (when the language is used as the target.) This approach contrasts with the more traditional one in which different grammars, usually written in different frameworks, are used for the two processes. The advantage of bidirectional grammars is that they have the potential to reduce the total cost of adding a new language (as both source and target) to an MT system. They can also reduce maintenance costs, since information is only represented in a single place. Bidirectional grammars are an important research topic within the larger international natural language processing community (for example, there was a workshop on bidirectional grammars at the 1991 ACL meeting in Berkeley), but they are only beginning to be explored in Japan, for example, by the SHALT2 and JETS projects at IBM [Takeda 90].

9.5 Generation

Most of the formal work on the use of linguistic knowledge in MT systems has focused on the use of that knowledge to aid in analyzing the source text. Generation into the target is usually considered a much easier problem. For example, at IBM we heard a second-hand quote from Professor Nagao that in doing Japanese to English translation, 80% of the errors occur in analyzing the Japanese source sentences. As a result, there is much less concern with improving the performance of the generation side of most MT systems than there is in improving the results of the analysis process. One consequence of this is that in most of the systems we saw, the English generation rules were not written by native English speakers, with the result that much of the output did not seem natural to us. There is beginning to be an increased concern with this issue, however, and many of the sites we visited expressed an interest in collaborating with the U.S. particularly in the area of developing English dictionaries and grammars.

There is also some work in the research labs on other aspects of the generation problem. The work on bidirectional grammars that we mentioned above is one example of this. So is some work, also at IBM Japan, on the use of the same chart mechanism for generation that is usually used in parsing. The advantage of the chart is that it prevents the same edge (constituent) from being generated more than once, so the overall of the efficiency of the system can be expected to increase.

---

[13]The English system GPSG [Gazdar 85] provided the initial basis for JPSG, so it too should be listed as a major influence on this work.

An interesting idea for the generation component of an interlingua-based system is to share a generator across similar languages and to represent the differences between the languages in the knowledge base and dictionaries. This approach is being pursued in the PIVOT system [Okumura 91].

9.6 Dictionaries

As shown in Chapter 4, comprehensive dictionaries play a very important role in the effectiveness of MT systems. Thus it is not surprising that all ongoing MT projects are devoting some of their R&D efforts to work on dictionaries. These efforts can be divided into four classes:

- Development of dictionaries (possibly in new subject domains) within the overall framework that has been defined for their existing MT system.

- Research with a goal of discovering new, more powerful dictionary structures.

- Tools that increase the productivity of dictionary builders.

- Construction of dictionaries for new languages.

The first of these was discussed in Chapter 4. The last was described in Chapter 3. This section will analyze the second effort — research that will lead to more powerful dictionary structures.

The Electronic Dictionary Project (EDR), mentioned briefly in Section 4.4, is conducting a large-scale, nine-year research effort whose goal is the construction of a set of machine-usable dictionaries that, taken together, will be able to serve as the basis for a large range of natural language processing applications, including MT [EDR 91].

Figure 9-5 (taken frm [EDR 91]) contains a schematic description of the EDR dictionary set, which is composed of the following four main pieces:

- A dictionary of individual words. Both general and technical terms are included. The current area of focus for the technical dictionary is information processing. The only languages that are being considered at EDR are English and Japanese, but CICC is extending this system to include other Asian languages as well. (See Section 9.9.) The word dictionary contains basic linguistic information about each word, as well as a set of pointers that describe the meanings of the words in terms of the concept dictionary. Each component of the word dictionary is monolingual; no bilingual information is stored there.

- A concept dictionary, which is not a dictionary in the conventional sense, since it is not a list of words. Instead, it contains a set of semantic concepts and a set of relationships among them. The concepts in this dictionary provide the basis for representing the meanings of sentences.   The concepts in this dictionary range from very general ones, such as *physical-object* and *action*, to very specific ones, such as *sparrow*.

- A co-occurrence dictionary, which provides information about surface co-occurrence relations between words. For example, since it is okay to say, "He drives a car," but not, "He drives a bike," this dictionary will contain the information that *car* can occur as the object of *drive* but *bike* cannot (while, on the other hand, *bike* can occur as the object of *ride* while *car* cannot).   This information can be used by a natural language generator to enable it to choose the correct wording for common concepts, such as, "control a vehicle so it goes to the right place," many of which have several different surface realizations (such as *drive*, *ride*, and *pilot*). It is worth pointing out that the need for a dictionary of this sort as part of an MT system seems to be quite widely recognized, particularly for transfer-based systems. So there are other similar efforts under way at other places including Mitsubishi [Suzuki 91] and NHK [Tanaka 91].

- A bilingual dictionary, which defines the correspondence between words in the Japanese

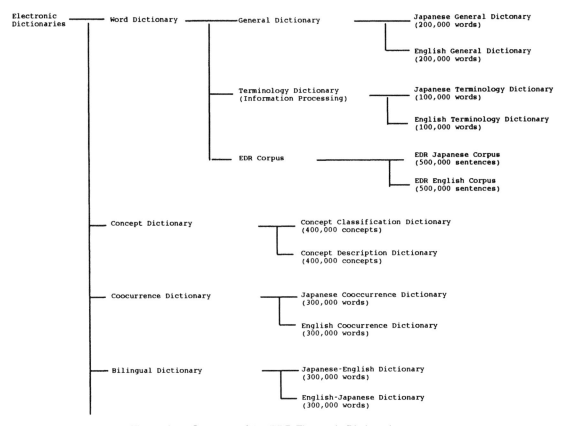

Figure 9-5: Structure of the EDR Electronic Dictionaries

word dictionary and words in the English word dictionary. Sometimes these correspondences relate words whose meanings are identical. But sometimes two languages do not have identical words. For example, the English word *horizon* has two corresponding words in Japanese, depending on whether the boundary is between earth and sky or between sea and sky. So the correspondences in this dictionary are marked as falling into one of four categories: equivalent, synonymous, broader (more general) than, and narrower (more specific) than.

Constructing dictionaries such as these so that they accurately reflect the languages that they are supposed to describe requires reliance on a large corpus of real texts. This is particulary important in the case of the co-occurrence dictionary. As a result, a side effect of EDR's dictionary building effort has been the construction of the EDR corpus, which is intended eventually to contain a half million sentences (consisting of both English and Japanese sentences).

The EDR dictionary is already being used in at least one important MT project, the Asian language effort at CICC (which will be described in more detail in Section 9.9). Thus the initial work in English and Japanese is being extended to Chinese [Zhu 89], Thai, Malay, and Indonesian.

Since the goal of the EDR effort is to support a wide range of natural language activities, EDR has stated the following policy on the distribution of their work:

In principle, all the results of the EDR project will be sold at reasonable prices. The same conditions regarding the usage of the EDR Electronic Dictionaries will be applied to all users no matter whether they are domestic or overseas users. It is expected that the prices will be somewhat lower than those of machine-readable dictionaries that are currently on sale. Special measures will be arranged for those users for academic purposes, such as universities and public research institutions. [Yokoi 91]

The dictionary interface description was published in January 1991. The interface itself, including the word list for both English and Japanese, has been announced as being available for the price of copying and shipping, and we know of some U.S. institutions that have received it. The first editions of the word and bilingual dictionaries are expected to be completed soon, but their release dates have not yet been determined.

9.7 Discourse-Level Issues

Japanese natural language processing researchers have been concerned for a long time with analyzing properties of Japanese texts and dialogues above the sentence level. Much of this work is based on discourse theories that were originally developed for English, but because Japanese discourses are structured very differently from English ones, a substantial amount of original work must be done. Examples include: work at ICOT on a model of the use of honorifics in Japanese [Sugimura 86] (based on Situation Semantics [Barwise 83]); an alternative treatment at ATR [Maeda 88] of the same phenomenon based on HPSG [Pollard 87] and Discourse Representation Theory [Kamp 84]; work at ETL [Ishizaki 88] on quantitative measures of the complexity of Japanese sentences (which is intended to serve as a basis for the evaluation of MT systems); and work at NTT [Shimazu 90] on analyzing Japanese sentences using an argumentation system based on defeasible reasoning [Konolige 88].

But in the more specific area of MT, there is much less work on issues that cross sentence boundaries. All the production MT systems that the JTEC team saw translate a single sentence at a time. In the research labs, there is also very little work on discourse-level phenomena. Instead, MT is largely viewed as a single sentence at a time process. For example, [Ikehara 89] claims that about 90% of Japanese written sentences in practical use can be translated in isolation and without any domain knowledge. As a result, he argues for ignoring both discourse issues and world knowledge. Despite this view, however, there is some work on discourse phenomena.

The one MT system we know about that is not organized primarily around the translation of individual sentences is the CONTRAST [Ishizaki 89a, Ishizaki 90] system at ETL. CONTRAST's task is to translate short newspaper stories. It makes use of a set of stored, script-like objects called contextual representational structures. These structures correspond to common, newspaper story situations, such as hijacking and kidnapping. They differ from scripts in that they do not depend solely on a small number of very low-level primitives as their basic units. The analysis part of CONTRAST uses the title of the story to find the correct contextual structure. Then it analyzes the rest of the story and fills in values that correspond to the details of the particular incident that is being described. The generation component then takes the complete instantiated structure and generates a description of it in the target language. Thus there is no guarantee that the structure of the target paragraph will be the same as the structure of the input, and in fact one goal of this effort is to enable translation between languages in situations where the conventions for organizing information are very different. Although CONTRAST is very ambitious in its structure, it is still a small prototype, which has only five stored contextual representational structures and which works only on short newspaper stories about those five things.

One of the most widely studied discourse phenomena in Japan is ellipsis, which is the process by which a necessary sentential element is omitted from the surface form with the expectation that it can be recovered from the discourse context. A simple example of ellipsis occurs in the English sentence, "Let's try again to loosen the screw, this time using a wrench." The phrase, "using a wrench" modifies a verb phrase that is missing. But it is intended to be "to loosen the screw," which can be picked up from an earlier phrase in the same sentence. Often, though, ellipsis can only be resolved by appeal to earlier sentences, so a general treatment of ellipsis must consider a larger discourse context. Ellipsis is even more common in Japanese than it is in English (for example, see the dialogue in Figure 9-6), so it is a very important issue, particularly for J/E systems. As a result, there is a long tradition of Japanese work on this problem. (See, for example, [Nagao 76].) The most common general-purpose approach to ellipsis resolution is to look back through prior sentences to try to find a constituent that is of the appropriate type (both syntactic and semantic) to fill the current gap. In the specific case of elided subject, which is very common in Japanese, the most common approach is to use the English passive in the translation. This can be done without any recourse to discourse context since the missing constituent is omitted in the English sentence also. This technique is used in many J/E MT systems, but it often leads to unnatural sounding translations.

Research on other techniques for the treatment of ellipsis is being done in several places, but most of it is primarily theoretical rather than implementation oriented; several of the efforts do not use any extrasentential context even for this problem. Work at NTT focuses on the use of rules to avoid generating unnatural translations for elliptical constructions [Nakaiwa 90]. And work at ATR takes advantage of the fact that they are working in a limited domain (telephone conference registrations, see Section 9.10) and so the form of each sentence can be used to determine what dialogue function it is serving (e.g., a request for information or a promise to do something) [Dohsaka 91]. The dialogue function then is used as a basis for filling in the missing constituents. In particular, facts about the way in which honorifics have been used can sometimes help to determine whether the speaker or the hearer is the intended subject of the sentence.

Another area in which some discourse-oriented work is being done is the use of task and domain knowledge as a basis for building a model of a task-oriented discourse. We discuss ATR's work in this area later, in Section 9.10, in the context of ATR's larger goal of building a translating telephone. But we should point out here that although there is work at ATR on learning about the structure of task-oriented dialogues, the primary MT system that is being built there still operates on a single sentence at a time.

A final area we will mention is the treatment of anaphora (expressions, such as pronouns, that necessarily derive at least some part of their meaning from some other linguistic expression on which they depend). We found very little work on anaphora, although some groups, such as the SHALT2 team at IBM and the group at NTT, indicated that they intend to extend their system to handle anaphora in the future.

9.8 Better Tools for Users

The JTEC team saw a substantial amount of work on the development of better tools for users. The bulk of this was aimed at reducing the cost of pre-editing. For example, JICST is just completing a system that performs about ten kinds of style checks automatically during pre-editing. See Section 6.1.1 for a more complete list of sites that are doing work in this area. There is much less work on tools for postediting, but we saw one system under development at Ricoh (as described in Section 6.3.)

One idea that appears to be gaining popularity is a move away from a black-box, batch-mode translation system and toward a system that interacts incrementally with a user throughout the translation process. This may be an improvement over the traditional approach in at least two ways. It may beat pre-editing, in which users have to anticipate where the problems are likely to occur. As a result, they may waste time in places where there would not have been a problem anyway, or they may miss a place where there is a serious problem and they could easily have helped. The interactive approach can also beat postediting because it allows the user to give some advice. Then the system picks up the advice and propagates it through the rest of the translation process. This contrasts with postediting, where, if users make changes, they must fix the entire translation if it depends on the change. This interactive approach to the overall translation process is being investigated in several labs, including Matsushita and Fujitsu. The JAWB interactive parser described in Section 9.4 is another example of this approach.

Another way to solve the imperfect translation problem is to give up on the idea that the MT system should output a single "best" translation. Instead, it can display several alternatives to the user, whose job is just to click on the right one. This is a lot simpler than the standard postediting task in which some of the MT system's output must be rewritten. This idea is being exploited in Ricoh's English/Japanese MT system, as well as in Catena's STAR.

9.9 Extension to Other Languages

As described in Chapter 3, the first generation of Japanese-built MT systems focused on the problem of translating between Japanese and English. We are now beginning to see, however, a broadening of the scope of the Japanese MT effort to include other Asian languages as well as European ones. Most of the efforts represent extensions of existing systems to new language pairs. The work at CICC is different, though, since it is an entirely new MT effort.

CICC began a six year project in 1987 with Overseas Development Assistance (ODA) funding. The technical goal of the project is to build a demonstration prototype of an MT system for Japanese, Chinese, Thai, Malay, and Indonesian. This system is aimed at technical texts, with an initial focus on information processing. The political goal is to develop strong connections between Japan and the emerging Asian marketplace. As a result, this is a strongly collaborative effort, with most of the work on the non-Japanese languages being done in the native countries.

The CICC system [Tanaka 89, Tsuji 90] is firmly grounded in prior Japanese work on MT. The syntactic analysis component of the system currently contains three parsers taken from three existing commercial MT systems: ATLAS-II (from Fujitsu), HICATS (from Hitachi), and PIVOT (from NEC). The plan is to integrate them into a single system. The system is interlingual [Ishizaki 89b], with the EDR concept dictionary serving as the basis of the interlingua. This project is thus an interesting test case for the EDR concept structure, which was initially developed to support processing Japanese and English. Of course, if the concept structure is truly language-independent, then no changes will be necessary to use it to process a new language. But no one expected that it would be language-independent in this extreme sense. The CICC team estimates that the size of the change to the concept structure required to add a new language is 10%. Of all the advantages of the interlingual approach described in Section 9.1, one is of particular significance for this effort. Because each language is defined separately, it is possible to spread out the development effort, with each language being worked on in its home country.

Because of the important structural differences that exist among the languages addressed by this project, a wide range of technical problems will need to be solved. One example of this that was mentioned during the JTEC visit is the fact that it is very difficult in Chinese to determine the part of speech of a word since there are no inflectional markers, as there are in many European languages, nor are there postpositional markers as there are in Japanese. Another example is that Thai not only has no word boundary markers; it has no sentence boundary markers either.

The prototype system is written in the programming language C. The performance goal for the system is to be able to translate more than 5,000 words per hour with an accuracy of more than 90% on grammatically correct texts all of whose words are in the dictionary. The dictionary is expected to contain 50,000 basic words in each language, plus 25,000 additional words in the domain of information processing. At the time of the JTEC visit, the system could translate a corpus of 500 sentences between the five languages, using dictionaries with 20,000 word vocabularies. The CICC team also expressed a strong interest in adding English to their system.

9.10 Speech-to-Speech Translation

The vision of a speech-to-speech translation system is widespread in Japan. Work on various aspects of this problem is being done in several labs, such as Matsushita, where they are building a Japanese/English system that includes a speech system based on the widely used idea of a Hidden Markov Model (HMM) [Rabiner 89].

The two largest efforts, though, are at NEC and ATR. NEC's vision is of a hand-held, speech-to-speech MT system. They have already produced a prototype E/J and J/E workstation-based system that can recognize a 500 word vocabulary for continuous speech and a 5,000 word vocabulary for isolated words. The typical time required for a short sentence is about five seconds for recognition and another ten seconds for translation.

But the most substantial effort in this area is being conducted at ATR, which has been working since 1986 on a planned 15-year project. One system is currently under development, and others are planned for the future.

The goal for the current effort is a 1500-word, speaker-independent, real-time, limited-domain, English/Japanese and Japanese/English system with greater than 75% accuracy. The task domain for the system is international conference registration. The prototype implementation, SL-TRANS [Kurematsu 91], is operational on a small set of example dialogues, such as the one shown in Figure 9-6 (taken from [Kogure 90]). Figure 9-7 shows the top-level architecture of SL-TRANS.

The speech recognition part of SL-TRANS is based on an HMM, with some enhancements (e.g., [Hanazawa 89]) that have emerged from this project. An LR phrasal parser is used to predict the next phoneme in the speech input [Kita 89]. Unfortunately, this combination is not powerful enough to determine a unique interpretation for each phrase, so a semantic filtering technique [Morimoto 90] is applied and early experiments suggest that it can reduce the number of candidate interpretations to less than a third of the original number. Once this hybrid procedure has produced an interpretation of the spoken input, that interpretation is passed to an analysis procedure, just as the typed input is in a conventional MT system. As described in Section 9.4, this analysis procedure is based on an HPSG/JPSG grammar and is performed using an active chart parser. The transfer component of this

	Japanese Input Utterances	English Output Utterances
1	Moshimoshi Sochira wa kaigijimukyoku desu ka.	Hello. Is this the office for the conference?
2	Hai Sou desu.	Yes. That is right.
3	(Watashi wa) kaigi ni moushikomi tai no desu ga.	I would like to apply for the conference.
4	(Anata wa) tourokuyoushi o sudeni o-mochi deshou ka.	Do you already have a registration form?
5	Iie mada desu.	No. Not yet.
6	Wakari mashi ta. Soredewa (watashi wa anata ni) tourokuyoushi wa o- okuri itashi masu. (Anata no) go-jusho to o-namae o onegai shi masu.	All right Then, I will send you a registration form. Your name and your address, please.
7	Juusho wa Oosaka-shi Kita-ku Chaya-machi nijuu-san desu. Namae wa Suzuki Mayumi desu.	The address is 23 Chaya-machi Kita-ku, Osaka. The name is Mayumi Suzuki.
8	Wakari mashi ta. Torokuyoushi wa shikyu okura se te itadaki masu. Wakara nai ten ga gozai mashi tara, itsudemo (watashi ni) o-kiki kudasai.	All right. I will send you the registration form immediately. If there will be a question, please ask me at any time.
9	Arigatou gozai masu. Soredewa shitsurei itashi masu.	Thank you. Good-bye.
10	Doumo shitsurei itashi masu.	Good-bye.

The odd numbered utterances come from the questioner; the even numbered ones come from the conference secretary. Parenthesized phrases are not expressed explicitly.

Figure 9-6: An Example of a Task-Oriented Dialogue

system is interesting because, as we mentioned in Section 9.1, it is a hybrid transfer/interlingua-based system.

The work at ATR differs from most of the other MT efforts that we looked at in its focus on two-person, interactive dialogues rather than on static text. This difference manifests itself both at the individual sentence level (where, for example, one sees sentences such as the ones in blocks 1, 2, 5, 9, and 10 above, which would be very unlikely to show up in a written text) and at the level of larger discourse units. As we said in Section 9.7, however, very little attention is currently being paid to phenomena at this larger level. But there is some work at ATR on such issues as analyzing the larger structure of task-oriented dialogues (e.g., in the NADINE system [Kogure 90]) and looking at patterns of interruptions in real telephone conversations [Myers 90], presumably to lay the groundwork for later efforts to exploit the larger dialogue context during the translation process.

Other work at ATR is aimed at exploring alternative approaches to parts of the speech-to-speech MT problem that may serve as the basis for future systems. For example, there is work on a neural net-based speech recognition system and another effort that is exploring the use of a hybrid symbolic/subsymbolic, massively parallel system for both speech and natural language processing [Tomabechi 90]. And, as described in Section 9.2, there is work on a new approach to translation that is driven by a large database of translated examples. Some of the work at ATR relies on international collaboration with institutions such as Carnegie Mellon University in the U.S. and the University of Manchester in the U.K.

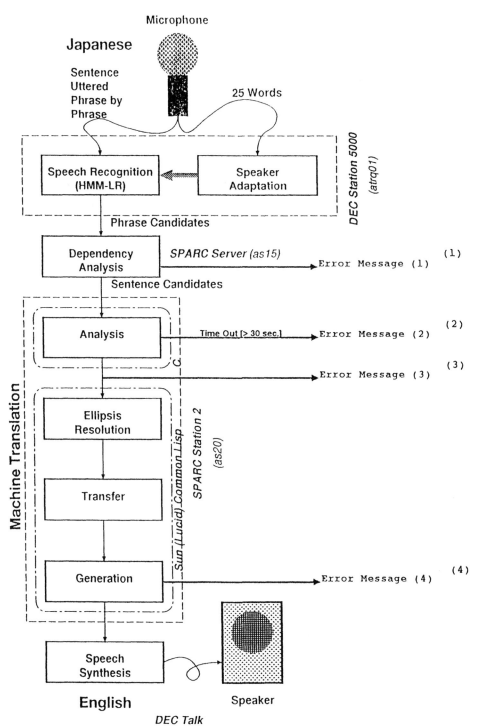

Figure 9-7: The Architecture of the SL-TRANS Speech-to-Speech MT System

9.11 Embedded MT Systems

As we pointed out in Chapter 6, there is a widespread appreciation in Japan of the potential role of MT as a component of larger information processing systems. So although it can be very useful as a stand-alone translation engine, it can also be embedded in database systems, electronic mail programs, and document production environments. Given this perspective, it is not surprising that many of the MT sites are working on prototypes of these kinds of MT systems. We described some of those applications in Chapter 6. We mention a few others here.

For example, at Fujitsu the JTEC team saw a demonstration of a system that allows German- and English-speaking users to retrieve texts from a Japanese text database. The user can enter key words in German or English, and they are translated into Japanese. The retrieval against the Japanese database is then done, and the titles of the articles that are returned are translated into German or English and displayed. Entire articles can also be translated at the user's request. We also saw demonstrations of an MT system embedded into an electronic mail system at both Fujitsu and Oki.

Toshiba has developed a system that embeds ASTRANSAC [Hirakawa 91], their J/E and E/J MT system, into a larger system that includes an OCR front end and an interface to a document processing system. The OCR front end scans the source document and creates a structural description of it (which means, for example, that pictures can be separated out and reintroduced later after translation has occurred.) The translation process then takes place using the structured document, and the software deals appropriately with the structure codes. The goal of this work on an embedded MT system was partly to make MT available to a wide array of end users. To make the system even more accessible to these users, ASTRANSAC offers several end-user customization capabilities, including: the ability to specify default values for various linguistic parameters in the system (including formality, rules for translating articles, and rules for choosing between active and passive voice); the ability to modify the dictionary; a tool for using the set of lexical items that occur in user-selected texts in the target language to bias lexical choice during translation; and the ability to use multiple occurrences of an ambiguous phrase in the source text to help resolve the ambiguity. One particularly interesting thing about all of these features is that they have been designed so that it will be easy to merge end-user customizations with vendor supplied upgrades without one invalidating the other.

The JTEC team was also informed of work on integrating MT into larger, document-processing environments at Hitachi, NEC, Toshiba, Matsushita, Oki, and others.

9.12 Massively Parallel Hardware

There is a substantial amount of research in Japan on massively parallel hardware. MITI's New Information Processing Technology (NIPT) plan (sometimes known as the Sixth Generation Project) is backing this effort. Also, most of the major computer companies are building high performance parallel machines, including Fujitsu, Hitachi, IBM Japan, Matsushita, Mitsubishi, NEC, NTT, Oki Electric, Sony, and Toshiba. There is also work at ICOT, ETL, and several university laboratories. Although this work is not directly related to MT, we mention it here because of the potential for exploiting this technology as a platform for future MT systems.

Partly as a legacy from the ICOT Fifth Generation Project, some of these machines are specifically targeted toward artificial intelligence applications, including representing and manipulating knowledge structures, such as semantic nets, that are playing an increasing role in MT systems as they move toward the use of conceptual structures as their intermediate representations (as described in Section 9.1). ICOT is now focusing a substantial amount of effort on the development of parallel natural language processing systems, and there is already some work on the use of massive parallelism for MT, for example at ATR, which bought a Connection Machine (from *Thinking Machines* in the U.S.), and is using it for MT research. Particularly because of the overlap between the companies that are involved in MT and those that are building parallel machines, there will be excellent opportunities to exploit this combination of technologies.

9.13 The Future

A very substantial amount of research, both on basic natural language processing and on machine translation, is being conducted in Japan. This section has provided an outline of some of the major trends. One key one, that was articulated by Professor Nagao, is that there will be a gradual shift toward knowledge-based (A.I.-based) systems for MT. On the other hand, some interesting possible trends are significantly absent. For example, other fundamental representational techniques, such as subsymbolic (or connectionist/neural net) systems, appear to be receiving very little attention. Despite all the research effort in MT, there was a consensus at the JEIDA roundtable held at the end of the JTEC visit that there are unlikely to be any significant research breakthroughs in MT during the next five years. Instead, it is reasonable to expect steady progress toward more powerful systems. This is not surprising in view of the fact that most of the work we saw is being conducted within well-established research traditions. There does, however, seem to be a clear consensus that the delivered MT systems of five years from now will be more robust, more usable, more accurate, and more widely exploited than they are today.

10. Future Directions in Machine Translation

Elaine Rich

The fundamental basis for any projection of future MT development in Japan lies in the recognition of MT as a key technology, particularly within the larger context of the information processing society of the future. Most of the major vendors of information processing technology (including both computer and communication companies) are involved in MT efforts in Japan. There is a clear symbiosis between these two efforts. The MT systems of today make available information that facilitates the development of the technology of the future. And that future technology will be the platform on which more powerful MT systems will run.

Perhaps because of the large distance between Japanese and most other major world languages, or because of their roots as an island culture, the Japanese well recognize that isolation is not in their long-term interest. Reducing isolation and increasing the ability to communicate globally will give the Japanese enhanced ability to achieve major national objectives. Not only is their exporting of goods and services facilitated by MT, but also their ability to import strategic information is enhanced. Thus, there is a consensus of industry, academic, and government leaders that the significant MT achievements of the 1980s must be continued through the 1990s and beyond the year 2000. Indeed, the vision of automated speech-to-speech interpretation is targeted for achievement in 2015.

While MT technology will continue to be pushed, the pull of thousands of Japanese users will ensure market development. These users already exist, both within the major companies that are participating in MT efforts, as well as within the wide range of organizations that make use of the MT services that are offered by commercial translation service bureaus. And this base of users is increasing. Just in the one week that the JTEC team was in Japan, we heard about several new MT services that had been or were about to be announced both by the major vendors and by the service bureaus. Each of them has the potential to bring in substantial numbers of new users. This is clearly a very dynamic arena.

Integration of MT with related technologies will probably accelerate so that optical character recognition (OCR), voice recognition, word processing, desktop publishing, office automation, document management, database use, electronic mail, language instruction, and other such technologies will be increasingly seen in products in the 1990s. Newer MT applications of existing MT technology, such as gisting and scanning large text databases to find relevant documents, will also become more common. Spin-offs such as software for pre-editing and small bilingual dictionaries for word processors and pocket translators are already on the market as separate products, and this trend is expected to continue. Since short-term profitability is not the determining factor, these longer term investments in innovative products will continue.

While no major technology breakthroughs are expected in the next five years, steady improvement will be seen in vital areas. At the wrap-up session at JEIDA at the end of our visit, we mentioned four areas of potential improvement: translation quality, better integration of MT systems with other applications, lower cost, and better user interfaces. We asked the Japanese representatives at the meeting (most of whom represented the MT manufacturers and a few of whom came from universities) which of these areas they felt was most important from the point of view of MT users. Of the 17 people, 13 said higher quality, three said a better user interface, one said better integration, and no one mentioned lower cost.

These views appear to be driving ongoing research and development efforts, most of which are focused on the creation of systems that exploit greater amounts of knowledge (in the form of grammars, dictionaries, examples, context models, and domain knowledge bases) in an attempt to produce higher quality translations.

As knowledge bases grow in quantity, quality, and comprehensiveness, the sharing of these intellectual properties will become more common, both for research and commercial purposes. International collaboration on MT research and development will be enhanced by this knowledge-sharing. There is a widespread recognition in Japan that international collaboration is particularly important in the development of knowledge bases for MT systems, since dictionaries and grammars can best be developed by native speakers of the languages that are being described. So, although most of the current Japanese MT systems have been developed with very little involvement by native speakers of languages other than Japanese, this situation will probably change considerably over the next five years.

User interfaces are also improving, partially as a result of feedback from the growing community of MT system users. This is, of course, a positive feedback loop, and as the interfaces improve, the user community grows, more feedback is available, and so forth. As a result, the Japanese fully expect to see a return on the substantial investment that they have made and are continuing to make in MT.

11. References

11. References

[Aizawa 90]   Aizawa, T., T. Ehara, N. Uratani, H. Tanaka, N. Kato, S. Nakase, N. Aruga, &
                 T. Matsuda.
                 A Machine Translation System for Foreign News in Satellite Broadcasting.
                 In *Proceedings of COLING '90*, pages 308-310. 1990.

[ALPAC 66]   Automatic Language Processing Advisory Committee (ALPAC).
                 Language and Machines: Computers in Translation and Linguistics.
                 Division of Behavioral Sciences, National Academy of Sciences, National Research
                     Council Publication 1416, Washington, 1966.

[Amano 88]   Amano, S., H. Nogami, and S. Miike.
                 A Step Towards Telecommunication with Machine Interpreter.
                 In *Proceedings of the Second International Conference on Theoretical and
                     Methodological Issues in Natural Language Processing.* 1988.

[Amano 89]   Amano, S., H. Hirakawa, and H. Nogami.
                 The TAURAS Design Philosophy.
                 In *Proceedings of MT Summit II*, pages 36-41. 1989.

[Ashizaki 89]   Ashizaki, T.
                 Outline of the JICST Machine Translation System.
                 In *Proceedings of MT Summit II*, pages 44-49. 1989.

[Bar-Hillel 71] Bar-Hillel, Y.
                 Some Reflections on the Present Outlook for High-Quality Machine Translation.
                 In W. Lehmann and R. Stachowitz (editors), *Feasibility Study on Fully Automated High
                     Quality Translation.* Rome Air Development Center, Rome AFB, Rome, N.Y., 1971.

[Barwise 83]   Barwise, J. and Perry, J.
                 Situations and Attitudes.
                 M.I.T. Press, 1983.

[Becker 84]   Becker, A.L.
                 Biography of a Sentence: A Burmese Proverb.
                 In E. M. Bruner (editor), *Text, Play, and Story: The Construction and Reconstruction of
                     Self and Society.* American Ethnological Society, Washington, D.C., 1984.

[Bennett 85]   Bennett, W. S. & Slocum, J.
                 The LRC Machine Translation System.
                 Computational Linguistics 11(2-3), 1985.

[Bostad 90]   Bostad, D. A.
                 Aspects of Machine Translation in the United States Air Force.
                 In *Benefits of Computer Assisted Translation to Information Managers and End-Users,
                     AGARD Lecture Series No. 171.* North Atlantic Treaty Organization, Advisory
                     Group for Aerospace Research and Development, Neuilly-sur-Seine (France),
                     1990.

[Bresnan 82]   Bresnan, J. (editor).
                 The Mental Representation of Grammatical Relations.
                 MIT Press, Cambridge, Mass., 1982.

[Brown 89]   Brown, et. al.
                 A Statistical Approach to Machine Translation.
                 Technical Report, IBM Research Division Technical Report in Computer Science RC
                     14773 (#66226), T. J. Watson Research Center, Yorktown Heights, N.Y., 1989.

[Chandioux 89]   Chandioux, J.
METEO: 100 Million Words Later.
In D. L. Hammond (editor), *Coming of Age: Proceedings of the 30th Annual Conference of the American Translators Association*. Learned Information, Medford, N.J., 1989.

[Dohsaka 91]   Dohsaka, K.
Interpretation and Generation through Efficient Representations.
Natural Language SIG Reports of the IPSJ , March 15, 1991.
(in Japanese).

[EDR 90]   EDR.
An Overview of the EDR Electronic Dictionaries.
Technical Report, Japan Electronic Dictionary Research Institute TR-024, 1990.

[EDR 91]   EDR.
Proceedings of the International Workshop on Electronic Dictionaries.
Technical Report, Japan Electronic Dictionary Research Institute TR-031, 1991.

[Estival 90]   Estival, D.
Generating French with a Reversible Unification Grammar.
In *Proceedings of COLING '90*. 1990.

[Farwell 90]   Farwell, D., & Wilks, Y.
ULTRA: a multilingual machine translator.
Technical Report, Computing Research Laboratory, Las Cruces, New Mexico MCCS-90-202, 1990.

[Gazdar 85]   Gazdar, G., E. Klein, G. K. Pullum, & I. Sag.
Generalized Phrase Structure Grammar.
Harvard University Press, Cambridge, Mass., 1985.

[Grimaila 91]   Grimaila, A. with J. Chandioux.
Machine Translation in the Real World.
In J. Newton (editor), *Computers in Translation: A Practical Appraisal*. Routledge, London, 1991.
(In press).

[Gunji 87]   Gunji, T.
Japanese Phrase Structure Grammar.
D. Reidel, Dordrecht, 1987.

[Hanazawa 89]   Hanazawa, T., T. Kawabata, & K. Shikano.
Recognition of Japanese Voiced Stops Using Hidden Markov Models.
Journal of the Acoustical Society of Japan 10:776-785, 1989.

[Hasegawa 90]   Hasegawa, T.
A Rule Application Control Method in a Lexicon-Driven Transfer Model of a Dialogue Translation System.
In *Proceedings of the 9th European Conference on Artificial Intelligence*. 1990.

[Hirakawa 91]   Hirakawa, H., H. Nogami, S. Amano.
EJ/JE Machine Translation System ASTRANSAC - Extensions toward Personalization.
In *Proceedings of MT Summit III*. 1991.

[Hutchins 86]   Hutchins, W. J.
Machine Translation: Past, Present, Future.
Ellis Horwood, Chichester, England, 1986.

[Ichiyama 89]   Ichiyama, S.
                   Multi-lingual Machine Translation System.
                   Office Equipment and Products 18(131):46-48, August, 1989.

[Ikeda 89]   Ikeda, T.
                   On an Interlingua Representation.
                   Natural Language SIG Reports of the IPSJ , June 30, 1989.
                   (in Japanese).

[Ikehara 89]   Ikehara, S.
                   Multi-Level Machine Translation Method.
                   Future Computing Systems 2(3), 1989.

[Ikehara 91]   Ikehara, S., S. Shirai, A. Yokoo, and H. Nakaiwa.
                   Toward an MT system without Pre-Editing -- Effects of New Methods in ALT-J/E.
                   In *Proceedings of MT Summit III.* 1991.

[Ishizaki 88]   Ishizaki, S. & H. Isahara.
                   Extraction of Qualitative and Quantitative Characteristics of Complexity Included in
                       Japanese Sentences.
                   Natural Language SIG Reports of the IPSJ , July 22, 1988.
                   (in Japanese).

[Ishizaki 89a]   Ishizaki, S.
                   Machine Translation System Using Contextual Information.
                   In M. Nagao, H. Tanaka, T. Makino, H. Nomura, H. Uchida, & S. Ishizaki (editors),
                       Proceedings of Machine Translation Summit I. Ohmsha, Tokyo, 1989.

[Ishizaki 89b]   Ishizaki, S. & H. Uchida.
                   On Interlingua for Machine Translation.
                   Natural Language SIG Reports of the IPSJ , January 20, 1989.
                   (in Japanese).

[Ishizaki 90]   Ishizaki, S., H. Isahara, T. Tokunaga, & H. Tanaka.
                   Steps toward a Machine Translation Using Context and World Model.
                   Japanese Artificial Intelligence Journal 4(6), 1990.
                   (in Japanese).

[JEIDA 89]   Japan Electronic Industry Development Association.
                   *A Japanese View of Machine Translation in Light of the Considerations and
                       Recommendations Reported by ALPAC, U.S.A.*
                   JEIDA, Machine Translation System Research Committee, Tokyo, 1989.

[JEIDA 91]   JEIDA.
                   Revised Outlines of MT Systems.
                   1991.

[Johnson 85]   Johnson, R.L., M. King, and L. des Tombe.
                   EUROTRA: A Multi-lingual System under Development.
                   Computational Linguistics 11:155-169, 1985.

[Kaji 88]   Kaji, H.
                   Language Control for Effective Utilization of HICATS/JE.
                   In *Proceedings of MT Summit II*, pages 72-77. 1988.

[Kamp 84]   Kamp, H.
                   A Theory of Truth and Semantic Representation.
                   In J. Groenendijk, T. Janssen, & M. Stokhof (editors), *Truth, Interpretation, and
                       Information.* Foris, Dordrecht, 1984.

[Kaplan 89]   Kaplan, R. M., K. Netter, J. Wedekind, and A. Zaenen.
                 Translation by Structural Correspondences.
                 In *Proceedings of the 4th Conference of the European ACL, Manchester.* 1989.

[Kita 89]   Kita, K., T. Kawabata, & H. Saito.
                 HMM Continuous Speech Recognition Using Predictive LR Parsing.
                 In *Proceedings of the International Conference on Acoustics and Speech Signal
                      Processing.* 1989.

[Kogure 89]   Kogure, K.
                 Parsing Japanese Spoken Sentences Based on HPSG.
                 In *Proceedings of the Int. Workshop on Parsing Technology.* 1989.

[Kogure 90]   Kogure, K., H. Iida, T. Hasegawa, & K. Ogura.
                 NADINE: An Experimental Dialogue Translation System from Japanese to English.
                 In *Proceedings of the InfoJapan'90 Computer Conference Organized by IPSJ to
                      Commemorate the 30th Anniversary.* 1990.

[Konolige 88]   Konolige, K.
                 Defeasible Argumentation in Reasoning about Events.
                 In *Proceedings of the International Symposium on Machine Intelligence and Systems.*
                      1988.

[Kudo 90]   Kudo, I.
                 Local Cohesive Knowledge for A Dialogue-Machine Translation System.
                 In *Proceedings of the 28th Annual Meeting of the ACL.* 1990.

[Kurematsu 91]   Kurematsu, A., H. Iida, T. Morimoto, & K. Shikano.
                 Language Processing in Connection with Speech Translation at ATR Interpreting
                      Telephony Research Laboratories.
                 Speech Communication Journal 10:1-9, 1991.

[Maeda 88]   Maeda, H., S. Kato, K. Kogure, & H. Iida.
                 Parsing Japanese Honorifics in Unification-Based Grammar.
                 In *Proceedings of the 26th Annual Meeting of the ACL.* 1988.

[Maruyama 90a]   Maruyama, H.
                 Structural Disambiguation with Constraint Propagation.
                 In *Proceedings of the 28th Annual Meeting of the ACL.* 1990.

[Maruyama 90b]   Maruyama, H., H. Watanabe, & S. Ogino.
                 An Interactive Japanese Parser for Machine Translation.
                 In *Proceedings of COLING '90.* 1990.

[Melchuk 63]   Melchuk, I.
                 Machine Translation and Linguistics.
                 In O. Akhmanova, I. Melchuk, R. Frumkina and E. Paducheva (editors), *Exact Methods
                      in Linguistic Research.* R-397-PR. The RAND Corporation, Santa Monica, 1963.

[Morimoto 90]   Morimoto, T., K. Shikano, H. Iida, & A. Kurematsu.
                 Integration of Speech Recognition and Language Processing in Spoken Language
                      Translation System (SL-TRANS).
                 In *Proceedings of the International Conference on Spoken Language Processing.*
                      1990.

[Muraki 89]   Muraki, K.
                 PIVOT: Two-Phase Machine Translation System.
                 In M. Nagao, H. Tanaka, T. Makino, H. Nomura, H. Uchida, & S. Ishizaki (editors),
                      Proceedings of Machine Translation Summit I. Ohmsha, Tokyo, 1989.

[Myers 90]   Myers, J. K.
               Methods for Handling Spoken Interruptions for an Interpreting Telephone.
               Natural Language and Communication SIG Reports of the Institute of Electronis,
                 Information and Communication Engineers 90(44), 1990.

[Nagao 76]   Nagao, M., J. Tsujii, and K. Tanaka.
               Analysis of Japanese Sentences, by Using Semantic and Contextual Information–
                 Content Analysis.
               Joho Shori 17(1), January, 1976.
               (in Japanese).

[Nagao 84]   Nagao, M.
               A Framework of a Mechanical Translation between Japanese and English by Analogy
                 Principle.
               In A. Elithorn & R. Banerji (editors), *Artificial and Human Intelligence*, pages 173-180.
                 North Holland, 1984.

[Nagao 85]   Nagao, M., Tsujii, J. & Nakamura, J.
               The Japanese Government Project for Machine Translation.
               Computational Linguistics 11(2-3), 1985.

[Nagao 86]   Nagao, M. J. Tsujii, & J. Nakamura.
               Machine Translation from Japanese into English.
               In *Proceedings of the IEEE*. 1986.

[Nagao 87]   Nagao, M.
               Role of Structural Transformation in a Machine Translation System.
               In S. Nirenburg (editor), *Machine Translation: Theoretical and Methodological Issues*.
                 Cambridge University Press, Cambridge, 1987.

[Nagao 89]   Nagao, M.
               Machine Translation: How Far Can It Go?
               Oxford University Press, Oxford, 1989.

[Nakaiwa 90]   Nakaiwa, H.
               Natural Form English Generation of Supplemented Case Elements in Japanese to
                 English Machine Translation System.
               In *Proceedings of the 4th National (Japanese) Conference on Artificial Intelligence*.
                 1990.
               (in Japanese).

[Okumura 91]   Okumura, A., K. Muraki, and S. Akamine.
               Mult-lingual Sentence Generation from the PIVOT Interlingua.
               In *Proceedings of MT Summit III*. 1991.

[Pollard 87]   Pollard, C. & I. A. Sag.
               An Information-Based Syntax and Semantics, Vol. 1.
               Technical Report, CSLI Lecture Note Number 13, 1987.

[Rabiner 89]   Rabiner, L.
               A Tutorial on HMMs and Selected Applications in Speech Recognition.
               Proc. of IEEE 77, 1989.

[Sakurai 91]   Sakurai, K., M. Ozeki and Y. Nishihara.
               MT Application for a Translation Agency.
               In *Proceedings of MT Summit III*. 1991.

[Sato 89]   Sato, S.
               Practical Experience in the Application of MT Systems.
               In *Proceedings of MT Summit II*, pages 125-127. 1989.

[Sato 90]   Sato, S. & M. Nagao.
                 Toward Memory-Based Translation.
                 In *Proceedings COLING '90*, pages 247-252. 1990.

[Shimazu 90]   Shimazu, A.
                 Japanese Sentence Analysis as Argumentation.
                 In *Proceedings of the 28th Annual Meeting of the ACL.* 1990.

[Smith 89]   Smith, B.
                 The Art of Machine Translation; Japanese to English.
                 IBM Research Magazine 27(4), 1989.

[Stanfill 86]   Stanfill, C. & D. Waltz.
                 Toward Memory-Based Reasoning.
                 Communications of the ACM 29(12):1213-1228, 1986.

[Sugimura 86]   Sugimura, R.
                 Japanese Honorifics and Situation Semantics.
                 In *Proceedings of COLING 86.* 1986.

[Sugimura 88]   Sugimura, R. H. Miyoshi, & K. Mukai.
                 Constraint Analysis on Japanese Modification.
                 In V. Dahl & P. Saint-Dizier (editors), *Natural Language Understanding and Logic
                     Programming, II.* Elsevier Science Publishers B.V., 1988.

[Sumita 90]   Sumita, E., H. Iida, & H. Kohyama.
                 Translating with Examples: A New Approach to Machine Translation.
                 In *Proceedings of the Third International Conference on Theoretical and
                     Methodological Issues in Machine Translation of Natural Language.* 1990.

[Sumita 91]   Sumita, E. & H. Iida.
                 Experiments and Prospects of Example-Based Machine Translation.
                 Natural Language SIG Reports of the IPSJ :82-85, March 15, 1991.

[Suzuki 91]   Suzuki, K. & T. Dasai.
                 A Processing of Co-Occurrence in Japanese English Machine Translation.
                 Natural Language SIG Reports of the IPSJ , March 15, 1991.
                 (in Japanese).

[SYSTRAN 91]   Systran.
                 SYSTRAN Company Handout.
                 1991.

[Takeda 90]   Takeda, K.
                 Bi-Directional Grammars for Machine Translation.
                 In *Proceedings of Seoul International Conference on Natural Language Processing.*
                     1990.

[Tanaka 89]   Tanaka, H., S. Ishizaki, A. Uehara, & H. Uchida.
                 Research and Development of Cooperation Project on a Machine Translation System
                     for Japan and Its Neighboring Countries.
                 In *Proceedings of Machine Translation Summit II.* 1989.

[Tanaka 91]   Tanaka, H. & T. Aizawa.
                 A Method for Translation of English Delexical Verb-Deverbal Noun Phrases into
                     Japanese.
                 Natural Language SIG Reports of the IPSJ , March 15, 1991.
                 (in Japanese).

[Toma 76]   Toma, P.
                  An Operational Machine Translation System.
                  In R. W. Brislin (editor), *Translation: Applications and Research*, pages 247-259.
                      Gardner, New York, 1976.

[Tomabechi 90]   Tomabechi, H.
                  Symbolic and Subsymbolic Massive-Parallelism for Speech-to-Speech Translation:
                      Hybrid Time-Delay, Recurrent, and Constraint Propagation Connectionist
                      Architecture.
                  In *Proceedings of an International Conference Organized by the IPSJ to
                      Commemorate the 30th Anniversary.* 1990.

[Tsuji 90]   Tsuji, Y.
                  Multi-Language Translation System at Using Interlingua for Asian Languages.
                  In *Proceedings of an International Conference Organized by the IPSJ to
                      Commemorate the 30th Anniversary.* 1990.

[Uchida 89a]   Uchida, H.
                  ATLAS.
                  In *Proceedings of Machine Translation Summit II*, pages 152-157. 1989.

[Uchida 89b]   Uchida, H.
                  Interlingua: Necessity of Interlingua for Multilingual Translation.
                  In M. Nagao, H. Tanaka, T. Makino, H. Nomura, H. Uchida, & S. Ishizaki (editors),
                      Proceedings of Machine Translation Summit I. Ohmsha, Tokyo, 1989.

[Uemura 86]   Uemura, S.
                  On Early Japanese Research Activities on Mechanical Translation.
                  ETL Bulletin 50(7):78-89, 1986.
                  (in Japanese).

[Valigra 91]   Valigra, L.
                  Japan Shows Progress in Machine Translation.
                  The Institute (news supplement to IEEE Spectrum) , May/June, 1991.

[Vasconcellos 91] Vasconcellos, M. and D. A. Bostad.
                  MT in a High-Volume Translation Environment.
                  In J. Newton (editor), *Computers in Translation: A Practical Appraisal.* Routledge,
                      London, 1991.
                  (In press).

[Vauquois 84]   Vauquois, B.
                  Automated Translation at GETA.
                  Technical Report, Grenoble: GETA, 1984.

[Wang 90]   Wang, Q., X. Wang, Y. Huang, & H. Yasuhara.
                  The Generation of Chinese Text from the Case Relations.
                  Natural Language SIG Reports of the IPSJ , November, 22, 1990.
                  (in Japanese).

[Weaver 55]   Weaver, W.
                  Translation.
                  In W. N. Locke and A. D. Booth (editors), *Machine Translation of Languages.* MIT
                      Press, Cambridge, Mass., 1955.
                  Originally published in 1949 and later reprinted in this collection.

[Wilks 91]   Wilks, Y.
                  SYSTRAN: It Obviously Works, but How Much Can it be Improved?.
                  Technical Report, Memorandum in Computer and Cognitive Science, MCCS-91-215.
                      Computing Research Laboratory, New Mexico State University, Las Cruces, N.M.,
                      1991.

[Yamauchi 88]   Yamauchi, S.
                 Ricoh English-Japanese Machine Translation System RMT/EJ.
                 BIT , September, 1988.
                 (in Japanese).

[Yokoi 91]   Yokoi, T.
                 Collaboration and Cooperation for Development of Electronic Dictionaries - Case of the
                     EDR Electronic Dictionary Project.
                 In *Proceedings of the International Workship on Electronic Dictionaries.* Japan
                     Electronic Dictionary Research Institute TR-031, 1991.

[Zhu 89]   Zhu, M, & H. Uchida.
                 Chinese Dictionary for Multilingual Machine Translation.
                 Natural Language SIG Reports of the IPSJ , March 18, 1989.
                 (in Japanese).

Appendix I: Japanese Sites in Part III Report

We list here all of the major Japanese sites that are mentioned in this report. There is a standard form for each entry. The name of the institution is given first, followed by the name(s) of the major MT system(s) that have been developed there. Notice that sometimes the name of the system is just the name of the company that developed it. Not all of the sites that we mention have developed a system, so the list will be empty for them. For sites that are not developers or that are unusual in some other way, there is an additional comment field that explains the site's role in this report. Most of the sites on this list were visited by one or more panel members. There are, however, a few sites that were not visited but that are mentioned in this report. Asterisks appear at the end of the entry line for those sites.

Advanced Telecommunications Research Institute International (ATR)

SL-TRANS, NADINE

Bravice International

MICROPAK

The panel has been told that Bravice went out of business in the first quarter of 1991.

Canon

LAMB   ****

Catena-resource Institute

STAR, The Translator (Macintosh version of STAR)

CBU

HANTRAN   ****

Center of the International Cooperation for Computerization (CICC)

      CICC

CSK

      ARGO

Digital Equipment Corporation (DEC), Japan

The panel looked at DEC only as a user of MT systems.

Electronic Dictionary Research Institute (EDR)

Not doing any MT development but they are producing a dictionary that is intended to support MT.

Electro Technical Laboratory (ETL)

      CONTRAST   ****

Fuji Electric

We visited Fuji to see their OCR system.

Fujitsu

      ATLAS-I, ATLAS-II

Hitachi   HICATS

IBM Japan, Ltd.

      SHALT, SHALT2, JETS

International Business Service (IBS)

IBS is a translation service bureau that uses some MT systems.

Institution for New Generation Computer Technology (ICOT)

ICOT is doing work in general NL processing but has no active MT project.

Inter Group

Inter Group uses MT systems.

Japan Electronics Industry Development Association (JEIDA)

The Japan Electronic Industry Development Association has an active committee on MT. Its members are drawn from companies, academia, and government organizations.

Japan Information Center of Science and Technology (JICST)

JICST

Kyoto University

Research on several MT and NLP projects, including a major contribution to the MU system.

Matsushita Electric Industrial Company

PAROLE

Ministry of International Trade and Industry (MITI)

The Japanese Ministry of Trade and Industry has shown a great deal of interest in MT.

Mitsubishi

      MELTRAN   ****

NEC

      PIVOT

Nippon Hoso Kyokai (NHK)

NHK uses the Catena STAR system.

Nippon Telegraph and Telephone (NTT)

      ALT-J/E

Oki Electric

      PENSEE

Ricoh

      RMT

Sanyo Electric

      SWP-7800 Translation Word Processor

Sharp

      DUET

Systran

SYSTRAN

Toshiba

ASTRANSAC

Appendix II: Biographies of Panel Members

Jaime Carbonell

Jaime G. Carbonell is Professor of Computer Science and Director of the Center for Machine Translation at Carnegie-Mellon University. He received his B.S. degrees in Physics and in Mathematics from MIT in 1975, and his M.S. and Ph.D. degrees in Computer Science from Yale University in 1976 and 1979, respectively. Dr. Carbonell has authored some 140 technical papers, and has edited or authored several books, including *Machine Learning: An Artificial Intelligence Approach*, volumes 1 and 2, and *Machine Learning: Paradigms and Methods and Knowledge-Based Machine Translation*. He is executive editor of the international journal, *Machine Learning*, and serves on several editorial boards, including that of *Artifical Intelligence*. He has also served as chair of SIGART (1983-1985), the special interest group on A.I. of the ACM, served on several government advisory committees, including that of the NIH human genome project, and is a founder and director of Carnegie Group, Inc.

Dr. Carbonell's research interests span several areas of artificial intelligence, including: machine learning, natural language processing, planning and problem-solving, knowledge-based machine translation, analogical reasoning, knowledge representation, and very large knowledge bases. In particular, Dr. Carbonell leads the PRODIGY project, an integrated architecture for planning and learning in complex domains, and also leads a multilingual high-accuracy machine translation research project.

David E. Johnson

David E. Johnson is a research scientist in the Theoretical and Computational Linguistics group, Mathematical Sciences department, IBM T. J. Watson Research Center, Yorktown Heights, New York. He received his Ph.D. in linguistics from the University of Illinois (Champaign-Urbana) in 1974 and has taught linguistics at the University of Illinois and at Yale University. His numerous publications include two books on linguistic theory: *Toward a Theory of Relationally-Based Grammar* (Garland Publishing: 1979) and *Arc Pair Grammar* (Princeton University Press: 1980) [with Paul M. Postal].

Dr. Johnson has had extensive experience in natural language processing. From 1974 to 1978 and again from 1982 to 1987, he was involved in the development of IBM's prototype natural-language database query system, TQA, whose leading-edge linguistic processing technology contributed significantly to IBM's product LanguageAccess. From 1987 to 1989, he was a staff manager in the Japanese Processing group at the IBM Japan Tokyo Research Laboratory, where he designed and oversaw the development of the English generator used in the JETS Japanese-English machine translation system, and participated in the development of the transfer component.

Elaine Rich

Elaine Rich is Director of the Artificial Intelligence Lab in MCC's Advanced Computing Technology (ACT) Program, where she has been responsible for the development of a knowledge-based natural language processing system. This work is now being used as the basis of an interlingual MT system. She was an assistant professor of computer sciences at the University of Texas at Austin prior to joining MCC.

Dr. Rich received an A.B. in linguistics and applied mathematics from Brown University in 1972 and a Ph.D. in computer science from Carnegie-Mellon University in 1979. She has published extensively, including the best-selling textbook *Artificial Intelligence* (McGraw-Hill: 1983, 1991).   She also has extensive experience as a consultant to several major corporations in the areas of AI.

Dr. Rich is a Fellow of the American Association for Artificial Intelligence.   She serves on advisory committees for such government organizations as the National Science Foundation and the Office of Technology Assessment.   She is Editor of *AI Magazine*, and serves on the editorial boards of several other AI journals.

Masaru Tomita

Masaru Tomita is an Associate Professor in the Computer Science Department at Carnegie Mellon University, where he is also the Associate Director of the Center for Machine Translation.

He holds a Ph.D. and a Master's Degree in Computer Science from Carnegie Mellon University (1985 and 1983, respectively) and a Bachelor's Degree in Mathematics from Kelo University (Yokohama, Japan, 1981.)   During 1984, he was a Visiting Scientist in the Electrical Engineering Department at Kyoto University (Kyoto, Japan).

Dr. Tomita's research interests are in the area of natural language processing, including machine translation, parsing, natural language interfaces, computational linguistics and speech recognition.   He has published three books, and authored or co-authored over 40 reference papers.   In 1988 he received a Presidential Young Investigators Award from the National Science Foundation.   He is an editorial board member of two international journals: *Computational Linguistics* and *Machine Translation*.

Muriel Vasconcellos

Muriel Vasconcellos has been professionally involved in translation, with focus on machine translation, for 27 years.   As chief of the translation program at the Pan American Health Organization, a UN-family agency, she has directed the development and practical implementation of MT since 1977.

Dr. Vasconcellos' studies have been in linguistics, in which she holds the Bachelor's (1958), Master's (1982), and Ph.D. (1985) degrees from Georgetown University.   Her graduate specialization was in theoretical linguistics, and her thesis was on translation theory.   For 11 years she lectured on translation at Georgetown, where she taught a course on machine translation (1980-1988) and was co-presenter of intensive workshops on MT in 1985 and 1987.

Dr. Vasconcellos has more than 50 articles on machine translation and translation theory to her credit, as well as the book *Technology as Translation Strategy* (SUNY Press: 1988), and she serves on the editorial boards of several journals, including *Machine Translation*.

She has been active in professional translator associations throughout her career.   She is currently president of the Association for Machine Translation in the Americas and secretary of the International Association for Machine Translation.

Yorick Wilks

Yorick Wilks is Director of the Computing Research Laboratory at New Mexico State University, a center for research in artificial intelligence and its applications. He received his doctorate from Cambridge University in 1968 for work on computer programs that understand written English in terms of a theory later called "preference semantics": the claim that language is to be understood by means of a search for semantic "gists," combined with a coherence function over such structures that minimizes effort in the analyser.

This has continued as the focus of his work, and has had applications in the areas of machine translation, the use of English as a "front end" for users of databases, and the computation of belief structures. He was a researcher at Stanford AI Laboratory, and then Professor of Computer Science and Linguistics at the University of Essex in England before coming to New Mexico. He has published numerous articles and five books in the area of artificial intelligence, of which the most recent is *Artificial Believers* (Lawrence Erlbaum Associates: 1991) [with Afzal Ballim].

Dr. Wilks is also a Fellow of the American Association for Artificial Intelligence, on advisory committees for the National Science Foundation, and on the boards of some fifteen AI-related journals.

Appendix III: Abbreviations Used in Part III

ATN	Augmented Transition Network
ATR	Advanced Telecommunications Research Institute International
CICC	Center of the International Cooperation for Computerization
DARPA	Defense Advanced Research Projects Agency (in the U.S.)
DEC	Digital Equipment Corporation
DS	Dependency Structure
EBMT	Example-Based Machine Translation
EC	European Community
EDR	Electronic Dictionary Research Institute
ETL	Electro Technical Laboratory
GPSG	Generalized Phrase Structure Grammar
HPSG	Head-driven Phrase Structure Grammar
HT	Human Translation
IBS	International Business Service
ICOT	Institution for New Generation Computer Technology
JEIDA	Japan Electronics Industry Development Association
JICST	Japan Information Center of Science and Technology
JPSG	Japanese Phrase Structure Grammar, a Japanese version of the English HPSG
JTEC	Japanese Technology Evaluation Center
LFG	Lexical Functional Grammar
MAT	Machine Aided Translation
MITI	Ministry of International Trade and Industry (in Japan)
MT	Machine Translation
NHK	Nippon Hoso Kyokai
NL	Natural Language
NLP	Natural Language Processing
NP	Noun Phrase
NTT	Nippon Telegraph and Telephone
OCR	Optical Character Recognition
PP	Prepositional Phrase
PS	Phrase Structure
S	Sentence
SL	Source Language
TDMT	Transfer-Driven Machine Translation
TL	Target Language
VP	Verb Phrase

Part IV

Advanced Computing
in Japan

M.A. Harrison, Chairman
E.F. Hayes
J.D. Meindl
J.H. Morris
D.P. Siewiorek
R.M. White

The information in Part IV was originally prepared in 1990, and certain portions are now out-of-date. However, it is included in this book as it provides substantial background information.

1. Executive Summary

Michael A. Harrison

To assess Japanese technology in advanced computing, the Panel began by dividing the subject into six basic areas. Detailed outlines of the areas were prepared and the Panel obtained a baseline of U.S. accomplishments in these areas through reading literature, attending conferences, visiting laboratories, and discussion with specialists.

The Panel visited Japan for one week. During this period, visits were made to five university sites, sixteen industrial sites, one consulting company, and nine government laboratories. Wherever possible, we tried to send at least two people to a given site. Our hosts were gracious, forthcoming, and even eager to show us the results of their efforts. We have prepared detailed reports on selected areas of specialization which form the main chapters of this report. Chapter 2 contains a summary of these evaluations, often in tabular form, which assesses where the U.S. and Japan stand in the selected areas.

The Technical Bottom Line

A one table summary of the U.S. and Japan positions in advanced computing is shown in Table 1.1.

A number of additional conclusions are presented below.

- Japan has made a significant long term commitment to information technology in all its aspects from research through commercialization.

This commitment extends back over thirty-five years and has been announced publicly in many places. In [1], Professor Moto-oka wrote:

> "Suffering from a shortage of land and natural resources, it is impossible for Japan to be fully self-sufficient in food, and her ability to supply her own

Area	Position[a]	Rate of Change[b]
Electronic Components	+	↑
Data Storage	○	↑
Computer Architecture	−	↗
Software	−	→
Scientific Calculations & Supercomputers	○	↗
Computer/Human Interface	−	↘
Multimedia	+	↗

Table 1.1: The Overall Comparison.

[a]This denotes position. A plus (minus) means that Japan is ahead (behind) the U. S.
[b]This represents the rate of change. A ↑ means Japan is pulling away from the U. S., while → means that the relative position is not changing.

energy and oil needs is the lowest among the developed countries. On the other hand, we do have one precious asset, that is, a highly educated, diligent and top quality labor force, our human resources. It is desirable to utilize this advantage to cultivate information itself as a new resource comparable to food and energy, and information – related knowledge – intensive industries should strongly be promoted to make possible the processing and management of information at will.

Such an effect would not only serve to help our country meet international competition, but would also enable us to make international contributions through knowledge–intensive technology."

To implement these goals, Japan has had a variety of national programs over this extended period of time. Industrial strategies have been coordinated, and even as this report was being prepared, MITI has introduced yet another multi-year plan devoted to achieving excellence in information technology [2].

- Success in information technology requires strong industries in all the allied technologies.

Advanced computing technology cannot be built without advanced semiconductors, chip-making technology, data storage devices, etc. Japan, both at the government and industrial level, has strongly supported these allied industries.

- The success of Japan in the computer industries has led to significant market share. The profits from this market share have been plowed back into R&D spending to a remarkable extent. In addition, Japanese capital expenditures remain high.

While our summaries show that Japan is ahead in some areas of advanced computing, these results do not yet show the effect of additional recent research and development as well as capital expenditures. The supporting data on R&D spending and on capital expenditures needed to maintain the short-term marketshare are provided in the next chapter. Thus the Japanese competitive position should remain strong over the next five years. The competitive position of the U.S. with respect to Japan during this period will depend, in part, on whether the U.S. is willing to match this rate of investment.

- Japan has been and remains relatively weak in software, but effective in software engineering.

There is a serious shortage of talented software people who can be hired to work in the large high technology Japanese companies. Part of this stems from the financial community which offers higher salaries, so the best young people choose careers there. Some of this loss of personnel is mitigated by the effective software factories whose employees have a lower educational level than the graduates from the major universities. However, there is nothing in Japan yet to compare to the strong community of creative and talented software people in the United States.

- Japanese universities remain substantially weaker than their American counterparts.

This is due to the lack of large projects in the universities of the type supported by DARPA in the United States. Japanese students graduate from the universities with a good conceptual education. The companies then provide continuing education programs which train them in design, production, etc. The comparable mechanism in the United States is much less intensive and effective because of employee mobility.

- A key theme in Japan is internationalization.

Japanese companies are using the profits from their success in consumer electronics and other information industries to establish themselves in the United States and elsewhere. Specific companies are establishing their own research and development laboratories, product development laboratories, manufacturing facilities, as well as sales and distribution centers in the United States. Within a period of ten years, there will undoubtedly be technologies conceived in these research laboratories and converted to products at local development labs. These products will then be manufactured and sold in the United States. This strategy appears to be mutually beneficial and will integrate the interests of both countries to a substantial extent. While profits may flow abroad, there will be new domestic jobs created, new technologies imported, and different management techniques demonstrated.

2. Computing in Japan

Michael A. Harrison

2.1 Organization

There has been a succession of studies on Japanese high technology in general and on the computer field in particular. One of the first was the National Research Council (NRC) report [3] in 1982 which pointed out the need for closer monitoring of the foreign literature and activities. A second phase of that study took place in which a large panel covered both microelectronics and computer science mainly in Japan and Western Europe. Although a final report of that study was not formally released, the principal findings were included in the first JTECH study [4]. These evaluations led to more specialization in the evaluation process, and the JTEC sequence of panels was established as shown in Table 2.1.

The current study began as an attempt to survey the "outer envelope" of advanced computing in Japan. The Panel members were chosen to cover key areas such as electronics components, data storage and recording, architecture, software, and scientific computing. At the kick-off meeting on July 11, 1989 at the National Science Foundation, the areas to be covered were discussed. It was decided to add an additional application area consisting of multimedia as well as computer and human interaction. This area was chosen as an important application which brings together a number of key technologies.

A detailed outline was produced for each area indicating its scope. Each panelist was asked to begin investigating his assigned area to determine the state of art in that subject. As a consequence of these investigations, which involved extensive consultations with fellow researchers, a list of designated Japanese establishments and individuals was assembled. Dr. Alan Engel of International Science and Technology Associates used this list to schedule visits for the Panel. During a one-week stay in Japan, the Panel visited five university laboratories, and sixteen industrial laboratories, one consulting company,

Topic	Chairman	Year
Computer Science	David Brandin	1984
Mechatronics	James Nevins	1985
Opto- and Microelectronics	Harry Wieder	1985
Telecommunications	George Turin	1986
Advanced Computing	Marvin Denicoff	1987
ERATO	William Brinkman	1988
CAD/CIM for Semiconductors	William Holton	1988
Sensors	Laurie Miller	1988
High Definition TV Systems	Dick Elkins	1990

Table 2.1: JTEC panels related to computing.

and nine government sponsored institutes or laboratories. The Panel's itinerary appears in Appendix A on page 165.

After returning to the U. S., a presentation of our findings was given at the National Science Foundation on December 8, 1989. The comments of the attendees at both meetings mentioned here were influential in drafting the final report.

2.2   Preview of the Report

The first JTECH study [4] started the tradition of using tables to explain which group was ahead in a given technology. While such tables and simple summaries destroy information and are no substitute for the reasoned analysis in the individual chapters, we will use them as a very concise summary.

The notation used in the tables given in this chapter is based on that used in [4]. The entries represent the absolute Japanese position with respect to the U.S. position as well as the rate of change of that position. The notation of Table 2.2 will be used.

Electronic Components

Turning to electronic components, we present the data in a tabular form. Since Japan is so strong in this area, Table 2.3 indicates the number of years in which Japan is ahead in various areas. A minus sign indicates the U. S. is ahead as described in Table 2.2. A few comments and other points are in order.

- In DRAM's, U.S. merchant vendors lag behind their Japanese competitors by 3-4 years and are losing ground.

Key

Absolute position vs. U.S.		Rate of change	
>	Far ahead	↑	Pulling away
+	Ahead	↗	
○	Even	→	Holding position
−	Behind	↘	
<	Far behind	↓	Slipping quickly

Table 2.2: Explanation of the notation.

Device	Gap
SRAM's:	≈ +2 years (high density)[a]
DRAM's:	≈ +3 years
NVRAM's:	≈ 0 years
Gate Arrays:	≈ +1, 2 years(high density)
Microprocessors:	≈ −2 years or more
Gallium Arsenide:	≈ +2 years
Packaging:	No U. S. presence
Infrastructure	Eroding[b]

Table 2.3: Electronic components summary.

[a]The symbol ≈ stands for "approximately equal to".
[b]Position of the U.S. Semiconductor Equipment Manufacturers as evaluated by the National Advisory Committee on Semiconductors [5].

Magnetic Recording

	Position	Rate of Change
Heads	−	↗
Media	−	↗
Head to Disk Interface	○	→
System	−	↗

Optical Recording

Optical Media	+	↗
Lasers	+	↗

Table 2.4: Data storage summary.

- In gate arrays (or ASIC's), U.S. merchant vendors lag behind their Japanese competitors by 1-2 years and are losing ground.

- In microprocessors, U.S. merchant vendors are ahead of their Japanese competitors by 2-3 years and appear to be holding this lead in a stable position.

- In packaging, captive U.S. suppliers such as IBM appear to be ahead or at least even with their Japanese competitors. However, the merchant market is dominated by a single Japanese supplier, Kyocera. Consequently, estimating a U.S. merchant position is hardly an issue.

A qualifying note regarding Table 2.3 is that the interval between an R&D announcement and commercial production typically has been smaller for U.S. companies than for their Japanese counterparts. This tends to exaggerate the gap between the U.S. and Japanese positions to some degree.

Data Storage

Turning to the data storage area, Table 2.4 shows the comparative status of the two countries.

Most of the Japanese industrial research appears to be focused on near-to-medium term issues. There is an enormous amount of exploratory work on alloys for thin film media, tribology, magnetoresistive sensors, etc. In the U.S. these efforts appear to be more fragmented. The U.S. does support more adventurous research, however. Examples include the holographic storage at MCC and attempts to exploit high resolution scanning microscopy. In Japan, NEC and Hitachi continues to pursue the Bloch line memory, which has revolutionary potential.

An interesting indication of the scientific vitality in the U.S. is the development of the technique known as SEMPA, which stands for Scanning Electron Microscopy with spin Polarization Analysis. Electron Microscopy provides one with sub micron resolution. Yet, except for Hitachi, there are no SEMPA instruments in the companies visited. However, except for IBM, no U.S. companies possess this capability either. But it does exist at four American universities.

There are very few universities in Japan that offer training in the field of recording. When asked about how their technologists are trained, most said that it is done "on the job" by the company. The American graduate research university is an engine with enormous potential. It is certainly not being effectively utilized to support the U.S. recording industry.

Another observation is the fact that all the Japanese companies that offer storage devices are (1) vertically integrated, and (2) have substantial research efforts (50 to 100 people) that encompass all the options.

One of the aspects of vertical integration was the ability of each company to prototype systems in order to evaluate the components. In the U. S. we have excellent university research efforts in magnetic modeling, tribology, encoding, thin films, etc. as well as venture-capital-funded component sources. But there is no mechanism for integrating these technologies into real systems. IBM is the only organization with this capability. This observation would suggest that the U.S. recording industry consider complimenting one of its university recording centers with the capability to prototype complete systems. This might be done in conjunction with an advanced manufacturing engineering program, which some universities are beginning to consider.

In comparison to Japan, only a few U.S. system companies are vertically integrated in recording. Vertical integration also has the potential of being more efficient. U.S. component suppliers, for example, complain of being misled by drive manufacturers who "multiple-order". If one has access to a strong vendor base then one can compete with vertical integration. However, the U. S. component suppliers are neither numerous nor healthy.

Related to vertical integration is the fact that most of the Japanese companies are also active in the consumer market. In the past, new technology was introduced into high-end products and then "trickled down" to consumer products. Today this paradigm is reversed. We often see the most advanced technology in consumer products first. The 8mm video and the R-DAT technologies are examples of consumer technologies that could have a major impact on digital systems.

To summarize, the U.S. recording industry will find it increasingly difficult to compete in the next one, and certainly two, generations of products. The failure to make significant

R&D investment now will mean less familiarity with the technology later, increasing the likelihood of design errors. Unless U.S. companies take a longer term view and improve their utilization of the university research community, the Japanese will eventually dominate data storage devices. The existing university recording efforts, in order to survive will be tempted to admit Japanese sponsors who have demonstrated that they are effective at transferring technology. The result will be that the research community will receive strong, long term support, the consumer will receive high performance storage, but the U.S. will have lost another high technology industry segment.

Computer Architecture

From its inception, computer architecture has been an experimental science. Systems have to be built and analyzed in order to further develop new theory. Over the past three decades a taxonomy of computer architecture has been evolving. If American and Japanese architectural projects are plotted on this taxonomy versus time several observations can be made.

First, the Japanese are experimenting with a vast number of computer architectures. Second, while the root of each subtree of the taxonomy was formed by an American architecture, the gap between the root of a subtree and the first Japanese project has narrowed from over a decade (i.e., from the American Illiac IV in the mid-1960s to the Japanese PAX in 1977) to less than a year (i.e., hardware simulation engines). Third, while the number of advanced architectural projects is roughly equivalent in the United States and Japan, the sheer volume of Japanese projects initiated since 1980 is very impressive.

The United States is generally ahead of the Japanese in computer architecture. However, the Japanese are strong and growing stronger in: hardware, prototyping, vector processing and pipeline design, dedicated hardware simulation architectures, multimedia workstations, and technology transfer between research and products.

Much of the advantage Japan has in hardware prototyping derives from a different notion of critical mass than the U.S. In the case of a mainframe data processor manufacturer, there were approximately 200 to 300 mainframes and 600 minicomputers supported by approximately 600 people to design, develop, and maintain this broad range of products. Compare these numbers to a typical U.S. start-up company with approximately 200 people but serving only a single product. The variety of products versus the number installed appears to be large. In other words, Japanese critical mass to undertake a project is considerably smaller than US projects.

Smaller critical mass indicates that the Japanese can produce a large variety of hardware products. A visit to a random consumer electronics store revealed an entire floor displaying over 300 models of personal computer of which over 100 were portables with LCD displays. The TRON project has already produced three implementations of the TRON chip [6]. The Fifth Generation project has developed two generations of PSI (Personal Inference Engine) and two generations of parallel processors (Multi-PSI and PIM). If computing moves from a mass production to a specialized product marketplace, Japan's ability to rapidly prototype with a small critical mass will be a distinct advantage.

The Japanese are very prolific experimenters. Can the rate of experimentation be maintained and what gain can be derived from duplication of effort? Two possible scenarios come to mind.

Convergence. The NTT mainframes are comparable to IBM mainframes. The packaging, semiconductor chips, cooling, and power distribution are all based on each manufacturer's technologies. Only a small number of custom chips had to be designed. NTT is currently working with other companies to unify the application interface while still maintaining each unique operating system. One can speculate that future integration and sharing between companies, perhaps around CTRON, could reduce duplication further freeing up resources to focus on higher level applications.

Integration. By having diverse groups intimately involved with the process of computer design, these groups will be in a better position to produce innovative systems in their area of expertise (such as computers and communications in the case of NTT).

Software

Traditionally, Japan has been weak in software, with the single exception of software engineering. A recent ADAPSO study projects sharp growth in the Japanese software industry by the year 2000; e.g. from \$6.893B in 1990 to \$33.123B in 2000 and points out that this is a major opportunity for U.S. industry. Japan alone cannot supply the demand.

While Japan has improved significantly in certain software areas like graphics, logic programming and AI applications, so have the rest of the international communities. A number of organizations, e.g. SIGMA follow the latest international software trends. Large Japanese companies are purchasing off-shore companies or individual pieces of software technology.

There are many problems in software for the Japanese including their preference for customized applications, a manpower shortage because of the loss of software engineers to the financial industry, and the lack of big software projects at the universities which prevent them from becoming a training ground.

Research management, particularly in software, is not easy. Japan appears to lack this skill in software and we have seen examples of companies carefully studying U.S. performance in this area, even hiring foreign consultants, and then repeating the same mistakes made in the U.S.

Thus, software remains a significant U.S. strength as Table 2.5 shows.

	Position
Programming Languages	−
Operating Systems	−
Artificial Intelligence	−
Data Bases	−
Software Engineering	+

Table 2.5: Software.

	Position	Rate of Change
CSCW[a]	−	↓
Hypertext	−	↓
Electronic Books	−	↘
Multimedia		
Components	+	↗
Workstations	◯	↗
MM Mail	−	↘
User Interfaces	−	↘

Table 2.6: Multimedia and human interfaces.

[a]Computer Supported Collaborative Work.

The lead of Japan in Software engineering is ironic. There is better research on Software Engineering in the U.S. but the Japanese apply the (U.S.) methods in a more disciplined fashion and achieve impressive results [7, 8].

Multimedia, Computer and Human Interfaces

In the area of computer and human interfaces, the U. S. is significantly ahead although there are signs that the Japanese are beginning to concentrate efforts here.

In multimedia systems, the Japanese are ahead in hardware technology because of their significant consumer electronics industry the U. S. is far ahead in software applications. Table 2.6 shows our current rankings.

Supercomputers

Table 2.7 records the Panel's impressions of Japanese supercomputers.

	Position	Rate of Change
Hardware	○	↗
Architecture	−	↗
Systems Software	−	↗
Monitoring tools	+	−
Vectorization	○	?

Table 2.7: Supercomputing.

The number of Japanese researchers in most areas of computational science and engineering is smaller than in the U.S. by a considerable margin. However, the numbers are growing in each of the fields surveyed as part of this study.

For the next five years the U.S. will continue to have more researchers in the main areas comprising supercomputers and scientific calculations. In the past, these larger numbers of researchers have stimulated more creative computational approaches to solving significant research problems. Thus, if we assume that U.S. researchers will continue to have access to adequate amounts of state-of-the-art supercomputers, it seems likely that the leadership the U.S. has provided in developing new approaches, algorithms and software will continue.

In terms of access to significant amounts of needed resources (e.g., megaflops, fast IO, graphics and visualization workstations) the situation over the next few years may actually favor Japanese researchers. Most knowledgeable investigators recognize that the Hitachi S-820/80 is, for most applications, the fastest single processor supercomputer. However the multi- processor capabilities of the CRAY Y-MP can provide better overall throughput and achieve better parallel computing speed for some applications [9]. Issues such as the number of supercomputers in use and their accessibility may be of more importance than which single machine is fastest.

Based on the quality of the results being published in the literature during the past year, none of the Japanese or U.S. supercomputers seem to have a decisive lead. In the future the situation may shift. The NEC SX-3 is projected to have a maximum speed of 22 GF, while the Cray-3 and the Cray C-90 are projected at about 16 GF. Thus, as we look ahead to the next releases of supercomputers and their projected capabilities there is a possibility the Japanese machines will make somewhat greater strides relative to the projected U.S. machines, but for scientific and engineering applications the most important issues are likely to continue to be ease of use and the amount of resources that can be allocated to a significant problem.

While we had very little actual "hands-on" experience with Japanese software, what follows appears to be true.

- The software products available on the Japanese supercomputers are as good or better than those available from Cray Research, but there are not so many of them.

- The monitoring tools provided by the Japanese vendors that are available to the scientific applications programmers appear to be as good or better than those available from Cray research.

- Applications software being developed by Japanese researchers may be better vectorized as a result of the better tools and vendor supplied software.

- Japanese supercomputer centers seem to be having little if any difficulty obtaining access to the best U.S. developed applications software.

Here are some general observations:

- The U.S. appears to be preeminent in all basic research areas of computational science and engineering.

- The Japanese are making significant strides as the current generation of researchers matures in their use of supercomputers and a younger generation is trained in computational science and engineering.

- There is a debate in the U.S. community about the future of high performance machines for scientific computing. The traditional users prefer machines such as those from Cray Research while others see advantages in the "killer micros" which are typically high performance, multiprocessor workstations, which run UNIX and which offer nice graphics for visualization. Without taking sides, we note that almost all of the U.S. manufacturers have a strong commitment to UNIX. It is estimated that the U.S. has at least a two year lead over Japan in this aspect of supercomputer software. As of this writing, Fujitsu's UTS (UNIX Timesharing System) presently runs on their M-680 but not the VP2600. The SX-UX for the NEC is not due until late 1991.

Technical Summary

Table 1.1 is a concise statement of our conclusions and provides data for both optimists and pessimists about the U.S. position. Japan is ahead in the basic building blocks like chips and components. We have not studied more specialized hardware in this report like flat panel and liquid crystal displays, lasers etc. in which Japan excels. If one compares revenues for manufacturers of electronics, etc. with the software areas where the U.S. is predominant, there is no comparison. The revenue is in producing chips and "iron", not software. Japan will continue to have both marketshare and profits which in turn fund

R&D. The Japanese have shown the willingness to invest in future R&D in microelectronics and computing.

On the other side, the U.S. investment in R&D for advanced computing is unimpressive. With a focus on "Big Science", with NSF's budget not increasing as projected, and with uncertainty clouding the future of DARPA, industry is left with an increasing responsibility for funding computer-related R&D. IBM has taken a leadership position in trying to form cooperative ventures, but some collaborative ventures such as U.S. Memories, Sematech, and MCC have not lived up to expectations. The U.S. Federal High Performance Computing Initiative could make a difference.

Therefore, we see Japan's position in advanced computing hardware becoming dominant unless new initiatives are undertaken.

2.3   Science and Technology

The basic structure of science and technology in Japan is well known [4, 10] and the key components, the elementary and high schools, the universities, industry, and government are all important. In Japan, the elementary and secondary school system produces good graduates, but other countries such as Korea and the United Kingdom do even better [11]. The Japanese universities have been traditionally weaker than their U. S. counterparts, but the situation seems to have improved over the past decade. Japan's government has played a consistently supportive role in science and technology. This includes government projects for funding new areas of research, minimizing the harassing effects of litigation, encouragement of exports, etc. Cf. [10, 12] for background. An example of this governmental support can been seen in Table 2.8 which displays some Japanese national projects in information technology. It does not include the latest MITI plan [2].

Japanese industry is the dominant force in computing. The large vertically intergrated companies are very competitive with each other and with foreign companies. The companies fund research and development generously. Table 2.9 shows the data for the top ten Japanese electronics companies. Table 2.10 shows the corresponding U.S. industrial R&D spending [13].

Certain points should be emphasized:

- The top 10 Japanese electronics companies invest as much in R&D as the top 100 U. S. companies combined.

- The U.S. government supports 47% of American R&D while Japan supports only 22% of its R&D [11, 14].

- NEC's R&D expenditures alone are roughly one third more than the total NSF

	Title	Period	Budget in Millions of Dollars
(1)	Very High-Performance Computer Systems	1966–1971	71
(2)	Pattern Information Processing Systems (PIPS)	1971–1980	156
(3)	VLSI Technology	1976–1979	213
(4)	Basic Technology for Next Generation Computer Systems (Fourth Generation Computer Systems)	1979–1986	156
(5)	Optical Measurement and Control Systems (Optoelectronics Application Systems)	1979–1985	128
(6)	Basic Industrial Technology for the Next Generation	1981–1990	714
(7)	Very High-Speed Scientific Computing Systems (Supercomputers)	1982–1989	164
(8)	Fifth Generation Computer Systems (FGCS)	1982–1991	714
(9)	Robotics for Work in Extreme Conditions (JUPITER)	1984–1990	142
(10)	Software Industrialized Generator and Aids (SIGMA)	1985–1989	178
(11)	Interoperable Database Systems	1985–1992	142

Table 2.8: Major R&D projects for future information technology.

Company	Percent of Revenue	R&D Spending in Millions ($)	Growth (over FY87)
NEC	16%	3,685	+12%
Fujitsu	10%	1,871	+30%
Sony	7%	1,076	+10%
Hitachi	6%	2,830	+13%
Matsushita	6%	2,418	+14%
Toshiba	6%	1,745	+6%
Sharp	6%	519	+13%
Canon	6%	496	+15%
Ricoh	6%	352	+10%
Omron	6%	171	+10%
Total	—	15,163	+14%

Table 2.9: Top Japanese R&D spenders.

Company	Percentage of Revenue	R&D Spending in Millions ($)	Growth (over FY87)
Digital Equipment	11%	1,307	+29%
IBM	10%	5,925	+9%
AT&T	10%	3,500	0%
Hewlett Packard	10%	1,019	+13%
Control Data	9%	336	−14%
Motorola	8%	665	+27%
Texas Instruments	8%	494	+15%
Xerox	7%	794	+10%
Unisys	7%	713	+19%
NCR	7%	416	+17%
Total	—	$15,169	+13%

Table 2.10: Top U.S. R&D spenders.

budget[1].

- NEC spent about two thirds as much on R&D as IBM although NEC is about 40% of the size of IBM

- Growth rates have slowed in both R&D funding and production of scientists and engineers in the U.S. with NSF reporting a 1% growth rate for the development and applied research component of R&D from 1986 to 1989 [11].

- The capital expenditures of the top 10 spending Japanese companies is about the same as the top 100 capital spenders in the U.S.

- The effect of the additional Japanese capital expenditures and R&D investments have not yet been felt. If the U.S. expenditures are not increased, the Japanese position will strengthen.

These numbers come from Japanese company reports for FY88 [13]. Since the dollar/yen ratio fluctuated during this period, the Japanese companies all used the same exchange rate of 132 yen to the dollar. There are 152 yen to the dollar as this is written (June 1990).

The situation with capital expenditures is also of interest [15]. The pattern here is for even more aggressive spending by Japanese companies. In one case, Ricoh invested 146% of its net cash flow in new plants in the U. S., Europe, and Japan. Tables 2.11 and 2.12 tell the story in more detail [13].

Statistical arguments about the relative strength of the two economies require careful analysis as [16] explains clearly. For example, in 1987, R&D spending (in billions of dollars of purchasing power) would indicate that the U. S. spent 2.6 as much as Japan ($121.3 to $46.1). But most of the U. S. spending was not in the commercial sector while most of Japan's spending was.

The gross national product per worker in 1988 was about the same in Japan as in the U.S. Japan's overall productivity is lowered by its performance in the service industries and agriculture. There has been a long term (40 years) decline in U.S. productivity. The Japanese rate of growth in productivity is twice that of the U.S. [16]. Readers interested in another perspective on productivity are referred to [17].

Productivity in science itself is often measured in terms of papers produced, presented, and/or published [18]. Another frequently used measure of creativity is the number of patents applied for, granted, etc. According to [11], the U.S. share of the world scientific and technical articles in engineering and technology dropped 10% from 1981 to 1986. The Japanese scientific position, measured by papers produced, has been rising 0.5% per year.

---

[1]The fact that NSF is supporting education and research in a broader range of sciences such as astronomy, earth sciences, etc. makes the comparison even more striking.

Company	Total in Millions ($)	Growth (over FY87)	Percentage of revenue	Cap. Exp. to net cash flow
Hitachi	$3,901	+38%	8%	99%
Matsushita	2,465	+42%	6%	81%
NEC	2,165	+14%	9%	128%
Fujitsu	2,157	+49%	12%	131%
Toshiba	2,027	+26%	7%	92%
Sony	1,633	+61%	10%	115%
Mitsubishi	1,587	+46%	8%	103%
Canon	629	+31%	8%	94%
Sharp	612	+46%	7%	93%
Ricoh	509	+75%	9%	146%
Total	17,685	+38%		

Table 2.11: Top Japanese capital expenditures for 1988.

Company	Total in Millions ($)	Growth (over FY87)	Percent of revenue	Cap. Exp. to net cash flow
IBM	5,390	+25%	9%	71%
Digital Equipment	1,518	+103%	13%	83%
Xerox	1,399	+49%	9%	168%
Motorola	873	+33%	11%	97%
Unisys	670	−7%	7%	60%
Hewlett–Packard	648	+28%	7%	58%
Texas Instruments	628	+36%	10%	94%
GM Hughes	533	+14%	5%	56%
Intel	478	+58%	17%	72%
NCR	420	+8%	7%	66%
Total	$12,557	+32%		

Table 2.12: Top U.S. capital spenders.

Category	NTT	AT&T
Technical employees in R&D	6,200	24,000
Total employees in R&D	7,100	29,000
R&D expenditures–FY '88	$1.454B	$3.5B
Total revenues–FY'88	$45.297B	$36.1B
Patent applications in 1988	3,500	
Patents issued in 1988		1,257
Papers presented domestically 1988	260	
Papers accepted in foreign Soc. & Journals	270	
Papers released for publication		3200

Table 2.13: Comparison between NTT and AT&T.

Between 1970 and 1983, the annual number of U.S. patents granted to U.S. inventors went from 46,000 to 34,000, but rose in 1988 to 45,000. However, the fraction awarded to foreigners of all successful patent applications rose from 30% in 1970 to 48.5% in 1987. Japanese inventors were most active in increasing the number of U.S. patents. Their awards increased from 11,000 in 1983 to 19,000 in 1988 [11]. By 1984, Japanese inventors obtained more U.S. patents than inventors in the United Kingdom, France, and West Germany combined, with the gap widening since then. It is concluded in [18] that Japan is a technological powerhouse, while its scientific position is improving but is far less potent.

To get a better grip on technical productivity in advanced computing technologies, we have attempted to compare NTT and AT&T. Unfortunately, the data categories do not match precisely. Table 2.13 provides such data as we have. The reason for the large difference in the number of employees at NTT and AT&T is that NTT does not have a manufacturing division. Moreover AT&T is in the computer business while NTT is not, although this may be changing.

2.4   Advice for Future Panels

It is impossible to do justice to such a large topic such as "advanced computing" with a Panel of this size in one week, no matter how talented and well prepared the Panel is. The length of the stay for panels should be extended to two weeks when the scope of the study is very large and adequate on-site support should be provided. Pre-trip orientation for those not already familiar with Japan would be desirable.

In the three panels on which this writer has served, there has been some sort of general computerized search of the Japanese literature. This has generally been of marginal utility.

It might be more helpful to have a translator available and some mechanism for obtaining specific papers requested by panelists.

By and large, the suggestions made in [4] for panel operations are still valid.

2.5   Acknowledgements

Many individuals besides the Panelists contributed to our study and report. We received a great deal of help from various individuals in the United States in doing our baseline studies of the various disciplines. We especially want to thank Mr. Mark Eaton of MCC for sharing his personal knowledge and providing information from his data base. We had tremendous support from the JTEC staff, ably directed by Dr. Duane Shelton and also including Dr. George Gamota, Dr. Allen Engel and Ms. Kaori Niida of ISTA, and Mr. Geoffrey Holdridge.

Planning our visits to Japan was greatly assisted by the help of many of our friends there. The Panel is especially appreciative of the efforts of Professor M. Nagao of Kyoto University, Professor Hideo Aiso of Keio University, Mr. K. Kishida of SRA, Dr. Nori Suzuki of IBM Tokyo Research Lab, Dr. H. Hirokoshi of Hitachi, Dr. Iwao Toda of NTT, Mr. M. Kato, Mr. S. Sato of Fujitsu, Dr. M. Sujimoto of Fujitsu, Mr. M. Mitsugi of Fujitsu, Dr. H. Mizuno of MEI, Dr. S. Miki of MEI, Mr. K. Nishitani of MEI, Mr. S. Moriyama of MEI, and Mr. Charles Wallace of NSF Japan.

Dr. Iwao Toda, Dr. Kenji Naemura of NTT and Mr. Umino of NTT America provided a great deal of valuable information as well as statistical summaries of certain research activities. At AT&T, we had the support of Mr. Alan T. English of Bell Laboratories. Ms Heidi Hijikata of the Department of Commerce provided additional insights into the TRON issues.

The Panel benefited from reviews of the preliminary draft of the report. Major reviews were done by Dr. Alfred V. Aho of Bell Telephone Laboratories, Mr. Mark Eaton of MCC and Mr. George Lindamood of the Gartner Group. The following people were also very helpful: Mr. Masaharu Araki of NTT, Mr. Noboru Akima of the Information Technology Promotion Agency, Professor Eiichi Goto of the University of Tokyo, Mr. Masako Komir-jama of Hitachi, Dr. Raul Mendez of the Institute for Supercomputing Research, Professor Ken Sakamura of the University of Tokyo, and Mr. Shigeru Sato of Fujitsu.

The preparation of this report was greatly assisted by the efforts of Mr. Michael van de Vanter who provided a great deal of background information on multimedia and human interfaces. Mr. Ethan Munson was kind enough to help with a number of computer issues including solving various problems having to do with bibliographic data bases. Both he and Michael van de Vanter had to deal with the thorny problems of incompatible data formats. Professor James Demmel of the University of California at Berkeley provided detailed information about certain supercomputers. Ms Toni Gritz had the opportunity to learn LaTeX while doing much of the typesetting of this report. Her patience, perseverance, and good humor and good humor were much appreciated.

3. Electronic Components, Chips and Packaging

James D. Meindl

3.1 Introduction

A new world is dawning in our lives. Its emergence is the single most important event of the 20th century. This genuinely new way of life is the information society [19].

More than any other artifacts, advanced computers epitomize the information society because they represent the most powerful tools yet devised by man. The principal driving force of advanced computers has been their electronic components and, more specifically, the astounding semiconductor integrated circuit or microchip. In 1958 the year of its invention, the microchip contained only a single transistor or electronic switch. Today, a typical microchip consists of a rectangle of semiconductor silicon, about half the dimensions of a dime, containing a complete functional circuit including more than one million transistors fabricated in-situ along with a multilevel network of interconnecting wires. The price of a modern microchip ranges from several dollars to several hundred dollars. This price range has remained rather constant since 1960 despite a doubling of the number of transistors per chip every 12 to 18 months over the same period. The number of transistors per microchip is conservatively projected to reach one billion by the year 2000! Cf. [20, 21]. Today, the principal types of integrated circuits used in advanced computers can be broadly categorized as:

1. silicon memory chips and

2. silicon logic and microprocessor chips. In addition,

3. gallium arsenide memory and logic chips are emerging as complements/competitors to silicon, and

4. chip packaging technology has become co-equal with semiconductor chip technology per se in determining the performance limits of advanced computers.

The U.S. was the undisputed world leader in semiconductor microchip research and development until 1980. Since that time Japan has surpassed the U.S. in most subcategories of semiconductor R&D and the gap between U.S. and Japanese capabilities and expenditures is widening. This chapter provides an assessment of the comparative status of semiconductor and packaging R&D in the U.S. and Japan on the basis of an analysis of current open literature and a limited set of visits in November 1989 to leading Japanese industrial laboratories. In this chapter "R&D" refers predominantly to applied research and new product development conducted in industry and only peripherally to basic research conducted in universities.

3.2   Discussion

This discussion is divided into four segments:

1. Silicon (Si) memory chips, [22, 23, 24, 25]

2. Si logic and microprocessor chips,

3. Gallium arsenide (GaAs) chips, and

4. chip packaging.

In each segment the comparative status of U.S. and Japanese R&D is evaluated.

3.2.1   Silicon Memory Chips

Typically, an advanced computer includes a multilevel hierarchical memory system consisting of three principal levels:

1. cache memory, the smallest capacity, highest speed and most expensive (per bit) level of memory usually implemented with static random access memory (SRAM) chips,

2. main memory, usually implemented with dynamic random access memory (DRAM) chips which offer larger capacity, lower speed and less cost (per bit) than SRAM chips,

3. bulk storage which is implemented with rotating magnetic, and more recently optical, disks which offer still larger capacity, lower speed or access time and less cost (per bit) than DRAM chips. In addition, many computers use reels of magnetic tape for off-line archival memory whose capacity is practically unlimited.

A key difference between SRAM and DRAM semiconductor memory chips and magnetic disk memories is that the former are volatile (i.e., the information stored in memory is lost if electrical power is terminated) while the latter are not. Consequently, one of the key thrusts of current semiconductor research is to enhance the properties of non-volatile random access memory (NVRAM) chips which themselves are further subdivided into categories depending largely on the erasure capabilities of a chip.

The dominant feature of semiconductor memory R&D over the past 15 years is that the number of bits stored in a single chip has increased by four times every three years. This rate is likely to continue until the mid–to–late 1990's at which time it is projected (by the author) to decline but still remain appreciable at about two times every three years.

Static Random Access Memory

Although SRAM chips are usually limited to use in smaller capacity cache memories in advanced computers, top–of–the–line supercomputers have used SRAM chips for the entire main memory as a result of their speed advantage over DRAM's. The current status of U.S. and Japanese SRAM R&D is reflected in Table 3.1. The first 1 Mb SRAM's were announced by Sony, Hitachi, Mitsubishi and Toshiba in 1987 all using CMOS technology. (CMOS technology involves the use of both N-channel, i.e., negative carrier, and P-channel, i.e., positive carrier , or Complementary Metal–Oxide–Semiconductor field effect transistors.)

In 1988 IBM and Phillips announced 1 Mb CMOS SRAM's along with Mitsubishi, Hitachi and Fujitsu. In 1989, Texas Instruments and Toshiba announced 1 Mb SRAM's using a more advanced technology BiCMOS which adds a vertical NPN Bipolar Transistor (BT) to CMOS technology and Sony announced the first 4 Mb SRAM chip. Preliminary information indicates that NEC, Toshiba, Hitachi and Mitsubishi will announce 4 Mb CMOS SRAM's in 1990 while Motorola will announce a 256 Kb CMOS SRAM [26] and Micron Technology, a 1 Mb CMOS SRAM.

The foregoing results suggest the U.S. merchant semiconductor[1] industry is roughly two–to–three years behind Japan in high density (i.e., relatively large numbers of bits/chip) SRAM R&D. This gap is projected to increase in the future due especially to superior Japanese manufacturing capabilities which result in relatively large yields and, therefore, low cost in high density chips.

The market for SRAM chips whose bit density is at the forefront of commercial products in volume production tends to be limited to a rather small number of organizations

---

[1]The term *merchant* is used to exclude the captive manufacturers like AT&T and IBM.

Name	Year[a]	Add. Acc.[b]	Min.[c]	Chip[d]	Cell[e]	I/O[f]	Power[g]	Package	Technology[h]
U.S.									
IBM, Burl.	1988	29	0.7	8.48×10.6	58.2	TTL	25	28pin, SOJ	CMOS, 5V(3.3V), 2/1/1, 6T
T.I.	1989	8	0.8	8.5×14.1	5.2×14.6	ECL	7	28pin, 600mil, DIP	BiCMOS, -4.5V, 1/0/2, 4T
Japan									
Sony, Kanag.	1987	35	1.0	8.0×13.65	6.4×11.6	TTL	10, 25	32pin, 600mil, DIP	CMOS, 2/0/2, 4T
Hitachi, Tokyo	1987	42	0.8	5.64×14	5.2×8.6		20, 10	32pin, 600mil, DIP	CMOS, 1/2/1, 4T
Mitsubishi, Ita.	1987	34	0.8	5.52×14.78	8.0×5.5		200, 10	32pin, 600mil, DIP	CMOS, 2/1/1, 4T
Toshiba, Kanag.	1987	25	0.8	6.86×15.37	5.6×9.5		20, 10	32pin, 600mil, DIP	CMOS, 1/1/2, 4T
Hitachi, Tokyo	1988	15	0.8	6.15×15.21	5.2×8.5		12.5, 7, 0	28pin, 400mil, SOJ	CMOS, 2/0/2
Fujitsu, Kawas.	1988	18	0.7	7.5×12	4.8×8.5		11.7,10, 000	28pin, 400mil, DIP	CMOS, 2/1/2, 4T
Mitsubishi	1988	14	0.7	5.51×15.7	8.0×5.2		12.5,100, 00		
*Sony, Kanag.	1989	25	0.5	7.46×17.41	3.6×5.87	TTL	10.8, 230		*CMOS, 1/1/2, 4T
Hitachi, Tokyo	1989	9	0.5	5.3×10.3	3.5×6.0	TTL	9.1,75, 000		CMOS,3/0/2, 6T, polyPMOST
Toshiba, Kawas.	1989	8	0.8	6.5×16.5	5.6×8.9	ECL	10,		BiCMOS, 2/0/2, 4T
Europe									
Phillips, Eindhoven	1988	25	0.8	7.7×12.1	5.0×12.0	TTL	7.5,		CMOS, 0/1/2, 6T

Table 3.1: 1&4* Mb SRAM R&D announcements.

[a]Year of Announcement
[b]Add. Access Time [nanosec]
[c]Minimum Feature Size [microns]
[d]Chip Size [mm]
[e]Chip Area [microns]
[f]I/O Interface
[g]Power Drain Active, Standby mw/MHz, microwatts
[h]Technology type, supply voltage, interconnection layers, cell type

(e.g. 1 Mb × 1 or 256 Kb × 4) and pin-outs. In contrast, the market for high performance SRAM's of lower bit density (e.g. 1 Kb, 4 Kb, 16 Kb & 64 Kb) is highly fragmented. U.S. "R&D" for these chips is conducted most successfully in smaller companies such as Performance Semiconductor Corporation, Cypress, Micron Technology and IDT, where cutting edge performance and not large volume manufacturing capability is the key ingredient for success.

Sony, a relative newcomer to the merchant semiconductor market, was the first corporation to announce a 4 Mb SRAM.

Dynamic Random Access Memory

A SRAM cell which stores one bit of information usually requires four N-channel MOS transistors (NMOST's) and two very high value polycrystalline silicon resistors or two P-channel MOS transistors (PMOST's) for a total of 6 devices per cell. These two alternatives for the cell are often referred to as the "4T" and "6T" cells where T signifies Transistor. If power is not interrupted, an SRAM chip retains a stored bit pattern indefinitely without refreshing it. In contrast, a DRAM cell consists of two devices, a storage capacitor which is either charged or discharged and a co-located MOST switch which serves to connect or disconnect the capacitor from the peripheral address/read/write circuits surrounding the array of memory cells. Because the storage capacitor is not perfectly isolated from its environment, its charge tends to leak continuously. Therefore, unless the bit pattern of a DRAM is periodically refreshed, via peripheral circuits, the stored information eventually will be lost. This need for refresh is the origin of the term Dynamic in DRAM. Because DRAM cells require only two devices and SRAM cells require six, DRAM chips of a given generation store four times the number of bits (or are four times more dense) than their SRAM counterparts. This larger density of DRAM's leads to lower cost per bit which in turn causes DRAM's to be the main memory of choice in all but the most expensive computers. Consequently, the largest volume semiconductor products are DRAM's both in terms of unit shipments and dollars.

The current status of U.S. and Japanese DRAM R&D is reflected in Table 3.2. The first 4 Mb DRAM's were announced by NEC, Toshiba and Texas Instruments in 1986 with the T.I. design substantially slower in access time (performance). In 1987, Mitsubishi, Hitachi & Oki, as well as IBM announced 4 Mb DRAM's while NTT announced a 16 Mb DRAM about two years ahead of an "expected" announcement for this chip. In 1988 Matsushita, Toshiba & Hitachi announced 16 Mb DRAM's and Siemens announced a 4 Mb chip. Most recently in 1989 Mitsubishi, Toshiba and NEC announced 16 Mb DRAM's without any corresponding announcements from U.S. or European companies. Preliminary information indicates that IBM will announce a 16Mb CMOS DRAM in 1990 [26] and that Micron Technology will announce a commercially available 4 Mb CMOS DRAM.

The foregoing observations suggest that the U.S. merchant semiconductor industry is

Company	Year[a]	Time[b]	Size[c]	Size[d]	Area[e]	I/O Interface	Power[f]/	Package	Technology Type, cell, supply voltage, interconn.
U.S.									
T.I.	1986	170	1.0	9.8×10.2	2.6×3.4	TTL	500, 40		CMOS,Trench C&T,1/0/2
IBM	1987	65	0.8-0.9	78-87 [mm]²	11-12.5 [micrn]²		365,6.6		CMOS,Trench, 3.3V,1/0/2
Japan									
NEC	1986	95	0.8	6.2×16.0	2.3×4.6		425,15	18pin,350mil,DIP	NMOS,0/2/1
Toshiba	1986	80	1.0	7.84×17.48	3.0×5.8		300, 2.5	400mil ceramic, DIP	CMOS,2/1/1
Mitsubishi	1987	90	0.8	4.85×14.91	4.2×2.6		300, 2.5	300mil, DIP	CMOS,1/2/1
Hitachi	1987	65	0.8	6.38×17.38	2.2×6.7		225, 0.5		CMOS,1/0/2
Oki	1987	65	1.0	8.75×17.07	2.88×5.85		325, 5	32pin,600mil,DIP	CMOS,BSC, 3/0/1
Matsushita	1987	60	0.8	4.54×17.78	1.74×4.6	TTL	250,3.0	300mil,DIP	CMOS,2/1/1
Fujitsu	1987	70	0.7	4.84×13.16	7.5 micrn²	TTL	200,4.5	300mil,18 pin, DIP	CMOS,3/1/1,stacked cell
Toshiba	1987	60	0.9	6.9×16.11	2.5×5.5	TTL	250,1.0		CMOS,2/1/1,trench
*NTT	1987	80	0.7	8.9×16.6	1.5×3.25	TTL	500,		CMOS,3.3V, 1/1/2
*Matsushita	1988	65	0.5	5.4×17.38	1.5×2.2		450, 5	20pin,300mil, DIP	CMOS,5V(4V,3V), 2/1/2
*Toshiba	1988	70	0.7	12×17.5	1.7×3.6		600,		CMOS,5V(4V), 3/1/2
*Hitachi	1988	60	0.6	8.2×17.3	1.3×3.2		420, 15		CMOS,5V(3.3V), -/-/2
*Mitsubishi	1989	60	0.5	7.7×17.5	1.5×3.2		300, 0.66	400mil, SOJ	CMOS,3.3V, -/-/2,BIST
*Toshiba	1989	45	0.6	7.87×17.4	1.6×3.0		325, 2.5		CMOS,5V(4V), 3/0/2
*NEC	1989	55	0.55	8.2×15.9	1.5×2.7		400, 10		CMOS,5V(3.3V),2/0/2,BIST
Europe									
Siemens	1988	60	0.9	6.5×14.05	2.3×4.6		350, 5	SOJ 26/20, 350mil	CMOS, 2/1/1

Table 3.2: 4&16* Mb DRAM R&D announcements.

[a]Year announced.
[b]Access time in nanoseconds
[c]minimum feature size in microns
[d]Chip size in mm.
[e]Cell area in microns.
[f]Power drain: Active, Standby [mw]

more than three years behind Japan in DRAM R&D. Compared with U.S. captive suppliers of semiconductor chips (i.e., IBM), the Japanese position clearly is less advanced. For example, IBM is known to be producing 4 Mb DRAM's in volume using 8 inch wafers while current Japanese production apparently is still limited to 6 inch diameter Si wafers. With a larger number of chips per wafer at larger wafer diameters, lower cost per chip is anticipated. Since Japanese companies have captured more than 80% of the world market for DRAM's, the urgency of increased market share for U.S. merchant companies is clear.

One notable fact is that the first 16 Mb DRAM announcement came from NTT in 1987, a corporation with perhaps the most powerful electronics research capability in Japan but without a role in volume production. No U.S. corporation has yet announced a 16 Mb DRAM; six Japanese companies have done so. The most probable future course for American corporations to afford access to world-class DRAM technology is cooperation with foreign partners. The market for DRAM's is so massive that these products are not just the principal drivers of semiconductor technology. Rather, DRAM's tend to dominate the entire development–manufacturing–profit– investment cycle of the worldwide semiconductor industry. DRAMS are also the proving grounds for design and production technologies that are subsequently used in other circuits, e.g. microprocessors, ASICs, etc.

Nonvolatile Random Access Memory

The original nonvolatile semiconductor memory was called a Read Only Memory (ROM). In essence, a ROM consists of an array of transistors surrounded by peripheral addressing/sensing circuits. By convention, if a one transistor cell is electrically connected to its X-Y address lines, the cell is said to store a binary "1" if the cell is not connected it is said to store a "0". The operation of connecting or not connecting all cells in an array is executed during the later stages of manufacturing of a wafer/chip by customing the design of a contact mask to allow or not allow a specific pattern of electrical connections. Thus, such ROM's are often referred to as "mask programmable". Once a bit pattern has been programmed into the chip during manufacture, it cannot be altered or "erased" thereafter.

The two distinct disadvantages of not being able to program a ROM except during manufacture and of total inability to erase a ROM led to a brilliant invention in the early 1970's, the electrically programmable read only memory or EPROM. The salient feature of an EPROM cell is that its single MOS transistor includes a "floating" gate positioned between the normal control gate and the source–to–drain channel in the Si substrate. A cell in an array is programmed electrically by applying terminal voltages to generate "hot" or high energy electrons flowing in the channel to pass through the insulator separating the channel and floating gate and then to reside on the floating gate to turn off the transistor and store a "0", whereas storing a "1" merely entails omitting application of appropriate terminal voltages and, therefore, not generating hot electrons. Moreover, a cell can be "erased" by exposing it to ultraviolet (UV) radiation through a quartz window in the package of the chip. The UV radiation simply accelerates enormously via photoemission the rate of leakage of charge from the floating gate. EPROM's currently comprise the largest class of NVRAM's. They are extensively used as "firmware" to implement the control programs of embedded micro and minicomputers.

The major disadvantage of an EPROM is that the chip usually cannot be erased in situ, that is, while it is actually in place within its natural operating environment. Rather, it must be removed and inserted into special hardware for exposure to UV radiation under appropriate conditions to erase and then re-program. Secondarily, the number of erase/program cycles which can be imposed on a given chip is limited typically to 100–1000 cycles, the "endurance" of the EPROM cell. To overcome the major disadvantage of UV EPROM's, the Electrically Erasable Programmable Read only memory (EEPROM) was invented. As the name implies, this chip can be electrically programmed (typically by generation of cool electrons which tunnel from the MOST drain to the floating gate). An individual EEPROM cell can be electrically erased by reversing the tunneling process. The use of cool tunneling electrons for both programming and erase typically increases the endurance of an EEPROM cell to 10^4 to 10^5 cycles. Although EEPROM's can be electrically programmed and erased on a cell–by–cell basis, essentially a cell consists of three transistors. A "normal" MOS transistor is used for reading, a second normal MOS transistor for programming and erasure, and a third floating gate MOS transistor for storage. Consequently, the density and cost of EEPROM's suffer in comparison to EPROM's. Nevertheless, in applications where a high degree of flexibility for reprogramming is important, EEPROM's offer significant advantages. In particular, the use of EEPROM's in combination with analog circuits and sensors to perform electronic "trimming" functions under microprocessor control opens a myriad of applications.

To respond to the density and cost shortcomings of EEPROM's, the flash EEPROM (or FEEPROM) was invented. In essence, it combines the fast programming via hot electrons that is characteristic of the EPROM with erasure via cool tunneling electrons that is characteristic of the EEPROM. Moreover, the FEEPROM uses only a single transistor per cell so that its density is nearly equal to that of the EPROM. This transistor is a "super-integrated" device essentially incorporating a control gate for reading and programming, an erase gate and a floating gate for storage in a single MOS transistor. In comparison to the EEPROM, the comparative disadvantage of the FEEPROM is that electrical erasure of cells must take place in large blocks, which is often no penalty at all. This block or simultaneous erasure feature is the origin of the term "flash". The high density and potential low cost of FEEPROM's open a vast new range of potential applications, perhaps even exceeding the size of the market for DRAM's. In particular, FEEPROM's are strong candidates to replace rotating magnetic disk storage systems initially in low end applications such as lap top computers.

The current status of U.S. and Japanese NVRAM R&D is reflected in Table 3.3. The cited announcements are selected in order to be representative yet brief. The overall picture

Company	Year	Type	Density	Access[a]	Prog.[b]	Erase[c]	Min.[d]	Chip[e]	Cell[f]	Technology[g]
U.S.										
T.I.	1987	EPROM	1Mb	150	2,000		1.5	7.31×7.31	3.67×3.67	CMOS, 2/0/1, 12.5V,
Seeq	1987	EEPROM	256Kb	150	100				4.5×12.0	CMOS, 2/0/1, 17V, 10^6
Intel	1988	EPROM	4Mb	90	10		1.0	9.5×8.78	3.4×3.5	CMOS, 1/1/1M, 12.5V,
Intel	1988	FEEPROM	256Kb	110	100	200	1.5	4.87×4.87	6×6	CMOS 1/1/1M, 12V, 10^4
Seeq	1989	FEEPROM	1Mb	120			1.5	6.2×8.2	5.6×4.4	CMOS, 2/0/1,
Intel	1989	FEEPROM	1Mb	90	10	900	1.0	6.23×6.23	3.8×4.0	CMOS, 1/1/1, 10^5
Japan										
Toshiba	1987	EPROM	4Mb	120	10		0.9	5.86×14.92	3.1×2.9	CMOS, 2/0/1, 10.5V,
Hitachi	1988	EPROM	1Mb	55	25		1.3	6.12×6.98	4.3×4.3	CMOS, 1/1/1,12.5V,
Toshiba	1989	ROM	16Mb	120		1.0		7.10×16.55	2.16×1.44	CMOS, 1/0/1
Toshiba	1989	FEEPROM	4Mb	1600		8	1.0	10.7×15.3	3.6×3.6	CMOS,3/0/1,5V(17V),10^4, "NAND" cell
Mitsubishi	1989	EEPROM	1Mb	120		1.0		7.73×11.83	3.8×8	CMOS, 2/1/2,
Europe										
SGS-Thomson	1988	EPROM	1Mb	70	50		1.0	7.2×6.35	4.3×4.4	CMOS, 1/1/1, 12.5V

Table 3.3: NVRAM R&D announcements.

[a] Access Time in ns.
[b] Prog. Time microns/B
[c] Erase time in ms.
[d] Minimum Feature Size in microns.
[e] Chip Size in mm.
[f] Cell Area in mm.
[g] Technology Type, interconnection layers, prog. voltage, endurance

can be interpreted as follows.

- Japan is several years ahead of the U.S. in high density ROM R&D as suggested by the Toshiba 1989 16 Mb ROM which apparently has no comparable U.S. "response." However, the importance of (masked) ROM's is diminishing.

- The U.S. appears to be about one year behind Japan in high density EPROM's as reflected by the Toshiba 1987 and Intel 1988 4 Mb EPROM's. In addition, preliminary information indicates that NEC will announce the first 16Mb EPROM in 1990.

- The U.S. appears to be about even with Japan in FEEPROM's as suggested by the 1989 Seeq & Intel 1 Mb as well as the Toshiba 4 Mb FEEPROM announcements. This is an area where process, device and circuit innovations are perhaps less straightforward than in SRAM's or DRAM's.

- Japanese companies appear to be ahead in high density EEPROM's. Interest in this chip has waned in the U.S., if not worldwide, during the past several years due to the success of FEEPROM's. However, a definite niche exists for EEPROM's which is being pursued by smaller U.S. companies.

Overall, in NVRAM R&D announcements, U.S. semiconductor merchant companies are apparently "closer" to Japanese corporations than in SRAM and DRAM announcements. A Japanese lead of less than one year is estimated.

3.2.2   Silicon Logic and Microprocessor Chips

The most powerful semiconductor technology "drivers" are memory chips. The massive revenues generated by these chips can support the substantial R&D and the staggering manufacturing investments needed for each new generation of technology. Once a technology becomes available a variety of additional categories of microchips can be economically implemented. Currently, these categories include microprocessors and coprocessors, semi-custom gate arrays, data communications and telecommunications integrated circuits, digital video and image signal processing circuits, A/D and D/A converters and analog micro circuits. In the following discussion, only semi-custom gate array and microprocessor R&D announcements are addressed since these categories, following memory chips, are the most indicative of the impact of semiconductor technology on advanced computing [22]. The trend over the past decade or so has been to use bipolar transistor gate arrays to implement the CPU chips for high end or mainframe computers and MOS transistor single chip microprocessors to implement the CPU of a personal computer or workstation.

Semi-Custom Gate Arrays

The majority of Application Specific Integrated Circuits (ASIC's) are implemented with semi–custom gate arrays (GA's). Cf. [22, 23, 24, 25, 27]. Basically a gate array consists of a cell typically including six–to–eight transistors arranged in a geometric pattern which allows them to be interconnected or wired in virtually any desired circuit configuration. A very common configuration for the transistors within a particular cell is a so-called gate circuit which performs one of several elementary logic functions which are the "atomistic" building blocks of all computers. A chip merely consists of a large matrix of such cells or gates and hence the term gate array. In the manufacture of a gate array, a wafer of chips/cells is processed to the stage that all transistors are finished but no interconnection metal or wiring is yet in place. The wafer is placed in inventory until an order is received for a particular configuration of gates. Then, the wafer is removed from inventory and its manufacture is completed by adding the specific multilevel wiring pattern needed for the ordered configuration of gates. The predominant advantage of this semi–custom approach, for example, is that often only the final 10–25% or about four of the 12–20 masks needed for manufacturing a particular chip are specific to it. All other (earlier) masks are common to all wafers produced with a given manufacturing process. Consequently, both cost and response time can be drastically reduced to great advantage in producing a logic circuit via a semi–custom gate array.

Historically, the seminal gate array R&D was conducted by IBM in the late 1970's. Today, Si gate arrays fall into two distinct classes. The first class consists of cells whose transistors are both N–channel and P–channel or complementary MOS field effect transistors (FET's) as previously mentioned in the discussion of SRAM's; these are CMOS gate arrays. The second class consists of cells including NPN bipolar transistors and resistors usually configured in the fastest form of (non–saturating) bipolar digital circuits or Emitter Coupled Logic (ECL). In general, ECL circuits are faster than CMOS chiefly because the larger transconductances (i.e., the ratio of output current change to input voltage change) of bipolar transistors (BT's) permit them to charge and discharge wiring capacitances more rapidly than MOSFET's.

The current status of U.S. and Japanese gate array R&D is reflected in Table 3.4. NTT in 1989 was the first company to announce a large BiCMOS array consisting of 20,000 gates in a sea–of–gates (SOG) configuration which fills the entire chip (exclusive of bonding pad areas) with gates without reserving area specifically for wiring channels. Also, in 1989 both Hitachi and Mitsubishi announced CMOS gate arrays including approximately 1.5 million transistors; and both Fujitsu and Mitsubishi announced BT ECL gate arrays including about 200,000 transistors and resistors. Perhaps the leading U.S. merchant supplier of CMOS gate arrays has been LSI Logic Inc. which announced a 940,000 transistor CMOS SOG array in 1989 following a 400,000 transistor CMOS SOG array announcement in 1988. In addition, preliminary information indicates that in 1990 Fujitsu will announce a 200,000

Company	Years[a]	Number[b]	Number[c]	Feature[d]	Chip[e]	Gate[f]	Number[g]	Technology
U.S.								
LSI Logic	1988	50	400	1.5, 3.75	15×15	0.40		CMOS, 1/0/2, SOG
IBM	1988	20	110	0.5, 1.0	7.5×7.5	0.20		CMOS, 0/1/2, SOG
LSI Logic	1989	235	940	1.0, 2.5	15×15	0.25	200/512	CMOS, 1/0/2, SOG
Japan								
Hitachi	1988	65	630	1.0,1.9	13×13	0.80(L)	264/	CMOS,1/0/3,SOG
NTT	1989	20	235	0.8	8.36×12.22	0.45(L)		BiCMOS, SOG
Hitachi	1989	130/38	1400	0.8,1.3	14.5×14.5	0.35	400/	CMOS,1/0/3
Mitsubishi	1989	200	1600	0.8,1.2		0.16		CMOS,1/0/2, SOG
Fujitsu	1989	50	144	0.35,1.0	7.8×8.2	0.04	180/	ECL,1/1/3
Mitsubishi	1989	12/36	209	0.60,1.5	14.5×13.0	0.11	272/	ECL,0/1/2
Europe								
Thomson-Mostek	1988	60	640	1.2,	13.4×13.4	0.30	320/	CMOS,1/0/2,SOG

Table 3.4: Gate array R&D announcements.

[a]Years of Announcements
[b]Number of Gates/Bits × 1000
[c]Number of Transistors × 1000
[d]Feature Size [microns]
[e]Chip Size [mm]
[f]Gate Delay [ns]
[g]Number of Pins/Pads

gate BiCMOS SOG array.

As reflected in Table 3.4, Japanese merchant vendors of high density gate arrays are more numerous than their U.S. counterparts and offer larger arrays with smaller minimum feature sizes thereby providing the means for superior performance. These advantages in gate arrays for semi–custom chips are derived directly from the superior Japanese position in standard (DRAM & SRAM) memory chips. As in the case of memory chips, Japanese companies again lead their U.S. merchant competitors in the timing of R&D announcements regarding gate arrays although the lead time is smaller (i.e., 1–2 years) for gate arrays. An important distinction between memory and gate array chips arises in their specific application. Use of a powerful set of software design tools is an integral part of the application of a gate array chip but rarely of a memory chip. Leadership of U.S. companies in this software helps to reduce the gap between American and Japanese applications of gate arrays. In "field programmable" gate arrays which combine gate arrays and EPROM technology, U.S. "start-up" companies currently are ahead.

Microprocessors

The combination of ever increasing storage capacity for memory chips and computing capability for microprocessor chips, [22, 23, 24, 25] and [28, 29, 30, 31, 32, 33], has been responsible for the birth and revolutionary progress of the personal computer. Essentially, a microprocessor embodies most of, and sometimes all of, the central processor unit (CPU) of a computer within a single silicon chip. Competing microprocessors commonly have drastically different architectures, which is rarely if ever the case for competing memory chips. For example, software designed for an Intel microprocessor is totally incompatible with (i.e., it will not run on) a Motorola microprocessor. In contrast, a 1 Mb DRAM from Texas Instruments usually can be expected to be a pin-for-pin replacement for a competing Hitachi or Toshiba part.

The original microprocessor was a 4–bit design announced by Intel in 1971 which became widely available as the 4004 in 1972. An abbreviated summary of the growth in complexity of Intel microprocessors from 1971 through 1989 is given in Table 3.5. CF. [28, 29].

Currently, the two most widely used microprocessor families are referred to as "complex instruction-set computers" (CISC's). They are:

1. the Intel 80x86 series of chips used in MS-DOS PC's marketed by IBM, Compaq and others, and

2. the Motorola 680x0 series of chips used in Apple Macintosh PC's.

The TRON microprocessor is the first Japanese CPU chip to become generally visible, although the Toshiba T88000 chip was used in that company's commercial UNIX workstations as early as 1983. Preliminary information [30] indicates that Toshiba will announce

Year	Chip	Number of Transistors
1971	4004	2,300
1974	8080	5,000
1978	8086	20,000
1982	80286	130,000
1985	80386	275,000
1989	80486	1,200,000

Table 3.5: Intel Microprocessor trend.

a 32-bit, 1.2 million transistor, 33 Million–Instructions–Per–Second (MIPS) TRON VLSI RISC chip in 1990. The TRON project is quite ambitious as reflected by formation of the TRON Association including more than 100 major Japanese corporations. Chapter 8 contains more information on this chip and the TRON project.

Although CISC's have dominated the computer world since the 1950's, a new architecture, the reduced instruction–set computer (RISC) has taken hold so strongly in recent years that nearly every major computer manufacturer is planning new products around this technology [31]. In essence, a RISC architecture significantly reduces the number of instructions built into the hardware of a computer by as much as a factor of 10. The prototype RISC machine, the 801 built by IBM in 1975 demonstrated RISC viability. MIPS Computer Systems with the R3000 chip and Sun Microsystems with the SPARC chip are among the most prominent new ventures which have strongly committed to RISC's. Among the larger computer companies, Hewlett-Packard with its Precision Architecture, DEC with its 3100 and 5000 series of workstations, and IBM with its RS/6000 series have announced major RISC products. Both Intel and Motorola also have powerful RISC processors in the 860 and 88000 respectively.

Two representative groups of microprocessor R&D announcements during 1987 and 1989 are summarized in Table 3.6. As suggested by Table 3.6, U.S. companies have been more aggressive than their Japanese competitors in pioneering successful new microprocessor architectures. In addition, preliminary information indicates this situation will continue during 1990 with the announcements by Hewlett Packard of a 90MHz CMOS RISC CPU and by MIPS Computer Systems of an 85 MHz ECL RISC CPU with two-level cache memory control [34]. Overall, it appears that U.S. companies are ahead of their Japanese competitors by at least two–to–three years in microprocessor R&D announcements. This situation contrasts strongly with the status of memory chip announcements (and sales) where Japanese companies predominate as reflected in Tables 3.1 and 3.2. Another interesting point of comparison between Tables 3.1 and 3.2 on one hand and Table 3.6 on the

Company	Year	Description	Number[a]	Clock[b]	Feature[c]	Chip[d]	Power[e]	Pads[f]	Technology
U.S.									
DEC	1989	50MIPS(Peak)32/64b RISC Microprocessor	294	50	1.5	14.5×9.5	9.0	224/	CMOS,0/1/2
DEC	1989	32 bit CPU(Cache controller, FPA, Clock Generator)	320 (650)	35	1.5	12×12	6.0	157(8)/	CMOS,3.3v,0/1/2
HP	1989	30MIPS Precision Architecture CPU	183	30	1.5	14×14	28	447/408	NMOS,1/0/3(2W,1Al)
DEC	1989	20MIPS Sustained,32b, Microprocessor 64b Data	180	100	1.5	7.76×6.21	3.0	176/168	CMOS,5.0V,0/1/2
GE	1989	40MHz 64b Floating Point Coprocessor	17	40	1.2	10×11.0		/132	CMOS,1/0/2
DEC	1989	50HMz Pipelined 64b Floating Point Arithmetic Processor		50	1.5	11.1×12.7			CMOS,
Intel	1989	1,000,000 Transistors 64b RISC on a Chip (i860)	1,000	50	1.0	10.0×15.0			CMOS,0/1/2
HP	1987	15MIPS 32b Microprocessor	115	30	1.7	8.4×8.4	10.0	251/272	NMOS,1/0/3(2W,1Al)
HP	1987	32b CMOS Single Chip RISC	164	8			1.0	92/84	CMOS,
DEC	1987	32b CMOS Microprocessor	135(180)	20	2.0	9.7×9.4	2.5	/84	CMOS,0/1/2
AT&T	1987	32b,13Kb Cache, Pipelined Microprocessor	172	16	1.75	10.35×12.23	0.5	140/125	CMOS,1/1/2
TI	1987	32b LISP Processor	553	25	1.25	10×10		/224	CMOS,1/0/2
Japan									
Matsushita	1989	64b RISC Microprocessor for Parallel Computer System	440	40	1.2	14.4×13.5	1.3	172/	CMOS,0/1/2
Mitsubishi	1989	50MHz 24b Floating-Point DSP	300	50	1.0	7.02×8.64	0.6	/135	CMOS,0/1/2
Mitsubishi	1989	40MFlops 32b Floating-Point Processor	85		1.3	13.28×12.55	0.7	/209	CMOS,0/1/2
NEC	1989	80b, 6.7MFlops, FPU with Vector/Matrix Instructions	433	20	1.2	11.6×14.9	1.5	/68	CMOS,0/1/2
Matsushita	1987	32b CMOS Microprocessor	372	50	1.0	9.74×9.45	1.7	/120	CMOS,
NTT	1987	32b LISP Processor	80	16.67	2.0	15×15	1.0	/208	CMOS,0/1/2

Table 3.6: Microprocessor R&D announcements.

[a] Number of Transistors in thousands.
[b] Clock Frequency in MHz.
[c] Feature Size in microns.
[d] Chip Size in mm.
[e] Power in watts
[f] Pads/Pins

other is that the number of transistors per memory chip tends to be many times larger than the number per microprocessor. Moreover, the minimum feature size for a microprocessor tends to lag that for memory by more than three years. These later two comparisons strongly reflect the predominant role of memory chips as semiconductor technology drivers. In addition, they reflect the importance of architecture and software capabilities in microprocessor development.

It is doubtful that the existing U.S. leadership in microprocessors can be sustained over the long term without reasonably prompt access by U.S. companies to competitive semiconductor processing technology as reflected by chip transistor density and minimum feature size for memory. This is a compelling concern of U.S. computer companies, particularly because future advances in performance of CPU's will become increasingly dependent on the inclusion of large amounts of SRAM cache memory within the CPU chip itself.

3.2.3   Gallium Arsenide Chips

The singular motivation for pursuing GaAs and other compound semiconductor electronic devices is the potential advantage in speed which they offer in comparison with Si devices. Cf. [22, 25] and [32, 35, 36, 37].

The magnitude of this advantage is not simply defined. To begin, at room temperature the mobility of electrons in pure GaAs crystals is well known to be about six times larger than the mobility of electrons in Si. Mobility is defined as the carrier velocity per unit of electric field strength or driving force for small field strengths. However, as electric field strength increases Si and GaAs behave qualitatively differently. In Si, carrier velocity monotonically increases with field strength and gradually saturates at its peak value. In GaAs, carrier velocity first increases to a peak value and then decreases, and finally gradually saturates at a value about 50% of the peak and approximately equal to the saturation velocity in Si. Consequently, if – as is usually the case for high speed devices – devices are operated at relatively large field strengths, the six times mobility advantage of GaAs typically diminishes to a two–to–three times velocity advantage. A further factor to consider is electron behavior in devices whose dimensions are comparable to the mean free path, or distance between collisions with lattice ions, of an electron which behaves ballistically between collisions. Although mean free paths of electrons are appreciably larger in GaAs than in Si, at sufficiently small device dimensions, electrons conceivably could traverse the entire active region of a device as ballistic carriers and thereby be "unaware" of many otherwise differentiating features of their host crystal.

In terms of materials technology, Si has a decided advantage over GaAs in that it is an elemental as opposed to a compound semiconductor. Achieving stoichiometric and defect free Si crystals is an easier task than the corresponding one for GaAs.

Another noteworthy point of comparison between Si and GaAs is that hole or positive carrier mobility is approximately equal in the two materials. In Si electron mobility is about three times greater than hole mobility and electron saturation velocity is less than twice the saturation velocity of holes. The closer match of electron and hole mobilities and velocities in Si, compared with GaAs, offers advantages in complementary circuits using both N(electron)–channel and P(hole)–channel field effect transistors (FET's).

Moreover, the high quality of the interface between a Si crystal and its native oxide (SiO$_2$) enables the fabrication of fully insulated gate complementary FET's which have not yet been demonstrated in any other semiconductor material. The fact that such circuits can be designed for virtually zero standby power drain is a major advantage of CMOS technology compared to any other, because low power drain implies larger packing density and, therefore, higher speed for a given cooling technology.

The most recent technological surge in Si microchips has focused on the combination of NPN bipolar transistors (BT's) and complementary MOSFET's. This technology is referred to as BiCMOS. The notable advantage of BiCMOS technology is that it combines an NPN BT with a transconductance (i.e., ratio of output current change to input voltage change or G_m) that is 5–10 times larger than offered by GaAs FET's [37], for example, with the low standby power of CMOS. Because the speed of high density chips is dominated by wiring capacitance whose rapid charging and discharging demands large transconductance, the combination of NPN BT's and complementary MOSFET's in BiCMOS may well offer speed advantages in comparison to GaAs FET circuits.

The most widely practiced form of GaAs technology is referred to as Enhancement Depletion Metal Semiconductor Field Effect transistor or E/D MESFET technology. It includes normally–off or enchancement and normally–on or depletion mode MESFET's. MESFET's are similar to MOSFET's with the critical difference that the input electrode of a MESFET consists of a metal–semiconductor diode that becomes highly conducting in the forward direction for input voltages larger than 0.7–0.8V, whereas the input electrode of a MOSFET consists of a metal–SiO$_2$–Si capacitor that simply does not conduct for input voltages smaller than the typical minimum 7–8V breakdown voltage of the SiO$_2$ insulator. The more favorable input characteristic of the Si MOSFET and the availability of complementary Si MOSFET's offer significant circuit advantages over GaAs E/D MESFET circuits.

To improve on the performance of GaAs MESFET's, the MODulation doped FET (MODFET) or high electron mobility transistor (HEMT) was invented. In its most simple form the MODFET consists of a relatively narrow energy band gap substrate (e.g. undoped or very low conductivity GaAs) on which a thin layer of a relatively wide energy band gap crystal (e.g., heavily doped or very high conductivity AlGaAs) has been epitaxially deposited to form a heterojunction. The electrons provided by the heavily doped AlGaAs layer become contained in a thin potential or quantum well within the GaAs substrate at the heterojunction. Because the GaAs is free of doping impurities, the electrons within the potential well exhibit the largest possible mobility for electrons in GaAs, particularly if a thin undoped "spacer" layer of AlGaAs is sandwiched between the GaAs substrate and the highly doped surface layer of AlGaAs. MODFET's have little advantage over MESFET's at room temperature (300°K) since lattice ion vibrations dominate carrier mobility at 300°K but offer substantial advantages at liquid nitrogen temperature (77°K) where dopant impurity scattering dominates carrier mobility. For example, MODFET transconductances at 77°K are 2-3 times greater than MESFET transconductances at 300°K [37]. Moreover, more advanced heterojunction FET's and BT's can be expected in the future through innovative fabrication processes.

Although Si devices and circuits are very strong competitors of GaAs for relatively large scale digital circuits where high packing density and, therefore, small signal propagation times are essential for very fast machine cycle times, in some applications the intrinsic speed advantage of GaAs can be effective. For example, in machine–to–machine communication links where small-to-medium scale integration is sufficient, GaAs chips offer advantages. This is especially so in comparison to the highest speed Si BT circuits, emitter coupled logic (ECL), since GaAs FET circuits offer equal or greater speed at substantially reduced power levels and, therefore, cooling needs. Most importantly, in OptoElectronic Integrated Circuits (OEIC's) where, for example, one may wish to combine high speed switching transistors with a laser diode, compound semiconductors such as GaAs and InP and there ternary and quaternary derivatives enable opportunities that are impossible using Si devices. This is particularly the case for OEIC's which interface with optical fiber or photonic interconnections.

It is important to point out that in addition to performance/speed advantages over Si, GaAs devices also exhibit greater radiation hardness. This is a particularly valuable property of GaAs devices for applications in satellites and space probes as well as in nuclear reactor environments. The current status of U.S. and Japanese GaAs SRAM R&D announcements is reflected in Table 3.7. In 1987 McDonnell-Douglas, Fujitsu and Hitachi announced 4Kb SRAM chips, all using different GaAs technologies. The Fujitsu and Hitachi chips are 20 and 10 times faster, respectively, than the McDonnell-Douglas SRAM which was designed for low power and large radiation resistance. In 1988 Gigabit Logic announced a 4Kb SRAM a factor of 3-6 slower than the Hitachi and Fujitsu chips both of which use a more advanced technology than Gigabit Logic. The overall position of U.S. merchant suppliers of GaAs SRAM's compared to their Japanese counterparts appears to be leading by 1–2 years in terms of actual commercial products, but lagging by 2–3 years in terms of demonstrated technology as discussed later in this section in connection with gate arrays.

Another interesting point of comparison is between the 4Kb and 16Kb GaAs SRAM's described in Table 3.7 and the 1Mb Si CMOS and BiCMOS SRAM's described in Table 3.1. The sub–10 nanosecond access times of the 1 Mb Si SRAM's are slow in comparison to a 1 nanosecond access time for a 4Kb GaAs SRAM. However, it is remarkable that 256 of the 4Kb GaAs chips are required to provide the same storage capacity as a single 1Mb Si chip. This is explained in part by the fact that the areas of the Si memory cells are more

Company	Year[a]	Number[b]	Access[c]	Min.[d]	Chip[e]	Cell[f]	I/O Interface	PowerDrain[g]	Technology
U.S.									
Rockwell	1987	16Kb	20	1.0,2.0	7.3×7.0	40×40		1.0	D MESFET, 4t-2d-6R cell
McDonnell-Douglas	1987	4Kb	10	1.0,2.0	3.9×4.9			0.2	C JFET
Gigabit Logic	1988	4Kb	3.0	1.0,		40×35	ECL	1.9	E/D MESFET, MIS C, Cermet R
McDonnell-Douglas	1988	16Kb	22.5		8.2×5.6	32×49		.68	C JFET, 6T cell
Vitesse	1988	1Kb	3.0/4.0		2.7×2.25	35×26	ECL/TTL	1.5	E/D MESFET
Japan									
Fujitsu	1987	4Kb	0.5	0.5,1.5	2.8×3.0	25×23	ECL	5.7	E/D HEMT,DCFL,HBE
Hitachi	1987	4Kb	1.0	0.7,	3.7×4.7	25×47	ECL	1.6	E/D MESFET, DCFL, 0/1/2
Mitsubishi	1987	16Kb	7.0	1.0,1.5	5.8×4.7	32×24		1.0	E/D MESFET, DCFL
Mitsubishi	1988	4Kb	7.0	1.0,	4.8×4.6	35×29		0.85	E/D MESFET,DCFL,Radiat. Hard
Mitsubishi	1989	16Kb	7.2	0.7,1.5	7.41×7.16	36×23		2.1	E/D MESFET,DCFL,Radiat. Hard
Europe									
Phillips	1987	1Kb	2.0	0.7,2.0	1.9×2.3	42×28		0.21	E/D MESFET

Table 3.7: GaAs SRAM R&D announcements.

[a] Year of Announcement
[b] Number of Bits
[c] Access Time [ns]
[d] Minimum Feature [microns]
[e] Chip Size [mm]
[f] Cell Area [microns]
[g] Power Drain [watts]

than an order of magnitude smaller than the areas of the GaAs cells which suggests the large handicap GaAs technology has to overcome in future competition with Si BiCMOS SRAM's.

A comparison of U.S. and Japanese GaAs gate array R&D announcements is presented in Table 3.8. The U.S. appears to be ahead by about 1-2 years in terms of actual commercial products. In the author's view, this assessment must be carefully qualified. Japan clearly leads the U.S. in GaAs materials technology, particularly for use in lasers for compact disk audio systems. Japanese companies have not been active in the GaAs digital integrated circuit (i.e. gate array and SRAM) market, presumably because of its small size and uncertain prospects for significant growth relative to silicon. However, if the market does develop, Japanese superiority in GaAs materials and semiconductor manufacturing equipment will offer an enormous advantage in competition with existing U.S. "start-up" companies (e.g., Vitesse, TriQuint and Gigabit Logic). Moreover, GaAs chip R&D announcements by large vertically integrated Japanese corporations (e.g., Fujitsu, Hitachi and Toshiba) have described "demonstrated technology" that is 2–3 years ahead of that of U.S. merchant companies.

Although an attempt has been made in the preceding discussion to compare the relative status of U.S. and Japanese GaAs microchip technology, a final caveat must be added. Because the commercial markets for GaAs microchips are in such a primitive state relative to Si, the volatility or uncertainty of relative positions of competing enterprises in GaAs is much greater than the corresponding situation in Si.

3.2.4   Chip Packaging

The four major functions of a chip package are protection, power distribution, signal distribution and heat dissipation [38, 39]. The disciplines involved are many and diverse. Moreover, the chip package or "module" constitutes the first level of an electronic packaging hierarchy. The number of levels within the hierarchy depends on the totality of packaging needs of a specific application. For example [39], in mainframe computers using single–chip modules, the second level of packaging is a "card" including multiple layers of wiring. Many modules and possibly other components are assembled on a card, (which in simple systems such as a pocket calculator may be the only level of packaging beyond the module.) The third level of the packaging hierarchy consists of multilayer printed-circuit "boards" often containing pluggable connectors to accept a group of cards. The fourth and final level of packaging, in this example, consists of an assembly of boards interconnected by pluggable cables for signal distribution and by heavy wires for power distribution and arranged to enable high-velocity air or liquid cooling. This fourth level of packaging is sometimes referred to as a "frame" [39].

The key issue at the first level of packaging is the single chip versus the multi-chip module. Handling a bare chip exacerbates testing and repair problems. Handling a module

Company	Year of Announcement	Number [a]	Feature [b]	Chip Size [c]	Gate Delay [d]	Technology
U.S.						
T.I.	1986	4	2.0,	5.8×5.8	0.04	HBT,I²L
Rockwell	1987	7	3.0,		0.30	D MESFET, BFL
Vitesse	1989	15	0.8,		0.17(L)	E/D MESFET, 0/0/3
AT&T	1989	2	1.0,	5×5	0.12	E/D MODFET
Rockwell/IBM	1989	1.1	1.4,2.5	4×4.5	0.07	HBT ECL, 0/0/2
Japan						
NEC	1986	3	,2.5	7.5×7.4	0.056	D MESFET, BFL, 0/1/2
Fujitsu	1986	1.5	1.2,2.0	5.5×5.6	0.085	E/D HEMT, DCFL
Toshiba	1987	6	1.0,2.0	8×8	0.76	D MESFET, SLCF, 0/1/2
NTT	1989	0.25	0.4,1.5	2.8×2.5	0.00003	E/R MESFET, LSCFL, 0/0/2

Table 3.8: GaAs gate array R&D announcements.

[a] Number of Gates × 1000
[b] Feature Size[microns]
[c] Chip Size[mm]
[d] Gate Delay[ns]

including only one chip eases these problems but introduces others. For example, the typical disparity in size between a single chip and its package increases both the distance between chips on a card and the associated signal propagation delays and consequently computation time for a given program. Multichip modules reduce the distance between chips and improve performance at the expense of increased manufacturing and replacement costs per module.

The use of a multichip module essentially combines the first and second levels of packaging by including the entire contents of a card within a multichip module, which can be inserted directly into a board. Historically, the most common substrates for multichip modules have been co-fired multilayer ceramic structures with as many as 30 or more levels of metallization isolated from each other by intervening layers of ceramic. The relentless quest for ever increasing wire density or smaller interconnect pitch in multichip packages has led to the introduction of silicon wafers as the substrates for multichip modules. The use of a Si wafer enables the deposition on it of a very dense multilevel wiring network consisting of copper conductors and polyimide insulators, for example. The patterning of this wiring can be accomplished using essentially the same high resolution processes that enable the internal high density multilevel interconnection networks of the chips themselves.

In their draft report of late 1989, the Committee on Materials for High-Density Electronic Packaging of the National Research Council states [38]:

> "Packaging is now approaching a turning point at which single-chip packages cannot be assembled directly onto conventional circuit boards without impairment of performance. A new level of packaging, the multichip module (MCM), is coming into prominence. MCM's consist of inorganic base layers, to provide power, ground and decoupling capacitances, and signal interconnect patterns fabricated of high conductivity metals and low-dielectric-constant organic polymer dielectrics. *The individual chips are assembled on top, either in unencapsulated form or in low impedance single chip packages.* The signal interconnection density achievable is very high, owing to the fineness of the patterns. Two layers of (in) MCM's can replace dozens of layers in conventional PWB's (printed wiring boards). Materials support for MCM designs must be strongly encouraged in the U.S."

The sentence which is italicized by this author suggests a high degree of flexibility in MCM features.

The IBM thermal conduction module (TCM) represents a (if not the) salient example of an advanced multichip module that has proven itself in the field [39]. A typical TCM uses a 90×90 mm ceramic substrate. The substrate consists of up to 33 molybdenum metallized alumina layers that are required for power distribution, for impedance controlled interconnections to 12,000 chip pads, and for wiring to the 1800 module pins that are brazed to the backside of the substrate for connection to a printed-circuit board (PCB). A typical substrate contains 350,000 vias for layer-to-layer connections and 130 meters of wiring. The substrate includes 100 chip sites. The "flip" chips (i.e. chips mounted up side down) themselves are connected to the substrate via "solder bumps" using a controlled collapse process that permits a full area array. (To illustrate only, for a 10×10 mm chip and a 51 micron pad pitch, a perimeter configuration would allow 784 pads while an area array would allow 38,809 pads [39].) Each chip in the TCM can dissipate up to four watts. Pistons contact the back of each flip chip to provide the main thermal path to a water cooled housing. The TCM is filled with Helium, without which each chip would be limited to less than half of the design power level. The TCM has been used extensively in the IBM 308x and 309x computer families.[2]

Apparently, the closest Japanese counterpart to the TCM is the NEC liquid cooled module (LCM) used in the SX-2 scientific/super computer and in NEC mainframes as well. The LCM chips are packaged in a single–chip carrier called a flip–tab–carrier. Each chip dissipates about 7 watts. A chip is tape automated bonded (tab) to a ceramic multilayer substrate face down utilizing 176 peripheral leads. The substrate translates the leads to an areal array of bumps on the bottom of the 14 mm flip–tab–carrier. A metal cover is soldered to the substrate which provides hermetic sealing and a thermal path to the piston of the LCM. Thirty six flip–chip–tab–carriers are mounted on a 100×100 mm multilayer ceramic substrate with thin film wiring for chip-to-chip interconnection. The module, which is similar to the TCM, is plugged into a planar board utilizing an areal array connector with 2,177 pins.

Comparing the TCM and the LCM leads one toward the conclusion that at least one U.S. corporation, IBM, is ahead or even with Japanese multichip packaging technology. A full R&D announcement of the TCM was made by IBM in 1983, while the corresponding NEC announcement came in 1985. Clearly, this assessment applies to vertically integrated corporations which do not "sell" packaging technology per se as a product.

The competitive situation with regard to merchant vendors of single chip and multichip packages is quite at variance with the preceding IBM–NEC comparison. Excluding low cost plastics, the worldwide market for chip packaging is absolutely dominated by a single Japanese corporation, Kyocera which does not have a major competitor. For this reason, packaging R&D announcements by smaller U.S. merchant vendors are difficult to assess in terms of their ability eventually to deliver competitive commercial products in volume. However, the growing importance of multi-chip modules in low cost consumer products such as pocket dictionaries and notebook computers, in moderate cost commercial products and in high cost-high performance supercomputers and telecommunication equipment is attracting increasing effort in a variety of packaging technologies in both Japan and the

---

[2]These figures have already been improved as this report goes to press. Now the dissipation is up to 20 watts and universal oil has replaced Helium.

Types of Microchip	U.S. Position Relative[a] to Japan	Rate of Change of U.S. Relative to Japan
1) SRAM's	Behind 2-3 years	Losing
2) DRAM's	Behind 3-4 years	Losing
3) NVRAM's	Behind 0-1 years	Losing
4) Gate Arrays/ASIC's	Behind 1-2 years	Losing
5) Microprocessors	Ahead 2-3 years	Stable
6) Gallium Arsenide SRAM's	a) commercial products Ahead 1-2 years	?
	b) demonstrated technology Behind 2-3 years	
7) Gallium Arsenide Gate Arrays	a) commercial products Ahead 1-2 years	?
	b) demonstrated technology Behind 2-3 years	
8) Packaging	U.S. Lacks Market Presence	?

[a]Note: This summary estimates the positions of U.S. merchant suppliers relative to their Japanese competitors. Inclusion of U.S. captive suppliers (e.g. IBM) would improve the U.S. positions for several types of chips. See text for further explanation.

Table 3.9: Summary of U.S. position in semiconductors.

U.S.

The current early use in Japan of AlN as a replacement for Al_2O_3 in ceramic packages offers a significant advantage due to the seven times larger thermal conductivity of AlN.

The brief comments on chip packaging provided in this chapter are intended to serve as an overview only. A current in–depth comparison of relevant U.S., Japanese and European packaging capabilities prepared by a highly focused group of experts is contained in [38]

3.3   Summary

An overall summary of the relative status of U.S. and Japanese semiconductor microchip and packaging technology is given in Table 3.9. These estimates are based on R&D announcements in published literature and on a limited set of private discussions with both

U.S. and Japanese semiconductor experts. The information is not comprehensive. It focuses on a selected group of major types of integrated circuits used in advanced computers. In particular, emphasis is placed on high density chips which incorporate the largest number of transistors per chip of a given type at a given time. Although previous Tables 3.1–3.8 have included IBM R&D announcements, Table 3.9 does not. It reflects the positions and rates of change of positions of U.S. merchant suppliers relative to their Japanese competitors.

The salient estimates summarized in Table 3.9 are:

1. In high density SRAM's, U.S. merchant vendors lag behind their Japanese competitors by 2-3 years and are losing ground.

2. In DRAM's, U.S. merchant vendors lag behind their Japanese competitors by 3-4 years and are losing ground.

3. In NVRAM's, U.S. merchant vendors lag behind their Japanese competitors by 0-1 years and appear to be losing ground more slowly than for DRAM's.

4. In gate arrays (or ASIC's), U.S. merchant vendors lag behind their Japanese competitors by 1-2 years and are losing ground.

5. In microprocessors, U.S. merchant vendors are ahead of their Japanese competitors by 2-3 years and appear to be holding this lead in a stable position.

6. In Gallium Arsenide (GaAs) SRAM's, the merchant market is in a very primitive state compared to that for Si SRAM's. Consequently, the confidence level one can attach to estimates of the U.S. position relative to Japan is less for GaAs than for Si SRAM's. However, based on available information, U.S. merchant vendors appear to lead their Japanese counterparts by 1-2 years in commercial products but lag behind by 2-3 years in technology demonstrated in R&D laboratories.

7. Although the current commercial market for GaAs gate arrays (or ASIC's) apparently is larger than that for SRAM's, again, the primitive state of the GaAs market compared with Si makes estimating positions even more tenuous. Based on available information, U.S. merchant vendors are estimated to be one or two years ahead in GaAs gate arrays – perhaps largely due to the reluctance of Japanese vendors to enter this market due to its small size and – two or three years behind in technology demonstrated in R&D laboratories.

8. Finally, in packaging, captive U.S. suppliers such as IBM appear to be ahead or at least even with their Japanese competitors. However, the merchant market is dominated by a single Japanese supplier, Kyocera. Consequently, estimating a U.S. merchant position is hardly an issue.

A qualifying note regarding the summary of the relative U.S. position presented in Table 3.9 is that the interval between an R&D announcement and commercial production typically has been smaller for U.S. companies than for their Japanese counterparts. This tends to exaggerate the gap between the U.S. and Japanese positions to some degree.

The alarming impact of America's continuing loss of world leadership in semiconductor technology has been described cogently in the recent report to the President and the Congress from the National Advisory Committee on Semiconductors [5]. Suffice it to say in this JTEC report that a healthy U.S. semiconductor industry is strategic to America's economic and military security because of the paramount role of semiconductors in modern computer, communications, control and measurement systems, which constitute the heart of the information revolution – the most significant event of our lifetime and possibly of the entire 21st century [19].

3.4   Projections for the Future

Perhaps the most interesting question regarding the future of semiconductors in advanced computing is, "Which technologies will be the winners?" Five stimulating points of view that were captured during this study are succinctly summarized as follows:

1. Continued aggressive scaling of CMOS technology with ECL compatible inputs and outputs (I/O's) and smaller power dissipation, via reduction in supply voltage from 5.0V to 3.3V, will enable high density CMOS technology to continue to narrow the CMOS-ECL performance gap and become the most widely used technology for advanced computers.

2. SRAM's for advanced computers will be dominated by BiCMOS technology. The fast cycle times of advanced computers will demand multi-chip modules using BiCMOS ECL for cache memory, multi-processor, co-processor, control and bus interface chips. Therefore, BiCMOS ECL will be the winning technology for advanced computers.

3. Essentially zero dislocation density GaAs wafers can now be produced via the fully liquid encapsulated Czochralski growth process. Using this starting material and a mature ion implanted E/D MESFET process will enable fabrication of high density high speed GaAs SRAM and logic chips that will represent the winning technology for advanced computers.

4. High electron mobility transistors (HEMT's) or modulation doped FET's (MODFET's) are the fastest semiconductor triodes yet produced. Using immersion cooling in liquid nitrogen E/D MODFET technology will be the winner for advanced computers.

5. Multichip modules (MCM's) with high density multilevel interconnections and excellent heat removal capabilities are an essential complement to all of the preceding
semiconductor technologies.

More generic projections of the future of semiconductor technology have identified the
following expectations for the year 2000 [20, 21]:

- a one billion transistor chip,

- a 0.25 micron or smaller feature size,

- approximately a 35×35mm die size.

The principal enabling technologies for this continued exponential development of semiconductor chips are likely to be:

- electron beam pattern generation,

- deep UV optical followed by x-ray lithography

- ion implantation, organo-metallic chemical vapor deposition (OMCVD) and molecular beam epitaxy (MBE) for introduction of semiconductor dopant impurities and
other additive processes,

- multi-chamber/stage etching/deposition for subtractive processes,

- multi-chamber/stage chemical and physical vapor processes for additive processes.

A critical point to recognize is that as a generic class these enabling technologies are
implemented with a diverse set of tools collectively referred to as semiconductor manufacturing equipment (SME). The U.S. SME industry is highly fragmented and rapidly
becoming non–competitive or is being acquired by foreign competitors. This erosion of
the infrastructure of the U.S. semiconductor industry is the most severe threat "from
within" to its future health. The fall of the domestic semiconductor industry, in turn,
will place U.S. computer, communication, control and measurement companies in a highly
vulnerable position relative to their foreign competitors. Finally, U.S. manufacturing and
service industries, all of which depend critically on electronics, computers, communication,
control/automation and measurement, will become handicapped relative to their foreign
competitors. In short, the SME industry and related materials industries represent the
lowest level of a "food chain" which reaches to the highest levels of the U.S. economy and
underscores emphatically the importance of healthy domestic SME and semiconductor chip
industries.

4. Data Storage

Robert M. White

4.1 Introduction

The data upon which computer systems operate spends most of its time encoded in a magnetic medium, be it a disk or a tape. The various storage systems are illustrated in Table 4.1.

We are all aware of the important role that semiconductors play in computing. But without the large, low-cost capacities provided by secondary storage high performance computing would be impractical. It is estimated that the secondary storage needed to support a computer system is between 10 to 50 times the semiconductor memory capacity. The tertiary, or archive, level must hold another factor of 10 to 50. The mass storage architecture of Lawrence Livermore Lab's Cray system, for example, consists of two Storage Technology 4400's, each consisting of 6000 cartridges holding 1200 Gigabytes. Magnetic

System	Disk Storage	Archival/Backup
Supercomputers (Cray)	8"-14", > 1 GB	3480 Cartridges
Minisupercomputers (Convex)		
Mainframe (IBM)	8"-14", > 500 MB	3480 Cartridges
Superminis (VAX)		
Workstations (SUN)	5.25", 300 MB-1GB	Data Cartridge
PC's	2.5"-3.5", 20 MB-100MB	Data Cartridge

Table 4.1: Secondary and archival storage in support of computer systems.

storage is an essential part of every computer system and likely to remain so.

Tape systems evolved from Europe. They were literally brought to the U.S. at the end of WWII and employed in commercial broadcasting. The U.S. was in an ideal position to develop consumer tape systems but for a variety of reasons declined to do so, leaving the market to the Japanese. The Betamax-VHS story is well known. Control of the consumer market is very advantageous for it enables one to amortize new technology development across a large volume. The Japanese developed the so-called cobalt-modified iron oxide particles which are used in many systems today, including disks. They have also introduced barium ferrite particles and perpendicular media into the consumer market.

The disk drive is very much American. It was first introduced by IBM, in 1954 and IBM continues to be the preeminent manufacturer of drives. And just as there has always been a market for IBM-look-alike computers, a plug-compatible disk drive market also evolved. As personal computers and workstations appeared this created a demand for drives that was met by venture capital-funded startups, generally by technologists whose roots could be traced back to IBM. As any computer user in the early 80's would tell you, the disk drive was the "weak link" in the system. It is therefore not surprising that the Japanese entered this market on the merits of their quality. Japanese market share grew rapidly while the U.S. manufacturers developed new manufacturing skills. Over the past two years the U.S. OEM disk drive manufactures have in fact regained market share. The reason for this, I believe, is that as recording technology has improved it has enabled smaller "form factors", i.e. box sizes, from 14 inches to 8 inches to $5\frac{1}{4}$ inches to $3\frac{1}{2}$ inches and now, apparently, $2\frac{1}{2}$ inches. Each new form factor has largely been pioneered by venture capital. This is supported by Figure 4.1 which shows that the Japanese now dominate the higher capacity systems which involve the larger diameters.[1]

New technology has also been supported by U.S. venture capital. One of the technology components of a drive is the media itself. For many years rigid disk drive media consisted of an aluminum substrate coated with magnetic particles in an epoxy. As higher recording densities called for thinner media it became obvious that one would eventually have to go to thin metallic coatings. It was American entrepreneurs that led the way. The top four suppliers of rigid media in 1988 were all American:

- Xidex

- Nashua

- Komag

- Domain Technology

Unfortunately this story has a sad ending. Xidex has been bought by Hitachi, Komag is partially owned by Asahi, and Domain has declared bankruptcy. This year the top four

---

[1]Source: Disk Trend '88.

(U.S. vs. Japan/Others)

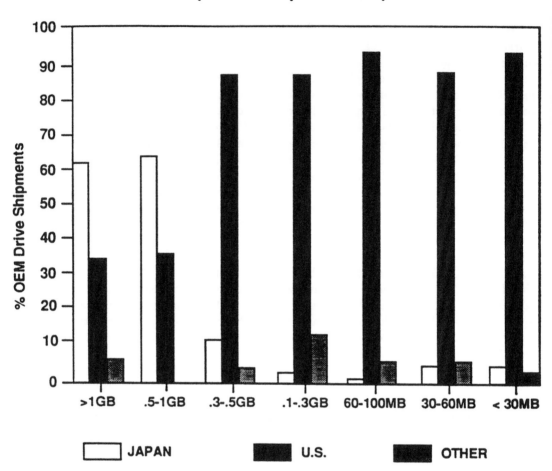

Figure 4.1: Percent of OEM shipments in different capacity categories.

Suppliers
TDK
Sony
Hitachi Maxell
3M

Table 4.2: The four leading suppliers of video cassettes.

United States	Japan
Applied Magnetics Corp. (AMC)	Matsushita
Read-Rite	TDR
PCI (Seagate)	Alps
Sunward	

Table 4.3: Head suppliers.

will likely include Denke and Mitsubishi. For reference, the top four suppliers of video cassettes are shown in Table 4.2.

The other major technical component of a drive is the "head", the electromagnet that writes and reads data to and from the disk or tape. For many years all heads consisted of a ferrite core with a hand-wound coil. In 1981 IBM introduced a thin-film head consisting of permalloy poles and a copper coil all fabricated by thin-film technology. The plug-compatible drive manufacturers were obligated to introduce their own thin-film heads. Control Data and Memorex joined forces while Storage Technology tried to do it alone, which was probably a contributing factor to their going into bankruptcy. The Japanese, however, continued to use ferrite heads because they had a lower cost. One of the advantages of the permalloy in a thin film head over a ferrite head is that it can generate a higher magnetic flux before its poles saturate. The Japanese, however, have neutralized this advantage by coating the tips of their ferrite heads with a metal that has a high saturation. These "metal-in-gap", or MIG, heads have inserted themselves in the technology chain between the conventional ferrite head and the thin-film head which has other advantages that may only become apparent at still higher recording densities.

Table 4.3 summarizes the sources for heads.

If one asks whether one can have an American computer if all the logic and memory chips come from Japan, one can also ask if there is an American disk drive if the heads and media come from Japan.

4.2   Disk Drive Technology

The measure of the recording efficiency of a disk drive is its areal density-the number of bits that can be stored per square inch. Figure 4.2 shows the growth rate of this indicator.[2]

The important point to note is that for drive suppliers to remain competitive they must double the areal density approximately every three years. Figure 4.3 shows that Japanese and U. S. technology is essentially equivalent.[3] However, the Japanese R&D investment is significantly greater as we shall indicate below.

Areal density is the product of both the track density and linear density along the track. Since the read signal is inversely proportioned to the track density, increases in tracks per inch must be accompanied by developments that compensate the reduced signal-to-noise ratio associated with the reduced signal amplitude. Narrower tracks also require a more accurate servo system to maintain track position as off-track tolerances become smaller with increased track density.

The signal in magnetic recording arises from the magnetic flux fringing out of the medium where the magnetization M_r, reverses direction. One way of increasing this signal is to increase the product $M_r d$ where d is the thickness. As we shall see below, increasing thickness works against increasing linear areal density, however, increasing M_r, is very desirable. There are several other magnetic properties that must be maintained when one tinkers with the composition.

Another obvious way to increase the signal is to fly the head closer to the disk. This is also required to increase the linear density and is therefore one of the major avenues to higher densities. The head in a $5\frac{1}{4}$ inch drive today typically flies at 10 microinches or 1/4 micron! Not only must the surface be uniformly smooth on this scale, but the environment carefully controlled to reduce particle counts and sizes that would cause damage. Mastering the technology of flying at, say, four microinches (0.1 micron) is the greatest challenge facing drive manufacturers today. For American companies this issue will determine survivability in the nineties.

To understand what influences the linear density consider the voltage induced in a head by a flux reversal as shown in Figure 4.4. Notice that the width of the voltage pulse is a complex combination of geometrical factors: the size of the gap (or thickness of the pole in the case of perpendicular recording), the head-to-disk spacing, δ, the thickness of the medium, and the width of the transition. We now see that making the medium thick spreads out the pulse thereby restricting interpulse separation, or linear density. Furthermore this result shows that reducing any one of these factors alone will not result in a narrower pulse – they must all be reduced together. We have already discussed

---

[2]Source: N. Talsoe, Seagate.
[3]Source: Disk Trend '88.

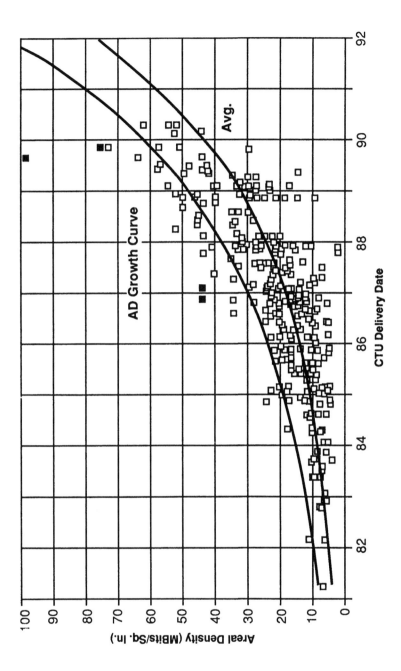

Figure 4.2: Historical growth of recording areal density.

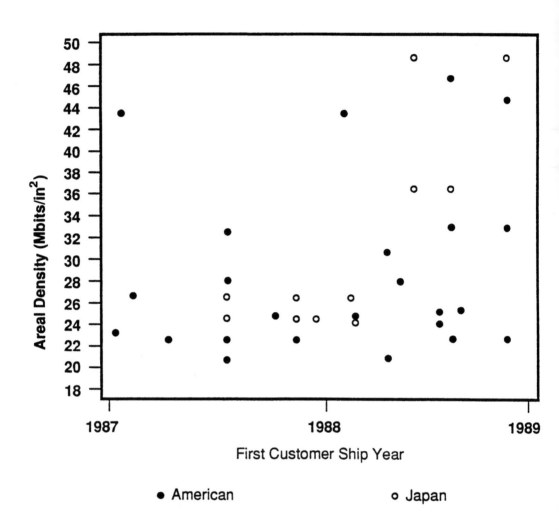

Figure 4.3: Growth in $5\frac{1}{4}$ inch areal density in the U.S. and Japan.

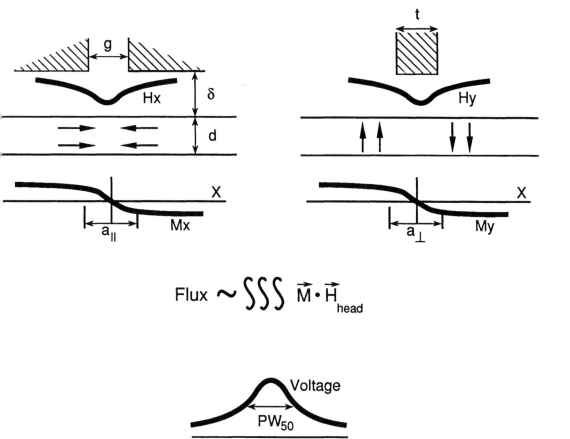

$$\text{Flux} \sim \int\int\int \vec{M} \cdot \vec{H}_{head}$$

$$PW_{50} = \sqrt{g^2 + 4(d+a)(d+a+\delta)}$$

Figure 4.4: Dependence of the output voltage on the recording geometry.

the difficulty in reducing the flying height. The thin film media used in today's drives is about 500 Å thick. Computer data cannot tolerate more than one error in 10^{12} bits. In older drives defects in the media were mapped so that such regions could be avoided during operation. Today's standards are such that few defects are tolerated on a disk. We thus have the challenge of manufacturing, with high yield, disks having a 500 Å or thinner coating that is comparatively free of pinholes as well as any variations in magnetic properties on a submicron scale.

Finally, consider the transition length, a. Such a width arises from the "magnetic charge" density that accompanies a spatial variation, $\nabla \cdot M$. This charge density is reduced by spreading the transition over a larger width. This spreading is resisted by the coercivity, H_c, of the material. The result is that the transition length is given by $a = 4M_s d/H_c$. Since decreasing $M_s d$ also decreases the signal, the best way to achieve a smooth transition length is to increase the coercivity of the materials. As a practical matter the coercivity cannot be larger than the field produced by the head in the writing process. Notice that if the magnetization is perpendicular to the direction of the reversal $\nabla \cdot M = 0$. That is, there is no demagnetization field and the transition length could be infinitely sharp. This is what makes perpendicular recording attractive. However, as we noted above, having a zero transition length does not buy higher density unless the other geometrical factors are also small. This is why perpendicular recording is first being introduced in contact formats such as tape and diskette. Japan championed perpendicular recording, largely due to the efforts of one Professor Iwasaki.

4.3   Recording in Japan

The JTEC visit included the following organizations involved in recording:[4]

NTT. The Nippon Telephone and Telegraph Company has recently undergone "privatization". However, it is still restricted from manufacturing. Consequently its research on recording continues to be directed at setting the requirements for drives that its suppliers such as Fujitsu and NEC must meet. The latest "target" was the GEMMY drive announced in 1988. This drive had an areal density of 40 Mb/in^2 using thin film media (either metallic or sputtered oxide) and thin film heads. Mr. Isamu Sato of NTT described current work on perpendicular recording. When asked how they plan to fly at 0.1 micron, he referred to new low-mass sliders. At NTT we were also shown a magnetooptic jukebox. Almost every company we visited demonstrated some form of magneto-optical recording.

NHK. We visited the Science and Technical Research Laboratories of Japan Broadcasting Corporation (NHK) because it is playing a leading role in HDTV, and has joint

---

[4]Cf. [40] through [154] for additional information.

development projects with electronics manufacturers on recording equipment. Mr. Taiji Nishizawa, Director, of the Advanced TV Systems Research Division confirmed that they plan to go directly to digital HDTV. The data rate this requires is 1.2 Gbits per second. Dr. Hiromichi Shibaya, who has had a long history of wide band recording head design, described their 8–channel rotary head.

NEC. NEC's recording effort, described by Drs. Esho and Gokan, involves about 50 people and covers the gamut of recording options. They still support plating for horizontal thin film media but are developing sputtered CoCrTa for perpendicular. They are enthusiastic about their self-loading, negative air pressure bearing for low flying heights. In optics they are covering all the bases by working on phase change media as well as magnetooptics. They have an M-O system for a banking application which sidesteps the direct overwrite problem by employing two lasers per channel. NEC is still pushing Bloch line technology [155] and hopes to have a modest density system operational in two years that will demonstrate all the functional aspects.

Hitachi. Mr. Y. Tsunoda, Manager of the "6th Department", described a large research effort that covers virtually all the recording areas-MR heads, perpendicular recording, high B_s, tribology, etc. Hitachi appears to have more "basic" research underway such as switching dynamics. Perhaps related to this is the fact that they have recently initiated a visiting scientists program -they pay salary and travel to Japan. There are about 30 "foreigners" in the Central Research Labs at present. In optical recording there are many options being explored. Their approach to the M-O overwrite is to use a magnetic head that "flys" at 10 microns. They also have an acousto-optic deflector scheme for achieving a 10 msec access for an optical head - but the coarse seek actuator is **big.** Hitachi also mentioned what was heard elsewhere, that shorter wavelengths for recording will soon be practical through frequency doubling with high-power lasers.

Fujitsu. Figure 4.5[5] shows Fujitsu's own projection of areal density. They are providing Gemmy drives for NTT and are working on a 100 Mb/in^2 $5\frac{1}{4}$ inch drive called "super-Humming". Yoshimasa Miura, Manager of their File Memory Laboratory described their work on perpendicular recording and MR heads. Fujitsu has used sputtered oxide media in its 10 1/2 inch Eagle drives, but these will be replaced by smaller formats that will use thin film metallic media. Koichi Ogawa described their work on magnetooptics which has been implemented in a drive containing eight nonremovable disks. This is targeted at the optical jukebox market. Ogawa pointed out that their scheme for passivating the TbFeCo M-O media by creating a Tb-oxide coating is very effective.

---

[5]Source: Fujitsu

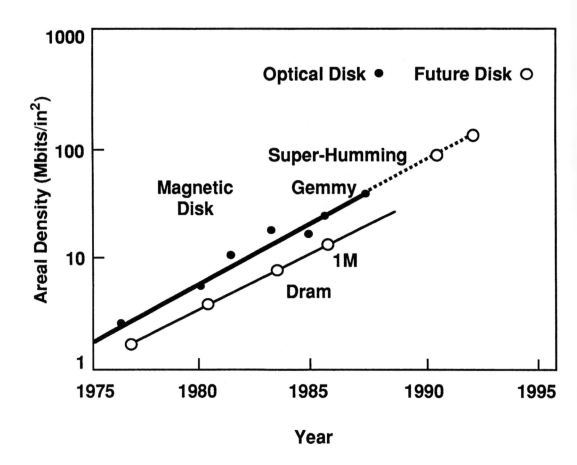

Figure 4.5: Projected area densities. Source: Fujitsu.

	Ba-f	MP	ME
Structure	Coated	Coated	Evaporated
	$(3.0\mu m)$	$(3.0\mu m)$	$(Co\text{-}Ni{:}0.2.0\mu m)$
			Prot.Layer
			$(SiO_2{:}0.02.0\mu m)$
Surface Roughness	Good	Good	Excellent
High-Density Output	Excellent	Good	Excellent
Anti-Corrosion	Excellent	Poor/Good	Poor
Lubrication	Good	Good	Poor
Head Contact	Good	Good	Poor
Producibility	Good	Good	Poor

Table 4.4: Comparison of properties for three types of media, Ba-f, MP and ME.

Toshiba. Toshiba has been working on barium ferrite since 1978. Both of my hosts, Dr. Toshiyuki Suzuki and Dr. Tatsu Fujiwara were students of Professor Iwasaki. Therefore it is not surprising that they are employing barium ferrite in many recording modes: a 16 MByte flexible disk drive, DAT, tapes, and rigid disks. The other Japanese drive manufacturers are not convinced, citing the poor overwrite as one reason. But Toshiba's view is summarized in Table 4.4. To support their claim on surface roughness they provided me the texture profiles shown in Figure 4.6. This shows profiles of flexible disks employing barium ferrite particles compared with two grades of iron oxide (DD and HD).

Sony. I regard Sony as a leader in recording. They have done a great deal to develop metal particle media and, recently, metal evaporated media for 8 mm video. Sony's so-called high-band 8mm film has a smoothness that enables a recording wavelength of 0.5 micron (Figures 4.7 and 4.8). Although Sony is primarily in video recording, it is important to remember that many of the technologies currently used in data storage came from video. This migration is illustrated in Figure 4.9. Thus Sony is in an excellent position to play a leading role in data storage.

Matsushita. I was impressed with the breadth and depth of Matsushita's activities. They seem set on becoming a major supplier of components (also under the names Panasonic or National). In the media area they are developing a metal particle-based 3 1/2 inch floppy disk capable of holding 12 to 16 Mbytes for Sony and NEC. They are also working on a perpendicular Co-Cr tape for future VCR products such as HDTV VCRs. They offer monolithic, mini composite, MIG, and thin film heads. They are

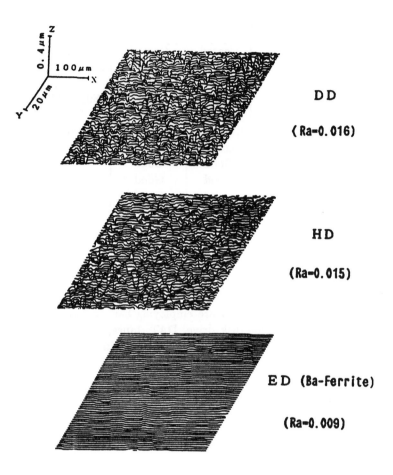

Figure 4.6: Surface profiles of flexible disks.

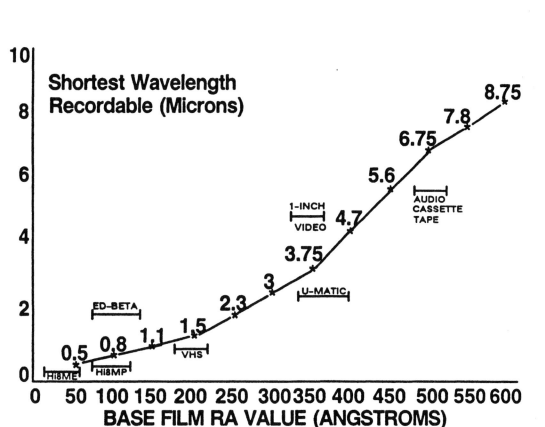

Figure 4.7: Dependence of recording wavelength on surface smoothness.

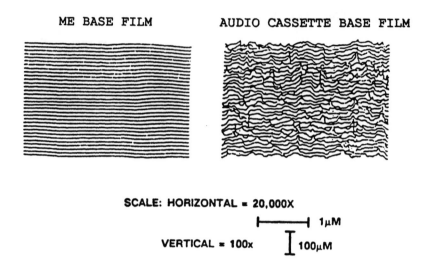

3 layers (TDK)

Figure 4.8: Comparing PET film base surface characteristics.

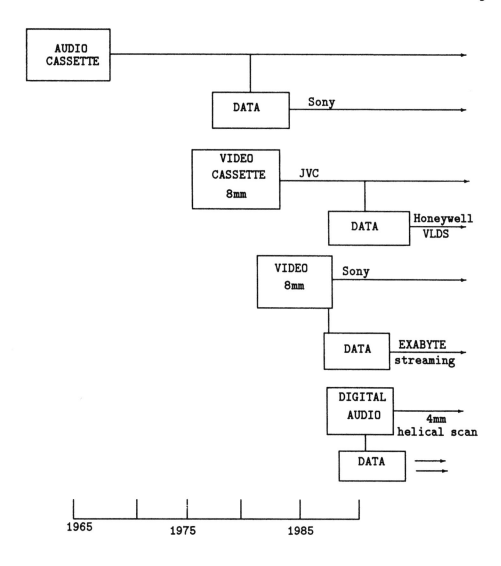

Figure 4.9: Migration of consumer recording technologies to data storage. After D. Mee of IBM.

working on soft materials for heads employing 200 Å nitride superstructures. They also have an effort on MR heads. Matsushita is the largest proponent of phase change erasable optical media.

4.4   Overview

If one steps back and looks at the recording activities in Japan one observes several things. First of all, most of the industrial research appears to be focused on near-to-medium term issues. One exception is NTT [155] which has a photon-echo storage project which is indeed a long-range concept (Cf. a recent report in Physics Review Letter [152] on this work.) In the U.S. we see more adventurous research such as the holographic storage at MCC, or the attempts to exploit the high resolution of scanning tunneling microscopy, or Recording Physics' "fluidized" drive. NEC continues to pursue the Bloch line memory, which has revolutionary potential. This may be viewed as an extension of magnetic bubble technology. Hitachi also has a long-standing project in Bloch line memories [156, 157, 158, 159, 160, 161].

An interesting indication of the scientific vitality in the U.S. is the development of the technique known as SEMPA, which stands for Scanning Electron Microscopy with spin Polarization Analysis. The U.S. National Institute for Standards and Technology (NIST) has done a great deal towards making this technique practical. Electron microscopy provides one with sub micron resolution. The spin polarization enables one to measure the magnetization with the same resolution. Since recording wave lengths are already in the submicron range such a technique should prove invaluable for understanding the recording process. Yet, except for Hitachi, there are no SEMPA instruments in the companies visited. However, except for IBM, no U.S. companies possess this capability either. But it does exist at the following universities with the indicated industrial ties:

- MIT

- Stanford/IBM

- CMU

- U. of Minnesota (Honeywell/Seagate)

There are very few universities in Japan that offer training in the field of recording. When asked about how their technologists are trained, most said that it is done "on the job" by the company. In fact, many of the "researchers" do not have Ph.Ds at first. But, they get them later under the *ronbun hakase* system. The American graduate research university is an engine with enormous potential. One only has to look at what it did for

	Fujitsu	Hitachi	NEC	Sony	Matsushita	Toshiba
Disk Drives	X	X	X	X	X	X
Tape Drives	X	X	X	X	X	X
Disks	X	X	Plated, Sputtered	X	X	X
Tapes	–		–	X	X	X
Heads	X	X	TF, Ferrite, MIG	TF	X	X
M-O Drives	X	X	X	X	X	–
M-O Media	X	X	X	X	X	–
Lasers	–	X	X	X	X	–

Table 4.5: Vertical integration in the Japanese recording industry.

	NTT	Fujitsu	Hitachi	NEC	Sony	Matsushita
Metallic media	X	X	X	X	X	X
Barium ferrite	–		X	–	X	X
M-O media	X	X	X	X	X	X
Phase change media	X		X	X	–	X
MR heads	–	X	X	X	X	X
Tribology	X	X	X	X	X	X
Air bearings	X	X	X	X	X	X
Coding	X	X	X	X		X
Perpendicular recording	X	X	X	X	X	X
SEMPA		–	X	–	–	–
Tunneling Microscope	X		X	X		X

Table 4.6: Vertical integration in research in recording in Japanese companies.

biotechnology. It is certainly not being effectively utilized to support the U.S. recording industry.

Another observation is the fact that all the Japanese companies that offer storage devices are (1) vertically integrated, (Table 4.5) and (2) have substantial research efforts (50 to 100 people) that encompass all the options (Table 4.6).

One of the aspects of vertical integration that struck me was the ability of each company to prototype systems in order to evaluate the components. Take Fujitsu's "Hero" drive, for example. It is not clear whether there is a real market for this "optical RAMAC", but they have a drive that is of beta-test quality. In the U. S. we have excellent university research efforts in magnetic modeling, tribology, encoding, thin films, etc. And, as we mentioned above, we do have venture-capital-funded component sources. But we have no mechanism for integrating these technologies into real systems. IBM is the only organization with

	IBM	AT&T	DEC.	Unisys	HP
Disk Drives	X		X	X	X
Tape Drives	X		X	X	X
Disks	X		X	X	X
Tapes	X			X	
Heads	X		X	X	
MO Drives	X				
MO Media	X				
Lasers					

Table 4.7: Recording activities by U. S. computer system manufacturers.

this capability. This observation would suggest that the U.S. recording industry consider complementing one of its university recording centers with the capability to prototype complete systems. This might be done in conjunction with an advanced manufacturing engineering program, which some universities are beginning to consider.

In comparison to Japan, only a few U.S. system companies are vertically integrated (Table 4.7) in recording. Ordinarily, vertical integration becomes financially advantageous when one's volumes exceed some level. One can then reinvest the savings in new technology, further enhancing one's technical edge. Vertical integration also has the potential of being more efficient. U.S. component suppliers, for example, complain of being misled by drive manufacturers who "multiple-order". Such practices are more easily controlled by vertical integration. If one has access to a strong vendor base then once can compete with vertical integration. However, the U. S. component suppliers are neither numerous nor healthy.

Related to vertical integration is the fact that most of the Japanese companies are also active in the consumer market. In the past, new technology was introduced into high-end products and then "trickled down" to consumer products. Today this paradigm is reversed. We often see the most advanced technology in consumer products first. The 8mm video and the R-DAT technologies are examples of consumer technologies that could have a major impact on digital systems.

In terms of covering alternative options, I found the Japanese all preparing for the eventual transition to perpendicular recording in rigid disk systems. They are seriously targeting flying heights below 0.1 micron. Most U.S.manufacturers regard perpendicular recording as too long range. As we mentioned above, U.S. drive manufacturers tend to rely on head and media suppliers for their components. There are very few sources of perpendicular media or heads in the U.S. Most of the major Japanese drive companies are developing in-house expertise with perpendicular Co-Cr films.

Another "option" under development by nearly all the Japanese companies visited is reversible optical storage. This is generally magnetooptic, although Matsushita is no longer the only one looking at phase change media. Hitachi, for example, claims to have found a fast crystallizing material suitable for single-beam overwrite. Again, vertical integration assures these efforts with their own state-of-the-art solid state lasers. Optical storage has been a long time coming. Part of the reason for this has been the lack of standards. As a result, one of the advantages of optical storage, its removable media, becomes a disadvantage. However, once magnetooptical systems achieve data rates and access times comparable to magnetic systems the fact that they are not plagued by the low flying height requirement will make them very attractive. The level of U. S. effort in this technology is woefully inadequate, considering its potential.

Another benefit of the sheer size of some of these Japanese companies is their ability to support sophisticated design capabilities. Both NTT and Hitachi described integrated MCAD/ECAD systems. Advanced manufacturing techniques are also being exploited.

To summarize, I feel that the U.S. recording industry will find it increasingly difficult to compete in the next one, and certainly two, generations of products. The failure to make significant R&D investment now will mean less familiarity with the technology later, increasing the likelyhood of design errors. Unless U.S. companies take a longer term view and improve their utilization of the university research community I predict that the Japanese will eventually dominate data storage devices. The existing university recording efforts, in order to survive will be tempted to admit Japanese sponsors who have demonstrated that they are effective at transferring technology. The result will be that the research community will receive strong, long term support, the consumer will receive high performance storage, but the U.S. will have lost another high technology industry segment.

5. Computer Architecture

Daniel P. Siewiorek

5.1 Overview

From its inception, computer architecture has been an experimental science. Systems have to be built and analyzed in order to further develop new theory. There is a strong coupling between architecture and technology. For example, Charles Babbage had developed a substantial theory of computation but the mechanical technology of the mid 1800's was inadequate. The theory stagnated until vacuum tubes became available in the mid 1900's. Thus experimentation is a key to advancing the theory of computer architecture.

In the later 1960's, Professor Michael Flynn introduced a taxonomy for computer architectures that can be used as a first order approximation for categorizing new computer systems. Figure 5.1 depicts the classical uniprocessor composed of a memory, data operator, and controller. Data and instructions are stored in memory and operated upon by the data element under directions from the controller. The data operation (e.g., arithmetic and logic unit) and controller are often paired together and called a processor. In Flynn's taxonomy this is a single instruction stream, single data stream (SISD) system since the processor interprets a single instruction at a time to operate on data stored in the memory. Higher performance can be obtained by replicating one or more of the basic elements of this computer (e.g., memory, data, or control). If the data and memory element are replicated the result is a single instruction stream, multiple data stream (SIMD) system as depicted in Figure 5.2. The data operator memory pair is often referred to as a processing element. Instructions are interpreted by the control unit and broadcast to the processing elements. The single instruction is executed on data in the local memory by all of the processing elements. All the processing elements must complete before the next instruction is issued, hence these architectures proceed from instruction to instruction in "lockstep"

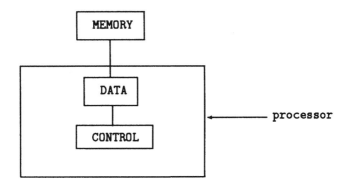

Figure 5.1: SISD: single instruction stream, single data stream.

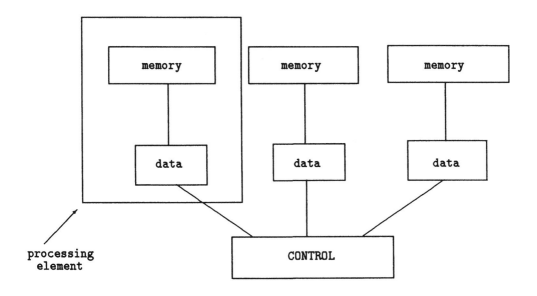

Figure 5.2: SIMD: single instruction stream, multiple data stream.

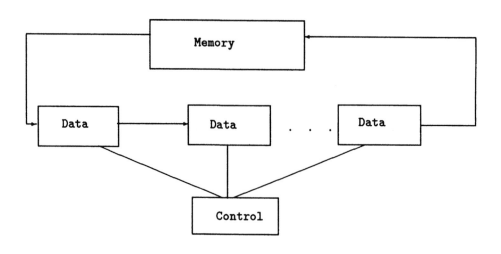

Figure 5.3: Vector data stream.

fashion. SIMD architectures excel on applications which can break their data into subsets, parceling a portion of the data to each processing element. The data in each processing element can essentially be operated upon independently.

If only the data operators are replicated the result is a pipelined or vector processor as depicted in Figure 5.3. Here data arranged in a one-dimensional array can proceed through the data operators in assembly line fashion. The controller instructs each data operator independently. While a significant architectural concept, pipelined processors do not fit into the classic Flynn taxonomy.

Finally, if the data operators and controller (i.e., processors) are replicated the result is a multiple instruction stream, multiple data stream (MIMD) architecture. If each processor shares a global memory the resultant architecture is called a "tightly-coupled" multiprocessor as depicted in Figure 5.4. If, however, memory is placed local to a processor (resulting in a complete computer) the MIMD structure is termed a "loosely-coupled" multicomputer as depicted in Figure 5.5. In tightly-coupled multiprocessors the processors synchronize with one another and share data in a common memory. Interprocessor communication is highly efficient. Multicomputers, on the other hand, typically intercommunicate through

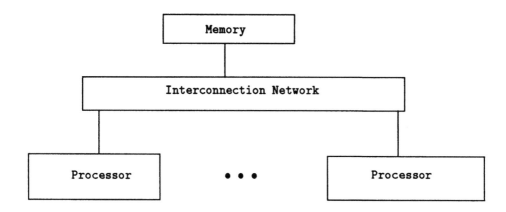

Figure 5.4: MIMD, tightly coupled.

messages which require operating system software intervention and larger latency than achieved in tightly-coupled multiprocessors. A more detailed discussion of this taxonomy can be found in the last section of this chapter which is entitled "A Survey of Computer Architectures".

The Japanese are currently experimenting with a vast number of computer architectures. Figure 5.6 is a more complete taxonomy of computer types based upon expanding the classical Flynn taxonomy. Representative American and Japanese architectural projects are listed. As we can see, the Japanese are experimenting with architectures in a majority of the taxonomy branches, especially in the multicomputer branch. Specifications for the Japanese projects can be found in tables presented later in this report. It is more enlightening to review the time-rated change of introduction of architectures. Figure 5.7, provided by NEC, shows a chronological evolution of computer architectures. The main branch is represented by SISD machines. In the mid 1960's two major sub-branches occurred corresponding to SIMD (processor array) and MIMD (multi-mini processors). Subsequent refinements of these major partitions occurred. In general, the root of each branch was formed by an American architecture. In the case of the SIMD branch, the Illiac-IV preceded the Japanese PAX project by over a decade. (Note however that a single Illiac-IV configuration was constructed whereas the PAX architecture has gone through five generations since 1977.) However, as we approach the 1980's the gap between the root of a subtree and the first Japanese project has narrowed to only a year (for example, see the CAD machines with the Yorktown Simulation Engine—YSE—at the root closely followed by the Japanese HAL project). While the number of advanced architectural projects is

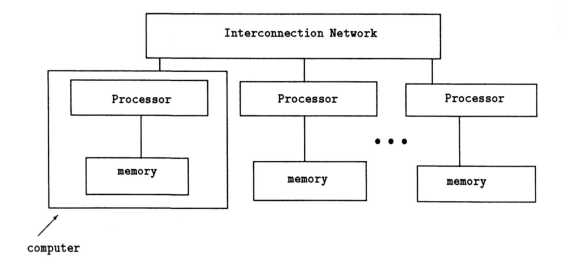

Figure 5.5: MIMD, loosely coupled.

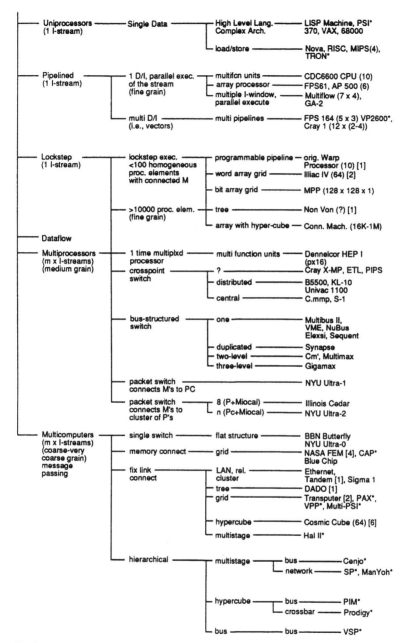

P: = Processor, M: = Memory, D: = data operation
I: = Instruction; the numbers in parentheses represent [link to node ratio, i.e., connectivity]; (degree of parallelism)
* = Japanese projects

Figure 5.6: Taxonomy of computer types. Source: C. G. Bell and D. P. Siewiorek

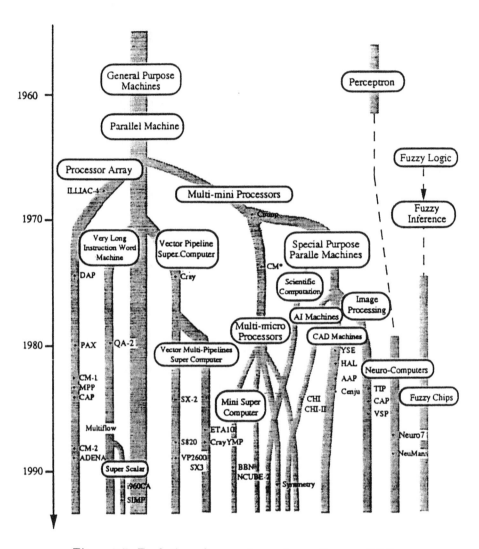

Figure 5.7: Evolution of computer systems. Source: NEC.

roughly equivalent in the United States and Japan, the sheer volume of Japanese projects commencing in approximately 1980 is very impressive. Furthermore, the Japanese are particularly active in the branch labeled special-purpose parallel machines, especially artificial intelligence machines.

The Japanese research projects can be divided into roughly three categories: short, medium, and long term. In general near term projects are composed of approximately four to ten processing elements with performance in the range of 0.1 to 10 billion [1] operations per second. The medium term projects are composed of roughly 20–100 processing elements with a performance in the range of 0.5 to 50 billion operations per second. Long term projects are experimenting with systems composed of 100 to 1000 processing elements.

Table 5.1 summarizes the systems currently in production or those whose research is mature enough to be converted into near term commercial products. General purpose mainline computing in Japan has focused on vector processing with a small number (i.e., four) of processing elements. Peak processing rates of 5 billion floating operations per second (FLOPS) have been obtained. These supercomputers are on a par with anything produced by the United States. Using specifications supplied by others, NTT has produced a mainframe computer which compares favorably with the IBM 3090 class [162]. NTT has also produced storage subsystems [163] and relational database processing hardware to compete with large IBM database systems. A third class of near term machines are dedicated to logic simulation. These systems composed of approximately 64 processing elements have been used to simulate the designs of the mainline supercomputers [164].

The medium term projects are summarized in Table 5.2. Except for the Fujitsu HPP (High-speed Parallel Processor) composed of 16 VP 2000 vector processors, and a few university projects the focus of the medium (and long) range projects are on dedicated applications. Dedicated machines for image processing, logic simulation, and logic programming [165] dominate the current thinking. When questioned about the focus on special-purpose processors one researcher responded that research teams were typically small in scope (five to ten researchers) which was insufficient manpower to produce a completely general-purpose operating system and application software. By the time a general-purpose research machine had reached demonstration stage, the feeling was that the main line of commercial general-purpose computing would have achieved parity thus obsoleting the research architectures. It was impressive that small groups of researchers could produce hardware systems composed of a hundred or more processors using the latest hardware

---

[1]Operations could be measured as instructions, floating point operations, or logical inferences. A common measure is in terms of millions of operations per second. For example, a 1 MIPS computer would execute a million instructions per second where each instruction represents either an integer operation or a program control flow operation. MFLOPS represents a million floating point operations per second and are composed of floating point arithmetic operations such as add, subtract, multiply, and divide. MLIPS represents a million logical inferences per second and are used in artificial intelligence systems as a measure of the number of symbolic decisions performed.

Name	Organization	PE's	Interconnect	Application	Performance
SX3	NEC	4		General	5.5 GFLOPS each
VP2600	Fujitsu	1		General	5 GFLOPS 128-2048 MB
DIPS E Series	NTT	4	Multiported Memory, Fiber loops	General	200 MIPS 512 MB
Rinda	NTT			Relational Database	10-100 times speedup on non-indexed searches
CMSS (Compact Mass Storage System)	NTT		Cross strapped	Backing store, Earthquake proof	60-670GB
Sigma-1	ETL	128	32 local networks tied to a global network	Data Flow FEA	170 MFLOPS
EM-4	ETL			Data Flow	
Hal II	NEC	64	Multistage	Logic Simulation	
Cenju	NEC	72 micro processors	Bus per Cluster, multistage between clusters	Logic Simulaton	
SP	Fujitsu	64	Hierarchical,multistage network	Logic Simulation (more than 10 built)	30 BIPS, 32 MB

Table 5.1: Systems in production or mature research prototypes.

Name	Organization	PE's	Interconnect	Application	Performance
HPP (High-speed Parallel Processor)	Fujitsu	16			Each PE a VP2000
DP (Display Processor)	Oki			3 D parallel geometry calculator	
VSP (Video Signal Processor)	NEC	126	16 processor cluster tied to I/O switch matrix broadcast bus	HDVT image, image processing	4MFLOPS 128-2048 MB
ManYoh	NEC		Loop structured multistage	Mixed Level logic simulator	
QA2	Kyoto Univ.		VLIW		
SIMP	Kyushu Univ.		Superscalar		
TIP	NEC	128	Dataflow pipeline, Ring structured	Image Processing	
CHI 2	NEC				500 KLIPS 64 Mwords

Table 5.2: Systems under development or underdeveloped commercial market.

fabrication technology. Hardware and software fabrication could be subcontracted to manufacturing organizations or independent third party companies. In essence, proliferation of experimental computer architectures is largely made possible by the ease with which hardware prototyping can be done.

The long term projects are summarized in Table 5.3 and focus primarily on parallel processors with up to 1000 processing elements. Again, image processing and simulation applications predominate. A major exception is the focus on parallel logic programming machines [166] and neural network research.

There is equally active experimentation in processor chips as depicted in Table 5.4. While the TRON (The Real-time Operating system Nucleus) [6, 167, 168] focuses on real-time applications across a broad range of business, industrial, and communications applications, the other chips are dedicated to narrower areas such as signal processing and LISP-structured programming languages [169, 170, 171].

The architectures presented in Tables 5.1 through 5.4 are grouped by application area in Table 5.5. The heavy emphasis on image processing and neural networks [172] is very apparent. Equally striking is the fact that each of the major computer manufacturers are experimenting with architectures in each of the major branches of the taxonomies depicted in Figures 5.6 and 5.7. Table 5.6 maps the architectures observed on this trip as represented by the parent organization against the major branches of the taxonomy. Note that Fujitsu, NEC, and Toshiba have experimental architectures in every major branch of the computer structures taxonomy.

Researchers receive basic training at the university and specialized training at their company. The lifetime employment with the company has a consequence that there is "living documentation" in that when a system is revised the original designers are available to "relive" the design decisions. Innovation is produced by moving people between departments and by moving research ideas into production with the researcher accompanying his prototype into product. Not only is a better technology achieved, but people are also kept fresh.

This observer feels that Japanese are especially strong in:

- hardware prototyping

- vector processing and pipeline design, vectorizing software

- dedicated hardware simulation architectures

- technology transfer between research and products

- experimentation with neural networks and incremental learning

- multi-media workstations including text, graphics, voice, and video

Name	Organization	PE's	Interconnect	Application	Performance
CAP	Fujitsu	256 Intel 80186	Grid	Graphics, CAM, Image processing	16 MFLOPS,50 MIPS two built in 1986, 512 Mbytes
QCDPAX	Univ Tsukuba.	432	2-D Torus, Mesh	QCD	12.38 GFLOPS (peak)
DPP (Dedicated Parallel Processing System)			Satellite Image processing, plasma simulation, weather		> 100 MFLOPS
FX	Fujitsu	1000		Astronomical calculations	
VPP (Variable Processor Pipeline)	Toshiba	64	2D mesh composed of slotted rings	Satellite image processing	
PSI-II (Sequential inference machine)	ICOT/Mitsubishi	128	2DByte wide	Logic programming	400 Klips 16MB
Multi-PSI	ICOT	128	2D Byte-wide mesh	Logic programming, Natural language, Parser, Shortest path Solver, Puzzle packer	10-20 MLIPS, 5-10GB
PIM (Parallel Inference Machine)	ICOT/Fujitsu internal/external instructions	1000 hypercube between buses	8 PE's/bus,	Logic programming	256 MB/bus shared 2 MB/processor local
Neuro-7	NEC		PC accelerator		
NeuroMan	NEC				
AI WS	Toshiba			Lisp, Prolog	
Prodigy	Toshiba	16 to 512	8×8 crossbar connected cluster, cube between clusters	AI, Neural Networks	Each PE 68000,2 MB

Table 5.3: Systems under development or with at best long term commercial prospects.

Name	Organization	Application	Performance	Notes
TRON		Real Time	8 MIPS Matsushita 7 MIPS Hitachi 7 MIPS Mitsubishi 17 MIPS Fujitsu 5 MIPS Toshiba	Culturally compatible with M68000, VAX, instruction sets
AI Chip (IP 1804)	Toshiba	Prolog, LISP	1MLIPS	ISC extended for AI, macroinstructions in ROM
Digital	Hitachi	Speech Recognition, Character Recognition, Expert System, Robotics	1.2 times SUN 4	6 neurons/chip to be assembled into 1000 chip machine
Analog Neural Chip	Fujitsu			1 neuron/chip
DSP	Toshiba	Medical electronic Image Processing, Space		
VSTEP	NEC		Parallel, 2D computations	Direct optical to digital memory vertical to surface Transmission Electro-Photonic Device

Table 5.4: Chips.

Database	Logic Simulation	Image Processing	Logic Programming	Neural Networks
DIPS	HAL	VSP	PSI	NEUROMAN
RINDA	Cenju	TIP	PIM	AIWS
	SP	CAP		Prodigy
	ManYoh	DPP		Digital
		DSP		Neural chip
		VPP	PIE64	

Table 5.5: Dedicated applications and representative machines.

Microprocessor	Special/ Processor/Chip	Pipeline	Hierarchical/ Mesh/Cube/ Multistage	Multistage
Fujitsu	Fujitsu	Fujitsu	Fujitsu	Fujitsu
NEC	NEC	NEC	NEC	NEC
Toshiba	Toshiba	Toshiba	Toshiba	Toshiba
Hitachi				
Mitsubishi				
Matsushita				
Oki				

Table 5.6: Classes of machines and representative manufacturers.

5.2   Response to Questions

A number of questions formed the basis of our interviews with various organizations in order to determine their views as to the future directions of computer architecture (the list of questions are reproduced in Appendix B.7). Most respondents either agreed with the premises provided by the questions or had no substantial further comments. There seemed to be a strong "compartmentalization" of expertise (e.g., one organization provided a dozen architects to cover individual segments of the questionnaire). "Cross cutting" questions that went between disciplines solicited few responses. Perhaps the questions were abstract enough to encounter a language barrier. The fact that most respondents were in industry which traditionally even in the United States has a narrower focus and do not have adequate opportunity to explore the broader issues, perhaps curtailed responses. One component that seemed to be uniformly missing from the people interviewed was that of quantitative analysis. While the papers provided to us indicated substantial gate-level simulation and some architectural simulation (such as used in cache design), these techniques did not seem to be universally applied. In addition, knowledge about application-level requirements and typical usage profiles were not encountered.

The Japanese excel at incrementally improving architectural concepts. For example Toshiba's Prodigy project was basically a cube except an eight by eight crossbar chip was used to reduce interconnection cables as well as to improve data transfer rate (e.g., byte parallel as opposed to bit serial). In the area of neural networks the Japanese are focusing on hardware architectures (e.g., analog/digital/optical neuro devices, neural network emulators on large parallel machines) [172] and applications. Each parallel processing project seemed to have one application being a neural net solving either speech recognition, character recognition, or serving as a knowledge base for an expert system [170]. However, the Japanese did not seem to be working on fundamental theory and models for neural networks. At least one researcher observed that the fundamental computational model was still speculative and thus he would rather focus on applications and tools which were much better defined.

The consensus response to the architectural questions included:

Instruction Sets. It is unclear whether RISC or CISC is better and research is progressing in both. Current silicon technology is suited for RISCs. However there were CISC-based chips dedicated to LISP language processing or to object management (such as the OZ project [173]) which were comparable or up to 50% faster than RISC instruction sets on the same application. The conclusion is that if you know the primitives, and that the primitives do not disturb the uniformity of one instruction per clock tick, then support for higher level languages can be introduced into the instruction set architecture [169, 174]. Examples include support for data structures such as linked list and arrays. One researcher felt that VLIW [175, 176] computers could replace RISC approaches for improving performance. IBM apparently thinks so too. Cf. the IBM RS/6000.

Parallel Processing. There is much work which needs to be done and it will be a long time before there are automatic parallelizers which are as effective as contemporary vectorizing compilers. Parallel languages also need to be developed. A few researchers however, felt parallelism was ready for commercialization. Several researchers criticized hypercubes as being unbalanced between node computation power and the interconnection network bandwidth. MIMD machines need a low ratio of FLOPS to communication time. Another researcher observed that multi-stage networks had severe latency restrictions but could be good for special selected applications in computer to computer structures (i.e., the multi-stage network is not used to connect processors with their main memory).

Pipelining, Multiple Functioning Units, and Vector Processing. Vector processing will remain the mainstream supercomputer technology for at least five years and probably ten. Superscalers have a maximum of three to four parallelism available for general-purpose programs thus will be limited and unable to surpass vectors machines. Some of the data flow applications have achieved a low level parallelism of ten. The future would be a combination of parallel and vector architectures [177].

Special-Purpose Architectures. As noted above, the Japanese are strongly focused on special-purpose architectures.

Influence of Software and Hardware. There were no real strong opinions in this area except that single language environments will not be able to survive except for supporting special fields such as signal processors.

Systems Issues. Not enough thought has been given to input/output. The focus has been on producing the correct interconnect structure for various applications. Once this has been determined the input/output problem will be worked. By the year 2000 the computing environment will be a mixture of architectures supported by at least a 10 Gbit/sec network. Users will map their applications onto the architecture best suited for their problem. Furthermore, there may be variations of the same architecture available to more finely match the application to the architecture (e.g., a highly-vectorizable application might be shipped to a vector processor with four pipelines while a lesser pipelineable application might be shipped to another model of the vector architecture with perhaps only one vector pipeline). The concept of servers in the environment will be maintained with not only compute servers, but also database servers.

5.3   Interactions Between Japanese and Foreign Researchers

Several organizations have pre-existing programs for interaction with international researchers. In particular:

ICOT. A formal agreement was signed in June of 1986 between ICOT and the National Science Foundation whereby US visiting researchers selected by NSF could visit ICOT. To date, only one US researcher has been so positioned and his year-long stay ended in October, 1988. ICOT has also entertained visitors from France, The United Kingdom, Israel, West Germany, Canada, Sweden, Italy, Australia, and Austria. ICOT has funded over 50 researchers to visit from these countries for up to one month at ICOT expense.

Toshiba. Toshiba has employed graduate students from MIT, Stanford, and Penn State. Students have also been supported from France and Scotland. There is a Toshiba Fellowship program for a term of from one to two years for British scientists from British government institutes that has supported eight researchers so far. Toshiba also has an Interim Employment of Post-Doctoral Research Fellows program whereby a student with a Ph.D. or equivalent experience will be paid to be a one to two year limited- term employee. The major restriction is that the limited-term employee not engage in the same type of work for any company during the term of employment or six months thereafter without written permission from Toshiba.

5.4   Computing Environment in Japan

A survey of 320 businesses by SEA (Software Engineers Association) (52% of which were software houses) indicated that the most frequently used computing environment shifted from mainframes and minicomputers (65%) in 1983 to an even split (46%) between mainframes and minicomputers and workstations (42%) in 1988 as summarized in Table 5.7. The survey also indicated that over that same five-year time period, the Unix/C environment grew from 10% to 40%, workstations improved the accessibility of computing (decrease from six persons per terminal in 1983 to two persons per terminal in 1988), and use of networking increased (40% of the computers were networked in 1988). The growth in the use of C came from decreased use of assembler (−16%), FORTRAN (−12%), and PL/1 (−8%). Some observers attribute these choices to the influence of the SIGMA project.

The computing environment at SRA, one of Japan's leading software development houses, featured a variety of workstations (i.e., SUN, Sony, NeXT, VAXStation) running

	1983	1988
Mainframe	37	30
Minicomputer	28	16
Workstation	20	42
PC	9	10

Table 5.7: Percentage change in the composition of Japanese computing.

Unix in multi-media (text, graphics, and video) windows. Unix-based commercially available parallel processors (e.g., Encore, Sequent) and parallel, super workstations (e.g., Ardent, Stellar) are relatively unknown. However, several Sequent machines were observed in use as simulators for PIM software.

5.5   Detailed Observations

Parallel architectures in Japan have evolved from first generation homogeneous interconnect structures (e.g., two dimensional networks) to second generation hierarchical structures (e.g., mixture of buses and interconnection networks). Figure 5.8 depicts the archetypical second generation parallel structure. The processing elements (PE's) in a cluster are tightly coupled and communicate over a high speed bus to shared memory. Private caches minimize the PE demand for the shared resources (i.e., bus and memory). The PE's can range from general-purpose microprocessors; to microprocessor/coprocessor pairs; to special purpose, custom VLSI chips [178]. The number of PE's per cluster is typically eight to sixteen. Clusters intercommunicate via messages through networks such as multistage switches or hypercubes. Typically there are eight to sixteen clusters. Thus the second generation hierarchical structures support 64 to 256 PE's.

It is interesting to note how the Japanese have taken the structures in the classical taxonomy and innovated to produce new structures. For example, consider the CAP image processing system by Fujitsu as depicted in Figure 5.9. Each "cell" is composed of an Intel 80186 and two megabytes of memory to form a computer. The cells are interconnected with north, east, south, and west neighbors in a classical mesh structure usually employed in SIMD architectures. An image can be broadcast to the cells via the video bus. High-level functions to operate on the image are issued by the host computer over the command bus. These commands trigger extensive computations in each of the cells. The resultant image can be sent back over the video bus to be displayed on a color monitor. A single controller and nearest-neighbor mesh connection are reminiscent of classical SIMD machines. However, instead of operating on single instructions broadcast by the host computer, the

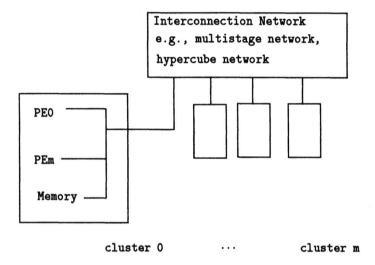

Figure 5.8: Hierarchical interconnect structure.

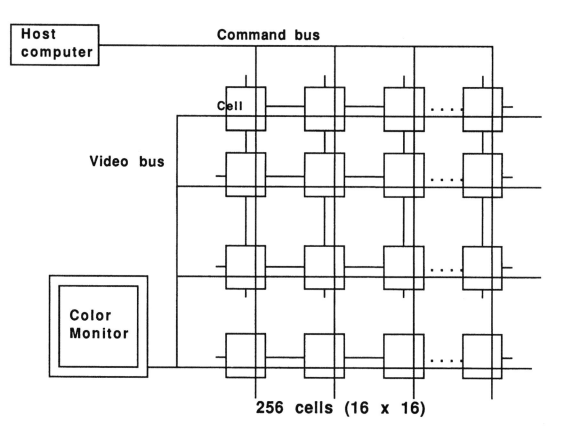

Figure 5.9: The CAP image processing system.

computer cells perform substantially more complex computations. Another example is the parallel inference machine (PIM [166]) depicted in Figure 5.10. Each cluster is composed of a shared memory multiprocessor. Half of the processors are connected through one routing network into the intercluster network while the other half of the processors use a different router. These routers form corners of a cube in n-space as depicted in Figure 5.11. Thus two different nodes in n-space can closely cooperate in the cluster while having more remote access to other clusters.

The visit with NTT (Musashino) Storage Systems Laboratory indicates that high-performance parallel systems are not yet generally considered as targets for their disk input/output systems. The NTT Gemmy disk drive can be configured into a storage system composed of dual storage directors attached to different block multiplexor channels. Each storage director handles two disk controllers. Each disk controller handles up to 16 disk drives. Finally, each disk drive is attached to two disk controllers. While this configuration provides numerous redundant paths for reliability, questions about parallel (stripping of data files) and distributed (distributing data files to allow concurrent data base accessing) processing to improve performance were not considered for NTT disk systems. (Note that this is compatible with the mission of a telecommunications system where reliability is the major concern.)

5.6   Observations, Impressions, and Scenarios

Based upon the small sampling of Japanese projects and researchers visited, it can be dangerous to jump to conclusions and to quickly stereotype any perceived patterns. Never-the-less, some phenomena were observed more than once which left definite impressions and led to speculation about the future. These observations, impressions, and scenarios are recorded here with a strong caution to the reader that they could just as easily be shallow research on the interviewers part, misinterpretations, and fiction.

5.6.1   Compartmentalization of Knowledge

In discussions with several organizations there appeared to be a strong compartmentizing of knowledge. Detailed questions were frequently answered with a "don't know" or deferred to another specialist in the room. This may have been due to a desire to be totally accurate or to politeness "to defer to the expert." Cross cutting questions, such as comparison of one architectural style versus another, were often left unanswered. One might speculate whether the same type of response might have occurred in U.S. industry from designers "down in the trenches" who did not have the luxury to take the long view as university researchers can. Perhaps, the Japanese are more reluctant to "wing it" than their American counterparts. Questions about quantitative performance measurements to spot

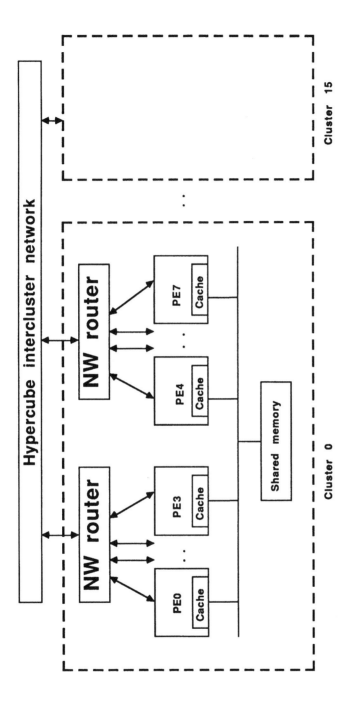

Figure 5.10: PIM system configuration.

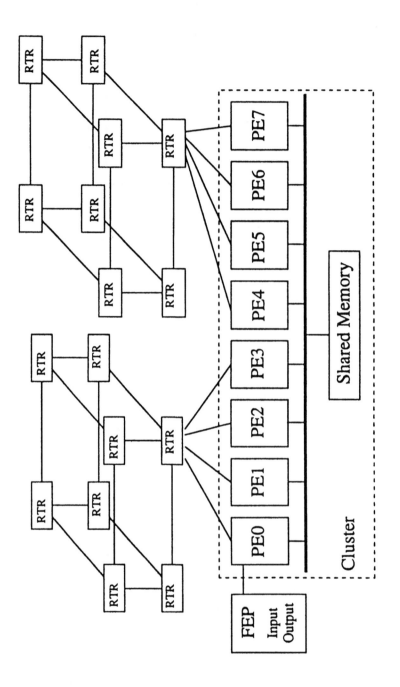

Figure 5.11: Intercluster network structure.

"bottlenecks" and tune systems accordingly were left unanswered. Either the quantitative architectural approach currently popular in the U.S. is missing or the right specialists were not present in the meetings.

5.6.2   Critical Mass

Consider the case of a mainframe data processor manufacturer. There were approximately 200 to 300 mainframes and 600 minicomputers supported by approximately 600 people to design, develop, and maintain this broad range of products. Compare these number to a typical U.S. start-up company with approximately 200 people but serving only a single product. The variety of products versus the number installed appears to be large. In other words, Japanese critical mass to undertake a project is considerably smaller than US projects.

Other observations indicate that the Japanese can produce a large variety of hardware products. A visit to a random consumer electronics store revealed an entire floor displaying over 300 models of personal computer of which over 100 were portables with LCD displays. The TRON project has already produced three implementations of the TRON chip [6]. The Fifth Generation project has developed two generations of PSI (Personal Inference Engine) and two generations of parallel processors (Multi-PSI and PIM).

5.6.3   Scenarios

The Japanese are very prolific experimenters. Several questions come to mind including can the rate of experimentation be maintained and what gain can be derived from duplication of effort? Two possible scenarios come to mind.

Convergence. The NTT mainframes are comparable to IBM mainframes. The packaging, semiconductor chips, cooling, and distribution are all common to NTT, Amdahl, and Fujitsu (with Fujitsu manufacturing the machines). Only a small number of custom chips had to be designed. NTT is currently working with other companies to unify the application interface while still maintaining each unique operating system. One can speculate that future integration and sharing between companies, perhaps around CTRON, could reduce duplication further freeing up resources to focus on higher level applications.

Integration. By having diverse groups intimately involved with the process of computer design, these groups will be in a better position to produce innovative system in their area of expertise (such as computers and communications in the case of NTT). Note, however, this scenario is in conflict with the compartmentalization observation above.

5.7   A Survey of Computer Architectures

This section is based upon an earlier survey prepared by C. Gordon Bell and the author. It describes the state-of-the-art in computer architecture through the use of a taxonomy. Four basic approaches have been utilized and are being evolved to increase performance through parallelism. The five main branches of computer structures (ignoring data flow) are given in Figure 5.6 and can be summarized as:

1. Simple uniprocessor computer (base case) – Single Instruction Single Data – the processor interprets a single instruction stream to operate on data stored in a common memory.

2. Pipelined, multiple execution unit uniprocessor for scalar and vector processing – Single and Multiple Statement execution architectures – the processor interprets a few machine instruction to operate, in parallel, on several scalars or on multiple data (e.g., several numbers or a vector) stored in common memory. These machines exploit a low degree of fine grain parallelism by either a prior knowledge of the program at compile time or simple hardware interlocks on processor registers at instruction execution time.

3. Lockstep uniprocessor – one instruction execution unit, many processing element/data memory pairs – a single machine instruction controls the simultaneous execution in a large number (100-100K) of processing elements on a lockstep basis. Each processing element has an associated data memory. Intercommunication is via fixed paths among the processing elements. Message passing occurs either on an explicit program routing basis as in Illiac IV or an implicit hardware routing basis as in the Connection Machine. The lockstep processor is targeted to exploit fine grained parallelism.

4. Multiprocessor – many instruction execution units operating on many data memories – each simple uniprocessor accesses programs and data stored in common memory. Processors synchronize with one another and share data within a set of statements (e.g., a loop or block). These machines exploit medium and coarse grain parallelism and distributed processing via local area networks.

5. Multicomputer – many computers are connected via a range of switches such as a high bandwidth switch (e.g., a Banyan switch or Omega network) a fixed switch structure (e.g., tree or hypercube). These machines support coarse grain parallelism as well as very coarse grain parallelism and distributed distributed processing via LANS.

The uniprocessor which operates on single data items from a single instruction stream forms the first class. Note that the distinguishing feature is the complexity of the instruction set. The speed of execution is inversely proportional to this complexity since a microprogrammed interpreter is required to carry out various data-type operations. The LISP machine is the most complex because data types must be type checked (and converted). A complex instruction set like the VAX-11 has four floating point, three string, and four integer/boolean vector data types that demand a large microprogrammed interpreter. The load/store architecture reappeared in the form of the hardwired interpreter of reduced instruction set (e.g., RISC) in order to match the logic speed of a processor with semiconductor memory speeds. Several instructions can be processed by a fetch, decode, execute pipeline to give parallelism of 2 to 4. An instruction is executed every 1 to 2 clock periods.

The multiple function unit, uniprocessor increases parallelism on the order of 4 to 10 by operating on several instructions from the stream using multiple execution units. These include the CDC 6600, "array" processors which operate on 4 to 6 data items and addresses in a parallel and pipelined fashion, and the proposal for a much more parallel instruction which can operate on 10 processing elements concurrently (Yale's ELI and Multiflow's Trace architecture). The TI ASC , CDC STAR and Cray 1 added vector data types to enable pipelining by explicit operations. The Cray 1 has 12 pipelines of 2 to 4 stages. The Systolic Processor is basically a programmable pipeline.

The lockstep uniprocessor uses a simple instruction decoder to process many data items in parallel. The Solomon and Illiac IV were the first, followed by the Goodyear STARAN and MPP. The latter unit operates on bits across many words and provides associative memory operations with parallelism of about 100. With VLSI, the idea of having thousands or millions of processing elements was inevitable, using every conceivable topology to interconnect the processing elements from the trees (non Von) to grids with more connections (Connection Machine). No general purpose lockstep processors are in common use, and it is doubtful that such systems will be useful over the next decade because they are unlikely to be cost-effective, efficiently programmed, or able to support I/O except for a few applications.

Multiprocessors have been built in every technology beginning in 1960. The initial multiprocessors used distributed cross-point switches with about four ports in each memory module (m) to enable multiple processor (p) access via $m \times p$ cables. With MSI technology, the cost of switching could be drastically reduced by having a central switch and only $m + p$ cables; 16 processor systems were built by BTL, CMU, and others. Dennelcor used several fast physical processors, each of which multiplexes across several instruction streams in the same fashion that the CDC 6600 PPUs were implemented. Today, a single "Unibus"-type structure provides a cost-effective switching for microprocessors. Caches, coupled with bus watchers to ensure cache coherency, support up to 20 processors on a single bus. By cascading multiprocessors together in a hierarchical fashion with caches at each level, up to 1000 processors can form a single multiprocessor (the Encore Gigamax). Another approach to interconnect processors is an interconnected set of simple 2 to 4 port switches such as a Banyan, Omega, or perfect shuffle network. Due to the cost and interconnection topology (i.e., cables), the switch width is limited and hence the networks are inherently slow due to serial packet transmission.

Multicomputers can be interconnected in three ways: via a separate switching structure such as an Omega network (the BBN Butterfly), in a grid using shared memory at the intersection of the computers, or with fixed links among the computers.

The uniprocessor branch is limited in performance range and scaleability. Branches 2 and 3 exploit the known structures of problems and are usually applied to a single problem at a time. These structures are difficult to apply to ill-structured problems or multiple, simultaneous problems. Branches 4 and 5 have the greatest potential for performance range and scaleability.

Since a multiprocessor using n processors can always emulate a multicomputer of n computers, the multiprocessor is a more general structure. The multicomputer is inherently difficult to use on any general basis due to the problem of allocating programs, data, and I/O to the computer. In addition to the allocation problem on a multicomputer, multiprogramming[2] introduces further complications in I/O, scheduling, and synchronization. The grain size is coarse, and since the connectivity is low, the intercommunication time is long. i.e., on the order of thousands of instructions.

Table 5.8 defines two main attributes of parallel applications. Grain size is the period between synchronization events for multiple processors or processing elements. Synchronization is necessary in parallel processing to initialize a task, parcel out work, and merge results. Lockstep processors are fine grain since all processing elements synchronize at the end of each instruction. Very coarse grain computation on multicomputers is synchronized every few thousand instructions. Another parameter, data connectivity, specifies the amount of data that can be transferred among the separate parts of a process per synchronization point. With the lockstep processor, connectivity is usually poor and the transmission time among the elements is long. For multiprocessors, processors can be synchronized every 50–500 instructions and data is immediately sharable through common memory on an instruction-by-instruction basis.

5.7.1   Research Trends

The decades of the 1960's and 1970's were devoted to generating new architectural concepts as exemplified by SIMD/MIMD, vector processing, multiple functional units, and fault-tolerant transaction processors. The designs were typical technology driven (i.e., take what technology would provide) and guided by the intuition of the architect. There were many memorable failures but also a sprinkling of notable successes.

The research of the 1980's has attempted to put computer architecture on a quantitative basis. Faster processors made it feasible to gather instruction traces from nontrivial

---

[2]A multiprocessor can exploit multiprogramming by assigning individual processors specific tasks until the tasks are completed.

Grain size	Language construct Parallelism	Sync.[a]	Data[b]	Computers[c]
Fine	Intra statement	1	1 [10–1000]	FPS (4–8)[d] Cray 1 (12×4), Systolic Array (10 ×5), Illiac IV (64), MPP (128), Connection Machine (16K–1M)
Medium	Program block single process, context	50–500	1–20 [1]	ELEXS1 (6)[e], Dennelcor (16)
Coarse	inter process, O/S call, message pass.	500–5000	10–100 [100-1K]	DADO, Hypercube (64–256)[f], BBN Butterfly
Very Coarse	task, program, Distributed proc.	5K–1M	10–1K [5K]	LAN e.g. Ethernet (1K)[f], VAX Clusters

[a]Synchronization interval in instructions.
[b]Data connectivity in (words) and [time in instructions].
[c]to support granularity.
[d]Numbers indicate the degree of parallelism. Parallelism by replicated processing elements, only one program counter.
[e]Parallelism in the number of processors.
[f]Parallelism in the number of computers (processor-primary memory pairs) which send messages to each other.

Table 5.8: Applications grain size and characteristics versus computer type.

benchmarks. Instruction and addressing mode usage frequency data triggered the instruction set design debate. The quantitative analysis then switched to cache designs. Currently the focus is based on multiple buses/hierarchical caches. It should be noted that this quantitative research is based upon a relatively small number of actual traces, each of a limited length (typically a million instructions). The benchmarks are typically scientific-oriented and compute bound. The length of the traces precludes operating system intervention or multiprocessing effect.

The increase in quantitative awareness can be documented by observing the increase in the frequency of papers containing quantitative numbers at the annual Computer Architecture Symposium. However, since raw data is so difficult to collect, the architectural features explored have been rather focused and narrow. For example, over 30% of the papers of the 1989 Symposium on Computer Architecture dealt with caches. Other important areas, such as input/output (only one paper at the 1989 symposium) have been forgotten or ignored. It would be desirable to have a more balanced approach to computer architecture research.

6. Progress in Software and Software Engineering

James H. Morris

6.1 Introduction

The Japanese have developed significant strength in software by applying the same methods that have served them in traditional engineering areas. Their approach is embodied in organizations called Software Factories. These organizations are unlike the typical U.S. ones. They

- employ thousands of workers, who spend their entire careers with the same company,

- continually predict, measure, and modify the performance of individuals and organizations,

- emphasize the quality of delivered products,

- make great efforts to reuse previous work,

- use sophisticated software tools, and

- depend less upon university computer science education.

These organizations demonstrate measurable superiority in the creation of custom systems for mainframes and minicomputers: 70% more lines of code per worker with less than half the errors [7]. This difference has not had any market impact in the U.S. because, so far, Japanese software groups focus their attention on local machines and customers.

	Japan	U. S.	
Total Revenues (billions)	$34.1	$70.4	
Hardware	62%	65%	
Large Systems	25%		13%
Medium Systems	10%		12%
Small Systems	15%		12%
Personal Computers	12%		28%
Software	38%	35%	
Shelf products	4%		19%
Custom Software	29%		14%
Other	5%		2%

All percentages are relative to total revenues.

Table 6.1: Japan-U.S. industry comparison, 1987.

Japan lags the U.S. in the development of a personal computer software industry. It also lags in the creation of innovative software, both in novel product design and traditional computer science areas like programming languages and operating systems. There are indications, however, that they may excel in the integration of video and computing.

This brief report is based upon observations made in Japan during November of 1989 and the observations of other students of the Japanese software industry, notably Yoshihiro Matsumoto of Kyoto University, Stuart Feldman and Robert Martin of Bellcore, Michael Cusumano of MIT, and Hide Tokuda of Carnegie Mellon.

6.2   The Computer Business

Most software in Japan is produced by the large computer manufacturers, NEC, Hitachi, Fujitsu, and Toshiba. Each has software factories which specialize in particular kinds of systems. We are aware of only three independent software houses, CSK, SRA, and ASCII, and they are very small by U.S. standards.

There are significant structural differences between the U.S. and Japanese computer business as Table 6.1, based on 1987 data, shows: [179, 180] The U.S. market is twice the size of the Japanese market. Personal computer hardware is not a large segment of Japan's industry, and most Japanese software is created for custom applications rather than sold off the shelf.

The lag in personal computer hardware might be partly due to the slowness of Japanese business to adopt word processing because of the intrinsic difficulties of the Japanese

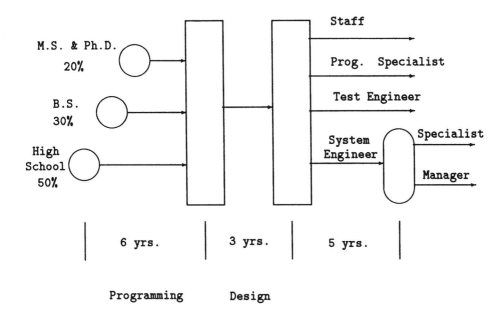

Figure 6.1: Career paths for a software professional at Toshiba.

alphabets. However, the situation is evolving to be more like the U.S. The leader in PC sales is NEC while the more expensive workstation market is led by SUN Microsystems and Sony.

The emphasis on custom software is partly due to the lack of a PC hardware base, which would require off-the-shelf software, but is also due to differences in customer-vendor expectations. Each large bank, for example, will expect to have a unique system developed in partnership with a vendor. In the U.S. one would expect many banks to buy the same basic system and adapt it to its own operation. In Japan, however, the vendor is expected to perform the adaptation and the companies therefore emphasize the reuse of software from one system to the next.

6.3   The Life of a Software Professional

Figure 6.1 shows the some of possible career paths for a Japanese software professional at Toshiba [181].

The most notable fact is that the average professional is a high school graduate who is trained by his company. In the U.S., a programmer is more often a university-trained Computer Science graduate. This particular statistic is probably an extreme case and is based on older information. For example, the data in [182] are five five years old and suggest that the Japanese software professional has had exposure to a higher technical school. Even the average high school graduate in Japan, as well as those going on to the higher technical schools have the mathematical and scientific training of a U.S. college sophomore. In any case, as Japanese universities improve their Computer Science education, this difference is diminishing. However, the brightest computer-knowledgeable university graduates in Japan go to work for banks and insurance companies because they pay more. Computer manufacturers get second choice. Software houses get third choice because they have little prestige.

The career pattern is similar for a U.S. software engineer. The progression from programmer to manager takes about the same amount of time. However, it is significant that this diagram represents a plan; and it is highly likely that he will pursue it within the company for his whole career. In the U.S. a software professional is more likely to change companies several times in a career.

The general style of Japanese working conditions – longer hours and minimal creature comforts – strike visitors immediately. In the words of one observer the conditions are "Dickensian". Even though there is a perceived shortage of programmers, there seems to be little move to attract them through better working conditions or higher pay. The Japanese system of keying everyone's pay to their age prevents major financial incentives. However, it seems clear there are more desirable jobs, as Figure 6.1 shows, and that better performers get them.

6.4   Tools

The companies we visited used a variety of conventional software tools for the management of software projects. For example, Toshiba employs a "Software Workbench" derived from the UNIX system [8].

There were more aggressive ideas in the area of support for common programming. They are attempting to transcend conventional programming through the use of very high level, partly graphical languages called applications generators. At Fujitsu, they use a tool, YPS, that generates COBOL from structured diagrams. They also have a few more experimental projects that attempt to use tools early in the requirements setting process.

We saw instances of machine support for the Structured Analysis and Design methodology. We did not see use of so-called fourth generation languages.

Despite the generally regimented operation of the Software Factories, they are constantly experimenting with new methods. Recently at Toshiba, a transmission line fault diagnosis project was undertaken using Prolog and C. The original version of the program was written in Prolog and tried on sample cases. Then the final version was produced by a semi-automatic translation process. The system was eventually 600,000 line of code and is now used by electric power companies.

The SIGMA project has been discussed extensively elsewhere [183]. It is a major effort to develop a software engineering environment based upon UNIX and networking. This requires: good computing machines (mainly workstations, but not necessarily), good tools, networking for effective information transmission as well as distributed software development environment. SIGMA was to develop a common system interface (including Operating System) for tool portability on the machines from the various vendors. Its major output is a System V based operating system specification that all members of the consortium are expected to support. It has also produced an extensive set of software tools in various languages. We saw debugging and performance tools demonstrated on an OMRON machine in a FORTRAN programming environment. We heard nothing of the networking or database parts of SIGMA, although they figured prominently in the early planning.

The first phase of SIGMA is ending. The various UNIX standards have been decided upon — System V.3 GKS, X.11, etc. — and the individual manufactures are building to them at their own places. In future they will conform to other standards – e.g. MOTIF – emerging from the US. There is an operational phase of SIGMA planned for the 1990's. All the companies we asked about SIGMA adopted a wait-and-see attitude. The fact that SUN and Sony, both supplying non-SIGMA systems, are the market leaders now indicates that SIGMA's impact has not been felt.

The results of the Sigma project were passed to a newly established company called SIGMA Systems, Inc. The company has, at present, 50 shareholders and 75 member companies.

6.5   Methodology

The foremost U.S. expert on software factories is Michael Cusumano who is completing a major book on the subject, based on several years of study [184]. He kindly made several preliminary working papers available to me for purposes of preparing this report.

An early report was based upon a survey of several Japanese and U.S. companies [185]. He conceptualized a range of work methods including job shop, a rigid factory, and a flexible factory. He designed and administered a questionnaire to test the sophistication of a company's software enterprise both in terms of tools and methods. A sample question is, "Do you monitor how much code is being reused?". The general result is that there is a wide spectrum in the sophistication of software process on both sides of the Pacific but, generally, the Japanese companies are ahead. This claim is generally accepted at the "journeymen" level, but is disputed at the "wizard" level.

The explicit conclusions of the study are

- The survey scores of all the facilities in the sample follow a normal distribution.

- There is no significant difference in the average scores for technology infrastructure between Japanese and U.S. facilities.

- The average Japanese score for methodology sophistication is significantly higher than the comparable U.S. scores.

- Facilities farther toward the total factory model exhibit control characteristics one might expect to find in a large factory-type organization: fewer defects (bugs) reported by users and more precise project scheduling. However, they do not conclusively exhibit tighter cost control.

- Facilities that exhibit another characteristic one might expect to find in a large factory-type organization – greater use of standardized components, i.e. higher rates of reusability of code – also appear to score high on the total factory criteria.

A similar study by Humphrey [186] on U.S. defense contractors and my informal observations tend to support these conclusions.

6.6   Measured Performance

A subsequent study by Cusumano and Kemerer produced more quantitative information about the actual performance of software organizations [7]. They studied forty different projects in both countries covering a spectrum of companies. Generally, the projects were custom software systems, not shelf products. Their major conclusions are listed below.

- Although there were differences in the programming languages and tools used in the two countries, there is no significant difference in the level of sophistication in tools.

- The relation of experience to responsibility of software engineers in the two countries are similar. An average programmer has 3.5 years of experience, a designer 4.5 years, and a manager 7 years.

- Japanese projects spent a smaller percentage of the total effort coding (25%) than U.S. projects (36%) and correspondingly more effort designing and testing. Part of this may be due to the significant number of field engineers who work directly with the customer. In the U.S. such people might be called sales support staff and not be counted in the software effort.

- Japanese projects employed full-time testing organizations more often (86%) than U.S. projects (61%). This runs counter to the claim that the Japanese eschew separate quality control organizations in favor of distributing responsibility to the producers, but it helps explain the better quality of Japanese code.

- The average Japanese project took 18% of its code from previous projects while the average U.S. project took 9%. Lifetime employment gives software factories access to "living documentation". When a company begins a new project that bears similarities to previous ones, they can simply call on the memories of people who worked on those projects to spot potential for reusing code or ideas. Software reuse is generally felt to be a key to productivity, and the Japanese companies work very hard to encourage it. It should be noted, however, that productivity can also be achieved selling an identical package many times, as some U.S. producers do.

- Japanese organizations produced 12,400 lines of code per person year while U.S. organizations produced 7,300 lines. Part of this difference can be explained by the higher reuse rate. On the other hand, the lower percentage effort spent on coding indicates that the relative coding rate for dedicated programmers is even higher. There is much anecdotal evidence that a typical Japanese programmer works longer hours than his U.S. counterpart, but official documentation does not support that view.

- The Japanese projects averaged 2.0 failures per 1,000 lines in first year after delivery while U.S. projects averaged 4.4.

While these results are based upon extensive data gathering, most are not statistically significant because there is great variance in both countries.

6.7   Speculations

The foregoing results are the strongest indication we have yet seen of an advantage the Japanese have over the U.S. in software production. Naturally, the question arises of why this possible superiority has not translated itself into a market advantage. There are Japanese software organizations in the U.S., but their primary customers are Japanese companies operating here.

Like us, the Japanese suffer from a shortage of programmers. Since they are unable to fulfill the needs of domestic customers, they have not yet considered exporting software services in the way that the Indians have. The Indians also have the advantage of being more facile with English.

The software factories are always focussed on the hardware platforms and markets of the parent company. At the moment, those markets are different because the PC and workstation markets are less developed. More significantly, most of the software is done as custom projects for single customers.

These differences are important, because the software game is played differently in the shrink-wrap, PC world. Mainframes are in the realm of big projects involving specifications, bids, contracts, and delivered systems – the well-known waterfall model. The consumer PC market works differently. The customer doesn't write specifications, he reads computer magazines and samples the running systems to decide what to buy. He does not normally respond to errors by reporting them; he stops buying products. Thus getting the specification right is less important, but getting the errors out of a released products is much more important.

How will the Japanese companies navigate the passage from customized software to shrink-wrapped software? This is a risker software business.

- The specifications are changing as fast as the competition. You won't get paid simply for meeting a written specification. A team developing a software product must make sure it is competitive.

- Errors are less correctable. Although all major software producers attempt to register and update the purchasers of their product; their ability to correct problems that occur in the field are limited by the widely dispersed customer base.

- Expensive marketing efforts must be mounted to get the product on the shelves.

Most clearly, the Japanese superiority in quality – errors per thousand lines – will make them strong competitors, if they can conceive the right products for the PC market. The need to respond to new developments and market effectively are less easily adapted to by software factories. Quickly adding a new feature to one's product to counter a competitor's announcements doesn't sound like what a software factory does best.

6.8   Operating Systems

A few places are exploring the fundamentals of operating systems for distributed systems.

We received an overview of Fujitsu's mainframe operating system development. A new idea is the introduction of system storage to overcome disk bottlenecks. This system storage appeared to be some sort of semiconductor memory that could be shared among many different processes.

The Sony Computer Science Research Group is of a very high educational caliber and is designing a completely new operating system based on distributed objects. They are re-thinking everything from the ground up, somewhat in the style of Argus. The Sony lab, consisting of some 12 researchers, has no plans to launch into the UNIX OS wars. We were told that they will distribute their software freely.

A group at Kyoto University's Research Institute for Mathematical Sciences has begun work on a new operating system called ToM, for Threads on Modules. It is undertaken in the general spirit of the Mach operating system, but differs in some important details. ToM's goals are: to provide programming model which is suited for distributed environment, to provide uniform environment for various machines connected by networks, to be able to easily change its network configuration, to provide high security and a convenient user interface, to enable users to customize their environment, to be compatible with UNIX 4.3 BSD, and to produce public domain software so that researchers can use it to test new facilities. The Kyoto group has support from Sony, Toshiba, SUN, and several other places. This is the group that produced an implementation of Kyoto Common LISP that was good enough to be adopted at several places in the U.S. Previously, they also produced a well-engineered window manger (GMW) which is still used by SIGMA. This group was created by Reiji Nakajima whose interests are primarily theoretical, but they seem to continue to produce interesting state-of-the-art software systems.

6.9   Programming Languages

Hitachi has built a Common LISP *product*. The system is 90,000 lines of code and took 250 man months to build. It does type inference and inline expansion.

NTT Software Labs developed the Elis machine, a LISP machine that seems to have performance better than Symbolics machines. They have sold about 200 of these machines to various places. They are developing NUE, the new universal environment, with its programming language TAO which allows one to program in LISP, Prolog, or Smalltalk styles interchangeably. I saw all this working. This work shows they understand the current programming language ideas thoroughly, but doesn't seem to go beyond them, except in unifying them.

6.10   General Attitudes

Japanese appear to look at Information Technology more romantically and hopefully than we do.

- As one takes the escalator to baggage claim at Narita airport he sees a billboard with the now-familiar NEC advertisement showing a multi-racial crowd and a motto "Worldwide understanding through computers and communications". It is reminiscent of Dupont's slogan from the 1950's, "Better living through chemistry".

- An elder university professor, Yoneji Masuda, has written books promising effective democracy and wide-spread self-realization through the use of computers [187].

- A young professor at Tokyo University, Ken Sakamura, runs a project called TRON which designs everything from microchips to cities – including operating systems, user interfaces, lamps, toilets, houses, and buildings. A repeated theme in his professionally produced publicity material is the possibilities that computers will make life better. Chapter 8 contains more detailed information about this project.

Most computer professionals dismiss such phenomena as silly, but I think they indicate something important about the Japanese competitiveness in computing. The fact that such idealistic goals are widely disseminated, if not universally accepted, suggests that many young Japanese will consider computing careers.

Shortly after my return from Japan I attended a meeting with some fund-raising professionals at my university. They described many charitable foundations that granted money to universities, but pointed out that computing was not on the list of things considered supporting to achieve their social goals.

6.11   Recommended Further Studies

- The excellent work by Cusumano should be supplemented by other, similar studies. His findings should be complemented by people with different perspectives.

- Software production methods in the banking and insurance industry should be studied. Those organizations apparently spend more extensively on salaries and equipment.

- Analyze a few specific software products. While we have seen studies of the differences among software processes among U.S. and Japanese organizations, we need to complete the picture by looking at some end products of those processes. This may be impeded by proprietary considerations, but needs to be done.

- Someone could attempt to set up a joint software factory somewhere in the U.S., although the cultural conditions would make it very difficult.

7. Multimedia and Human Interfaces

Michael A. Harrison and James H. Morris

7.1   Introduction

Over the last several years, it has become clear that many problems need to be solved in the areas of human interfaces to computer systems. In addition, whenever there is a significant advance in I/O technology, there is a corresponding surge in the entire computing field. For example, the advent of bit-mapped displays on personal computers and relatively cheap laser printers led to the explosion in workstations and in desktop publishing.

It is about to happen again as critical communication technologies (networking) and consumer electronics (facsimile products, modems, audio, video, etc) blend with software. These are important research areas because of the potential to dramatically improve the way computers are used. A popular vision of a future in which computers are integrated with a variety of media may be found in [188].

The major Japanese companies dominate consumer electronics, and moreover Japan is investing heavily in the infrastructure to install ISDN. The U.S., in contrast, seems to generate creative applications and to excel at solving the software problems. For these reasons, the Panel decided to investigate the current Japanese research and development work in the areas of multimedia and human interfaces.

Since these fields are less well known, we digress briefly to mention the key parts of these fields.

Computer supported cooperative work, CSCW. The idea is to use computers to assist in performing cooperative work and to assist in group decision-making. For example, one group in a Palo Alto software research laboratory was able to work closely with another research laboratory in Portland. Two-way live video, special-purpose hardware, and software systems are needed. One needs a large information display or perhaps individual workstations so that file sharing is possible and even a simulated common desktop. There is a need to have an electronic blackboard and to be able to do electronic voting. A rather complete survey is available in [189] in which the following six basic technological components are discused.

- Electronic Boardroom
- Teleconferencing Facility
- Group Network
- Information Center
- Decision Conference
- Collaboration laboratory

Much of the early work in this area was done at the Xerox PARC [190, 191, 192, 193]. Although CSCW systems have failed to achieve their promise as yet, the area is receiving more attention. Recently announced special purpose hardware will provide significant boosts in performance and reductions in cost.

Hypertext and Multimedia. The vision of hypertext consists of a system in which a user reads an electronic document or book. There are links in the system so that a reader may select an entry and follow the link for more information. Combined with multimedia, each system can become a potent educational tool. For example, a student reading a text on opera can get more information on a specialized composer, say Mozart, then continue to access more information on *Le Nozze di Figaro* and even hear the finale of Act II using the high quality audio facilities of a multimedia workstation. Work on electronic encyclopedias is currently being pursued [194, 195, 196].

The concept of hypertext dates back to Vannevar Bush [197, 198] and an early prototype was done by Doug Engelbart [199]. The first important commercial hypertext system was *Hypercard* on the Macintosh. Xerox's NoteCards should also be mentioned in passing [200, 201, 202, 203, 204]. Another interesting system is Superbook [205, 206]. The evaluation of SuperBook in [207] is worth reading. Other work of interest may be found in [208, 209, 210, 211, 212, 213, 214].

The multimedia area is attracting a great deal of commercial attention at this time. While there have been a number of interesting experiments, robust software systems are needed to exploit the hardware capabilities. Multimedia mail systems are desirable and their wide-spread use depends on issues of networking and standards [215, 216, 217, 218, 219].

User Interface Management. About ten years ago, it was widely recognized that it was not enough for engineers to just build a workstation and then to seat a user in front of it. Designers had to plan carefully to ensure that the interface between the human and the machine was harmonious and that communication was effective. Developing this software is quite different than building ordinary system software and is challenging. One example of poor design is the interface to most VCRs. In our interaction with software people, we inquired into how proficient these experts were in programming their VCRs. Judging from our casual poll, the VCRs of Japan and the U.S. are mostly displaying 12:00 and are blinking. The programming error rates for these devices is amazing.

In the last decade, there has been extensive research into tools that assist user interface design and that help evaluate the resulting designs. Cf. [220] which includes a long list of such tools and a nice discussion of the issues. Other papers of interest include [215, 221, 222, 223, 224, 225]

Japanese work in these areas can be broken down into several subareas; multimedia workstations, networking, video related research, collaborative work, and software (both techniques and applications). Much of the work appears to be in the industrial laboratories including the major project FRIEND21 which is somewhat distributed.

7.2   Japanese Industrial Work

Multimedia workstations are being developed by several major corporations, namely Canon, Fujitsu, Hitachi, Matsushita, NEC, and Sony. For example, the Fujitsu FM Townes system has a CD ROM player with 550Mb. The system handles audio, voice, and scanned images. Sony NEWS workstations were displayed at a business conference in the summer of 1989 in Tokyo running FDDI and with interfaces to high quality video and audio.

ISDN is in limited operation in parts of Japan. The major cities are already wired. A number of organizations have leased lines but actual ISDN traffic is fairly small. It is unknown what the business traffic will be in ISDN systems. The ISDN services which have been proposed include: LAN interconnections, video phones, video conferencing, and desktop conferences. A number of related projects are underway with an emphasis on a real time aspects of the net and human interfaces.

Fujitsu

Fujitsu is involved in a plan to utilize computers to facilitate office work, namely the reading and writing of (paper) documents. The idea is to eliminate the defects of paper documents by providing video, voice and animation; allowing non-linear access through hypertext links; sharing of information; rapid searching, multiples representations, and network delivery of data and sources [226]. It is interesting to note in passing that Fujitsu is doing joint work in these areas with Bellcore.

The potential benefits of merging computer and television technologies has been obvious for some time. Fujitsu Laboratories is working in a number of aspects of HDTV and applications to video conferencing [227, 228]. One HDTV set is equivalent to five regular computer screens at the level of NTSC and so compression is a topic of some importance. These techniques are being used in a joint project with Sony to build improved video tape recorders.

An effort is also being undertaken to investigate electronic magazines. The latter work is done in collaboration with the Japanese publishing companies.

We observed a number of applications of neural net technology to various problems at Fujitsu. Ms. Nishijima has developed a neural network and created an interface with a (musical) drummer. That is, a live drummer tries to have a jam session with a multimedia system using this neural network. The drummer trains the system by playing several rhythms. The system "learns" what the drummer is doing and then plays back the material with some variations. After a training session of some three hours, the computer system has developed to the stage where the two can have a jam session. It is a very interesting application and a video tape was shown indicating the training sequence and the resulting final session [229].

This is but one of many applications of neural net technology in Japan. It is not clear where this technology is going and whether anything besides small examples can be made to work. This Fujitsu project is perhaps the most creative we saw in terms of being a novel application. To me, this seems to be an example of the new openness that the Panel discovered on this trip to Japan. On previous trips, we had observed very little opportunity for "unrestricted research". This looks like an example of somebody with a clever new idea who was given the freedom to experiment and it worked.

NEC

NEC is very serious about multimedia applications in general and has two laboratories responsible for multimedia with a total of some 300 people. There are between 20-30 full time people devoted to multimedia specialists. NEC is interested in CSCW and will start work on a networking project to achieve this very soon. The work in this laboratory is quite interesting and compares well with similar work in the United States. On the other hand, we saw applications here toward product design and evaluation which seem missing in U. S. organizations.

One of the most interesting projects concerns the electronic or video book [230, 231]. To seriously develop this concept, requires work on authoring, data base, information retrieval, media processing, representations, system integration and of course a circulation method. NEC is working on all aspects of these problems. In addition to making the base technologies work, they are developing tools for multimedia scripts, an authoring system and a graphics editing system. Interactive training programs are being built as well. In authoring, they are concentrating on character recognition, layout recognition, and automatic key word extraction. Like everyone else in this area, there is concern about document exchange. They also work on multimedia data bases and information retrieval. An object oriented multimedia data model is being developed. NEC researchers are concerned with image retrieval from such a system and developing "clues" which one might give to the system to aid in retrieval. Like other Japanese manufacturers, NEC researchers have found that neural nets work very well for a number of character recognition problems. Their automatic character recognizer is 99.9% accurate if the font is being used is registered with the system.

At the NEC Central Research Labs, they have a good prototyping tool, INTERA, based on 286-based machines. It simulates button panels on screen. It uses a graphically presented finite state machine model for programming. The user can press buttons on the screen which represent the various actions that would make sense for a VCR. Confusing programming instructions could be identified and the interface changed or simplified.

NEC has a human factors group that video tapes and analyzes users of NEC products under development. A small number of psychologists are involved in user interface testing. They demonstrated experimental prototype multi-media dictionary that used sound to give English and Japanese pronunciation and used video clips to explain usage. There is just one word in the system: "go". We heard about a video book project that experiments with color maps and performs color anti-aliasing. It is based on a Hue-Saturation-Brightness color model.

NEC has a well equipped laboratory for product evaluation. Three TV cameras are placed to record people, hand operations, and screen response. The data are rather carefully analyzed. Three or four subjects per product are used and each video tape that is made is one hour long. It then takes one month to analyze the tapes and a current focus of effort is to shorten the evaluation time. The NEC researchers claim that their methods are novel.

IBM Tokyo Research Laboratory

At the IBM Tokyo Research Lab, we saw a demonstration of MODES, a multi-media data base working on the example of a personnel data base complete with pictures and maps. This seemed the same system from 1987, but now runs on smaller machines.

Mugen System is a system which allows the customization of environments. Mugen is meant to be a customer programming environment which is targeted towards the use of personal computers. This means that users may be facile with application packages but not necessarily good programmers. The idea is that there is a customer programming technique which captures the users operations and generates new application programs from them. The idea is that one should be able to create a new application without having to write a real machine code. The system includes story editing and events programming. The system intercepts all commands to the window system so that it has sufficient control. There appears to be some sort of relational data base built into the system. Actually, this includes relational objects but it is not clear whether a full fledged data base system is available, further details are available in reference.

7.3   Japanese Government Projects

Much of the work in these application areas is being conducted at industrial labs. The presence of substantial Japanese governmental support shows up in two areas. One is the Advanced Telecommunications Research Institute International (ATR) and the other is the Friend21 project.

ATR

The Advanced Telecommunications Research Institute International, ATR for short, is located in the Kansai Science City, near Nara. The institute is housed in a new spacious modern building which is furnished in a high tech style. Laboratories are very well equipped.

ATR, the parent company, is organized as a research institute. In turn, the institute has four laboratories:

1. ATR Communications Systems Research Laboratories.

2. ATR Interpreting Telephony Research Laboratories.

3. ATR Auditory and Visual Perception Research Laboratories.

4. ATR Optical and Radio Communications Research Laboratories.

As of October 1, 1989, ATR had a total of 159 regular and an additional 22 other invited researchers. Of these, twelve were foreigners. Total funding was $361.4M with $198.4M spent on R&D. The latter consists of $12.9M from ATRI, $138.6M from the Japanese Key Technology Center and $46.9M from other private companies like NTT and KDD.

The visitor to ATR is struck by how quiet the working facilities are. Perhaps this is because there seems to be excess space. The target number of researchers is 240 while only 178 are in residence.

ATR's research program includes a "wish list" of difficult problems in the area of communications. These include:

- Intelligent Networks

  - High security communications
  - User friendly communications
  - Automatic generation of communications software
  - Effective use of visual information

- Automatic Telephone Translating System

  - Speech Recognition
  - Machine Translation
  - Speech Synthesis

- Man/Machine Interface

  - Visual Pattern Perception & Recognition
  - Speech Perception & Recognition

- Optical & Radio Communications

  - Optical Intersatellite Communications
  - Research for Communications Devices
  - Basic Technological Research for Mobile Communications

Our group toured a large variable reverberation chamber with excellent fine grained control of the amount of reverberation.

We also saw a demonstration of an automatic translator, using CMU speech recognizer technology, and a speech synthesizer system. One starts with Japanese input which is pronounced phonetically from Romaji text. The material is translated to English and then "pronounced" by using a commercial ASCII to acoustic device, namely DECTalk. While the principal examples are time consuming, the researchers are optimistic.

ATR has a specification for G3 FAX available in hypertext form. Another issue of some interest is the use of encryption and decryption techniques applied to images. A variety of standard techniques are being utilized for these purposes, such as RSA and running key generators [232].

A number of projects are underway using neural net techniques.

Our group was received courteously and all of our questions were answered. Yet management was strangely reluctant to volunteer anything not specifically requested. The individual researchers were more outgoing but the social interactions were perplexing and were noted by all three members present.

To summarize, ATR is a new laboratory in an outstanding facility. It has a broad participation from the industry, government, and its board contains well known individuals.

Friend21

The Friend21 project is sponsored by MITI and involves some fourteen companies working together in the center of Toranomon. The project started in 1988 with a plan of operating for six years. The budget is 13 billion Yen or $92 million. FRIEND21 stands for "Future Personalized Information Environment Development for the 21st Century". It involves all of the major companies and proposes the Metaware and Agency Model for a new human interface architecture. MITI, realizing the potential of this area, wanted printing and publishing companies to be added to the list of sponsors. A video tape was shown describing the idea of the project. This video tape had symbolic descriptions of what should be done rather than any specifics or prototypes which is reasonable at this stage of the project. No project director had been selected. A number of the items included in the forecast of future work included personalized news and video services, interaction with high definition TV, although our host conceded that that was likely to occur in the 21st Century. There will be friendly interfaces to data bases. While voice input is a desirable feature the Hitachi group is not optimistic about that occurring. Key notions at the more abstract level includes metaphone and metaware which are sort of "on screen" persona. The agency model was discussed. This consists of multiple blocks of agents workings in some abstract area called a "Studio". A key point is cooperative execution. Thus the system envisions something like a script using what is commonly called the "Blackboard Model" in western AI circles. This requires some sort of personal information agency which has all the user parameters. There was a discussion of how one communicates in multi-media and they proposed sending what is called a "multi-media map with script" this is sort of like sending a video tape by mail.

Another rather obvious application which is interesting is the ability to have homes connected over high speed networks to centralized repositories. For example, if one purchases "TV Guide" and then such a guide is printed with barcodes inside, a family that wishes to view a certain movie can simply use the bar code to order the movie and this can be downloaded over the network in the background so that the family will have a copy for its own viewing. In other words, this eliminates video tape rentals and allows a central repository to provide copies. Another way to think of this is perhaps as a programming interface with VCRs. When we discussed implementation, the response was somewhat vague but the idea seemed to be based on the "blackboard model" described earlier. While the discussion of human interfaces in multimedia was interesting and informative, most of this comes from the FRIEND21 project and is public information.

While the plans for Friend21 are interesting we did see or hear any novel ideas not already being carried out in the U.S.

Universities

Some interesting related work is taking place in the Japanese Universities. There is multimedia work being performed as part of the TRON project which is reported on in more depth in Chapter 8. Also cf. [233, 234, 235, 236, 237].

7.4   Conclusions

While there is more creative software work in the multimedia and CSCW areas in the U.S., Japan is well positioned to challenge in this area with its strength in consumer electronics. Close cooperation between hardware and software people is essential to develop these technologies successfully. Japan's focus on product development may provide a distinct tactical advantage.

Longer term research ideas are freely available from western R&D laboratories although curiously, the Media Laboratory, so glowingly depicted in [188], routinely receives harsh criticism from respected MIT scientists [238, 239]. Attempts to acquire additional information from the Media Laboratory in order to evaluate the actual research accomplishments were not successful.

Future JTEC panels might consider the following points.

- ATR should be monitored. It is focusing on sophisticated Computer-Human Interaction research.

- The area of video and computing should be monitored. As the MITI-sponsored ICOT and SIGMA projects wind down, projects like Friend21 may attract heavy funding. A super SIGMA program is just beginning.

8. TRON

Michael A. Harrison

8.1   Introduction

The newspapers and trade books which discuss Japanese science and technology present a homogeneous picture of closely coordinated activities in industry and academia smoothly orchestrated by the Japanese government represented by MITI, the Agency for Science and Technology, and the Ministry of Education. The TRON project simply does not fit this model. TRON stands for the Real-time Operating System Nucleus which is part of the vision of Professor Ken Sakamura of the University of Tokyo. Professor Sakamura, whose expertise is mainly in computer architecture, started the TRON project in 1984.

The idea is that the world of the future will be even more computerized than today. Professor Sakamura has designed specifications for a standard chip, a family of operating systems, and other devices to work together to support this computerization at all levels. TRON is an open project in which the university-developed specifications of both hardware and software are completely open, and the specifications are available to all companies for exploitation [240, 241, 242]. Industry is encouraged to adopt these specifications. It takes a great deal of hard work to "encourage" the adoption of any design for an industrial standard, independent of the technical merits of the design. We were amazed to see how well publicized the TRON project is. For example, in our interview with Professor Sakamura, he began by showing us a twenty minute video tape promoting the ideas of the TRON project. This particular video tape is aimed at the population with a high school education. The literature on TRON is extensive. Cf. [6, 167, 168, 243, 244, 245, 246, 247, 248, 249, 250, 251, 252, 253, 254, 255, 256, 240, 241, 242, 257, 258, 259].

On March 14, 1988, a TRON Association was formed. Its newsletter started publication the following November. The association has a distinguished board of directors, and the

Manufacturer	Name	Performance
Hitachi	GMICRO/200	7 MIPS at 20 MHZ
Mitsubishi	GMICRO/100	7 MIPS at 20 MHZ
Toshiba	TX1	5 MIPS at 25 MHZ
Fujitsu	GMICRO/300	17 MIPS at 25 MHZ
MEI	MN10400	8 MIPS at 20 MHZ

Table 8.1: TRON chips.

newsletter is full of detailed information. There are over 140 corporate members in the TRON Association including many major foreign and Japanese companies. A few of its members are AT&T, DEC, Fujitsu, Hitachi, IBM, MEI, Melco, Motorola, NEC, NTT, Olivetti, Siemens, Sony, and Toshiba. A full corporate membership, which includes a seat on the Board of Directors, costs over $23,000.

Using specifications provided by Professor Sakamura and others, five TRON chips have been produced so far [251, 255]. Fujitsu, Hitachi and Mitsubishi have produced GMi-cro microprocessors [247] which are 32-bit devices for engineering workstations based on TRON [247, 260]. There are other support facilities on the same chips. The performance of the TRON chips is shown in Table 8.1. Toshiba has a 32-bit TRON chip with twenty-five floating point and eleven decimal instructions on the chip rated at 33 MIPS peak and at 15 MIPS on the average [6]. The chip is fabricated using a 0.8 micron CMOS technology and has 16 kilobytes of cache memory on the chip which is divided evenly between instructions and data. There are some 1.2 million transistors on the chip.

In software also, TRON is supposed to be a universal system. It has multilingual support through TULS or the TRON Universal Language System. There are many flavors of the TRON operating systems. BTRON, which stands for Business TRON, is a version for multimedia systems and other business applications [245, 252, 256]. There is a software vendors group for BTRON consisting of some twenty companies. There is also CTRON (centralized or communications) for servers and communication interfaces [257, 259, 261]. ITRON is to provide basic software for intelligent objects [258, 255]. There is also an MTRON for Macro TRON which is to be used for distributed environments.

What is the actual interest of the Japanese companies in TRON, and how important is the system? There is no doubt that the individual companies have some real interest in the project and have been working on various parts of it. For example, Mitsubishi has developed a Micro ITRON operating system for single chip 16-bit computers, which are widely used in robotics. Matsushita has produced a BTRON machine. The computer comes with a main unit, a special TRON keyboard designed by Professor Sakamura, a color monitor, and a laser disk drive. The MEI machine is based on a 16-bit 80286 processor rated at 8 megahertz with one wait cycle. The system has 2 megabytes of main memory as well as two $3\frac{1}{2}$ inch floppy disk drives. The monitor is 15 inches and has 640×400 dots per inch. The monitor can use any of sixteen colors from a choice of 4,096 [252].

One of the TRON application projects is the construction of a TRON house. Sixteen firms have provided funding to build a TRON house in Roppongi, a neighborhood of Tokyo. The house has an area of 372 square meters with three floors plus a basement. There are some 380 embedded computers in the house. Items such as refrigerators, pots and pans, are stored in the basement and recalled to the kitchen upon pressing buttons. There is complete computer control over the environment, e.g. ventilation, temperature and humidity controls, etc. While these computerized services are pleasant for average inhabitants, they are essential for the handicapped. The TRON Association is sensitive to the problems of the physically impaired.

A TRON intelligent building is being planned which will incorporate some 10,000 microprocessors. There are even future plans for a TRON city. Some twenty companies have already signed up for this project which will be known as the Chiba Computer City. The city will include a multi-story office building, a residence for technicians, a hall for international conferences and concerts, and commercial facilities. It is anticipated that one thousand people will live in the city while the total number of people working there will be between five and six thousand people.

There has been a successful public relations campaign to make TRON known as the system of the future. Articles about TRON and Professor Sakamura appear in the international media [167]. In spite of all this publicity, it is not clear that TRON will gain wide acceptance. Thus, we made a conscientious effort to explore this issue at some length. We asked questions about TRON at all the Japanese companies we visited. The answers were very guarded. Our impression is that the companies are mildly interested in TRON, and most of the sponsors are putting up a small amount of money just to make sure they are informed of any future breakthroughs. Of all the companies, perhaps MEI is the most committed. Even personal discussions with top MEI executives have led us to believe that the support in the company is quite tentative. The problem appears to be that TRON is a monolithic world of its own. No manufacturer is willing to devote major resources to TRON at the expense of more proven approaches, but the vision is too interesting to ignore.

8.2   TRON and Trade Friction

TRON became a *cause célèbre* when it received attention from the United States Trade Representative's (USTR) office. As part of the Super 301 law, the USTR *lists* barriers to international trade. Areas of concern are monitored and discussed. At a later time, a practice may be *cited* as a priority practice under Super 301 which can lead to serious penalties under the law. The Government of Japan's involvement with TRON was listed [262]. We quote from the 1990 listing [263] which is more current.

"The United States is concerned about the potential for Japanese government intervention to support the recently introduced TRON (The Real–Time Operating System Nucleus) project. This is an effort initiated in the Japan Electronics Industry Development Association. Although some U.S. companies are members of the TRON association, no U.S. manufacturer is in a position to sell TRON–based PCs or telecommunications equipment.

With Japanese government support, however, several Japanese companies have pursued development of such products. Thus specification of TRON capabilities can give Japanese manufacturers a significant competitive advantage.

In August 1989, NTT announced its plans to use TRON architecture to upgrade its next generation digital communications network although no company yet manufactures it. NTT officials have subsequently explained that NTT will specify that suppliers provide a TRON interface for certain equipment, but that NTT has no plans to specify a TRON operating system.

NTT issued a request in November 1988, for joint development of a high-speed packet multiplexing system stating that TRON will be used for system management. NTT has also issued contracts to Japanese companies to modify TRON for use in certain specific NTT applications.

The NTT market for which TRON will be specified has not yet been estimated. In mid–1989, NTT announced that TRON will be used for system management in all future NTT digital switches.

The United States will closely monitor the procurement of personal computers for Japanese schools. Those procurements will be jointly funded by the local prefectures and Japan's Ministry of Education which received $30 million for this purpose in (Japanese) FY 1989.

At one point the Japan Center for Educational Computing had reportedly considered issuing recommended specifications which would favor TRON computers. However, it now appears the Center will not limit its recommendation to TRON–oriented specifications.

On September 9, 1988, the United States expressed its concern about possibly discriminatory school computer procurement. In two subsequent meetings Japan provided some limited additional information on the procurement. During 1989 reviews of the U.S.–Japan NTT agreement, the United States requested additional information on the NTT procurement specifications requiring TRON and TRON–related contracts. Additional information on the TRON project is also being sought from the Japanese government through technical level consultations."

Professor Sakamura, responding to the 1989 listing of TRON [262], criticized the USTR's position [243]. He suggested that Japanese must act like the economic super-power it is and

> "must be prepared to slug it out ...
> ...
> The TRON project is one of the risks Japan must take."

Although Professor Sakamura supplied us with reference [262], he subsequently sug-gested that the translation into English distorted the nuances of his statement. His version follows:

> "The image is not one of boxing, as the expression "slug it out" would suggest, but is drawn from the world of sumo. In sumo, when someone reaches the top rank of yokozuna, he is expected to fight with the honest dignity befitting that rank. He has a responsibility to win consistently, but also to fight fairly and confront his opponent directly, not resorting to any tricks or taking the easy way out. Another way of putting it is that a yokozuna must use his superior strength for the honor of the sport as a whole. This is quite a different image from "slugging it out", as though TRON were a kind of power play designed to batter the rest of the world. Rather, we see TRON as a contribution to the world that fulfills the responsibility of a nation that has grown economically strong."

While TRON was listed as a potential trade problem, it was never *cited* as a Super 301 trade practice. In correspondence concerning these matters with Professor Sakamura, an official in the Department of Commerce and myself, it appeared that the strong reaction on the Japanese side was due to a misunderstanding between the technical and informal uses of the word "cite."

Are the TRON technical designs and specifications superior to what is otherwise avail-able in the market place? The designs are competent, but not at the state of the art. The specifications are slightly different from existing commercial products. For example, the TRON chip specification is very similar to Motorola's 68000 in a number of respects. The Japanese manufacturers themselves do not seem terribly interested in committing a lot of support to TRON until it has proven that it is technically superior or has a large potential market. When we asked Professor Sakamura about the acceptance of his systems in Japan, he professed disappointment as well. He said that the Japanese manufacturers are simply too conservative and do not want any system that has not established some marketshare.

The controversy about TRON may or may not have been productive. The U.S. De-partment of Commerce position of encouraging new technologies but opposing Japanese government interference in the marketplace ignores that the U.S., through the Department of Defense (DOD) does become involved in the marketplace. For example, DOD acted as a venture capitalist for Gazelle and also created a market to support the introduction of some promising highly parallel technology.

Since the Japanese companies are themselves not very interested in TRON, perhaps Professor Sakamura might have brought the technology to the U.S. where eager venture capitalists might have funded it, making this an opportunity for the U.S. to develop technology invented in Japan, to use it here, and even re-export it to Japan.

On the other hand, the discussion of the TRON incident has led to a decision of the Japanese government not to specify BTRON for procurements of computers for the Japanese schools. Now that procurement is open to both TRON computers and other architectures which may be supplied by U.S. vendors. This is in accord with international standards on government procurement which prohibits design specifications as opposed to performance specifications.

8.3   Summary

To summarize, the TRON project is a truly unique one. Historically, TRON might have been the first commercially viable Japanese microprocessor design. We are unaware of any single project developed in a university or industrial laboratory here which has generated so much attention and public interest. This project deserves further observation.

9. Advanced Scientific Computing in Japan

Edward F. Hayes

9.1 Introduction

The focus of this report is on the current status of advanced scientific and engineering applications in Japan. The study of this important topic has been a stimulating undertaking for me because of my long-term interest in high performance computing and networking in the U.S.[1]

Since the job of assessing high performance computing research in all fields of science and engineering is clearly beyond what one person can hope to accomplish in a six month period, I decided early on to try to focus on those areas that were in one way or another related to the "Grand Challenges" [264]. Significant progress in each of these research areas is likely to require all the computing resources and good ideas that the world community can generate. So it is important to try to understand what role the Japanese computational science and engineering community is likely to play over the next five to ten years.

Figure 9.1, which is taken from the OSTP report, lists some of the grand challenges and their projected computational requirements. To make progress towards the solution of these grand challenges we are going to need significant improvements in high performance computing hardware and software. Moreover, brilliant new and innovative computational approaches will be needed as well.

On the hardware side, it may be informative to compare the current capability of the three Japanese supercomputers to the U. S. supercomputers (see Table 9.1). If we accept

---

[1]The author was chair of the National Science Foundation Task Force that was charged with the design and implementation of the present supercomputing centers and networking activities.

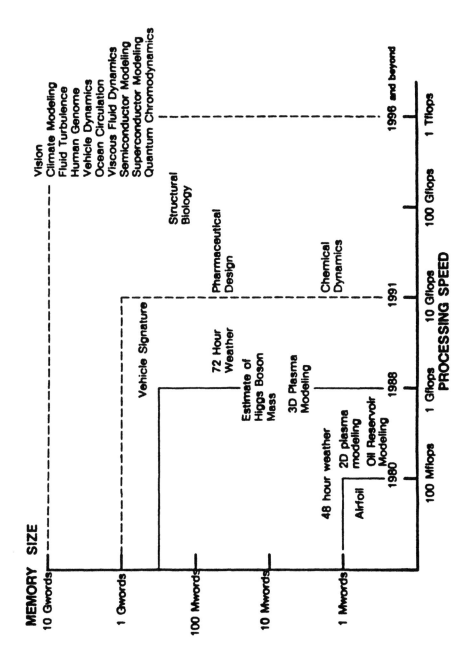

Figure 9.1: Some grand challenges.

Supercomputer	Peak Performance (GFLOPS)	Memory Capacity (MW)	Number of Processors
Hitachi S-820/80	3.0	64	1
NEC SX-2	1.3	128	1
NEC SX-3[a]	22.0	256	4
Fujitsu VP-400E	1.7	32	1
Fujitsu VP-2600/20[a]	5.0	256	1
CRAY X-MP	0.94	64	4
CRAY Y-MP	2.7	128	8
CRAY-2	1.95	128	4
CRAY-3[a]	16.0	1024	16
CRAY C-90	16.0	256	16

[a]These are projected parameter values.

Table 9.1: Supercomputer parameters.

the projections for the next generation of Cray and Japanese supercomputers, it seems clear that Japanese scientists and engineers who have access to these machines will be strategically positioned to make significant contributions to the solutions of one or more of these grand challenges.

On the human resource side of high performance computing, if we look at the situation at the Department of Energy (DOE) national laboratories, the National Science Foundation (NSF) supercomputer centers and National Center for Atmospheric Research (NCAR), and at the National Aeronautics and Space Administration (NASA centers), the number of high quality researchers and the number of significant research results is very impressive.[2] In the U.S. the unique combination of significant amounts of time on state-of-the-art high performance computers, quality software and documentation, expert training and consulting, and convenient networking access has contributed significantly to this strength.

In Japan the number of computational researchers and the amount of fundamental basic research activity are much smaller than in the U.S. This appears to be true in all fields of computational science and engineering. In the past the differences in the level of activity have been so large in some fields that U.S. researchers did not pay very much attention to what their Japanese counterparts were doing.

The situation in Japan is improving, however. In several computational research ar-

---

[2]See, for instance [265, 266, 267, 268, 269, 270].

Manufacturer	Number	Percentage
Cray	14	10.07
ETA	1	0.72
Fujitsu	69	49.64
Hitachi	32	23.02
NEC	23	16.55
Total	139	100.00

Table 9.2: Installed supercomputers in Japan as of September 1989.

eas the Japanese have made significant recent progress and the Japanese computational research work is reaching the quality, if not the quantity, of current work here in the U.S. Increasing numbers of Japanese computational scientists and engineers are gaining access to significant amounts of state-of-the-art supercomputer time and the software environment in Japan is improving as well.

Thus, over the next five years it is reasonable to expect challenges to the current U.S. preeminence in most areas of computational science and engineering. You can get some measure of the current Japanese investment in supercomputers from Table 9.2. As of August, 1989 there were 125 supercomputers installed in Japan. About 30 of these supercomputers were installed at academic centers.

The organization plan for this chapter is as follows. The next section contains a brief overview of the high performance computing centers in Japan that support significant amounts of basic research. The following section is a brief status report on computer networking in Japan, followed by more detailed discussions of a few of these academic centers. The final section contains some qualitative comparisons between U.S. and Japanese scientific and engineering research activities that use high performance computers as a tool.

9.2   Overview of Academic Supercomputer Centers

Since the focus of this report is on basic research applications using supercomputers, no attempt was made to cover high performance computing centers in industry. As noted above, only 30 of the 125 supercomputers in Japan as of August 1989 are in academic research environments.

There are four categories of supercomputer centers that allocate a significant amount of their time to fundamental basic research:

• National university centers

- National Center for Science Information System (NACSIS)

- Interuniversity institutes

- Special centers

Each of these categories of centers plays a unique and important role in Japanese high performance computing research.

The national universities have supercomputer centers that are basically service bureaus for academic researchers. These centers currently provide computing services to over 20,000 researchers. Charges are set to recover a small amount of the total cost of providing the computer time. These centers have no direct research support. The Ministry of Education provides direct operational support, but researchers must obtain their own research support for workstations and for computer charges. The seven National University Centers are located at the following sites.

- Hokkaido University

- Tohoku University

- Tokyo University

- Nagoya University

- Kyoto University

- Osaka University

- Kyushu University

Table 9.3 indicates the kinds of supercomputers at each of these sites. There are two NEC, two Hitachi, and four Fujitsu supercomputers at these seven centers. The Tokyo University Center will be discussed in more detail below.

The National Center for Science Information System (NACSIS) is the second kind of center. NACSIS was inaugurated in 1986 as the center for accessing scientific data bases (e.g., Science Citation Index). While it does not have a supercomputer, this center is a significant resource for Japanese researchers and it is beginning to play an important role in computer networking both within Japan and networking to the U.S.

The centers at the four Interuniversity Institutes constitute a third kind of academic supercomputer center. The orientation of each of these centers is apparent from their titles.

- Institute for Molecular Sciences (Okasaki)

- Institute for High Energy Physics (Tsukuba)

University	Hokkaido	Tohoku	Tokyo	Nagoya	Kyoto	Osaka	Kyushu	NACIS[a]
Location	Sapporo	Sendai	Tokyo	Nagoya	Kyoto	Osaka	Fukuoka	Tokyo
Mainframe	HITAC M-682H	ACOS 2020	HITAC M-680H M-682H×2	FACOM M-780/20	FACOM M-780/30	ACOS 2020	FACOM M-780/20	HITAC M-682H M-684H ACOS 1000/10[b]
Supercomputer (GFLOPS)	S-820/80 (2)	SX-2N (1.1)	S-820/80 (2)	VP-200 (0.5)	VP-400E (1.7) VP-200 (0.5)	SX-2N (1.1)	VP-200 (0.5)	
Manufacturer	Hitachi	NEC	Hitachi	Fujitsu	Fujitsu	NEC	Fujitsu	Hitachi NEC
Permanent Staff (Staff Scientist)	28 (5)	37 (11)	49 (10)	31 (9)	48 (7)	30 (6)	30 (8)	76 (16)
Related Educational Organizations	53	45	274	66	57	132	93	
No. of Users (Approximate)	1600	1800	7000	1700	4200	1600	2100	
Director	Prof Tagawa Ryozaburo	Prof Noguchi Shoichi	Prof Goto Eiichi	Prof Shimazu Yasuo	Prof Nagao Makoto	Prof Yamada Tomoharu	Prof Sagara Setsuo	Prof Inose Hiroshi

[a]NACIS: National Center for Science Information System
[b]Used for electronic mail.

Table 9.3: Status of Japanese computing facilities in June 1989.

- Institute for Space and Astronautical Science (Tokyo)

- Nuclear Fusion Institute (Nagoya)

These Institutes all have significant research supercomputing centers. They do not charge users for computer time. They tend to have smaller numbers of users (hundreds rather than thousands) and researchers are able to undertake projects that require significant allocations of computer time (i.e. thousands of hours). The research support for these centers has also included necessary funds for workstations needed for advanced graphics and visualization. Activities at the Institute for Molecular Sciences will be discussed in more detail below.

The final set of supercomputer centers includes four special centers that might be of particular interest to U.S. computational scientists and engineers.

- Protein Engineering Research Institute (Osaka)

- Institute for Laser Fusion (Osaka)

- Institute for Computational Fluid Dynamics (Tokyo)

- Institute for Supercomputing Research (Tokyo)

Each of these centers has a special research mission and the Protein Engineering Research Institute and the Institute of Computational Fluid Dynamics will be discussed in more detail later.

9.3   Networking in Japan

There are five basic elements to the networking environment in Japan that are important for high performance computing:

- Science Information Network (768 Kbps)

- Satellite Link to National Science Foundation (9.6 Kbps)

- MFENet Connections (9.6 Kbps)

- WIDE Project (2-3 64 Kbps)

- PACCOM Network - Science Internet

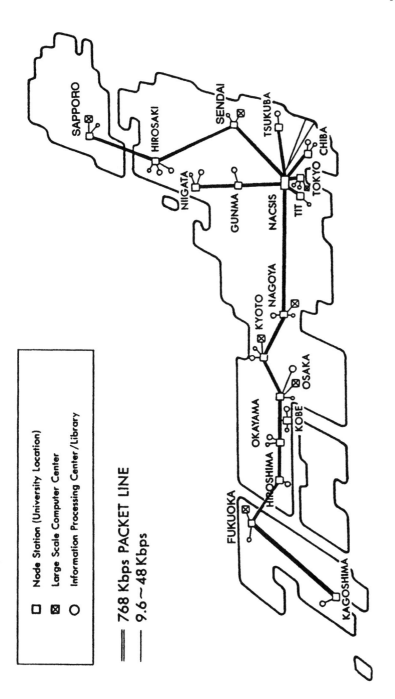

Figure 9.2: Science information network as of June 1989.

Since 1987 all of the national university supercomputer centers and NACSIS have been connected to each other by the Science Information Network (See Figure 9.2). The Institute for Molecular Sciences was connected to the network in July 1989. The backbone of the Science Information Network is a 768-Kbps packet line. The network uses the $N-1$ protocol and provides time sharing and batch processing services. While the network does provide convenient access to the NACSIS data bases, the network does not appear to be used heavily for remote access to supercomputers. According to Professor Eiichi Goto, director of the Tokyo University Supercomputer Center, the strategy in Japan has been to put money into additional supercomputers rather than into building better computer networks like we have in the U.S.[3] This works out reasonably well for access within Japan, since Japan is a small country from a geographic perspective. The Science Information Network has been connected via satellite to the NSF since the beginning of 1989.

The connection to the Department of Energy supported MFENet is shown in Figure 9.3. Currently this connection is only at 9.6 Kbps. According to Dr. Tetsuo Kamimura, director of the National Institute for Fusion Research at Nagoya, the MFENet-IPPJNet link has greatly facilitated collaboration between the U.S. and Japanese fusion researchers.[4] The existing link, which of course could be better than 9.6 Kbps, facilitates joint work on code development and usage, and data analysis, while minimizing the necessity for long exchange visits or frequent foreign travel by collaborating scientists. David Baldwin, Director of the Texas Institute for Fusion Studies, also echoed the importance of the network link to the overall success of the U.S.-Japanese program in plasma physics. Both Baldwin and his colleague Wendell Horton,[5] who manages the U.S.-Japan technical exchange program, indicated that the Japanese program in plasma physics has developed strength in the innovation of advanced computer simulation techniques, especially the pioneering particle simulation work of Kamimura [271]. Thus they were interested in the extent to which the network link will improve joint code development and, importantly, lead to needed improvement in the documentation of the Japanese codes. From this perspective there seems to be a good case for upgrading this network connection in the near future.

The WIDE project (Widely Integrated Distributed Environment) [272] was initiated in April 1988 by Professor Jun Murai (University of Tokyo). Its aim is to create a backbone network for all academic networks in Japan, as well as a research testbed for ISDN (voice and data transmission) and OSI (operating systems) studies. The backbone for the WIDE

---

[3] Professor Eiichi Goto's view that in Japan networking is not as important as in the U.S. was also supported in a letter from Professor Makoto Nagao who is the director of the supercomputer center at Kyoto University. Even if the lack of this infrastructure is not a problem for researchers within Japan, it may limit U.S.-Japanese collaborative research efforts in computational science and engineering.

[4] Dr. Tetsuo Kamimura's comments on the importance of the MFENet - IPPJNet link were supported by Wendell Horton, manager of the U.S.-Japanese technical exchange program in plasma physics, and by Dr. David Baldwin, director of the Texas Institute for Fusion Studies.

[5] Dr. Wendell Horton's report to DOE, titled "Basic and Applied Plasma Physics in Japan," provides an excellent overview of these cooperative research activities.

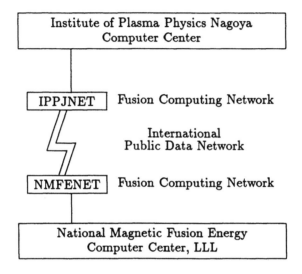

Figure 9.3: U.S. – Japan data linkage.

network is two to three 64 Kbps lines. The number of users is quite small (about 2000).

Networking in Japan is in its early stages of development. A number of the centers (e.g., the Protein Engineering Institute) are not currently connected to either the WIDE network or the Science Information Network. According to Bill Gale, visiting researcher at the Institute for Supercomputing Research, "... the rate of network growth in Japan appears slowed by lack of inter-agency government cooperation and by government regulations, absent in America since the deregulation of the telephone industry" [272].

The PACCOM project funded by NSF and NASA in 1988, aims to construct a network infrastructure in the Pacific region. The primary focus of PACCOM in Japan is the WIDE network. A number of the Japanese researchers expressed interest in improved networking within Japan and to the U.S. Science Internet. Such developments have the potential to enhance U.S.-Japanese collaborative projects in many research areas.

9.4   Institute for Molecular Sciences

According to Will Lepkowski [273], "The Institute for Molecular Sciences (IMS) in Okazaki is a prime example of Japan's institutional future. If Japan really plans to internationalize its basic research by attracting more foreign scientists to the country, IMS is probably the model of such an effort."

IMS has twenty research laboratories, each staffed by a full professor, an associate professor, two research associates and a few technical associates. Three of these laboratories have foreign visiting professors. The twenty laboratories are organized into five departments and one facility for coordination chemistry.

- Department of Theoretical Studies

- Department of Molecular Structure

- Department of Electronic Structure

- Department of Molecular Assemblies

- Department of Applied Molecular Science

- Coordination Chemistry Laboratories

IMS has 6 specialized research facilities.

- Computer Center

- Low-Temperature Center

- Instrument Center

- Chemical Material Center

- Equipment Development Center

- Ultraviolet Synchrotron Orbital Radiation Center

IMS has no undergraduate students. Since the faculty members have no undergraduate teaching duties, they are able to maintain very high levels of research activity.

Professor Keiji Morokuma, an internationally known quantum chemist, is the Director of the IMS Computing Center. His research in molecular electronic structure theory is well known in the U.S. and around the world. His recent "ab initio MO Study of the Full Catalytic Cycle of Olefin Hydrogenation by the Wilkinson Catalyst $RhCl(PR_3)_3$" [274] has succeeded in clarifying the potential energy profile for the full catalytic cycle of ethylene hydrogenation.

The IMS Computing Center has a Hitachi S-820/80 supercomputer with 256MB of memory. The 4-GB of extended memory allows the input/output (I/O) of intermediate data at a speed of about 2 GB/second. This capability has had a major impact on their code designs for molecular integrals. Since the number of integrals that must be manipulated in a Linear Combination of Atomic Orbitals (LCAO) molecular orbital calculation scales as the number of atomic orbitals (AOs) to the fourth power, the amount of IO required for a 100 AO calculation is considerable. On a Cray the IO associated with the manipulation of the molecular integrals can become the rate controlling step in a Self Consistent Field (SCF) calculation – this has led some researchers in the U.S. to attempt to circumvent the IO problem by recalculating the integrals for each SCF iteration [275]. Morokuma reports that with the extended memory IO is not a bottleneck for large SCF calculations.

The IMS Computing Center has an extensive program library which includes the following:

- IMS Molecular Packages – about 200 investigator-supplied programs.

- Quantum Chemistry Program Exchange Programs – all (500) QCPE Programs have been purchased and are available.[6]

- NUMPAC Library – extensive numerical calculation program library (about 1,000 subroutines) obtained from Nagoya University.

Unlike the situation at the national university computing centers the IMS Center has extensive graphics and visualization capabilities. The color video that Professor Iwao Ohmine made of his molecular dynamics calculations of water may be the most extensive anywhere in the world [276]. Some of this work was carried out in collaboration with Peter

---

[6]The Quantum Chemistry Program Exchange, the University of Indiana, Bloomington, Indiana is a source for the programs.

Wolynes of the University of Illinois. Wolynes spent about seven months at IMS while on sabbatical leave from the University of Illinois. Wolynes is one of the top U.S. theoretical chemists.

One of the features of the IMS Computing Center that is attractive to international visitors such as Wolynes is that it is possible to undertake significant computational problems (i.e., the combination of the raw computing power and the modest number of users facilitates the highest quality computational studies). Currently Wolynes is back at Illinois, but Fred Mies of the National Institute for Standards and Technology (previously the National Bureau of Standards) is at IMS collaborating with Professor Hiroki Nakamura, an internationally known atomic and molecular scattering theorist.

The initiative of such U.S. researchers to go to the IMS is an indication of the quality of the research program there.

Unlike the U.S. supercomputer centers, the IMS center does not have any computer operators or systems staff. The computers run completely unattended.[7] The Hitachi software package provided to IMS has been designed to facilitate this mode of operation. When system fixes are necessary Hitachi is called in to do the job. This environment makes running a supercomputer center relatively easy, according to Morokuma. The operations overhead is low and they can allocate their time and efforts to computational research problems. The IMS Computer Center has a total staff of six (one associate professor, one research associate, and four technical staff members). With this size staff the IMS center is not able to mount major software development projects like those at the NSF supercomputer centers.

9.5   University of Tokyo Computing Center

This Center is the largest of the seven National University Centers. All computer equipment at the center is rented, not purchased. The annual rental is about $10 M. The rental approach enables the center's computing capacity to be expanded or upgraded as needed. The history of the center's upgrades is as follows:

- 1966

    - Hitachi 5020E (256 KB)

- 1973

    - Hitachi 8800/8700 (3 MB)

---

[7]This is true of most Japanese supercomputers and mainframes. The Mean Time Between Failures (MTBF) of Japanese supercomputers is roughly 5,000 hours while a typical Cray X-MP reportedly has a MTBF of 200 to 400 hours.

- 1980

    - Hitachi M-200H (16 MB)
    - VAX11/780 (4 MB)

- 1981

    - Hitachi M-200H × 4 (64 MB)
    - VAX11/780 (4 MB)

- 1982

    - Hitachi M-280H × 2 (64 MB)
    - VAX11/780 (4 MB)

- 1983

    - Hitachi M-280H × 3 (96 MB)
    - S-810/20 (128 MB)
    - VAX11/780 (4 MB)

- 1989

    - Hitachi M-682H × 2 (384 MB)
    - M-680H (128 MB)
    - S-820/80 (512 MB)
    - VAX8600 (20 MB)

The center has maintained state-of-the-art supercomputers for over a decade.

Professor Eiichi Goto, the director, is a distinguished, internationally known developer of computers [277]. While he is an effective director for the center, his real professional love seems to be his ERATO Quantum Magnetoflux Logic Project, which is aimed at building the fastest single-processor scalar computer using quantum flux parametron (QFD) devices [278].

The center currently has a Hitachi S-820/80 supercomputer with a 512-MB memory. In addition, it has three Hitachi M68xH high speed mainframe computers, each with an attached Integrated Array Processor, not shown in the 1989 equipment list above.

At present about 7,000 researchers use the center. It has about 50 permanent staff of which 10 are classified as research scientists - somewhat smaller than at the NSF supercomputer centers.

According to Professor Goto, the center receives no support for research projects. This is one of the reasons that the center does not have the complement of advanced graphics and visualization facilities found at most supercomputer centers in the U.S. The center currently provides only limited support for graphics; they have a small number of Suns and VAXes.

Of the 16,611 CPU hours used in FY 1988, about 40 percent was for science research projects and 52 percent for engineering projects.

The center seems to be run very efficiently, but the resources available to any single user are limited. This apparently leads to many small projects and a few large projects. Some users claim that buying their own advanced workstation may be a better investment of limited funds. If supermini-computers become available to current users in large numbers, this could result in significant changes in the user mix.

My impression based on published research results in several fields is that although this center supports many researchers, the integrated quality of the research is lower than that at the NSF supercomputer centers or at the other types of supercomputer centers in Japan. Charging for time and trying to serve too many researchers tends to drive out excellent major projects - the ones that supercomputers are needed to solve. However, the center meets an important need for high performance computing cycles for academic research.

9.6   Protein Engineering Research Institute

The Protein Engineering Research Institute (PERI) was founded in April 1986. The organizational structure of PERI is as follows:

- Structural Analysis of Proteins (X-ray, NMR, and Cryo-EM)

- Structure-Function Correlation and Design of New Proteins

- Protein Synthesis

- Isolation, Purification, and Characterization of Proteins

- Database and Computer Analysis

While all of the divisions use the computing facilities in their research, almost all the researchers of the second and fifth divisions are focusing on computer analysis. Also, in the first division, the researchers first obtain data from measurements and then use computers extensively to determine the structure of various proteins.

The PERI Computing Center has a Fujitsu VP-400E supercomputer with a 768-MB main memory. It is used primarily for molecular mechanics, molecular dynamics, and

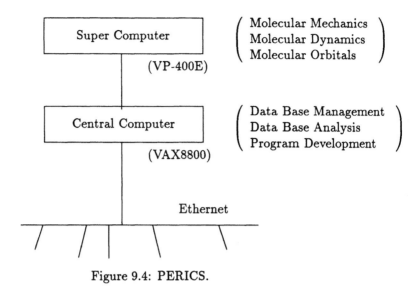

Figure 9.4: PERICS.

molecular orbital studies of protein structure and function. Figure 9.4 shows how the supercomputer is attached to other computing equipment (i.e., VAX 8800 and various workstations). According to Mr. Toru Yao, director of the Database and Computer Analysis Division, there are about 50 users of this computing facility.

Peter Kollman, University of California at San Francisco, and Andy McCammon, University of Houston, both know key people at PERI including Haraki Nakamura who Kollman believes is doing some very important work on long range electrostatic interactions similar to the work of Barry Honig at Columbia University. Both McCammon and Kollman indicated that Professor Nobuhiro Go is probably the top person in Japan in the simulation of protein dynamics and structure. His recent work with Akinori Kidera [279] at PERI using the normal mode space for Monte Carlo simulation of X-ray diffraction data looks very promising based on their recent human lysozyme test.

In preparing this section, I consulted with Professor George Phillips, Rice University, and Professor Florante Quiocho, Baylor College of Medicine. They are experts in protein structure and dynamics and know about the research activities at PERI. They indicated that PERI is probably the top laboratory in Japan for protein engineering research.

The program software available at the PERI Computing Center includes the most advanced program software in the field. The main codes in their program library are listed in Table 9.4.

Molecular Calculations Codes

AMBER   CHARMM
DISCOVER   FEDER
PRESTO   Gaussian86
JAMOL4

Data Base Analysis Codes

BION   IDEAS
DSSP   Original Programs

Codes for Prediction of Structure

HOMOLO   PRDSEC
N14PRDG   NJM

Codes for Determination of Structure

PROTEIN   FRODO
PROLSQ   GROMOS
DISGEO   DADAS

Table 9.4: Software available at PERI.

Much of this software has been ported from outside Japan, particularly the U.S. For example, FRODO is a code for displaying protein structures that was developed by Professor Florante Quiocho from the Baylor College of Medicine. The Japanese-developed software includes PRESTO, which is a PERI-developed program; the JAMOL program from IMS, and DADAS developed by Professor Nobuhiro Go for NMR analysis.

While the researchers are making extensive use of imported software for determination of protein structures there did not appear to be significant efforts to develop new, innovative methods for determining structures. PROTEIN is a suite of crystallography programs developed by Huber in Germany, and FRODO and PROLSQ are both from the U.S. The only major program that they do not seem to have is Professor Alex Brunger's program EXPLOR.

The software development projects directed at database analysis have resulted in several original program codes. This seems to be the main focus of their software development activity.

The laboratory is very well funded by MITI (70 percent) and by 14 private companies (30 percent). They have state-of-the-art X-ray, and nuclear magnetic resonance (NMR) facilities. They also have excellent graphics and visualization capability. Their video movie of protein dynamics (human lysozyme) is comparable to protein dynamics videos generated by researchers in the U.S.

9.7   Institute of Computational Fluid Dynamics

The Institute of Computational Fluid Dynamics (iCFD) is a private organization that is owned and operated by Professor Kunio Kuwahara. Kuwahara is an associate professor in the Research Division for Space Systems Engineering of the Institute for Space and Astronautical Science. iCFD company currently operates four supercomputers (see Table 9.5). According to Dr. Hideo Yoshihara, formerly with the Office of Naval Research, Liaison Office Far East, the total computing power represented by these computers exceeds, for example, that of the National Aerodynamic Simulator at the NASA Ames Research Center [280].

Kuwahara indicated that he established the iCFD to obtain access to the large amounts of supercomputer time necessary to carry out fundamental fluid flow studies. Support for this company comes mainly from Japanese automotive manufacturers. iCFD research is centered on the calculation of complex unsteady incompressible turbulent flows over bluff bodies such as automobile configurations.

According to Professor Steve Orszag of Princeton University, Kuwahara's research is having a major impact on the very much smaller computational fluid dynamics research community in Japan. While his earlier work was not up to the standards of the leading researchers in the U.S., his current simulations are approaching those standards in terms

Computer	CPU Speed (GFLOPS)	Memory (MB)
Fujitsu VP-200	0.533	256
VP-400E	1.7	512
Hitachi S-820/80	3.0	512
NEC SX-2	1.3	256
Total	6.5	1,536

With the total peak speed and memory of the 8-CPU Cray Y-MP/832 being 2.67 GFLOPS and 32MW (or 256 MB), it follows that the iCFD computers are approximately equivalent to 2.6 Y-MPs on the basis of CPU speed and to 6 Y-MPs in terms of memory size.

Table 9.5: Power of iCFD computers.

of mesh size and time scale segmentation.

Kuwahara has sponsored three computational fluid dynamics meetings in Japan (1985, 1987, 1989). These meeting brought together (by invitation only) some of the top U.S. and Japanese researchers in the field. As a result, many of the top U.S. researchers in computational fluid dynamics are familiar with Kuwahara's research.

Kuwahara has assembled an impressive array of workstations including the Ardent Titan and Stellar graphics workstations. His color video tapes of complex flows are impressive. iCFD has developed a scientific visualization system for production of high resolution video movies. Their color videos showing particle path lines, streamlines, and pressure levels are probably among the best in the world.

Currently, the iCFD staff can rapidly generate simulated wind tunnel results for sections of cars and airplanes. For instance, a single Navier-Stokes simulation of sidewall effects of two dimensional transonic wind tunnel using 1.5 million grid points (necessary for good three dimensional detail) took about 25 hours on the VP-200.

9.8   Comparisons between U.S. and Japan

The number of Japanese researchers in most areas of computational science and engineering is smaller than in the U.S. by a considerable margin. However, the numbers are growing in each of the fields surveyed as part of this study. These fields are:

- Chemistry

- Fluid Dynamics

- Protein Engineering

- Plasma Physics

- Laser Fusion

The quality of the Japanese efforts in the first three fields has been described in the previous sections. A discussion of the Japanese plasma physics and laser fusion efforts has not been included here. These fields are already a strong component in the current U.S.-Japan bilateral research program, and reports already exist on these activities that are available within DOE. My investigation of these two areas is consistent with the findings in these reports.

It seems likely that for the next five years the U.S. will continue to have the larger numbers of computational researchers in each of the fields listed above. In the past, these larger numbers of researchers have stimulated more creative computational approaches to solving significant research problems. Thus, if we assume that U.S. researchers will continue to have access to adequate amounts of state-of-the-art supercomputers, it seems likely that the leadership the U.S. has provided in developing new approaches, algorithms and software will continue.

In terms of access to significant amounts of needed resources (e.g., megaflops, fast IO, graphics and visualization workstations), the situation over the next few years may actually favor Japanese researchers. Before visiting Japan, I talked with a number of people about the benchmarks that have been made of the U.S. and Japanese supercomputers (Ann Hayes at Los Alamos National Laboratories (LANL), Bob Borchers at Lawrence Livermore Laboratories (LLL) and Dave Kuck at the University of Illinois). A common theme in these conversations was that, while there has been a great deal of interest in benchmarking, the information available from benchmarking studies only give semi-quantitative predictions on the relative performance of various supercomputers. Benchmarking is fraught with challenges and problems.[8]

Nevertheless, it may be informative to report the benchmark results obtained recently by K. Fujii and H. Yoshihara for an unsteady Reynolds-averaged Navier/Stokes code [283, 284]. This code is nearly 100 percent vectorizable. The benchmark results for the Japanese and U.S. supercomputers are given in Table 9.6. Cf. [283]. Comparison of the actual speeds achieved for single processors shows that the actual GFLOPS achieved by the Hitachi S-820/80 is ahead of all the others. However, if one looks at the elapsed time comparisons in Table 9.7, it is clear that the eight-processor capability of the Cray Y-MP/832 wins out in terms of the shortest processing time.

In Table 9.7, there are three cases of interest.

---

[8]See, for example [281] and [282]

Computer	Peak GFLOPS	Actual GFLOPS	Actual/ Peak
Cray Y-MP/832	0.334	0.175	0.524
Fujitsu VP-400E	1.7	0.395	0.232
Hitachi S-820/80	3.0	0.602	0.201
NEC SX-2A	1.3	0.414	0.319

Table 9.6: Benchmark results – Fujii/Obayashi Navier/Stokes Code.

Case 1 Calculations with the code as furnished using standard compilers.

Case 2 Code as furnished, but permitting additional Fortran- compatible compiler tuning including use of compiler directives.

Case 3 Same as Case 2, but modifications of the algorithms and changes in the programming permitted.

While such benchmarks are not representative of the full range of supercomputer applications, most knowledgeable investigators recognize that the Hitachi S-820/80 is, for most applications, the fastest single processor supercomputer. However, the multi-processor capabilities of the CRAY Y-MP can provide better overall throughput and achieve better parallel computing speed for some applications [9].

From an applications researcher's perspective, benchmarks are interesting, but what really matters is what research results can be obtained and published in the literature. So the important question is what difference in supercomputer speed actually gives a researcher a significant advantage in solving a real research problem (i.e., what percentage difference in speed is important?). Based on the quality of the results being published in the literature during the past year, none of the Japanese or U.S. supercomputers seem to have a decisive lead. Any relative speed advantages in the current generation of supercomputers do not appear to be conferring particular advantages on researchers that cannot be overcome by better applications codes, greater allocations of time, creativity of the investigator in changing the basic approach, or better system and mathematical software.

In the future the situation may shift. The SX-3 is projected to have a maximum speed in excess of 22 GFLOPS, while the Cray 3 and the C-90 are projected at about 16 GFLOPS. Thus, as we look ahead to the next releases of supercomputers and their projected capabilities, there is a possibility the Japanese machines will make somewhat greater strides relative to the projected U.S. machines, but for scientific and engineering applications the most important issues are likely to continue to be ease of use and the amount of resources that can be allocated to a significant problem.

Computer		CPU (min)	Elapsed (min)	CPU/ Elapsed
Cray Y-MP/832				
1:	(200 iter./1 CPU)	57.57	57.58	1.00
	(200 iter./8 CPU)	66.42	46.37[a]	1.43
2:	(200 iter./8 CPU)	52.22	7.97	6.93
3:	(200 iter./8 CPU)	55.07	8.15	6.76
	(2,000 iter./8 CPU)	550.40	77.92	7.06
Fujitsu VP-400E[b]				
1:	(200 iter.)	25.51	28.17	0.91
	(2,000 iter.)	254.60	258.41	0.99
Hitachi S-820/80				
1:	(200 iter.)	16.75	17.80	0.94
3:	(200 iter.)	16.32	18.43	0.89
	(2,000 iter.)	161.98	163.63	0.99
NEC SX-2A				
1:	(200 iter.)	24.33	24.79	0.98
3:	(200 iter.)	20.12	20.52	0.98
	(2,000 iter.)	200.80	201.20	1.00

[a]This autotasker anomaly was circumvented by directives in Case 2.
[b]No changes were found to be necessary in Cases 2 and 3.

Table 9.7: Benchmark results - elapsed time.

During my visits to the Japanese supercomputer centers, I attempted to develop a perspective on the software, programming environments and programming tools available on Japanese supercomputers. Since I was not in Japan long enough to use any of the Japanese supercomputers myself, I had to rely on information from researchers who had. This can be a risky situation, but with that as background what follows appears to be true.

- The software tools available on the Japanese supercomputers are as good or better than those available from Cray Research.

- The monitoring tools provided by the Japanese vendors that are available to the scientific applications programmers appear to be as good or better than those available from Cray Research.

- Applications software being developed by Japanese researchers may be better vectorized as a result of the better tools and vendor supplied software.

- Japanese supercomputer centers seem to be having little if any difficulty obtaining access to the best U.S.-developed applications software.

The final comparison deals with the quality of the computational research results. White it would be presumptuous to suggest that I am able to do this reliably for fields outside my own specialty of computational chemistry. However, I have read a good deal about what is going on at the U.S. supercomputer centers and at least have attempted to gain a perspective. So here are my general observations:

- The U.S. appears to be preeminent in all basic research areas of computational science and engineering.

- The Japanese are making significant strides as the current generation of researchers matures in their use of supercomputers and a younger generation is trained in computational science and engineering.

Appendix A: Personnel and Agendas

A.1   Biographical Sketches

A.1.1   Michael A. Harrison

Michael A. Harrison is a Professor of Computer Science at the University of California at Berkeley. He received his B.S. and M.S. in Electrical Engineering from Case Institute of Technology and his Ph.D. degree from the University of Michigan at Ann Arbor. Since 1963, he has been a faculty member at Berkeley and spent his academic leaves at MIT, Stanford, Frankfurt, and the Hebrew University at Jerusalem.

Professor Harrison has worked on a wide range of topics in computer science and electrical engineering including switching theory, discrete systems, formal languages, and security issues for operating systems. His current research interests are in software, particularly software environments, user interfaces and electronic publishing.

Professor Harrison was a member of the National Research Council's Computer Science and Technology Board and was chairman of an NRC Panel on International Developments in Microelectronics and Computer Science. He also served on the first JTEC Panel study. He is the author of five books and over one hundred technical publications in the areas of mathematics, electrical engineerings, and computing.

Professor Harrison has held a Guggenheim Fellowship, been a National Lecturer for the Association for Computing Machinery, and a distinguished visitor of the IEEE Computer Society. He is an editor of numerous journals, has held a number of positions in the Association for Computing Machinery, including the Vice Presidency of that Association, and is a Director or Trustee of several other organizations.

A.1.2   Edward F. Hayes

Edward F. Hayes is Vice President for Graduate Studies, Research and Information Systems at Rice University. Prior to returning to Rice 1987, he was at the National Science Foundation as Head of the Physical Chemistry and Dynamics Section (1976-80), Head of the Chemistry Division (1982-83; 1985-87) and Controller (1983-1985). Dr. Hayes was on Special Detail to the Office of Management and Budget, Executive Office of the President during 1980-82. He received a B.S. degree from the University of Rochester and M.A. and Ph.D. degrees from The Johns Hopkins University.

Dr. Hayes has received the Meritorious Executive Award in the Senior Executive Service of the United States Government in 1986 and the Distinguished Service Award from the National Science Foundation in 1985. He is a Fellow of the American Association for the Advancement of Science and the American Physical Society.

Dr. Hayes has over seventy publications on quantum theory of molecular structure, application of electronic computers in quantum chemistry, intermolecular interactions and scattering theory.

A.1.3   James D. Meindl

James D. Meindl in Senior Vice President for Academic Affairs and Provost of Rensselaer Polytechnic Institute in Troy, New York. From 1967 through 1986 he was with Stanford University where he was John M. Fluke Professor of Electrical Engineering, Associate Dean for Research in the School of Engineering, Director of the Center for Integrated Systems, and Director of the Electronics Laboratories and the Integrated Circuits Laboratory. He is a Co-Founder of Telesensory Systems, Inc., the principal manufacturer of electronic reading aids for the blind, and served as a member of the Board from 1971 through 1984. From 1965 through 1967 he was Director of the Integrated Electronics Division at the Fort Monmouth, N.J. U.S. Army Electronics Laboratory. He received his B.S., M.S. and PhD degrees in electrical engineering from Carnegie Mellon University in 1955, 1956 and 1958 respectively. He is the author of a book on micropower circuits and over 300 technical papers on ultra large scale integration, integrated electronics, and medical electronics. Dr. Meindl is a Fellow of the IEEE and the American Association for the Advancement of Science. He is a member of the National Academy of Engineering, the American Society for Engineering Education, and the Academic Advisory Council of the Industrial Research Institute. He is the recipient of the IEEE 1990 Education Medal "for establishment of a pioneering academic program for the fabrication and application of integrated circuits." He was the recipient of the 1989 IEEE Solid-State Circuits Award for contributions to solid-state circuits and solid-state circuit technology. At the 1988 IEEE International Solid-State Circuits Conference, he received the Beatrice K. Winner Award. In 1980 he was the recipient of the IEEE Electron Devices Society's J.J. Ebers Award for his contributions to the field of medical electronics and for his research and teaching in solid-state electronics. From 1970-1978 Dr. Meindl and his students received five outstanding paper awards at the IEEE International Solid-State Circuits Conferences, along with one received at the 1985 IEEE VLSI Multilevel Interconnections Conference. His major contributions have been a) new medical instruments enabled by custom integrated electronics, b) projections and codification of the hierarchy of physical limits on integrated electronic, and c) leadership in creation of environments promoting high quality academic research. His current professional interests are academic administration and ultra large scale integration (ULSI).

A.1.4   James H. Morris

Dr. James H. Morris is a Professor of Computer Science at Carnegie Mellon. He received a Bachelor's degree from Carnegie Mellon and an M.S. and Ph.D. in Computer Science from M.I.T. He taught at the University of California at Berkeley and worked at the Xerox Palo Alto Research Center where he was a Research Fellow. From 1983 to 1988 he directed the Information Technology Center at CMU, a joint project with IBM which developed a prototype university computing system, Andrew. His research interests include programming languages and computer-mediated communication. He is a principle investigator of the NSF's EXPRES and PREP Editor projects. He is the president of the MAYA Design Group, a consulting firm.

A.1.5   Daniel P. Siewiorek

Daniel P. Siewiorek was born in Cleveland, Ohio on June 2,1946. He received the B.S. degree in Electrical Engineering (summa cum laude) from the University of Michigan, Ann Arbor, in 1968, and the M.S. and Ph.D. degrees in Electrical Engineering (minor in Computer Science) from Stanford University, Stanford, California, in 1969 and 1972, respectively.

Dr. Siewiorek is a professor in the School of Computer Science and the Carnegie Institute of Technology Department of Electrical and Computer Engineering at Carnegie Mellon University, where he helped to initiate and guide the Cm* project that culminated in an operational 50-processor multiprocessor system. He has designed or been involved with the design of nine multiprocessor systems and has been a key contributor to the dependability design of over two dozen commercial computing systems. His current research interests include computer architecture, reliability modeling, fault-tolerant computing, modular design, and design automation. He has conducted research and served as a consultant to several commercial and government organization, including Digital Equipment Corporation, Jet Propulsion Laboratory, the Naval Research Laboratory, Research Triangle Institute, and United Technologies Corporation. Dr. Siewiorek has published over 200 technical papers and five books, including "The Theory and Practice of Reliable System Design."

Dr. Siewiorek was recognized with an Honorable Mention Award as Outstanding Young Electrical Engineer in 1977, awarded by Eta Kappa Nu (National Electrical Engineering Honorary Society); was elected an IEEE Fellow in 1981 for "contributions to the design of modular computing systems," and has served as chairman of the IEEE Technical Committee on Fault-Tolerant Computing. He was also awarded the 1983 Frederick Emmons Terman Award by the American Society for Engineering Education for Outstanding Young Electrical Engineering Educator and the 1988 ACM/IEEE Eckert-Mauchly Award for "outstanding contributions to the field of computer architecture." Dr. Siewiorek was the Founding Director of the Center for Dependable Systems and is now the Director of the CMU Engineering Design Research Center's Design for Manufacturing Laboratory. He is a member of the IEEE, ACM, Tau Beta Pi, Eta Kappa Nu, and Sigma XI.

A.1.6   Robert White

Robert M. White has recently been appointed Under Secretary of Commerce for Technology. In this position he is responsible for managing the Technology Administration which includes the National Institute of Standards and Technology. Prior to this he was Vice President and Director for Advanced Computing at MCC.

From 1984 until 1989 Dr. White was Vice President of Control Data, initially responsible for data storage advanced technology, later as Chief Technical Officer. Prior to CDC, he spent 13 years with Xerox at its Palo Alto Research Center. From 1965 until 1970 he was Assistant Professor of Physics at Stanford, and has maintained a Consulting Professorship of Applied Physics ever since. He received his B.S. in physics from MIT and a Ph.D., also in physics, from Stanford. He is the author of four books, including Introduction to Magnetic Recording, and over 100 papers dealing with condensed matter physics and storage technologies. He is a member of the National Academy of Engineering, a fellow of both the American Physical Society and the IEEE and the recipient of an Alexander von Humboldt prize. His major contributions have been in the areas of nonlinear phenomena and optical properties of magnetic materials and the physics of magnetic recording.

A.2   Itinerary of JTEC Panel in Japan

Date	Lab	Panel Members Visiting
November 6	Hitachi CRL	Harrison, Morris, Shelton
November 6	IBM Japan	Harrison, Morris
November 6	SRA	Harrison, Morris
November 6	NTT (Musashino)	White
November 6	University of Tokyo	Siewiorek, Meindl
November 6	Denki Kagaku Kogyo	White
November 7	NEC	Harrison,Meindl,Morris, Shelton, Siewiorek
November 7	Fujitsu (Kawasaki)	Harrison,Meindl,Morris,Siewiorek
November 7	SONY	White
November 7	National Institute Fusion Research (Nagoya)	Hayes,Shelton
November 8	SONY	Harrison, Morris, Siewiorek Meindl
November 8	NTT (Yokosuka)	Harrison, Meindl, Siewiorek
November 8	NTT Musashino	Morris
November 8	Fujitsu (Atsugi)	White
November 8	NHK	White
November 8	Inst. Computer Fluid Dynamics	Hayes, Shelton
November 8	University of Tokyo	Hayes, Shelton
November 9	ICOT	Merrill, Siewiorek
November 9	SIGMA Project	Harrison, Morris
November 9	University of Tokyo	Harrison, Morris, Siewiorek
November 9	Toshiba (Kawasaki)	White
November 9	Hitachi CRL	White
November 9	Institute Supercomputing Research	Hayes, Shelton
November 9	Institute Molecular Science	Hayes
November 10	PERI	Hayes
November 10	Laser, Nuclear Fusion Center	Hayes, Shelton
November 10	Kyoto University	Harrison, Morris
November 10	Matsushita (Osaka)	White
November 10	ATR	White, Harrison, Morris
November 10	ETL (Tsukuba)	Meindl, Siewiorek
November 10	University of Tsukuba	Meindl, Siewiorek

A.3   Agenda of Kickoff Meeting, July 11, 1989

JTEC Advanced Computing Panel Kick-off Meeting

July 11, 1989

2000 L Street, NW, Washington, D. C. Room 613

AGENDA

9:30	Continental Breakfast	
10:00	Introductions	Gamota
10:10	Overview of JTEC	Shelton
10:25	Overview of NSF's Interests	Huband
10:35	Overview of DOD Interests	Schwartz
10:45	Panel Chairman's Remarks	Harrison
11:00	Panel Discussion on Study Scope and Allocation of Tasks	
12:30	Working Lunch	
	Administration of Study	Holdridge
	Report and Workshop	Gamota
	Literature Support and Japan Trip	Engel
1:15	Panel Support Requirements	
1:45	Overview of DOE Interests	Nelson
2:00	Additional Panel Discussion	
3:15	Meeting Adjourns	

A.4   Agenda of Oral Report Meeting, December 8, 1989

JTEC Advanced Computing Workshop
December 8, 1989

1800 G. Street, NW, Washington, D. C. Room 540

AGENDA

9:30	Continental Breakfast	
10:00	Welcome to NSF	
10:10	Review of JTEC	Huband
10:30	Overview of Study	Harrison
11:10	Electronic Components for Computer Architecture	Meindl
11:50	Software Factories	Morris
1:00	Video Tape from ICFD	Shelton
12:30	Lunch (served in meeting room)	
1:20	Data Storage and Related Technologies	White
2:00	Computer Architecture and Systems	Siewiorek
3:20	Trends (TRON video tape)/Summary/Options	Harrison
4:00	Open Discussion	
4:30	Adjournment	

Appendix B: Trip Report

R. D. Shelton

B.1 Introduction

I accompanied the panel on this trip as a representative of the sponsors and the Japanese Technology Evaluation Center. One needs a detailed knowledge of the experiences of these panels in Japan to competently manage the Center. I last went to Japan with the second JTEC group to go there – the Denicoff computer panel in October 1986. Our advance arrangements then were done by Raul Mendez, and I was interested in comparing first hand the kind of access we were now able to get. I do have some expertise in computers and could understand most of what was presented, but I cannot assess its position relative to the cutting edge of U.S. research. As it turned out, I was able to fill in for some appointments in Tsukuba that would have otherwise had to be cancelled and to smooth over a misunderstanding with Paul Spee of the Japanese Government's ERATO project. Otherwise I mostly accompanied Ed Hayes to help gather information on scientific applications of supercomputers.

My purpose here is to provide some personal perceptions of what I saw in the Japanese laboratories which might be used to remind the panelists of some points to be made in their assessments. The substantive points are in the bullets, the text is mostly a travelogue for context. The references are to papers I was given to support the briefings we received.

B.2 Monday November 6

An organization meeting at breakfast was held at the Ginza Tokyu Hotel with Mike Harrison, Jim Meindl, Dan Siewiorek, Jim Morris, and Robert White. In the morning I went with Harrison and Morris to the Hitachi Central Research Lab (HCRL) in Kokubunji where we got "the boardroom treatment" – some interesting presentations in a fancy conference room. The company brochure [285] indicated that Hitachi had sales of $22.8 billion in the fiscal year ending March 31, 1989 and invested $2.08 billion (9.1%) of it in research. Since 1984 their gross sales have been fairly flat–increases in information and communications systems and electronic devices (to 44% of sales in 1988) have made up for declines in all other sectors of their business. They had 78,400 employees of whom 12,100 were engaged in R&D – about 1/3 at the corporate research laboratories (including HCRL) and 2/3 in the Business Groups. This is a big company, almost entirely in electrical and electronic products.

Several members of the 8th Department of HCRL (computer systems, advanced information processing, and the computer center) made presentations on some of their results. Some high points were:

- Their participation in the MITI FRIEND21 project was summarized, and an animated videotape was shown to simulate the personalized human interface that the project is intended to develop. The project is budgeted at 13 billion yen for a six-year period. Most of the large Japanese electronics firms are participating, Toshiba, NEC, Mitsubishi, Matsushita, Sony, Hitachi, Fuji Xerox, Sharp–as well as several major printing firms, Iwaniami, Dainipon, and Topan. The project consists of a set of software standards that allows information transmission and display applications ("agents") to be handled within a 'studio' environment. They gained a lot of ideas from the Blackboard System. No specific hardware platform has been considered yet. Hitachi had only 8 researchers on this project now, but until September they had 14. Results to date were reported in an international symposium in August 1989.

- They are researching parallel computers with the objective of "making parallel computers the supercomputers of the future" – such as their MIMD-type H2P parallel processor. The detailed results that Naoki Hamanaka presented were on interconnections of processors, specifically a "hyper crossbar" network. Simulation results were presented to determine the optimum number of dimensions in the hypercube. For a total of 256 PEs, the results indicate that 3 dimensions are optimum. They stated that the corresponding result for the 4000 PE case was 5 dimensions, and they thought that their simulation methodology might scale up to 16,000 PEs [286].

- Mamoru Sugie showed some research results on dynamic load balancing on a 16-cluster parallel inference machine – each cluster had 8 PEs. He examined six strategies for balancing the load on clusters by looking at normalized processing time as a function of dispatching rate. He concluded that the optimum strategy is one which determines the dispatch target at random but aborts the dispatch if the target has more load than the sender. A strategy where the cluster with the maximum load dispatches to the cluster with the minimum load was actually better on part of the graphs shown, but he said this strategy did not produce stable results [287].

B.3   Tuesday November 7

The entire group (Ed Hayes arrived Monday night) went to NEC Central Research Lab in Kawasaki. The NEC annual report [288] stated that the company had sales of $23 billion in the year ended March 31, 1989 (up 17%)–almost entirely in electronic device (19%), communications (26%) and computer (43%) products. In April 1989 they announced the world's most powerful computer to date, the four processor SX-3 expected to perform at 22 GFLOPS (peak) when delivered in 1990.

Ed Hayes and I met with Ken Hayami and Shun Doi who are supervisors in their Information Basic Research Lab.

- They showed us two color still photos of the wind flow lines around the NEC office tower in Tokyo showing the beneficial effects of a wind cutout in the structure in reducing velocity and turbulence at the sidewalk. The pictures were presented as an example of what could be done in the visualization of supercomputer output.

At 11:30 Dr. Hayes and I left to visit the Institute of Plasma Physics (IPP) at Nagoya University. We made it via Shinkansen 20 minutes early. We met with Dr. Tetsuo Kamimura, the director. He gave us one copy of several papers, which Dr. Hayes took back.

- Their computer center provides services on FACOM VP-200 and VP-200E supercomputers and a FACOM M-380 mainframe to IPP. They also support (via a 256 Kbaud network) the Institute of Laser Engineering (Osaka U.), the Plasma Physics Lab (Kyoto U.), the Plasma Research Center (Tsukuba U.), the Plasma Physics Center (Kyoto U.), and the Institute for Fusion Theory (Hiroshima U.) – which is to be absorbed into IPP. They are also linked to the interuniversity network in Japan [289].

- The U.S.-Japan Fusion Research Cooperation Program was signed in May 1979, and has just been renewed. It involves linkage with the MFEnet and the U.S. fusion communities and could serve as a model for future cooperative projects under the S&T treaty. It took five years to get the agreement set up, but it is now working smoothly. Since 1985, it has included a physical link (at 9600 baud) between the MFEnet at Livermore and their computer center. There have been 24 joint research projects to date (exchanging computer programs and data), joint workshops, and six exchange visitors at IPP. There are a number of joint committees to coordinate the arrangements [290]. Dr. Kamikura knows David Nelson, who is charged with implementation of this part of the treaty, and Jim Leighton (JFL@CCC.MFENET) is his primary contact in the U.S. If this existing infrastructure was used to implement new joint research efforts, Dr. Kamikura would like to see improvement of the network with extensions to Unix and a higher data rate for the link to the U.S.

- He stated that their machine was free to all users, so there did not seem to be a strong economic incentive to optimize supercomputer code. They do monitor vectorization of their users' programs (using software from Fujitsu) and make recommendations for program improvement or transfer to a M380 mainframe. He mentioned typical vectorization percentages of above 95%. He said that they could use a more powerful machine at the University of Tokyo, but they would have to pay for those services.

B.4   Wednesday November 8

We met Fred Fendeis at ONR/Tokyo. He asked one of his staff, Dr. Hideo Yoshihara, to guide us to the Institute for Computer Fluid Dynamics. Dr. Kuwahara's Institute turned out to be the highlight of the trip for me. It was my first opportunity to visit a Japanese home – Dr. Kuwawawa has his office in the living room of his house. It seemed to be very Japanese to me with the slippers to wear, the delightful Japanese garden in the front yard, and Mrs. Kuwahara serving us tea. So I was surprised when Dr. Yosihara told us that this was considered to be a Western-style house.

- Dr. Kuwahara is the ultimate gadgeteer – no other private individual owns a super-computer; he has four of them in the large garage attached to his house. He also has a lot of smaller machines like Titans and Stellar minisupers and some impressive peripheral equipment for making motion pictures from the supercomputer output. His staff of twenty or so had about three workstations per person. While Dr. Kuwahara's wealth (from Tokyo real estate) has made all this possible, his Institute can also be viewed as similar to an American university spin-off. He is an associate professor at the Institute of Space and Astronautical Science at Sagamihara and intends his Institute to become a profit-making enterprise – by selling supercomputer cycles and CFD solutions.

- He showed us his VP 200, VP 400, SX-2, and 820–all in unmanned machine rooms where they required virtually no maintenance and operators. He said he had experienced only one hardware crash, and the electrical power service hardly ever failed. Software crashes were fairly common however. He is planning on upgrading to the SX-3 and VP 2000 when they become available, and buying an IBM 3090 VP for CAD/CAM applications.

- Dr. Kuwahara's then showed us some CFD visualization results on a 300mm laser disk he had mastered–apparently as a form of art. The color motion pictures showed supercomputer results from two and three dimensional calculations of the flow of a fluid over cylinders or more complicated objects like aircraft wings or automobiles–the kind of thing that can be done experimentally in a wind tunnel. There were also some images of rods stirring liquid, heat produced by a stove, etc. Displays included flow lines, particles released in the input flow, different colors for temperatures, pressure, velocity, clockwise and counter-clockwise vortices, etc. It was an impressive demonstration of what can be done to visualize supercomputer output, and he gave us a VHS tape version.

- He had a small wind tunnel to attempt to validate his computational results, but it was very difficult to prove that the simulation produces the same results.

- He gets a very high degree of vectorization with CFD algorithms. He said that NASA Ames was doing some similar work in the U.S. and mentioned John Kim there.

We had a nice American lunch with Dr. Fendeis at the New Sanno Hotel which is open to those traveling on DOD travel orders. It is a good place to stay if one can get the approvals, and Fred can do so. We then went to NSF/Tokyo at the embassy – Fred wanted to deliver a copy of the draft JTEC superconductivity report. I had attached copies to my ONR proposal so he had read it.

Dr. Hayes and I then visited Professor Eiichi Goto of the University of Tokyo at his ERATO project office near the University of Tokyo. Professor Goto is one on Japan's most distinguished computer pioneers. His technical manager of the ERATO project office was Dr. Yasuo Wada who had come to the U.S. to attend the JTEC superconductivity workshop in 1989 [291]. His ERATO – Quantum Flux Parametron (QFP) project consists of 25 scientists and technicians in three research groups, extending from 1986–1991 [292]. After discussion of his ERATO project, Dr. Hayes asked some questions on the Japanese supercomputer network, and Dr. Goto escorted us to the University of Tokyo Computer Center which he also serves as Director.

- Professor Goto was interested in promoting the QFP technology because of its very fast (1 ps/gate) and extremely low power dissipation (1 nW/gate) characteristics. He thought that it was more promising than Fujitsu's approach as implemented in their Josephson Junction 4-bit microprocessor. They have been able to make QFP circuits more tolerant to external magnetic fields, and the shielding group has been making good progress [293].

- He did not think that parallel computers would come into the mainstream of supercomputing soon because some problems were inherently sequential. Thus a general purpose machine must have a fast scaler processor and a strictly parallel machine built of slower processors would not be suitable.

- He was asked if interconnection of their supercomputer network with NSFnet would be an attractive way to implement the S&T treaty. He said that some Japanese Institutions (National Astronomical Observatory, etc.) were already connected via the fibre optic cable to Hawaii, and that seven major national university supercomputer centers are connected via 64 Kb/s lines. Professor K. Miyoshi of Hokkaido University had prepared a brochure [294] on their supercomputer network Connection of these two networks is under discussion.

B.5   Thursday November 9

Dr. Hayes and I went to the Institute for Supercomputing Research (ISR) to visit Raul Mendez, the director. As mentioned, Mendez organized a previous JTECH trip to Japan, and worked with me on the program committee of the last Computer Science Conference where he was able to get several distinguished Japanese scientists to give invited papers. Dr Mendez has a great deal of experience in benchmarking most of the competing Japanese and U.S. supercomputers. Because of the sensitivity of these issues, some of his results have been controversial.

- ISR consists of 15 people who do computing research on the five supercomputers operated by the famous Recruit company–primarily to provide computing services to clients. They have a Cray XMP at Osaka, a Cray XMP at Yokohama, a VP-200 at Tokyo, and an SX-2 and a VP-400 at Kawasaki. They also have a number of alternatives to supercomputers: Titan 2s, an Alliant FX/8, an iPSC machine, an 32-processor MiPAX parallel machine, etc [295].

- Dr. Hayes asked about typical vectorization percentages. Mendez stated that some applications like CFD could get 90% or more, people like the Japanese Atomic Energy Research Institute (JAERI) more commonly got percentages more like the 50% quoted as typical in NSF supercomputer centers. The Fujitsu compiler produces the best vectorization results–a little ahead of Cray's. The state-of-the-art in vectorization tools is FORGE from Pacific Sierra Research in Placerville, CA which emulates the Cray compiler and runs on a workstation. Fujitsu also has an interactive vectorizer.

- When asked who had the fastest supercomputer, Mendez responded that it is difficult to compare an 8-processor Cray YMP to a fast uniprocessor like the Hitachi 820-80. Clearly the Cray is better for throughput and the 820 is better for the fastest single-job response time.

- The new TPC-3 optical fibre undersea cable was completed this summer and provides three 64 Kbaud channels to a Hawaii gateway to the U.S. ISR and the Universities of Tokyo and Keio are now on the Internet via this cable, which is heavily utilized for file transfer, E-mail, and remote log-on.

- When asked about parallel computer research in Japan, Mendez said: (1) ICOT can now be viewed as primarily a parallel architecture project. (2) Hoshino at Tsukuba has his PAX machines. (3) Fujitsu, NEC, and NTT have some research underway. (4) The MITI Superspeed National Project included the SIGMA-1 dataflow machine.

- His general assessment of the position of the U.S. versus Japan in supercomputer technology was (1) In components the Japanese are far ahead. (2) In architecture the Japanese are behind but are gaining ground in research, (3) In software the U.S. is ahead, especially in applications. For example the PAM CRASH program is only available for the Cray–from a French company called Mecalog. It is a automobile crash simulation used by all the automobile manufacturers and was based on public domain code from LLNL. He thought that Cray would be able to maintain its position in competition with the three Japanese companies for at least five years. Some reviewers of this report disagree with this conclusion.

B.6   Friday November 10

I took the bus to Tsukuba City to the Electrotechnology Lab (ETL) of the Ministry of International Trade and Industry (MITI). In 1988 ETL had 559 scientists and engineers with 134 administrators and staff for support. Its budget was about 9.5 billion yen ($70 million). They are participating in ten of MITI's national projects including the Sunshine and Moonlight energy projects; the Advanced Robot Technology and Interoperable Database System information technology projects; the Basic Technologies for Future Industries electronics project; and the Peaceful Utilization of Nuclear Energy, Human Frontier Science Program, High-Speed Computer System, Pollution Control Technology, and Observation System for Earth Resources interdisciplinary projects. I met with the directors of three of ETL's 14 divisions, but I spent most of my time talking about their parallel computation research projects with Dr. Akio Tojo, director of the Computer Science Division, and his staff.

- The ETL SIGMA-1 was based on the data flow structure concept of J. B. Dennis at M.I.T. They like to describe it as the world's fastest non-Von Neumann machine. It was demonstrated in 1987 to achieve 170 MFLOPS average and 427 MFLOPS peak performance for a particular benchmark program [296]. They are now working on an improved version, the EM-4, which will use a single chip processing element, the RISC-type EMC-R, permitting a machine with more than 1000 PEs. The PE contains 50K gates and achieves 12.5 MIPS. They are currently building a prototype with 80 PEs on which they expect to achieve a peak of 1 GIPS. They were rating this machine in instructions per second instead of floating point operations per second because they designing it for symbolic manipulation problems – they hope to add floating point processors later [297]. Dr. Shimada was a enthusiastic advocate for the data flow approach to massively parallel architectures. He believes that the concurrency must be transparent to the user and that it should be easier to do this with data flow machines than the Connection Machine. But such systems software is not now available for the data flow machine.

- I saw an interesting demonstration of their OZ (object-oriented open distributed) system. The idea is to develop a methodology for distributing applications over several processors connected by a network, using an extension of the notions of object oriented languages – by allowing internal data and interchange messages to be objects with type inheritance, as well as the communicating entities themselves [288]. The demonstration system included three LAN segments and about six workstations. LAN segments are based on OSI connectionless stacks up to the presentation layer including a token-bus broadband physical layer of IEEE 802.4 type. The demonstration program was the familiar Tower of Hanoi program distributed over the network, but with a nice twist: the output of the program drove a robot arm which moved the rings on the pegs of a real toy. The project is a part of MITI's Interoperable Database National Project which is nearing completion. Database research could be the focus of an entire JTEC panel next year in support of the S&T treaty which lists the database area as a candidate for joint projects [298].

- There was some discussion of the Semantic Network Machine, IXM, which includes 32 Transputer processors connected to 126K (40-bit) words of associative main memory. Such a system can be effective in suppressing the computational explosion in large semantic network processing. Logical operations can also be done in parallel on the associative memory, resulting in a maximum of 1880 MOPS for the less-than operation. The machine is programmed in IXL which is a superset of Prolog. They are expanding the system to 64 PEs and experimenting with interconnection topologies. [299]

- I heard a little about a project to investigate an optical bus for interconnection of processors using a cylindrical mirror to create an optical broadcast medium. At the moment this appears to be a theoretical study. [300]

- ETL is doing a considerable amount of electronic device and semiconductor manufacturing technique research. I was able to get a little information, but most of our time was spent discussing the parallel computing research above. Two of the appropriate division directors were available: Dr. Toshio Tsurushima attended my briefings, and Dr. Susumu Takada stuck his head in (with a couple of reprints). I visited Dr. Yukata Hayashi, a former associate of Dr. Meindl, in his laboratory, and he gave me his forecasts of the developments that will be necessary to reduce integrated circuit feature size to 1/40 micron, taking ICs to the ULSI level. The transistor devices themselves will need radical changes since the number of dopant atoms in the gate region will be reduced to 25 or so, leading to inadequate performance. They are developing inversion layer and X-MOS transistors as candidates for the smaller devices needed. Dr. Takada's group has developed a superconducting integrated circuit technology using refractory Josephson tunnel junctions, including a demonstration 1Kbit RAM chip [301].

- Dr. Siewiorek had given me some questions, reproduced in the next section, to try to get some responses from the staff at ETL and from Professor Hoshino. They responded to the ones numbered below:

  1. Dr. Shimida felt that very long instruction word, VLIW, computers could take the place of RISC approaches in further performance improvement at the register- transfer level.

  2. Dr. Tojo thought that higher level language support in hardware had not been very successful in the past and was not familiar with much efforts in direct instruction set support. OZ is an example of a architecture project inspired by higher level language concepts.

  3. They are designing instruction sets for the data flow machine (EM-4).

  4. Dr. Tojo said the main bottleneck in parallel computing is communications. One measure of a parallel architecture is based on the ratio of FLOPS to communication time. For the Connection Machine the ratio is about 1000, implying that it is not suitable as a MIMD architecture – it must be used as a SIMD machine. The SIGMA-1 has a ratio of 2-7 so that it is much more suitable as a MIMD machine. Good compilers are the key to use of parallel machines; the users should not have to specify parallelism explicitly (but should be able to if needed). They cited a couple of examples of extensive software development efforts that were necessary to convert programs to run on the Connection Machine.

  5. They are interested in the data flow approach, of course, and the associative memory approach of IXM. Tojo thought that neural nets would be useful for only special applications.

  6. The development environments for parallel computers are clearly inadequate. A user-friendly environment like Unix is needed to interact with the parallel system.

7. Some Japanese designers believe that uniprocessors are limited to about 1-5 GFLOPS, thus faster machines must come from parallel approaches. IBM compatibility constrains uniprocessor designs. The Japanese have access to the fastest chips; Cray does not.

8. Their parallel architecture research is outlined above.

9. They agree that fast scalar processors are essential for supercomputers. Supercomputer centers often have low vectorization results.

10. Their data flow machine sometimes achieves a low- level parallelism of 10 simultaneous operations. The "Multiflow" VLIW machine can also achieve more than three or four.

11. Levels of parallelism can be mixed on a data flow machine.

12. No such research at ETL.

13. Dr. Tojo said that they are seeing more special purpose processors but that such processors can be considered to be peripheral processors of a general purpose machine.

14. Their IXM content addressable machine can be considered to be special purpose architecture. They have performed some basic research on neural nets.

15. The RISC trend seems to be in the direction of less feedback from software convenience to hardware design. As mentioned, OZ was inspired by software considerations.

16. They are investigating the software/hardware interaction for data flow machines.

17. Dr. Tojo expects that the computer environment ten years from now will look like an improvement of personal computers–with much more powerful processors, much better displays, and high speed networking. large computers will be limited to compute and database servers.

In the afternoon I visited Professor Hoshino at the University of Tsukuba to see the latest version of his parallel computer, the QCDPAX. I visited him in 1986 with the Denicoff panel, so I had some feel for his progress. He had some difficulty in getting funds for the next PAX generation until he teamed up with some physicists doing quantum chromodynamics research. Monbusho decided to support the QCDPAX since its lattice interconnection is well suited for the algorithms involved. Indeed Norman Crist at Columbia [302] has surveyed six similar joint parallel computer/QCD projects underway worldwide. He says that Dr. Hoshino's PAX-32 was the first project to construct highly parallel combinations of (32) microprocessors and floating point chips for physics calculations.

- The present QCDPAX machine is the fifth version since 1977 [303, 304, 305]. It is based on a custom processing element Professor Hoshino designed using the Motorola 68020 CPU and the L64133 floating point unit, including custom microcode. One such PE can achieve 33 MFLOPS theoretically and has been measured at 28.65 MFLOPS. It is a vector processor in the sense that once the CPU has started a vector operation, the FPP can continue processing elements using DMA without intervention by the CPU. The QCDPAX with 1 to several 100's PU's is now commercially available from the Anritsu Corporation.

- The present version of the QCDPAX has 288 such PEs. It has a theoretical peak performance of $288 \times 28.65 = 8.25$ GFLOPS. In March they will have 480 PEs installed for 13.75 GFLOPS. Most of the grant went for this hardware, and there was not much left for software. They developed a C++ extended compiler for the machine but it is not stable, so they are mostly programming in assembler [306]. They have five physicists, two computer scientists, and ten graduate students working on the project.

- I went over Dr. Siewiorek's questions with him and he was willing to respond to a few:

    4. The PAX is directed toward minimizing response time, because some of the simulations they run take ten hours or more.

    5. Parallel computing is becoming more of a mature science. He is editor of Parallel Computing and felt that many of the papers were not really new. The field is ready for commercialization. But, Mitsui is not presently selling the earlier versions of PAX. Japanese mainframe manufacturers think that parallel machines are ready for commercialization, but that the market is not large enough.

    6. The development environment is OK for experts but not for the general user.

    12. Computer scientists are ready to share research but physicists are very competitive. They are competing for the Nobel Prize.

    13. Yes, he sees a trend toward special architectures.

    15. PAX was inspired by certain algorithms.

    17. Unix as a basis for open systems has its problems, particularly security. Distributed systems are harder to maintain. He thinks that parallel computers will become commercially successful when they get good general purpose compilers or applications programs.

B.7   Appendix – A Computer Architecture Survey

Daniel P. Siewiorek

These questions formed the basis for interviews with various Japanese computer architects.

Instruction Sets

1. Over the past decade there has been substantial research in "stream lining" instruction sets (i.e., RISC-reduced instruction set computers) to increase performance.

   (a) Do you feel there is any more research required on "stream line" instruction sets? If not, are there further gains to be obtained through careful engineering or has the concept reached a point of diminishing returns and is not worthy of further exploration?

   (b) Has the focus on "stream lined" instruction sets gone too far and ignored support for higher level software abstractions?

2. "Stream lined" instruction sets have focused on the Unix operating systems, C programming language, and workstation environments. What do you see as the role of direct instruction set support for other environments such as object-oriented, functional programming, direct higher level language execution?

3. Are you conducting research into instruction set design? If so, could you share with us what topics you are exploring?

Parallel Processing

4. With the advent of high-performance microprocessors, numerous research and commercial parallel processors have been built. Yet most of these systems have been devoted to increasing throughput (i..e., increasing the number of independent jobs produced per unit time) rather than increasing speedup (i.e., devoting the entire structure to one task and decreasing its execution time). Do you feel this observation is true? If so, what do you feel is the major bottleneck for applying parallel architectures to increasing speedup? What research do you feel needs to be accomplished to make parallel processing routinely available to the programmer/user?

5. Many different parallel processing architectures have been proposed such as SIMD (single instruction, multiple data), MIMD (multiple instruction, multiple data), systolic, and neural networks. Are there other new architectures that should be considered? What are the relative merits of each architecture? Do you foresee one architecture as becoming dominant?

6. Are current programming environments adequate for tapping the potential of parallel processors? What should the programming environment look like?

7. Which do you feel is better, a high-performance uniprocessor or a parallel processor composed of lower performance processors? Why?

8. Are you conducting research into parallel processing? If so, could you share with us what topics you are exploring?

Pipelining, multiple function units, vector processing

9. Concurrent and overlapped operation of independent modules has been used to enhance performance from the dawn of the electronic computing age. Even microprocessors employ multiple function units and pipelining as they strive to execute more than one instruction per clock tick. Some have argued that vector processors are too costly for the amount of speedup achieved and that a fast scalar processor achieves nearly the same performance for a fraction of the cost. Do you feel there is a future for vector processing? If so, what form will vector processing take in the future? Currently vector processing is restricted to large machines. Will this ever be applied to smaller computers such as microprocessors? Are there any hardware or software research topics that need to be pursued to make vector processing more cost-effective?

10. It has been observed that the amount of low level parallelism in conventional programs is limited to about three or four. This would limit the expected number of functional units that could effectively be used in an architecture. Do you foresee a limit to the number of instructions that can be executed per clock tick? Could this limit be raised? If so, how?

11. Pipelining/multiple function units/vector processing/SIMD structure take advantage of "fine grain" (sometimes called inter- statement) parallelism. Parallel processing typically takes advantage of "medium grains" (sometimes called task level) parallelism. Distributed processing (in multicomputers such as cubes and networks) takes advantage of "coarse grain" (sometimes called process level) parallelism. Can these architectural concepts be intermixed? Do they complement or compete with each

other? Will one form of parallelism dominate? Is any research required to answer these questions? If so, what research topics do you see that need to be pursued?

12. Are you conducting research into pipelining/multiple function units/vector processing and/or their interaction with parallel processing? If so, could you share with us what topics you are exploring?

Special Purpose Architectures

13. Historically there have been special architectures devoted to a small range of applications such as data bases, transaction processing, fault-tolerant computing, real-time computing and data flow computing. Do you feel there is an increasing trend towards specialized systems or do you feel that these functions will be taken over by "general purpose" machines?

14. Are you conducting research into special purpose architectures? If so, what is your application area and/or what new techniques are you exploring?

Influences of software on hardware

15. Historically, hardware architects have provided a system that software designers have had to program. Occasionally hardware architects have provided support for software concepts such as objects, direct execution of high-level language statements, and operating system runtime support. These experiments have met with marginal success due to the overhead of imposing one computational model on all software. So far the main exception has been the interaction of compiler writers and streamlined instruction set design (and to a lesser extent, trace-driven scheduling of multiple function units). Do you agree with this observation? If not, why not? What do you feel are the most important research topics in the area of the software/hardware interaction?

16. Are you conducting research into the interaction of software on hardware? If so, could you share with us the topics you are exploring?

Systems issues

17. Contemporary computing environments are composed of a mixture of personal computers, workstations, minicomputers, and main frame computers interconnected by one or more networks. More of the computing is moving into the personal computers and work- stations with the larger computer structure turning into resource servers

(i.e.,file, compute, print servers). What do you foresee as the computing environment of the year 2000? Will it change? If so, how? Are network bandwidths adequate? What bandwidth will be required? Will heterogeneous distributed system replace symmetric, homogeneous parallel systems? What form will input/output take? Are current input/out architectures adequate? If not, what will be required of the new input/output architectures? What research topics need to be pursued to support computer systems architecture of the year 2000?

18. Are you conducting research into systems architectural issues? If so, could you share with us what topics you are exploring?

Bibliography

[1] T. Moto-oka. Challenge for knowledge information processing systems. In T. Moto-oka, editor, *Fifth Generation Computer Systems*, pages 3–89, Amsterdam, 1982. JIPDEC, North Holland Publishing Co.

[2] Comprehensive feasibility study of advanced computing. Report of the Recent Information Processing Technology Investigation Committee, Industrial Electronics Division, MITI, March 1990.

[3] Carl Hammer, Tania Amochaev, Albert Traynham, Robert Dewar, David Gries, Hisashi Kobayashi, H. T. Kung, George Lindamood, Tadao Murata, V. Sadagopan, Norihisa Suzuki, and Valentin Turchin. International developments in computer science. NRC Report, National Research Council, Washington, D.C., 1982.

[4] David H. Brandin, Jon Bentley, Tom Gannon, Michael A. Harrison, John Riganati, Fred Ris, and Norman Sondheimer. JTECH Panel Report on Computer Science in Japan. Japanese Technology Evaluation Program JTECH-TAR–8401, Science Applications International Corporation, San Diego, December 1984.

[5] *A Strategic Industry at Risk*. National Advisory Committee on Semiconductors, Nov. 1989.

[6] 1.2 Million Transistor, 33-MIPS TRON VLSI CPU to debut in 1990. TRON News & Information, February 1989. TRON Association, Number 4.

[7] Michael Cusumano and Chris Kemerer. A quantitative analysis of U.S. & Japanese practice & performance in software development. *Management Science*, 1990.

[8] Matsumoto and Yoshihiro et al. SWB-II: a software test system for realtime control system. *IEEE Newsletter, Distributed Processing Techniques Committee*, Vol. 7(No. 2):17–21, Oct. 1985.

[9] Ichizo Ninomiya et al. Performance of NUMPAC mathematical library package on supercomputers. In *Proc. Symp. Super Computing, Grant-in-aid for Cooperative*

Research (A) "Research on Effective Use of Super Computers", pages 23–31, Tokyo, January 1990. The Ministry of Education, Science and Culture. In Japanese.

[10] David H. Brandin and Michael A. Harrison. *The Technology War*. John Wiley and Sons, New York, NY, 1987.

[11] National Science Board. Science & Engineering Indicators—1989. Washington, DC: U.S. Government Printing Office, 1989. (NSB 89-1).

[12] Clyde V. Prestowitz, Jr. *Trading Places*. Basic Books Inc., New York, 1988.

[13] Paula Doe. Japan spends aggressively and builds for the future. *Electronic Business*, April 16 1960.

[14] Neil Gross. Hustling to catch up in science. *Business Week*, pages 74–82, June 15 1990.

[15] David E. Sanger. Japan Keeps Up the Big Spending to Maintain Its Industrial Might. The New York Times, VOL CXXXIX, No. 48,202, April 11, 1990.

[16] Peter Passell. America's position in the economic race: What the numbers show and conceal. The New York Times, March 4 1990.

[17] Michael L. Dertouzos, Richard L. Lester, and Robert L. Solow. *Made in America*. MIT Press, Cambridge, MA, 1989.

[18] Francis Narin and J. Davidson Franc. The Growth of Japanese Science and Technology. *Science*, 245(11):600–605, August 1989.

[19] J. D. Meindl et al. Brief Lessons in High Technology. Stanford Alumni Association, 1989.

[20] J. D. Meindl. "Ultra-Large Scale Integration". *IEEE Trans. ED*, ED-31(11):1555–1561, Nov. 1984.

[21] J. D. Meindl. "Chips for Advanced Computing". *Scientific American*, 257(4):78–89, Oct. 1984.

[22] Digest of Technical Papers. IEEE ISSCC, Feb. 1987.

[23] Digest of Technical Papers. IEEE, 1983-1989. IEEE Symposium on VLSI Technology.

[24] Digest of Technical Papers. IEEE, 1987-1989. IEEE Symposium on VLSI Circuits.

[25] Technical Digest. IEEE IEDM, Dec. 1980-1989.

[26] T. Sugano, Y. Okabe, and K. Asada. University of Tokyo, Japan. Annual Research Review, No. 24.

[27] J. Kofard. Private Communication. LSI Logic Inc.

[28] P. Gelsinger et al. Microprocessors circa 2000. *IEEE Spectrum*, 26(10):43–47, Oct 1989.

[29] G. Parker. Private Communication. Intel Corp.

[30] TRON News & Information. Tron Association, Feb. 1989. No. 4.

[31] The Battle Royal in Chips. Business Week, Nov. 1989. p. 192.

[32] J. Moll. Private Communication. Hewlett Packard Corp.

[33] What to do with 100 Million Transistors. Electronic Engineering Times, June 1989. Vol. 544, p.1.

[34] Advanced Program. IEEE ISSCC, 1990.

[35] G. Baldwin. Private Communication. Hewlett Packard Corp.

[36] Technical Digest. IEEE, 1986-1989. IEEE Gallium Arsenide Integrated Circuits.

[37] Paul M. Solomon. A comparison of Semiconductor Devices for High Speed Logic. *Proc IEEE*, 70(5):489, May 1982.

[38] National Research Council. *Materials for High-Density Electronic Packaging & Interconnections*, Washington, D.C., 1989. National Academy Press. Report of the Committee on Materials for High-Density Electronic Packaging.

[39] Microelectronics Packaging Handbook, 1989.

[40] O. Kubo et al. Properties of Ba-ferrite particles for perpendicular magnetic recording media. *IEEE Trans. on Magnetics*, MAG-19(6), 1982.

[41] O. Kubo et al. Particle size effects on magnetic properties of $BaFe_{12-2x}Ti_xCo_xO_{19}$ fine particles. *J. Appl. Phys.*, 57(8), 1985. Part IIB.

[42] T. Ido et al. Cooercitivity for Ba-ferrite superfine particles. *IEEE Trans on Magnetics*, MAG-22(5), 1986.

[43] Magnetization reversal for barium ferrite particulate media. IEEE Transactions on Magnetics, 1987. 23(5).

[44] S. Kurisu et al. Surface effect on saturation magnetization of Co and Ti substituted Ba-ferrite fine particles. *IEEE Trans. on Magnetics*, MAG-23(5), 1987.

[45] O. Kubo et al. Improvements in the temperature coefficient of coercivity for barium ferrite particles. *IEEE Trans. on Magnetics*, MAG-24(6), 1988.

[46] O. Kubo et al. A study on substitution elements for barium ferrite particles for perpendicular magnetic recording. *Journal of Magnetic Society of Japan*, 13(S1), 1989.

[47] T. Fujiwara et al. Recording performances of Ba-ferrite coated perpendicular magnetic tapes. *IEEE Trans. on Magnetics*, MAG-18(6), 1982.

[48] T. Fujiwara. Barium ferrite media for perpendicular recording. *IEEE Trans. on Magnetics*, MAG-21(5), 1985.

[49] M. Isshiki et al. Relations between coercivity and recording performances for Ba-ferrite particulate media. *IEEE Trans. on Magnetics*, MAG-21(5), 1985.

[50] T. Fujiwara. Magnetic properties and recording characteristics of barium ferrite media. *IEEE Trans. on Magnetics*, MAG-23(5), 1987.

[51] K. Yamamori et al. Orientation effects of barium ferrite media. *Journal Magnetics Society of Japan*, 13(S1), 1989.

[52] K. Yamomori et al. High density recording characteristics for Ba-ferrite flexible disks. *IEEE Trans. on Magnetics*, MAG-22(5), 1986.

[53] M. Imamura. Barium ferrite perpendicular recording flexible disk drive. *IEEE Trans. on Magnetics*, MAG-22(5), 1986.

[54] M. Kusunoki et al. Peak shift characteristics for barium ferrite flexible disk drive. *IEEE Trans. on Magnetics*, MAG-23(5), 1987.

[55] T. Yamada et al. A 16MB 3.5 inch Ba-ferrite disk drive with dual track following servo modes. *IEEE Trans. on Magnetics*, MAG-24(5), 1987.

[56] K. Yamamori et al. Overwrite characteristics in partial penetration recording. *IEEE Trans. on Magnetics*, MAG-24(6), 1988.

[57] T. Suzuki et al. Perpendicular magnetic recording and its application to digital recording. *ICASSP 86*, 1986. Tokyo.

[58] N. Ohtake et al. Magnetic recording characteristics of R-DAT. *IEEE Trans. on Consumer Electronics*, CE-32(4), 1986.

[59] T. Suzuki. Anhysteretic magnetization process for perpendicular Ba-ferrite tapes used for DAT magnetic contact duplication. *Journal Magnetics Society of Japan*, 13(S1), 1989.

[60] T. Suzuki. Barium ferrite tape for DAT magnetic contact duplication. *IEEE Trans. on Magnetics*, MAG-25(5), 1989.

[61] K. Yamamori. Perpendicular magnetic recording performance of double-layer media. *IEEE Trans. on Magnetics*, MAG-25(5), 1989.

[62] T. Suzuki et al. Magnetization transitions in perpendicular magnetic recording. *IEEE Trans. on Magnetics*, MAG-18(2), 1982.

[63] T. Fujiwara et al. Perpendicular magnetic recording of analog signals by means of pulse width modulation. *IEEE Trans. on Magnetics*, MAG-18(6), 1982.

[64] T. Suzuki. Perpendicular magnetic recording-its basics and potential for future. *IEEE Trans. on Magnetics*, MAG-20(5), 1984.

[65] Y. Sonobe et al. Spacing loss and change in wave length of perpendicular magnetic recording in the narrow spacing region. *IEEE Trans. on Magnetics*, MAG-24(6), 1988.

[66] K. Yamamori et al. Perpendicular magnetic recording floppy disk drive. *IEEE Trans. on Magnetics*, MAG-19(5), 1983.

[67] M. Sagoi et al. Film structure and magnetic properties for Co-Cr sputtered films. *IEEE Trans. on Magnetics*, MAG-20(5), 1984.

[68] M. Sagoi et al. Microstructural inhomogeneity and magnetic properties in Co-Cr sputtered films. *IEEE Trans. on Magnetics*, MAG-22(5), 1986.

[69] Y. Tanaka et al. Inclining columnar structure in Co-Cr films prepared by roll magnetron sputtering. *IEEE Trans. on Magnetics*, MAG-23(5), 1987.

[70] M. Sagoi. Influence of impurity gases on properties of Co-Cr sputtered films. *Journal Vac. Science Technology*, A7(2), Mar/Apr 1989.

[71] M. Sagoi et al. Phase-diagrammatic behavior of Co-Cr sputtered films. *Journal Applied Phys.*, 66(7), 1989.

[72] M. Kanamaru et al. Pass wear durability and defect behavior for Co-Cr thin film media. *Journal Magnetics Society of Japan*, 13(S1), 1989.

[73] N. Inoue et al. The magnetic anisotropy and columnar structure of obliquely sputtered Co-Cr films. *Journal Magnetics Society of Japan*, 13(S1), 1989.

[74] Toshiba review. International edition, 1985. No. 154, Winter.

[75] F. Goto, H. Tanaka, M. Yanagisawa, N. Shiota, M. Kimura, Y. Suganuma, and T. Osaka. Proceedings of the symposium on electrochemical technical in electronics. In *Recent Development of Plated Magnetic Disks*, 1988.

[76] T. Maruyama, K. Yamada, T. Tatsumi, and H. Urai. Soft-adjacent-layer optimization for self-biased MR elements with currentshunt layers. *IEEE Transactions on Magnetics*, Vol. 24(No. 6), 1988.

[77] K. Yamada, T. Maruyama, M. Ohmukai, T. Tatsumi, and H. Urai. CoZrMo amorphous films as a soft adjacent layers for biasing magnetoresistive elements with a current shunt layer. *J. Appl. Phys.*, 63(8), 1988.

[78] Katsumichi Tagami, Hideki Tamai, Toyoko Arai, and Hiroshi Hayashida. Pass wear durability of CoCrTa perpendicular flexible disks. *Journal of The Magnetics Society of Japan*, Vol. 13(S1), 1989. Supplement.

[79] Toyoko Arai and Katsumichi Tagami. Friction characteristics for double-sided perpendicular recording flexible disks. *Tribology and Mechanics of Magnetic Storage Systems*, VI(SP-26), 1989. STLE Special Publication.

[80] K.Tagami, H. Tamai, H. Hayashida, and T. Arai. Pass wear resistance for perpendicular recording media. *IEEE Transactions on Magnetics*, 24(6), 1988.

[81] Masahiro Yanagisawa. Slip effect on thin liquid film on a rotating disk. *J. Appl. Phys.*, 61(3), 1987.

[82] M. Yanagisawa. Depletion of liquid lubricants on magnetic recording disks. Tribology and Mechanics of Magnetic Storage Systems. Volume IV.

[83] Masahiro Yanagisawa. Observation of thickness profiles on lubricants during sliding tests. *Japanese Journal of Applied Physics*, 27(9):L1609–1611, 1988.

[84] M. Yanagisawa and Y. Tsukamoto. Fatigue life of thin film materials for magnetic storage devices. Preprint.

[85] M. Yanagisawa, Y. Tsukamoto, and F. Goto. Wear mechanism on thermal oxidation film for plated magnetic disks. Preprint.

[86] Morishige Aoyama, Takayuki Takeda, Hideki Tamai, and Katsumichi Tagami. Bit error rate characteristics for a Co-Cr-Ta single layer perpendicular recording medium. *Journal of The Magnetics Society of Japan*, 13(S1), 1989. Supplement.

[87] Katsumichi Tagami, Hiroshi Gokan, and Masahito Mukainaru. Magnetic anisotropy of perpendicular media on grooved structure substrate. *IEEE Transactions on Magnetics*, 6, 24. reprinted.

[88] Hideki Tamai, Katsumichi Tagami, and Hiroshi Hayashida. Ta additive effect on RF magnetron sputtered CoCr films. *IEEE Transactions on Magnetics*, 24(6), 1988.

[89] Katsumichi Tagami and Hiroshi Hayashida. Corrosion rate activation energy of sputtered CoCr perpendicular media. *IEEE Transactions on Magnetics*, MAG-23(5), 1987.

[90] F. Toto, T. Osaka, I. Koiwa, Y. Okabe, H. Matsubara, A. Wada, and N. Shiota. Electroless plated disks for perpendicular magnetic recording. *IEEE Transactions on Magnetics*, MAG-20(5), 1984.

[91] T. Sekiguchi, H. Kato, Y. Sasaki, T. Arimura, H. Inada, T. Iwanaga, K. Toki, and M. Okada. High bit rate digital video recording using magneto-optical disks. Preprint.

[92] Toshiaki Iwanaga, Satoshi Sugaya, Hiroshi Inada, and Tadashi Nomura. Magneto-optic recording readout performance improvement. *Applied Optics*, 27:717, 1988.

[93] Y. Yamanaka, K. Kubota, H. Fujii, K. Kobayashi, T. Suzuki, and H. Gokan. High density magneto-optical recording using 0.67 m band high power laser diode. *IEEE Transactions on Magnetics*, 24(6), 1988.

[94] M. Okada, Y. Sasaki, T. Iwanaga, K. Toki, M. Nakada, H. Inada, T. Sekiguchi, and H. Gokan. High C/N magneto-optical disks using plastic substrates for video image applications. *IEEE Transactions on Magnetics*, MAG-23(5), 1987.

[95] M. Okada, T. Habara, H. Chikugo, A. Okada, K. Toki, O. Okada, H. Inada, and H. Gokan. Bit error analysis for magneto-optical disks under accelerated aging conditions. *NEC Research and Development*, (94):49–56, 1989.

[96] K. Koumura, F. Takizawa, T. Iwanaga, and H. Inada. High speed accessing using split optical head. Optical Data Storage Topical Meeting, January 1989.

[97] T. Aikawa, H. Mutoh, and T. Sugawara. An experimental study of signal equalization for thin film heads. *IEEE Transactions on Magnetics*, MAG-2(5), 1986.

[98] Hitoshi Kanai, Takao Koshikawa, and Akira Kakehi. A study of D50 and W50 on thin film magnetic heads. Fujitsu Laboratories, Ltd.

[99] M. Kanamine, H. Kanai, and K. Hata. Stability of magnetic domains in narrow strip laminated CoZrCr films. *IEEE Trans. Magn.*, 24(2045), 1988.

[100] H. Kanai, K. Hosono, and H. Takagi. The effects of head configuration and bias current on the read sensitivity profiles of MR head. *IEEE*, 1989. reprint.

[101] G. Ishida. Sputtered γ - Fe_2O_3 thin film disks. Fujitsu Ltd., October 1989. ECS 178th Meeting, Hollywood, Florida.

[102] T. Yamada and D. B. Bogy. Load-unload slider dynamics in magnetic disk drives. *IEEE Transactions on Magnetics*, 24(6), 1988.

[103] Y. Mizoshita, K. Aruga, and T. Yamada. Dynamic characteristics of a magnetic head slider. *IEEE Transactions on Magnetics*, MAG-21(5), September 1985.

[104] K. Aruga, Y. Mizoshita, T. Yamada, and S. Yoneoka. Spacing fluctuation of flying head sliders in track accessing (forced vibration analysis using finite element method). Fujitsu Laboratories, Ltd.

[105] T. Yamada, Y. Mizoshita, and K. Aruga. Spacing fluctuation of flying head sliders in track accessing (measurement using optical interferometer). Fujitsu Laboratories, Ltd.

[106] S. Yoneoka, T. Yamada, K. Aruga, T. Ooe, and M. Takahashi. Fast take-off negative pressure slider. *IEEE Transactions on Magnetics*, AMG-23(5), September 1987.

[107] S. Yoneoka, T. Owe, K. Aruga, T. Yamada, and M. Takahashi. Dynamics of inline flying-head assemblies. *IEEE reprint*, 1989.

[108] Minoru Takahashi. A signal analysis of piezoelectric transducers furnished on head sliders. In Japanese.

[109] T. Yamamoto, Y. Imada, and K. Nakajima. The effect of grain size on the wear behavior of Mn-Zn ferrite. *IMechE*, 1987.

[110] K. Aruga, Y. Mizoshita, M. Iwatsubo, and T. Hatagami. Acceleration feedforward control for head positioning in magnetic disk drives, May 1989. International Conference on Advanced Mechatronics.

[111] Kazuo Kobayashi, Junzo Toda, and Tayayuki Yamomoto. High density perpendicular magnetic recording on rigid disks. *FUJITSU Scientific and Technical Journal*, 19(15), 1983.

[112] K. Kobayashi and Fujitsu Laboratories. Analysis of output voltage in perpendicular recording. In Japanese.

[113] Takao Koshikawa, Eiichi Kanda, Michiaki Kanamine, Kazumasa Hosono, and Hitoshi Takagi. Edge-noise evaluation of single-pole thin film magnetic head. *Journal of The Magnetics Society of Japan*, 13(S1), 1989.

[114] Kazuo Kobayashi, Junzon Toda, Takayuki Yamamoto, Hitoshi Takagi, Yoshio Takahashi, and Kunio Hata. Thin film head of perpendicular magnetic recording. In Japanese.

[115] T. Koshikawa and H. Takagi. Edge-noise simulation of single-pole thin film magnetic head. In Japanese.

[116] Katsumi Kiuchi, Hiroaki Wakamatsu, Fumitake Suzuki, and Michiaki Kanamine. Effects of underlayer thickness and external fields on noise in perpendicular double-layered media. *Journal of The Magnetics Society of Japan*, 13(S1), 1989.

[117] K. Kiuchi, H. Wakamatsu, F. Suzuki, and H. Takagi. High-energy Co-Cr thin films sputtered on glass disks for perpendicular recording. *IEEE Transactions on Magnetics*, 24(6), 1988.

[118] K. Kiuchi, H. Wakamatsu, and F. Suzuki. Noise characteristics on double-layered perpendicular media. Fujitsu Laboratories. In Japanese.

[119] H. Wakamatsu, K. Kiuchi, and F. Suzuki. Correlation between S/N and magnetic anisotropy of NiFe underlayer on double-layered perpendicular media. In Japanese.

[120] Ryousuke Kudou, Hiroshi Ichi-i, and Akio Futamata. Facom 6443 magneto-optic disk drive subsystem. *FUJITSU 39*, 3(06):237–243, 1988.

[121] M. Moritsugu, S. Arai, A. Futamata, F. Abe, and K. Ogawa. New optical head for magneto-optic library units, January 1989. Proceedings of SPIE-The International Society for Optical Engineering.

[122] F. Abe, M. Moritsugu, A. Futamata, and K. Ogawa. Fast access rewritable magneto-optical disk library. International Conference on Advanced Mechatronics.

[123] M. Moribe, Y. Hashimoto, M. Maeda, K. Itoh, and S. Ogawa. Bit-error reduction in magneto-optical disks. *SPIE*, 899, 1988.

[124] M. Miyazaki, I. Shibata, S. Okada, K. Ito, and S. Ogawa. A new protective film for magneto-optical TbFeCo media. *J. Appl. Phys.*, 61(8), April 1987.

[125] Yoshimasa Miura, Masao Suzuki, and Junshiro Sugihara. Facom 6425 disk subsystem and future disk storage technology. *FUJITSU Scientific and Technical Journal*, 23(4), December 1987.

[126] Shinji Ohtaki Ken-ichi Itoh, Mitsuru Hamada. Replication master for optical disk substrates. *FUJITSU Scientific and Technical Journal*, 23(1), March 1987.

[127] I. Sato, A. Terada, and S. Ohta. Magnetic recording media for large-capacity fast-access magnetic disk storage. *Review of the Electrical Communications Laboratories*, 36(1), 1988.

[128] Y. Koshimoto, T. Mikazuki, and T. Ohkubo. Magnetic head design for large-capacity fast-access magnetic disk storage. *Review of the Electrical Communications Laboratories*, 36(1), 1988.

[129] S. Takanami, M. Mizukami, and T. Kakizaki. Large-capacity fast-access magnetic disk storage. *Review of the Electrical Communications Laboratories*, 36(1), 1988.

[130] S. Hirono, K. Nonaka, and I. Hatakeyama. Magnetization distribution analysis in the film edge region under a homogeneous field. *J. Appl. Phys.*, 60(10), November 1986.

[131] J. Kishigami, A. Tago, and Y. Koshimoto. Domain analysis of amorphous CoZrRe film. *IEEE Transactions on Magnetics*, MAG-23(5), September 1987.

[132] J. Kishigami, K. Itoh, and Y. Koshimoto. Three-dimensional pole edge effect on narrow track film heads. *IEEE Transactions on Magnetics*, 24(6), 1988.

[133] I. Sato, K. Otani, S. Oguchi, and K. Hoshiya. Characteristics of heat transfer in a Helium-filled disk enclosure. *IEEE Transactions on Components, Hybrids, and Manufacturing Technology*, 11(4), December 1988.

[134] T. Ohkubo and J. Kishigami. Accurate measurement of gas-lubricated slider bearing separation using visible laser interferometry. *Journal of Tribology*, 110, 1988.

[135] T. Ohkubo and J. Kishigami. Accurate measurement and evaluation of dynamic characteristics of flying head slider for large-capacity fast-access magnetic disk storage. *IEEE Transactions on Magnetics*, MAG-23(5), September 1987.

[136] T. Ohkubo, S. Fukui, and K. Kogure. Static characteristics of gas-lubricated slider bearings operating in a helium-air mixture. *Journal of Tribology*, 111, 1989.

[137] K. Mochizuki, I. Sato, and T. Hayashi. Detection of a impulse force in head-disk media contact using small piezoelectric transducer. *Progress in Acoustic Emission IV, The Japanese Society for NDI*, III, October 1989.

[138] T. Miyamoto, I. Sato, and Y. Ando. Friction and wear characteristics of thin film disk media in boundary lubrication. *Tribology and Mechanics of Magnetic Storage Systems*, 5, STLE SP-25, 1988.

[139] T. Miyamoto, I. Sato, and Y. Ando. Lubrication performance of melamine cyanurate composite lubricant for thin film disk media. *IEEE Transactions on Magnetics*, MAG-23(5), September 1987.

[140] R. Kaneko and T. Miyamoto. Friction and adhesion forces on magnetic disk surfaces. *IEEE Transactions on Magnetics*, 24(6), November 1988.

[141] T. Ohkubo and Y. Koshimoto. Feasibility study on perpendicular rigid disk. *Journal of The Magnetics Society of Japan*, 13(S1), 1989.

[142] T. Kato, R. Arai, and S. Takanami. Write-current equalization for high-speed digital magnetic recording. *IEEE Transactions on Magnetics*, MAG-22(5), 1986.

[143] T. Kao, S. Takanami, S. Hirono, and I. Sato. A study on signal processing for enhanced density in vertical recording systems with mig head. NTT Applied Electronics Laboratories. Japan.

[144] S. Hirono and A. Furuya. Enhanced perpendicular coercive force of CoCr film formed on a very thin initial sublayer. *IEEE Transactions on Magnetics*, 24(6), 1988.

[145] M. Saito, T. Takeda, and K. Itao. 90-mm optical disk subsystem using high-speed digital control techniques. *Optical Data Storage, 1989 Technical Digest Series*, 1, January 1989.

[146] M. Saito, T. Takeda, and K. Itao. Optical micro-disk subsystem using optimum error control strategy. NTT Applied Electronics Laboratories. Tokyo.

[147] T. Takeda, M. Saito, and K. Itao. System design of optical micro-disk subsystem. In *Proceedings of SPIE-The International Society for Optical Engineering*, pages 12–15, Los Angeles, CA, January 1988. The International Society for Optical Engineering, The International Society for Optical Engineering. Vol. 899.

[148] H. Nakanishi S. Hara and T. Yoshizawa. Hardware design for high performance 130-mm optical disk storage system. *Review of the Electrical CommunicationsLaboratories*, 36(2), 1988.

[149] A. Watabe, M. Yamamoto, and K. Katoh. High-speed recording technology for optical disk compatible between write-once and magneto-optical media. *Review of the Electrical Communications Laboratories*, 36(2), 1988.

[150] K. Nishimura and S. Murata. 5-channel magneto-optical recording using a laser diode array. NTT Applied Electronics Laboratories, Tokyo.

[151] S. Murata and K. Nishimura. Improvement in thermal properties of a multi-beam laser diode array. NTT Applied Electronics Laboratories, Tokyo.

[152] M. Mitsunaga, R. Kachru, E. Xu, and M. K. Kim. cw photon echo. *Physical Society Review Letters*, 63(7), August 1989.

[153] M. Mitsunaga and N. Uesugi. 248-bit optical data storage in Eu3+:YA1O3 by accumulated photon echo. NTT Basic Research Laboratories, Tokyo, to be published.

[154] M. Mitsunaga, M. K. Kim, and R. Kachru. Degenerate photo echoes: simultaneous storage of multiple optical data. *Optics Letters*, 13:536, June 1988.

[155] Yashuaru Hidaka. Bloch line pair generator using the flank wall near the stripe domain head. *IECE*, 1:1–224, March 1986.

[156] Y. Maruyama, R. Suzuki, and Konishi. Generation, propagation, and detection of Bloch line pairs. *IECEJ*, 1:159, March 1987.

[157] Y. Maruyama, K. Fujimoto, and R. Suzuki. Characteristics of Bloch line propagation by field–access scheme in the case of stripe domain stabilization by film grooving. *IEICE*, 5:5–13, March 1989.

[158] K. Fujimoto, Y. Maruyama, and R. Suzuki. Bloch lines observation by high-frequency wall oscillation. *IEICE*, 5:5–14, March 1989.

[159] Y. Maruyama, K. Fujimoto, and R. Suzuki. Characteristics of read operation for Bloch line memory using I_m bubble garnet film. *IECEJ*, 5:5–15, March 1990.

[160] K. Fujimoto, Y. Maruyama, and R. Suzuki. Characteristics of Bloch line pair propagation at the corner of stripe domains using field access scheme. *IECEJ*, 5:5–16, March 1990.

[161] R. Suzuki. Bloch line memory prototype which is a possibility of 1 G bit memory. *Denshi Zairyo*, 25(12):97–99, December 1986.

[162] Shizuo Shiokawa, Yoshitsugu Obashi, and Akira Nagoya. DIPS-11/5E Series Mainframes. *Review of the Electrical Communications Laboratories*, 35(6):633–641, 1987.

[163] Kiyoshi Itao, Tadashi Hirono, and Shigefumi Kosokawa. Automated Magnetic Tape Memory System: System Design. *Review of the Electrical Communications Laboratories*, 34(5), 1986.

[164] Shigeru Takasaki, Fumiyasu Hirose, and Akihiko Yamada. Logic Simulation Engines in Japan. *IEEE Design & Test of Computers*, pages 40–49, 1989.

[165] Nakashima Hiroshi and Katsuto Hakajima. Hardware Architecture of the Sequential Inference Machine:SI-II. *IEEE*, 1987.

[166] Akira Hattori, Shinogi Tsuyoshi, Kouichi Kumon, and Atuhito Goto. PIM/p:A hierarchical parallel inference machine.

[167] The Man behind TRON – A New Computer for the '90's. Business Tokyo, October 1989.

[168] A new keyboard for the coming information age. TRON News & Information, July 1989. 6–8,TRON Association, Number 9.

[169] Tsukasa Matba, Takeshi Aikawa, Kenichi Maeda, Mitsuyoshi Okamura, Kenji Minagawa, Takeshi Takamiya, and Mitsuo Saito. Twin Register Architecture for an AI Processor.

[170] Shigeru Kawakita, Mitsuo Saito, Yasuo Hoshino, Yoshiaki Bandai, and Yasuhiro Kobayashi. An Integrated AI Environment for Industrial Expert Systems. *IEEE*, pages 258–263, 1988. IEEE International Workshop on Artificial Intelligence for Industrial Applications.

[171] Mitsuo Saito, Takeshi Aikawa, Kenichi Maeda, Yoshinobu Sano, and Yasuo Hoshino. An AI Processor: RISC Architecture with Hardware Support for AI Languages. *IEEE Tokyo Section*, (27):39–43, 1988. Denshi Tokyo.

[172] Chikara Tsuchiya, Yoshihide Sugiura, Hiroshi Iwamoto, Hideki Yoshizawa, Hideki Kato, and Kazuo Asakawa. The First Commercial Neurochip: Analog Time-Division Processing Reduces the number of wirings, June 1989.

[173] Michiharu Tsukamoto, Yutaka Sato, Hideki Shitanda, Noguo Yoshie, Nobuhiko Funato, Nobuaki Tanaka, Shogo Nakagome, and Akio Tojo. The Architecture of OZ: Object-Oriented Open Distributed System. *INTAP*, 1988. Proceedings of the Second International, Symposium on Interoperable Information System.

[174] Mitsuo Saito, Takeshi Aikawa, Tsukasa Matoba, Mitsuyoshi Okamura, Kenji Minagawa, and Tadatoshi Ishii. Architecture of an AI Processor Chip (IP1704).

[175] Kemal Ebcioğlu, Kemal, and Toshio Nakatani. A New Compilation Technique for Parallelizing Loops with Unpredictable Branches on a VLWIT Architecture.

[176] Toshio Nakatani and Kemal Ebcioğlu. "Combining" as a Compilation Technique for VLIW Architectures.

[177] Atsushi Inoue and Akora Maeda. The Architecture of a Multi-Vector Processor System, VPP. *Parallel Computing 8*, pages 185–193, 1988.

[178] Shuichi Sakai, Yoshinori Yamagughi, Kei Hiraki, Yuetsu Kodama, and Toshitsugu Yuba. An Architecture of a Dataflow Single Chip Processor. *ISCA*, 1989.

[179] Computer Industry Report: The Gray Sheet. International Data Corporation, December 1988. p. 3.

[180] Japan Computer Industry: Review and Forecast, 1987-1992. International Data Corporation, January 1989.

[181] Yoshihiro Matsumotoa. A software factory: An overall approach to software production. *IEEE reprint EH0256-8/87/0000/0155501.00*, 1987.

[182] Human resources for software in the year 2000 – who is resonsible for fostering education for a highly computerized society? Report of the Committee for Studying Industrial Structure, Working Group for the Computer Industry, Study Group for Computer Engineers, MITI, 1985.

[183] SIGMA News. Information-Technology Promotion Agency, Vol. 1, 1986. Japan.

[184] Michael Cusumano. *Japan's Software Factories.* Oxford University Press, 1990.

[185] Michael Cusumano. The 'Software Factory' reconsidered. Technical report, Sloan School of Management, MIT, 1987. Working Paper No. 1885-1987.

[186] Watts S. Humphrey, David H. Kitson, and Tim C. Kasse. The state of software engineering practice: A preliminary report. Technical report, Carnegie Mellon Software Engineering Institute, February 89.

[187] Masuda and Yoneji. *The Information Society as Post-industrial Society.* World Future Society, 1980.

[188] Stewart Brand. *The Media Lab.* Viking Press, New York, 1987.

[189] Kenneth L. Kraemer and John Leslie King. Computer-based systems for cooperative work and group decision making. *ACM Computing Surveys*, 20(2):115, June 1988.

[190] G. Foster and M. Stefik. Cognoter, theory and practice of a Colab-Orative tool. In *Proceedings Computer-Supported Cooperative Work*, Austin, TX, December 1986.

[191] Lucy A. Suchman and Randall H. Trigg. A framework for studying research collaboration. In *Proceedings of the Conference on Computer Supported Cooperative Work*, Austin, December 1986.

[192] M. Stefik, D. G. Bobrow, G. Foster, S. Lanning, and D. Tatar. Wysiwis revised: Early experiences with multiuser interfaces. *ACM Transactions on Office Information Systems*, 5(2):147, April 1987.

[193] Mark Stefik, Gregg Foster, Daniel G. Bobrow, Kenneth Kahn, Stan Lanning, and Lucy Suchman. Beyond the chalkboard: Computer support for collaboration and problem solving in meetings. *Communications of the ACM*, 30(1):32–47, January 1987.

[194] Steven A. Weyer. The design of a dynamic book for information search. *International Journal of Man-Machine Studies*, 17:87–107, 1982.

[195] Alan Borning, D. B. Lenat, D. McDonald, C. Taylor, and Steven A. Weyer. Knoesphere: Toward a searcher's guide to encylocpedic knowledge. In *International Joint Conference on Artificial Intelligence-83*, 1983.

[196] Stephen A. Weyer and Alan H. Borning. A prototype electronic encyclopedia. *ACM Transactions on Office Information Systems*, 3(1):63–88, January 1985.

[197] Vannevar Bush. As we may think. *Atlantic Monthly*, 176(1):101–108, July 1945.

[198] Vannevar Bush. Memex revisited. In Vannevar Bush, editor, *Science Is Not Enough*, pages 75–101. William Morrow, 1967.

[199] Douglas C. Engelbart and William K. English. A research center for augmenting human intellect. In *AFIPS Proceedings, FJCC*, volume 33, pages 395–410, Fall 1968.

[200] Randall H. Trigg, Lucy A. Suchman, and Frank G. Halasz. Supporting collaboration in notecards. In *Proceedings of the Conference on Computer Supported Cooperative Work*, Austin, December 1986.

[201] Frank G. Halasz, Thomas P. Moran, and Randall H. Trigg. Notecards in a nutshell. In *Proceedings SIGCHI Conference on Human Factors in Computing Systems*, pages 45–52, Toronto, Canada, April 1987.

[202] Randall H. Trigg and Peggy M. Irish. Hypertext habitats: Experiences of writers in notecards. In *Proceedings Hypertext '87*, page 89, Chapel Hill, NC, November 1987.

[203] Randall H. Trigg, T. P. Moran, and Frank G. Halasz. Adaptibility and tailorability in notecards. In *Proceedings of INTERACT '87*, Stuttgart, West Germany, 1987.

[204] Frank G. Halasz. Reflections on notecards: Seven issues for the next generation of hypermedia systems. *Communications of the ACM*, 31(7):836, July 1988.

[205] Joel R. Remde, Louis M. Gomez, and Thomas K. Landauer. Superbook: an automatic tool for information exploration-hypertext? In *Proceedings Hypertext '87*, page 175, Chapel Hill, NC, November 1987.

[206] Dennis E. Egan, Joel R. Remde, Thomas K. Landauer, Carol C. Lochbaum, and Louis M. Gomez. Behavioral evaluation and analysis of a hypertext browser. In *Proceedings SIGCHI Conference on Human Factors in Computing Systems*, page 205, Austin, TX, May 1989.

[207] Dennis E. Egan, Joel R. Remde, Louis M. Gomez, Thomas K. Landauer, Jennifer Eberhardt, and Carol C. Lochbaum. Formative design evaluation of superbook. *ACM Transactions on Information Systems*, 7(1):30, January 1989.

[208] Jeff Conklin. Hypertext: an introduction and survey. *Computer*, 20(9):17–41, September 1987.

[209] Edward Barrett, editor. *Text, Context, and Hypertext*. MIT Press, Cambridge, MA, 1988.

[210] Jeff Conklin and Michael L. Begeman. Gibis: a hypertext tool for team design deliberation. In *Proceedings Hypertext '87*, page 247, Chapel Hill, NC, November 1987.

[211] Jeff Conklin and Michael L. Begeman. Gibis: a hypertext tool for exploratory policy discussion. *ACM Transactions on Office Information Systems*, 6(4):303, October 1988.

[212] Jeff Conklin and Michael L. Begeman. Gibis: a tool for all reasons. S P-252-88, Software Technology Program, MCC, Austin, TX, August 1988.

[213] Theodor H. Nelson. Dream machines: New freedoms through computer screens - a minority report. In *Computer Lib: You Can and Must Understand Computers Now*. Hugo's Book Service, Chicago, IL, 1974.

[214] Steven Feiner. Seeing the forest for the trees: Hierarchical display of hypertext structure. In *PROC Fourth ACM-SIGOIS Conference on Office Information Systems*, pages 205–212, 1988.

[215] Matthew E. Hodges, Russell M. Sasnett, and Mark S. Ackerman. A construction kit for multimedia applications. *IEEE Software*, 6(1):37, January 1989.

[216] Joyce K. Reynolds, Jonathan B. Postel, Alan R. Katz, Greg G. Finn, and Annette L. DeSchon. The darpa experimental multimedia mail system. *Computer*, 18(10):82, October 1985.

[217] Jonathen B. Postel, Gregory G. Finn, Alan R. Katz, and Joyce K. Reynolds. An experimental multimedia mail system. *ACM Transactions on Office Information Systems*, 6(1):63, January 1988.

[218] Robert .H. Thomas, Harry C. Forsdick, Terrence R. Crowley, Richard W. Schaaf, Raymond S. Tomlinson, and Virginia M. Travers. Diamond: a multimedia message system built on a distributed architecture. *Computer*, 18(12):65–78, December 1985.

[219] H. Lison and T. Crowley. Sight and sound. *UNIX Review*, 7(10):76–86, 1989.

[220] Brad A. Myers. User-interface tools: Introduction and survey. *IEEE Software*, 6(1):15, January 1989.

[221] James Foley, Won Chul Kim, Srdjan Kovacevic, and Kevin Murray. Defining interfaces at a high level of abstraction. *IEEE Software*, 6(1):25, January 1989.

[222] Gerhard Fischer. Human-computer interaction software: Lessons learned, challenges ahead. *IEEE Software*, 6(1):44, January 1989.

[223] David J. Kasik, Michelle A. Lund, and Henry W. Ramsey. Reflections on using a uims for complex applications. *IEEE Software*, 6(1):54, January 1989.

[224] William D. Hurley and John L. Sibertl. Modeling user interface-application interactions. *IEEE Software*, 6(1):71, January 1989.

[225] John C. Thomas and Wendy A. Kellog. Minimizing ecological gaps in interface design. *IEEE Software*, 6(1):78–86, January 1989.

[226] Hajime Kamata, Tsuneo Katsuyama, Toshimitsu Suzuki, Yu Minakauchi, and Katsutoshi Yano. Communication workstations for b-isdn: Monster (multimedia oriented super terminal). Proc. Globecom'89, November 1989. Fujitsu Laboratories Ltd., 1015, Kamikodanaka, Nakahara-ku, Kawasaki, 211, Japan.

[227] Toshitaka Tsuda, Kiichi Matsuda, and Takeshi Okazaki. A consideration of TV-conferences using HDTV signals. Fujitsu Laboratories Ltd. 1015, Kamikodanaka Nakahara-Ku , Kawasaki 211, Japan. pp 495-502.

[228] Takeshi Okazaki, Shin ichi Maki, Takashi Itoh, Kiichi Matsuda, and Toshitaka Tsuda. Implementation of a hdtv codec using a hybrid quantizer. Globecom '87, Fujitsu Laboratories LTD. 1015 Kamikodanaka, Nakahara-ku, Kawasaki, 211 Japan, pp 421-425.

[229] Masako Nishijima and Yuji Kijima. Learning on sense of rhythm with a neural network - the neuro-drummer-. pages 77–80. The First International Conference on Music Perception and Cognition. Kyoto, Japan, October 17-19 1989.

[230] Nicole Yankelovich, Norman Meyrowitz, and Andries van Dam. Reading and writing the electronic book. *Computer*, 18(10):15–30, October 1985.

[231] Nicole Yankelovich, Bernard J. Haan, Norman K. Meyrowitz, and Steven M. Drucker. Intermedia: the concept and the construction of a seamless information environment. *Computer*, 21(1):81–96, January 1988.

[232] Shu Tezuka. A new class of nonlinear functions for running-key generators (extended abstract). pages pp 181–185, 1988. Presented at Eurocrypt 88.

[233] M. Maekawa, K. Sakamura, C. Ishikawa, and T. Shimizu. Multimedia machine. Technical Report 83-08., Tokyo University Info.Sci.Department, 1983.

[234] M. Ohta et al. Multimedia workstation - PIE. Technical Report 85-17, University of Tokyo, Department of Information Science, 1985.

[235] M. Ohta et al. Multimedia information processing based on a general media model. Technical Report 85-18, University of Tokyo, Department of Information Science, 1985.

[236] M. Ohta et al. The implementation and experience of multimedia workstation - PIE. Technical Report 87-04, University of Tokyo, Department of Information Science, 1987.

[237] M. Maekawa, M. Ohta, and K. Shimizu. Garbage collection for multimedia processing. Technical Report 87-01, University of Tokyo, Department of Information Science, 1987.

[238] Edward Dolnick. Inventing the future. *New York Times Magazine*, CXXXVI(47,240):30–33,41,59, August 23 1987.

[239] Senior MIT Faculty Members. Private communication, June 1990.

[240] Ken Sakamura. *TRON Project 1987–Open Architecture Computer System*. Springer–Verlag, 1987.

[241] Ken Sakamura. *TRON Project 1988–Open Architecture Computer System*. Springer–Verlag, 1988.

[242] Ken Sakamura. *TRON Project 1988–Open Architecture Computer System*. Springer–Verlag, 1989.

[243] Ken Sakamura. Helping incompatible computers get together, Nihon Keizai Shimbun, July 8 1989.

[244] Ken Sakamura. Computer projects in Japan. *IEEE Micro*, 9(3), June 1989.

[245] Ken Sakamura. An overview of the BTRON–286 specification. *IEEE Micro*, 9(3), June 1989. This issue includes related articles on the BTRON–286 hardware and video image handling.

[246] Ken Sakamura. A floating–point VLSI chip for the TRON architecture; an architecture for reliable numerical programming. *IEEE Micro*, 9(3), June 1989. This issue includes a related article on floating–point standards.

[247] Hideo Inayoshi, Ikuysa Kawasaki, Tadahiko Nishimukai, and Ken Sakamura. Realization of Gmicro/200. *IEEE Micro*, 8(2), April 1988.

[248] Ken Sakamura, Ryoichi Sano, and Kazuhiko Honma. Introducing TOBUS: the system bus in the TRON architecture. *IEEE Micro*, 8(2), April 1988.

[249] Ken Sakamura, Kanehisa Tsurumi, and Hiro Kato. Applying the μbtron bus to a music LAN. *IEEE Micro*, 8(2), April 1988.

[250] Ken Sakamura. The TRON project: An open–system computer architecture. *IEEE Micro*, 7(2), April 1987.

[251] Ken Sakamura. Architecture of the TRON VLSI CPU. *IEEE Micro*, 7(2), April 1987. The open architecture of the TRON microprocessor.

[252] Ken Sakamura. BTRON, the business oriented operating system. *IEEE Micro*, 7(2), April 1987. This issue includes related articles about the MMI subproject, which deals with man–machine interfaces and about the TRON keyboard unit.

[253] Ken Sakamura. The TRON project. *Microprocessors and Microsystems*, 13(8), October 1989.

[254] Ken Sakamura and Tatsuya Enomoto. 32–bit microprocessors based on the TRON specification. *Microprocessors and Microsystems*, 8(13), October 1989.

[255] Hiroshi Takeyama and Ken Sakamura. Design and implementation of the ITRON specification. *Microprocessors and Microsystems*, 13(8), October 1989.

[256] Masahiro Shimizu, Yoshiaki Kushiki, and Ken Sakamura. Operating system based on BTRON specifications. *Microprocessors and Microsystems*, 13(8), October 1989.

[257] Toshikazu Ohkubo, Tetsuo Wasano, and Ichizo Kogiku. Configuration of the CTRON kernal. *IEEE Mirco*, 7(2), April 1987.

[258] Hiroshi Monden. Introduction to ITRON, the industry–oriented operating system. *IEEE Micro*, 7(2), April 1987.

[259] Tetsuo Wasano and Yoshizumi Kobayashi. Application of CTRON to communication networks. *Microprocessors and Microsystems*, 13(8), October 1989.

[260] Misao Miyata, Hidechika Kishigami, Kosei Okamoto, and Shigeo Kamiya. The TX1 32–bit microprocessor: Performance analysis and debugging support. *IEEE Micro*, 8(2), April 1988.

[261] NTT applying CTRON specification based operating system, August 2 1989.

[262] Staff of the United States Trade Representative. 1989 national trade estimate report on foreign trade barriers. Technical report, Office of the United States Trade Representative, Washington, DC, 1989.

[263] Staff of the United States Trade Representative. 1990 national trade estimate report on foreign trade barriers. Technical report, Office of the United States Trade Representative, Washington, DC, 1990.

[264] The Federal High Performance Computing Program. Executive Office of the President, Office of Science and Technology Policy, September 1989.

[265] Annual Report to the National Science Foundation from the National Center for Supercomputing Applications, 1987.

[266] National Center for Atmospheric Research Annual Report, 1988.

[267] New Dimensions of Insight – Science at the San Diego Supercomputer Center, 1988.

[268] Projects in Scientific Computing, Pittsburgh Supercomputing Center, 1988-89.

[269] Science at The John von Neumann National Supercomputer Center, Annual Research Report, 1988.

[270] Supercomputing Review. Eamonn Wilmott Publisher, San Diego, October 1989. Norris Parker Smith, Ed.

[271] D. C. Barnes, T. Kamimura, J. N. Leboeuf, and T. Tajima. Implicit particle simulation of magnetized plasmas. *J. Comput. Phys.*, 52:480–502, 1983.

[272] B. Gale. The 3rd ISR supercomputing workshop. *Vector Register*, 3:11–15, 1989.

[273] W. Lepkowski. Japan's science and technology aim toward globalization. *C&EN*, pages 7 – 14, May 8, 1989.

[274] C. Daniel, K. Koga, J. Han, X. Y. Fu, and K. Morokuma. Ab initio MO study of the full catalytic cycle of olefin hydrogenation by the Wilkinson catalyst RhCl(PR$_3$)$_3$. *J. Am. Chem. Soc.*, 110:3773–3787, 1988.

[275] M. Haser and R. Alrichs. Improvements on the direct SCF method. *J. Comput. Chem.*, 10:104–111, 1989. See other references in this paper.

[276] I. Ohmine, H. Tanaka, and P. G. Wolynes. Large local energy fluctuations in water. II cooperative motions and fluctuations. *J. Chem. Phys.*, 89:5852–5860, 1988.

[277] K. F. Loe and E. Goto. *DC Flux Parametron - A New Approach to Josephson Junction Logic*, volume 6 of *Series in Computer Science*. World Scientific Pub. Co., Philadelphia, PA, 1986.

[278] E. Goto, T. Soma, and L. Fock. Fluxoid Josephson computer technology,. In *Proceedings of the 3rd, 4th, and 5th Riken - Erato*, Philadelphia, PA, 1988. World Scientific Pub. Co.

[279] A. Kidera and N. Go. Normal mode debye-waller factor in protein x-ray crystallographic refinement. In *Proceedings of the Second International Conference, Protein Engineering '89*, August 20-25, 1989.

[280] H. Yoshihara. Professor Kunio Kuwahara's Unique Institute of Computational Fluid Dynamics. *ONRFE Sci. Info. Bul.*, 14:115–119, 1989.

[281] O. M. Lubeck. *Supercomputer Performance: The Theory, Practice, and Results*, volume 27 of *Advances in Computers*, pages 309–362. Academic Press, 1988.

[282] M. Berry, D. Chen, P. Koss, D. Kuck, S. Lo, Y. Pang, L. Pointer, R. Roloff, A. Sameh, E. Clementi, S. Chin, D. Schneider, G. Fox, P. Messina, D. Walker, C. Hsuing, J. Schwarzmeier, K. Lue, S. Orszag, F. Seidl, O. Johnson, R. Goodrum, and J. Martin. The perfect club benchmarks: Effective performance evaluation of supercomputers. *Int. J. Supercomp. Applications*, 3:5–40, 1989.

[283] K. Fujii and H. Yoshihara. A Navier/Stokes benchmark for Japanese and U.S. supercomputers. *ONRFE Sci. Info. Bul.*, 14(2):69–74, 1989.

[284] Office of Naval Research Far East Sci. Info. Bul., 1989. 14(2).

[285] Hitachi Central Research Laboratory. Hitachi, June 1989.

[286] Hitachi Central Research Laboratory. The parallel processor H2P. Hitachi Central Research Laboratory, November 1989. Briefing Notes.

[287] Mamoru Sugie. Load dispatching strategy on parallel inference machines. Hitachi Central Research Laboratory, November 1989. Briefing Notes.

[288] M. Michiharu, Y. Sato, H. Shitanda, N. Yoshie, N. Funato, N. Tanaka, S. Nakagome, and A. Tojo. The architecture of OZ: Object-oriented open distributed system, 1988. Proceedings of the Second International Symposium on Iteroperable Information Systems 1988.

[289] October 1986. Computer Center. Institute of Plasma Physics, Nagoya University Japan.

[290] Institute of Plasma Physics, October 1986. Computer Center (Brochure). Nagoya University, Nagoya 464, Japan.

[291] Mildred Dresselhaus. JTEC Panel Report on "High Temperature Superconductivity in Japan". JTEC, Japanese Technology Evaluation Center, Baltimore, MD, November 1989.

[292] William Brinkman. JTEC Panel Report on "The Japanese Exploratory Research for Advanced Technology (ERATO) Program". JTEC, Japanese Technology Evaluation Center, Baltimore, MD, December 1988.

[293] W. Brinkman and D. Oxender. JTECH panel report on japanese exploratory research for advanced technology (ERATO) program. Japanese technology evaluation program, Science Applications International Corporation, December 1988.

[294] February 1989. Computer Center. University of Tokyo, Japan.

[295] Institute for Supercomputing Research. ISR Two Year Report. Also ISR Vector Register Newsletter–about 5 issues a year since 1987.

[296] T. Shimada, K. Hiraki, and S. Sekiguchi. A dataflow supercomputer for scientific computations: The SIGMA - 1 system. Vector Register, November 1988.

[297] S. Sakai, Y. Yamaguchi, K. Hiraki, Y. Kodama, and T. Yuba. An architecture of a dataflow single chip processor. ACM, 1989. International Symposium on Computer Architecture 1989.

[298] W. Graham. U.S.- Japan agreement on cooperation in research and development in science and technology, June 1988. Memorandum from the Executive Office of the President, Office of Science and Technology Policy, Washington, DC.

[299] T. Higuchi, T. Furuya, H. Kusumoto, K. Handa, and A. Kokubu. The prototype of a semantic network machine IXM, 1989. International Conference on Parallel Processing.

[300] M. Suzuki, H. Tajima., Y. Hamazaki, Y. Okada, and K. Tamura. Experiments on an optical bus using holography. *ETL Report No OQE85 - 175*, pages 3–17, 1989. Electro Technical Laboratory, Japan.

[301] S. Takada. A superconducting IC technology based on refractory Josephson tunnel junctions. advances in superconductivity, August 1988. Proceedings of the 1st International Symposium on Superconductivity.

[302] N. Christ. QCD machines. In *Nuclear physics B*, pages 549–556, September 1989.

[303] T. Hoshino, Y. Sato, and Y. Asamoto. Parallel Poisson solver FAGECR - implementation and performance evaluation on PAX computer. Journal of Information Processing, 1988.

[304] T. Hoshino. Development of super parallel computer PAX and its applications, 1990. SNA '90, International Conference on Supercomputing in Nuclear Applications.

[305] T. Hoshino, R. Hiromoto, S.Sekiguchi, and S.Majima. Mapping schemes of the particle-in-cell method implemented on the PAX computer. Parallel Computing, December 1988.

[306] T. Shirakawa, T. Hoshino, Y. Oyanagi, Y. Iwasaki, T.Yoshie, K. Kanaya, S. Ichii, and T. Kiwai. QCDPAX - an MIMD array of vector processors for the numerical simulation of quantum chromodynamics, November 1989. Presented at the Supercomputing '89 Conference.

Printed and bound by CPI Group (UK) Ltd, Croydon, CR0 4YY

08/05/2025

01864823-0003